QUEENS
CONSORT

QUEENS CONSORT

ENGLAND'S MEDIEVAL QUEENS

LISA HILTON

PEGASUS BOOKS
NEW YORK

QUEENS CONSORT

Pegasus Books LLC
80 Broad Street, 5th Floor
New York, NY 10004

First Pegasus Books cloth edition 2010

Library of Congress Cataloging-in-Publication Data is available.

ISBN: 978-1-60598-105-5

10 9 8 7 6 5 4 3 2 1

Printed in the United States of America
Distributed by W. W. Norton & Company, Inc.
www.pegasusbooks.us

For Patrizia Moro

CONTENTS

PART FOUR
DEPOSITIONS, RESTORATIONS

PART FIVE
LANCASTER AND YORK

LIST OF ILLUSTRATIONS

MAPS

GENEALOGICAL TABLES

England in the Twelfth Century

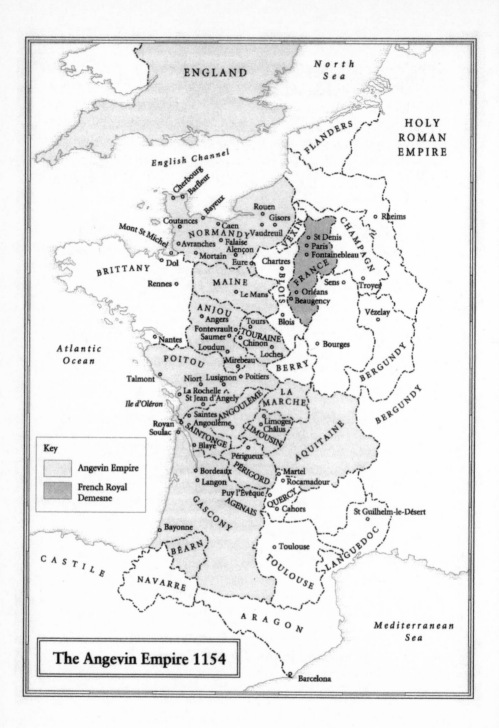

The Angevin Empire 1154

'Royalty is a government in which the attention of a nation is concentrated on one person doing interesting actions. A republic is a government in which that attention is divided between many, who are all doing uninteresting actions. Accordingly, so long as the human heart is strong and the human reason weak, royalty will be strong because it appeals to diffused feeling, and republics weak because they appeal to the understanding.'   Walter Bagehot *The English Constitution*

'It is to be supposed that Henry IV was married, since he certainly had four sons, but it is not in my power to inform the Reader who was his wife.'   Jane Austen *A History of England*

INTRODUCTION

Who is the Queen? The King's wife? Or something more than that? In the period between the Norman Conquest and the accession of Mary Tudor in the sixteenth century, no woman ruled England as queen in her own right. The role and status of king were constantly in the process of redefinition, an ongoing negotiation between royal, ecclesiastical and aristocratic powers, but they remained throughout essentially constitutional, their authority enshrined in and upheld by law. No equivalent constitutional role existed for the king's consort. Yet between the eleventh and fifteenth centuries, English queenship evolved an identity of its own, an identity predicated on, but not limited to marriage to the king. The story of England's medieval queens is composed of two entwined narrative strands: the first the development of queenly tradition and practice, the second the diverse lives of the very individual women who controlled, enlarged and manipulated their customary heritage. It is this combination of the abstract and the intimate, this synthesis of statecraft and the self, which makes the exploration of English queenship so exciting and so important to our understanding of the evolution of the country. The political, religious, administrative and cultural history of the emergent English nation cannot be fully considered without reference to the role of the queen; at the same time, queens are exceptional among women of the medieval period in that we can know them more throroughly as people than could almost any of their contemporaries.

The story of English queenship begins with a French princess. In the centuries after the collapse of Roman imperialism, Europe experienced a perpetually fluctuating regathering of territorial power. Put simply, such power was achieved by violence, but the role of kings was increasingly delineated and formalised by religious liturgy. While their status had yet to become institutional, much less constitutional, a similar process began to arise in the case of queens. As early as 751, evidence exists of the blessing of queens, while two ninth-century texts, *De Ordine Palatii* and *Liber de Rectoribus Christianis*, contributed to the understanding of a queen's duties. The queen orders the king's household and maintains his royal regalia, she distributes provisions and presides in his hall, dispensing rewards to his warriors and gifts to foreign emissaries. There is also an emphasis on the queen as a model of virtue and a prudent counsellor to her husband. Here already is a sense in which the office of queen is invested with authority; the 'rectrix' of *De Rectoribus* 'governs' and 'rules'. The first ceremony through which such authority was formally bestowed is the consecration of Judith, daughter of the French King Charles the Bald, on her marriage in 856 to Aethelwulf, the King of the West Saxons. The twelve-year-old bride was married to her middle-aged husband at Verberie-sur-Oise 'and after Bishop Hincmar of Reims had consecrated her and placed a diadem on her head he [Aethelwulf] formally conferred on her the title of queen, which was something not customary before then to him or his people'.[1]

Consecration, coronation. These are the processes which set a queen apart from other women in a mystery she shared only with her husband. The concept of 'God's anointed' seems antiquated, if not obsolete, in an age when royalty has become for many something of a tragicomic soap opera, but it is still possessed of tremendous potency even today. When millions watched the televised coronation of Queen Elizabeth II in 1953, the cameras turned reverently away at the moment of anointing, but one witness present described the Act of Dedication as 'the most wonderful thing I ever saw ... when she lifted the Sword and laid it on the altar ... She was putting her whole heart and soul to the service of her people'.[2] Though the ceremony broadcast that day from Westminster Abbey had developed in many ways, it was not in essence so different from the ninth-century rite celebrated in a field in northern France. Very few people may nowadays believe that royalty is semi-divine, but queenmaking connects us, even at this end of this century, with our most atavistic selves. The Christian appropriation of ancient beliefs about women's sacred fertility explicitly articulated the connection between queenship and earlier birth cults; consecration was thus apotheosis. The transformative power of coronation was noted in the eleventh century by Godfrey of Reims in reference to William the Conqueror's daughter Adela of Blois who, unlike her older siblings, born while their parents were a mere duke and duchess, is credited with 'fully royal blood'. An unruly twinge of reverence for such beliefs might now be dismissed as embarrassing sentimentality, but there existed no sense of the irrationality of such a contention for the period in question. Just as the Church was omnipresent for every individual, from peasant to magnate, so the idea of difference, of selection by God, coloured the concept of the medieval monarch. Though there is ample, touching, funny evidence for the humanity of medieval queens, it is essential to remember that they were isolated as well as elevated by consecration. They were unique, they were sacred, they were magical.

Marriage, however, was a much more prosaic matter. 'Marriages were matters of allies, claims, lands, treasure and prestige ... They were affairs between families rather than individuals, an instrument of policy rather than passion.'[3] Royal brides were essential diplomatic tools and personal feelings an irrelevance. Henry III set out the official line: 'Friendship between princes can be obtained in no more fitting manner than by the link of conjugal troth.' Yet noble and particularly royal women have too often been reduced to the status of animated title deeds, significant only in terms of the transmission of property. At first glance, the characteristic hostility shown towards women exercising any form of power seems to support this, but if queens were instruments, they were also instrumental. All politics was dynastic politics, that is family politics. The centre of power was the king and no one, in theory at least, was physically closer to the king than the queen. The absolute passivity demanded of royal women in accepting their mates should not blind us either to the degree of wealth, power or dynastic validation carried in the queen's body, or to the practical powers that individual women could exercise at every level of cultural and political life. More than anything else, it was birth, marriage and death that affected medieval power structures so, as mothers and wives, queens were the focus and the source of political stability.

These elements converged in the coronation ordo, which outlined two essential dynamics of queenship at the moment of consecration. Intercession and maternity were channelled through Christian emphasis on women's special dignity. In the twelfth century, Abelard wrote of women's extraordinary status as delineated by Christ, their loyalty during the Passion and their capacity for prophecy in 'a demonstration of female authority, precedence and exclusivity in religious life ... unsurpassed in the Middle Ages'.[4] The cult of the Virgin Mary, Marianism, was a device that sanctified childbirth – so much so that the opening blessing of the coronation ceremony has been called a 'fertility charm', allying the new queen's childbearing with that of the women of the elect Davidic line, including the Virgin herself. Maternity was in turn closely associated with intercession, the second dynamic upon which the ordo ultimately dwelled.

3

Intercession was in some senses a transgressive act, a means by which 'masculine' authority was diverted by the power of 'feminine' mercy. The Old Testament queen Esther, recast by the Church fathers in the mould of the Virgin, was a particularly important symbol of female intercession. A petition to Anne of Bohemia in the fourteenth century sums up the particular role of the queen: 'Let the Queen soften royal severity that the King may be forbearing to his people. A woman mellows a man with love; for this God gave her, for this, o blessed woman, may your sweet love aspire.'[5] The queen's merciful love could move her husband to show his human side in what was effectively a skilful division of psychological labour: she could melt the king's heart without making him appear weak or indecisive. Yet formal intercession became a ritual of queenmaking even as its real power to effect change declined: the progress (admittedly detrimental to queenly power) from a queen as counsellor or adviser to a queen as often merely symbolic intercessor, as in the case of the famous plea of Philippa of Hainault for the burghers of Calais, can be clearly charted over 500 years of medieval queenship.

How could a queen best make use of her sacred capital? What practical, as well as symbolic differences separated her from other women? Common law recognised three states of female existence, each of which was defined in terms of masculine authority: maiden, wife and widow. Only as widows could women be officially released from male guardianship to order their own affairs. Queens, however, enjoyed the status of *femmes soles* even while their husbands were living, and were therefore more independent before the law than any other married woman. They could sue and be sued, acquire property, grant land and witness its granting, preside over legal cases, hear oaths, appoint ecclesiastics and make wills. They could, and did, raise armies. This unique legal status could be employed to manage and expand their finances, create and control their children's inheritances and, in some cases, to fight wars. From the regencies of Matilda of Flanders and Matilda of Boulogne to the much-vilified money-grubbing of Eleanor of Castile, from the successful revolution of Isabella of France to Marguerite of Anjou's desperate fight for her son's crown, English queens used their position according to both temperament and the exigencies of circumstance. Salic law, whereby claimants descended from the female line could not inherit a throne, enshrined in France from the early fourteenth century and widely adopted across Europe, was never applied in England, making English queens exceptional even among their Continental counterparts. Stephen, Henry II, Edward IV and Henry VII owed some or all of their claims to their female ancestors, while those of Edward III and Henry VI, at the beginning and end of the Hundred Years War, were derived from their mothers.

Direct claims in the maternal line were the most obvious manifestation of the centrality of queens to royal power, but the skein of kinship that connected the intermarried royal families of Europe encompassed generations of women. Recent scholarly work on the importance of the maternal family of Eleanor of Provence and the granddaughters of Eleanor of Aquitaine permit a fresh perspective on trans-Continental networks of authority and patronage. The fostering of kinship, through marriage alliances, religious foundations, gift-giving and embassies, bore practical fruit when queens could call in their claims to broker treaties or raise funds and troops. Given the primacy of marriage in cementing such relationships, royal mothers had a particularly crucial role in negotiating advantageous matches for their children. Queen mothers could be exceptionally influential when their husbands were absent or deceased, and situations in which mothers literally had to fight for their children were confronted by Matilda of Boulogne, Marguerite of Anjou and Elizabeth Woodville.

Yet medieval royal motherhood is a contentious issue. Many English queens had to adjust to marriage in their teens, and consequently to exceptional numbers of pregnancies. Childbirth on progress or campaign was an occupational hazard, and queens had to compromise their personal maternal inclinations with the huge demands of their public role. Then, as now, 'working' women have been criticised for neglecting or damaging their children, and much retrospective psychologising has been devoted to castigating queens such as Eleanor of Aquitaine for their lack of involvement with their offspring. Such theorising fits neatly with a concept of medieval childhood that dismisses bonds of affection between parents and children and claims grandly that 'the family at the time was unable to nourish a profound existential attitude between parents and children ... [parents] cared about them less for themselves ... than for the contribution those children could make to the common task'.[6] Increasingly, evidence about medieval royal families contradicts this view, demonstrating that while royal women were little involved in the practical aspects of raising their children, entirely in accordance with their culture, they were extremely attentive to matters of education and upbringing. 'It is the natural bent of all human beings,' wrote Bernard of Anjou in 994, 'to believe that in this lies the largest part of their happiness.' Love of and delight in children is manifest even in the pragmatic details of account books, while evidence of maternal grief at the loss of sons and daughters is moving and poignant. Not all queens were perfect mothers, but nor were they all the cold, distant figures of a historiography that denies emotional reality. Tiny, intimate portraits such as Matilda of Scotland playing with her little boy in the grounds of Merton Priory, or Marguerite of France carefully choosing buttons for her sons' best coats, allow us a touching glimpse of royal motherhood beyond its symbolic and political role.

Such examples also reveal that a queen's private life was not necessarily loveless. Modern Western hostility to arranged marriages recoils at the notion that they might produce satisfactory relationships, but such evidence as there is suggests that several English queens did enjoy loving partnerships with their husbands. Love was certainly not necessary in a dynastic marriage, but it could and did grow, as between Matilda of Flanders and William the Conqueror, Edward I and Eleanor of Castile, Edward III and Philippa of Hainault. King Stephen was so eccentrically affectionate as to remain faithful to his wife. But a beloved queen was also a vulnerable one. Her sexual intimacy with the king was an exclusive power, but it also played on that deeply rooted Christian fear, fear of the corrupting woman, which in turn tapped into disquiet about foreignness, about the possibility of a spy in the royal bed. In the 400 years before the Conquest, only two English queens, Judith and Emma of Normandy, were foreign, compared with sixteen of twenty between 1066 and 1503. International marriages were crucial to the kingdom's stability and prestige, but outsiders also represented a threat. Queens were often forced to choose between their blood relatives and their marital kin, and excessive patronage of foreign connections led to frequent criticism or even, in the case of Eleanor of Provence, to revolt. Anxieties about the whispering, cajoling woman also militated against the efficacy of the queen's role as counsellor or adviser. The effectiveness of 'intimate persuasions' was noted by several writers, and Eleanor of Provence was not shy of advertising her influence over her husband in bed, but queens were simultaneously confronted with a culture that promoted silence and submissiveness in women. Sages from Aristotle to St Peter acclaimed the virtues of silence, the Virgin herself was associated with dumb fortitude and civic statutes such as Hertford's 1486 Ordinance on Scolds laid smalltown strife at the door of gossiping women. While ritual intercession was glorified, the confidence and trust that developed in a successful union could arouse profound suspicion.

The physical aspects of a royal marriage were thus a focus for both celebration and apprehension. Since the future of the realm was explicitly dependent on a queen's body, on her fertility, her marriage might also call the king's masculinity into question. What might be termed the folk memory of primitive fertility beliefs, in which fruitfulness was an assurance of virility and therefore of prosperity, was translated through the Christian sacrament of marriage into a reflection of the limitations of the sovereign himself. A barren marriage showed that God was displeased, and boded ill for the nation; conversely, an overly passionate relationship cast doubts on the king's masculinity: 'The nature of the king's marriage, or rather the extent to which the king's use of this sacrament was pleasing to God, was supposed to impinge on the welfare of the realm in a very material sense.'[7] The reputations of Eleanor of Aquitaine and Isabelle of Angoulême were blackened by interpretations of such misgivings, while Henry VI's manifest intellectual shortcomings prompted questions as to whether an inadequate sexual bond with his wife, Marguerite of Anjou, was responsible.

And what of love outside marriage? Infidelity was practically expected of kings, though troops of bastard children in the kinds of numbers produced by Henry I and John had diminished somewhat by the end of the period. The very presence of the queen and her ladies in the otherwise male-dominated precincts of the royal palace correlated with her unique symbolic status, but it also created a public ritual out of every moment of her life. Private acts such as prayer, eating and sleeping were ritualised into constant affirmations of power. Sexual pleasure, even within marriage, was viewed dubiously by the Church. Christine de Pisan noted that romance was perilous for women, recommending wholesome activities such as sewing and weaving as distractions for dangerously idle minds, and writer after writer warned against the sins of illicit love:

> A great hunger, insatiate to find
> A dulcet ill, an evil sweetness blind,
> A right wonderful, sweet-sugared error.[8]

And in the case of a queen, for whom adultery was treason, solitude was particularly threatening.

Much attention has been given to the position of queens in relation to the dominant literary genre of the period, troubadour poetry, or the school of courtly love. Until quite recently, such poems were interpreted as a sort of manifesto for the aspiring adulterer (medieval people, apparently, didn't do jokes), but courtly love is best understood as an extremely elegant and complex parlour game, very much a literary movement rather than an ideology. Evidence from ecclesiastical court cases and contemporary literature shows that adultery was consistently enjoyed by the general population, but troubadour literature, like Hollywood films today, tells us about people's dreams, not their lives, and the men and women of the period were certainly sophisticated enough to tell the difference: 'While literary texts offer fantasies of personal choice of spouse ... they largely reinforce a lay position that marriage is a family affair.'[9] Even so, Isabella of France, the only English queen to have lived openly with her lover, defied the Pope himself to pursue her extramarital relationship with Roger Mortimer. But perhaps a successful affair, like a successful murder, is the one that no one discovers. Eleanor of Aquitaine, Isabelle of Angoulême and Marguerite of Anjou were accused of adultery, while the romantic adventures of Catherine de Valois in widowhood had extraordinary consequences for the succession. Perhaps the most exceptional relationship of all was that between the relatively low-born Englishwoman Elizabeth Woodville and Edward IV. The handsome prince really did come for Elizabeth, but the outrage surrounding their love match proved that passion was best left to poets.

Elizabeth Woodville's marriage scandalised the nation, and her critics were quick to find proof of her unsuitability as a royal bride in her conduct. The pride and haughtiness which would have been expected in a better-born woman were swiftly translated in her case into evidence of parvenu arrogance. Similarly, criticism of Henry I's daughter the Empress Matilda focused on the aggressive 'masculinity' of her demeanour. The Empress's contemporary and opponent, Queen Matilda of Boulogne, *did* very similar things – she governed men, raised armies and fought for the crown – but she managed to do so while attracting praise. Both examples point to the centrality of correct behaviour and manners to effective queenship. In all aspects of their self-presentation, queens had to contend with the contradictory expectations contained in their anomalous political position, to tread extremely carefully between seemliness and excess. Beauty, for instance, was seen as the objective correlative of nobility. Indeed, so prodigally are compliments strewn about in the chronicles that it is very difficult to ascertain what royal women really looked like. All the same, it seems quite likely that beauty would have been pretty closely confined to the aristocracy, considering their access to better nutrition and hygiene. Given the appearance of much of the population, details like cleanliness or acceptable teeth could go a long way. The queen's looks were part of the king's magnificence, a manifestation of his power, yet praise of her physical charms also diminished her, by making apparent her status as a commodity: potential brides were routinely subjected to immodest physical inspections, and excessive beauty could ignite fear of the over-influential seductress. Since visible splendour was an essential political tool, gorgeous clothes and precious jewels were 'an attribute of the royal state, part of the drama of power'[10] and as such represented a positive obligation for women, yet the queen had also to be mindful of accusations of extravagance or rapacity.

As aristocratic elites across Europe began to forge a strong cultural identity, 'courtly' behaviour became a prop to the social order. Violence still governed the world, but it needed to be contained and controlled in order to be effectively deployed. Hence manners and courtesy, codified and romanticised in chivalric literature, were an essential means of manipulating behaviour. The minutiae of social conduct – how to sit, stand, enter a room, eat, wash, dance – became crucial signifiers of rank and prestige. The distinguished French historian Georges Duby described this process of coalescence as 'the fusion of the aristocracy',[11] and it was one in which women, particularly queens, had a central role. Walter Map depicted the sorry state of Henry II's court after the departure of Eleanor of Aquitaine for Poitiers: a squalid, filthy place where the food was uneatable and the wine so tainted that the wincing courtiers had to filter it through their teeth. Eleanor of Castile took a dim view of the discomforts of royal accommodation and quickly installed glass windows and gardens and promoted the consumption of fruit. Such 'women's touches' were not entirely superficial. The queen's presence demanded, in theory at least, a higher standard of manners and behaviour and, as the exemplar for the court, she was also in a position to fulfil her role as cultural ambassador. From the impressive promotion of vernacular literature by the Anglo-Norman queens at the beginning of the period to Elizabeth of York's familial involvement with the printer William Caxton at its end, English queens were particularly associated with literary innovation, but they were also influential on the way the court lived, dressed, ate and entertained. Matilda of Boulogne and Marguerite of Anjou proved that when it came to necessity, a queen could be no mean general, but military success was increasingly balanced by the status accorded to the civility of a court, in which art, music, poetry and deportment gave the measure of royal power.

From Saxon times, women had been especially connected with the memorialisation of the dead (as the Sachsenspiel laws under which Anne of Bohemia was raised makes explicit), so queens were able to continue the tradition of glorifying and sanctifying their ancestry by initiating and participating as patrons in the most prestigious of all manifestations of power: the establishment of religious houses. That the Church was the backbone of Western civilisation is no longer a very fashionable view, but tension between royal and ecclesiastical powers was a source of tremendous energy as well as dissent. In the founding of monasteries and the sponsoring of new orders such as the Dominicans and the Franciscans, queens found themselves at the heart of the intellectual debates of their times. They corresponded, and sometimes dared to quarrel, with popes and archbishops and promoted their own candidates to ecclesiastical sees. Their gifts to the Church not only advanced the arts but affirmed their own status as patronesses and provided a means of entering the political world even as the expansion of administrative courts reduced their direct opportunities to act as counsellors.

The briefest assessment of English queens consort demonstrates that they cannot be reduced to mere corollaries of their husbands. Nor are they easily categorised. As this book hopes to show, it is possible to establish a consistent picture of the development of queenship itself, but such a picture is constantly straining against individual women's responses to their position. What they were not was passive or powerless. What they were, by the nature of their position, is remarkable, in many senses aberrant. Here they are, an exceptional confederacy: magnificent, courageous, foolish, impetuous – splendid in their royal array.

A NOTE ON TERMINOLOGY

Dower and *dowry*: Dowry was the payment (in money, lands or both) provided by the bride's family that she brought to her marriage. Dower is the provision made by a husband for his wife after his death.

Princes and *princesses*: These titles were not until the fourteenth century widely applied to the children of kings, who were usually styled according to their birthplace, or as 'Lord' or 'Lady'. However, for the sake of clarity, the terms are sometimes employed anachronistically to make it clear that the children mentioned are royal.

Court: The date of the existence of a royal court, and of what precisely it consisted, are matters of much scholarly discussion. Here the term is used purely in a general sense to refer to the place where the king was, or to the circle around him.

Consistency of titles: Many of the figures in this book were known by a number of different titles in the course of their lives. To avoid confusion they are called by the first and last titles they held, where relevant, e.g., Henry of Bolingbroke/Henry IV, or simply by the last title they held.

Names: There is much discrepancy in medieval spelling and 'proper' names are a matter of taste as well as convention. In the following pages 'Eleanor' is used rather than 'Alienor' for Eleanor of Aquitaine, as the sound is similar but the anglicised version easier on the eye in the English language, while the French spelling of Marguerite of Anjou's name has been retained since it is doubtful that anyone in her lifetime called her Margaret. Joanna of Navarre is often known as Joan or Jeanne, but the contemporary pronunciation is preferred here, as is the traditional spelling of 'Woodville' rather than the more accurate but less easily pronounced 'Wydeville'. Isabelle of France and Isabelle of Angoulême have kept their French spelling, while Edward II's queen, another Isabelle of France, is distinguished as Isabella.

PART ONE

ENGLAND AND NORMANDY

NORMANS AND ANGEVINS

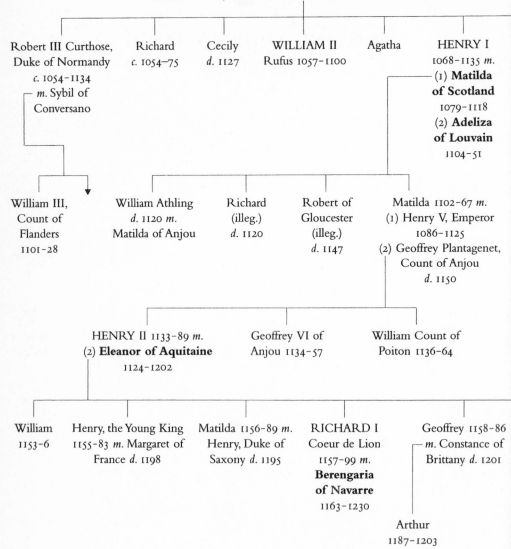

Adela *m.* Baldwin IV of Flanders

Matilda of Flanders 1031-83 *m.* WILLIAM I the Conqueror 1025-87

Robert III Curthose, Duke of Normandy c. 1054-1134 *m.* Sybil of Conversano

Richard c. 1054-75

Cecily d. 1127

WILLIAM II Rufus 1057-1100

Agatha

HENRY I 1068-1135 *m.*
(1) **Matilda of Scotland** 1079-1118
(2) **Adeliza of Louvain** 1104-51

William III, Count of Flanders 1101-28

William Athling d. 1120 *m.* Matilda of Anjou

Richard (illeg.) d. 1120

Robert of Gloucester (illeg.) d. 1147

Matilda 1102-67 *m.*
(1) Henry V, Emperor 1086-1125
(2) Geoffrey Plantagenet, Count of Anjou d. 1150

HENRY II 1133-89 *m.*
(2) **Eleanor of Aquitaine** 1124-1202

Geoffrey VI of Anjou 1134-57

William Count of Poiton 1136-64

William 1153-6

Henry, the Young King 1155-83 *m.* Margaret of France d. 1198

Matilda 1156-89 *m.* Henry, Duke of Saxony d. 1195

RICHARD I Coeur de Lion 1157-99 *m.* **Berengaria of Navarre** 1163-1230

Geoffrey 1158-86 *m.* Constance of Brittany d. 1201

Arthur 1187-1203

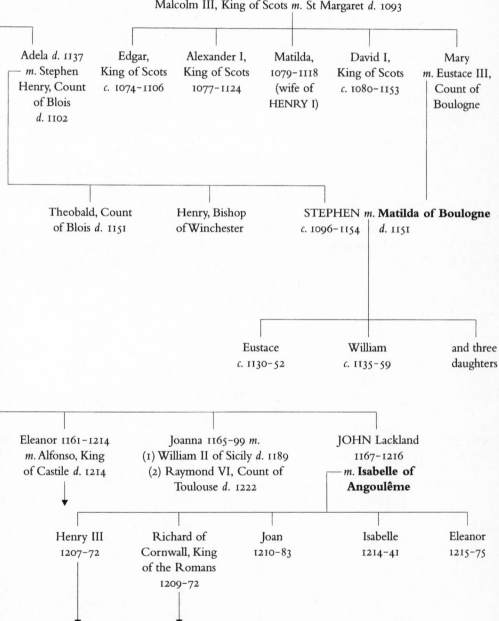

Malcolm III, King of Scots *m.* St Margaret *d.* 1093

Adela *d.* 1137
m. Stephen
Henry, Count
of Blois
d. 1102

Edgar,
King of Scots
c. 1074-1106

Alexander I,
King of Scots
1077-1124

Matilda,
1079-1118
(wife of
HENRY I)

David I,
King of Scots
c. 1080-1153

Mary
m. Eustace III,
Count of
Boulogne

Theobald, Count
of Blois *d.* 1151

Henry, Bishop
of Winchester

STEPHEN *m.* **Matilda of Boulogne**
c. 1096-1154   *d.* 1151

Eustace
c. 1130-52

William
c. 1135-59

and three
daughters

Eleanor 1161-1214
m. Alfonso, King
of Castile *d.* 1214

Joanna 1165-99 *m.*
(1) William II of Sicily *d.* 1189
(2) Raymond VI, Count of
Toulouse *d.* 1222

JOHN Lackland
1167-1216
m. **Isabelle of
Angoulême**

Henry III
1207-72

Richard of
Cornwall, King
of the Romans
1209-72

Joan
1210-83

Isabelle
1214-41

Eleanor
1215-75

CHAPTER 1

MATILDA OF FLANDERS

'The friend of piety and the soother of distress'

Matilda of Flanders never expected to be Queen of England. Initially, she was not much attracted to the idea of becoming Duchess of Normandy. A story in the Chronicle of Tours claims that when she learned Duke William of Normandy had proposed for her, she angrily declared she would never marry a bastard, upon which William forced himself into her bedroom in Bruges and soundly beat her. Another version has the illegitimate Duke dragging her from her horse and pursuing his rough courtship in the roadside mud. Matilda was apparently so overcome by this display of macho passion that she took to her bed and announced she would never marry anyone else. The tale 'may be regarded of more interest to the student of psychology than the student of history',[1] but as with many interpretations of medieval history, what contemporaries could believe had happened is sometimes as revealing as what actually did.

Matilda was descended from Charlemagne and the Saxon king Alfred the Great and her mother, Adela, was a daughter of the King of France. Her prospective husband may have been a duke, but his title gentrified a family that was only a few generations' distance from Viking marauders, whereas her own paternal line, the counts of Flanders, had ruled since the ninth century. But if Matilda objected to the match, her father, Count Baldwin IV, saw a Norman alliance as a contribution to Flanders' growing status as a political power. In the end, that alliance was to become more profitable than the Count could ever have imagined.

Yet when William and Matilda were betrothed in 1049, the status of both Duke and duchy might have made any bride apprehensive. The rights of the dukes of Normandy had been recognised in the early tenth century and William was a direct descendant of the duchy's first ruler, Rolf the Viking. After a splendid career of raiding and pillaging in France, Scotland and Ireland, Rolf (or Rollo) was baptised by the Archbishop of

Rouen some time before 918 and settled down to a new life as a Christian ruler. Five generations later, in 1034, Duke Robert, William's father, felt sufficiently detached from his pagan ancestors to set off on a pilgrimage to Jerusalem. He died on his return journey in 1035, leaving a seven-year-old boy as his heir.

The first years of William's minority rule saw a catalogue of anarchic and brutal violence. The archbishop of Rouen, Count Alan of Brittany and the lords Osbern and Turold had been appointed guardians to the boy, but the archbishop died in 1037, followed by Count Alan in 1040. The Count's replacement, Gilbert of Brionne, was murdered a few months later by assassins in the pay of the Archbishop's son. Turold was killed at the same time. Then Osbern, who acted as William's steward, 'unexpectedly had his throat cut one night … while he and the Duke were sound asleep in the Duke's chamber at Vaudreuil'.[2] The homicidal avarice of competing factions of the Norman nobility keen to take advantage of William's weakness to seize lands and power for themselves instilled such fear in the boy duke of the treachery within his own household that he was often reduced to sheltering in peasants' cottages.

William's personal survival was dependent mainly on the historical relationship between Normandy and the kings of France. The Norman dukes had been vassals of the kings since 968, and in 1031 King Henry I, Matilda's maternal uncle, had taken refuge at Rouen during a period of civil war. With the help of William's grandfather, Duke Richard II, he had managed to recover his kingdom. When, after a decade of bloody skirmishes, war broke out in Normandy in 1046, William appealed to Henry. Together they fought the first significant battle of William's distinguished military career, at Val-es-Dunes near Caen in 1047, against a rebel army led by William's cousin Guy of Burgundy. William won, but for the next thirteen years he was to find himself almost constantly at war.

The marriage between William and Matilda took place towards the end of 1051. In the beginning it was surrounded by controversy. Although it had been planned in 1049, the match was banned in the autumn of that year by Pope Leo IX at the Council of Reims on the grounds of consanguinity. Christian marriage as it was to be understood by future generations was a relatively new invention in the eleventh century, and as part of increasing reforms the Church was anxious to turn a custom into a regulated institution. Canon law forbade the union of individuals who were related in certain 'prohibited degrees', and William and Matilda were fifth cousins. Family connections were further complicated by a marriage contract between Matilda's mother, Adela, and Duke Richard III of

Normandy, William's uncle, before her marriage to Count Baldwin (pre-contract was another invalidating factor), and by the fact that after the death of Matilda's grandmother, Ogiva, her grandfather, Baldwin IV, had taken as his second wife Eleanor, a daughter of Duke Richard II of Normandy. Another theory relating to the papal objection is that Matilda herself was already married, to a man named Gerbod, by whom she had a daughter, Gundrada, who eventually became the wife of William of Warenne, first Earl of Surrey. This story has, however, been dismissed as 'in the highest degree impossible'.[3] Nevertheless, the union did not receive a retrospective papal sanction, from Nicholas II, until the second Lateran Council of 1059.

According to the chronicler William of Jumièges, Matilda's parents, Adela and Baldwin, did not consummate their marriage until 1031, which suggests that Matilda could have been no older than about nineteen when she married William. Since there is no evidence that she was the eldest of their four children, she might well have been considerably younger. Whatever her personal opinion of the match, both her father and her bridegroom were sufficiently keen on it to defy papal sanction, and Count Baldwin brought his daughter to Eu, where the wedding was celebrated. Afterwards the ducal couple travelled together to Rouen.

What were the motivations behind William and Count Baldwin's arrangement? Matilda's father was in the process of reorienting his small but strategically important country with the aim of distancing it from the German-controlled Holy Roman empire and forging stronger links with France, as evinced by his own marriage to the French princess Adela. Having become one of the principal vassals of the King of France, he saw his ambitions further consolidated by the marriage of Matilda's brother Baldwin to Richildis, the widow of the Count of Hainault, in 1049. Having fought unsuccessfully against Flanders in the settlement of Richildis's inheritance, and concerned by constant skirmishing along the Flemish-German border, the German Emperor, Henry III, was apprehensive about a Norman-Flemish alliance which would diminish his influence still further. (Since the current pope, Leo IX, owed his throne to the Emperor, it is unsurprising that he agreed to return the favour by opposing the marriage between William and Matilda.) Normandy could also prove a powerful ally against the English crown, which was at the time hostile to Flanders: King Edward had summoned a fleet to serve against Count Baldwin on the Emperor's side if necessary. In his turn, Duke William was conscious of his own hitherto vulnerable position, dependent as he was on the continued cultivation of the goodwill of the

French King and a small group of loyal aristocrats. He was frequently in conflict with the lords of Arques, Ponthieu and the Vexin, who periodically aligned themselves with Count Eustace of Boulogne, one of Count Baldwin's most rebellious vassals. The marriage with Matilda would thus provide both William and Baldwin with a mutual reinforcement of power to subdue the rebels whose territories lay between their lands. Further, it has been suggested that Matilda's impeccable bloodline went some way to enhancing William's own prestige and eradicating the stain of his illegitimacy.

That William was known to his contemporaries as 'the Bastard' and not 'the Conqueror' is not in doubt, but the implications of this status in terms of the eleventh century need to be examined carefully. The chronicler Orderic Vitalis's claim that William 'as a bastard was despised by the native nobility' may be dismissed as an anachronistic judgement from a later age. Contemporary perceptions did not necessarily stigmatise or even fully recognise illegitimacy. The regularisation of ecclesiastical marriage was still very much an ongoing process, and William's grandfather, Duke Richard II, had been the first of the line to make a Christian marriage, at the turn of the previous century. His sons continued to take concubines, as was still the prevailing custom, and William's father, Duke Robert, did not make a dynastic marriage. His concubine Herleva of Falaise, William's mother, was the daughter of Fulbert, 'the chamberlain', which was not necessarily a high office at the time. That William was sensitive on the subject of his birth was clearly known, as the soldiers of Alençon were to find to their cost, but this may have been more to do with his maternal grandfather's profession than his mother's unmarried status. Fulbert was a skinner, though he appears in some accounts as a 'pollinctor', which in Roman usage meant undertaker. When William besieged the castle of Alençon, the troops 'had beaten pelts and furs in order to insult the duke'[4] with his grandfather's dirty, menial origins. William had the hands and feet cut off thirty-two of them.

(The ancestry of the English kings was, incidentally, still good for a giggle a century later. Henry II, having quarrelled with the bishop of Lincoln, refused to greet him at a picnic one day. The King was mending a leather bandage on his finger with a needle and thread and the bishop, daringly trying to amuse him, remarked: 'How like your cousins of Falaise you do look.' Luckily for the bishop, Henry fell about laughing.[5])

Norman chroniclers do display discomfort with William's birth, as well as with his defiance of the papal ban on his marriage. Flouting the authority of the Pope was a highly risky form of disobedience, since it could provide rebels in the duchy with a religious sanction for political disloyalty. William, however, had been dodging traitors for most of his life, he was a brilliant military strategist and he was possessed of an extremely powerful will. William of Malmesbury recounts how, in the aftermath of his mother's life-threatening labour, the newborn William was left on the floor of Herleva's room while she was cared for. The tiny baby grabbed at the rushes covering the floor with such strength that his attendants predicted he would 'become a mighty man, ready to acquire everything within his reach, and that which he acquired he would with a strong hand steadfastly maintain against all challengers'.[6] So William wanted Matilda of Flanders badly enough to defy the Pope, and he got her.

The prestige of Matilda's ancestry was obviously considered a sufficient compensation for someone of William's relatively uncertain status, as she brought no dowry of land or titles to the union. The desirability of an elite bride was based on the power of her male relations, her wealth and her lineage, and the first two attributes did not necessarily outweigh the third. Ancestry – specifically maternal ancestry – was also to be the principal factor in the choice of the next English queen, the bride of Matilda's son Henry.

At the time of their marriage, William was in his early twenties and Matilda, as has been noted, probably in her late teens. He was a tall man by the standards of the day, about five feet ten, clean shaven and short-haired in the Norman style. Matilda, by contrast, was tiny, just four feet two inches tall. William of Jumièges describes 'a very beautiful and noble girl of royal stock' while Orderic Vitalis declared that she was 'even more distinguished for the purity of her mind and manners than for her illustrious lineage ... She united beauty with gentle breeding and all the graces of Christian holiness.' Conventional tributes such as these appear so frequently that it is difficult to attach much real meaning to them, but William and Matilda were sufficiently attracted to one another for their first child, Robert, to be born within three years of the wedding. They would go on to have three more sons and át least five daughters. Accounts concur that the marriage was happy, and that very happiness was crucially to affect the structure of political power in Normandy and, eventually, in England.

Aristocratic marriages were not made in the expectation of affection. Matrimony was the primary means of advancing family and dynastic interests. A woman of Matilda's status was required to marry as the concerns of her family directed, but this did not mean she would be merely handed about Europe like a diplomatic doll. All eleventh-century politics were family politics, and political legitimacy was dependent not only on military power but on claims of blood, and therefore on women. A particular emphasis was placed in dynastic marriages on the role of the wife as a 'peace-weaver', a mediator or intercessor. In the Anglo-Saxon poem 'Beowulf' a match is arranged is arranged between the children of two enemies, Hrothgar and Froda, 'to settle with the woman a part of his deadly feuds and struggles'. Even if women were no longer carried off as booty from the battlefield as they had been a few centuries previously, in an extremely violent society the grace and good manners of an aristocratic wife were vital to the domestic interactions of powerful men:

> The woman must excel as one cherished among her people and be buoyant of mood, keep confidences, be open-heartedly generous with horses and with treasures, in deliberation over the mead, in the presence of the troop of companions, she must always and everywhere greet first the chief of those princes and instantly offer the chalice to her lord's hand, and she must know what is prudent for them both as rulers of the hall.[7]

The country where Matilda had grown up was considered an extra-ordinarily violent region even by the standards of the time. In comparison with France and England it was a primitive, backward area – Dudo of St Quentin claimed that when the Scandinavians were offered the province by Charles the Simple, they rejected it in favour of Normandy. A twelfth-century account, *The Life of St Arnulf*, describes the state of Flanders in the eleventh century: 'Daily homicides and spilling of human blood had troubled the peace and quiet of the entire area. Thus a great number of nobles, through the force of their prayers, convinced the bishop of the lord to visit the places where this atrocious cruelty especially raged and to instruct the docile and bloody spirit of the Flemings in the interest of peace and concord.'[8] These turbulent conditions hampered development. No town had a population of more than 5,000 and there were few stone buildings. Nevertheless, the mid-eleventh century saw the beginning of an increasing prosperity which would make Flanders one of the most important European centres of commerce and culture in the centuries to come. By the fifteenth century, it was 'completely founded on the fact and course of merchandise'[9] and the centre of mercantile activity was Bruges, already in Matilda's time a key port. In 1037, her parents had been in the city to greet a famous visitor, the exiled Queen Emma of England.

A dynastic connection between Flanders and England had been established in the ninth century. Judith, the daughter of Charles the Bald, became England's first consecrated queen in 856 on her marriage to Aethelwulf, King of the West Saxons. After Aethelwulf's death, Judith was briefly married to her own stepson before eloping with Baldwin 'Iron Arm', the first Count of Flanders. Their son, Baldwin II, married Aelfthryth of England, a daughter of Alfred the Great, the first monarch to be recognised as ruler of all England. Matilda was descended from both England's first anointed queen and one of its greatest kings.

When Emma, daughter of Duke Richard I of Normandy, married Aethelred of England nearly 150 years later, she was able to take advantage of the growing customary power attached to the role of queen. In 973, Aelfthryth, her mother-in-law, had been consecrated, and after her death the new queen became 'the axis around which English politics turned'.[10] Extraordinarily, Emma was crowned queen twice, as after Aethelred's death she married Cnut of Denmark, who reigned from 1016 to 1035. The conflicts between the children of these two marriages led to Emma's exile in Flanders and formed the background to Matilda's own coronation as queen of England.

Emma's marriage to Aethelred was influenced by the Viking descent of the Norman dynasty. Within a century of the 911 grant of Normandy to Rolf the Viking, Scandinavian language and customs had largely died out, and the duchy was Christian, but the Normans retained some loyalty to their seafaring, pillaging cousins. In 996, Richer of Reims was still referring to the Norman duke as '*pyratum dux*' and in the year 1000 a Viking fleet was permitted to shelter over the winter in Normandy before crossing the Channel to raid England in the spring. As late as 1014, a pagan horde led by Olaf and Lacman was received in Rouen to recover from its exertions in laying waste to a large area of north-western Gaul. The alliance created by Emma's marriage put a stop to such attacks on England, at least temporarily. By 1013, England was again under threat from a Danish force, and Aethelred, Emma and their sons, Edward and Alfred, took refuge in Normandy as the invaders swiftly overcame the north and east. Aethelred returned in 1014, but died two years later, in April 1016. As well as his two children with Emma, he left an elder son, Edmund, by his first wife. Edmund, who became known as 'Ironside' for his fierce resistance to the Danes. Edmund succeeded in driving the invaders north of the Thames, whereupon it was agreed that the kingdom would be thus partitioned. But Edmund himself died in November 1016 leaving Cnut, the newly elected Danish ruler, as king of England. The following summer,

Cnut married Emma. He also had two children with an Englishwoman, Aelfgifu, Swain and Harold 'Harefoot'. It was decided that the rights of the couple's previous children should be waived in favour of a son from the new marriage, and a boy, Harthacnut, obligingly appeared.

Emma is the first and only pre-Conquest English queen of whom an image survives. In the *Liber Vitae* of the New Minster, Winchester, Cnut and Emma present a gold cross to the abbey. Emma wears a diadem and is styled '*Regina*'. Her biographer sees the illustration as especially import-ant in the development of queenship, noting the 'special status of the king's wife, as queen, that is as a consecrated person and as an office holder'.[11] Until she became queen dowager, Emma was the richest woman in England, and established herself as a leading patron, commissioning illuminated manuscripts from Peterborough and her own (highly flattering) life story, the *Encomium Emmae Reginae*. In the frontispiece to this work, Emma is shown crowned and seated on a throne beside her sons Edward and Harthacnut, but her figure is larger than theirs. Enthrone-ment is quite uncommon in eleventh-century representations, usually reserved for Christ or other heavenly figures and only just beginning to be used for kings. Emma proved herself adept at managing the new status that the illustrations accord her, succeeding in placing both Harthacnut and Edward on the English throne.

When Cnut died in 1035, Emma suffered a blow to her ambitions when Harold Harefoot was chosen as regent while Harthacnut was absent in Denmark. Emma was able to maintain control for a time in the old capital of Winchester, where she retained Cnut's treasure and was sup-ported by Godwin, Earl of Wessex, who had become Cnut's most trusted adviser. Her sons by Aethelred, Edward and Alfred, chose this moment to sail from Normandy, where they had remained in exile following their father's death. Harold Harefoot did not even pretend to believe their claim that this was an innocent visit to their mother. Edward was prevented from landing at Southampton, but Alfred managed to get to Dover. At this point Earl Godwin switched his allegiance from Emma to Harold Harefoot and Alfred, 'the blameless Aetheling'*, was murdered at Ely.[12] *The Anglo-Saxon Chronicle* reports what happened next: 'Here Harold was everywhere chosen as king and Harthacnut forsaken because he was too long in Denmark, and his mother ... was driven out without any mercy to face the raging winter; and she then came beyond the sea to Bruges, and there Earl Baldwin received her well.'[13]

* Aetheling was the Anglo-Saxon usage for 'hereditary prince'.

The *Encomium Emmae* gives a fuller description of Emma's presence at Bruges, which suggests something of the city Matilda knew as a child: 'The latter town is inhabited by Flemish settlers and enjoys very great fame for the number of its merchants and for its affluence in all things upon which mankind places the greatest value. Here indeed [Emma] was ... honourably received by Baldwin, the marquis [sic] of that same province and by his wife.'

Emma was active in Bruges, working to establish Harthacnut's right to the throne. In 1039 he finally arrived, with a large fleet, to join her and they spent the winter as Count Baldwin's guests. When Harold Harefoot conveniently died in the spring of 1040, Emma and Harthacnut returned triumphantly to England. For two years, she once again enjoyed power as Mater Regis (queen mother), until Harthacnut died after a drinking session at a wedding celebration in Lambeth in 1042. Emma had always championed him above her other sons, but now she was obliged to negotiate a relationship with Edward, who had joined his younger brother in dual kingship a year earlier, and now became sole ruler of England. According to *The Anglo-Saxon Chronicle*, Edward had a low opinion of his mother's wavering loyalties, and deprived her of most of her wealth. Emma died at Winchester in 1052, just after Matilda of Flanders became Duchess of Normandy.

Matilda was perhaps no more than a tiny child when Emma visited Bruges, and there is no evidence that the Queen of England saw her, though, given the length of Emma's stay and the 'honourable' reception she received from Count Baldwin and Countess Adela, it is perfectly plausible that she was presented to their children. The triangular political relationships between Normandy, Flanders and England continued in the next decades, and Emma set a powerful example of what a politically astute and determined woman could achieve. She had effectively governed as regent in Wessex during Harthacnut's absence in Denmark, she had obtained wealth and position as a patron, and though her life ended rather flatly, she did live to see two of her sons crowned king.

Very little is known of Matilda's childhood in Flanders, but Queen Emma was not the only influential woman from whom she might have drawn an example. The last centuries of the first millennium witnessed an extraordinary concentration of women's power as part of the emerging dominance of the Christian church. Royal abbesses were at the forefront of the new monastic movement, both as a trans-European phenomenon and in the country of which Matilda would eventually be queen, where it is estimated that fifty religious houses appointed their first abbess from a royal family. Royal blood was an 'essential prerequisite' for sanctity.[14] Bede's eighth-century *Ecclesiastical History* observes the vital role played by Saxon women in the conversion of their male kin to Christianity, enumerating royal missionaries such as Bertha, wife of the Kentish King Aethelred; her daughter Aethelburh, who married and converted King Edwin of Northumbria; Eanflaed, Edwin's daughter, and Hilda, his great-niece. The foundation and patronage of abbeys was a potent symbol of royal authority, and far from being a retreat from the world, the religious life offered women an active role in dignifying the lineage of their houses. 'The holiness of such women redounded to the honour of their male kin and the lineage they shared . . . a daughter or a sister in a convent was not a woman "disposed of", but a woman put to work to add sanctity and legitimacy to newly, often nefariously acquired lordships.'[15]

A strong connection between the religious life and female scholarship was also current at the time. It was suggested to Matilda's daughter, Adela of Blois, that learning was one way in which daughters could surpass their fathers, devoting their leisure to cultivating knowledge and a love of books. Early education was very much a domestic, maternal responsibility, and one that was taken seriously. Throughout the medieval period, an extensive clerical literature advises mothers on proper childcare and education and as early as Asser's ninth-century *Life of King Alfred*, this was emphasised in Saxon England. The writer notes that 'with shame be it spoken, by the unworthy neglect of his parents . . . [Alfred] remained illiterate even till he was twelve years old or more'. But Alfred's mother, Osburgh, 'a religious woman, noble by birth and by nature', gave Alfred and his brother a book of Saxon poetry, saying, 'Whichever of you shall the soonest learn this volume shall have it for his own.' When Alfred succeeds, his mother 'smiles with satisfaction'.

The cult of the Virgin, which was to play such a resonant part in contemporary conceptions of medieval queenship, also connected royalty, sanctity and learning. An engraving from ninth-century Mercia shows the Queen of Heaven holding a book, connecting three dynamics which were to be central to Matilda's own conduct and the manner in which she raised her children. The northern, pagan concept of the queen as wise and judicious counsellor to her husband was absorbed, in Christian education, into St Paul's edict in I Corinthians on the duty of wives to influence their 'unbelieving husbands' – an obligation adopted by Matilda's Saxon predecessors with evident success, there was a new tension between the dynamic, evangelising role of the queen as a source and symbol of sacred power and the injunction, also found in St Paul, that Christian wives should be meek, passive and silent. Later stipulations on the education of women suggest that Matilda would also have been exposed to this new conception of her wifely role. In the influential manual *The Book of the Knight of the Tower*, Geoffrey de la Tour-Landry suggested that women's learning should be limited 'to the virtuous things of scripture, wherefore they may better see and know their salvation'. The fifteenth-century commentator Bartholomew Granville[16] stressed the importance of deport-ment to the well-bred woman's character. Her carriage should be erect, but her eyes modestly cast down; she should be 'mannerly in clothing, sober in moving, wary in speaking, chaste in looking, honest in bearing, sad in going, shamefast among the people'. Writers from the end of the period such as Giles of Rome and Christine de Pisan concurred that spinning, sewing and embroidery were ideal activities to keep girls from idle and potentially sinful imaginings.

Extrapolating from these two slightly variant traditions, it is not possible to do more than give a sense of the intellectual atmosphere in which Matilda of Flanders was raised, though evidence of her character and activities can be stretched to support the theory that she was successful in creating a role combining both active pious queenship and suitably modest personal conduct. Literacy in Latin had been a notable feature of the Flemish court, and since Matilda's daughters could certainly read the language, it seems likely that she too had some knowledge of it, which in turn suggests that her own mother had favoured a 'royal' education. Writing, however, was extremely uncommon among laywomen, and it is probable that Matilda, like her daughter-in-law, used a clerk for her letters. What other practical skills she acquired is not known, though the thirteenth-century French romance *Silence* suggests that appropriate accomplishments for girls of her class were music, particularly the harp and viol, and embroidery. Matilda's daughter-in-law, Matilda of Scotland, was to be a patron and promoter of the skills of English needlewomen, and while the nineteenth-century writer Agnes Strickland's assertion that the Bayeux Tapestry was made by Matilda of Flanders and her ladies has been proved false, Matilda did leave some fine work in her will, and her husband certainly patronised one Leofgeat of Wiltshire, who is recorded as making gold embroidery for the King's use. Saxon needlework is one example of the cultural validation that was as essential to the Norman project of conquest as military might, in that the Anglo-Saxon past was reclaimed and absorbed into a new tradition.

However profound were the wider implications of such activities, there was much more to Matilda's life than sitting around sewing. Aristocratic women were the principal managers of their family's households and estates, particularly in a time when their men were often absent for long periods on campaign. Their effectiveness in applying themselves to a role that might be seen as the equivalent of running 'a major business enterprise'[17] is borne out by the frequency with which they were named as executrixes in widowhood. Whatever the precise details of Matilda of Flanders' early training, it seems to have equipped her well for life as a ruling duchess and a successful, fully engaged consort.

Matilda appears as William's consort in a charter to Holy Trinity in Rouen in 1053. By then, the marriage had directed an important change in William's policy and family attitudes. As a minor, he had relied on the older generation for support, particularly his uncles, Mauger, archbishop of Rouen, and William of Arques. As William grew more confident and emotionally involved with Matilda, he began to redefine his family more intimately, in terms of his own growing children. In a pattern that would become a familiar problem to English princes, he also began to favour his own contemporaries over his senior relations. By 1052, both uncles were in open opposition to William and in 1053, William of Arques staged a revolt. Matilda was now faced with an experience common among aristocratic brides: a conflict between her husband and her natal family. William's relationship with Matilda's uncle, King Henry of France, had been an important motivation for their marriage, but this aspect of the alliance had turned sour when Henry reconciled with William's archenemy Geoffrey, Count of Anjou. Normandy was now isolated between hostile Angevin and French territory, and Henry was keen to profit from dissent within the duchy. In response to his uncle's opposition, William besieged the fortress of Arques, and Henry led a relief force to the rebels. William succeeded in forcing Henry to retreat, and William of Arques went into exile in Boulogne, where he died. Archbishop Mauger was obliged to retire after a Church council at Lisieux in 1054, and withdrew to Guernsey, but William's difficulties with Henry continued.

The French King made another attempt on Normandy in 1054, sending a divided army to the north and south of the River Seine. William faced Henry in the south, sending his cousin Robert of Eu to confront the northern column. Robert achieved a spectacular victory at Mortemer and once again Henry was repelled, but he continued plotting with Geoffrey of Anjou and in 1057 Normandy was attacked yet again. The French and Angevin forces invaded from the south and pressed towards the Channel, laying waste to the countryside en route. William met them at the estuary of the River Dives at Varaville, where a high tide split the enemy forces. Their battalions cut in half, Henry and Geoffrey could only stand helplessly on the bank and watch as William massacred their army. Both Henry and Geoffrey died in 1060, by which point William had already begun a long campaign to secure Maine as a border province.

Such a compression of military events might give the impression that William and his peers spent most of their time hacking at one another on the battlefield, but this would be to misunderstand the nature of medieval warfare and to neglect the significant cultural and economic development of Normandy in the 1050s. Despite the near-permanent military commitments of the duke, he was not engaging in pitched battles on a regular basis. Europeans were notoriously cautious in war, as a twelfth-century Arab commentator noted,[18] and it was prudence as much as bravery that won campaigns. So when diplomacy failed, siege warfare – taming the enemy by hunger and isolation, or strategies such as taking important hostages – was tried. Outright armed combat was avoided as far as possible: it was only as a last resort that a commander would risk his men's lives in large numbers or, worse, that of his prince.

So while the Normandy Matilda knew was certainly dominated by her husband's armed struggles to control his aristocracy and expand and secure his borders, it was able concurrently to develop peacefully and profitably. A distinct 'Norman', as opposed to Scandinavian or French, identity was becoming clearly established. The towns of Rouen, Bayeux and Caen were expanding – a Jewish community of artisans and merchants was founded in Caen around 1060 – and the duchy was profiting from the wine-growing regions to the south as tuns were shipped down the Seine to supply Britain and the north. There was also something of a religious revival. Normandy had been Christian as far back as the fifth century, but owing to the Viking incursions, by the first decades of the tenth, there were no monasteries remaining. William's grandfather, Duke Richard, restored the monastery of St Michel in 965, and by the eleventh century, Benedictine abbeys were flourishing at Préaux, Lyre, Corneilles, Conches and St Georges-de-Boscherville, in addition to William and Matilda's own foundations at Caen. St Stephen and Holy Trinity were created in response to the papal recognition of William and Matilda's marriage in 1059. The papal edict was revoked on condition that William and Matilda each performed a penance of building and endowing a monastic house 'where monks and nuns should zealously pray for their salvation'.[19] Matilda's foundation, Holy Trinity, was functioning under its first abbess (appropriately named Matilda), by the end of the year, with a choir of nuns to sing the daily offices. The abbey was finally consecrated in 1066.

That year is, of course, the one that everyone knows: 1066, the year of Hastings, the year that English history really 'began'. Throughout the first fifteen years of Matilda's marriage, the manoeuvrings and manipulations that led to the battle of Hastings were fitting gradually into place. Edward the Confessor, the English King, had married Edith, the daughter of the powerful Earl Godwin, in 1045, but by 1051 the marriage was still childless. Having spent much of his life in Normandy, the King's loyalties to the duchy were strong, and he began to build up a faction of Norman retainers at the English court, possibly as a check on Godwin's influence. Nevertheless, in September 1051, Godwin was confident enough to openly defy Edward and events came to a head. The Godwin family was outlawed, Godwin himself fled to Flanders, continuing the tradition of the province as a refuge for disaffected English ambition, and Edward repudiated his wife, leaving the English throne without even the possibility of a successor.

Some historians accept that William of Normandy visited England at this juncture, and while there is very little reason to believe that such a visit took place, it is agreed that Edward offered William the English crown. Robert, the former abbot of Jumièges in Normandy and subsequently, as part of Edward's pro-Norman policy, archbishop of Canterbury, passed through Normandy on his way to Rome, bringing the promise of the succession and hostages to confirm it. (These hostages were Wulfnoth, Earl Godwin's son, and Haakon, his grandson, and they were to remain in Normandy for thirteen years.) Later stories included the presentation of a ring and ceremonial sword. There were, however, other strong contenders for the throne. The children of Edward's sister Godgifu, Countess of the Vexin, had an interest, as did the descendants of Edmund Ironside, whose son Edward 'The Exile' returned to the English court in 1057 but died shortly afterwards, leaving a son, Edgar Aetheling, as the claimant for the house of Wessex. And it was still possible that Edward might have children of his own.

In 1052, everything changed again. Godwin was begrudgingly restored to favour and Queen Edith was fetched out of the convent. Godwin died the following year, and his son Harold became Earl of Wessex, assuming his father's role as the second man in the realm. It was too early for William to risk a confrontation, and for him the decade was one of consolidation. He waited patiently for his chance and, in 1064, the winds of opportunity finally blew.

They blew Earl Harold and his party to the coast of Ponthieu, a neighbouring county of Normandy, where they were immediately imprisoned by the local lord, Count Guy. The purpose of Harold's journey is unknown, despite the claim of later Norman sources that he had been sent as an envoy to reaffirm Edward's promise to William and retrieve the hostages. When storms deposited Harold at Ponthieu, William was conveniently able to deliver him from captivity, and the two men spent the summer together. Though Harold was effectively a prisoner, everyone politely maintained that this was a friendly visit. Whatever might have been in the two men's hearts, there was no outward manifestation of rivalry, indeed 'there is every likelihood that a good time was had by all'.[20] William was anxious to impress his guest with his status as a great prince and his jewels, silks, furs and plate were much on display. He also took the opportunity to introduce Harold to Norman military tactics in a short campaign against Brittany, in which Harold acquitted himself admirably. But beneath the displays of amity, William was intent on furthering the purpose he had been harbouring for over a decade. At some point before his return to England, Harold swore an oath to uphold William's claim to the English crown, an oath which also included the promise of marriage to one of William and Matilda's daughters. The scene is depicted in the Bayeux Tapestry, with Harold placed between two altars holding sacred relics, which he touches with his hand as William, seated on a throne and holding a sword (the sword supposedly sent by King Edward?) looks on.

Harold's estimation of the value of his oath was demonstrated when King Edward died on 5 January 1066. The next day, the newly consecrated royal abbey at Westminster saw the funeral of one king and the coronation of another: Harold. He took Ealdgyth, sister of Morcar, the Earl of Northumbria, as his wife. It was a smooth succession, suggesting it had been arranged in advance, but Harold was immediately beset by challenges. At stake was not only the future of the English crown, but the orientation of the country towards either Scandinavia or Latin Europe, and the consequent balance of both ecclesiastical and political power in western Europe as a whole. The crucial figures involved were Harold himself, his brother Tostig, Harald Hardrada, King of Norway, and Duke William of Normandy.

By the summer of 1066, William was preparing for war. The English expedition brought new and important responsibilities for Matilda, who was to act as his regent in the duchy in his absence, in the name of their son Robert, who was now fourteen. Something of William's long-term plans for the attempt on the English throne may be discerned in the fact that he had officially designated Robert as his heir in 1063, suggesting that he knew he was to risk his life and hoped to ensure a trouble-free succession. Three years later, as the troopships were under construction in the shipyards and the massive organisation of men, horses and supplies was underway, William called a great assembly where he proclaimed his son as his heir before his chief magnates and extracted an oath of fidelity. Three counsellors were appointed to guide Matilda in William's absence, Roger of Beaumont, Roger of Montgomery and Hugh d'Auranchin. Matilda was to demonstrate her political capabilities more fully in the future, but it is significant that during the critical period of the expedition, Normandy, 'a province notoriously susceptible to anarchy'[21] suffered no major disturbances, despite being left in the nominal charge of a young woman and a boy. Matilda also contributed directly to the venture with the gift of the *Mora*, the large and brightly decorated ship in which William himself set sail for the English coast.

Harold was aware of the challenge to his crown being mobilised across the Channel, but he was faced with more immediate problems. Tostig had been made Earl of Northumbria in 1055 after his father's reconciliation with King Edward. He was deeply unpopular, and ten years later the Northumbrians rebelled against him. Tostig was exiled to Flanders and replaced by Morcar, soon to become Harold's father-in-law. Shortly after Harold's succession, Tostig attempted to revenge himself by mounting a series of raids along the English coast, but was driven up to Scotland, where he made a treacherous alliance with one of Harold's far more powerful rivals, the King of Norway. Harold Hardrada now proclaimed himself the rightful heir of King Cnut and set out with a huge fleet to make a bid for the throne. Tostig swore allegiance to him and their combined forces managed to take possession of York in September 1066. Harold moved his army northwards with spectacular speed and attacked the invaders at Stamford Bridge, to the north-east of the city. It was a magnificent victory. Tostig and Harold Hardrada were killed and only twenty-odd Viking ships were left to limp back to Norway.

Yet once more, Harold had to move fast. The Norman forces had landed at Pevensey on 28 September and were now encamped at Hastings. There was no option but to swing his exhausted men round and make for the south coast. The two armies met on 14 October.

The only contemporary account of the battle to have survived in English is the 'D' version of *The Anglo-Saxon Chronicle*. It is a brief and poignant description of the passing of a world:

Then Earl William came from Normandy into Pevensey, on the eve of the Feast of St Michael, and as soon as they were fit, made a castle at

Hastings market town. This became known to King Harold and he gathered a great army and came against him at the grey apple tree. And William came upon him by surprise before his people were marshalled. Nevertheless the King fought very hard against him with those men who wanted to support him, and there was great slaughter on either side. There was killed King Harold and Earl Leofwine his brother, and Earl Gyrth his brother and many good men. And the French had possession of the place of slaughter.

King William I was crowned at Westminster on Christmas Day 1066. The ceremony was a crucial reinforcement of the legitimacy of his right to the throne. William needed to show that he held the crown not only by right of conquest, but as the true heir to an unbroken line of succession. The choice of the Confessor's church at Westminster was a part of this declaration of legitimacy, and Westminster became the coronation church for almost every subsequent English monarch. The tenth-century Saxon rite was employed, with two notable modifications. The congregation was asked, by the archbishop of York in English and the bishop of Coutances in French, for its formal assent to William's rule, a question that was incorporated into following coronations. And the *Laudes Regiae*, a part of the liturgy that had been used at the coronation of Charlemagne and on the highest Church holidays ever since, were sung. Pre-Conquest, William had been named in the *Laudes* as 'Duke of the Normans', after the French king. Post-Conquest, he is referred to as 'the most serene William, the great and peacegiving King, crowned by God, life and victory'. Life and victory, *vita et Victoria*, is a Roman formulation, while *serenissimus* is the antique imperial title: William was evoking the most ancient authorities to support his new status. No mention was made in the post-1066 *Laudes* of the king of France, implying that he and William were now equals. As William's consort, Matilda of Flanders was associated in this declaration of majesty, and thus the queen's role was publicly formalised as never before.

William sailed back to Normandy in 1067. At Fécamp in April, he displayed the English royal regalia and had the *Laudes* performed at the most splendid Easter court the duchy had ever seen. He returned to his new kingdom the following year and sent for Matilda, who arrived with the bishop of Lisieux as her escort and was crowned by archbishop Aldred at Westminster on the feast of Pentecost, 11 May 1068. Once again the *Laudes* were sung, and Matilda was anointed as well as crowned. The use of holy oil on the monarch's person marked a moment of apotheosis, of spiritual consecration. Unction symbolised the unique relationship between the anointed and God. The coronation ordo used for Matilda incorporated three important new phrases: *'constituit reginam in popolo'* – the Queen is placed by God among the people; *'regalis imperii ... esse participem'* – the Queen shares royal power; and *'laetatur gens Anglica domini imperio regenda et reginae virtutis providential gubernanda'* – the English people are blessed to be ruled by the power and virtue of the Queen.[22] The power of English queens consort was always customary rather than constitutional, but Matilda's coronation reinforced the rite undergone by her ancestor Judith, which transformed queenship into an office.

A counterpoint to Matilda's arrival in England was the departure of the mother figures of the two most important Anglo-Saxon dynasties. Gytha, the mother of King Harold, and the Confessor's queen, Edith, sailed to St Omer in Flanders with 'the wives of many good men',[23] while Agatha, the widow of Edward Aetheling, and her daughters Margaret and Christina left for Scotland after Matilda's coronation. The 'D' version of *The Anglo-Saxon Chronicle* juxtaposes the departure of the Englishwomen and the arrival of the new Norman queen in a manner which highlights the significance of blood ties and marriage to political legitimacy. For the Saxons, 1066 represented 'an almost total dispossession and replacement of the elite',[24] and that dispossession was marked not only by the redistribution of lands to William's supporters but by the dislocation of the carriers of Saxon blood, the women themselves. The 'D' Chronicle anticipates the role of women in disseminating the bloodline of the conquerors through marriage, Orderic confirms that Matilda travelled with an entourage of Norman noblewomen and a study of post-Conquest nomenclature shows that the process of melding Saxons and Normans into a new race was well advanced by the end of the twelfth century, by which time nearly all English people bore 'Continental' names. (The major chroniclers of the period, William of Malmesbury, Henry of Huntingdon and Orderic Vitalis himself were all products of 'mixed' marriages.) Thus the picture painted by *Chronicle* 'D', of the sorrowing Saxon womenfolk making way for the wives and mothers of the next Norman generation, becomes a symbol of victory and defeat which emphasises the centrality of women in dynastic power structures.

As the stark description of 'D' makes clear, the Conquest was a domestic as well as a military triumph. Marriage to Saxon heiresses was a significant means of obtaining greater control of Saxon lands. The Domesday Book records that 350 women held lands in England under the Confessor, their combined estates amounting to 5 per cent of the total area documented.

Two per cent of this was held by Queen Edith, the Confessor's wife, and his sister Godgifu, and the majority of the rest was divided between thirty-six noblewomen. For women who chose not to go into exile, the convent offered a refuge from marriage to an invader. The archbishop of Canterbury, Lanfranc, was concerned about the number of Englishwomen who had gone into hiding in religious houses. Matilda of Scotland, the granddaughter of Edward Aetheling, spent much of her childhood in two convents, perhaps as a means of protecting her from Norman fortune-hunters, though the possibility of her having betrayed an implied vocation was to cause controversy in her marriage to Henry I. The eventual ruling of the archbishop of Canterbury on the matter was based on Lanfranc's judgement that women who had taken the veil to protect themselves 'in times of lawlessness' were free to leave the cloister.

At the time of her coronation Matilda was pregnant with her fourth son, Henry, the only one of her children to be born in England. She and William went back to Normandy for Christmas 1068, but the Norman victory in his kingdom was still insecure. A huge uprising, headed by Edgar Aetheling, broke out in Northumbria, and William had to return to deal with it. That Matilda, now heavily pregnant, joined him on the expedition is proved by the birth of Henry at Selby in Yorkshire. The 'harrying of the north', as the campaign became known, appalled con-temporaries with its ruthlessness. *The Anglo-Saxon Chronicle* reports variously that William's troops 'ravaged and humiliated' the county, 'wholly ravaged and laid waste to the shire', or just 'completely did for it'. Matilda showed great fortitude and loyalty in accompanying her husband at this dangerous time, and the journey she made shortly after her son's birth all the way back to Normandy, where she took office as William's regent, attests to her physical bravery and determination. Normandy would prove to be the main focus of Matilda's activities for the rest of her life, but she did take an interest in her newly acquired English lands. With the aid of her vice-regal council she managed her estates effectively, granted charters and manors – including two, Felsted in Essex and Tarrant Launceston in Dorset, in 1082, to provide the nuns at Holy Trinity, her monastic house at Caen, with wardrobes and firewood – and founded a market at Tewkesbury.

The manor of Tewkesbury provided the setting for another legend. Before the Conquest, Tewkesbury was held by the Saxon lord Brictric, who was said to have caught Matilda's eye at her father's court in Flanders while on an embassy from Edward the Confessor. Apparently Brictric did not return her interest, but Matilda neither forgave nor forgot and, after

Hastings, supposedly demanded the manor from her husband and proceeded to throw Brictric into prison at Winchester, where he died in
mysterious circumstances two years later. That Brictric owned the property, and that it passed to Matilda, who granted it to Roger de Busci
before her death, may be ascertained from the Domesday Book, but this
also confirms that Brictric (who, since he inherited the manor in 1020,
might be assumed to have been rather old on his presumed 'embassy' in
the 1050s) had died before the lands were granted to the Queen. Another
story that portrays Matilda as sexually jealous and vengeful tells of William
dallying with a woman, and Matilda having 'the lady in question ham-
strung and put to death'.[25] Again, it is hard to imagine that Matilda might
forget herself so far as to murder a mere mistress, and indeed William was
reputedly faithful to her. All the same, these tales, like that of Matilda's
feisty refusal of William's suit, suggest the perception of a certain force of
character, and it is deliciously tempting to imagine the mighty Conqueror
quailing before the temper of his tiny queen.

There is no doubting the strength of character revealed by Matilda's
determination to use her position as regent of Normandy to fight for
justice in her homeland. In 1067, her father had died and was succeeded
by his son, Baldwin VI, who successfully annexed the Hainault inheritance
of his wife, Richildis. Matilda's younger brother Robert had married
Gertrude, the widowed Countess of Frisia, several years before, and on
Baldwin VI's death in 1070 he invaded Flanders, which was being held
by Richildis, as regent, for her son Arnulf. Since Normandy and Flanders
were both French vassal states, Matilda united with the King of France to
go to her nephew's aid, sending Anglo-Norman troops under the
command of William FitzOsbern, Earl of Hereford. This was very much
a Norman initiative: William did not intervene in his capacity of king of
England. On 22 February 1071, Robert defeated his nephew and sister-
in-law, and little Arnulf was killed on the battlefield at Cassel. Matilda was
outraged by what she saw as Robert's cruelty, and she blamed him for
the loss of her commander, FitzOsbern. However, though Hainault was
granted to Arnulf's younger brother Baldwin, since Philip of France now
accepted Robert as Count of Flanders, she was obliged to concede defeat.
Robert the Frisian remained a thorn in William of Normandy's side.
Along with Geoffrey Martel, Count of Anjou, and Conan, Duke of
Brittany, Robert 'hatched many plots against me, but though they hoped
for great gain and laid cunning traps they never secured what they desired,
for God was my help'.[26] William might have tried to claim Flanders for
his wife, as her inheritance, but given the continued struggle to hold

Normandy and England, and the grudging support of the French for Robert the Frisian, he judged that a campaign in Flanders would overstretch his resources.

Like all contemporary rulers, Matilda lived a peripatetic life, moving constantly through her lands with her own household, hearing petitions, overseeing her accounts and convening courts. Her progresses may be followed through her charters, the number and frequency of which are evidence of her personal power. Matilda's special place in confirming and adding her approval to William's grants confirm her unique superiority over even the most powerful male magnate. However, business activities did not prevent her from taking considerable interest in her children's education. Matilda and William had four sons: Robert, Richard (who died in 1075), William, known as William Rufus for his red hair, and Henry; and five daughters: Agatha, Cecily, Adela, Constance and Matilda. All were remarkable for their level of education – Matilda clearly did not believe that learning should be confined to men. Adela, who married Stephen of Blois in 1083, became a noted literary patron, displaying her skills at the transportation of the relics of the Empress Helen, the mother of the first Christian Roman Emperor, Constantine, in 1095, when she read aloud the inscription on the new reliquary for the company. William Rufus and possibly Henry were tutored by Archbishop Lanfranc, and Henry ensured that his own daughter, the Empress Matilda, was educated enough to understand government documents written in Latin.

Matilda's daughters were educated at her Holy Trinity foundation at Caen and received instruction from a monk who was a well-known orator. Cecily entered Holy Trinity as a novice in 1075, eventually becoming abbess in 1113. Holy Trinity's brother house, William's foundation of St Stephen's of Caen, provided a link with the reforming tendencies in Church practices championed by Lanfranc, first as abbot of St Stephen's and then as archbishop of Canterbury. Lanfranc's ardent faith was spiritually inspiring to William and his queen. Matilda's household, like her husband's, was strict in its observances, and Matilda heard Mass every day. She and William were enthusiastic supporters of Lanfranc's mission to revitalise the Church, which William recognised as a potentially significant means of uniting his new realm. Between 1072 and 1076, Lanfranc organised a series of reforming councils to regulate the English Church according to Norman practices, forbidding simony (the sale of church offices), ruling against clerical marriage and determining episcopal sees. William's martial persona is so overwhelming that his spiritual side is often neglected, but it was relevant in his marriage to Matilda in that 'this ever devout and eager worshipper'[27] believed in the Church teachings on marriage propagated by Lanfranc, and broke with four generations of family tradition by never producing a bastard.

Sharing her husband's piety, assisting in his government and managing his Norman lands, Matilda was in many ways an exemplary queen and the sense of her marriage is of a strong and successful partnership. However, she was also prepared to defy her husband and set her own political judgements against his. In 1077, Matilda's eldest son, Robert 'Curthose', rebelled against his father, and Matilda secretly supported him. Robert's discontent stemmed from what he saw as unfair treatment following the Conquest. In 1063, Matilda and William had witnessed the charter for 'Robert, their son, whom they had chosen to govern the regnum after their deaths',[28] a strategy for affirming the loyalty of William's magnates to his heir of which his own father had made use in 1034. In 1067, Robert effectively became 'acting' duke of Normandy, but when, in 1071, William began to make annual visits to the duchy after a four-year absence, Robert resented his father's resumption of his ducal powers. Orderic described Robert as a 'proud and foolish fellow', but his mother loved him enough to involve herself in the quarrel. In 1077, Robert took his grievance to the King of France, who granted him the castle of Gerberoy as a base to fight a campaign against his father. William besieged him there for three weeks in 1079, but returned unsuccessfully to Rouen, the two were reconciled and Normandy was regranted to Robert. Matilda sent money from her own revenues to help Robert, and a Breton monk, Samson, later told Orderic Vitalis that he had been dispatched to William by Matilda to try to persuade him of Robert's case. The family were reunited at Breteuil in 1080 for the betrothal of Matilda's daughter Adela to Stephen of Blois, an event which marked not only the alliance between Blois and Normandy against the threat of the Angevins, but the end of the rebellion, the castellan of Breteuil having been one of Robert's backers.

William does not appear to have held Matilda's support for Robert against her; indeed, such maternal loyalty was laudable, if unwise. Orderic Vitalis recounts her speech to her husband in words that, though unlikely to have been recorded verbatim, convey a sense of the devotion expected of royal mothers: 'O my lord, do not wonder that I love my first-born with such tender affection. By the power of the most high, if my son Robert were dead and buried seven feet in the earth and I could bring him back to life with my own blood, I would shed my lifeblood for him!'

In 1082, Matilda accompanied her husband to meet his half-brother,

Odo of Bayeux, at Grestain, where their mother Herleva was buried, to make arrangements for an abbey there. Odo had been a longstanding ally since his appointment to the bishopric in 1052 and had played an essential role in the Conquest. He was a swashbuckling churchman of the pre-reform era, enormously rich, a father and a mace-wielding warrior. William relied on him greatly, and had given him the earldom of Kent and the vice-regency of England in the 1060s and 1070s, but by 1082, Odo was becoming a threat. Having built up a strong personal faction in England, he came up with a plan to get himself elected pope and began spending huge amounts of money to achieve his ambition. After the meeting at Grestain, Odo left for England to embark for Rome, a journey William had expressly forbidden. The King himself arrested his brother as he was about to sail from the Isle of Wight, and Odo spent the rest of his life in the Tower of Rouen. William was quite prepared to be ruthless with members of his own family, and Odo had been a far more loyal servant to him than his son Robert. So was his reconciliation with Robert, who had gone as far as to take up arms against him, perhaps an indication of Matilda's pacifying influence?

The King and Queen were back in Normandy early in 1083 for Adela's wedding. Matilda did not live to see the marriage of another daughter, Constance, to Alan of Brittany in 1086. By the summer of 1083 she was ill, and that November she died. William was with her as she dictated her will and made her confession. Matilda left the contents of her chamber, including her crown and sceptre, to Holy Trinity, where she wished to be buried. She also gave generously to the poor from her deathbed, an example William followed in 1087. He had not married Matilda with the expectation of making her a queen, and it has been suggested that had he not taken a wife until after 1066 he might have sought a more illustrious match, yet their marriage had in some ways been instrumental to the Conquest. Without Matilda's alliances and, more importantly, her blood, William may not have been able to retain Normandy so effectively, or to prosecute so vigorously his claim, and that of his legitimate sons, to England. And without her capable regency, he might not have been able to hold both his realms post-Conquest.

William was reportedly wretched at her death. Despite the bride's early objections, the marriage of William the Bastard and Matilda of Flanders was undoubtedly a success, both emotionally and practically. It also per-mitted Matilda to establish a model of active queenship so influential on her immediate successors that the consorts of the Anglo-Norman kings are seen to this day as representing the zenith of English queenly power.

CHAPTER 2

MATILDA OF SCOTLAND

'Enduring with complacency'

Edith of Scotland was a true Anglo-Saxon princess. Her mother, Margaret, was the daughter of Edward 'the Exile', son of Edmund Ironside, and his wife Agatha. Edith's grandparents had left their Hungarian refuge for Edward the Confessor's court in 1057, and though Agatha had been widowed shortly afterwards, she remained in England with her children, Edgar, Margaret and Christina, through the events of 1066. *The Anglo-Saxon Chronicle* implies that they were present for the coronation of Matilda of Flanders at Pentecost in 1068, as it was not until the summer that the family departed the uncertain atmosphere of Westminster for the protection of King Malcolm of Scotland. Malcolm persuaded Margaret to become his wife. She resisted at first, declaring she preferred to remain a virgin, the better to serve God, but eventually overcame her reluctance and, in spite of sacrificing her virginity and producing eight children, still achieved sainthood after her death. Edith, the fifth child and her first daughter, was born in 1080. Queen Matilda of Flanders and her son Robert Curthose were her godparents. Like William of Normandy, Edith supposedly asserted her regal ambition early: during her baptism she grabbed at Queen Matilda's veil and tried to pull it towards her own head, a gesture which, with hindsight, was naturally considered to have been an omen.

Edith's childhood can be glimpsed through the *Life of St Margaret of Scotland*, a biography of her mother which she commissioned as queen. Evidently Margaret was an extremely pious woman, but she and her siblings were also sophisticated, bilingual and educated, and she had a great influence on the somewhat rustic Scottish court. Margaret loved books and studied the Bible diligently, and though her husband was illiterate, there is a touching image in the *Life of St Margaret* of King Malcolm holding his wife's book as she reads. He surprised her with gifts of rich bindings for her books, and while she 'delighted more in good works than the possession of riches'[1] she was mindful of the show of magnificence required by her station. She encouraged foreign merchants to visit Scotland with previously unheard-of luxury goods, decorated the royal halls with hangings and rich gold and silver plate and smartened up both the appearance and the manners of the King and his retinue, forbidding his men to go plundering when they rode out with her husband.

The picture of Margaret as a mother is sketchy, but unusually intimate for a royal woman of the time, suggesting that her daughter contributed her own recollections to the memoir. Margaret admonished her children and had her steward beat them if necessary, but as a result they reputedly had very good manners, and were brought to their mother 'very often' for religious instruction in simple language that they could understand. The *Life* also shows Queen Margaret sitting the children of the poor on her knee and feeding them mashed-up food. Edith's tremendous regard for her mother creates a strong image of a warm and happy early childhood.

This changed, however, in 1086, when Edith and her younger sister Mary left for the abbey of Romsey to be educated under the supervision of their aunt Christina. Edith spent the next six or seven years 'in fear of the rod of my Aunt'[2] who treated her harshly, slapping and scolding her cruelly, and constantly made her feel as though she were in disgrace. Christina also stirred up a great deal of future trouble for her niece by forcing her to wear a heavy black veil. Edith reported that 'That hood I did indeed wear in her presence, chafing and fearful ... but as soon as I was able to escape out of her sight I tore it off and threw it in the dirt and trampled on it. This was my only way of venting my rage and the hatred of it that boiled up in me.'[3]

There is something delightful in this picture of the cross little princess stamping on the symbol of her stern aunt's authority, but Edith had the self-discipline and intelligence to keep her rebelliousness sufficiently in check while she acquired an extremely good education. Before 1093, the girls moved to Wilton Abbey, gratefully leaving Aunt Christina behind to grow old at Romsey. Both convents were centres of women's learning and literacy, where, according to William of Malmesbury, 'letters were trained into the female heart'. At the turn of the twelfth century, Wilton accommodated between eighty and ninety women and had a distinguished association with the daughters of the old Anglo-Saxon aristocracy. Edward the Confessor's queen, Edith, had retired there before her death in 1075, as a contemporary of the well-known 'English poetess' Muriel. Among the abbey's treasured relics were a nail from the True Cross, a portion of the Venerable Bede and the body of St Edith, which made it a popular destination for pilgrims. The house had been rebuilt in stone by the Confessor's queen, and St Edith's shrine boasted an impressive alb embroidered with gold thread, pearls and coloured stones. Anglo-Saxon needlework was highly prized, and in later life Edith continued to patronise the art with which she had grown up in the convent.

Edith's education at Wilton was not confined to traditionally feminine activities. The convent's rigorous intellectual tradition may be seen in the reading list prepared for Eve of Wilton, who went on to become a well-known anchoress, or holy recluse, in France. Eve began her training in 1065, aged seven, and when she left as a young woman was considered capable of reading St Augustine and Boethius, among many others, in Latin. Edith's first language was English, but she perfected her French at Wilton, and she, too, learned some Latin. She read both the Old and New Testaments, the books of the Church fathers and some of the major Latin writers, familiarity with whom she was later to demonstrate in her letters. The house was a sort of cross-cultural finishing school where the daughters of conquered and conquerors met – Gunnhildr, the daughter of King Harold and his gloriously named mistress Eadgyth Swan-Neck, was also a pupil there, and the training Edith received was a good preparation for the new Anglo-Norman world in which she would be required to move.

By 1093, it seems, Edith's parents considered her ready to enter this world, as they betrothed her to the Breton magnate Alan the Red, Count of Richmond. Before the marriage could take place, however, politics intervened. In the August of that year, Edith's father, King Malcolm, was present at the dedication of Durham Cathedral, after which he was summoned to Gloucester by William Rufus to hold a council with him. 'But then when he came to the King, he could be entitled to neither speech with our King nor to the covenants which were earlier promised him.'[4] Affronted by such disrespectful treatment, Malcolm returned to Scotland, stopping to visit his daughter at Wilton on the way. William Rufus had been at the convent the same week and had seen Edith dressed as a nun. When her father arrived to find his daughter wearing the veil, he ripped it from her head, tore it into pieces and trampled it to the ground, declaring he would have her marry Count Alan rather than become a nun. He rode off to Scotland with her immediately, where they arrived to find Queen Margaret unwell. Still smarting at the English King's behaviour, Malcolm then 'gathered his army and travelled into England, raiding with greater folly than behoved him'.[5] A party led by Robert Mowbray, Earl of Northumbria, surprised him, and both Malcolm and his son and heir Edward were killed. When Queen Margaret heard the news, her illness worsened and, on 16 November, within three days of losing her husband and son, she, too, was dead.

Edith was now an orphan and, it appears, a runaway. Her husband-to-be, Alan the Red, had also visited Wilton that turbulent summer, and it is not known whether he saw Edith there. It is quite possible she had already left, as, perhaps to console himself, he ran off with King Harold's daughter Gunnhildr. Anselm, the archbishop of Canterbury, now stepped in to take charge of this scandalous situation. Gunnhildr had confessed to him that she had decided to become a nun, and the Archbishop wrote to her threatening her with damnation if she did not go back to Wilton. Although Alan the Red died before he and Gunnhildr could make it to the altar, she was obviously determined that the religious life was not for her, since she married his brother, Alan the Black, instead. Edith, mean-while, perhaps inspired by Gunnhildr's obstinacy, also refused to return to the convent. Although she had been seen in the veil on several occasions, she always maintained that she had never intended to profess herself a nun. When Anselm instructed Osmund, bishop of Salisbury, to see that this 'prodigal daughter of the King of Scots whom the devil made to cast off the veil'[6] was retrieved for the Lord, she defied him.

Edith did not return to Wilton, and between 1093 and 1100 she disappears from the chronicles. After her father's death, the Scottish crown was claimed by his brother, Donald, whose son Duncan seized the throne before being murdered by Donald's supporters. In 1096, Edith's uncle, Edgar Aetheling, led an army against Donald and succeeded in placing her brother Edgar on the throne as Edgar I. Edith's whereabouts during these dangerous times are unknown. It has been suggested that she may have spent time at the court of the English King, William Rufus, who had perhaps considered her as a possible wife during her time at Wilton. And when she re-emerges, it is no longer as the prodigal princess but indeed as a royal bride, and with a new, Norman-friendly name: Matilda. Her husband-to-be, however, was not Rufus, but his younger brother Henry.

The division of the Conqueror's inheritance had left Henry in an ambiguous position. He received a large sum of money and an interest in the lands of his mother, Queen Matilda, but no marriage had been arranged for him and he had no clear political role. He supported his elder brother William who, though not the Conqueror's first-born son, had been his choice to succeed him as king, in his ambition to reunite the

Anglo-Norman realm, an aim William went some way towards achieving when Robert Curthose departed from Normandy on the first crusade in 1095. Robert and William had already recognised each other as heir if either should die without a son, and now William took the opportunity to govern Normandy in Robert's absence in exchange for a large loan to support his expedition. Henry had been periodically in conflict with William, but at the time of the Normandy agreement they had made peace, and he appears as a member of William's household, leading a squadron of knights in one of the endless Norman border skirmishes. Despite the apparent accord between the brothers, more than one commentator has claimed that Henry planned to murder his brother, and that, in the summer of 1100, he grabbed his chance.

What is not in doubt is that William Rufus was killed in a hunting accident in the New Forest on 2 August, and that by the next day, Henry had persuaded the officials of the King's castle at Winchester to give up both the castle and the royal treasure it contained, then ridden hard for London, where he was crowned king at Westminster by the bishop of London and issued a 'Charter of Liberties' which promised just government. One of Henry's first acts as king was to send for Archbishop Anselm, who was in exile. Another was to propose to the princess of Scotland.

Perhaps it is Henry's very decisiveness that has subsequently cast suspicion on his conduct. His swift response to the crisis of William's death preserved the throne for the Norman dynasty without conflict, and it is tempting for historians to argue that this speedy reaction must have been part of a calculated coup. Yet fatal hunting accidents were commonplace – Henry and William's own brother Richard had died this way, as had one of Robert Curthose's illegitimate sons – and none of Henry's contemporaries suggested that there had been anything untoward in William's death. At the time the only controversy was the new King's proposed marriage.

Both Williams had been kings of England but, thanks to his Yorkshire birth, Henry was an English king. A marriage to a descendant of the ancient Wessex line would not so much legitimise the Norman claim as augment the perception of a continuity of rights being fostered by the Norman chroniclers. The nine-month reign of 'Earl' Harold, to which rank he had been demoted, was being presented as an aberration, a brief usurping of the crown, with William of Normandy signifying a return to the 'true' line of English royalty through his claim as Edward the Confessor's designated heir. In terms of Norman propaganda, a marriage between Henry and Edith should have been understood as the union of two members of the same house, not as the representative of a conquered dynasty bestowing her royal bloodline on the conqueror, which was, of course, what it was. Whatever the official line, Henry was aware that Edith's blood would transmit powerful rights to an heir and enhance his popularity with his English subjects. The Norman magnates, having 'adopted' Edward the Confessor as their forebear, could hardly object without undermining their own presence. Edith's Scottish connections increased the chances of a truce on the perennially troublesome northern border, which would release funds and men for service in Normandy and the Welsh marches.

The political motivations for the match were sound enough, but the chronicler William of Malmesbury kindly suggests that Henry was actually in love with Edith. If Edith had indeed spent time at William Rufus's court, it is possible that Henry could have met her there. It is also suggested that Henry's education included a period at Salisbury, as a pupil of Bishop Osmond, who was charged with retrieving the runaway princess, and that Edith might have attracted his attention at this time. William of Malmesbury is understated about Edith's looks – her beauty was 'not entirely to be despised' – but Henry loved her so much that 'he barely considered her marriage portion'. The objection to the match was Edith's purported commitment to become a nun.

Edith's self-confessed rejection of the hated veil forced upon her by her Aunt Christina makes it clear that, however pious she might have been, she was determined to take up a place in the royal world to which she was born. But the evidence of witnesses who had seen her wearing the veil counted against her. It was Edith herself who took the initiative of arranging a meeting with the newly returned Archbishop Anselm. Disgusted by the idea that a genuine religious vow might be broken, he declared he 'would not be induced by any pleading to take from God his bride and join her to any earthly husband'.[7] The two met at Salisbury and, after hearing Edith's own account, Anselm agreed to call an ecclesiastical council to decide the matter, and representatives were sent from Canterbury and Salisbury to make enquiries. A significant factor in the council's decision was the ruling by the previous archbishop, Lanfranc, that Anglo-Saxon women who had taken refuge in convents at the time of the Norman Conquest were not to be held as sworn nuns when they emerged from hiding. The council concluded that 'under the circumstances of the matter, the girl could not rightly be bound by any decision to prevent her from being free to dispose of her person in whatever way she legally wished'.[8]

On 11 November 1100, the Anglo-Saxon princess became a Norman queen. When exactly Edith became Matilda is uncertain, but the adoption of her godmother's name signalled her intention to break with the past and reinforce her closeness to her new marital family. She and Henry were married by Anselm on the steps of Westminster Abbey. Before he performed the ceremony, the archbishop recounted the story of the religious controversy and invited any objections. According to Eadmer, 'The crowd cried out in one voice that the affair had been rightly decided and that there was no ground on which anyone ... could possibly raise any scandal.'

From a contemporary perspective, fertility was perceived as a sign that a marriage was blessed by God, and in February 1102, Matilda (having earlier suffered a miscarriage) gave birth to a daughter, also named Matilda, at the royal manor of Sutton Courtenay. A son, William, was born before the end of September the next year. A prophecy made on William of Normandy's deathbed made the birth of the prince especially joyous to the new royal family. Archbishop Anselm recorded that in 1066 England had been about to be delivered to its enemies as a punishment for the sinfulness of its people (an interpretation shared by *The Anglo-Saxon Chronicle*). The realm would only be secure when 'a green tree shall be cut through the middle and the part cut off being carried the space of three acres, shall without any assistance become united again with its stem, burst out with flowers and stretch forth its fruit, as before, from the sap again uniting'. The green tree represented the royal house of England, the three acres Harold, William and William Rufus, and the reunification was the marriage of Henry and Matilda, its fruit the new baby boy. The prophecy recalls the stark image of the hoary grey apple tree on the battlefield of Hastings, the reminder of so much death being transformed into an emblem of new and promising life.

In twelfth-century England, ownership of land was of paramount importance in the acquisition of wealth and prestige. The records of lands held by Matilda of Scotland permit much greater insight into the customs that would be established for English queens than do those of Matilda of Flanders. Surprisingly, in that she was the sister of a reigning king and the daughter of another, William of Malmesbury suggests that Matilda brought little or no dowry to Henry, though since she did possess some lordship rights in the north, this may have been exaggerated to emphasise Henry's disinterest in the financial element of their marriage. Matilda's dower estates were principally granted from those lands held by Queen Edith,

Edward the Confessor's widow. Though it has been argued that there was no consistent pattern of grants to Anglo-Saxon queens, there was a perceived tradition that certain properties were the prerogative of the queen, and the fact that Henry chose to grant such properties to Matilda suggests he wished to incorporate her into that tradition.

Matilda's ability to control and manage her estates set a vital precedent for queenly power. One such estate was the abbey of Waltham, which was worth £100. The abbey remained part of the queen's holdings well into the century – both Matilda and Eleanor of Aquitaine drew servants from among its canons, while Isabelle of Angoulême and Eleanor of Castile made use of its revenues. Matilda of Scotland was personally involved in the abbey's dealings; indeed, the charter by which Henry granted the property to her mentions the 'queen's court' held there. Charters and land exchanges were conducted in Matilda's name and between 1108 and 1115 she gave permission for the canons to hold a fair. Another property that became associated with English queens was the convent of Barking, which was granted to Matilda of Boulogne in the next reign and provided Eleanor of Provence with five months' worth of revenues during her widowhood. Matilda of Scotland received rents and tithes from Barking, improved the nearby roads and made the house responsible for the upkeep of a bridge she had constructed, assigning the revenues of her nearby manor of West Ham to pay for its maintenance.

Matilda was also the owner of substantial property in London. Henry's grants to her in the capital may also have had a political motive, since some Londoners had not forgotten their allegiance to Matilda's uncle Edgar Aetheling at the time of the Conquest and remained emotionally loyal to the Wessex line. As a representative of that line, Matilda would be better able to retain their support, and her management of her London possessions was astute in this respect. A charter of donation to Westminster Abbey explicitly states that the gift was made 'at the prayer of Queen Matilda', a site near Aldgate was made available in 1107–8 for a new house for the Augustinian canons, and sixty shillings per year from dock revenues were diverted to build a hospital for lepers at St Giles. These docks acquired the name of Queenshithe, which remains today. Later queens followed Matilda's example by using their rights to the toll on disembarked goods to fund charitable projects. Adeliza of Louvain endowed Reading Abbey with one hundred shillings per year from her Queenshithe revenues, while Matilda of Boulogne contributed from them to her hospital foundation St Katherine by the Tower.

Leprosy was a particular focus for Matilda's compassion. She was the benefactress of a 'leprosarium' at Chichester and possibly the patron of the hospital of St James at Westminster (textual sources attribute the foundation to Henry II, but archaeological evidence dates the building earlier than his reign), while her leper hospital at St Giles was still caring for fourteen sufferers at the time of the dissolution of the monasteries in 1539. Matilda's parents had publicly washed the feet of several hundred paupers as part of their Lenten devotions, and Matilda followed in their footsteps in her own humble ministrations to lepers. Her brother David described a scene in her apartments at Westminster:

> The place was full of lepers and there was the Queen standing in the middle of them. And taking off a linen cloth she had wrapped around her waist, she put it into a water basin and began to wash and dry their feet and kiss them most devotedly while she was bathing them and drying them with her hands. And I said to her 'My lady! What are you doing? Surely if the King knew about this he would never deign to kiss you with his lips after you had been polluted by the putrefied feet of lepers!' Then she, under a smile, said 'Who does not know that the feet of the Eternal King are to be preferred over the lips of a King who is going to die? Surely for that reason I called you, dearest brother, so that you might learn such works from my example.'[9]

There is something a little too didactic about this anecdote for it to be entirely authentic, perhaps, but it tells us something about both Matilda's reputation among her contemporaries and their expectations of their queen. It illustrates the connection between piety and that other important element of queenship, the role of intercessor or 'peace-weaver', the Christian duties of compassion and charity mingling with the role of mediator with the earthly representative of God's power, the king. Matilda showed that it was possible for a queen to combine a public demonstration of religious devotion with an effective political function.

Matilda played a significant part in the development of the Anglo-Norman Church, which was undergoing a period of problematic evolution in relation to the papacy that was to become known as the Gregorian or investiture controversy. While it centred on the issue of ecclesiastical investiture, it had far broader implications for the relative roles of spiritual and temporal powers in England and throughout Europe. The eleventh century had seen many attempts to clarify and consolidate canon law, of which the sacrament of secular marriage that influenced the subsequent reputation of William the Conqueror was one. Other disputes concerned clerical marriage and the sin of simony, or the sale of Church offices. As early as 1059, the papal see had decided that secular leaders had no right to determine the election of popes, since the Church was founded on the authority of God alone. Traditionally, rulers had had the power to invest prelates, and to receive homage from them for their temporal powers, that is, the lands and revenues they controlled. Henry I's involvement in this controversy was further complicated by the variance between Norman and English practices. Archbishop Anselm had gone into exile to avoid conflict with William Rufus and, although Henry had recalled him on his accession, Anselm, who had attended the Council of Rome in 1099, felt morally unable to condone the prevailing conventions of investiture in England and Normandy. In 1102, a compromise was reached whereby Henry was able to appoint bishops so long as Anselm himself was not required to consecrate them, but this soon broke down. Matilda's own chancellor, Reinhelm, gave back his ring and staff of office rather than accept what he saw as uncanonical consecration, while William Giffard, a candidate for the see of Winchester, refused to allow the ceremony to proceed. In spring 1103 Anselm felt obliged to leave once more for Rome to seek papal advice.

During the two and a half years of Anselm's absence, Matilda corresponded with him. Her letters are the earliest in existence known to have been written by an English queen. Though they are not in her own hand – a clerk wrote them on her behalf – they display 'a scholarship rare among laymen and quite exceptional amongst laywomen'.[10] Her efforts to mediate between the archbishop, her husband, and the Pope, Paschal II, required not only a sophisticated understanding of the theological questions at issue and their political repercussions, but also a great deal of diplomatic discretion. Matilda signalled her support for Anselm just before his departure for Rome, when she witnessed a charter at Rochester which she signed '*Matildis reginae et filiae Anselmi archiepiscopi*', but she was also aware that she could not afford to alienate Henry. The King had claimed the revenues of Canterbury for himself when Anselm left, on the grounds that the see was vacant, but Matilda was able to get him to set aside a personal allowance for the archbishop. However, when Henry extracted further sums of money from the clergy a few years later and they begged the Queen to intervene, she wept and insisted she could do nothing. She knew that success meant concessions, that she could not afford to overplay her hand without losing her influence over Henry.

Anselm confirmed his awareness of that influence when he wrote: 'Counsel these things, intimate these things publicly and privately to our

Lord the King and repeat them often.'¹¹ The perceived intimacy of husband and wife was one of the most powerful (and occasionally feared) elements of queenly power, and Matilda declared herself ready to make use of it. She encouraged Anselm: 'Farther, frequent, though secret consultation promises the return of the father to his daughter ... of the pastor to his flock.' She claimed that she was 'skilfully investigating' Henry's heart and had discovered that 'his mind is better disposed towards you than many men think; and I favouring it, and suggesting wherever I can, he will become yet more courteous and reconciled towards you'. Matilda appeared confident of her power to persuade her husband. 'As to what he permits now to be done, in reference to your return, he will permit more and better to be done in future, when, according to time and opportunity, you shall request it.'

Henry's understanding of the investiture issue was that it represented a diminishing of the royal prerogative,.and he was reluctant to give way. In 1104, the Pope threatened to excommunicate him. Matilda had written to Paschal, describing the 'lugubrious mourning' and 'opprobrious grief' the realm of England was suffering from the lack of its 'dearest father', Anselm, and pleading in high-flown classical rhetoric for the archbishop's return. Now, as excommunication was mooted, Anselm urged Matilda to 'beg, plead and chide' Henry to change his position. A compromise was eventually agreed in which Henry gave up his powers to invest prelates but retained the right to receive homage for 'temporalities', a concession in ecclesiastical terms, but one in which the secular powers of the crown were arguably augmented.

Matilda's involvement in the investiture controversy demonstrates a degree of confidence between King and Queen that is reinforced by the political responsibilities Henry assigned to her. The first six years of his reign were dominated by his ambition to retain control of Normandy. In 1101, he had made peace with his brother Robert in the treaty of Alton, but in 1105 he began the conquest of the duchy in earnest. After the battle of Tinchebrai in 1106, where Robert was taken prisoner, Normandy was his. It has been estimated that Henry spent 60 per cent of his time in Normandy,¹² and Matilda, the designated head of his curia, or council, frequently acted as regent of England during his absence. That a woman should fulfil such a role was not perceived as odd by contemporaries: 'The sources reveal the Queen intimately and actively involved in the public affairs of the kingdom, and none of the writers of these sources exhibit any surprise or dismay that this should be the case.'¹³

Charter evidence is particularly important in ascertaining Matilda's status. Her earliest public attestation took place in 1101, at the same time as Henry granted her the abbey of Waltham. Matilda pardoned the canons of Waltham the sum they had previously paid to the see of Durham for work on the cathedral there. In the sixty-five charters she witnessed during the first eighteen years of Henry's reign, her name is placed above that of the bishops, second only in status to the King himself (the only exception being a charter to the Conqueror's foundation of St Stephen's Caen, where Matilda appears after two kings, Henry and her brother Edgar King of Scots). Many charters feature clauses concluding with the words '*per reginae Matildis*', which has been interpreted as an indication that the Queen supervised the document between the council and the clerks' office to ensure that its contents accorded with what had been decided.[14] Matilda also issued at least thirty-three charters of her own, and a smaller group 'clearly shows the Queen acting with what amounts to vice-regal authority', sending out writs in her own name. The second-ever mention of the English exchequer, in the *Abingdon Chronicle*, describes a sitting of the exchequer court at Winchester in 1111, presided over by Matilda while Henry was in Normandy. As in the case of Matilda of Flanders, the cross-Channel division of property in the Anglo-Norman realm made shared rule both necessary and natural, and Matilda of Scotland's career represents a high point in the opportunities for medieval women to exercise public power.

Cultural patronage was a vital element of such powers, and one of Matilda's first demonstrations of this was the commissioning of the *Life* of her mother, St Margaret of Scotland, which may have had a didactic as well as a hagiographic purpose, serving as a 'mirror' (in the sense of model or guide) of the virtues of the perfect princess for the young queen to emulate. Matilda certainly succeeded in imitating Margaret in her piety and her desire to regulate the Church, but she seems to have been less successful at reconciling her own inclinations towards simplicity and humility with the grandeur that was both expected of her and indeed obligatory as a manifestation of royal authority. In a pre-literate, highly visual culture, opulence and magnificence were essential badges of power, and as such were considered necessary virtues. St Margaret herself had recognised this in her attempts to spruce up the Scottish court, and Matilda may have been aware of the example of her erstwhile namesake, St Edith of Wilton, a holy Kentish princess who dressed splendidly even as a nun. When St Aethelwold reprimanded her for her worldliness, Edith replied that spiritual purity could sit just as well under silks as rags and continued to show off her beautiful gowns. Matilda, though, was 'possibly somewhat uninspired in matters of style'.[15] In fact, her Norman courtiers thought her rather a bore.

The glamour and sophistication associated with royal courts naturally led to their condemnation by moralists as places of licentious behaviour. Margaret of Scotland had been aware of their potential for scandal and kept it in check: 'None of her women were ever morally degraded by familiarity with men and none ever by the wantonness of levity.'[16] The showiness and self-indulgence of the Anglo-Saxon court, it was implied, constituted one of the 'sins' for which the English had paid at the Conquest. William of Malmesbury draws an unflattering comparison between the clean-shaven, 'delicate' and economical Normans and the 'fantastically appointed English', who adorned themselves with masses of gold jewellery, drank to excess and sported tattoos. Forty years later, though, the contrast was less apparent: long hair was in, absurdly pointed shoes were fashionable for men and women's gowns required extravagant amounts of fabric, their sleeves trailing on the ground. Elegant ladies painted their faces and bound their breasts to achieve a slimmer figure. In the midst of this finery the Queen seemed dowdy. Marbod of Rennes ventured tactfully: 'You, o Queen, because you are, fear to seem, beautiful,' but the outfit Matilda wears on her seal had been out of style for a generation before she was crowned. (The dress shown on the seal is probably a copy of one belonging to Matilda of Flanders, and it is similar, too, to a gown in which Henry's sister Cecily, the abbess at Caen, is depicted elsewhere.)

The atmosphere at Henry and Matilda's court was very different from the racy environment of the unmarried Rufus's reign, and William of Malmesbury suggests that Matilda was blamed for the change. Although Malmesbury's 1066 portrait sneers at the English for their extravagant appearance and behaviour, it was Matilda's Englishness that was now perceived as dull. At their traditional crown-wearing at Westminster a few weeks after their wedding, Henry and Matilda were nicknamed Godiva and Godric, two unambiguously English names that would have had old-fashioned and stuffy connotations. The fact that Matilda's first language was English may have been a positive advantage to Henry, whose own grasp of the tongue is uncertain, but French was the language of social status, of the elite, and the very fact that Matilda spoke English at all provided the snobbish with a reason to look down on her.

The difficulty of reconciling piety and the sophisticated behaviour expected of a courtier had formed part of the background to Matilda's education at Wilton. 'Courtly love', the term used to describe the elegant, mildly licentious literature that had such tremendous cultural influence in Europe from the twelfth century onwards, is particularly associated with the legend of a later English queen, Eleanor of Aquitaine, but long before Eleanor supposedly presided over her 'courts of love', the ideas, if not the form of the literature were being discussed in the Anglo-Norman kingdom. There are as many definitions of what precisely its ethos was as there are scholars to debate it, but in essence the genre is concerned with the idealisation of a married mistress by the poet, who worships his beloved and performs all manner of elaborate deeds in an attempt to win the merest mark (sometimes considerably more) of regard. The tradition later melds with the cult of chivalry and knightly honour, producing a romantic dreamworld of valiant knights and beautiful ladies that maintains a vague but potent grip on modern-day perceptions of medieval life. Muriel, the poetess who was particularly honoured by her burial next to the relics of the Venerable Bede at Wilton, was described in a pre-1095 poem addressed to her by Baudri de Bourgueil as a beautiful young noblewoman who eschewed marriage and wealth to devote herself to virginity in the convent. A monk poet, Serlo, wrote to Muriel praising her choice and explaining the conundrum that a lady in 'society' could not be both elegant and virtuous since, in a world where marriages of convenience ruled, a woman who did not take a lover would be looked down on as ill-bred or provincial. This was precisely the dilemma ritualised by the troubadour poets. Given the veneration of Muriel's memory at Wilton, it is likely that Matilda encountered this conundrum during her training there. Much to the disappointment of the court, Matilda inclined to virtue, but the connection with Wilton and Muriel strengthens the association of Matilda with a prototype of the courtly lady who was to become such a significant cultural entity in the following centuries.

Her contemporaries may have considered her a failure in the glamour stakes, but Matilda's intellectual legacy is satisfactorily enduring. One of her passions was architecture, and if her taste in clothes was conservatively 'English', the buildings she loved were uncompromisingly Norman in their awe-inspiring grandeur of scale. She has links with the abbey at Waltham, rebuilt by architects whose style was influenced by the designers of Durham Cathedral, Abingdon Abbey, Selby Abbey, Merton Priory and the church at St Albans, all either Norman foundations or rebuilt in the Norman style after the Conquest. Neither her Augustinian foundation of Holy Trinity Aldgate, of which the Queen's confessor, Norman, was the first prior, nor her leper hospital survive, but contemporary accounts note their fashionable style and size. While 'it is unquestionably true that

Matilda shared the Norman passion for erecting large buildings',[17] she also took an interest in projects of a more domestic scale, building the first arched bridge in England, over the River Lea at Stratford-le-Bow, where previously there had been only a dangerous ford. The bridge was endowed with land and a mill to keep it in repair and was still in use in the nineteenth century. At Queenhithe, Matilda added a bathhouse with piped-in water, along with a set of public lavatories – appealingly pragmatic, if not exactly the sort of undertaking normally associated with courtly ladies.

More conventionally, Matilda was a keen patron of music and literature, the former being among her main enthusiasms, according to William of Malmesbury. The musician William LeHarpur was given tax relief on lands granted to him by the King, and the Norman minstrel Rahere, who had performed for William Rufus, continued to work under Henry. Henry himself has preserved an historical reputation for learning, his nickname, Beauclerc, attesting to his literacy, but 'it has long been recognised that the epithet ... is something of an exaggeration, and that the credit for court sponsored literary and artistic activity in the first quarter of the twelfth century belongs to Henry's wives rather than the King himself'.[18]

The context of Matilda's own literary interests is that of the 'Twelfth-century renaissance', 'the first age since classical antiquity when the intellectual emerges as a driving force'.[19] As with the later, best-known Renaissance, there is a good deal of dispute about when this new intellectual current began to flow, of what exactly it consisted and the degree to which contemporaries were aware that they were part of it, but essentially, as the cohesive concept of 'Christendom' emerged after the Gregorian reforms, both Church scholars and the secular elite had a 'lively awareness of doing something new, of being new men'.[20] The authority of the Church fathers was being challenged by a modern sensibility to the possibilities of analysing rationally the natural world and man's place in it as the link between the created universe and the divine power. Christian humanism was beginning to take form. This exciting intellectual energy manifested itself in systematised administrative and canon law, a rapidly expanding interest in books and libraries, developments in vernacular literature such as the courtly romance, a sense of historical writing as a discrete genre (this particularly strongly in the new Anglo-Norman kingdom with the works of Malmesbury, Orderic Vitalis and Geoffrey of Monmouth), the development of the famous 'schools' at Laon, Chartres and Paris and increasing opportunities for exposure to Jewish, Arabic and Greek science after the reconquest of Toledo from the Moors in 1085.

Man's relationship with Christ was also reconfigured, with the Saviour considered for his human as well as divine qualities, and hence a greater emphasis was placed on His suffering and sacrifice. Such radical ideas often led to accusations of heresy, but the figure of Christ as Redeemer contributed to the development of the cult of Marianism, which became a particularly dominant motif in the representation and understanding of English queenship. Anselm was one of the innovative churchmen who popularised such thinking and Matilda was also close to his pupil, Gundulph of Rochester. Gundulph revered Mary Magdalene and promoted Marianism, celebrating the Feast of the Immaculate Conception before it was universally recognised. The celebration of the women in Christ's life highlighted a gentler, more compassionate Christianity, but Marianism also elevated the simple village girl of the New Testament to a Queen of Heaven, frequently depicted in the glorious raiments of her earthly counterparts.

While patronage and religion were closely linked, the world of international scholarship was closed to women. Latin was the official language of scholarship as well as of government and the Church, and though Matilda and her sister-in-law Adela of Blois did have some knowledge of Latin, the everyday language of the ruling class was French. So the area in which noblewomen were best able to participate in the new sensibility was that of vernacular culture. Matilda commissioned a French translation of a Latin poem, 'The Voyage of St Brendan', which has been described as a 'Celtic version of the classical odyssey poem'[21] and is the earliest surviving example of literary Anglo-Norman. 'St Brendan' was performed in a cycle of three episodes at the Easter court of 1107–8. Matilda's desire to celebrate the memory of her mother's achievements is reflected in the eight poems written for the Queen which mention Margaret, demonstrating that contemporary writers were alert to Matilda's interests and how best to attract her attention. Matilda was the first patron of Philippe de Thaon, who went on to work for her successors Adeliza of Louvain and Eleanor of Aquitaine, but her most famous literary association, in addition to the *Life of St Margaret*, is with William of Malmesbury, who wrote *The Deeds of the Kings of England* at her request.

Malmesbury, however, leaves a curiously unflattering depiction of the cultural ambitions of his patroness, suggesting that her desire for intellectual distinction – and the recognition that embracing new artistic developments would add to her reputation, and thus that of England – resulted in harsh management of her estates:

Her generosity becoming universally known, crowds of scholars, equally famed for verse and singing, came over, and happy was he who could soothe the Queen's ears with his song. Nor on these only did she lavish money, but on all sorts of men, especially foreigners, that through their presents they might proclaim her dignity abroad ... Thus it was justly observed that the Queen wanted to reward as many foreigners as possible, while others were kept in suspense, sometimes with effectual but more often with empty promises. So it arose that she fell into the error of prodigal givers; bringing many claims to her tenantry, exposing them to injuries and taking away their property, but since she became known as a liberal benefactress, she scarcely regarded their outrage.[22]

This is a long way from the benign image of 'Good Queen Maud' which pertained after Matilda's death. Matilda was reprimanded by Anselm for her punitive taxation of her lands, which did not exempt Church properties, and her promotion of 'foreigners' also attracted criticism among Norman churchmen. Yet promotion of the arts was a means of remaining directly involved in the liturgy, placing as it did the tangible evidence of a patron's generosity within the Church itself. Matilda's presentation of a pair of bells to Chartres, or the ornate candlesticks, 'trees of brass fashioned with wondrous skill, glittering with jewels as much as with candlelight'[23] she gave to Le Mans, engaged her in a triple cycle of patronage between the artisans she encouraged, whose productions were the marks of her favour, the churchmen who sought that favour and the capacity of the latter to spiritualise the physical objects bestowed on them in acknowledgement of the Queen's regard. Writing to Adela of Blois, Bishop Baudri of Dol requested an elegant cope (complete with fringe), as his return for publicising her literary discernment. In a letter to Matilda, Hildebart of Lavardin, bishop of Le Mans, declared that in offering Christ those jewelled candlesticks she was associating herself with the women who witnessed the crucifixion and brought precious spices to His tomb.

Such opportunities for patronage were especially attractive to women at a time when overt political action was a receding possibility. If the ascendance of the formalised, Latinised and thus masculinised administrative kingship for which the reign of Henry I is noted was in part responsible for this diminution in political potential for noblewomen in general, it served to emphasise the significance of a particular woman, the Queen, in her traditional role as intercessor. As new structures of government made direct, informal approaches to the King more difficult, the intimacy of his relationship with his wife made her a target for those who wished their petitions to be heard. Once again, Matilda was able to link this form of patronage with her support for the Church, as with Henry's charter for Westminster, which states that his donation is made 'at the prayer of Queen Matilda', or in the case of the nuns at Malling, who received the right to a weekly market 'for the love of and at the request of my wife Queen Matilda'.

Henry may have loved his wife, but he was certainly not faithful to her. He was a walking baby boom, producing over two dozen extramarital children. Matilda appears to have accepted this with equanimity, 'enduring with complacency, when the King was elsewhere employed', as Malmesbury discreetly put it, and it may have been that it suited her pious leanings to stop having sexual relations with her husband after she had done her duty of providing him with children – Malmesbury adds that she 'ceased either to have offspring or desire them'. After Henry's visit to Normandy in 1104, Matilda spent much of her time at Westminster, where eight of her twenty-two charters whose place of issue is identifiable were drawn up. Henry apparently conducted his goings-on at Wooodstock, a town there is no evidence she ever visited, which suggests a certain care for her dignity. It seems that they achieved an arrangement that was satisfactory to them both, and if Henry was sexually estranged from his wife, he continued to involve her in government. Nor did her 'retirement' at Westminster mean that Matilda had ceased to be publicly active. The lively, scholarly atmosphere of her London court has been noted, and when Henry departed once more for Normandy in 1106, he left the realm under her regency. Matilda herself crossed to Normandy that year, issuing a charter at Lillebonne and witnessing another at Rouen, and she may have enjoyed a private concert by Adelard of Bath, who played the cithera for her.

In 1109, Matilda participated in the Whitsun court described by Henry of Huntingdon as the most magnificent of the reign, where the contracts for the marriage of Henry and Matilda's daughter were drawn up. In 1110, eight-year-old Princess Matilda left for Germany, to be educated at the court of her betrothed, Henry V of Germany and Holy Roman Emperor. It was a momentous marriage, validating the importance of England's new ruling dynasty and giving young Matilda the title of Empress by which she was known for much of her life. A letter to Queen Matilda from the Emperor attests to how her influence with her husband ensured the matter went smoothly: 'We have from experience come to know of your zeal in all those things that we ask from your lord.'

Henry was abroad again the next year, when Matilda presided at the exchequer court and was also present at St Peter's, Gloucester to witness a gift of lands to the house. In 1114 the Queen took her son William to visit the new foundation of Merton Priory. There is very little evidence of Matilda's day-to-day involvement with her children, though it is possible that young Matilda was raised in her mother's household, but the visit to Merton gives a sense of Matilda trying to inculcate piety in her son with the same sweetness and understanding of children's nature that her own mother had displayed. She hoped that the happy memory of the visit, of playing with her at Merton, would encourage William to regard the house favourably when he became king. Matilda also succeeded in persuading Henry to agree to the marriage of her brother David to the King's ward, Matilda of Senlis. David became King of Scotland in 1124 and was to play an important role in the life of his niece the Empress, but at the time his prospects of succeeding to the crown seemed slight, and the marriage meant he could take the title of Earl of Huntingdon in right of his wife. The wedding was celebrated before Christmas 1113, while the King was in England. Matilda was regent again in 1114–15 and 1116–18. The latter period shows her involving her son William in her activities, obviously in preparation for his own succession. Together they issued three writs on the business of a ship belonging to the abbot of St Augustine's, Canterbury.

Matilda may have fallen ill in 1114, as her correspondent the bishop of Le Mans wrote to her asking after her condition and enclosing a prayer to St John the Evangelist for her recovery. She did recover, as her activities in the following four years demonstrate, but her family had a sad reputation for dying young. Matilda's last act as regent of England was made in Oxford, for the protection of a chapter of hermit monks, and on 1 May 1118 she died at Westminster. The Church had questioned her right to marry, and now there was a quarrel over the right to bury her. The monks of Trinity Aldgate claimed it, and when Henry returned from Normandy they lodged a complaint, via the canons of St Paul's, against the monks of Westminster, who had taken the body. Henry confirmed all Matilda's donations to Trinity and compensated the order with a gift of relics from the Byzantine emperor, and Matilda was laid to rest at Westminster. The King gave money to maintain a perpetual light by her tomb, which was still being paid in the reign of Matilda's great-great grandson Henry III, while her brother David organised an annual memorial Mass.

Despite the controversy over her marriage and the criticism she had attracted in the management of her lands, Matilda died a beloved queen. Soon after her death reports of miraculous signs occurring at her tomb began to circulate, and a cult to her quickly grew up at Westminster. Over the next decade her grave attracted as many papal indulgences for pilgrims to Westminster on St Peter's Day as did that of Edward the Confessor. Her official epitaph was inscribed on her tomb during the reign of her grandson Henry II, but the *Hyde* chronicler summed up the popular mood: 'From the time England first became subject to kings, out of all the queens none was found to be comparable to her, and none will be found in time to come, whose memory will be praised and name will be blessed throughout the ages.'[24]

CHAPTER 3

ADELIZA OF LOUVAIN

'The Fair Maid of Brabant'

Matilda of Scotland did not live to experience the disaster of the *White Ship* in 1120, a tragedy for the Norman dynasty which had massive repercussions not only on the life of her daughter Matilda but on the future of England. After his mother's death, William continued to act as regent in England for a year before joining his father in Normandy for his marriage to yet another Matilda, this one the daughter of Fulk of Anjou. King Henry had been threatened in the duchy since 1111 by an alliance between the French, Angevins and Flemings, but William's marriage and Henry's significant defeat of Louis VI of France at Bremule in 1119 secured his rule for the time being, and the following year William paid homage to Louis as his father's nominal overlord for Normandy. The royal party sailed for England in November, but the ship in which William was a passenger – along with his illegitimate half-brother Richard, half-sister Matilda, Countess of Perche, and many of the heirs to the great estates of England and Normandy – was wrecked on a rock at the harbour of Barfleur. According to Orderic Vitalis, the captain, Thomas Fitzstephen, struggled to the surface, but when he heard that the heir to the throne had drowned he allowed the waves to claim him rather than face the King. None of the young nobles in William's party was saved – indeed, the only survivor was a butcher from Rouen. Even for a man with as many children as Henry, the loss of three at once was personally shattering; the implications for the succession, moreover, were disastrous.

Henry's second marriage, to Adeliza of Louvain, has conventionally been seen as a response to the urgent need for a legitimate heir in the aftermath of the shipwreck, but negotiations for his new wife may have begun as early as 1119. Adeliza's father Godfrey 'The Great', landgrave of Brabant, Count of Louvain and Duke of Lower Lorraine, was a vassal of Henry's son-in-law, the Holy Roman Emperor, and if the supposition that Henry met his daughter Matilda on the Continent in 1119[1] is correct, she may have been involved in arranging the match, which accords with the marriage contract having been agreed in April 1120, before the loss of the *White Ship*. Godfrey's second wife, Clemence, whom he married after the death of Adeliza's mother, Ida of Chiny, was the mother of the Flemish Count Baldwin VII, who had fought for the French as part of the anti-Norman alliance in 1118. When Baldwin died, Clemence and Godfrey, whose lands bordered with Flanders, strongly opposed the succession to the state of his cousin Charles. Henry I had come to terms with Charles after Bremule but, as part of a policy of containment, a union with the daughter of Charles's enemy was an intelligent precaution.

Henry announced the marriage in council on 6 January 1121, and sent a party to Dover to meet Adeliza, who had already embarked for England. The wedding took place at Windsor on 29 January, barely two months after William's death. Given the time needed for Adeliza's preparations and the journey itself, it is clear that Henry intended to marry her even before he lost his son. William's new bride, Matilda of Anjou, remained in England for some months after the disaster, presumably waiting to see if she was pregnant, but was retrieved by her father the same year. While she took the veil at Fontevrault, Henry kept her dower, much to Fulk's indignation.

Eighteen-year-old Adeliza, known as the 'Fair Maid of Brabant', was reportedly quite beautiful. Considering her fifty-three-year-old bridegroom's reputation as a womaniser, lust, as well as politics, and of course the distinction of her descent from Charlemagne, may have played a part in his choice. She was crowned on 30 January 1121, but from the beginning it was plain that Henry wanted her queenship to follow a very different model from that of Matilda of Scotland. Adeliza has often been viewed as a rather passive, ineffectual queen, since there is little evidence of her undertaking independent projects or embracing any political role, but this was less to do with her personal capacities, whatever they may have been, than with the fact that, as far as Henry was concerned, her purpose was to bear him sons. To this end, he kept his wife with him on his travels, leaving her scant opportunity to participate in government.

Many of Adeliza's charters were witnessed as a co-signatory to the King, including her first, a grant to the monks of Tiron in September 1121. As we have seen, witnessing was in itself a politically charged act, as it emphasised the queen's elevated status not only in relation to other women (who appear rarely as co-signatories in royal charters) but also to men, as the queen's name would come after the king's and before those of the other witnesses. Queenly witnessing was thus an expression of power rooted in office. Adeliza's frequent appearances as a witness to Henry's charters also enable us to track her movements with her husband. After their marriage they went to Winchester, then to Westminster, for a crown-wearing ceremony at the Whitsuntide court. Adeliza surfaces again in a grant to Merton Priory in December, but witnesses no more documents with Henry until the confirmation of a grant to St Peter Exeter at Easter 1123, while the court was at Winchester. Henry travelled energetically in England throughout 1122. He was at Northampton at Easter, then Hertford, Waltham, Oxford, a two-day pause at Windsor, Westminster for Whit Sunday. After a visit to Kent, it was back to Westminster, then north to York, Durham and Carlisle, York again for the Feast of St Nicholas, Nottingham and Dunstable for Christmas. He kept up this pace for another six months before he and Adeliza sailed from Portsmouth for Normandy in June 1123. In the light of such a timetable, the Queen's lack of independent charter activity becomes more understandable. It was not until 1126 that she issued her first as principal signatory, a grant to the canons of Holy Trinity at Christchurch London, which was drawn up while she was in residence at Woodstock.

The court in Adeliza's time was structured along the lines Henry had been establishing for the first twenty years of his reign, which stood in a marked contrast to the roistering, undisciplined culture that had prevailed under William Rufus. The new, more sober tone had led to Henry and Matilda of Scotland being mocked for their stuffiness, but since, according to Eadmer, William Rufus's courtiers had rampaged about the countryside boozing stolen wine, destroying crops and making improper advances to respectable women, the people, at least, appreciated Henry's reforms. He prohibited the requisitioning of goods, set fixed prices for local purveyance and stipulated allowances for the members of his household, including forty domestic staff. As well as her constant proximity to the King, another obstacle to any meaningful political activity on Adeliza's part may have been the regulated system of 'administrative kingship' that was one of the main achievements of Henry's rule. This system, outlined in the Constitution Domus Regis, which lays down the hierarchy of offices, from chancellor through to stewards, butlers, chamberlain and constables, functioned on both sides of the Channel, with a limited entourage of officials accompanying the King and a larger group remaining permanently in either England or Normandy. In England the most important of these officials was Roger, bishop of Salisbury, who acted as regent when the King was in Normandy. As well as vice-regency, Henry introduced a body of travelling agents, inaugurated the exchequer (although in this period it was essentially an accounting procedure rather than a separate office), and insisted on more thorough record-keeping, all of which contributed to the stabilisation of government as England adjusted to the new patterns of landholding imposed by the Norman Conquest. As regent and collaborator with the king's officers, Matilda of Scotland had played an important role in the implementation of Henry's reforms, but their very efficiency left less room for Adeliza.

Cultural patronage, as Bishop Baudri had reminded the Conqueror's daughter, was one sphere in which a woman might hope to outdo her husband or father, and which could compensate for diminishing influence in the political realm. As has been noted, women were especially influential in the development of vernacular literature (indeed, the production of 'Old French' works in France is minimal during the period in comparison with the blossoming of vernacular writing in the Anglo-Norman realm). Here, at least, Adeliza did make her mark. The rededication of 'The Voyage of St Brendan' to her after Matilda's death shows that she was ready to participate in this tradition; she is recognised, too, in the mention of 'the Queen of Louvain' in Gaimar's *Estoire des Engleis*, commissioned by Constance FitzGilbert, a Lincolnshire noblewoman. Adeliza herself commissioned an account of Henry's reign from the poet David (now lost), which was set to music, as well as receiving the dedication of Philippe de Thaon's 'Bestiary', the oldest surviving French example of the genre. Adeliza's literary interests continued into her widowhood, during which she patronised the poet Serbo of Wilton. Her facility in French evinces a certain level of education, as, given her birthplace, it was unlikely to have been her first language. It is not known, though, whether, like Matilda, she spoke English. She might have availed herself of one of the new dictionaries, such as that attributed to Alexander, archdeacon of Salisbury, with its Anglo-Norman glossary of Old English words. Bi- and trilingual texts were also appearing, of which the most famous example is the Eadwine Psalter, produced at Canterbury in the mid-twelfth century.

Another novelty associated with Adeliza is the payment of 'queen's gold', which was to form an important part of the income of queens consort in the coming centuries. Queens-gold was a tax of an extra 10 per cent on any fine to the crown over the value of ten marks, as well as on tax paid by Jews. One origin of the custom is the dispute for primacy between the sees of York and Canterbury. Hugh the Chanter records that the bishop of Durham, Ralph Flambard, offered 1,000 marks of silver to Henry I and a hundred to Matilda of Scotland to favour the candidacy of

York. Flambard, who had been treasurer to William Rufus, was apparently familiar with the 10 per cent balance of such payments. It has been claimed that 'it is almost certain that Eleanor [of Aquitaine] was the first English queen granted the right to claim queens-gold',[2] and the practice was standardised during Eleanor's queenship, but Adeliza is the first example of a queen receiving a proportion of a licence fine. She was given twenty silver marks from forty-five paid to Henry I by Lucy, Countess of Chester. (With a gold-silver ratio of 1:9, this represents a larger proportion [approximately two-fifths] of the total than was ratified under Henry II as one gold mark to the queen for every hundred silver marks received by the king.)

Henry was also generous to Adeliza in assisting her to make the best of her dower lands. As well as lands which had been part of Matilda's holdings, such as Waltham and the Queenhithe revenues, Adeliza had estates in Essex, Hertfordshire, Bedfordshire, Middlesex, Gloucestershire and Devon, on which Henry granted her exemption from land tax for demesne (untenanted) holdings in the 1130 Pipe Roll. He also made her a gift of a portion of the royal estate at Berkeley, and the entire county of Shropshire, for which she was not obliged to return accounts at the biannual royal exchequer.

Even though Adeliza was well provided for financially, it could not compensate for the fact that her marriage failed in its primary objective. She and Henry had no children. The reason is uncertain (it was not for the want of trying), as neither of them was infertile. A letter to the Queen from Hildebert of Lavardin, archbishop of Tours, suggests that Adeliza had expressed her unhappiness to him. 'If it has not been granted to you from Heaven that you should bear a child to the King of the English,' wrote the archbishop consolingly, 'in these [the poor] you will bring forth for the King of the Angels, with no damage to your modesty. Perhaps the Lord has closed up your womb, so that you might adopt immortal offspring ... it is more blessed to be fertile in the spirit than the flesh.'[3] Thus Hildebert encourages Adeliza to identify herself with the face of pious queenship, hinting that her lack of children might be turned into a form of holy chastity, such as that practised by her predecessor Matilda after she 'ceased to desire offspring'. This may have been small comfort. Adeliza made no significant religious foundation of her own, though she was a witness to Henry's 1125 charter for the foundation of Reading Abbey and also a patron of Waltham, Winchester Cathedral, Osney, Eynsham, St Sauveur in the Cotentin and the orders of the Templars and Cistercians. In later life she assisted in the foundation of the small priory of Pynham on the causeway at Arundel and of a leprosarium at Wilton, where she lived for a time in her first widowhood.

Adeliza was in Normandy with Henry until September 1126. On their return to England, they were accompanied by Henry's newly widowed daughter, Matilda the Empress, his only surviving legitimate child. Politically, the two women had been connected even before Adeliza's marriage, as Matilda's husband, Henry V, had assisted her father in the recovery of his duchy of Lorraine, and Adeliza had attended the Imperial court as a young woman (the Empress was a year or so older than her stepmother). During the Christmas court at Windsor, which was attended by all the leading magnates as well as by David of Scotland, Matilda's uncle, the Empress lived in Adeliza's household, where she remained until she departed for her second wedding in May the following year. Henry was making plans for the succession, and though this was clearly necessary, it was a humiliating public declaration of Adeliza's failure.

Henry left for Normandy in 1127. Adeliza was with him there in 1129, returning in July and keeping Christmas at Winchester before sailing back across the Channel in the early autumn of 1130. She witnessed her last grant with the King at Rouen before July 1131. They were in England again in August, again with the Empress, who had already quarrelled with her new husband, Geoffrey of Anjou, and Matilda stayed with the Queen until the disagreement was patched up. She was reunited with Geoffrey in September. Adeliza may be presumed to have remained with the King during his English peregrinations until his return to Normandy in August 1133, but she is not mentioned as a charter witness between this point and Henry's death in 1135, nor as being present at his deathbed, which was attended by his illegitimate son Robert of Gloucester and the bishop of Rouen. The nineteenth-century biographer Agnes Strickland claims Henry was bitter and cruelly ill-tempered about Adeliza's infertility, but the tax grant of 1130 and the fact that Adeliza was by his side until 1131 suggests that their relationship was civil, even hopeful, at least up to that point, and there is no evidence, other than her absence from the records, that it deteriorated afterwards. Henry's prolongation of his stay in Normandy is attributed by Henry of Huntingdon to the continuing quarrels between the Empress Matilda and her husband. There were, apparently, at least three occasions when he wished to leave for his kingdom due to concerns about rebellions in Wales.

On 1 December, Henry died at Lyons-la-Forêt, of a seizure supposedly brought on by a surfeit of lampreys, his body 'much weakened by strenuous labours and family anxieties'.[4] If there is any hint of reproach towards

Adeliza, it can only be these 'anxieties', which centred on the uncertain succession. And if Henry was eager to return to England there is nothing to indicate that it was not in part to rejoin his wife.

Henry's body was interred at Reading, the abbey he had founded in 1125 in a conscious celebration of his dynasty 'for the salvation of my soul and that of King William my father and King William my brother and William my son and Queen Matilda my mother and Queen Matilda my wife'. There was no place for Adeliza in this vaunting of Norman blood. After a year of mourning, some of which she spent at the convent of Wilton, Adeliza granted the monks of Reading the manor of Aston in Hertfordshire, an annual payment of one hundred shillings and lands 'to provide for the convent and other religious persons coming to the Abbey on the occasion of the anniversary of my lord King Henry'. Perhaps in imitation of Henry's tribute to Matilda of Scotland, she also ordered a perpetual light to be maintained at his tomb.

Adeliza, too, chose to be buried at Reading, but if she was keen to maintain her royal associations in the next life, she was not yet ready to spend the rest of her earthly existence as a mourning queen dowager, and in 1138, she married for love. Her romance with William d'Aubigne was played out against the dramatic backdrop of the seizure (or usurpation, depending on one's party) of the crown by Henry I's nephew, Stephen of Blois. D'Aubigné's father had been butler to Henry I – this was a court office rather than a domestic post and hence not such a disparagement as it might appear – and William himself held the lordship of Buckenham in Norfolk. He was from the first a loyal adherent of King Stephen, who granted him the earldom of Lincoln just after his marriage to Adeliza. William built the aptly named Castle Rising in newly fashionable stone, though during his marriage to Adeliza they lived mainly at her dower castle of Arundel on the Norfolk coast, where she had installed her half-brother Joscelin as castellan in 1136 (she also assisted him in making a good marriage, to the northern heiress Agnes de Percy). William and Adeliza had at least seven children (Adeliza is the ancestress of two other queens, Anne Boleyn and Catherine Howard) and together they founded two Augustinian houses.

Some years before her death, Adeliza decided to leave her husband, with his consent, and devote herself to prayer. She spent five years in the Benedictine abbey of Afflighem, of which her Louvain family had been patrons since 1085. Upon her death there, however, she requested that she be buried next to Henry at Reading.

Despite the success of her second marriage, it was as a queen that

Adeliza chose to identify herself in death. Given the civil war through which she lived, and in which her second husband played a significant role, it would have been surprising if she had not reflected on the consequences of her barren royal union. That she achieved a degree of contentment, and left her mark on the literary and pious tradition of Anglo-Norman queenship, demonstrates that while though she obviously suffered as a consequence of her failure to provide Henry with an heir, there was more to Adeliza than that failure. Her legacy is less regal than that of Matilda of Scotland, but it is royal nonetheless.

CHAPTER 4

MATILDA OF BOULOGNE

'Ennobled by her virtues as by her titles'

The queenship of Matilda of Boulogne has been largely overshadowed by the career of her more celebrated cousin, the Empress Matilda. The story of the Empress has made her a champion to many modern writers: hers is a dramatic tale of a woman bravely fighting for her rights after her throne was usurped by Stephen, Count of Mortain. Yet the two Matildas had more in common than their name. They were both descended through their mothers from the royal Anglo-Saxon line, both heiresses in their own right, both married to power-hungry men and both determined to defend the patrimony of their sons. Events gave the victory to the Empress's cause, but it is arguable that Matilda of Boulogne was the greater queen. Interpreted in the light of representations of ideal feminine behaviour, a comparison of their activities emphasises the importance of conduct for royal women, whose power to command was tempered by the manner in which they elected to present their deeds. Matilda of Boulogne thought and fought like a man, but she never made the mistake of acting like one, in contrast to the Empress, whose demanding, dictatorial behaviour cost her her chance of the throne.

Matilda of Boulogne was selected by Henry to be the bride of his nephew Stephen as part of his dynastic policy following the disaster of the *White Ship*. Stephen was born around 1096, the third child of Adela, daughter of William I and Matilda of Flanders, and her husband Stephen, Count of Blois, whose lands lay between the troubled borders of France, Normandy and Anjou. Stephen's elder brothers were provided with lands and lordships, and when their father died on crusade in 1102, it made sense for Countess Adela to look to her brother's court to secure her third boy's fortune. Stephen became Count of Mortain after Henry's success at the battle of Tinchebrai in 1106, and the King continued to grant him large endowments in England and Normandy over the next decade, making him one of the most significant landholders in the realm.

When Henry's heir William was drowned in 1120, Stephen's status was heightened. If the King's new marriage to Adeliza of Louvain produced no heirs, and his daughter Matilda and her husband, the Emperor Henry, remained childless, then Stephen and his brothers would have a strong claim to the English crown. Five years later, when neither Adeliza nor Empress Matilda had provided a child, Henry came to an agreement with Matilda's father, Eustace of Boulogne. Eustace, Henry's vassal for the lands he held in England, was also his brother-in-law: Mary, the Countess of Boulogne, was the younger sister of Matilda of Scotland. Eustace was a pious man, drawn to the spiritual life, and he wished to retire from the world and spend the rest of his days as a monk at Cluny. Since he had no son (the *Gesta Stephani* meanly describes the Countess of Boulogne as 'barren', even though she was a mother), Eustace consented to invest Stephen with his English lands and his county of Boulogne. After the wedding, Count Eustace said a private goodbye to his daughter at Romilly, took his vows and disappeared into the cloister. The marriage took place early in 1125 – the lack of an exact date is a tantalising omission, given how closely it bound the lives and ambitions of the two Matildas.

Henry I had numerous reasons for choosing Matilda for his favourite nephew. Stephen's elder brother Thibault had just succeeded to the lands of Champagne, adding them to his county of Blois, which made him an increasingly significant player in Continental politics, and a man Henry needed to cultivate in order to keep the northern border of Normandy secure. The King may also have wished to compensate Stephen for the loss of the Montgomery holdings in Normandy, originally confiscated from the family and given to Stephen, but which he had been obliged to return during a period of military unrest. The Boulogne inheritance was a rich one, incorporating the county of Lens as well as the city itself, a staging post on the trade routes that led to Paris.

However, neither of these reasons is as powerful as that of the future of the crown, and this is where the date of the marriage becomes so significant. On 23 May, the Emperor Henry died at Utrecht, leaving his widow, the Empress Matilda, in a position to take up her claim as her father's direct heir. Matilda of Boulogne was, like her cousin, descended through their grandmother, Margaret of Scotland, from the ancient kings of England. She had a further dose of royal blood through her father Eustace, also a descendant of Aethelred II. Her marriage with Stephen would therefore associate another potential claimant to the crown with Henry's house, and in this respect the marriage may be seen as part of 'the dynastic chess game designed to make the Empress her father's successor'.[1] However, as the marriage took place *before* Emperor Henry's death, it is highly possible that Matilda's royal connections were being deployed to strengthen Stephen's claim.[2] The latter argument gives some insight not only into Stephen's perception of his uncle's intentions, which wavered confusingly at the end of the King's life, but also into Matilda's. In arranging her marriage early in 1125, Henry, on some level, gave her to understand that he had designated her the next queen of England. So, while the perseverance shown by Matilda of Boulogne in the defence of her husband's rights was no more than would have been expected of a loyal wife, her tenacity and courage might also have been motivated by the sense that she was fighting for her own position as a rightfully anointed queen.

How, though, could Matilda of Boulogne have believed this when the claim of the Empress Matilda seemed so clear-cut? In 1127, *The Anglo-Saxon Chronicle* describes Henry's Christmas court at Windsor, where 'He caused archbishops and bishops and abbots and earls and all the thegns that were there to swear to give England and Normandy after his death into the hand of his daughter.' King David of Scotland swore first, followed, after an undignified scuffle over precedence, by Stephen, then the King's illegitimate son Robert, Earl of Gloucester. It would be wrong, however, to attribute Henry's insistence that his magnates swear fealty to Matilda to a desire to circumvent Stephen's claim. In 1127, the King's anxiety was focused on William Clito, the son of his disgraced and dispossessed brother, Robert Curthose, who had been his prisoner since Tinchebrai. Clito's claim was strong, and arguably, on the grounds of his sex, weightier than the Empress Matilda's. He had the support of many Norman barons and, worse, for Henry, that of Louis VI of France. In March 1127 Clito, with Louis's support, succeeded to the title of Count of Flanders, to which he had some rights through his grandmother Matilda of Flanders. With this move, the French King hoped to destroy the traditional alliance between England and Flanders, and to worry Henry's ever-harassed Norman borders. The threat from Clito was short-lived. After he attacked Boulogne that summer, Henry and Stephen bullied and bribed the Flemings to rebel, and Clito was caught up in a war with another candidate for the Flanders title, Thierry of Alsace, in which he conveniently died the following July.

By then, though, Henry had attempted to shore up his daughter's power by marrying her to Geoffrey of Anjou. The Empress herself appears to have objected to this match with a boy ten years her junior, and felt it as a disparagement, since Geoffrey barely had even a comital title, but in 1127, with Clito and Louis plotting against him, Henry had deemed an alliance with Anjou a necessity. Negotiations were rushed through, and the wedding took place at Le Mans in June. The marriage secured Henry's southern Norman border against incursions from the French, but it made his nomination of his daughter more controversial, as it was unclear what role Geoffrey was intended to play when his wife inherited the crown. The Durham chronicler, the *Le Mans* Chronicle and Henry of Huntingdon suggest there was some understanding that Geoffrey would share a joint rule, a possibility of which William of Malmesbury was also aware. Huntingdon and Malmesbury claim that a further oath-swearing took place in 1131. Nevertheless the unpopularity of the marriage among the English magnates was used by some as a way of levering themselves out of their promise.

Matilda's concept of her own queenship, then, should not be measured against a simple model in which the rightful heiress was dispossessed of her claim. In the rapidly changing political climate of Henry's last decade the King's motivations and contingencies were constantly shifting, and the position of the Empress remained less a legal reality than a matter of opinion, even at her father's deathbed.

When Henry I of England died at Lyons-la-Forêt on 1 December 1135, the validity of the oaths was questioned by pro-Stephen chroniclers, while even pro-Empress commentators conceded that the King had to some extent changed his mind as he was dying. William of Malmesbury maintained that he nominated Matilda, but not Geoffrey – 'He assigned all his lands on both sides of the sea to his daughter in lawful and lasting succession' – adding that he had recently been angry with Geoffrey, which suggested that Henry had originally envisioned shared rule but had had doubts at the end. John of Salisbury quotes the leading magnate Hugh Bigod as declaring that the lords were absolved from their oath by the King; the *Gesta Stephani*, which is hostile to the Empress, went further, claiming that the oath had been extracted under duress and was therefore invalid, though, unlike Salisbury, the *Gesta*'s author did not record that Henry named Stephen. That no official announcement was made is shown by the account of Orderic Vitalis, who describes the anger and confusion of the Norman barons. They continued to argue about what to do for some weeks, having no idea which candidate they were supposed to support. From both pro-Empress and pro-Stephen writers, then, it is evident that there was some equivocation about the succession, indeed, enough to conclude it is 'beyond question that [Henry] chose to die without committing himself to any successor'.[3] So why did Henry, who had apparently been so keen to assure the Empress's succession, lose his resolve in his last hours? Did he perhaps feel that the Angevin marriage had been a precipitate error, now that fate had disposed of Clito? According to Malmesbury the bishop of Salisbury maintained he had sworn the original oath only on condition that Henry did not give his child in marriage to 'anyone outside the kingdom without consulting himself and the other chief men', and while the second oath-swearing of 1131 would technically have overridden such objections, the very need for it shows that Henry was aware of the sensitivity of the situation. It is quite possible that he was in pain, confused and afraid, and thus unable to make his wishes clear; on the other hand, it is just as likely that he had expressed those wishes privately during the week it took him to die.

Ultimately, what Stephen did mattered more than what Henry said. Henry himself had understood the necessity of speed in securing the crown, and his nephew followed his example. When the King died, Stephen and Matilda were in Boulogne and the Empress in her husband's lands in Anjou. Within four or five days, Stephen and a small band of supporters had arrived in London. Most of Henry's leading magnates remained in Normandy, attending Henry's corpse, a factor which eased Stephen's progress considerably, and on 22 December the new King was crowned at Westminster. It was a bloodless coup.

Matilda stayed in Boulogne with her family for the first months of 1136. She and Stephen had five children: Eustace, William, Baldwin, Matilda and Mary. If Stephen could succeed in holding the crown, their prospects, as well as her own, would be radically different. From Boulogne, she was in a position to keep a close eye on events in Normandy. In early December, Stephen's elder brother Count Thibault had been invited by the Norman lords to receive the dukedom from them, but as they met the news arrived from England that Stephen had already been acknowledged by the people of London as king. Speculatively, we might consider that Thibault's acceptance of this fraternal treachery (he was, after all, Countess Adela's elder child and therefore had a stronger claim than Stephen if the Empress was to be overlooked) points to Henry's having privately named Stephen before he died. Further, the invitation of the Norman magnates suggests that Stephen's usurpation was not a simple matter of his having swiped the crown from under the nose of a defenceless woman, but a decision enacted in an environment where, if the lords were clear on anything, it was that they did not wish a woman to govern them. That the Normans summoned Thibault so swiftly makes it clear they preferred a man.

The Empress, meanwhile, had also acted quickly to consolidate her power as far as she was able. She and Geoffrey were on the Norman borders in the first week of December, laying claim to the castles she had been given as dower, but she received no further support from the Norman lords, another confirmation that their wishes lay elsewhere. Matilda had achieved a little peninsula of power in the duchy, which would be crucial in years to come, but for the moment her attempts to prosecute her claim were contained within the southern marches.

Matilda of Boulogne's own coronation at Westminster at Easter 1136 was an important step in reinforcing her husband's status. She was the second English queen to descend directly from the Anglo-Saxon royal line after her aunt Matilda of Scotland and, since Stephen's claim was bolstered by his wife's heritage, her own connections, as Henry I had recognised, were significant in lending him legitimacy. The coronation, and the court held afterwards at Oxford, was Stephen's first major display of regal power, intended to impress his kingship on the people in a way his unavoidably rushed coronation could not do. Henry of Huntingdon recorded excitedly that 'never was there one to exceed it in numbers, in greatness, in gold, silver, gems, costume and in all manner of entertainments'. Among the guests was Henry of Scotland, Matilda's cousin through her uncle King David, who had paid homage in his father's name to Stephen at York, and who was now seated on the King's right, a mark of the speed with which the Scottish monarch had submitted to the new rule in England. Three archbishops, five earls and more than twenty-four barons attended the court, as did Matilda's eldest son Eustace, now the heir to the English throne.

All of Matilda's children were now royal, and almost immediately their future marriages became matters of state. Her two-year-old daughter Matilda was betrothed to the thirty-one-year-old Count Waleran of Meulan, the second-greatest landowner in Normandy and, along with his stepfather and cousin, one of the leaders of an important group of magnates. Little Matilda even went through some sort of marriage ceremony. But her parents' hopes of cementing Waleran's loyalty suffered a setback when Matilda and her brother Baldwin died in London the following year. The Queen chose to bury her babies at Holy Trinity Aldgate, a house to which she had formed a particular attachment since her marriage and which, as a foundation of Matilda of Scotland, also had a place in the emergent spiritual traditions of English queens. The tiny coffins were interred on either side of the high altar, and records from the priory describe the King and Queen grieving together over their double loss.

The royal couple sought solace in their faith, and piety seems to have been one of the cornerstones of their relationship. They shared an intellectual interest in developing variants of belief, from the simple, mystical spirituality of hermits and anchorites to the elaborate splendours of high Cluniac ritual. As queen, Matilda was able to both witness and participate in one of the most prolific periods of monastic expansion since the Conquest. During the twelfth century, over a hundred religious houses were founded for women where, in 1066, only nine had existed. The vigour of this renaissance was characterised by an unusual degree of co-operation between the sexes as men and women worked together the better to serve their God, a mood that was reflected in the pious collaborations of Matilda and Stephen.

The tensions between the worldly and spiritual elements of her new role were brought home to Matilda when she visited a holy hermit, Wulfric, as she travelled from Corfe Castle to Exeter the summer after her coronation. Wulfric was a favourite of King Stephen, who had visited him some years before and heard him prophesy that King Henry would die in Normandy and he, Stephen, would succeed him, but now Matilda found herself being scolded by the holy man for having taken too high-handed a stance in the case of a Somerset noblewoman who had attended her court at Corfe. Chastened, Matilda later chose to patronise her own, female hermit, Helmid the nun, who was provided with an acre of land to build a cell in the domains of the abbey of Faversham, Kent, founded by Stephen in the hope that it would become a family resting place, as Reading had been for Henry I.

Matilda's provision for Helmid shows that she was attentive to a religious movement that represented a revolution in human consciousness, a new concept of meditative, inward-looking spirituality which appears for the first time in texts such as the *Ancrene Riwle*, a guide for anchoresses produced at the beginning of the thirteenth century. Anchorites were voluntarily walled up to spend their lives in prayer for their communities, many of them remaining in tiny cells (Eve of Wilton's was just eight feet square) for as long as fifty years. Matilda's attraction to this extreme, isolated spirituality was shared by Stephen, and together they patronised the Savignac movement, inspired by the wandering saint Vitalis, who had established a community in the wild lands of Savigny in Stephen's county of Mortain. Matilda founded a Savignac house at Coggleshall in Essex, and Stephen endowed three, at Furness in Lancashire, Buckfast in Devon and Longvilliers, across the Channel in Montreuil.

Matilda and Stephen also continued their close family association with the Cluniac order, which had received Matilda's father and to which Stephen's mother, too, had retired before her death. Matilda's mother, Mary of Scotland, was buried in the Cluniac house at Bermondsey in 1115, and when Stephen came to endow Faversham, a colony of the faithful was sent from Bermondsey to inaugurate the community. Another strand of the reformed Benedictine order was the Cistercians, whose house at Clairmarais also enjoyed royal patronage. Matilda was also interested in the crusading traditions of her own and her husband's families, and she supported the order of the Templars, who protected and financed the crusaders. The first documented English grant to the Templars was made by Matilda's father, Eustace, and the Queen herself founded Cressing Temple in Essex in 1137 and Temple Cowley in Oxfordshire in 1139. The grand master of the order, Osto of Boulogne, witnessed two of Matilda's charters as well as the treaty which eventually ended the civil war. Providing for the crusades was an active form of piety that appealed to Matilda's 'dauntless and decisive nature ... accustomed to command. If she could not lead the knights of Christ against the enemies of the Church, she could at least provision them.'[4]

Religion was central to the lives of all aristocrats at the time, and daily attendance at Mass was a feature of the royal household, but Stephen and Matilda's mutual enthusiasm for exploring new spiritual movements suggests that their religious life was very much a shared one, gesturing towards their closeness as a couple. As well as their religious affinities, both families had a strong tradition of educating their women. Stephen's grandmother Matilda of Flanders had ensured that her children were well schooled, and Countess Adela, his mother, was a notable patron, praised by the poet Godfrey of Reims, who went as far as to suggest that God had arranged the battle of Hastings in order that she might become a princess. Adela corresponded with her husband when he was on crusade; she wrote, too, to Archbishop Anselm, from whom she requested prayers in manuscript, and Hugh de Fleury, who dedicated his *Historia Ecclesiastica* to her. She also demonstrated publicly that she was able to speak Latin. Adela combined intellectualism and spirituality with the capacity for government she had inherited from both her parents and, after the death of her husband, she was active in ruling Blois, Chartres and Meaux until her retirement. Matilda's mother, Mary of Scotland, had enjoyed the same excellent education at the convents of Wilton and Romsey as her sister and, probably at her instigation, Matilda of Boulogne was also educated in England. Her own daughter Mary eventually became abbess of Romsey, linking the women of Matilda's family over three generations with this centre of feminine piety and scholarship. Stephen, then, was accustomed to the company of cultivated women, and his consistent reliance on his wife's advice and diplomacy indicates both trust and a respect for her intelligence.

Other evidence of the intimacy between Stephen and Matilda is the fact that Stephen, unlike the spectacularly promiscuous Henry I, is known to have been faithful to his wife. He had taken a mistress, as was almost expected of young aristocrats, before his marriage, and had a child by her in 1110, but he showed himself uxorious even in his arrangements for sin. 'Damette', or 'Little Lady', as his mistress was referred to, was firmly paid off when Stephen married, but their son, Gervase, was educated and entered the Church, eventually becoming abbot of Westminster. The only whiff of scandal attaching to the liaison came when Gervase arranged for his mother, ostensibly a woman of modest means, to rent the abbey's manor at Chelsea at a cheap rate. When she took possession of the property, however, she was recorded as owning forty shillings and a valuable silk cloth, which suggests that Stephen had maintained her honourably for some years.

The strength of Stephen's marriage was perhaps one of his greatest assets as a king, and Matilda's active support became indispensable to him very early in his reign. In 1137, she accompanied him on a five-month military and diplomatic journey through Normandy, resulting in a three-year truce with Geoffrey of Anjou, who was still aggressively pushing his wife's cause. It was a busy period for Matilda: of the total of fifty-eight charter attestations she made as queen, fifteen fall into the two-year period from 1136 to 1138. Peace in Normandy was essential if Anglo-Norman society was to hold together. For magnates with interests in both countries, a division of their fealty, and their privileges, between two lords was unacceptable, and if the Angevins gained ground in the duchy, it would strengthen the Empress's case there. Stephen unwisely returned to England in November 1137 – and brought civil war with him.

In the summer of 1138, a series of rebellions broke out across England. The Empress Matilda had been sending envoys to potential pro-Angevins, and a number of lords now set themselves against the King. While Stephen occupied himself with risings in the Welsh marches, Matilda had her first experience of military activity as she took personal responsibility for an outbreak of unrest in Kent. Her Boulogne inheritance proved its worth in this conflict and in many more to come. Her father's territories had included the port of Wissant, a vital – and wealthy – centre for the Anglo-Flemish wool trade and a resource for channelling money and mercenaries to England to assist the King. Paid Flemish troops were a crucial royal weapon, and Matilda is credited with having had the foresight, in the wake of William Clito's death, to make peace with Thierry of Flanders in order to facilitate the provision of these Flemish soldiers. Generous grants to Thierry's foundation of Clairmarais may have sealed the truce. Thus, when Dover rebelled, Matilda was able to call out 'friends, kinsmen and dependents of Boulogne'.[5] Using troops from Boulogne and Flanders under the command of her illegitimate cousin Pharamus of Boulogne, she successfully besieged Dover Castle. (She was not, incidentally, the only active female military leader at the time: Ludlow Castle was being mobilised against Stephen by Lady FitzJohn, the widow of the castellan, though Stephen chivalrously left Ludlow out of his campaign that year.)

Meanwhile, the Scots, whose ruler, King David, had been persuaded by his niece the Empress to abandon his truce with Stephen, invaded in April, and by the end of July had pillaged their way to Yorkshire. In August, a royalist army defeated them at Northallerton, decimating the rebels, though King David himself escaped. From September, peace negotiations were held and after Christmas, Matilda was appointed to treat with David, who was, of course, her uncle as well as the Empress's. The papal legate Alberic of Ostia had originally approached Matilda to ask for her help in convincing a reluctant Stephen of the necessity for a truce, and in the end the Queen's 'shrewdness and eloquence triumphed'.[6] An agreement was reached at Durham on 9 April 1139 according to which Henry of Scotland was created Earl of Northumbria. Matilda and Henry travelled south together to ratify the treaty at Nottingham. Matilda had emphasised that the newly created county of Northumberland was not to be an extension of Scotland, but would remain part of England, retaining its English laws and customs. She thereby succeeded in creating a 'buffer zone' on the Scottish border by investing a Scottish prince with an interest in keeping an English peace.

Interestingly, this development may represent a new strategy for the governance of English comital lands which connects Matilda's Scots initiative with her predecessor, Adeliza of Louvain. The Scots initiative was the first in a series of attempts by Stephen to regulate the administration of the country by incorporating the magnates into a hierarchy of local government. Particular towns or castles would be held for the King by officials (some of whom were given earldoms for the purpose) who would co-operate with regional military government on behalf of the crown to defend against or anticipate attack. This system was not a consistent feature of Norman or French comital administration, but it had been employed in Adeliza's father's territories of Brussels and Louvain. When Adeliza had invited her brother Joscelin to England and invested him as castellan of Arundel, she was following the model of her father, the Duke of Brabant. Introduced by Adeliza in 1136 and imitated by Matilda and Stephen in 1139, this is 'the only directly proveable example of foreign innovation in administration in Stephen's reign', and its source is a queen.[7]

When Stephen seized power, he initially received the support of Henry I's illegitimate son, Earl Robert of Gloucester, but in May 1138, Robert withdrew his homage from Stephen and declared for his sister Empress Matilda. If Robert had held his peace since 1136 out of prudence, his decision now was a matter of ambition but also, apparently, one of conscience. The correspondence of Gilbert Foliot, the abbot of Gloucester, with Brian FitzCount, an ally of Robert's, shows that the earl sought biblical justification for his change of allegiance. According to Foliot, Robert was influenced by the passage in the Book of Numbers about inheritance by women: 'It seemed to some that by the weakness of their sex they should not be allowed to enter into the inheritance of their father. But the Lord, when asked, promulgated a law, that everything their father possessed should pass to the daughters.' Foliot's claim has been disputed, but Robert's change of heart made an immediate and crucial difference to the Empress's prospects. With Robert on her side, she was strong enough to make her attempt on the throne.

In September 1139, the Empress, her brother and a company of Angevin knights landed on the Sussex coast. Robert rode straight away for Bristol and the west country, circumventing the King's army on the way. The choice of Sussex for the launch of the Empress's campaign was dictated in part because the Queen Dowager, Adeliza of Louvain, had shown support for her cause. According to William of Malmesbury, Adeliza and the Empress had been in correspondence for some time, and Adeliza now defied her second husband, William d'Aubigne, a staunch Stephenite, to offer the Empress protection at their seat at Arundel Castle.

Diplomatically, this placed Stephen in an awkward position, as the Empress and Queen Adeliza had anticipated it would. Adeliza and Stephen, Orderic Vitalis corroborates, had up to this point enjoyed a cordial relationship. If Stephen were to attack Arundel, it would be a mark of grave disrespect to a lady who was highly thought of in the kingdom. And Stephen was always gallant where women and children were concerned. To the consternation of Orderic, who suggested he would have been better to act 'after the fashion of his ancestors', Stephen permitted a safe-conduct for the Empress and Earl Robert's wife, Mabel, to leave the castle. William I would have had no truck with such chivalrous gestures.

It is possible that Stephen, unlike Orderic, had a fuller understanding of what appeared to some contemporaries as a conspiracy between the two women. Adeliza hoped to make peace between the rival claimants. Stephen had visited her at Arundel in 1138, around the time of her marriage to d'Aubigne, and he had confirmed the grants to Reading she had made at the memorial Mass for King Henry in 1136. Adeliza was thus assured of his goodwill, and she chose to make her move towards nego-tiation when the Empress's cause was weak. Very few rebel outposts remained in England and the Empress had no significant champion in the country. By hosting her at Arundel, Adeliza could work alongside her husband to try to bring about a settlement, with herself and d'Aubigne as mediators. This was a risk, as Adeliza was gambling with her husband's standing in the event of displeasing the King. That Adeliza's conventional adoption of the queen's 'peace-weaving' role could be construed by contemporaries as disingenuous, if not treacherous, shows something of the poisonous, paranoid mood of the country at the time.

One of the Empress's main aims on her arrival in England was to disseminate the moral rightness of her cause. Just as commentators had been keen to chart the intellectual progress of Robert of Gloucester's decision to declare for his sister, now both royalist and Angevin parties concerned themselves not only with results on the battlefield but with their ethical justification. Might had to demonstrate that it was right. The more sophisticated atmosphere of the court of Henry I and Matilda of Scotland had inspired a more scrupulous attention to political ideology: 'Stephen's accession started a long-running aristocratic seminar on the subject which did not end until 1153 ... In these arguments, the synods and the conferences of the intervening years, we see the stirrings of the effects of literacy on the closet group of the Anglo-Norman aristocracy: its developing tendency intellectually to justify its pragmatic actions ... Those at the top of society had begun to feel that they needed to occupy the moral high ground.'[8] For an increasingly literate Norman ruling class, conflict now required something other than military resolution, it necessitated an evaluation of theoretical perspectives which could stand up to scrutiny.

As Gloucester's dilemma had shown, one such area of theoretical concern was inheritance rights, specifically those of women: 'In particular the inheritance rights of women mattered to them in determining where their allegiance ought to lie.'[9] The royalists were in no position to argue against the idea that women could inherit or transmit claims, since their own King's right to the throne was based on it (though one attempt to circumvent this was the revival of the old claim that Empress Matilda was illegitimate, as her mother Matilda of Scotland had been professed as a nun before her marriage to Henry I). There is little proof, however, that inheritance rights in general were one of the causes of the civil war.

One theory used to explain Stephen's desertion by his barons is the 'tenurial crisis' whereby uncertainties in inheritance law that were not regulated until the next reign threatened many magnates with dispossession. Yet the three leading magnates who prosecuted the conflict, Robert of Gloucester, Miles of Gloucester and Brian FitzCount, were in receipt of Stephen's confirmation of their holdings as granted under Henry I and the contention that inheritance law was not ratified in England until Henry II has been challenged. Nor, beyond the Empress's own claim, did they themselves have any particular interest in women's inheritance. Anxieties about what was very much a gender issue might be read on another level: that the war was not fought to determine the rights or wrongs of a specific view of land transmission, but as a manifestation of scruple, in which self-interest came to require a bulwark of ideology.[10]

Yet if 'no concerns about inheritance customs pre-programmed men to defect from Stephen',[11] and they were therefore not hoping for reform of those customs under the Empress, it does not automatically follow that the magnates were sanguine about the future implications of such a precedent. Another way of looking at the gender aspects of the debate about the Empress's rights and comparing her position with that of Matilda of Boulogne is to consider the way in which their *conduct* was perceived. As the *Life of St Margaret of Scotland* demonstrates, women who wielded power could be lauded, rather than perceived as transgressive, provided that power was modified within a context of appropriately feminine piety and submissiveness. Gilbert Foliot's praise of the Empress emphasises precisely such qualities (the italics are this writer's):

In accordance with her father's wishes she crossed the sea ... married there *at her father's command* and remained there carrying out the duties of imperial rule virtuously and piously until, after her husband's death, not through any desperate need or feminine levity, but *in response to a summons from her father,* she returned to him. And though she had attained such high rank ... she was in no way puffed up with pride, but *meekly submitted to her father's will* and on his advice took a second husband ... In all this you will not find any cause why she should have been disinherited.

Implicitly, Empress Matilda's fitness to rule is grounded here in her obedience, meekness and submissiveness to her father (and, the repeated emphasis conveys, to her Heavenly Father), and it follows that in pursuing her claim she was not acting with a 'masculine' lust for power, but motivated by the 'feminine' qualities of compliance and duty. The *Gesta Stephani* provides an interesting counterpoint. In this instance, even the usually antipathetic writer of the *Gesta* is compelled to praise Empress Matilda for her bravery. However, he does so by highlighting her masculine qualities: 'The Countess of Anjou, who was always above feminine softness and had a mind steeled and unbroken in adversity ...' It was these traits – which, as Marjorie Chibnall has so rightly pointed out, would not have been as greatly criticised had they been displayed by a man – that were to prove disastrous to the Empress's hopes.

Initially, the Empress had cause for optimism. After just one month in England, her supporters had organised and taken control of the southern marches and the Severn Valley. On 7 November 1139, Robert of Gloucester successfully attacked Gloucester. Meanwhile, Stephen was busy putting down sporadic uprisings throughout the country. He and Matilda kept Christmas together at Salisbury, and in February Matilda travelled to France for a ceremony that had great propaganda value for the royalists: the betrothal of her fourteen-year-old son Eustace to Constance, the sister of Louis VII of France. This strengthened the alliance agreed between the French and English kings in 1137, and was obviously a powerful demonstration of the French King's faith in the future of Stephen's dynasty. Matilda's role in negotiating this marriage has been seen as establishing a precedent for the involvement of queens in the alliances of their children.[12]

The following August, Matilda was once more employed as her husband's diplomatic representative at a putative peace conference in Bath. She and Archbishop Theobald of Canterbury represented the royalist party, while Robert of Gloucester spoke for the Empress. Bishop Henry of Winchester, King Stephen's younger brother, then took the proposals to King Louis, who was now concerned for the future of his sister as well as his own rights as the overlord of Normandy. Stephen himself found them too disadvantageous and rejected them. His unwillingness to come to terms exacerbated the unrest in England, but it was not until the siege of Lincoln the following year that the Empress decisively gained the upper hand.

Stephen's actions between August 1139 and February 1141 have been criticised for incoherence, but though it may at first appear that he rushed about the country desperately fighting fires, his policy of 'administrative' earldoms theoretically left him free to lend his presence where it was most urgently required. When Ranulf, Earl of Chester seized the castle of Lincoln just before Christmas 1140, Stephen's response was to try to create a similar role for him. In return for the settlement of a land claim in the region, the earl and his brother were left in charge of the castle. But Stephen did not trust Ranulf and a month later he reneged on his promise. No chronicler offers a precise reason for his change of heart, but John of Hexham gives an account of a quarrel between Ranulf and Henry of Scotland over disputed rights in Carlisle and Cumberland. According to this story, Queen Matilda, advised that Ranulf was planning to kidnap Henry, arranged for him to travel safely back to Scotland with a strong bodyguard. There is little more to this version of events than rumour, though it is notable that it acknowledged the significance of the Queen's intervention. However, it does hint at an awareness that Ranulf was generally belligerent. His ambitions in Lincolnshire were highly threatening to other magnates, and Stephen may have retracted the concessions he had granted him after a hostile reaction from other lords at his Christmas court.

The battle for Lincoln was one of the most decisive events of the civil war. Orderic Vitalis notes that two women were closely involved in the original seizure of the castle by the Earl of Chester. The countesses of Chester and Lincoln, Matilda and Hawise, distracted the castellan's wife while Ranulf entered the castle as though he planned to do no more than collect his wife from her visit. A small detail, but one that illustrates how even women not possessed of queenly authority were able to do more to support their husbands' strategies than standing by as anxious spectators. Stephen attacked Lincoln Castle on Candlemas, 2 February. It was considered an inauspicious day for a battle, as the feast marks the change in the Church calendar from the celebrations of the Nativity to the anticipation of the sorrows and privations of Lent. In the procession to morning Mass before the King rode out on his raid, Stephen dropped his candle and it broke. Such an interruption in the carefully choreographed liturgy was seen as another bad omen, but Stephen was determined. He made a good show in the mêlée, fighting with first his axe and then his sword, but he was ignominiously laid low by a well-aimed rock (so much for the glamour of chivalry), and taken prisoner.

Stephen was removed to Gloucester, where he met his cousin the Empress a week later, and then detained at Earl Robert's fortress at Bristol. Matilda of Boulogne was campaigning in the south. She was in London in April, which suggests she had turned back in an attempt to hold the capital. There the Queen 'made supplication to all, importuned with prayer, promises and fair words for the deliverance of her husband'.[13] The Empress held an Easter court at Oxford, then progressed to Winchester, where she received a royalist delegation from London which included Matilda's clerk, Christian. The Londoners petitioned for the King's release, but the Empress slyly insisted that he was not a prisoner – how could a king be held prisoner by his own vassals? Matilda countered this by claiming that the archbishop of Canterbury would never accept the Empress without the specific permission of the King. Yet Stephen's liege-men were turning to the Empress in increasing numbers. Crucial defectors were Earl Geoffrey de Mandeville, Hugh Bigod of Essex and Aubrey de Vere, the future Earl of Oxford. Mandeville's declaration for the Empress, in return for which he was granted substantial concessions and rewards, particularly affected the Queen, as he held custody of the Tower of London, which Matilda was forced to quit in mid-May. Her new daughter-in-law Constance, though, was obliged to stay behind. Matilda retreated to Kent, which was safer and well positioned for communication with her county of Boulogne.

After a second conference with a party from London in June at St Albans, the Empress proceeded to Westminster. Initially, the citizens had been reluctant to receive her, as Matilda of Boulogne's forces, under her Flemish captain William of Ypres, were laying waste to the land on the Surrey shore, but De Mandeville's change of sides, and thus the possession of the Tower, smoothed the Empress's path and she began to make plans for a crown-wearing ceremony at Westminster. It was at this point that she adopted the title of 'Lady of the English'. The *Gesta Stephani*, however, considered her behaviour at Westminster far from ladylike. The crown appeared to be within reach, but it was her *conduct* that allowed it to slip from her grasp. To the Londoners, her behaviour seemed discourteous and stubborn, even downright pig-headed. She demanded large sums of money from the city and insulted its representatives when they turned her down. On her arrival at the palace, she had received petitioners, as was customary for a ruler, including envoys from Matilda of Boulogne who requested that Eustace be allowed to inherit King Stephen's Continental holdings if he were not to become king. Failing to appreciate that a show of clemency and 'feminine' pacifism would win her vital support, the Empress refused outright. By 24 June, the Londoners had had enough of her, and decided to declare their loyalty to Queen Matilda. The city bells were rung as a signal to the people to storm the palace, and the Empress and her entourage made such a hasty escape that they were obliged to abandon their dinner.

At first King Stephen's brother Bishop Henry had been prepared to come to an accommodation with the Empress, but the Westminster debacle was so distasteful to him that he withdrew his support. It was rumoured that the Empress was planning to make an illegal gift of the county of Boulogne to one of her champions, and the Bishop met with Matilda to reassure her, promising to work for the King's freedom. To recover from the embarrassment of London and to stage a show of strength, the Empress held a court at Oxford, moving on in August to Winchester, where Bishop Henry had immured himself in Wolvesey Palace. Matilda rushed to her brother-in-law's defence, arriving on 12 August to besiege the besiegers. Her supporters were now swelled by the earls of Essex and Pembroke, who had returned to the royalist camp, bringing a contingent of Essex and Suffolk barons with them, and after two days the Empress and Robert of Gloucester were hounded out of the city, the Empress riding astride her horse like a man for greater speed. She managed to reach Devizes, but Earl Robert, fighting in her rearguard, was taken by the Earl of Warenne.

Matilda of Boulogne now had a vital hostage of her own and the rival campaigns had reached a stalemate. Once again, women took the diplomatic lead. Matilda communicated with Robert's wife Mabel, Countess of Gloucester, through messengers to negotiate an exchange of prisoners. Mabel, anxious for her husband's safety, proposed easy terms for his return, while Matilda suggested that if Stephen were released, Earl Robert could be appointed royal justiciar. William of Malmesbury saw this as an attempt to bribe Robert into changing sides, but the Earl himself rejected both plans, his wife's because it was motivated by her 'too eager affection', according to Malmesbury, and the Queen's because his sister would never countenance it. Nevertheless, Matilda and Countess Mabel were able to come to an agreement about the fates of the two most powerful men in the country without their conduct being portrayed as arrogant or excessively ambitious. 'It is striking that there is no disparaging comment, only recognition of their actions as peacemakers and indeed power brokers, involved in careful diplomacy.'[14] They finally brokered a complex deal in which Matilda and her younger son William went to Bristol, remaining with Mabel as hostages for Stephen. Meanwhile, the King was liberated to travel to Winchester, where he freed Earl Robert. Robert then returned to Bristol to release the Queen, leaving *his* son William at Winchester with the King, who freed him when his own wife and child were released. During this exchange, Stephen and Gloucester had time for a polite, rather sportsmanlike chat, agreeing that neither should take the situation personally.

Support for the Empress among the barons now began to decline. A general proposition for their disenchantment has been termed 'neutralism', meaning that the self-interest of the magnates was no longer felt to be secure with the Empress and that they thought it wiser simply to withdraw. They had not come to her side out of chivalry, and they were not gallant now. 'Matilda had shown at the height of her power that she had neither the political judgement nor the understanding of men to enable her to act wisely in a crisis.'[15] The Empress was also dealing with a cunning politician in Matilda of Boulogne. To recover the loyalty of Geoffrey de Mandeville, Matilda granted him a charter at Canterbury, promising that he could retain the advantages bestowed on him by the Empress if he returned to the King's side. Although Queen Matilda was an experienced diplomat who had commanded military campaigns, she was always careful to present herself as a supplicant: a mother seeking justice for her son, a loving wife concerned for her husband. She was conciliatory where the Empress was harsh, and she knew that a display of apparent weakness could count as a strength. As she sat beside him in her gold crown at their Christmas court at Canterbury, Stephen had every reason to be grateful for the intelligence and fortitude of his wife.

The King relied even more heavily on Matilda early in the next year, 1142. Although the Empress's hopes had received a serious setback, the uprisings continued. Stephen and Matilda made a progress to York, where they were reconciled with Ranulf of Chester, but the King was ill through-out much of the spring and summer, suffering from lassitude and depression. A great army was mustered at York and then had to be sent home again because the King was too listless to determine how they should advance. Faced with her husband's debilitation, Matilda became more active than ever. She travelled alone across the Channel and on 23 June held a court at Lens, in her county of Boulogne, in an attempt to raise funds and men. By the autumn, Stephen had recovered sufficiently to besiege Oxford, where the Empress was staying. He was no longer in a position to be gentlemanly, as he had been at Arundel three years before. The siege continued until December but the Empress made yet another escape, creeping out of the wintry city in a white cloak, invisible against the snow, and making her way to Abingdon accompanied by just a handful of knights. The Empress Matilda may have had unappealing manners, but she was gloriously brave.

From 1141 to 1147, Matilda of Boulogne based herself mainly in London. Her presence was important in retaining the loyalty of the city, and she was conveniently close to Dover to ensure that the crucial communications between Dover and Wissant remained accessible. During this period, 56 per cent of Matilda's attested and independent charters were made within forty miles of London and none more than eighty miles away. While Stephen trailed from siege to siege, Matilda supervised government business, and it has been judged probable that she was also responsible for the collection of revenues at the Westminster exchequer.

Oxford had surrendered after the Empress's escape, but still the war dragged on. The next summer Stephen was defeated at Wilton by Earl Robert, who now controlled the territory to the west of Winchester. In Normandy, the King's imprisonment after Lincoln had prompted the magnates to seek terms with the Empress's husband, Geoffrey of Anjou, who was still pushing her cause along the duchy's borders. Geoffrey campaigned stolidly in Normandy every year, and in 1144 he took Rouen and had himself invested as duke in April. The loss of Normandy was a bitter blow, and the only comfort Stephen could take from it was that gradually, the barons on both sides were losing interest in the fight for England.

Historians have suggested two dates, 1148 and 1150, as the beginning of the 'magnates' peace', but Earl Robert's death in October 1147 lends support to the earlier year, as his demise marked the collapse of even nominal party adherence. One by one, the lords simply gave up fighting. The Empress lingered on for four months with her small garrison at Devizes, where she had fled after her escape from Oxford, but early in 1148 she was back in Normandy. So irrelevant had she become by now that only one source mentions her departure. Gervase of Canterbury's clerk reported approvingly that she had returned, a humbled wife, 'to the haven of her husband's protection'.

The careers of Matilda of Boulogne and the Empress Matilda had mirrored each other in many ways. Both women now chose to retreat from active politics and, following the example of their mothers, Matilda and Mary of Scotland, in the tradition of pious female royalty, they elected to live apart from their husbands and to embrace religious seclusion. The Empress opted for the priory of Nôtre-Dame-du-Pré, outside Rouen, for her retirement; after 1147 Matilda of Boulogne lived mainly in Canterbury at the monastery of St Augustine. It seems that Matilda had long felt the call of the contemplative life. As early as 1141, during the negotiations for Stephen's release, she had proposed an unusual solution: that Stephen might emulate her own father and retire to a monastery, in which case she could have decided to do likewise. Alternatively, Matilda suggested, the King could live as a sort of permanent pilgrim in the Holy Land, where she could have accompanied him. Her interest in crusading and the Templars made this an attractive idea, though it was never pursued, and Matilda settled for a less adventurous manner of drawing closer to God.

In spite of her decision to devote herself to the Church, Matilda remained busy. Some indication of her social character can be inferred from the fact that she complained of the boredom of living among the monks, who observed a rule of silence. One occupation was the supervision of the building of Faversham Abbey, seven miles west of the priory, which Stephen founded in 1147 as a dynastic monument to the house of Blois. Faversham had had royal associations since the fifth century, and a lodging house, the Maison Dieu, was built in the twelfth century for the use of royal travellers as they passed between London, Dover and Canterbury. Few buildings remain at Faversham, and those that survive are of a later date, but excavations have shown that the church, dominated by a massive central tower, was of the impressive proportions typical of Norman architecture, its nave measuring 370 feet by eighty. Faversham never achieved the prestige Stephen planned for it, any more than did his own dynasty, but Matilda, her husband and their eldest son Eustace were all eventually buried there.

Until the end of her life, Matilda was never able entirely to ignore the demands of her position as queen. Although the Empress had left England, the pursuit of the succession had passed to the next generation, in the person of her son Henry Plantagenet, known as Henry FitzEmpress, the future King Henry II. While the marriage between the Empress and Geoffrey of Anjou was emotionally distant, with neither seeming interested in the other's company beyond the requirements of duty, as a business partnership it was a success. The Empress offered Geoffrey the opportunity to consolidate and expand his Continental holdings and he supported her fully in Normandy. The couple had three sons, Henry, born at Le Mans in 1133, Geoffrey (1134) and William (1136), but did not live together after 1138. Henry was associated early with his mother's claims. Between the Westminster rout and the defeat at Winchester, when she was attempting to consolidate support among the barons, she offered lands not only in England but also Normandy in exchange for their loyalty, and a charter of 1141 to Aubrey de Vere begins: 'Henry, son of the daughter of King Henry, rightful heir of England and Normandy ...' Henry was seven when his mother sailed for England to make good her rights, and in 1142 he was brought over to join her, his presence a meaningful instrument in her campaign in that it demonstrated that should she achieve the crown, the succession was assured. When his father obtained the dukedom of Normandy in 1144, Henry returned to the duchy, where he remained until 1147. In March of that year, on his own initiative, the fourteen-year-old gathered a small party of knights and set off for England to fight for his mother, but his gallant gesture ended in embarrassment as he was forced to appeal unsuccessfully to both the Empress and Robert of Gloucester for funds. In the end, it was his uncle Stephen who, instead of imprisoning him, kindly bailed him out and he went back to Normandy in disgrace.

The Empress, her husband and three sons met at Rouen in 1148 to decide the next step in the Angevin strategy. If Henry wanted to make good his own claim after the Empress's return to Normandy, he would have to deal with the problem of the rival heir, Stephen's son Eustace. Eustace's parents had begun to lobby for their son's rights to be recognised. In 1147, when he was twenty-one, Stephen knighted him, and with Matilda's consent he was given possession of the honour and county of Boulogne. Eustace himself was insecure about his title to the kingdom, which may have been a consequence of his mother's request to the Empress at Westminster in 1140 that he should be granted at least Stephen's Continental holdings, implying that his inheritance was less than assured. In any event, when Henry arrived in England in spring 1149, Eustace took it as a personal challenge. One commentator, John of Hexham, noted that their personal rivalry was so intense that they seemed to be fighting a duel for the kingdom.

Henry FitzEmpress held his first English court at Devizes, which was still pro-Angevin, on 13 April. Presumably to Eustace's dismay, the Stephenite *Gesta* described Henry as the 'true heir'. The *Gesta* author was reflecting the mood of the country, which was increasingly inclined to the view that the Angevins would prevail. From Devizes, Henry moved to the court of his great-uncle, David of Scotland, at Carlisle, where, in the presence of a number of significant magnates, he was knighted. This may have been intended as a symbolic gesture, rather than as a declaration of war, but during Henry's return journey from Carlisle, Stephen ordered Eustace to garrison Oxford, and the two young men fought a campaign of skirmishes in the south-west. Eustace attempted to capture Devizes, and almost succeeded in taking Henry prisoner at Dursley, but Henry eluded him and managed to escape to Normandy in January 1150.

In response to the confrontation between Henry and Eustace, Stephen and Matilda took steps to have Eustace crowned in his father's lifetime, a custom which was unfamiliar in the England of that period, but which had precedents among the Anglo-Saxon kings and also in the Capet dynasty in France. Indeed, it was a policy that Henry II was to enact with his own son. It required the consent of Theobald, the archbishop of Canterbury, with whom the royal couple had until recently enjoyed good relations. Stephen had appointed Theobald to the see in 1138, in preference to his own brother Bishop Henry, and in 1147 Theobald had personally selected the Queen's confessor, prior Ralph of Holy Trinity Aldgate. In 1149, though, Theobald refused to consent to Eustace's coronation. His direction came from the papal curia, which had changed its policy towards Stephen's rule since 1136, when the King had received a vital gesture of support from Innocent II that effectively confirmed his right to the crown. The papacy had also been supportive when the Empress's adherents had tried to contest his claim at the Lateran Council of 1139. But Innocent's successors, Celestine and Eugenius, took a more neutral line. The official reasoning was that the curia accepted Stephen as de facto king, but did not necessarily recognise him as the rightful ruler. Eustace's coronation, establishing his right to inheritance, would contradict this piece of careful casuistry. Theobald had already displeased Stephen by attending a papal council at Reims the previous year against the King's express wishes and had been exiled for a while. Eugenius III had placed England under interdict, though Matilda still succeeded in hearing Mass at Canterbury, and she interceded with her husband for the archbishop, who lodged at the abbey of St Bertin outside Boulogne during his exile.

Matilda was particularly keen to see Eustace crowned, and after Theobald refused to be swayed she involved herself in the disputed election to the archbishopric of York. Stephen and the Pope had disagreed for some years over the installation to York of the papal candidate, Henry Murdac. The distinguished French cleric Bernard of Clairvaux had twice written to Matilda to ask for her intervention in the matter, the level of authority the Queen had achieved being shown in his reference to 'the glory of your kingdom', which acknowledged her as an equal partner with her husband. In order to mollify the Pope, Matilda persuaded Stephen to accept Murdac, who, in return, undertook to plead Eustace's cause. According to John of Hexham, he achieved some limited success at the Curia in 1151, but much of the energy behind the plan had been Matilda's, and when she died, it died with her. In the case of her second son, William, it does not appear even to have been considered.

Matilda's last diplomatic mission took place in Flanders in 1150. Now that Louis VII, and his Queen, Eleanor of Aquitaine, were returned from crusade, Stephen sought to renew their anti-Angevin pact, and Bishop Henry visited Paris as an ambassador on his way to Rome. Matilda accompanied him as far as the border of Flanders, and the alliance was proposed, though an unusually bitter winter prevented a campaign from being fought. Matilda's visit proved fruitful the next year, when Louis attacked Normandy from the north. However, the French king fell ill and the combined push against the Angevins collapsed when Geoffrey of Anjou and Henry FitzEmpress agreed a truce with France in 1151. Stephen held a great council in London at Easter 1152, which Matilda attended to try to rally support. The magnates were persuaded to swear an oath to Eustace, but both the King and the Queen knew how much that was worth. Increasingly, it seemed that only Henry FitzEmpress could unite the weary country.

Matilda was spared the inevitable collapse of her hopes for her husband and son when she died, at Headingham Castle on 3 May 1152, while on a visit to her friend and former lady-in-waiting Euphemia, Countess of Oxford. It was obvious that the Queen's illness was fatal, but there was just enough time to summon her confessor, the prior of Holy Trinity Aldgate, who administered the last rites, and Stephen himself, who confirmed a grant to Holy Trinity on her behalf from Headingham. Matilda's body was transported in state to London, then on to Faversham. Hers was the first royal burial at the abbey she and Stephen had hoped would celebrate the founding of a new English royal dynasty. She was joined there the next year by Eustace, who died of a seizure – some said brought on by rage – in August 1153.

King Stephen and Henry FitzEmpress met at Winchester on 6 November 1153. Henry paid homage to Stephen and was designated his heir. William of Boulogne, Matilda's second son, paid homage to Henry, who swore to provide for him honourably. (Mary, the surviving royal daughter, had not married: she became a nun at St Sulpice, Rennes.) Stephen and Henry then travelled together to Westminster, where they were received by rapturous crowds who could hardly believe that peace had descended at last. The two enemies kept Christmas together, then travelled to Oxford, Dunstable, St Albans, London and Canterbury, where they heard Mass. Every stage of their journey was marked by public celebration and as much magnificence as Stephen's drained resources could muster. In March Henry returned to Normandy. All he had to do now was wait for Stephen to die.

Perhaps it is not going too far to suggest that Stephen's acquiescence in bestowing the kingdom on Henry was in some way related to his wife's death. He was susceptible to depression, as his illness ten years before had shown, and 'what Stephen could not replace was the Queen's steadfastness of purpose and steady judgement'.[16] Politically, there were sound and complex reasons why the Winchester agreement made sense, but after Matilda's death and the shocking loss of Eustace, Stephen no longer had the emotional resources or purpose to go on struggling. He did not display any bitterness, and outwardly remained cheerful and active, but he was exhausted and grieving, and in October 1153 he began to suffer from a disease of the bowel and internal bleeding. He died at Dover on 25 October, attended by Prior Ralph and Archbishop Theobald, and was laid to rest with his wife and son at Faversham.

In many ways, Matilda of Boulogne was a model consort. As a regent, diplomat, warrior, counsellor and mother, she occupies a position along-side with her predecessors Matilda of Scotland and Matilda of Flanders at the apogee of English queenship, after which many historians concur that the power invested in the office began to decline. Yet she also lived in a period where writers were beginning to reconfigure their attitudes to feminine authority.

Anglo-Saxon commentators generally accept that women could par-ticipate in war and government, betraying 'not the slightest surprise ... when a woman is learned, devout, an able administrator or a brave fighter'.[17] Matilda of Boulogne was all of these things. However, post-Conquest attitudes to gender shift to a point at which any sign of such capabilities in remarked upon with astonishment and viewed as excep-tional. 'Masculinity', in terms of categorising the characteristics of women, becomes amorphous. In one sense it can be positive, in that if a woman does anything so unusual as to suggest she might have a brain it must be because she possesses 'manlike' qualities, but in another it can be negative, disturbing, unqueenly. The Empress Matilda found herself damned in the chronicles on both counts. Henry of Huntingdon reduces her brilliant escape from the siege of Oxford to 'a woman's trick', while William of Newburgh condemns her 'intolerable feminine arrogance' – intolerable, that is, in a woman. The *Gesta* author claims that she 'unsexed' herself:

'She began immediately to assume the loftiest haughtiness of the greatest arrogance – not now the humble gait of feminine docility, but she began to walk and talk more severely and more arrogantly than was customary, and to do everything herself.' Comportment that was acceptable, even demanded, in a powerful man, but derided in a woman.

What Matilda of Boulogne achieved was a means of regulating her conduct in comparison with her rival's in a way that successfully manipulated the new, post-Conquest model of queenly femininity. The *Gesta* describes her as '*astuti pectoris virilisque constantiae femina*' – having the virile, courageous breast of a man, but the constancy or fortitude of a woman. Like the Empress, her courage made her 'manlike', but her *conduct* was tempered by an acceptable level of conventional femininity. It is interesting to speculate what might have become of England's first putative queen regnant had she been possessed of Matilda of Boulogne's diplomatic feminine modesty during those tense days at Westminster. Neither the Empress nor Matilda succeeded in their ambitions, and Matilda's husband is one of the great, if misunderstood, failures of English kingship. Matilda herself, though, was never anything less than a great queen.

PART TWO

AN EMPIRE TO THE SOUTH

CHAPTER 5

ELEANOR OF AQUITAINE
'An incomparable woman'

Queenship was an extraordinary office and any woman who inhabited it was of necessity exceptional, but Eleanor of Aquitaine is the most famously exceptional woman of the medieval period. To some extent, the historical perception of her depends on a model which assumes that the stifling sexism of the Middle Ages was as apparent in everyday life as it seems to be in the history books; that Eleanor stands out because she defied, sexually, intellectually and politically, the limits placed around her gender. Yet Matilda of Flanders, Matilda of Scotland and Matilda of Boulogne were all women who exercised political influence in government and patronage, women in comparison with whom Eleanor seems rather less of an exception. Perhaps it would be more accurate to say that Eleanor of Aquitaine was an extraordinary person, in many senses a less successful English queen than her Anglo-Norman predecessors, who nevertheless stamped her image on a century.

During the summer of 1137, the thirteen-year-old Eleanor of Aquitaine was briefly one of the most powerful rulers in Europe. Her first taste of independence as Duchess of Aquitaine was sandwiched between the death of her father that April and her marriage to the Dauphin of France in late July. Eleanor has been called 'a creature of romance and legend, but not of history'.[1] She generated slanderous speculation in her lifetime and in the eight centuries since her death has been moulded to fit the moral, theoretical and literary fashions of the ages with imaginative abandon. Since speculation is something of a tradition where she is concerned, perhaps just one instance might be permitted here: that these few months of orphaned independence inspired Eleanor with a desire for autonomy in her own lands which coloured her judgement and actions for the rest of her life.

The Duchy of Aquitaine encompassed over a quarter of modern-day France. Though ducal authority differed according to region, being concentrated around Poitou, Eleanor's inheritance gave her overlordship of a vast tract of land incorporating Poitou to the north and Gascony to the south, the cities of Bordeaux and Bayonne and the counties of Saintonge, Angoulême, Perigord, Limousin, Auvergne and La Marche. Trade in wine and salt, varied agriculture, the control of Atlantic ports and the junctions of the pilgrim routes to Compostella as they merged towards the Pyrenean passes made Aquitaine rich, if not quite the idyllic rural paradise the Eleanor-legend contrasts so unfavourably with the chilly north where she spent the fifteen years of her first marriage. Since the time of her grandfather, Aquitaine had been an important artistic centre, the focus of the new troubadour literature that spread its influence through-out Europe, and whose codes would affect both contemporary culture and its future interpretation.

Eleanor's grandfather, William IX, was the first known troubadour poet. Eleven of his sophisticated, often erotic lyrics survive. He married Philippa of Toulouse (giving Eleanor a claim to the county which both her husbands would unsuccessfully prosecute) and, notably, left her as regent in Poitou when he went on crusade in 1099. He then arranged for their son, Eleanor's father, to marry Anor, the daughter of his mistress, the appropriately named Dangerosa, with whom he lived for years in flagrant double adultery. Philippa, the Duchess, departed for the abbey of Fontevrault in disgust, and William tastefully declared that he would found a rival abbey at Niort, to be served by whores, though this claim has now been confirmed as an allusion to a now-lost poem. William IX might have been as famous in his own time for his personal life as his poetry, but his son William X was a much more placid character. His main interest in life was eating, which gave Eleanor something in common with her future husband, whose father, the King of France, was nicknamed 'Louis the Fat'. William and Anor had three children, but Eleanor's only brother died in childhood, leaving her as heir. In 1136, William roused himself to make the pilgrimage to Compostella, but before departing he assembled his vassals and had them swear allegiance to his daughter. Aware that Eleanor's inheritance made her highly vulnerable to bride-snatchers, he also made her a ward of the French King and arranged her betrothal to the Dauphin Louis. Eleanor and her younger sister, Petronilla, accom-panied their father as far as Bordeaux before he set off to cross the mountains to Spain. He died at Compostella on Good Friday, 9 April 1137.

On the news that Eleanor had come into her inheritance, the King sprang into action. Though he was too sick and obese to rise from his bed, he insisted that his son should go immediately to claim his wife. Aquitaine was a tremendous prize in comparison with the comparatively meagre holdings of the French crown of the period, and the King was afraid it might be snatched from his grasp. So the seventeen-year-old prince – accompanied by 500 knights, his tutor, Abbot Suger of St Denis, the counts of Champagne and Vermandois and a sumptuous baggage train transporting precious tapestries, extravagant robes and chests of treasure – set off for the palace of Ombrière in Bordeaux, where Eleanor was living, surrounded by guards. He arrived at Bordeaux on 11 July, crossed the River Garonne by boat to join Eleanor and their marriage was celebrated on 25 July in the cathedral of Saint-André by the archbishop of Bordeaux. Appropriately, given her future reputation, the bride wore scarlet. After spending their wedding night at Taillebourg en route for Poitiers, they reached the city on 1 August, the same day that King Louis died. Their investiture at Poitiers as Count and Countess was also therefore a cor-onation, in which Louis was described by Orderic Vitalis as coming into possession of Aquitaine as well as the kingdom of France. Eleanor was later crowned queen at Bourges.

Louis had already been crowned at Reims, according to Capetian tradition, when he became Dauphin in 1131 after the death of his elder brother Philip. Until this point, he had been intended for the Church, and was greatly influenced by his mentor, Abbot Suger, under whose tutelage he had spent his childhood at the abbey of St Denis. He was not bad looking, and was later described by John of Salisbury as loving his queen 'almost beyond reason', but his piety often caused him to be torn between the conflicting demands of religion and statesmanship, and his reign has been described as 'a long career of energetic ineffectiveness'.[2] Although he was known for his pacific tendencies – which marked him out among his aristocratic contemporaries, for whom making war was part of the business of being – according to the *Chronique de Touraine* the celebrations of his marriage to Eleanor were marred by a violent incident. One of Eleanor's vassals, William de Lézay, had refused to attend the ceremony where oaths of loyalty were sworn to Louis as the new Duke of Aquitaine. He had also stolen some of Eleanor's precious white hawks. Full of bravado, Louis and his companions rode off to teach him a lesson, leaving behind their chain mail because of the summer heat. De Lézay ambushed the party, and Louis's men got the upper hand only after a nasty skirmish, culminating in Louis supposedly cutting off the thief's hands personally. This seems like a rather pathetic attempt on Louis's part to impress Eleanor with his prowess as a warrior, but the brutality to which he was prepared to resort in extremis reveals an unpleasant side to his character.

This explosive tendency was shamefully demonstrated at Vitry-sur-Marne in 1142 in an episode for which Eleanor was held to be partly responsible. The previous year, Louis had rashly decided to make an attempt on Toulouse, in right of Eleanor's claim on the county, without consulting his chief magnates. To his fury, several of them refused to send their obligatory liege of knights for the attack, including Theobald, Count of Champagne. The King's effort to attack Toulouse was an embarrassment: despite his confidence that the city could easily be taken by surprise, Louis found it well defended, and he was obliged to slink back to Poitiers, where Eleanor was waiting for him. To save face, they made a grand tour of Eleanor's lands, but as they progressed in a leisurely manner back to Paris, Eleanor's sister Petronilla inconveniently fell in love with the Count of Vermandois, who was married to the sister of the Count of Champagne.

The next twist in the story came when the archbishopric of Bourges became vacant and the cathedral chapter elected their own nominee, Pierre de la Chatre, over Louis's personal candidate, Carduc. In Rome, Pope Innocent II confirmed the chapter's choice and invested De la Chatre with the post. Petulantly, Louis denied the new archbishop entry to Bourges, despite the Pope taking the alarming step of placing the royal household under an interdict. The Count of Champagne stirred the pot by giving refuge to the homeless De la Chatre.

Meanwhile, the Count of Vermandois had abandoned his wife and children and was determined to marry Petronilla. Three tame bishops were found to pronounce an annulment and celebrate the wedding. The Countess of Vermandois took refuge with her brother, who fired off furious protests to Rome. The Pope excommunicated Vermandois and Petronilla and placed their lands under interdict. Louis sent an army to lay waste to Champagne, but when Theobald proved intractable, the King himself led a band of mercenaries to besiege the town of Vitry. Louis was not an effective military commander and the best that can be said of his choice of tactics is that it lacked foresight. The townspeople, terrifed by what they had heard of the previous French attacks, crowded into the wooden castle for protection. Louis's bowmen shot burning arrows over the walls as the mercenaries stormed the town, and soon the whole edifice was in flames. Desperately, the survivors, at least a thousand people, rushed to the sanctuary of the cathedral, but it was too late: the fire was out of control and the cathedral was burned to the ground with the loss of every soul inside it.

It is notable that the first inquiry into the legality of Eleanor's marriage to Louis took place in the aftermath of this horrific disgrace. The pretext for dissolving the marriage of the Count and Countess of Vermandois had been that they were related within the prohibited seven degrees. The influential cleric Bernard of Clairvaux asked how Louis dared to prosecute the annulment when he, too, was related to Eleanor within the degrees, as was demonstrated by a family tree drawn up by the Bishop of Laon. Subsequently, when the Count of Champagne sought to marry his daughters to two of Louis's more powerful magnates, Louis forbade what would have been a threatening conglomeration of power on the grounds of consanguinity, an action that Bernard again denounced as hypocritical. After Vitry, Bernard had written to Louis, warning him: 'Those who are urging you to repeat your former wrongdoings against an innocent person are seeking in this not your honour but their own convenience. They are clearly the enemies of your crown and the disturbers of your realm.' It was a commonplace to criticise kings indirectly by putting the blame on 'bad counsellors', but in this instance Bernard seems to be pointing the finger firmly at Eleanor, her sister and Vermandois. Bernard's chastisement, his raising of the consanguinity issue and the fact that Eleanor had not yet produced a child suggest that as early as 1143 there may have been doubts about her suitability as queen.

Eleanor and Louis were technically third cousins once removed, both being descended from King Robert II, but this had clearly not been considered relevant at the time of their betrothal since no dispensation had been sought from the Pope. Indeed, 'there was a well-established century long tradition of Capetians entering into incestuous unions without having those marriages dissolved'.³ Childlessness was seen as a sign of God's disapproval of an illegitimate marriage, so perhaps Louis's attempts to make reparation for the Champagne wars – which included restoring Theobald's lands, confirming De la Chatre as archbishop of Bourges and adopting monastic attire – extended to paying more zealous sexual attention to his wife. In any event, in 1145, Eleanor's first child, Marie, was born. After Bernard of Clairvaux had reassured her that if she worked to restore relations between Louis and Theobald she would finally be blessed with a child, Eleanor had been active in promoting peace, and it therefore seemed that in the arrival of Marie she had been granted a miracle.

Modern writers on Eleanor have often made much of an assumed sexual incompatibility between her and Louis. Eleanor herself was later to imply that she had been sexually frustrated, but this could simply have been a post-hoc justification. The fact that she did not give birth until eight years into her marriage is less surprising in the light of the confusion about her date of birth. Many writers have accepted an error on the part of an early twentieth-century scholar which placed her birth in 1122. More reliable evidence from a late thirteenth-century genealogy produced at Limoges corrects this date to 1124. Eleanor was therefore thirteen when she married Louis, and it is quite possible that she had not yet reached puberty. Estimates of the average age of menarche for medieval girls range from fourteen to seventeen, so if Eleanor was at the later end of the spectrum, she may not have been capable of conceiving for some years.[4] This is not to suggest that Louis was a less than attentive husband; it serves merely to illustrate that, as ever with Eleanor, the assumptions about her character have proved more persistent than the facts.

Now that she was a mother, Eleanor's position was validated, but there is little real evidence from the first decade of her marriage as to whether or not she was content in it. With hindsight, some writers have argued that she was unhappy with the repetitive ceremonial role she was obliged to play, that she found the French court austere and unrefined and that she was thwarted in her attempts to introduce southern customs. She was criticised for being extravagant – Bernard of Clairvaux disapprovingly pictured the queen and her ladies with their arms 'loaded' with bracelets, their earrings, long linen headdresses draped over the left arm, fur-trimmed cloaks and delicate gowns – but beyond this image there is simply no detailed account of her participation in Louis's court during this period. Nor does she appear in any of his charters, in contrast to her predecessors, who had been politically active. Perhaps she did try to exert influence over her husband in private, perhaps she did not. There is no record either way. To infer from this absence of information that 'these changes in the fundamental role of the queen consort, which came about *purely* [the italics are this author's] as a response to concern over Eleanor's influence, set a precedent for future queens of France, who mostly found themselves without power or political influence',[5] seems an excessive and inaccurate attempt to aggrandise what is more accurately described as Eleanor's non-influence. Similarly, the idea that Eleanor shrewdly tucked away the consanguinity argument to produce at a later date seems an idea informed more by a desire to cast her as the agent of events than to represent her eventual divorce as part of a broader political schema.

The romantic nonsense that trails Eleanor's image is greatly inspired by her experiences on crusade. In December 1144, the Christian colony of Edessa had fallen to Imad al-Din Zengi, the Turkish ruler of Mosul and Aleppo. Along with the kingdom of Jerusalem, the principality of Antioch and the county of Tripoli, Edessa made up the kingdom of Outremer, established after the First Crusade between 1099 and 1109. The recently elected Pope, Eugenius III, issued a bull in response, calling on Christendom to defend the Holy Land against a newly militant Islam. The bull, 'Quantum Praedecessores', was actually addressed to Louis, but even before he could have received it the King declared at his Christmas court at Bourges that he intended to 'take the Cross'. He received a rather lukewarm reception, but by Easter the next year France was alive with crusading fervour. This was largely due to the influence of Bernard of Clairvaux, who was closely connected with Outremer and who worked authoritatively with the Pope to achieve maximum recruitment for the expedition. The bull was reissued in March, and Louis called an assembly of magnates at Vézelay to hear Bernard preach. It was a deeply emotional, if carefully stage-managed occasion, with Louis sitting next to Bernard, displaying the fabric cross which symbolised his pledge and Eleanor coming forward to kneel and promise the allegiance of her vassals. Bernard then set off on a whirlwind tour to call the faithful to defend Jerusalem, and he was so successful that 'towns and castles are emptied, one may scarcely find one man among seven women, so many women are there widowed whilst their husbands are alive'.[6]

Evangelical zeal aside, the Church was offering an attractive package to crusaders: the remission of all confessed sins, immunity from civil lawsuits incurred after taking the Cross, exemption from interest on loans and the right to raise money by pledging land to churches or other Christians (a benefit that provided a cloak for a good deal of usury). These advantages, combined with Eleanor's charm and energy in persuading her liegemen to join, encouraged some of the greatest lords of southern France to take part in the Second Crusade, along with a number of aristocratic women. As well as the Queen of France herself, the countesses of Toulouse and Flanders, Mamille of Roucy, Florine of Burgundy and Torqueri of Bouillon accompanied their husbands. There were also at least 300 women who offered to travel as nurses, plus the ladies' attendants. The women and their baggage were later criticised as a frivolous distraction from the holy purpose of the crusade, not to mention a practical encumbrance, but as Eleanor sets off from Metz on 11 June 1147 on a silver-saddled horse, her flowing robe embroidered with the lilies of France, she is, for once, certainly captured as the epitome of the troubadour heroine: noble, pious, romantic and brave.

The crusade was a disaster for Christian Europe and for Eleanor's reputation. In many ways, reaching the Holy Land at all was a momentous achievement, given the enormous scale of the operation in terms of numbers, geographical span and cost, but a combination of 'bad timing, poor strategy, flawed diplomacy [and] catastrophic logistics'[7] made success unlikely even before the French army arrived at Constantinople. They were preceded by the other main part of the crusader force, the German army led by the Emperor Conrad. As they travelled onward, the German contingent was attacked by Turkish forces near Dorylaeum, and suffered a disastrous defeat at the hands of their mounted archers, so swift and lethal they were known as 'winged death'.

The French entered Constantinople on 4 October, and were given a magnificent reception by the Byzantine Emperor Manuel Comnenus, whose wife Irene had corresponded with Eleanor as the French forces progressed through Hungary. Louis enjoyed a private audience with the Emperor in the breathtaking splendour of the Boukoleon Palace, where he was granted the special privilege of being permitted to sit down, and was taken on a tour of the shrines and relics of the city, including the stone from Christ's tomb and the lance that pierced His side. Manuel courteously organised a joint celebration of Louis's personal saint, St Denis, where the Frenchmen marvelled at the singing of the Greek castrati, and treated his guests to a banquet which included frogs, caviare and artichokes (the French showed themselves rather provincial when they sniffed at these rose-strewn delicacies, suspicious of poison). They crossed the Bosphorus in mid-October, and it was as they left Nicaea on the twenty-sixth, ominously during a partial eclipse of the sun, that they learned of the German defeat. This was a devastating blow to morale, and as they crawled the 120 miles to Ephesus, a journey which took a month, the army began to splinter, wearied by changes in the route and dwindling supplies.

Eleanor was involved in one of the most dramatic of the five attacks the French army managed to repel during the next 200-mile stage to the port of Adalia. An examination of how she is portrayed as being responsible for this incident is a good example of the way in which her power has been overestimated and her influence manipulated into legend. In the conventional version of the story[8] the French army was travelling across Mount Cadmos at Honaz Daghi, with the Queen's party riding in the vanguard under the supervision of one of her own Aquitaine men,

Geoffrey, Lord of Rançon. Ignoring the King's instructions to make camp on the exposed plain, Geoffrey followed Eleanor's advice and escorted the women through a pass to what seemed to be a protected valley. The Turks, who were lying in wait for the main body of the French force, allowed Eleanor's party into the valley as a feint, and when the troops arrived, they fell upon them. Louis acquitted himself bravely, leading a charge of his immediate entourage of knights to safeguard the infantry and the large numbers of non-combatant pilgrims following behind. The attack is explained as one of the fundamental causes of the failure of the crusade, and that failure has its source in Eleanor, who 'by her undisguised flirtations had spread confusion and dismay and discord in the noblest host that ever went to the East'.[9]

Neither of the two accounts of Cadmos, Odo de Deuil's eyewitness description written up a month later, and William of Tyre's, which postdated events by thirty years, mentions Eleanor at all. The Queen's position at the head of the van and her influence over Geoffrey de Rançon in his flouting of Louis's orders is an invention by Richard, a much later writer. Yet even though Eleanor has been acquitted of blame by a scholar writing as long ago as 1950, Richard's version of events is still widely accepted. What is considered plausible in terms of Eleanor's legend tells us a good deal about its hold over contemporary perceptions, and about the preoccupations of modern historians, but, as always with Eleanor, one has to look carefully for the truth.

King Louis was courageous and well trained in handling weapons when he had to, but he was no strategist. The army limped on for another twelve days, surviving on horse meat, the desperate rations of the starving soldier. After a month of bickering over ships and supplies in Adalia, he succumbed to pressure from his magnates to press on to the Holy Land, abandoning his infantry. There were simply not enough ships available to carry the troops. In theory the men were to proceed overland to Tarsus under the command of Thierry of Flanders and Archibald of Bourbon, but the officers jumped aboard the first vessel that came into port, leaving the infantrymen to the mercies of the Turks. Thousands were killed and thousands taken as slaves, an outcome which did nothing for Louis's reputation. 'Here the King left his people on foot and with his nobles went on board ship,' recounts William of Tyre pointedly. Not only was Louis stupidly careless of the welfare of those who followed him, but the loss of his infantry was to prove a major handicap in the campaign for Damascus.

Finally, on 19 March 1148, Louis and Eleanor landed at St Symeon, ten miles downriver from the city of Antioch. They were met by a choir singing the '*Te Deum*' and received by Eleanor's uncle, Prince Raymond, the ruler of the province. Eleanor's behaviour in Antioch provoked scandalous charges from four of the principal chroniclers of the crusade and gave rise to ever more elaborate tales of her sexual perfidy in the years to come. John of Salisbury recorded:

The most Christian King of the Franks reached Antioch, after the destruction of his armies in the east, and was nobly entertained there by Prince Raymond, brother of the late William, Count of Poitiers. He was as it happened the Queen's uncle, and owed the King loyalty, affection and respect for many reasons. But ... the attentions paid by the Prince to the Queen, and his constant, indeed almost continuous conversation with her, aroused the King's suspicions. They were greatly strengthened when the Queen wished to remain behind, although the King was preparing to leave, and the Prince made every effort to keep her, if the King would give his consent. And when the King made haste to tear her away, she mentioned their kinship, saying it was not lawful for them to remain together as man and wife, since they were related in the fourth and fifth degrees.

William of Tyre confirms that Raymond 'resolved also to deprive him of his wife, either by force or secret intrigue. The Queen readily assented to this design, for she was a foolish woman. Her conduct before and after this time showed her to be, as we have said, far from circumspect. Contrary to her royal dignity, she disregarded her marriage vows and was unfaithful to her husband.' Gervase of Canterbury and Richard of Devizes are more cautious, but hint strongly at the same story: that Eleanor was suspected of committing adultery with Raymond. Louis was clearly disturbed by her behaviour and by the possibility of the illegitimacy of their marriage, which she had raised, as he confided in Abbot Suger, who wrote back to advise him to restrain his angry feelings until he had returned to France.

Whether Eleanor 'technically' committed adultery is a moot point (though it is worth remembering that to have done so while on the holy mission of crusade would have been a grave sin indeed). What matters is that her behaviour was sufficiently careless for those around her to believe she did. The hints from the chroniclers were undoubtedly affected by their knowledge of the subsequent royal divorce — none of them was writing less than fifteen years after the events they describe — and it may have been that Louis's huffy removal from Antioch had less to do with Eleanor than with a disagreement over strategy. Raymond was pushing for a concerted attack on Aleppo, the power base of Nur al-Din, but most of the crusaders wished to fulfil their vows by making for Jerusalem. Eleanor appears to have tried to talk Louis round to Raymond's view, which certainly made more sense from a military perspective, but Louis had two strong reasons to demur: his own sacred vow to lay the Oriflamme of France on the altar of the church of the Holy Sepulchre, and the more practical consideration that having left his infantry behind at Adalia, he had insufficient foot soldiers to mount an effective siege. Given that Louis's decision to leave Antioch proved crucial in the failure of the crusade, the adultery story and the fables it spawned are interesting in the context of 'the anxieties about gender, sexuality and sovereignty that continually surfaced in medieval definitions of queenship'.[10]

In the thirteenth century *Récits d'un Ménéstral de Reims* and the fifteenth-century *Chronique Normand*, it is claimed that Eleanor had an affair with Saladin himself and attempted to elope with him by boat. Both accounts emphasise her wealth, its loss to France in her subsequent divorce and her lack of a son. Saladin, the celebrated Muslim general who took Jerusalem in 1187, would certainly loom large in Eleanor's life, but these tales are patently fiction. What is important is the subtext: the linking of Eleanor's subversive sexual desire to failures in kingship and hence to a weakening of the sacred tie between the anointed king and God which validated – or not – the Christian assumptions of the crusaders. The traditional queenly role of intercessor is here perverted into something dangerous and threatening. Eleanor becomes the symbol of the seductress who can displace nations through her sexual power over the king, as was later the case with her daughter-in-law Isabelle of Angoulême. *Ménéstral* and *Chronique* are only two of many accounts that portray Eleanor as lascivious and promiscuous, but, again, they are of less interest in relation to the facts of her life than in the way they manipulate her image to discuss or warn against the combination of sexual and political influence that was the unique prerogative of queens.

Louis got his sight of the Holy City, and then agreed with Emperor Conrad to attack Damascus, where the army assembled on 24 July. Four days later, the crusaders retreated after the city repelled a shambolic attack. The defeat was all the more humiliating in that the army 'remained intact'.[11] Numerous theories were offered to justify this pathetic showing, the most acceptable being that the Christians had been betrayed, for a variety of complicated political reasons, by the barons of Jerusalem. A simpler explanation may be that they were afraid of becoming trapped between the city and the relief force sent out by Nur al-Din from Aleppo. Many commentators blamed the bungled expedition on the presence of women among the crusaders, while clerics, including Bernard of Clairvaux, saw it as a harsh lesson from God.

After Damascus, there could no longer be any doubt that the Second Crusade was a catastrophe. 'So great was the disaster of the army and so inexpressible the misery that those who took part bemoan it with tears to this very day,' declared Otto of Freising.[12] It had been a fruitless waste of life, and the majority of those who suffered were not great nobles, whose deaths were at least recorded for posterity with a degree of honour, but the nameless thousands who had pushed valiantly towards Jerusalem only to die anonymously in the dust. Nothing was left of the euphoria and nobility of purpose that had galvanised the crowds at Vézélay. Louis and Eleanor remained in the Holy Land until the following Easter, while the King attempted to recover some benefit by raising loans to defend the beleaguered kingdom of Jerusalem, then embarked for France in a fleet of ships hired from Sicily. Not only was Louis concerned about the collapse of his glorious mission and the consequent damage to his own reputation; now, as he returned to his kingdom, he had the state of his marriage to worry about.

John of Salisbury reports that Eleanor had raised the prospect of divorce at Antioch in 1148. Louis was apparently prepared to consider the proposal on the grounds of their consanguinity, but was advised against proceeding as it would be too shameful, on top of the ruinous crusade, if 'the King was said to have been despoiled of his wife or to have been abandoned by her'.[13] Since in 1148 the initiative lay with Eleanor, it has been frequently argued that the couple's eventual divorce in 1152 was the outcome of a long-term plan of hers; that she 'fashioned her marital situation to meet her own ends'.[14] Eleanor, it is claimed, manipulated her husband's conscience to gain her freedom. There are good reasons to doubt this theory, the first of which is that when the King explained the situation to the Pope, Eugenius, with whom he and Eleanor had a meeting at Tusculum on their return journey, he forbade them even to consider such a step. Eugenius threatened anathema on anyone who objected to their union and declared that it could not be dissolved on any pretext whatsoever. The Pontiff also offered some more intimate marriage counselling. He 'made them sleep in the same bed, which he had decked with priceless hangings of his own; and daily during their brief visit he strove by kindly converse to restore love between them'.[15] Louis accepted the Pope's judgement enthusiastically as, at this stage, according to John of Salisbury, he was still very much in love with his wife, and the birth of a second daughter, Alix, in 1150 shows that Eleanor had (whether graciously or not) submitted to her duty. It was the gender of this second child, rather than any protracted strategy of Eleanor's, that pushed Louis towards divorce in 1152. It is important to understand that the desire to present Eleanor as an auto-nomous heroine has neglected to take into account the legal and customary background of the ending of her first marriage. Eleanor and Louis had now been together for fifteen years, and she had not produced a son.

One of the factors contributing to the lasting success of the Capetian dynasty was the handing down of the crown from father to son from the tenth century until the beginning of the fourteenth. In a culture that did not sanction divorce, the Capetians were skilled at manipulating the canon laws on consanguinity to their own ends, either to remain in marriages the Church considered illegitimate or to dissolve others that had not supplied the requisite male child. Consanguinity was 'a marvellous excuse for cynics'.[16] The *miracle capetien*, this unbroken line of succession spanning hundreds of years, looks less of a miracle, and the 'scandal' of Eleanor's divorce less scandalous, when it is considered that every French king from Philip I (1060–1108) to Philip II (1180–1223) was divorced at least once. Both Louis's father and grandfather had had their first marriages dissolved on the basis of the prohibited degrees and had gone on to produce heirs with new wives. After Alix's birth, Louis was concerned that Eleanor might not give him a boy. Any suggestion that the King and Queen of France separated because of Louis's concern for his soul is contradicted by the fact that first, he had full papal dispensation to continue the marriage and secondly, when he remarried, he did so to a woman even more closely related to him, Constance of Castile. Eleanor's second husband was also related to her in the same degree.

The conservative Abbot Suger died in 1151, and it may have been the absence of his restraining influence that finally pushed Louis to move for an annulment. The archbishop of Sens was appointed to lead a council consisting of various barons, clerics and the bishops of Reims, Bordeaux and Rouen, which met at Beaugency in the county of Blois in March 1152. After three days of deliberation, the council predictably decided in favour of the King's wishes. No adultery claim was produced, and the consanguinity argument was unchallenged by either Eleanor or Louis. Marie and Alix were declared legitimate, since the marriage had been undertaken in good faith, and both parties were permitted to retain their

lands intact. Eleanor and Louis had kept Christmas at Limoges after a tour
of Eleanor's territories in the south and they were together at Bordeaux
in January 1152, but the next month Louis left Eleanor alone at Poitiers,
in anticipation of the council's ruling.

Eleanor had no means of independently instigating a separation from
Louis, but she made it clear that the annulment was agreeable to her. After
the crusade, William of Newburgh notes, she was 'greatly offended with
the King's conduct, even pleading she had married a monk, not a king'.
This allusion to Louis's supposed lack of virility has again been taken at
face value, as a rationale for Eleanor's choice of second husband. The
implication is that she was frustrated and needed a 'real man'. Perhaps she
was, and perhaps she did, but all we can know for certain of her motivations
relates to her political position as both an immensely powerful landowner
and a relatively vulnerable woman rather than to a heroine of chivalry
who married for love.

It has been suggested that Eleanor had come to a secret understanding
with the man who would become Henry II of England when, in 1151,
as Duke of Normandy, he accompanied his father, Geoffrey of Anjou, to
Paris to pay homage to Louis: 'It is said that while she was still married to
the King of the Franks, she had aspired to marriage with the Norman
Duke ... and for this reason she desired and procured a divorce'.[7] In the
summer of 1151, the French were at war with the Angevins in Normandy,
and according to this argument, Geoffrey of Anjou, knowing of the
clandestine arrangement, made the otherwise surprising decision to cede
part of the Vexin to Louis. Leaving aside the fact that any 'secret understanding' could only have been reached in Paris when Geoffrey and Henry
were there – that is, after they had agreed to the Vexin annexation, the
confirmation of which was part of the reason for their trip to the French
capital – a look at the situation in Normandy at the time shows that there
were good tactical reasons for Geoffrey's concession at this point which
had nothing to do with Eleanor.

England was in the last stages of the civil war that would see Henry
FitzEmpress crowned as the heir to the Empress Matilda. In 1151, Louis
was allied with King Stephen of England against the Angevins, and was
campaigning in Upper Normandy with Eustace of England, the husband
of his sister Constance. Geoffrey of Anjou was fighting in the south, but
was saved from a full assault by the French when Louis fell ill in Paris and
was unable to join the army mustered in the Mantois. Louis had already
lost Montreuil-Bellay to the Angevins, which had been the primary
motivation for his offensive, and the Angevins were keen to reach a truce

as they aimed to take the conflict out of Normandy and back to England. The stall in Louis's alliance with Stephen caused by his illness meant a peace was acceptable to both sides, and Geoffrey and Henry left Paris in the belief that Louis was temporarily mollified and planning to launch a new invasion across the Channel. Geoffrey's 'otherwise inexplicable'[18] change of heart is thus explained. Further, in 1151, however much Eleanor may have desired a divorce, she was hardly in a position to plot a new marriage unless she knew for certain that the annulment would proceed. Since she was still living with Louis until early the following year, this was prospective, not definite.

Still, Aquitaine was too precious to be left to the mercy of fortune-hunters, and Eleanor does seem to have decided very quickly what she needed to do. After saying her farewells to Louis at Poitiers in February, she appears to have withdrawn to Fontevrault, from where she set off for her own capital once the annulment was announced. On the very first night of her freedom, 21 March 1152, Theobald of Blois attempted to seize her on her southward journey. She escaped by travelling by water to Tours, but when she tried to cross the River Creuse at Port des Piles, she was warned of another ambush, this one set by Henry's younger brother, the junior Geoffrey of Anjou. She had to rush to the safety of Poitiers by back roads and once she arrived there she lost no time in sending to Henry in Normandy, asking him to come immediately to marry her. The speed of this development does suggest the existence of some kind of understanding between them, as by 18 May Henry was in Poitiers, where he and Eleanor were married discreetly at the cathedral of St Pierre. Misguided extrapolations from the political situation in Normandy do nothing to explain the alliance. A more measured account of Eleanor's career proposes simply that 'physical attraction and love of power seem to have drawn Eleanor and Henry together'.[19] That they met in Paris and that Eleanor kept Henry in mind in the event of achieving her freedom is perhaps the most that can be said of what transpired between February and May.

Eleanor's divorce meant that in principle, Aquitaine would now be released from French overlordship. After her marriage to Henry, the recovery of her beloved duchy was Eleanor's first priority. Her first independent charter as Duchess after her marriage is a reconfirmation of the rights of the abbey of St Jean Montierneuf in Poitiers, dated 26 May 1152. This was a standard act for any new lord coming into his lands, and Eleanor used it as a gesture to emphasise that she had regained sole control, stressing that her benefactions to the house followed in the tradition of her great-grandfather, grandfather and father. The next day, she revoked a grant of the forest of La Sèvre to the abbey of Saint-Maixent, which she had co-signed with Louis in 1146, then regranted it in her own right. These two acts are largely symbolic, indicating Eleanor's determination to govern her inheritance herself, but if she hoped to enjoy a degree of autonomy in Aquitaine with her new husband, that hope was short-lived. Louis, concerned for the rights of Marie and Alix, refused initially to relinquish his claim on Aquitaine and continued to use his ducal title until 1154, even though Henry assumed it in 1153. Eleanor continued to be a figure of power in the duchy, but by 1156, at which point Henry had settled his dispute with Louis and sworn fealty to him for his Continental possessions, Eleanor's position of independence had been eroded between the contending demands of both of the men who claimed the right to act on her behalf. At their Christmas court at Bordeaux, Henry accepted homage from Eleanor's Aquitainian vassals, and for the period 1157–67, she is not mentioned in any of the duchy's charters.

It was the same story in England. After the death of Eustace of Blois in August 1153 and the signing of the treaty of Winchester in November, Henry was finally poised to achieve his mother's thwarted ambition and inherit the English crown. In 1154 he and Eleanor travelled to Normandy to wait for news from England. On 25 October King Stephen died, and the new King set sail from Barfleur on 7 December. Eleanor was crowned at his side on 19 December at Westminster. After that, until 1168, she appears in the sources as little more than an ornament. Her reputation as a great queen stems from her later activities in Aquitaine and in the government of her sons. By contrast, the period she spent by her husband's side as queen of England is one of virtual invisibility. True, she did act as regent of the kingdom in Henry's absence until 1163, issuing writs and documents and presiding over at least one court at Westminster, as well as in Normandy, but in comparison with her predecessors Matilda of Flanders, Matilda of Scotland and Matilda of Boulogne, who 'exercised all the prerogatives of sovereignty',[20] evidence of Eleanor governing and man-aging her household and lands is scant. Her role was ceremonial and, in these years, reproductive: 'Summer and winter, crossing and re-crossing the Channel, almost always expecting another child; here she is, severely reduced to the strictest obligations of a feudal queen: other than the duty to produce numerous offspring for her husband, she must be present everywhere, at every moment, showing herself to the vassals at the plenary courts of Christmas or Easter, riding, sailing, riding again.'[21] This picture of Eleanor in the first phase of her English queenship highlights its two dominant demands: travel and childbirth. Eleanor and Henry had eight children between 1153 and 1166. William, their first son, died aged three in 1156, but Henry, Matilda, Richard, Geoffrey, Leonor, Joanna and John all survived to marry.

After William's death, Henry II focused his aspirations on his second son, known as the 'Young King' to distinguish him from his father. Young Henry underwent two coronation ceremonies in his father's lifetime, the French-style confirmations of inheritance that Matilda of Boulogne had failed to obtain for her son Eustace. In 1159, Henry married two-year-old Marguerite of France, King Louis's daughter by Eleanor's replacement, Constance of Castile. Despite a stipulation in the 1158 betrothal agreement that Marguerite would not be brought up by Eleanor of Aquitaine, the little girl entered Eleanor's household after her marriage. After Constance died giving birth to another daughter, Alys, who was betrothed to Eleanor's son Richard, Louis took a third wife, Adela of Blois. In 1165 she presented him with his yearned-for son, Philip Augustus. Like her sister, the Young Queen, Alys came to live with her new family. The previous year, Eleanor's daughters by Louis, Marie and Alix, had been married to two brothers, Henry and Theobald of Champagne, and though Eleanor had no part in these arrangements, she convened a council with the archbishop of Cologne at Westminster in 1165 to confirm the marriage of her daughter Matilda to Henry of Saxony. The next year mother and daughter travelled together to Dover, where Matilda embarked for her new life in Germany, and around the same time her brother Geoffrey was betrothed to Constance, the heiress to Brittany. Eleanor's involvement in her husband's marital strategies for their offspring, as well as the birth of her last child, John, in 1166, suggests that relations between them were at least functional at this juncture, but romance was about to distort her reputation once again.

In 1165, Henry II fell in love with Rosamund de Clifford, the daughter of a minor Norman knight. Their affair lasted a decade, and although Henry was only in England for three years or so during this period, it provided ample and enduring raw material for the weavers of Eleanor legend. From September 1165 to March 1166, the King stayed mainly at Woodstock, uncharacteristically for such an habitually peripatetic man, and failed to keep Christmas with his wife. He later built a garden at Everswell, near the royal palace, featuring ponds and bowers. The chroniclers were off. The besotted King had reputedly constructed a fantastic maze of 'Daedalus work' for his beloved (a description that appears for the first time in Higden's fourteenth-century *Polychronicon*) and the neglected Queen was murderously enraged. The rivalry between the two women was immortalised in stories and songs such as 'The Ballad of Fair Rosamond', though very little indeed is known of the real Rosamund and there is no evidence that the fantastic maze was ever built or that the Everswell garden had anything to do with her. In appropriately melodramatic style, Eleanor is supposed to have poisoned her rival, a tale that has received an unreasonable degree of attention given that Rosamund lived until 1176, by which time Eleanor had been in prison for three years.

The Rosamund episode has been used as an explanation for the fact that, by 1168, Henry and Eleanor had effectively separated but, once again, there was a simple, practical rationale behind an apparently emotional act. Eleanor's childbearing years were now over and it made perfect sense for her to relocate to Aquitaine to manage her perennially unruly vassals, leaving Henry with greater freedom to concentrate on his other lands. Eleanor may well have welcomed the chance of autonomy, not to mention a more gracious mode of living than that experienced by Henry's entourage, whose accommodation more often resembled a campsite than a court, but their marriage had always been based on business, and it was business that provided the primary reason for Eleanor's removal from England. That the Plantagenets were a spectacularly unhappy family would be proved time and time again on the battlefield in years to come, but Eleanor's presence in Aquitaine in 1168 was part of the loose administrative strategy through which Henry tried to govern his geographically and culturally disparate dominions. His territories – England, Normandy, Anjou and Aquitaine, which extended from the Scottish border to the Pyrenees – were collectively known as the Angevin empire, though they were never subject to imperial-style government. None of the Angevin kings called himself an emperor, all preferring to style themselves 'King of England, Duke of Normandy and Aquitaine and Count of Anjou', and while Henry did introduce similar administrative structures to this 'odd conglomeration of diverse powers',[22] he himself seems to have thought of, and intended to pass on, his lands as federated regional states rather than a single, centrally governed bloc. Royal authority varied greatly between the tightly controlled Anglo-Norman realm and the disparate, fluid and often mercurial loyalties of the south. Henry's decision that Eleanor should return to Aquitaine was an attempt to increase his hold on those southern aristocrats who were inclined to disregard their overlord when he was not facing them with an army; in short 'to calm and contain the Aquitainians, Henry gave them back *their* duchess'.[23]

In December 1168, then, Eleanor held her first independent Christmas court at Poitiers. This marked the beginning of the productive period during which she operated as governor of Aquitaine. Based at Poitiers, where she had refurbished the Maubergeonne Tower, the former lodgings of her grandfather's mistress Dangerosa, and surrounded by Poitevin, rather than Anglo-Norman counsellors, Eleanor was free to involve herself in the day-to-day management of her lands as she had never previously been able to do. Initially she was very much Henry's regent, but after the investiture of her son Richard as Duke of Aquitaine in 1170 she associated two thirds of her known acts with him. Assisted by her sensechal, Raoul de Faye, and her two clerks, Jordan and Peter, Eleanor busied herself with granting and confirming donations to religious houses, directing taxes, tolls and rights over customs and commodities such as wheat, salt and wine and confirming the loyalty of her lords by receiving their homage at Niort, Limoges and Bayonne.

Eleanor was also able to cement what was to become a sixty-years patronage of the abbey of Fontevrault, which she had first visited in 1152. The house, whose links with the dukes of Aquitaine dated back to the time of William IX, was notable for accommodating men and women, with the monks providing the manual labour and the nuns fulfilling a contemplative role, as specified by its founder, Robert d'Arbrissel. Both orders were governed by an abbess who, it was stipulated, must be a widow rather than a virgin who had never known the world. Henry, too, had ancestral ties with Fontevrault: the couple had founded Fontevrauldine cells in England, at Eaton, Westwood and Amesbury. In 1170 Eleanor granted lands, timber and firewood to the abbey and she went on to build the huge octagonal kitchen, with its five fireplaces, that may still be seen there today. Positioned where Eleanor's natal territories bordered Henry's, Fontevrault was to become both power base and retreat for her in later years, as well as – at Eleanor's designation, it has been convincingly argued[24] – the great dynastic memorial to the Angevin line.

At first, Eleanor in Aquitaine continued her policy of support of and co-operation with her husband. In 1169, Henry the Young King and Richard met Louis VII at Montmirail and agreed upon a treaty which would give Normandy, Anjou and England to the Young King, Brittany to Geoffrey, in right of his betrothal to Constance, and Aquitaine to Richard, the latter two grants to be held in vassalage to Louis. It was also confirmed that Richard would marry Alys, the sister of the Young King's wife and Louis's second daughter by Constance of Castile. Richard was invested as Duke in 1170, a very satisfying development for Eleanor, who used the occasion to demonstrate her own power and augment it by her association with the future duke. At the cathedral of St Hilaire on 31 May,

Eleanor wore the coronet of Aquitaine over a silk mantle and a scarlet cloak embroidered with the three leopards of Anjou. In her hand was the sceptre she had carried at her coronation as queen of England. The coronet was placed briefly on Richard's head, then substituted with a plainer silver circlet: Eleanor was making it clear that she was still in control. Richard was by her side at her Christmas court of 1171, and the next year they received King Alfonso of Aragon and King Sancho VI of Navarre on a diplomatic visit to discuss the county of Toulouse and the conditions of the Gascon-Pyrenean borders. Significantly, in three acts issued at Poitiers in 1172, Eleanor alters her previous form of address 'to the king's faithful followers and hers' – *fidelibus regis et suis* – to 'her faithful followers' *fidelibus suis*. In theory, her power in the duchy still devolved from Henry, and she was certainly limited geographically to a relatively small area around Poitiers, and economically by the fact that Aquitaine had no chancery of its own, but it does appear that during this period Eleanor was dissociating herself from Henry and reasserting her status as duchess in a manner whose significance would be revealed when the Angevin empire erupted in revolt the following year.

On the evening of 5 March 1173, the Young King crept out of the bedroom he was sharing with his father at Chinon and rode for Paris. From the Norman border, Henry II sent an envoy of bishops to ask Louis of France to return his son. 'Who is it that sends this message to me?' asked Louis, feigning bewilderment.

'The King of England,' they replied.

'Not so,' answered Louis. 'The King of England is here.'

It was a declaration of war. For years, Henry and Eleanor's beautiful son and heir had been chafing against what he saw as the unreasonable constraints placed upon him by his father. He might have been crowned twice, but all he had to live on were promises. Even his younger brother Richard had more power than he, while his father had cavalierly granted away his promised castles of Chinon, Loudun and Mirebeau as part of a planned marriage settlement for John without even asking his permission. Spoiled, lazy and greedy, the Young King refused to understand the exigencies under which his father was operating, and, encouraged by an opportunistic Louis, he was determined to fight for his rights. He was supported not only by the treachery of his brothers, Richard and Geoffrey, but by Eleanor, who chose to ally herself with her ex-husband against the father of her sons.

What were Eleanor's motivations for this extraordinary step? Some writers have claimed that the assassination in 1170 of the archbishop of

Canterbury, Thomas à Becket, provoked her beyond endurance, but this has been dismissed by others as a 'post-hoc contrivance'.[25] Eleanor had actively supported Henry in his struggle against Becket, with whom she had had a distant personal relationship, and though she would have been as shocked as any conventionally pious person by his murder, she was nothing if not a pragmatist. Becket was set for sainthood, but she could make little political use of that. Another theory is that Eleanor wanted to assert herself against Henry as a consequence of the frustrations of her marriage, in particular her resentment at being overshadowed by his mother, Empress Matilda. Again, this is implausible, because Eleanor had been living independently since 1168, a year after Matilda's death. These factors could well have informed her attitude to Henry, but why would she have waited five years to extract her 'revenge'? A popular charge is that Eleanor was so jealous of Rosamund de Clifford that she raised Poitou for spite, which is as absurdly melodramatic as suggesting that she murdered Henry's mistress. A likelier explanation is more prosaic: power. Eleanor loved Aquitaine and she wanted to ensure that it would pass intact to Richard. Her elder sons were respectively fourteen, fifteen and twenty, still young and in need of guidance. If Henry were to be defeated, Aquitaine, freed from his interference, would be much more governable, and Eleanor would have a considerably wider stage on which to exercise her control.

How far was Eleanor directly involved in the rebellion? William of Newburgh, Ralph Diceto and Roger of Howden all agree that she advised Richard and Geoffrey to ally themselves with the Young King and sent them to Paris to join him. Richard FitzNigel, too, asserts that Eleanor used her influence on the younger boys. A letter written to Eleanor by the archbishop of Rouen on Henry's instructions confirms that the English king believed his wife was responsible for turning his sons against him – 'the fact that you should have made the fruits of your union with our Lord King rise up against their father . . .' – and acknowledges her capacity to sway them: 'Before events carry us to a dreadful conclusion, return with your sons to the husband whom you must obey and with whom it is your duty to live . . . Bid your sons, we beg you, to be obedient and devoted to their father.'

Eleanor was threatened with the full anger of the Church if she did not obey, but she paid no mind to the archbishop. She was determined to see the struggle through. She was not, however, acting alone. Although Gervase of Canterbury presents the whole rebellion as being planned and carried out by Eleanor, Louis and it was claimed, Eleanor's seneschal,

Raoul de Faye, were also deeply involved. What Eleanor did was to skilfully manipulate a varied set of regional grievances against Henry into a concentrated movement, using the ambitions of the French King and the ever-turbulent lords of the south to bolster the strength of her sons. This was not revenge, but an exceptionally cold-blooded political gamble. Eleanor's readiness to make use of Louis, and to be of use to him, suggests that she did not permit emotion to play much of a part in her strategies. She could put aside whatever feelings she still had for Henry after twenty years together if disloyalty would get her what she wanted. The scandalous events of Eleanor's life have often led to her being depicted as a creature of emotion rather than reason, a portrayal that emphasises her 'feminine' willingness to allow her heart to rule her head. Nowhere is this more untrue than in her promotion of the 1173 rebellion. Eleanor was not jealous, or peeved, or frustrated: she was ruthless.

In May, she decided to join her sons at Louis's court, changing into men's clothes on her journey the better to avoid capture. Gervase of Canterbury mentions her arrest almost as an aside to his expressions of disgust at this transgression, the fact that Eleanor was prepared to adopt such a sinful disguise being yet more evidence of the lengths to which she would go to snatch power. It is not known where Eleanor was taken, but since four Aquitaine men, William Maingot, Porteclie de Mauzé, Hervé le Panetier and Foulques de Matha, all received grants of land from Henry, it is suspected that she was betrayed by people who were close to her, who could have fed information to Henry and informed him of her itinerary. Maingot and De Mauzé were ducal castellans who between them had witnessed seven of Eleanor's charters during her period in government of Aquitaine from 1168 to 1173. De Maingot was appointed to Le Faye's former post of Seneschal in 1174. If they were the traitors, Eleanor was hardly in a position to blame them.

It is intriguing to speculate how events might have gone had Henry not captured his queen so early in the game. The Young King and Louis had assembled an impressive force, including the counts of Flanders, Champagne, Boulogne and Blois, a number of lords from Anjou and Maine who had renounced their homage to Henry and a group of English barons. The Young King had made an unpleasant little deal with the King of Scotland, rashly promising him Northumbria in return for an attack from the north and, by September, the Count of Angoulême, Eleanor's crusading companion Geoffrey de Rançon and the powerful Poitevin lords Guy and Geoffrey de Lusignan had also joined the rebels. Henry was attacked by a hydra-headed enemy, facing over the course of eighteen months fronts in Normandy, the Vexin, the south-east of England and its northern marches, Poitou and the Atlantic coast of Aquitaine. He had the advantage of his swift army of Brabantine mercenaries, the loyalty and military skill of his bastard son Geoffrey and the tactical inadequacy of Louis, in command of the disparate rebel forces, who, though personally brave, was no general. Recalling Eleanor's complaints about Louis's monk-like tendencies, would she have advised the Young King differently had she been free?

By the end of September 1174 it was all over. The uprising had mostly consisted of sieges and castle-taking, and as usual the real victims were the peasants and townspeople, with Normandy being hit particularly hard. Henry's settlement with his sons, decided at Montlouis near Tours, was a combination of generosity and viciously brilliant diplomacy. He forced the King of Scotland to pay homage to him as a vassal and to surrender five important castles, gave half the revenues of Poitou and Brittany to Richard and Geoffrey respectively and granted the Young King a more substantial allowance and two castles in Normandy – but none of the power he craved. Richard was given the task of subduing the rebels in Aquitaine, where he began to acquire his magnificent martial reputation. Henry was magnanimous, however unwisely. It was only Eleanor who remained unforgiven.

That Henry had trusted Eleanor right up to the moment she betrayed him decisively by making for Paris is demonstrated by the fact that when he disbanded her court at Poitiers in May 1174, some of the most important young women in the Angevin realm had been staying there in her charge. Marguerite, the next queen of England; her sister Alys, Richard's betrothed; Geoffrey's fiancée, Constance of Brittany; John's prospective bride, Alice of Maurienne; Henry's illegitimate sister Emma of Anjou and Joanna, his daughter with Eleanor, had all been in her entourage. They all, along with Eleanor, sailed with Henry to England from Barfleur in July. Marguerite, Alys of France and Constance were sent to the castle at Devizes (probably along with Alice of Maurienne, who died shortly afterwards), while Emma was swiftly disposed of in marriage to a Welsh prince. Eleanor, who spent the first period of her captivity in an unknown castle, possibly Rouen, Chinon or Falaise, was isolated, and was to remain so for the next fourteen years.

The extent of her exclusion from court and political life is reflected in the sparse record evidence for this period. In Aquitaine, where she had been active until the rebellion, Eleanor is mentioned only twice. The English Pipe Rolls indicate that she lived at Winchester and Sarum, making brief visits to a limited number of other houses in the charge of Ranulf Glanville, a former Yorkshire sheriff and Ralph FitzStephen, a chamberlain in Henry's household. She was permitted two chamberlains of her own after 1180, but the only other named member of her staff is her maid, Amaria. An 1176 entry in the Pipe Rolls notes a payment of £28 13s 7d for two scarlet capes, two furs and a bedcover for 'the use of the Queen and her servant', suggesting that though Eleanor's living conditions were reasonable, they were not consummate with her status, as her clothes were no finer than a servant girl's and apparently she and Amaria had to share the same bed. As far as the English were concerned, Eleanor no longer existed. It was left to one of her Poitevin poets, Richard, to mourn her imprisonment in the style to which her reputation has become accustomed:

> Daughter of Aquitaine, fair, fruitful vine! Tell me, eagle with two heads, tell me, where were you when your eaglets, flying from their nest, dared to raise their talons against the King of the North Wind? ... Your harp has changed into the voice of mourning, your flute sounds the note of affliction and your songs are turned into sounds of lamentation. Reared with abundance of all delights, you had a taste for luxury and refinement and enjoyed a royal liberty. You lived richly in your own inheritance, you took pleasure in the pastimes of your women, you delighted in the melodies of flute and drum ... You abounded in riches of every kind. ... Eagle of the broken alliance, you cry out unanswered because it is the King of the North Wind who holds you in captivity. But cry out and cease not to cry, do not weary, raise your voice like a trumpet so that it may reach the ears of your sons. For the day is approaching when they shall deliver you and then you shall come again to dwell in your native land.

Eleanor was to spend the remainder of her days as Queen of England under house arrest, but the end of her reign by no means marked the end of her power. In widowhood, she continued to dominate the fortunes of the English crown until her death, in her eightieth year, and beyond. Her political influence cast its shadow across the fifteenth century, and the legend of her life ultimately outlasted even that.

CHAPTER 6

BERENGARIA OF NAVARRE

'A most praiseworthy widow'

On 3 September 1189, a new king was crowned at Westminster. Eleanor of Aquitaine's betrayal of Henry marked the beginning of a long series of cruel disappointments which marred the last period of his reign. A decade after Montlouis, the Young King and Geoffrey had rebelled against their brother Richard's rule in Aquitaine, but the uprising collapsed when the Young King died suddenly in June 1183. Three years later, Geoffrey, too, was dead: his heir, Arthur of Brittany, was born after his father's demise. All Henry II's strategies for the future seemed to be unravelling at once, a position he himself exacerbated by making Princess Alys, Richard's betrothed, his mistress. Alys's wily brother Philip Augustus, now King of France, took advantage of Henry's endless stalling over the marriage and marched into Angevin territories on the pretext of reclaiming Alys's dowry of Berry and the Vexin. Richard, who had long feared that Henry intended to designate his younger brother John as heir, threw in his lot with the French King, and for a time the two enjoyed a passioante friendship which was the wonder of the chroniclers. Richard and Henry were still at war when the King died a bitter and possibly unshriven death on 5 July 1189, shortly after witnessing the French armies burning his beloved birthplace of Le Mans to the ground.

One of Richard's first acts on learning of his father's death had been to dispatch William Marshal to England to release his mother, and Eleanor, now aged sixty-eight, was with her beloved son as he was anointed. She had made several public outings since 1183, prompting some historians to consider that Henry may have responded to the Young King's deathbed request for his mother to be set free, but effectively she remained a prisoner. She was permitted a progress through her dower lands in an attempt to forestall Philip Augustus's claim to them on behalf of his sister Marguerite, the widowed Young Queen, and was produced for several strategic appearances before returning to England in 1186, but her freedom was illusory: 'She was paraded abroad when it suited Henry and confined when it did not.'' As Richard's regent in England until his coronation, Eleanor was finally able to exercise the powers which had so long lain dormant. Matthew Paris noted that Eleanor's activities in this period made her 'exceedingly respected and beloved'. Her capabilities were particularly useful as Richard did not plan to spend any longer in his new kingdom than he had to. Since the battle of Hattin in 1187, in which the Muslim ruler Saladin had inflicted unbearable slaughter on the knights Templar and Hospitaller in the Holy Land, Richard had had only one object in mind: Jerusalem.

Before Richard's crusading plan could be put into action, there remained one last detail to be taken care of. Marriage was essential for two reasons: first to cement an alliance that would provide vital protection of the Angevin territories in the south during his absence, and secondly to attempt to secure the succession. If he were to die without a son, the competing heirs would be his nephew Arthur of Brittany and his brother John. When Richard arrived in France in December 1189, he renewed his longstanding pledge to poor, patient Princess Alys, but after a council held in Normandy in March 1190, which included the archbishop of Canterbury, John and Eleanor, he persuaded Philip Augustus to 'reconsider' the match. This diplomatic delaying tactic was designed merely to hold off Philip's anger for as long as possible – Richard had no intention of marrying the disgraced Alys, but he needed French support for the crusade and therefore thought it unwise to mention to his jilted fiancée's brother that he was already engaged to another woman.

Various dates are given for the betrothal of Richard of England to Berengaria of Navarre. Like his mother, Richard has in many ways become the victim of his own legend, and there is a tendency to romanticise the first meeting of the Spanish princess and the most romantic of kings. The high chivalric version has him falling in love with her during a tournament in Pamplona when he was still Count of Poitiers, possibly as early as 1177, even though at the time she was about seven and he was twenty. The marriage may have been mooted in 1185, but a more generally accepted date for the confirmation of the betrothal is 1188. In any event, Richard continued to play his double game with Philip until literally hours before Berengaria arrived for their wedding.

On 7 August 1190, Richard embarked at Genoa, rested for five days at Portofino, and continued down the coast of Italy, meeting Philip Augustus at Messina on Sicily on 24 September. Meanwhile, Eleanor set off from

Bordeaux across the Pyrenees to fetch the bride. Her destination, Navarre, was a small but geographically important kingdom on the Spanish side of the mountains, a nexus for pilgrim and trade routes as it controlled the two main passes of Sonpont and Roncesvalles.

Navarre might not have been large, but it was no provincial backwater. The population was Occitan-French, Basque, Jewish and Muslim as well as Navarrese, a blend reflected in (relatively) tolerant attitudes towards non-Christians and a sophisticated legal code. Like Richard, Berengaria was of mixed ancestry, and she already had family connections with the Angevin dynasty. Her cousin Alfonso VIII of Castile was married to Richard's sister Leonor and her aunt Margarita had married William the Bad, the Norman King of Sicily, in 1150, serving as regent for several years after his death on behalf of her son William the Good, the recently deceased husband of Richard's sister Joanna. Unlike Richard's, Berengaria's parents appear to have been happily married. They had five children in twenty-five years together, and after Berengaria's mother, Queen Sancha-Beata, died in 1179, her father, King Sancho El Sabio (the Wise), spent the remaining twenty years of his life without remarrying, a pattern that would be followed by both Berengaria and her sister Blanca.

Sancho El Sabio's reign was dominated by the power struggle between Navarre and the neighbouring kingdoms of Aragon, Castile and Leon. On at least two occasions Henry II had met the kings of Navarre, Aragon and Castile to arbitrate in these conflicts. King Sancho was allied with the King of Aragon against Richard's enemy, Raymond of Toulouse, so a Navarrese connection could provide vital support for the English king in southern Gascony, while Sancho would benefit from protection against his enemy the King of Castile. In April 1185, Richard had agreed to help the ruler of Aragon to persuade Sancho to return two castles, which suggested he already had some influence in Navarre, and it is notable that in that year Berengaria was given the *tenencia*, or fief, of Monreal near the favoured royal city of Tudela. Neither of her two sisters are known to have received a similar gift, and it is likely that the King of Navarre was thus enhancing his daughter's status with a view to her betrothal to Richard. In 1188, the troublesome troubadour Bertran de Born was gloating over Richard's rejection of Alys for Berengaria, and though neither the date nor place of Berengaria's birth are known for certain, it is estimated that she would have been about eighteen when her betrothal was confirmed.

Berengaria met her famous mother-in-law in Pamplona, where Sancho held a banquet at the Olite Palace before the two women set off to cross the Alps, descending into Lombardy, where Eleanor witnessed a charter at Lodi near Milan, and on to Pisa. Here they paused to wait for news from Richard, and since there was no ship available to take them directly to Sicily, Richard decided that they should continue along the coast to Naples, where they embarked in February, accompanied by the Count of Flanders, who was travelling to join the waiting crusaders at Messina. It was an arduous journey for these intrepid women to undertake, particularly in the case of the sixty-six-year-old Eleanor, but beyond this sparse itinerary, no record remains of the time they spent together. An Alpine crossing was particularly gruelling in winter, and Berengaria and Eleanor had no choice but to live in intimacy as they were carried in litters up the precarious passes, pausing to sleep in monasteries, or as their horses plodded through the dense, freezing mists of the Lombardy plain, but they do not seem to have developed a warm relationship. In charters given from Fontevrault in the years after Richard's death, Eleanor refers to her daughter-in-law as 'Queen Berengaria' without adding the affectionate 'dilectissima' or 'carissima' appended to the names of her daughters.

Three chronicle accounts emphasise Berengaria's 'wisdom', though so little is known of her early life that it is impossible to ascertain her education, and we can do no more than suppose it was similar to that of other girls of her class. Berengaria is sometimes described as a Basque, but again there is no evidence that she spoke the Basque language. Her mother tongue was possibly Castilian or, more likely, Romance (Aragonese-Navarrese), which had become the official language of the Navarrese chancellery in 1180. The language she was most likely to have had in common with Eleanor was Occitan, which was also spoken in Navarre. Mothers-in-law are often intimidating creatures, and Eleanor, the most famous woman in Europe, must at first have been a terrifying companion for a girl who had barely ventured outside her father's domains. Perhaps there were awkward silences.

As Berengaria and Eleanor moved slowly south, the tension between Richard and Philip Augustus became acute. The two kings had arrived in Sicily a day apart, in late September, and Philip immediately began seeking to weasel Richard's disagreements with the island's ruler, Tancred, to his own advantage. Tancred, the bastard nephew of William the Good, had succeeded in claiming the throne in defiance of the rights of Constance of Hauteville, the new bride of the German Emperor. His position was precarious, and he was deeply suspicious of the motives of the crusaders. Joanna, William's widow, was imprisoned in Palermo, and though Richard was swiftly able to secure her release, Tancred prevaricated about her dowry, claiming that the terms of William's will were void and trying to palm her off with a meagre cash payment. When riots broke out between the citizens of Messina and the crusaders, whose presence was imposing great strain on the city's resources, Richard saw an opportunity to demonstrate to Tancred that he meant business. He took Messina 'in less time than a priest could say matins',[2] set up a mobile fortress and established a strict set of rules to control the behaviour of his soldiers. Unsurprisingly, Tancred now showed himself amenable to negotiation. Philip Augustus, by this time desperate to force Richard to marry Alys, tried to persuade Tancred that Richard planned to betray him.

Though Richard had of necessity been discreet about Berengaria's arrival, Philip was aware of her journey, and that Eleanor had met the German Emperor at Lodi. It was easy for Philip Augustus to suggest that the English King was in league with the Emperor to overthrow Tancred, and for a while he was believed, but Richard had an ace to play. In March, he informed Philip bluntly that he had no intention of marrying Alys, since she had for years been his own father's mistress and had even had a child by him. If Philip insisted on imposing the damaged goods of the Capets upon him, he would produce witnesses to publicly affirm Alys's disgrace. The Treaty of Messina records Philip's helpless concession that 'the above mentioned King [Richard] may freely marry whomever he wishes, notwithstanding the former agreement made between us that he would take our sister Alys as wife'. Tancred had revealed Philip's poisonous suggestions, and Richard had satisfied him with a recognition of his crown – the promise of a betrothal between Richard's nephew Arthur of Brittany and Tancred's daughter – and a pact against invasion. Tancred provided another, larger payment against Joanna's dowry settlement and the two kings exchanged gifts. Richard got nineteen ships and Tancred received Excalibur. Tancred was obviously a gimcrack diplomat, but he was pleased with his magic sword, and certainly a happier man than Philip who, exposed as a liar and the brother of an adulteress, slunk off in disgust for Acre on 30 March 1191, just hours before Richard's new wife arrived.

Given the background to her entrance to Messina, the reports of Berengaria's reception are disappointingly low-key. Ambroise does his best to introduce a bit of romance: 'For the news had been brought to him that his mother had arrived there, bringing the King his beloved. She was a wise maiden, noble, brave and fair, neither false nor disloyal. Her name was Berengaria and her father the King of Navarre had handed her over to the mother of King Richard, who was longing for her to be brought to him. Then she was named as Queen. For the King had loved her very much; ever since he was Count of Poitiers he had desired her.'[3]

Other writers (none of them eyewitnesses) describe Berengaria as 'of renowned beauty and wisdom', 'a beautiful and learned maiden', 'nobly born', 'beautiful' and 'of splendid parage'.[4] Richard of Devizes strikes a discordant note amid this conventional praise with his contention that Berengaria was 'more wise than beautiful', though the Navarrese historian Mañuel Sagatibelza Beraza loyally suggests that if her wisdom surpassed even her beauty, Berengaria must have been wise indeed. The Berengaria scholar Ann Trindade suggests that even within the constraints of medieval literary convention, some of her 'distinctive personal qualities' may be discerned from these descriptions, notably in the repeated use of *'sage'* – wise – and Ambroise's interesting choice of *'preux'*, meaning brave, an unusual adjective to apply to a woman. Both these qualities were to be tested in the next stage of Berengaria's long journey to the altar.

Since it was Lent, the royal wedding could not be immediately celebrated in Sicily, so on the Wednesday of Holy Week the huge crusader fleet of 219 ships set off for the Holy Land. Eleanor had spent only three days in Sicily with her children. Berengaria and Joanna travelled in the same vessel, modestly separated from Richard. Off the coast of Crete, the fleet was scattered by storms and the ship containing the Dowager Queen of Sicily and the queen-to-be of England was driven towards the coast of Cyprus. Isaac Comnenus, the island's ruler, supposedly attempted to lure them ashore at Limassol in the hope of a fat ransom, and the *'Itinerarium'* imagines the two shipwrecked queens gazing longingly across the violent waves, yearning for rescue. Richard then obligingly appears in full Lionheart mode, charging up the beaches, sword in hand, imprisons the 'tyrant' Comnenus and liberates his fiancée. In fact, the conquest of Cyprus had always been on Richard's agenda, and the threat of shipwreck was merely an unmissable opportunity to add to the Lionheart legend.

One of Richard's greatest strengths as a military commander was his capacity for organisation away from the battlefield. He had already identified Cyprus as a vital staging post in the crusade supply line, and waiting until Philip Augustus had set off for the Holy Land before invading the island relieved him of the obligation to honour the agreement of a fifty-fifty division of spoils acquired in 'God's service'. On 6 May Richard appeared from Rhodes, where his own ship had docked, and within weeks he had control of Cyprus. Comnenus surrendered on 1 June, once he learned that Richard had taken his daughter prisoner, on the unusual condition that he not be bound in irons. Ever the gentleman, Richard supposedly had some silver chains made up. With his coffers fortified – Cyprus was an immediate source of revenue in the form of treasure and a tax levied on the inhabitants – Richard promptly sold the island to the order of the Templars for 100,000 Saracen bezants.

It is quite possible that Richard had had it in mind to hold his wedding on Cyprus, provided all went according to plan, rather than in the embarrassing presence of the French King in Palestine. Whenever he made the decision, on 12 May, while his men were sweeping over the island, he and Berengaria were married in Limassol at the chapel of St George.

The ceremony was performed by Richard's own chaplain, Nicholas, later bishop of Le Mans, before Berengaria was crowned Queen of England by John, bishop of Evreux. The groom wore a rose silk tunic accessorised with a scarlet cap, gold embroidered cape and sash and a gold and silver scabbard. The bride's outfit is not recorded. An English poem describes the wedding, suggesting it was celebrated in style:

> There King Ric spoused Beringer
> The King's daughter of Navarre
> And made there the richest spousing
> That ever maked any king.
> And crowned himself Emperor,
> And her Empress, with honour.[5]

Berengaria got a three-week honeymoon on the island of Aphrodite and then, on 5 June, husband and wife set sail once again. Berengaria and Joanna were now joined by the captured Cypriot princess, whom Richard had entrusted to his wife's care. Isaac Comnenus was deposited at the fortress of Margat on the Syrian coast before the fleet moved on to Tyre. Berengaria may have witnessed a sea battle when the rear of the fleet encountered a laden Muslim supply ship bound for the besieged garrison at Acre. Richard succeeded in taking the ship in a perfectly timed blow to Muslim morale.

On 8 June the new Queen of England arrived at Acre and, for the next two years, while Richard was making his reputation as the greatest warrior in the west, remained in a curious limbo, a queen without a country, with no outlet for any of the traditional activities associated with her position. Pierre de Langtoft describes Berengaria and Joanna as coming together 'like birds in a cage', a sad image which suggests something of the restricted existence they led. Together with the Cypriot princess, they were housed first at Acre, then at Ramleh and Jaffa, but both cities were dangerous and there was little opportunity to explore their exotic surroundings. Weaving, embroidery, board games, reading and prayer were likely pastimes, and they were able to enjoy music, as the writer Ambroise mentions the presence of minstrels. Mindful of Eleanor's dubious crusading reputation, Berengaria was bound to conduct herself discreetly and the silence of the chroniclers about Berengaria and Joanna suggests that their conduct was spotless: their lives were apparently so dull that there was nothing worth recording of them. One highlight was the Christmas court Richard held at Latrun, where the two queens proved a great attraction and Berengaria was able to perform the ceremonial role she had been led to expect would be required of her, at least for a short time. But for the most part Richard (again, perhaps recalling the failure of the Second Crusade, and the accusations that the presence of women had undermined it morally) was naturally inclined to keep them away from the action. We might imagine that sensually Berengaria's experience was novel and exciting – the scents of strange and wonderful flowers and spices, the sounds of an unknown language, the flavours of orange water and olives – but for her the Holy Land was a country only glimpsed from behind the leather curtains of a litter or through the narrow window of a fortress.

Berengaria and Richard said goodbye at Acre in September 1192. She and Joanna sailed for Europe on 29 September and the queen of England was not to see her husband again for nearly two years. After landing at Brindisi, their party made its way to Rome, where Berengaria stayed for six months. In April, she witnessed a charter on securing a loan, signing herself proudly as 'Queen of the English, Duchess of the Normans and Aquitainians, Countess of the Angevins'. It is just possible that her attempt to raise money might have been connected to the capture of Richard in December by his old enemy Leopold of Austria, who had taken him prisoner as he made his way home from the Holy Land and handed him over to the German Emperor, Henry VI. Richard's return to Europe had been complicated by the quarrels that had flared up during the crusade, and the coasts of southern France and Italy between Genoa and Pisa were barred to him. After a perilous journey on the high autumn seas, he reached Venice, from where he attempted to cross Austria. He was seized at Erdburg near Vienna, according to legend making a poor show of disguising himself as a cook. Richard's captivity was a great boon to both Emperor Henry and Richard's former friend Philip of France, and in February the King's ransom was set at the impossible sum of 100,000 marks.

It was not Richard's wife who busied herself working for his release, but his mother Eleanor – an opportunity for action that marks the beginning of the greatest period of her queenship, albeit now as dowager. Berengaria, meanwhile, left Rome in June 1193, escorted by Cardinal Melior and Stephen of Turnham, and travelled to Pisa, Genoa and Marseilles, accompanied first by her brother-in-law King Alfonso and then by Raymond of Toulouse to the Aquitaine heartlands of Poitou. As Berengaria continued her stately progress, Eleanor was frantically trying to prevent her youngest son John from usurping his brother's throne and to raise the enormous ransom for Richard's release. John had wasted no time in profiting from Richard's absence, manipulating the unpopularity of the chancellor, Walter Longchamp, to march on London to effect the officer's dismissal and the sequestration of his estates. He then set off on a series of progresses designed to win popularity and to convey, prematurely, the impression that he was Richard's heir-apparent. To some extent, Eleanor had condoned, if not supported, John's activities until this juncture. She approved of Walter of Coutances, archbishop of Rouen, who had been appointed head of the regency council in Longchamp's place, and had refused to receive the delegation of cardinals Longchamp had mustered in his support, even denying them safe conduct across Normandy. Now, though, John had gone too far.

Eleanor had kept her Christmas court of 1191 in Normandy where, in January, Philip Augustus launched an attack on Gisors, in flagrant defiance of the truce of God, the agreement by which crusading monarchs agreed not to wage war upon one another. When the assault failed, the French King turned to John. He offered him all Richard's French holdings if he would marry the abandoned Princess Alys (who, as no one knew quite what to do with her, was still languishing in the semi-custody of the English at Rouen) and surrender Gisors. John accepted with alacrity, but Eleanor managed to reach England just as he was preparing to sail for Normandy. She convened councils at Winchester, Windsor, Oxford and London to demand a renewal of the oath of loyalty to Richard and contrived to have John's castles confiscated if he attempted to leave the country. This contained him for a time, but when news of Richard's capture finally broke after months of puzzling silence, John lost no time in rushing to Paris to pay homage to Philip, claim Richard's Angevin lands and confirm that Arthur of Brittany would be excluded from the succession. In April 1193, Philip invaded Normandy and attempted to besiege Rouen. John, meanwhile, had raised a mercenary force in Wales and taken Windsor Castle; he had also hired mercenaries in Flanders. Gervase of Canterbury reports how, under Eleanor's orders, people of all social ranks, peasants, knights and nobles, manned the eastern coast of

England to successfully repel them. Still, as Eleanor had to raise a sum of money three times the annual expenditure of the English government to secure Richard's release, it was necessary to come to a swift accommodation with her treacherous son. John agreed to place the royal castles he had appropriated in Eleanor's temporary keeping, and Eleanor set about her campaign.

In the first of two extraordinary letters to Pope Celestine III, Eleanor recalls in no uncertain terms Henry II's support for the papacy during the recent conflict between Rome and the Emperor Frederick. 'Grief,' she reproaches him, 'does not recognise a master, is afraid of no ally, it has no regard for anyone and it does not spare them, not even you.' The Pope's reluctance to help Richard for fear of threatening the tenuous truce between Rome and the empire is 'a mark of criminality and disgrace'. In reminding him of her husband's loyalty in preserving the papacy, she remarks that Celestine's failure to intervene on Richard's behalf is bringing the Church into disrepute. 'Indeed, among the public it casts a shadow over the Church and excites a rumour among the people (and it considerably damages your standing) the fact that in such a crisis, amid so many tears ... you have not sent those princes even one messenger from those around you.' Eleanor's second letter is an impassioned outpouring of maternal grief, reinforced by references to her royal status and Marian imagery:

> I wish that the blood of my body, already dead, the brain in my head and the marrow of my bones would dissolve into tears, so much that I completely melt away into sorrow. My insides have been torn out of me, I have lost the staff of my old age, the light of my eyes; if God had assented to my prayers He would condemn my ill fated eyes to perpetual blindness so that they no longer saw the woes of my people ... why have I, the Lady of two kingdoms, reached the disgrace of this abominable old age?

Revisiting her previous charge that the Pope is being prevented from acting by worldly concerns, Eleanor has the temerity to ask: 'Is your power derived from God or men?' In her fury, she dares to accuse the Pope of being a coward, of keeping 'the sword of Peter sheathed'. Despite these taunts, the Pope continued to dither, so she set about raising the entire ransom herself.

Everyone in England, from the wealthy, who were taxed at 25 per cent, to the Cistercian monks, who had nothing to give but their sheep, was forced to contribute to the fund. Eleanor appointed a council of five to supervise the collections and the booty was stored in the vault of St Paul's. Collectors rode all over Anjou and Aquitaine and Eleanor personally dunned the abbot of St Martial at Limoges for 100 marks. The Pope eventually stirred from his lethargy, kindly offering to place England under interdict if Richard's beleaguered subjects did not melt down their plate fast enough, which was not quite the assistance Eleanor had been hoping for. But by the autumn, she was able to promise over two thirds of the ransom to the imperial envoys.

Eleanor left for Germany in December 1193. Rather wonderfully, the captured Cypriot princess was one of the ladies in her train. It has been suggested that she may have taken the oportunity to visit her first child, her eldest daughter with Louis, en route, as her journey took her through the northern regions of Champagne, and she and Countess Marie may have seen one another again at Meaux or Provins. Eleanor was in Cologne in time to keep the feast of Twelfth Night, and though John and Philip had offered the Emperor a last-minute bribe to delay Richard's release, she was reunited with her son at Mainz in February. On 12 March, the King of England landed at Sandwich. Richard was determined to put his upstart brother in his place and, after giving thanks for his deliverance at Canterbury and at a reception in London, he set off for Nottingham to besiege the castle John had garrisoned. In his swift execution of his task, he introduced Greek fire for the first time, a crusading device which combined sulphur, pitch and naptha to 'bomb' the walls. On 17 April, Richard was crowned again in the ancient capital of Winchester, but once more, it was Queen Eleanor, not Queen Berengaria, who witnessed his triumph.

Berengaria's apparent lack of activity during this period has been interpreted as a sign of a breach in the marriage, but it is difficult to see how she and Richard could actually have had time to fall out. Since the moment they had embarked for the Holy Land, they had spent only a few weeks in one another's company. Yet contemporary chroniclers such as Roger of Howden made it clear that there was something wrong with their relationship, and modern scholars have found a fruitful field of speculation in the supposed rift. The period of Richard's Austrian adventures and captivity is exceptionally rich in Lionheart legend, and Berengaria, too, finds a place in it. However dubious their veracity, an examination of these stories and of how they have been used and interpreted brings us closer to an understanding of both twelfth-century and modern perceptions of the mystery at the heart of their marriage.

The explanation, according to many modern commentators, is that there were two queens in the relationship. Despite being obliged to concede that there is 'no direct evidence to prove that Richard was homosexual, and some direct evidence to prove that he was not', a 'majority' of writers are determined to believe that the Lionheart was gay.[6] Richard had at least one illegitimate child, Philip of Cognac, acquired a reputation for less than gentlemanly behaviour with the wives and daughters of his enemies and apparently so affronted a Fontevrault nun with his attentions that she declared she would rather put out the beautiful eyes that had seduced him than submit, but none of this is in itself proof that Richard did not also enjoy sexual relations with men. That he did has been inferred from various chronicle accounts, the first of which deals with his relationship with Philip Augustus. Roger of Howden reports that during the period of their intense friendship in 1187, before the mutual alienation of the crusade, the two men 'ate from the same table and drank from the same cup and at night they slept in the same bed. And the King of France loved him as his own soul and their mutual affection was so strong that because of the vehemence of their mutual affection the Lord King of England was dumbfounded.'[7] Ann Trindade has highlighted the choice of the word 'vehemence', which is used by several writers in the course of describing sexual love, but there was nothing at all unusual about medieval men sharing either plates or beds, and if Richard was 'dumbfounded' it may well have been by the fact that he had achieved such friendship with his traditional enemy.

The second often-cited piece of evidence concerns the visit of a hermit in 1195. The holy man warned Richard to be 'mindful of the destruction of Sodom and abstain from unlawful things; or else God's just retribution will overtake you'.[8] Scholars disagree on the interpretation of the sins of Sodom. Some note that the term could be used to cover a range of sexually aberrant activities and is therefore applicable to Richard's adulterous heterosexual behaviour at this juncture; others insist on texts which refer 'consistently and unambiguously to male homosexual intercourse'.[9] Later Lionheart legends certainly pick up on the theme of Richard's sexuality. In the English romance *Richard Coeur de Lyon*, the imprisoned King falls in love with the King of Almain's daughter, and when her furious father releases a ferocious lion into his cell, he reaches down its throat and rips out its heart. This seems a straightforward bit of heroic fantasy, but it has also been interpreted as a 'defensive' anecdote, designed to counter the story of the hermit by casting Richard as aggressively heterosexual. The most famous of the legends concerning Richard's captivity is perhaps that of the minstrel Blondel, who sang piteously before a number of German castles before hearing the voice of his beloved master. The story appears in the thirteenth century, and in some versions Blondel is portrayed as a rival to Queen Berengaria for Richard's love. That it is entirely fictitious does not entirely dismiss the possibility that contemporaries thought Richard had love affairs with men and that the Blondel story could be a reformulation of collective rumours.

Academic obsession with dragging the Lionheart out of the closet may indicate no more than that to twenty-first-century eyes Richard was too convincingly straight for his own good, but what is interesting about the hermit story, the most compelling piece of evidence for some sort of extramarital antics, is the way it centres upon Richard's reconciliation with his Queen. That such a reconciliation was called for has led some scholars to believe that the marriage was never consummated, but there is no reason to believe this was so. According to Howden, the King initially disregarded the hermit's warnings, but during Holy Week he fell ill. He called for priests and confessed, then 'received his wife, whom he had not known for a *long time* [this author's italics], and renouncing unlawful intercourse, was united with his wife and the two became one flesh; then God gave him health of both body and soul'. This suggests that Richard had 'known' Berengaria at some point; that he had not done so for a long time is explained by the simple fact that he had not seen her. The King heard Mass, gave alms and ordered new church ornaments to replace those which had been impounded to raise his ransom. This pattern of reformation and reunion follows an earlier sequence in which Richard performed a similarly motivated penance in Sicily before departing on crusade, a penance capped by the arrival of Berengaria at Messina. Sin, sexual or otherwise, is followed by disease (a pious objective correlative), then repentance, symbolised by union with Berengaria, and a return to God. The point here is not the precise nature of the sins Richard committed, but the primacy given to the queen as a symbol of redemption and healing. Abuse of the sacrament of marriage leads to God's displeasure and disease; the proper use of the queen's body sets things right. In this light, the hermit story might be read as much as a celebration of the sanctity of sex within marriage as a hint of Richard's love for men without it.

A likely date for Richard and Berengaria's reunion is June 1194, at Loches. His English homecoming had been short-lived. In May, Richard and Eleanor sailed for Normandy, where Eleanor presided over a reconciliation between her sons at Lisieux. John prostrated himself before his brother and was forgiven – was Richard displaying the same kind of ill-judged leniency that had caused so many problems for his father Henry? – and after that it was back to business as usual, which for Richard meant war. Philip's incursions into Normandy had to be stopped, and it was this mission that occupied the last five years of Richard's life.

Berengaria was accompanied to Loches by her brother Sancho. Their father, Sancho El Sabio, died the following month and Berengaria's brother, who had proved himself staunchly committed to the English alliance, returned to Navarre. In Poitou, Berengaria had been keeping a small household, moving between the castles of Chinon, Saumur and Beaufort-en-Vallée, but the next Christmas she and Richard may have been together at Eleanor's palace in Poitiers. She was certainly present with him when Joanna was married to Raymond VI, the new Count of Toulouse, in Rouen in October 1196, in an ill-fated attempt to resolve the difficulties between the houses of Aquitaine and Toulouse. In 1195, the year given by Howden for the hermit's visit, she and Richard purchased land together at Thorée and built a house there. This single attempt at constructing a marital home certainly suggests that Richard was at this stage committed to Berengaria, though there is no evidence that they ever lived there together, and nothing of this modest property, with its mill and fish pond, stands today. In 1216 Berengaria made a gift of it to the brothers of the hospital of Jerusalem.

Richard was also preoccupied with a far grander building project: the castle of Château Gaillard at Les Andelys, a magnificent declaration of defiance to the French (the name means 'Saucy Castle'). Whomever else Richard loved, he loved his castle, even referring to it, rather sadly, as his 'child'. Though he spent much time at the château, again, there is no indication that Berengaria ever visited him here; indeed, it has been claimed that, despite the reconciliation reported in the chronicles, Richard was during this period considering repudiating Berengaria, primarily on the grounds of her childlessness but also because her brother, now Sancho VII 'El Fuerte', was 'insouciant about Richard's diplomatic concerns'.[10] In 1198, Richard had enlisted papal support to push Sancho over the matter of Berengaria's dowry castles, Rocabruna and St Jean Pied-de-Port, and the newly consecrated Innocent III had duly written to Sancho, who appeared to do little about the matter. This request has been construed as evidence that the Navarrese alliance was under strain, since Sancho was now more concerned with politics to the south of the Pyrenees, and at the same time gathering vassals in Gascony whose first allegiance ought to have been to Richard. Though there is truth in both of these points, Sancho's long-term policy towards the English suggests a continued relationship of mutual interest and support, indeed a certain dependence, which was later to become particularly relevant in the matter of Berengaria's disputed dowry. If Berengaria had 'outlived her usefulness',[11] it was biologically, rather than diplomatically. Whether or not Richard did experience sexual difficulties with women, he was fertile and had married in the hope of producing an heir. Berengaria did not provide one. The term 'barren' may be distasteful to modern ears, but as far as her contemporaries were concerned, Berengaria had failed in her primary duty as a queen, and when she was widowed in 1199, it became clear that the Angevin rulers, now represented by Eleanor of Aquitaine and John, had no further use for her.

Richard's struggle with Philip of France over the territories of the Vexin and Gisors, which occupied the last years of his life, amounted to little more than two bald men fighting over a comb. Perhaps this explains why the Lionheart legends attempted to invest Richard's pointless and premature death with one last bit of glamour by claiming that he went to besiege Chalus-Chabrol in search of buried treasure. In fact, the attack on Chalus, near Limoges, in March 1199 was a necessary part of the King's strategy in his ongoing struggle to maintain control of his vassals in Aquitaine. But the great warrior had grown a little careless. Strolling outside his camp on the evening of 26 March, protected only by his helmet and shield, Richard was hit in the arm by an arrow fired from the ramparts. His health had been sporadically poor as a result of the illnesses he had suffered on crusade, and even though the arrow head was wrenched from his flesh, it became clear that the wound was infected and that he was not going to recover. A messenger was dispatched to his mother Eleanor at Fontevrault, and she arrived at his bedside in time to be with him as he died, on 6 April. The castle fell the same day.

Berengaria, who was at Beaufort-en-Vallée, was not summoned to Richard's deathbed, supposedly because this would alert the French and allow them to take advantage of the situation. It is a measure of her political marginalisation that a visit from Eleanor should not have been considered suspicious, whereas Berengaria's arrival would have signalled an emergency. Instead Berengaria heard the news from Bishop Hugh of Lincoln, who had been en route to meet Richard when he was informed of the King's death. According to Adam of Eynsham, Berengaria was 'sorrowing and almost heart broken' and Hugh said Mass for her and was able 'to calm her grief in a wonderful way'. Hugh then departed for Fontevrault, where Richard was buried on Palm Sunday in the presence of Queen Eleanor. Although later chroniclers assumed that Berengaria was among the chief mourners, it appears that she did not attend the funeral, as she kept Easter at Beaufort with Bishop Hugh and her brother-in-law John. In response to an urgent message from Eleanor, John had rushed from Brittany to Chinon as Richard was dying to secure the royal treasure, then ridden on to Fontevrault, where he visited not only Richard's tomb but that of his father and Henry the Young King, before going on to Beaufort. Three days later Berengaria did visit the abbey, where she witnessed a charter issued by Queen Eleanor. Why did Berengaria not take up her rightful position at Richard's funeral? Was she too ill with grief to contemplate the journey? Or did she consider Fontevrault too much Eleanor's territory? In later life Berengaria maintained some correspondence with the abbey, purchasing land for her own foundation from the abbess in 1230, but she eschewed any connection with the royal mausoleum, unlike the next Queen of England, Isabelle of Angoulême. Berengaria had had little joy from her marriage, and John and Eleanor made it quite clear in the year after her widowhood that her concerns were of little importance to them. Her resistance to the Angevin way of death has something assertive about it, a little gesture of defiance towards the mother-in-law who was the most powerful woman of her age.

During her brief meeting with the grieving Eleanor at Fontevrault, Berengaria discussed with the papal envoy, Cardinal Pietro di Capua, the prospective marriage of her sister Blanca. The bridegroom was Thibaut of Champagne, Eleanor's grandson by her daughter Marie, who had succeeded to his brother's comital title two years earlier. Berengaria accompanied her sister to her wedding at Chartres in July and acted as witness to the ceremony. Marie, the former regent of Champagne, had died the previous year, but Berengaria's association with the Champenois court highlights a neglected link that hints at a spiritual affinity between Richard and herself, whatever disappointments their marriage brought them.

Until their deaths, Richard and his half-sister Marie had shared a confessor, Adam de Perseigne, abbot of the eponymous Cistercian abbey in the diocese of Le Mans. The Cistercians were much favoured by Berengaria's Navarrese family, a tradition she was to continue in her own foundation, and in her widowhood Adam remained a staunch supporter and friend to her. Unlike many clerics of the day, he sustained warm relations with women (though he was sharp on the frivolities of Blanca's court), and while none of his letters to Berengaria survive, he also corresponded with her sister and appears as a signatory and witness on several documents relating to Berengaria, as well as assisting in the establishment of her own Cistercian house and personally selecting his successor, Gautier de Perseigne. Richard and Marie had enjoyed a close relationship, the strongest attestation of which is a poem written in captivity by Richard addressed to his 'Countess sister'. The connection with Adam de Perseigne suggests that Berengaria was less marginalised among the second generation of Angevin royalty than has previously been assumed. Through him she was linked to one of the most significant female rulers of her day, and their friendship after Richard's death indicates that both husband and wife had confided and trusted in this astute, literary cleric. The interests and values they shared with Adam were clearly mutual, and such confidence implies a subtle degree of sympathy between Richard and Berengaria.

Blanca of Champagne herself was soon widowed: Thibaut died in 1201, leaving her the mother of one child and expecting another. Her court provided a refuge for Berengaria over the next few years, as both Eleanor and John were too absorbed in the upheavals of the Angevin succession to concern themselves with her welfare. Another sadness had come with Joanna's death late in 1199. Raymond of Toulouse had spent much of their marriage warring with his own barons, and had proved to be a neglectful and, it seems, cruel husband. Joanna had decided to leave him and turned to Richard for protection, but as she travelled to meet her brother, ill and pregnant with her second child, she received the news of his death from Eleanor at Niort. By August, she had managed to rejoin her mother and brother John, who were keeping court at Rouen, and when it was obvious that she was dying she asked to take the veil as a nun at Fontevrault. Eleanor was able to persuade the archbishop of Canterbury, Hubert Walter, to set aside canon law to admit this unconventional vocation, and though Joanna was too unwell to stand up in church to make her profession, she was able to ensure her entitlement to be buried as a veiled nun after her death. She was interred alongside her father and brother at Fontevrault. Her child, possibly born by Caesarian section, lived only a few hours. Joanna made no mention of Berengaria in her will, but then this princess who had been a queen had nothing to leave but 3,000 marks given in charity by her brother John, which she requested be distributed among the poor. The Cypriot princess who had shared Berengaria and Joanna's experiences of the Holy Land seems to have had a knack for being in the right place at the right time: she became the next Countess of Toulouse.

★

Eleanor of Aquitaine had spent much of the period between Richard's reconciliation with John at Lisieux in 1195 and his death in 1199 in relative seclusion at Fontevrault, where she still lived in royal style, albeit on a smaller scale. When, on his deathbed, Richard finally confirmed John, rather than Arthur of Brittany, as his heir, Eleanor knew she would have to intervene to ensure the succession. Richard's decision has been attributed to Eleanor's influence, but why was she so keen for John, who had repeatedly shown himself to be so disloyal, to inherit over Arthur, who, as Geoffrey's son, arguably had the better hereditary claim and could also add Brittany to the Angevin power bloc? One answer is Eleanor's powerful dislike of Arthur's mother, Constance of Brittany. Since Arthur was barely into his teens, a crown for the son would mean a regency for the mother. The reduction of the governance of a large area of Europe to a squabble among women is typical of the way in which Eleanor's legend has subsumed her political acumen. Underage kings were inevitably surrounded by destructive factionalism, and the aggressive tactics of Philip of France would require a strong opponent with a united baronage to oppose them. Moreover, John had effectively been king of England for some years, he was experienced and, with the backing of Eleanor's status in Aquitaine, stood a better chance of holding the Angevin lands together.

John was invested as Duke of Normandy on 25 April 1199 and crowned King of England at Westminster on Ascension Day the same year. The English and many of the Norman lords accepted his accession, but the situation on the Continent was far from clear. Arthur continued to behave as if his rights superseded John's, for example, in presuming to appoint William des Roches as seneschal of Anjou. Accompanied by Des Roches and his mother, he then led an army to the city of Angers, which promptly surrendered to him. The lords of Anjou, Maine and Touraine now came out in support for Arthur, and Eleanor was obliged to come out of retirement at Fontevrault to go to war. She selected Mercadier, one of Richard's most loyal military captains, as her general, and accompanied him to Angers. Constance and Arthur fled north and the city was sacked on Eleanor's orders as punishment for accepting Arthur. Eleanor then commanded that the surrounding countryside be laid to waste. If the dating of these incidents is correct, then it is an impressive example of Eleanor's energy at the age of seventy-three. In the space of a fortnight she had travelled from Chalus to Fontevrault after Richard's death, buried her son, campaigned in Anjou and arrived back at Fontevrault to make a grant to the abbey of St Marie de Turpenay for the celebration of Richard's anniversary, witnessed by Berengaria, on 21 April.

Eleanor could have rested for only a few days at Fontevrault, because on 29 April she was at Loudun, then at Poitiers on 4 May, Montreuil-Bonnin the next day, followed by Niort (where she broke the news of Richard's death to Joanna), Andilly, La Rochelle, St-Jean d'Andely, Saintes and Tours. By 1 July she was in Bordeaux, and in Rouen by the end of the month. The purpose of this progress was most obviously to consolidate support among her own people, but she also initiated a small political revolution when, at Tours in June, she paid homage to Philip Augustus of France for her Aquitaine dominions. This was an extraordinary act for a woman to perform independently. While it was not unknown for women to hold lands in their own right, Capetian tradition had always deemed that a man – a husband or a brother – paid homage as her proxy. To do so personally made a powerful symbolic statement about a woman's ability to wield authority. Moreover, it was a shrewd move in the campaign against Arthur. By paying homage herself, Eleanor was effectively separating Aquitaine and Poitou from the other Angevin dominions. Having already exchanged a series of charters with John designating him her heir, she was able to deprive Philip of France of any legal cause to invade her lands or interfere there to Arthur's advantage. To have acted so quickly, in such a compressed period of time and under the strains of bereavement and war shows not only an informed knowledge of the law but a remarkable ability to apply it.

Eleanor displayed similar ingenuity in her inauguration of communes or corporations in several towns, including La Rochelle. Based on a set of rules known as the Establishments of Rouen, these charters have some-times been seen as evidence of a proto-democratic strain in Eleanor's governance, but in fact by granting 'independence' to towns, Eleanor was incorporating the relatively new commercial power of the urban bourgeoisie more firmly into the older system of vassalage. The flattered burghers were permitted a mayor (subject to Eleanor's approval) and the freedom to order some of their own affairs, but along with the right to defend themselves and their customs came an obligation to participate in the levy when Eleanor summoned her vassals to war.

Swindled by Richard out of her dower properties, Berengaria was even-tually obliged to throw herself on the mercy of the French and spent the remainder of her life as Lady of Le Mans. From this point she no longer used any of the titles that had accompanied her signature in Rome over a decade before. Now she signed herself '*humilissima regina quondam Anglo-rum*' – 'most humble former queen of the English'. Berengaria had been a queen without a kingdom, but in the city of Le Mans and its suburbs, a total of thirty-seven parishes, she found her own small realm. She was permitted to appoint her own seneschal, Herbert de Tucé, and members of her household included Paulin Boutier, a knight, Pierre Prévot, her cantor, Simon and Garsia, her clerks, Adam and then Gautier de Perseigne, her chaplains, and her women, of whom one, Julianeta, was an embroideress. Thus established, she began to take an active and rather contentious part in local politics.

In Le Mans, Berengaria lived mainly at the palace of the counts of Maine and took a close interest in its church, St Pierre, which was constantly at odds with the rival cathedral chapter of St Julien. In 1204–6, two of Berengaria's servants, Martine and Luke, tried to exact a tax payment from one André, who claimed he owed the money not to St Pierre but to St Julien. In retaliation, the cathedral chapter excommunicated one of the servants. The next year, Berengaria ordered the seizure of André's goods and imprisoned him in the tower of Le Mans. The chapter promptly placed the city under interdict, but St Pierre defied them and successfully petitioned the papal curia to be allowed to celebrate low Mass with the church doors closed and no bellringing. The feud continued in 1218, this time over money Berengaria allegedly owed to St Julien, as Ann Trindade recounts:

> Several other canons, acting on the authority and instructions of the Chapter, had warned Queen Berengaria to see that the money that her servants had taken in contravention of the rights of the Chapter was returned. But she replied that she would not return the money because, as she said, this customary right was hers. They told her the Chapter was ready to grant a hearing to her representatives and those of the man she had imprisoned and pass judgement. She replied that she would have none of it and after she had been warned several times about this by the Chapter and still refused to do anything about it, the Chapter placed the church and the city under the interdict.[12]

Berengaria herself enjoyed special protection from the Pope during the interdict. In acknowledgement of her 'devotion to the Holy Roman Church and to our own person, and because of the universal obligation of our pastoral office, which charges us to exercise our case and concern with special favour towards the orphan and the widow'.[13] The interdict was eventually lifted in 1218 after which Berengaria, who had been living at Thorée, returned ceremonially to Le Mans. She finally handed over the money to St Julien in 1220. Given that the sum in question was five denarii of Tours, a paltry amount, the whole affair rings slightly of the bickerings of a suburban local council.

However, money was never far from Berengaria's mind. In 1213, she had sent envoys to John to try to make arrangements for the transfer of funds from properties that were hers by right, but John enjoined her to keep silent and reassured her that arrangements were in hand. He finally promised 2,000 marks in arrears and 10,000 pounds in two instalments, but then wrote the next year to regretfully inform his 'dearest sister' that he couldn't pay. In 1216, the Pope complained to the archbishop of Tours of the 'frequent acts of injury and theft' Berengaria had endured, but despite papal pressure it was left to John and Isabelle's son Henry III to settle the debt to Berengaria, agreeing to pay her 4,500 pounds over five years. The negotiations were still dragging on in 1226, more than a quarter of a century after Richard I's death.

One of the more blithely ridiculous claims to have been made about Berengaria is that, notwithstanding the view of many writers that she was the only English queen never to have set foot in England, 'in fact she was a frequent visitor to the court of King John, as is attested to by the numerous safe-conducts given to her and her servants … In 1216 she toured England after the King had given her permission to travel wherever she pleased in the realm and in 1220 she was amongst the vast throng gathered to witness the translation of Becket's bones.'[14] Safe-conducts were issued for Berengaria and her servants in 1215, 1216, 1219 and 1220, but there is absolutely no evidence that she undertook a pleasant tour of England during the barons' wars. Nor is there any confirmation that the conducts were even used, though they may have been intended to serve as passports through Aquitaine to Navarre, in the event that Berengaria was left so impoverished by her genial brother-in-law that she was obliged to return to her homeland.

Since John had well and truly cheated her, Berengaria was obliged to make the best of what resources she had. Her efforts to do so earned her a rather unpleasant reputation as 'a persecutor of the Jews'.[15] Le Mans had a significant Jewish community, and Berengaria, perhaps following Navarre's liberal tradition towards the Jews, had employed the services of Jewish moneylenders during her marriage. A record exists of her use of revenues from the queen's Cornish tin mines to pay a debt to an Italian Jew named Pontius Amaldi in 1199. But France was not Navarre and, as in England, Jews were liable to have their property confiscated without recompense, despite this being expressly forbidden in a papal bull of 1120.

Berengaria was prepared to exploit their degraded legal status, rewarding her servant Martin with a house and vineyard taken from two Jews, Desiré and Copin, in 1208, a gift he sanctified by selling one acre of the land to pay for a memorial Mass for Richard I's soul. Berengaria also profited from the sale of land by converted Jews and gave a former Jewish school building to her chapel. The signature of Adam de Perseigne on one such document, and her donations to the Dominican order, who made the conversion of Jews something of a speciality, may testify that she was interested in saving Jews as well as robbing them. Certainly Adam, her close friend and spiritual counsellor, disapproved of the ill-treatment of Jews, so his involvement suggests that at least some of Berengaria's trans-actions were conducted with a degree of probity. Such activities in any case hardly amount to persecution, and indeed were not considered illegal by the powerful, but in the light of Berengaria's readiness to plead her own vulnerable status as a widow to the Pope, they do seem somewhat hypocritical.

Since what dower rights Berengaria had managed to claw back were usufructuary – that is, only for her lifetime – she needed money to acquire land if she was to fulfil the project that dominated the last years of her life. Her plan was to found a house for the Cistercians, an order closely linked with her natal family and from whom she sought anniversary Masses for Richard and her sister Blanca after the latter's death in 1223. Berengaria bought land from the hospital of Coeffet and a vineyard from Fontevrault to fund her foundation of Nôtre Dame de la Pieté-Dieu at Epau. Louis VIII of France granted her forty-six acres of woodland with seven meadows and two gardens on the River Huisine, where she erected two watermills for the monks. Louis and his mother, Blanche of Castile, visited Epau to confirm the gift to their 'dearest relative and kinswoman' in 1230. That year, the first monks arrived and the abbey was confirmed by the Pope and consecrated by Bishop Geoffrey de Laval in January 1231. Sadly, Berengaria did not live to see her abbey sanctified, as she died the preceding December. She was buried at the abbey, in the choir, and, after being moved in the nineteenth century, her bones have now been restored to the chapter house.

Berengaria is one of England's least-known medieval queens and often considered one of the saddest, dwarfed by both her husband and her mother-in-law. Her marriage could not be called successful, yet it offered her an opportunity for experience and adventure which far exceeded the limitations of many women of her class, and her interactions with her powerful relatives specifically affected the alignment of power in Europe.

As Lady of Le Mans she continued to exercise authority and succeeded largely by her own efforts in raising an impressive monument to her memory. She was tenacious and, in a quiet way, refused to be dominated by the much larger characters of the Angevin rulers who became her marital family. The glory of the Third Crusade is Richard's, but it is worth recalling that had it not been for his last-minute wedding to Berengaria, it might never have happened at all.

CHAPTER 7

ISABELLE OF ANGOULÊME

'More Jezebel than Isabelle'

Eleanor of Aquitaine had given birth to John, her sixth child, in England in December 1166, when she was forty-two. Between the ages of about three and seven, he was raised at the abbey of Fontevrault along with his sister Joanna. Writers seeking to condemn Eleanor for her 'bad parenting' (and there are many), or to find a psycho-historical explanation for John's unpleasant personality traits in adulthood, have focused on this period of relative isolation from his immediate family as a stick with which to beat his mother and a source of John's 'cruel, miserly, extortionate, duplicitous, treacherous, mendacious, suspicious, secretive, paranoid and lecherous' character.[1] In both instances, they overstate the case. John's period at Fontevrault corresponds to Eleanor's absence in Poitou and Angoulême before the revolt of 1174, and represented 'a provision of child care for him'.[2] Fontevrault had a long history of association with the Aquitaine ducal house, and it was also a place of close family associations for his father, whose aunt, the widowed Matilda of Anjou, had become abbess there, and whose cousin, another Matilda, the child of Geoffrey of Anjou's sister Sibyl, was a nun at the abbey during the children's stay. Fontevrault was well placed for them to receive visits from both parents, and may simply have been a practical solution to the conflicting demands of government and family.

Eleanor's subsequent lack of contact with her younger son has also been blamed on her neglectfulness as a mother, which again seems unfair, as she was a prisoner until John reached his early twenties. Whatever their personal relationship, and despite the fact that Eleanor had come into conflict with John when he schemed to usurp his brother Richard's power, her commitment to him after Richard's death was unswerving. Her primary loyalty was to Aquitaine and the preservation of the Angevin lands, so when John inherited the crown her energies were directed at maintaining the duchy for him. Indeed, it became the focus of the last years of her life.

In 1176, Henry II had made John Count of Mortain in Normandy, and when Richard objected to John taking over Aquitaine in 1183 his father sent him instead to Ireland, where his eight-month stay proved a disaster. Henry had also hoped to create an appanage for his youngest son by marrying him to Isabella, the heiress to the Gloucester earldom, but the legality of the marriage was always dubious. Archbishop Baldwin of Canterbury challenged the union on the grounds of consanguinity and demanded that John appear at an ecclesiastical court, but the archbishop died before the Pope had had time to rule on the interdict against the marriage. John and Isabella continued to live together despite Baldwin's having forbidden them to cohabit, but when, on Richard's death, John's prospects changed so dramatically he began to consider a more advantageous dynastic match and to revive the idea of an annulment that he had been considering since 1196. His project had the support of the bishops of Saintes, Poitiers and Bordeaux, but the new Pope, Innocent III, objected to it. Nevertheless, in the absence of an appeal from John's wife Isabella (it is suggested that John simply bought her off), and because of the uncertainty as to whether the ten-year marriage had been legal in the first place, John was able to wriggle free.

If the losses of prestige and territory the English sustained under John are to be attributed to a woman, it is more fruitful to look to his second marriage than at any maternal inadequacies of Eleanor of Aquitaine. John's marriage to Isabelle, sole heiress to Ademar, Count of Angoulême, had its roots in the rivalry between the Angoulême dynasty and the Lusignans, another powerful Aquitaine house, over the territory of La Marche. The Lusignans had always been troublesome vassals until Richard developed a friendship with Hugh de Lusignan during the Third Crusade, after which he promoted the family at the expense of their rivals.

In 1200, Eleanor spent two months at the court of Castile, where she personally selected Princess Blanca from among her daughter Leonor's children as the bride of Louis IX of France. By April she was back at Fontevrault, but any thoughts she may have had of resuming her retirement were put paid to by the revolt of the Lusignans, who were once again laying claim to La Marche. Philip of France used the dispute as an excuse to break the recently signed truce of Le Goulet and Arthur of Brittany allied himself with the Lusignans against John. Eleanor left Fontevrault with the intention of establishing herself defensively against Arthur in Poitiers. Twenty miles to the north of her capital, she paused for the night at Mirebeau. Hugh de Lusignan was not far away at Tours with Arthur, and the pair planned to take Mirebeau and kidnap Eleanor. Fortuitously, John was marching his forces to Chinon when he heard that Mirebeau was besieged. By the time he arrived, Eleanor, who had attempted to stall Arthur with negotiations, had been reduced to shutting herself up in the keep. On 1 August, in the only truly impressive battle of his life, John stormed Mirebeau, captured Arthur and Hugh de Lusignan while they were enjoying a breakfast of roast pigeon, and liberated his mother. John was perhaps more delighted to have captured Arthur than to have freed Eleanor – he certainly capitalised on it by murdering his nephew as soon as he decently could.

After the kidnapping episode, John agreed to hand over La Marche to Hugh de Lusignan and to reject Ademar's claim. However, Ademar's daughter was betrothed to Hugh, a development that would ally the rival claimants and allow Hugh, on his marriage, to annex the Angoulême lands. Either John did not know of the betrothal or it had not been agreed when he handed over La Marche in 1200, but once he learned of it, he was confronted with the prospect of a dangerous Lusignan power bloc with serious implications for the ruling structure in the south: the combined territories would cut off Aquitaine by alienating the land between Poitou and Gascony. The obvious solution was to prevent the wedding and, according to the chronicler Roger of Howden, it was Philip of France, Ademar's overlord, who slyly suggested to John that he marry Isabelle himself.

John was at the time engaged in negotiations for a marriage to a princess of Portugal. Such an alliance would have protected the southern borders of the Angevin territories in much the same way as Richard's marriage to Berengaria of Navarre had done. But now he rushed into wedlock with Isabelle. His precipitousness attracted censure from Ralph of Diceto, who reported: 'Lord John, King of England, having in mind to marry a daughter of the King of the Portuguese ... sent from Rouen some great notables to bring her back to him. But he married Isabella, only daughter and heir of the Count of Angoulême, and he did this while they were on the journey, without having warned them, taking much less care for their safety than was worthy of the Royal Majesty.'

John's haste is here seen as unseemly, unkingly, and, given that Diceto was writing later, the consequences of his marriage are implicitly fore-shadowed in its hurried, thoughtless beginning. John's carelessness for the feelings of the princess of Portugal at the time may have been the result of his preoccupation with making Isabelle his wife before Hugh de

Lusignan got wind of the plan: on 5 July he was negotiating with Count Ademar and on 24 August he and Isabelle were married at Bordeaux. They were crowned together at Westminster on 8 October, then made a progress north, through Cumberland and Yorkshire, to meet the King of Scots, returning south to Guildford for Christmas and moving on to Canterbury for an Easter crown-wearing ceremony in March.

As Frank McLynn comments, 'Almost everything about John's union with Isabella has invited controversy: his motives, the murky circumstances of his engagement, the status of the marriage in canon law, the personality of the new queen and the reason for the excessive wrath of the Lusignans.'[3] John's motives have been attributed to no more than (a rather distasteful) lust, as chroniclers later remarked on his sexual enthralment to Isabelle. John was promiscuous, though certainly no more so than his father or his great-grandfather Henry I. His known mistresses included Hawise, the Countess of Aumale, and two women named Clementia and Suzanne. He had a bastard daughter, Joan, by Clementia, and other illegitimate children included Geoffrey, Osbert, Richard and Oliver, the latter two of whom were the sons of noblewomen. This was not particularly unusual, but within the accepted code of extramarital adventures it was considered bad form to target the wives and daughters of the aristocracy, and John's impolitic pursuit of well-born women was given as a reason for his later alienation by his barons. It does seem, then, that John allowed sexual passion to overrule prudence, but in the case of his wife it was more probably realpolitik – the desire to circumvent the creation of a united territory of Lusignan, La Marche and Angoulême, and to claim the succession of Angoulême for himself – that drove him.

John was notorious for a lack of respect for the Church, but if he was prepared to risk the anger of Rome, in this instance it was likely to be for his own strategic advantage rather than for sexual satisfaction, which he could easily find elsewhere. Legally, the Angoulême match stood on unsteady ground, as no divorce from Isabella of Gloucester was formally obtained; John merely capitalised on the uncertain status of his first marriage. Isabelle's age was another potential impediment to legitimacy, and her betrothal to Lusignan could also be seen as an obstacle in canon law. It was claimed that the bride had reached the legal age of twelve, but many contemporaries were doubtful of the truth of this. Isabelle's mother, Alice de Courtenay, could not have married Ademar before 1184, as she had only that year been divorced from her previous husband, the Comte de Joigny, on the grounds of consanguinity. She is first recorded as Ademar's wife in a document awarding a grant to the abbey of St-Armandde-Boixe in 1191. According to these dates, Isabelle may have been as old as fifteen, but she could equally have been no more than nine.

The Lusignans' disgust at the marriage points to her being at the younger end of this range. The betrothal to Hugh de Lusignan had been made with the support of King Richard, and the couple had exchanged the *verba de praesenti* which, in normal circumstances, was binding and could be broken only with a special dispensation, as had been granted in the case of Isabelle's mother. Roger of Howden maintains that because Isabelle had not reached the age of consent in 1200, Hugh de Lusignan was prepared to wait to marry her in church. Marriages were often contracted while the parties were under age, but it was common for such unions not to be formalised or consummated until the age of consent had been reached. John's sister Leonor, for example, had married Alfonso of Castile at eight but did not have intercourse with him until she was fifteen. So 'the suspicion remains that [Hugh's] bride was a pre-pubescent child in 1200 and that the King stepped in where . . . Isabelle's betrothed husband believed it indecent to tread'.[4] The fact that Isabelle did not bear a child until 1207, and then did so almost annually until 1215, also suggests that she had not reached puberty at the time of her wedding. Hugh, then, had not only been cheated of his wife and his inheritance; he also had to endure having his own integrity exploited by John.

Given the controversy surrounding his marriage, it is unsurprising that John wished to legitimise Isabelle's queenship as firmly as possible at her coronation. In a new addition to the coronation ordo, she was not only crowned but anointed 'with the common consent and agreement of the archbishops, bishops, counts, barons, clergy and people of the whole of the realm'.[5] Isabelle's prestige was thus further enhanced, but her status was not entirely dependent on her position as John's wife. She was more than the daughter of a provincial nobleman; indeed, the connection with her maternal ancestry arguably elevated her husband's status. Her mother was a granddaughter of Louis VI and cousin to the reigning French King, Philip Augustus. The De Courtenays also had marriage ties with the royal houses of Hungary, Aragon and Castile and the comital dynasties of Hainault, Namur, Nevers and Forez. Through Alice's brother Peter de Courtenay II, who in 1216 became the Emperor of Constantinople, the De Courtenays enjoyed links with the kings of Jerusalem and Cyprus and the counts of Champagne. Queen Isabelle had English relatives, too, in the Courtenays of Oxfordshire and Okehampton, and though the relationship was distant, it was strong enough for Isabelle's son Henry III to address Robert Courtenay of Okehampton as 'kinsman' in a letter of

1217. Isabelle might not have been a king's daughter like Berengaria of Navarre, but the antiquity and extent of her international family ties, as well as the strategic significance of Angoulême, made her if anything a more prestigious bride.

The primary consequence of the marriage was another Lusignan rebellion – one that would eventually lead to massive Angevin losses. Hugh and his brother Ralph of Eu took their grievance to the French King and Philip Augustus, as he had planned all along, espoused their cause as an excuse to declare John's lands forfeit. Isabelle had crossed to Normandy with John in May 1201 and, after a visit to the duplicitous Philip in Paris in July, had joined the Dowager Queen Berengaria at Chinon. The royal couple kept Christmas at Caen where, according to Roger of Wendover, John seemed oblivious of the worsening military situation and spent his time feasting and lying in bed late with his wife. Count Ademar of Angoulême died the next year, 1202, and Isabelle remained in the Angevin south, possibly with her mother, who was given a pension of over fifty livres a month in 1203 and governed the province until John took over comital duties in 1204, whereupon she retired to La Ferte. Isabelle was not at Falaise when John received Arthur there in his last court appearance in January 1203. It has been claimed that she was besieged at Chinon by Aimery de Thouars in the February of either 1201 or 1203. Since Aimery did not rebel until 1202, the later date is more plausible; it also tallies with Isabelle spending time with her bereaved mother in Angoulême. She was in England in December 1203, and may have passed through Chinon en route to join John. *The History of William the Marshal* recounts that John was desperately worried when he arrived at Le Mans to find the road to Chinon cut off, and that the Queen had to be rescued by a band of mercenaries headed by Peter de Preaux. This incident has been used to castigate John for his excessive love for Isabelle: after she was recovered he was accused of caring more for her bed than for the defeat of his enemies, and this charge, whether accurate or not, is likelier to refer to 1203, since in January 1201 the couple were still in England.

The King and Queen returned to England the following December and kept Christmas at Canterbury. In March Richard's pride and joy, the supposedly impregnable fortress of Château Gaillard, fell to Philip of France, and a month later, Eleanor of Aquitaine was dead. Mirebeau had been Eleanor's last great adventure. Afterwards she had returned to Fontevrault, this time for good. At the abbey she heard the news of Arthur's death, John's losses in Normandy and the storming of Richard's beloved castle. Perhaps all this did not grieve her as greatly as might be expected, because by the spring of 1204 she had sunk into exhausted senility. Having been admitted to the order of Fontevrault in 1202, she died in her nun's habit on 1 April 1204 and was buried in the crypt. Nothing of her activities save for her imprisonment had made her exceptional in England, though the legacy of Aquitaine continued to dominate English politics until the fifteenth century. Her ambitions and love for Aquitaine were the focus of her life, so it is as a very European, rather than simply an English queen, that she ought rightly to be remembered.

There were now two living queens of England, and their conflicting economic needs had a direct effect on the events of the following years, leading to the loss of Normandy and a drastic weakening of the English position in the Angevin territories. In 1201, Berengaria had met John at Chinon to discuss her dower arrangements, which were further complicated by his marriage to Isabelle. After Eleanor's death in 1204, her assigned lands should in theory have been available to Berengaria, but the Angevin castles that were hers by right were now under threat from Philip. In any case, John had no interest in Berengaria's future. To Isabelle, he committed land in Saintes and Niort in Poitou, Saumur, La Flèche, Beaufort-en-Vallée, Bauge and Château de Loir in Anjou, the last of which had been promised to Berengaria as early as 1191. On Eleanor's death, John also pledged her English and Norman inheritance – which included the towns of Exeter and Chichester, manors in Devon, Ilchester, Wilton, Malmesbury and two in Wiltshire, Queenhithe Dock, Waltham, the honour of Berkhamsted, Rockingham and the county of Rutland and Falaise, Domfront, and Bonneville-sur-Tocque – to Isabelle. Again, the Norman lands were technically Berengaria's property.

Berengaria's dower intersects interestingly with John's policies at two points during this time. Despite the claims that the Navarrese alliance had ceased to function effectively, Berengaria's brother Sancho had signed two treaties of support for John, in 1201 and 1202. With the expansion of the Castilians into the Basque country in 1199–1200, the King of Navarre was dependent on a Gascon port to provide access to the sea and in 1204 the town of Bordeaux swore allegiance to him, presumably with John's approval. This not only demonstrates a continued interdependence between Navarre and Aquitaine, but perhaps explains why John did not attempt to relieve himself of his obligations to Berengaria by pressing Sancho for the return of her two castles at Rocabruna and St Jean Pied-de-Port.

John's cavalier attitude to Berengaria's rights was to prove costly to his cause in Normandy. In the months after Eleanor's death, Philip Augustus had begun a round-up of Norman cities. Falaise and Caen fell, then Rouen on 24 June. Eventually the whole of Normandy, with the exception of the Channel Islands, was captured by France. Various theories have been put forward to explain the undermining of the English crown in the province. Paris was overtaking provincial capitals like Rouen and Chartres as a centre for intellectual and economic activity, and some Norman lords felt that the interest of the English kings in Normandy and its traditions was diminishing.[6] The Normans were also resentful about the ongoing costs of the wars between the English and French kings, and they were still bitterly paying off both Richard's crusading debts and his ransom. In these arguments, John's loss of Normandy is cast not as a personal failure but as bowing to a process of historical inevitability. Nevertheless, according to Frank McLynn, 'It is very difficult to see how any overarching historical process can excuse or mitigate John's egregious stupidity in farming out large sectors of Norman administration to mercenary captains.'[7]

This 'egregious stupidity' might well extend to John's treatment of his sister-in-law since, in 1204, as a consequence of John's favouritism of Isabelle, Berengaria was left with no choice but to go over to the enemy. Blanca of Champagne had already been obliged to appeal to the protection of Philip as her overlord during the regency she held for her young son. Now Berengaria, who had been lingering at her sister's court, felt compelled to do the same. Having exploited John's marriage to fan the quarrel with the Lusignans for his own purposes, Philip made use of it again and offered himself as the protector of the destitute English Dowager Queen. In August 1204 Berengaria acknowledged Philip as her overlord and in exchange for 1,000 marks and the rights to the battered city of Le Mans gave up to him her assigned properties of Falaise, Domfront and Bonneville-sur-Toque, removing them even further from the possibility of eventual recovery by John.

If Berengaria had been cheated, so was Isabelle. The rents of the Queen's dower went straight to the King, who spent lavishly on magnificent clothes and jewels for himself, as well as reputedly appropriating others' ornaments if they caught his fancy. Though he did present Isabella with robes and valuable cloth and gifts of wine and fish, financially, he treated her like a child. Of course, in the early years of their marriage she may well have been a child, and perhaps it was her tender age that gave John the bizarre idea that instead of having her own household, as was customary, the Queen might as well lodge with his first wife, Isabella of Gloucester who, until the birth of Isabelle's first son, Henry, in October 1207, was maintained in *her* own household at Winchester at the cost of eighty pounds a year. The first wife removed to Sherborne before the second gave birth in Winchester, and her allowance was reduced to fifty pounds. Had the thirty pounds' difference been for the Queen's upkeep? Between 1205 and 1206, at least, this was certainly the case. When Isabelle was not living with her husband's ex, she spent long periods at Marlborough, at the home of Hugh de Neville, whose wife was one of John's mistresses. (Lady de Neville was perhaps less than enthusiastic about her role as the royal lover, as she supposedly offered to pay a forfeit of 200 chickens to spend a night with her longsuffering husband.) After Henry was born, Isabelle lived for a time at Corfe Castle, but *The Canterbury Chronicle* refers to her as being 'in custody', which is an odd way to describe a new household, if that is what it was. In November 1207, John also declared that the queens-gold tax was to be paid not to Isabelle, but to the King's exchequer, making it probable that he, not she, had the benefit of it.

This treatment casts doubt on the chroniclers' accusations that John's reign was weakened by his extravagant uxoriousness. After Henry, he and Isabelle went on to have four more children, Richard, the first Earl of Cornwall (born 1209), Joan (1210), who married King Alexander of Scotland in 1221, Isabella (1214), who married Frederick, the Holy Roman Emperor, in 1235 and Eleanor (1215), whose first husband was William Marshal, Earl of Pembroke. The close succession of these births indicates that the marriage was functional, if not harmonious.

The scarcity of references to Isabelle in the chronicles has also been interpreted as evidence of a lack of discord, but there may be a more sinister interpretation of that. Isabelle is mentioned in only one of John's charters, a grant to Chichester in 1204, in marked contrast to the King's other religious grants, such as that to Beaulieu Abbey in 1205, in which the souls of John's relatives Henry II, Eleanor of Aquitaine, the Young King and Richard I are invoked, as well as his ancestors and heirs – a list that pointedly leaves out the Queen. Nor did Isabelle issue any charters in her own name. Though Berengaria had made only one as queen, the loan agreement in Rome on her return from the crusade, she had never actually lived in England. Eleanor of Aquitaine, of course, had issued many. Isabelle's lack of financial independence explains this to some extent, but it is also possible that John deprived her of her liberty as well as her income. During a stay at Devizes, *The Canterbury Chronicle* describes Isabelle as 'includitur', enclosed or confined, but given that this was at the time Richard was born, there is nothing exceptional about its choice of words: confinement, a queen's 'taking her chamber' before a birth, was an established and increasingly ceremonial custom. The *Chronicle*'s earlier description of her residence at Corfe is, however, aberrant. Was the Queen of England living under some sort of house arrest after bearing her first child? And if so, why?

During her first pregnancy, Isabelle had requested that her half-brother from her mother's earlier marriage, Pierre de Joigny, join her in England. Pierre and John were on good terms, even though Pierre's overlord was Philip of France. Since we know that Pierre had envoys at John's court in 1209, joined John in Poitou in 1214, was permitted to cross to England the next year and granted a pension of 200 pounds and returned to France only when the war was over, it has been concluded that, despite his French allegiance, Pierre had fought for his sister's husband. How does his loyalty to John, and John's favourable treatment of him, tally with the rumour that Pierre and Isabelle were having an incestuous relationship? In 1233, a man named Piers the Fair died in County Cavan, Ireland, and a local chronicle recorded that he was known as 'the son of the English Queen'. Piers, like Peter, is an anglicisation of Pierre. There is every reason to dismiss this story as nonsense from beginning to end, but it was not the only whisper of scandal that Isabelle attracted.

Isabelle was reputedly a beautiful girl, as was her mother – Alice had attracted the notice of both William the Marshal and the Young King at a tournament in Joigny in 1180 – and the fact that the mysterious Piers was 'fair' suggests that mere inherited good looks may have been twisted into 'evidence' that he was connected with Isabelle. The Queen's sexual allure was also exploited as part of the narrative of the failure of John's kingship. Matthew Paris, writing mid-century, recalls the account of Roger of London, whom John sent as an ambassador to the ruler of Morocco in 1211. According to Roger, Isabelle 'has often been found guilty of incest, witchcraft and adultery, so that the King, her husband, has ordered those of her lovers who have been apprehended to be strangled with a rope in her own bed'.[8] John could have been involved in establishing contacts in North Africa, but this particular embassy, and the story as a whole, are widely dismissed as a scandalous fabrication. Yet there are further allusions to her captivity.

In 1214, a mercenary named Terric the Teuton accompanied Isabelle with an armed guard and twelve horses from the coast at Freemantle, via Reading, to Berkhamsted. In December the Queen was moved to Gloucester, then Winchester in May 1215, Marlborough and Bristol in 1216. On 30 October King John wrote to Terric: 'We shall shortly be coming to the place where you are ... Keep your charges carefully. Let us know frequently about the state of your charge."[9]

These assertions and whispers – Isabelle's 'imprisonment', the incest rumour, the Paris story and Terric's custody of the Queen – have been used to manufacture a story of adultery and cruelty that sits well with the legend of 'Bad King John' and his suitably wicked Queen. The last of these, Isabella's movements under armed guard, is easily explained by events, though it serves also as a reminder of how a queen's unique position as a foreigner and sexual intimate of the king could be turned against her to provide a plausible, personality-driven narrative for broader events.

In 1206, a truce was agreed with France for two years, Philip retaining his Norman gains and John the troubled Angevin territories in the south. John's illegitimate daughter Joan had been married to the Prince of north Wales, Llewellyn ap Iorweth, the same year, and John received homage from the Welsh princes at Woodstock in 1209, but when a revolt broke out in 1210, Joan was sent to negotiate a peace. In 1212, Llewellyn abandoned the treaty agreed by his wife and allied himself with Philip of France. Amid a general atmosphere of unrest and fear, it was rumoured that Isabelle had been raped at Marlborough and the heir apparent, Henry, was taken away from his mother for his own protection. By 1213, Philip was planning an invasion. On 2 February John and Isabelle, accompanied by their son Richard of Cornwall and John's niece Eleanor of Brittany, sailed from Portsmouth, arriving at La Rochelle on the fifteenth. By 15 March they were at Angoulême, and then travelled through Limousin, reaching Angers on 17 June. In the intervening period, negotiations had been reopened with the Lusignans. Queen Isabelle's former fiancé, Hugh de Lusignan, had married her cousin Matilda, the daughter of her father's elder brother Wulgrim, who had died in 1181. As the child of an older brother, Matilda's claim to the Angoulême inheritance was arguably better than Isabelle's own, and she was not prepared to cede her rights at this point. John and Isabelle needed to come to terms with the Lusignans if Angoulême was to be retained, and Isabelle pushed for the betrothal of her four-year-old daughter Joan to Hugh de Lusignan X, Hugh and Matilda's son. The arrangement was agreed at Parthenay on 25 May. This seemed like a brilliant piece of diplomacy, and John entered Angers as a conqueror, but he had failed to consider the reaction of the Poitevin magnates, who now refused to come out and fight for him.

Since his Norman losses had begun to mount up in 1204, John had concentrated his energies on building up a series of alliances with which he could outwit Philip. His strategy in 1214 was to draw the French King to the south while his nephew Otto of Germany (the son of his sister Matilda and Henry of Bavaria) and their ally Ferand of Flanders surprised the French with their main force in the north. Things began to go wrong when, after two skirmishes with Philip, it became apparent that the southern magnates were simply no longer prepared to deliver their obligations to John. At Bouvines on 27 July Otto and Ferand were roundly defeated while John sulked in Aquitaine. Normandy, Brittany, Anjou, Maine and Touraine were swiftly mopped up. The loss of the loyalty of the Poitevin magnates had cost John his empire.

John and Isabelle returned to England in October, and it was at this point that she was collected from the coast by Terric the Teuton. The picture of the adulterous, imprisoned Queen now begins to look very different. The fears aroused at the time of the Welsh rebellion, and the conditions in England, reeling from the defeat of a campaign it had taken ten years and huge amounts of money to wage, made it natural that John would wish Isabelle to be protected. Until Bouvines, John and Isabelle had travelled together, sufficiently harmoniously for her to give birth to another child the following year. This is not to say that John had necessarily treated her well. Her 'custody' at Corfe in 1208 may have been due to the King's indifference to his wife's comfort after he had done his duty and sired an heir, and he had continued to be flagrantly unfaithful to her. In 1212, the accounts show a chaplet of roses purchased for a woman who was a 'friend' of the King, and Susan, a servant to either the same 'friend' or her sister, had been provided with a dress in 1213, suggesting that John was having at least one adulterous affair. But his unkindness is not proof of Isabelle's infidelity. The Matthew Paris tale is, as has been noted, viewed as a scurrilous fiction, and contrasts with Roger of Wendover's view that John was too much in love with his wife, but what these contradictory stories have in common is that they seek to smear Isabelle. After the failure at Bouvines, the likely reason for blackening Isabelle's reputation becomes clearer.

In Paris's report, Robert of London claims that John found Isabelle 'hateful' to him because he blamed her for the collapse of his attempts to regain his Continental power. This would make sense after 1214. Roger of Wendover's accusation that John preferred to make love to Isabelle than war on France depicts the King as emasculated, weakened by sexual desire. The chroniclers have played the old game of *chercher la femme* and found a source for John's failure in his relationship with Isabelle. As her 'foreignness' and her sexual intimacy with the King are perverted into the cause of national disaster, she becomes the sorceress who invites strangers to her bed and drains the King's virility. If John personally blamed Isabelle for her involvement in the Lusignan betrothal, this would account for an estrangement from a wife for whom he had never appeared to care deeply on anything but a physical level, while the conditions in England which pertained as a consequence of his Continental failure would require him to make some provision for her safety.

The historian Paul Strohm stresses that in considering the narrative context of historical texts the reader must be alert to the fact that perception, ideology and belief are as important as what actually took place; that texts are 'finally composed within history, if not within a sense of what did happen, at least within a sense of ... what commonly held interpretative structures permitted [people] to believe'.[10] Thus the treatment of Isabelle's reputation, her casting as incestuous, adulterous, even a witch, demonstrates the vulnerability of queens to a model where their unique source of power, their intimate relationship with the king, could be used to convey anxiety and provide motivation for the inadequacies of the king himself. Sexual deviance, as would prove the case with Edward II in the next century, was a powerful focus for such anxious commentary.

There is no real evidence that Isabelle of Angoulême was an adulterous queen, but her reputation as a seductress was coloured by what she did next. When John returned to England in October 1214, he met tremendous discontent among his magnates, who convened at Bury St Edmunds to try to force him to sign a charter guaranteeing their rights with regard to the crown. In a laughably hypocritical gesture, given his history with the papacy and his well-known abuses of the English Church, John promptly took the Cross, and unsurprisingly the Pope then found in his favour against the barons. On 3 May 1215, the now openly rebellious magnates (who included the cuckolded Hugh de Neville), announced that they had revoked their homage to the King and attempted to besiege the castle of Northampton. They moved on to Bedford and by 17 May were in London. John withdrew to Winchester, where Isabelle was staying with her guard. The Tower of London was still held for the King, but by early June Northampton and Lincoln had fallen to the rebels, and on 10 June John was obliged to meet their leaders near Staines. Five days later, John formally accepted the treaty which became famous as Magna Carta, at Runnymede between Staines and Windsor. On 19 June the magnates renewed their allegiance and a committee of twenty-five was established to ensure that the new agreement was enforced.

The provisions of the charter give some sense of the abuses the barons felt themselves to have been victim to for years. The crown was forbidden to make wrongful dispossession, to take over deceased persons' property and interfere in Church placements without writs being prepared by a sheriff and read in a court of assize. Royal exploitation of the law, such as denying trial, taking money to influence suits, profit from writs and depriving men of their rights where they had not broken the law, were forbidden. Magna Carta is obviously one of the most significant constitutional documents in history, but in 1215, John had no intention of abiding by it. He appealed to the Pope, who obligingly declared it to be eternally invalid and threatened to excommunicate anyone who attempted to uphold it.

John's rejection of Magna Carta initiated the conflict known as the first barons' war. The magnates were desperate to find a leader who could overthrow John and become the next king. Henry, John's eldest son, was still a child, and a long, potentially contentious regency could not save the country. Instead, as in the case of Henry II, a maternal claim was invoked as a solution to civil war. The magnates elected Louis of France, the son of Philip Augustus, who had an entitlement to the English crown in right of his wife, Blanche of Castile. Blanche, who was the daughter of John's elder sister Leonor and her husband Alfonso of Castile, had been chosen by her grandmother, Eleanor of Aquitaine, as Louis's bride in 1200. An embassy was sent to Louis, and meanwhile pandemonium raged in England. Ireland, Scotland and Wales seized the opportunity to rebel. John marched his troops from a muster at Dover to Rochester, then northwards via St Albans, Northampton, York and Newcastle to Berwick. The level of destruction wrought by the King's forces had not been seen since William the Conqueror's infamous harrying of the north. In January 1216, John swung his army back south for an equally destructive return, and though two bands of troops were sent from France, Prince Louis himself did not appear. John was back at Dover by the end of April, and on 21 May the French ships were sighted off the coast.

By the summer, the whole country was at war. Louis had entered London in June, and an army of Scots rebels joined him at Canterbury in September. The King hurried eastwards, reaching Lincoln on 28 September, but there is a strange and much-disputed gap in his movements at this time. At the greatest crisis of his life, he took time off to plunder a few abbeys. On 12 October, John's party was caught by high tides or quicksand in the Wash and, according to legend, the crown and royal regalia were lost. Although he was already suffering from dysentery and needed to be carried in a litter, John consoled himself with a feast of peaches and cider, which did nothing to improve his health. Reaching the castle of the bishop of Lincoln at Newark, he accepted that his illness was fatal, named his son Henry as his heir, extracted an oath of allegiance to him and appointed William Marshal, Earl of Pembroke, as regent and Guardian of the Realm. As John lay dying on 19 October, his household was reportedly more concerned with plundering than with mourning.

Isabelle was at Bristol when the news of her husband's death arrived. Magna Carta was reissued in the city and nine-year-old Henry was proclaimed King. Now that John was dead, there was no need for Louis, who had been defeated after a token battle with William Marshal at Lincoln on 20 May and had withdrawn to France 10,000 marks the richer for renouncing his claim to the throne. Isabelle had little chance of a place on her son's regency council which, under the guidance of Marshal, the bishop of Winchester and the papal legate, set the pattern for future royal minorities, with the exception of Edward III. Henry was already living in the household of the bishop, and his sister Eleanor joined him there after her father's death. Joan and Richard of Cornwall were given into the charge of Peter de Maulay and Philip Mark. Isabelle's plans seem to have been in place as soon as she was widowed. She made three grants for the salvation of John's soul – of the tithes of the mills at Berkhamsted, a confirmation of John's Chichester gift and a fair at Exeter for the monastery of St Nicholas, but thereafter she did not mention John in any of her acts for the rest of her life. Whether she had no interest in a political role in England or recognised that she was unlikely to achieve one, she was determined to go home.

Isabelle might well have been married when she was a child, she had been humiliated by her husband, slandered and kept in a state of demeaning dependence. She made it very clear that she did not care for England, and even her children were not enough to keep her there, but she was not prepared to leave without finally asserting her rights. She demanded that both her dower settlements, of 1200 and 1204, be honoured, insisted on being compensated for the loss of her French dower with properties in Devon and Aylesbury and claimed her interest in Saintes and Niort, even though she had agreed on Saintes as the dowry for her daughter Joan's marriage to Hugh X de Lusignan. That her complaints were vociferous may be inferred from the regency council's provision of a separate lodging for her in 1217, on the diplomatic grounds that those at Exeter Castle were unsuitable to her status. When Isabella left for Angoulême that year, she took with her only six-year-old Joan. Henry was King and his brother Richard, as the next in line, had to remain in England, but Isabelle could easily have taken her baby daughters Eleanor and Isabella. Eleanor of Aquitaine has been criticised as a neglectful mother, but her daughter-in-law was far more callous. She simply abandoned four of her children, and Joan saw her mother again only as a result of the Lusignan connection.

Isabelle had had quite enough of being pushed around and was now ready to go to extremes in her pursuit of power. Early in 1220, she married Hugh de Lusignan, her daughter's fiancé and the son of the man to whom she had once been betrothed. Not only was this a shocking way for a mother to behave towards her child, it was scandalously uncanonical: she had exchanged the *verba de praesenti* with the senior Hugh, which made her marriage to his son incestuous. Perhaps she was attracted to marriage with a man closer to her own age. Hugh was in his early thirties, while she herself could have been as young as twenty-five, and they had nine children in fifteen years, which suggests a degree of mutual enthusiasm. However, there was also a practical reason for her decision. Her cousin Matilda, now her mother-in-law, refused to give up her rights to Angoulême until 1233, and Isabelle required a strong ally to help her to retain her claims on the county. Her need of Hugh was greater than her daughter's, and Joan's feelings were hardly a factor.

Initially, Isabelle was concerned to paint her marriage as a sacrifice necessary to her son's interests. In a letter to Henry she explained that Hugh's friends had persuaded him against marrying Joan, who was too young, and instead to take a French wife. If he had done so, Isabelle writes, all Henry's lands in Poitou and Gascony would have been at risk, and 'therefore, seeing the great peril that might accrue if the marriage should take place . . . ourselves married the said Hugh . . . and God knows we did this for your benefit rather than our own'.

In England, the regency council feebly demanded the return of Joan and her dowry, but Isabelle refused, as she was not willing to give up her claim to Saintes. If the council had presumed that meek, malleable Isabelle, who had tolerated living with her husband's ex-wife and in the household of his lover, would act as a pro-English ambassadress in Angoulême, Isabelle had other ideas – and she had the English over a barrel. The alliance with Hugh had created precisely the situation John had hoped to avoid by marrying her in the first place. In 1221, the council confiscated her English dower lands, but Isabelle promptly threatened to make an alliance with the French and in 1222 the council restored the properties. She sought to expand her influence by invading Cognac, which the English had lost back in the 1180s. In her territorial disputes, Isabelle showed that she had learned something from the only political duty with which John had entrusted her. During the barons' war, she had had custody of the brother of Roger de Lacy, whose son John had been one of the rebel signatories to Magna Carta. When a local magnate named Bartholomew de Puy attempted to oppose her, she took him and his two sons hostage until they gave in to her demands. The bishop of Saintes was so disgusted by her unchivalrous behaviour that he excommunicated her.

Isabelle has been accused of using Joan as a hostage, too, but her reasons for keeping her daughter were no more mercenary than the council's wish to recover her. Joan's awkward position was resolved at a meeting between Henry III and Alexander, King of Scots in June 1220. As ever, the Scots were causing trouble and a marriage was proposed between Joan and Alexander. Having secured her own position, Isabelle now permitted Joan to leave, and the Princess sailed from La Rochelle to rejoin her siblings. She became Queen of Scotland in 1221 and was nicknamed Joan Make-peace for her part in yet another Anglo-Scottish peace agreement. Eventually, then, Joan made a more prestigious marriage than the one prefigured by the betrothal her mother had arranged and broken, though in her personal opinion, becoming a queen was poor compensation for life at the rather rough-and-ready Scottish court.

Isabelle knew the value of her own status as Dowager Queen of England and styled herself thus until the end of her life, using the royal seal that gave her full list of titles: Queen of England, Lady of Ireland, Duchess of Normandy and Aquitaine and Countess of Anjou. Her regal prestige was stamped into the coinage of Angoulême from 1224. But that was as far as her loyalty to England went. She repeatedly complained to the regency council about their lack of military support for her Angoulême projects and a debt of 3,500 marks she asserted John should have bequeathed to her. Continually frustrated, in 1224 she called England's bluff and defected to France. Philip Augustus died in 1223 and his son, the erstwhile champion of the English barons, was now Louis VIII. Hugh de Lusignan had sworn his allegiance to his stepson Henry of England, but when Louis invaded Poitou in 1224 he accepted the French King as his overlord. Louis made Isabelle an offer of 2,000 Paris livres in exchange for relinquishing her dower lands in England, the revenues of Langeais and dower rights in Saumur. Anxiously, the English made a counter offer, but she refused it. In 1226 she took Louis's gold and, although her son planned a meeting with her when he projected a French campaign, Hugh renewed his fealty to Louis in May of that year. When Louis was succeeded by his son with Blanche of Castile, Louis IX, Hugh and Isabelle perpetuated the alliance, for which they received a vast pension of 5,000 livres in 1230.

Isabelle was now at war with both her English sons. Not only was she an ally of Henry II's enemy (which gave the lie to her original justification to Henry for her marriage to Hugh) but Richard of Cornwall was fighting her husband for control of his territories. She did, however, retain some loyalty to Richard, who was perhaps her favourite child, and it resulted in difficulties in her hitherto successful relationship with Hugh. By 1230, Hugh and Isabelle had succeeded in creating a more centralised government and a powerful mini-state in what had once been the heartland of the Angevin empire. But their control was resented and from that year some of their vassals began to declare for Henry of England. Isabelle's allegiance also began to show signs of wavering again. In 1231 she gave control of her reconfiscated English dower holdings to Richard and in 1241, she quarrelled with King Louis.

Two reasons are given for Isabelle's anger. Louis held an oath-swearing at Poitiers, which she attended, but she was deeply offended at the affront to her dignity when the French Queen, the Countess of Chartres and the Countess's sister were given seats, while the Queen of England and Countess of Angoulême was expected to stand. Moreover, Louis announced that he was handing the comital title of Poitiers to his brother Alfonse, even though he had granted it to Richard of Cornwall in 1225. Isabelle's reaction was to remove her furniture and hangings from Hugh's seat at Lusignan and repair to her own castle at Angoulême, signifying that she felt he was somehow to blame for the proceedings. As her proxy at the oath-swearing, Hugh had allowed her to be insulted and her son deprived of his title. She declared she would leave her husband, or at least banish him from her bed, and when this threat failed to galvanise him she rounded up a coalition of barons to rebel against the French. Henry III was campaigning against Louis in Gascony and Hugh now declared his support for the English King in an attempt to pacify his wife.

The two sides met in the second battle of Taillebourg, where the English suffered such terrible losses that Henry himself was saved only when Richard of Cornwall sent a pilgrim's staff to the French camp across the River Charente and arranged a parley, which concluded with Henry being permitted to withdraw to Saintes. Hugh, terrified by the consequences of his disloyalty now that it seemed Louis had the upper hand, changed sides yet again and deserted. Within a week of the English defeat at Taillebourg, he and Isabelle tried to make peace with Louis, but it came at the price of their pension and the abandonment of Isabelle's claim to Saintes. They were also obliged to pay for the maintenance of French garrisons in three of their most important castles. Hugh's cowardly conduct provoked contempt among both the English and the French, and Isabelle had to face the fact that twenty years of military and diplomatic effort in building up her territories in Poitou had been wasted. She had not been capable of exploiting the situation her first marriage had prevented, and had ended up allowing the French to expand further into the south, just as the English had feared. She was reported to be so furious that she tried to stab herself.

Isabelle did not die of rage, but she did not live long after Taillebourg. She retreated to Fontevrault, where she passed away in May 1246, and where her effigy remains. One exceptional artefact commemorating her defiance still exists. Alice of Angoulême's first husband had a son by a previous marriage, Jean de Montmirail. Jean, who had served as a knight under King Philip Augustus, entered the Cistercian monastery at Long-pont, Picardy some time before 1217. By the 1230s he was being venerated as a saint. A coffer containing his bones, two feet long and six inches deep, and decorated with the badges of Hugh de Lusignan, Alfonse of Poitiers and Louis IX, was made at Limoges shortly after Taillebourg. Given the exceptional richness of Isabelle of Angoulême's cognatic connections, the gift of the coffer to the King suggests that she was involved in the peace negotiations between her husband and the crown, making use of her stepbrother's bones as a particularly appropriate relic. Those connections did not die with Isabelle. While her queenship had been dominated by the passionate tyrannies of her first husband, the children of her second marriage were to play a revolutionary part in the reign of her son Henry III. Isabelle had not been well treated by the throne of England. It might have been of some comfort to her to know that her Lusignan sons were to be a thorn in its side for many years to come.

PART THREE

PLANTAGENET QUEENS

THE PLANTAGENETS

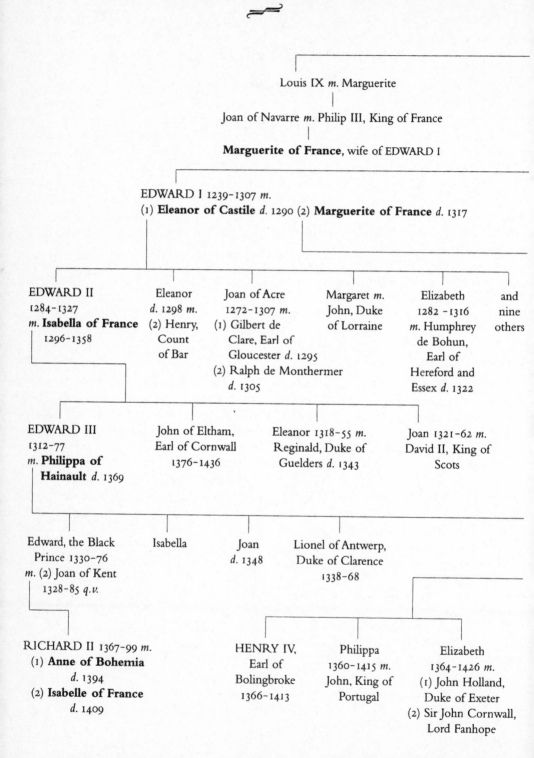

Louis IX *m.* Marguerite

Joan of Navarre *m.* Philip III, King of France

Marguerite of France, wife of EDWARD I

EDWARD I 1239-1307 *m.*
(1) **Eleanor of Castile** *d.* 1290 (2) **Marguerite of France** *d.* 1317

EDWARD II	Eleanor	Joan of Acre	Margaret *m.*	Elizabeth	and
1284-1327	*d.* 1298 *m.*	1272-1307 *m.*	John, Duke	1282 -1316	nine
m. **Isabella of France**	(2) Henry,	(1) Gilbert de	of Lorraine	*m.* Humphrey	others
1296-1358	Count	Clare, Earl of		de Bohun,	
	of Bar	Gloucester *d.* 1295		Earl of	
		(2) Ralph de Monthermer		Hereford and	
		d. 1305		Essex *d.* 1322	

EDWARD III	John of Eltham,	Eleanor 1318-55 *m.*	Joan 1321-62 *m.*
1312-77	Earl of Cornwall	Reginald, Duke of	David II, King of
m. **Philippa of**	1376-1436	Guelders *d.* 1343	Scots
Hainault *d.* 1369			

Edward, the Black	Isabella	Joan	Lionel of Antwerp,
Prince 1330-76		*d.* 1348	Duke of Clarence
m. (2) Joan of Kent			1338-68
1328-85 *q.v.*			

RICHARD II 1367-99 *m.*	HENRY IV,	Philippa	Elizabeth
(1) **Anne of Bohemia**	Earl of	1360-1415 *m.*	1364-1426 *m.*
d. 1394	Bolingbroke	John, King of	(1) John Holland,
(2) **Isabelle of France**	1366-1413	Portugal	Duke of Exeter
d. 1409			(2) Sir John Cornwall,
			Lord Fanhope

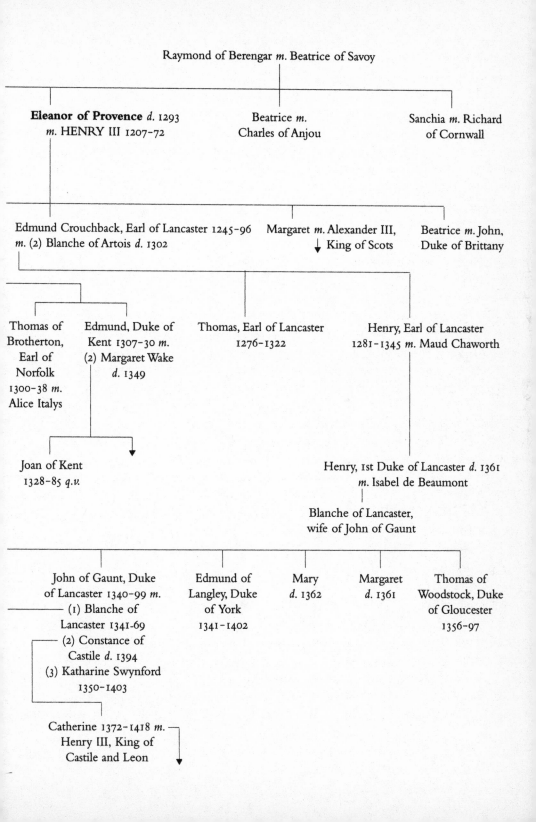

Raymond of Berengar *m.* Beatrice of Savoy

Eleanor of Provence *d.* 1293
m. HENRY III 1207–72

Beatrice *m.*
Charles of Anjou

Sanchia *m.* Richard
of Cornwall

Edmund Crouchback, Earl of Lancaster 1245–96
m. (2) Blanche of Artois *d.* 1302

Margaret *m.* Alexander III,
King of Scots

Beatrice *m.* John,
Duke of Brittany

Thomas of
Brotherton,
Earl of
Norfolk
1300–38 *m.*
Alice Italys

Edmund, Duke of
Kent 1307–30 *m.*
(2) Margaret Wake
d. 1349

Thomas, Earl of Lancaster
1276–1322

Henry, Earl of Lancaster
1281–1345 *m.* Maud Chaworth

Joan of Kent
1328–85 *q.v.*

Henry, 1st Duke of Lancaster *d.* 1361
m. Isabel de Beaumont

Blanche of Lancaster,
wife of John of Gaunt

John of Gaunt, Duke
of Lancaster 1340–99 *m.*
———— (1) Blanche of
Lancaster 1341–69
——— (2) Constance of
Castile *d.* 1394
(3) Katharine Swynford
1350–1403

Edmund of
Langley, Duke
of York
1341–1402

Mary
d. 1362

Margaret
d. 1361

Thomas of
Woodstock, Duke
of Gloucester
1356–97

Catherine 1372–1418 *m.* ——
Henry III, King of
Castile and Leon

CHAPTER 8

ELEANOR OF PROVENCE

'How high does the arrogance of woman rise if it is not restrained?'

Eleanor of Provence was the second daughter of Count Raymond-Berengar, who had ruled Provence as a vassal of the Emperor Frederick II since 1219, and Beatrice of Savoy. Eleanor's sisters Marguerite (born 1221), Sanchia (1228) and Beatrice (1231) were all to become queens, and each of their marriages was to be influential in shaping the direction of English policy abroad. In 1234, Marguerite joined the French monarchy as the bride of Louis IX, and it was this alliance that encouraged Henry III of England to consider Eleanor as a wife. Their union provides an exceptionally strong example of the significance of women in the dynastic strategies of Europe's royal houses as well as of the importance a queen's natal family could achieve in the politics of her adopted country.

On attaining his majority in 1227, Henry was anxious to begin the recovery of the Angevin lands lost under his father, John, and since the French crown would naturally oppose any such attempt, a marriage with Eleanor had the potential to counter the influence of her sister's. Both the French and English kings were interested in securing the support of the house of Savoy, which was powerful in the east and south of France. Raymond-Berengar was neither particularly rich nor likely to be able to leave his daughters any great territorial claims, and both Marguerite and Eleanor were selected as royal wives as much for their maternal family's connections as for their status as the Count's daughters.

Henry was keen enough to marry Eleanor to dissolve a previous arrangement with Joan, the heiress to the small but strategically placed county of Ponthieu on the Norman border. This agreement had progressed so far that in April 1235 Henry had written to her father asking for Joan to come to England, and had planned her coronation for the next month. The French King – or more specifically his mother, Eleanor of Aquitaine's granddaughter Blanche of Castile – strongly objected to the match, and by invoking a promise made by Joan s father that he would forfeit his lands if he married his eldest daughter without the King's permission, they were able to stop the marriage at the last minute. Henry's acceptance of their interference suggests that he was glad to have an excuse to renege on his pledge.

Apparently, Joan did not much mind being jilted by the King of England, and released Henry from his engagement. By October, Henry's envoys Richard le Gras and John of Gatesden were in Provence to inspect the new lady (who, like nearly all girls of her class, was complacently pronounced to be beautiful), while John FitzPhilip and Robert de Mucegros were charged with the negotiation of her dowry, which was settled at 10,000 marks. Eleanor's dower arrangements were more complicated – Isabelle of Angoulême was still living, and if Henry were to die before the new Queen and the Dowager Queen it would be difficult to provide for both of them – but the portion was provisionally fixed at fourteen English towns including Gloucester, Cambridge and Bath. With the business arrangements settled, in November the twelve-year-old Eleanor was married by proxy, with Robert de Mucegros standing in for the King at the castle of Tarascon, and, after travelling via Vienne, Dover and Canterbury, where her marriage was consummated, she was crowned at Westminster on 20 January 1236.

In just a few months, Eleanor's world had changed completely. It is not possible to extrapolate her 'real' feelings from the sources, but the fact that, nearly fifty years later she joined forces with her daughter-in-law Eleanor of Castile, who was married at fourteen, to persuade Edward I that his thirteen-year-old daughter was not yet ready for matrimony, suggests she herself may have found the transition difficult. Eleanor's subsequent and often ill-advised dependence on her Savoyard relatives may also have stemmed from a sense of personal isolation at the time of her marriage. Unlike many royal brides raised with the expectation of their future role, often in the country of which they would become queen, Eleanor had had to adjust to both marriage and queenship in a very short space of time. She was to display great ambition and a highly protective love for her children, but also a strong tendency to control, which was interpreted as 'arrogance' by her critics but which may well have had its source in self-preservation, in a need for the reassurance that came from feeling she was mistress of her own environment. She also demonstrated a certain impatience with what she saw as the provincial insularity of English politics, which compared so unfavourably with her own sophisticated, cosmopolitan background.

The Provençal court was culturally, if not financially rich, and Eleanor's father was a patron of troubadour literature. Eleanor herself spoke Occitan, French and the Norman French of Henry's court, as well as having some grasp of Latin, and though the north-south divide in European culture, which had been exaggerated even in Eleanor of Aquitaine's time, was now still less pronounced, it may still have seemed very marked to a young girl spending her first freezing winter far from home. Much like Eleanor of Aquitaine, Eleanor of Provence was a daughter of the south, 'a milieu of music, dancing, tournaments, knights-errant and fair damsels in distress, while Henry's dominions to the north symbolised sobriety and joylessness, the world of ... stubborn and irreducible facts, the boring domain of penny-pinching accountants, nit-picking lawyers and pedantic administrators'.[1] Eleanor's later career proved she could pick a nit as well as the next man, but Henry's initial treatment of his young wife suggests that he was eager to make the contrasts between old and new homes less jarring.

Henry was clearly aware that his new wife might find her English accommodation rather shabby, for he built or improved apartments for her in nine of the royal residences, including a chamber and chapel at Westminster and a room decorated with roses painted on a white ground in the Tower of London. At Clarendon, modern conveniences were installed: a 'fair privy chamber, well-vaulted' on both floors of her rooms, and glazed windows that could be opened in the chapel. Architecture was one of Henry's passions, and Eleanor benefited from his decision to show his welcome to her in buildings. All her life, she seems to have loved gardens. A walled garden was made at Clarendon and herb gardens at Kempton and Winchester, while at Woodstock, a favourite residence of the couple, a flower garden was laid for her outside her chapel, with another herb garden around the 'stew', or fish pond. Later, at Gloucester, a bridge was constructed to enable Eleanor to walk in the gardens of neighbouring Llanthony Priory. Most touchingly of all, one of the gardens laid out for her at Windsor was 'Provençal' in style. Henry was also thoughtful when it came to the initial appointments to Eleanor's household, choosing John of Gatesden and Robert de Mucegros, the two courtiers with whom she had had most contact before her wedding, as her wardrobe keeper and steward respectively. For the post of her doctor and tutor, he selected Nicholas Farnham, a scholar who eventually became bishop of Durham. Without reading too much into these gestures, it might be said Henry was mindful that his young wife was feeling insecure and lonely, and that he tried to make her surroundings comforting.

Despite Eleanor being twelve to her husband's twenty-eight, they had begun sleeping together straight away and, in a dramatic incident at Woodstock in 1237, it was Henry's intimacy with his wife that saved his life. In the middle of the night, a madman somehow broke into the royal bedroom, waving a knife and demanding the crown. He stabbed at Henry's bed, but luckily Henry wasn't in it, as he was with Eleanor in her apartments. When the intruder began searching for the King, the alarm was raised by one of Eleanor's ladies, Margaret Biset, who had stayed up late to read her psalter. Eleanor remembered Margaret's courage, and thirty years later Henry confirmed a property grant to the Biset family's leper foundation at Maiden Bradley on account of his Queen's 'great love' for the house.

In general, however, Eleanor's queenship was to be marked not by particular loyalty to her English servants but by her close and continuing associations with her Savoyard family. She has been described as the 'supreme example'[2] of the manner in which well-born women could maintain political power after marriage by manipulating the connections of their birth families. Her mother, Beatrice of Savoy, had five brothers, all of whom were impressively skilled diplomats. Together, the 'eagles of Savoy' were able to build up a network of alliances that extended their influence all over England and France and across the Alps into Italy. The brilliance of Eleanor's uncles lay in their capacity to engage in apparently conflicting policies while simultaneously working for their collective good. By 1240, two of these uncles, Thomas and Peter, were at Henry's court, and in 1244, a third, Boniface, was provided to the see of Canterbury. In Peter of Savoy, to whom she was especially close, Eleanor found a guide and a teacher as she began to negotiate her first steps in English politics.

Her political career really began after the birth of her first child, Edward, in 1239, when she and her uncles worked together to neutralise any threat posed to the baby prince's interests by King Henry's younger brother, Richard of Cornwall. Peter of Savoy had arrived in England while Richard was away on crusade and Henry was preparing for a military expedition in Poitou. If he were to be killed, Edward's position would be highly vulnerable, and Eleanor sought to associate the future of the Savoyards with his security. Henry ordered that, in the event of his death, the castles of the Welsh marches should be delivered to Edward, and in early 1242 he issued similar instructions for several fortresses, including Dover. Moreover, Eleanor's own importance was augmented at Richard's expense, since not only was he left out of any guardianship arrangements made for Edward, but it was also decided that any castle the Queen could not hold personally as regent would be delivered up to any of her uncles who were not in a position of fealty to France (which at this point meant Peter of Savoy). While these decisions went some way to ensuring that Edward would have powerful and loyal supporters in the event of his inheriting the crown, they obviously risked alienating Richard of Cornwall. The solution to this was a proposed marriage between Richard and Eleanor's sister Sanchia of Provence, which would dissipate any conflict between Prince Edward and his uncle by allying their interests. So in May 1242 Peter of Savoy was dispatched as an envoy to participate in a proxy marriage ceremony with Sanchia at Tarascon.

That summer, Eleanor accompanied Henry to Poitou on campaign. She had given birth to a daughter, Margaret, in September 1240, and was now in the last stages of pregnancy with her third child. They landed at Royan in Gascony and while Henry set off to confront his brother-in-law Louis on the battlefield, Eleanor was delivered of another girl, Beatrice, at Bordeaux. The expedition was a failure, largely as a result of the defection of Hugh de Lusignan after the English and French forces met at Taillebourg, a disastrous battle for the English, and one in which, as we have seen, Henry himself was saved from capture only by the quick thinking of Richard of Cornwall, who rode into the enemy camp and negotiated a retreat to Saintes. Impulsively, Henry promised Gascony to his brother in return for his rescue, which did not suit Eleanor's plans at all. It is possible that her reaction to Henry's gesture resulted in Richard being deprived of Chester, as on 17 August 1243, a month before the royal party returned from Gascony, some of Eleanor's dower lands were exchanged for the county in a document witnessed by yet another Savoyard uncle, Philip. Richard was then persuaded to renounce Gascony in return for lands worth 500 pounds a year.

Despite the failure of Taillebourg, Henry put on a magnificent show when Beatrice of Savoy and Sanchia arrived for the wedding proper, which took place at Westminster on 23 November. Beatrice's visit was diplomatic as well as celebratory: she aimed to convince Henry to lend her embattled husband 4,000 marks on the security of five castles in Provence, which were to be held for the use of the King and Queen of England. The inclusion of Eleanor in this contract emphasises the importance of her right of inheritance in Provence, which was a means for Henry to acquire strategic strongholds in the province. The smoothness of these arrangements was not, however, appreciated by the English people, who already perceived the marriage between Richard and Sanchia as evidence of Eleanor's excessive power over the King. 'The whole community in England,' wrote Matthew Paris, 'taking it ill, began to fear that the whole business of the kingdom would be disposed of at the will of the Queen and her sister.'

The devious devices of the Savoyards were further exposed when Eleanor's father Raymond-Berengar died in 1245. As the sole unmarried sister, Beatrice was to inherit, but Blanche of Castile, the Dowager Queen of France (and mother-in-law to Eleanor's sister Marguerite) had no intention of letting such a prize escape French clutches. She conspired with the Pope, Innocent IV, to marry Beatrice to Charles of Anjou, King Louis's younger brother. Shockingly, this plan was faciliated not only by Eleanor's mother, whose allegiances were quite evenly divided, but also by Philip of Savoy and Archbishop Boniface. However, if the Savoyards took, they also gave. Even as Henry was being relieved of his stake in the Provençal inheritance, Peter was negotiating a deal with Eleanor's fifth uncle, Amadeus, the ruler of Savoy, whereby Amadeus became Henry's vassal and awarded him four castles in exchange for a pension of 200 marks and a downpayment of 1,000. A further clause was the marriage of Amadeus's granddaughter to a royal ward. Having accepted these conditions, Henry was then unwise enough to permit a number of marriages between Savoyard girls and eligible English aristocrats, among them Edmund de Lacy, heir to the Earl of Lincoln, Richard de Burgh, heir to the Irish lordship of Connacht, William de Vescy, heir to Alnwick, Alexander Balliol and Baldwin, heir to the Earl of Devon, who married Queen Eleanor's first cousin Marguerite, the daughter of Thomas of Savoy. Naturally, English magnates with daughters of their own to provide for greatly resented this plague of Savoyard brides, and though the policy was Henry's much of the blame was laid on Eleanor.

In total, 170 Savoyards are known to have enjoyed royal patronage, though the majority of them were clerks and fewer than eighty-five remained permanently in England. Thirty-nine did receive grants of land, and at the top of the scale Eleanor's uncles, notably Peter, received massive gifts of land and money. Matthew Paris was quick to point out the resentment this provoked, a resentment not confined, in his account, to the immediate circle of the court. So why was Eleanor so insensitive to the effect of this favouritism on her own reputation and her husband's popularity? One answer may be found in the legacy of another English queen, Isabelle of Angoulême. Isabelle had five children by her second husband, Hugh de Lusignan: William de Valence, Geoffrey, Guy and Aymer de Lusignan and Alice. Despite the treachery of their father, in 1247 Henry invited all his half-siblings to join him in England. Immediately, the Lusignans set themselves up as a counter-faction to the Savoyards. In particular, they were jealous of the affinity of interest Eleanor had created between Edward (who was their nephew, too) and her Savoyard family. Almost immediately, conflict between the rival groups began to focus on Eleanor, so it might be concluded that she was prepared to ignore the negative consequences of Savoyard patronage in the interests of the valuable bulwark it provided against the Lusignans who, from the start, she seems to have perceived as her enemies.

In 1244 Eleanor gave birth to a second son, Edmund. Henry, determined that this child should be a boy, had had 1,000 candles set before the altar of Becket's shrine at Canterbury and 1,000 more at the church of St Augustine. He told the abbot of St Edmund's that if he had a son he would name the child for the saint and had the monks chant the Antiphon of St Edmund while Eleanor was in labour, so the result of his efforts was highly satisfactory. The birthdates of Eleanor's first four children (1239, 1240, 1242 and 1244) indicate that she and Henry had been sleeping together regularly (the fact that no baby is known to have been born earlier suggests that she might not have fully reached puberty at the time of her marriage), but she was not to have another child until 1253. While she may have suffered miscarriages or unrecorded stillbirths, this absence of documented pregnancy may point to an estrangement between a couple whose married life had begun so successfully. That Eleanor and Henry were at odds in these eight years is clear from their actions, and their difficulties may have stemmed from Eleanor's increasing appetite for power and her antipathy towards the Lusignans.

In addition to her lands and queens-gold, Eleanor raised funds through the incomes of royal wardships, whereby the estates of a minor were managed to the profit of the holder until the heir came of age. Gifts of such wardships were a convenient means for a king to increase his wife's income without impinging directly on the crown estates, and they were to become a significant part of the financial endowments of English queens. (For the period between 1257 and 1269, for example, Eleanor raised an average of over 750 pounds a year from wardships.) Among numerous similar arrangements, Eleanor had received wardship of the De Toesny lands in 1242. Her De Toesny grant explicitly excluded advowsons, or the right to present a chosen candidate to a Church living, so when, some years later, she placed a churchman, William of London, in a De Toesny benefice to which she had no right, she found herself in conflict with her husband. Henry dismissed her choice and attempted to appoint his own man, Artaud de St Romain, to the post. Eleanor saw this as a public humiliation and, with the support of Robert de Grosseteste, the sheriff of Buckinghamshire, the dispute was brought to court. At this point, Eleanor was clearly angry enough with Henry to risk openly embarrassing him, and since her candidate won (at least, he was still in office in 1274), the case would have made the King seem shamefully henpecked. It may have been this incident that prompted Henry to take a strong line against Eleanor's meddling when, in 1252, the Lusignan-Savoyard rivalry spilled over into ecclesiastical matters.

The archbishop of Canterbury, Eleanor's uncle Boniface, found himself in conflict with Aymer de Lusignan, who had been appointed archbishop elect of Winchester, over the appointment of a prior to the hospital of St Thomas at Southwark. Aymer installed his own candidate while Boniface was travelling abroad, but Boniface's official, Eustace de Lenn, excommunicated the new prior on the grounds that Boniface had to confirm the election. When the prior defied him, Eustace had him imprisoned at Maidstone, and Aymer promptly sent a group of armed men to release him. They set fire to the archepiscopal manor and kidnapped Eustace. Both Eleanor and Henry were furious at this undignified pettiness, but Eleanor saw in the situation an opportunity to strike against the Lusignans. When he learned that she had tried to interfere, Henry packed her off to Guildford in disgrace, took over control of her lands and deprived her of her right to queens-gold. Peter of Savoy was also forced to leave the court for a time. This seems an exceptionally stern reaction, but Henry's patience had been sorely tried. As well as the embarrassment of the court case, Eleanor's involvement with one of his most difficult subjects, his brother-in-law Simon de Montfort, had been plaguing him for years.

While the Lusignan-Savoy conflict can be seen at the simplest level as two competing families struggling for royal favour, De Montfort had been an ongoing source of a variety of problems for Henry since 1239. Simon de Montfort senior had been the leader of the crusade against the Albigensian heresy in the Languedoc, and though he had acquired a reputation for greed and cruelty, his high standing in England was reflected in the promotion of his son, who was given a share of the earldom of Leicester. De Montfort junior had made a scandalous secret marriage to Henry's sister Eleanor, the widow of William Marshal. Eleanor had taken a vow of chastity in the presence of the archbishop of Canterbury after her first husband died, but De Montfort persuaded her into a clandestine ceremony at Westminster. Henry and his brother Richard were deeply angered by the offence to themselves, to the Church and to their sister's dignity, but De Montfort was shameless. He cavalierly used the King's name as security for loans and there was an ugly incident at the churching ceremony for

Queen Eleanor after the birth of Edward when Henry, having discovered that De Montfort had borrowed 20,000 marks from Thomas of Savoy against his name, rounded on Simon and Eleanor, calling them fornicators. For a time the couple were forced into exile, but by 1247 De Montfort had been restored to favour and appointed governor of Gascony, with Eleanor's support: it is possible that she feared Richard of Cornwall still had designs on the province, which she was determined would form part of Edward's apanage, hence her desire to have her own man in place.

In 1249, Eleanor persuaded De Montfort to free a rebel lord, Gaston de Béarn, a cousin of hers, requesting a pardon and the restoration of his lands. De Béarn did homage to both Henry and Edward, but raised another rebellion as soon as he was released, leaving Eleanor's strategy of appeasement looking very foolish. In 1251, another family occasion provided the arena for a public quarrel. The wedding of eleven-year-old Princess Margaret and ten-year-old Alexander III of Scotland, to whom she had been betrothed since the age of four, was spoiled by Henry and De Montfort falling out over money. Henry had undertaken to reimburse De Montfort for the maintenance of the royal castles in Gascony, but De Montfort's administration was proving expensive and ineffective, and now Henry refused to pay up. Mindful of the safety of her eldest son's inheritance, Eleanor nagged Henry into handing over the money. The next year, Henry's mistrust of De Montfort was confirmed when his brother-in-law was put on trial to answer charges of corruption and incompetence brought by Gascon landowners and churchmen. The King was enraged when Peter of Savoy spoke up for him and the English lords cleared him of the charges.

By 1252, then, it appeared that the rather trivial dispute over the prior of St Thomas's was only one of a series of situations in which Eleanor had put her own interests above her husband's wishes, and in which she had not been afraid to use her powerful family, whom Henry himself had supported, against him. The apparent eight-year gap in their sexual relationship puts this incident at the climax of a dispute which had been going on for some years, and Henry's exasperation might be seen more as a reaction to Eleanor's presumption over a long period than a specific response to a single event.

Eleanor's punishment lasted only two weeks. She returned to court at Clarendon fifteen days after the incident and her queens-gold was restored ten days later. She and Henry kept Christmas at Winchester, spent a few days at Westminster and travelled together to Windsor in January. Chastened, Eleanor exchanged New Year gifts with the Lusignans. Since the days of the Anglo-Saxon kings, such gifts had been part of the pageantry of English royalty, combining an impressive display of wealth and patronage with a certain mystical symbolism, and in January 1253 Eleanor gave more than sixty of them at a cost of over 200 pounds. She presented sixty-one rings, ninety-one brooches, thirty-three ornamented belts and ten gilded goblets. Geoffrey de Lusignan and William de Valence were among the recipients and Eleanor accepted a gift of plate from Aymer de Lusignan. Magnificent jewels and plate were a component of the largesse a queen was expected to dispense as a courteous demonstration of her status, but often, as was the case with the Lusignans, they carried a diplomatic message (echoed, in the aftermath of the St Thomas's quarrel, by the kiss of peace exchanged by Aymer and Boniface at a council held at the end of January). The distribution of plate and goblets was a particularly symbolic act for a queen, recalling the Anglo-Saxon emphasis on the king's wife as the 'peace-weaver' celebrating concord by acting as a cup-bearer for the king and his lords.

One outcome of Eleanor's reconciliation with Henry was her last child, Katherine, born in the November of that year. Another was that when Henry was obliged to return to Gascony to quell a rebellion in the province that spring, Eleanor was appointed regent, a position she held for ten months between August and May. As a measure of her status, she was awarded a large increase in her dower and the right to bequeath 3,000 marks beyond her own possessions in her will, while Peter of Savoy, who had also been returned to favour, was awarded 15,000 marks. During this period Eleanor attended two Parliaments, met foreign embassies, sat in council and in meetings of different sections of the Westminster administration and took a close interest in the financial arrangements for Henry's campaign, all while either pregnant or newly delivered. In her husband's absence, she organised her own banquet for her churching after Katherine's birth, a reminder that as regent she was responsible not only for the execution of royal power, but for the maintenance of the splendour of the crown as demonstrated in formal state occasions.

Eleanor was also prepared to make use of her sexual relationship with Henry to get what she wanted. She had inherited the patronage of two previous queens' institutions, the hospital of St Katherine by the Tower and the Augustinian house of Holy Trinity, which had charge of the hospital. In 1253, the prior of Holy Trinity installed his own candidate as master of the hospital, and the hospital appealed to Eleanor. She wrote to the bishop of London, Henry Wingham, a former royal chancellor, and the prior of Holy Trinity, threatened by Wingham with the consequences of Eleanor's anger, was forced to back down. The canons of Holy Trinity complained to the Pope, who expressed his disapproval, but Eleanor grandly ignored him and in 1273 gave the hospital a new charter of endowment, providing for a master, three brothers, three sisters and twenty-four poor men, of whom six were to be scholars. Eleanor's secret weapon was the canons' description of her as the King's 'nicticorax', or 'night bird', the implication being that her influence over Henry in bed might provoke him to punish Holy Trinity if the prior would not relent. Eleanor bequeathed the patronage of St Katherine's to all future queens and dowager queens of England, and the foundation still exists today, as the Royal Foundation of St Katherine – still in the gift of the queen consort and still abiding by the rules so imperiously set down by Eleanor.

In the spring of 1254, Eleanor was preparing for another visit to Gascony, this time with a happy prospect in mind. Edward was to be married to another Eleanor, the thirteen-year-old sister of Alfonso X, King of Castile. The background to this match stretched as far back as 1152, when Eleanor of Aquitaine had first made her duchy part of the Angevin possessions on her marriage to Henry II. When Eleanor's daughter Leonor became Queen of Castile, her husband, Alfonso VIII, maintained that she had been promised Gascony as a dowry, and though there was no formal confirmation of this assertion, he had used it as a pretext to invade the province in 1206, when King John was being assailed by Philip Augustus's encroachments to the north of the Angevin lands.

Now the Gascon question had flared up again as Alfonso X began to claim Aquitainian magnates, including the restless Gaston de Béarn, as his vassals. When he started to proclaim himself the heir of the murdered Arthur of Brittany, Henry III even suspected that he had designs on the English throne. After Henry's successful suppression of the 1253 rebellion support for Alfonso in Gascony declined, but a marriage between the heir of England and the Spanish princess would consolidate the resolution of the dispute and accordingly Henry began proceedings that May, which is when Eleanor of Castile's name first appears in English records.

Eleanor of Provence's new daughter-in-law was the child of her former rival for Henry's hand, Joan of Ponthieu, and Ferdinand III of Castile. Ferdinand already had seven sons by his first marriage, so had hardly been short of an heir, but his mother Berengaria (the sister of Blanche of Castile and another granddaughter of Eleanor of Aquitaine) was concerned that he would fall into immoral ways if he did not remarry, and together she and Blanche had arranged the match with Joan. Ferdinand and Joan had five children, of whom Eleanor, born in 1241, was one of three to survive beyond infancy. In February 1254, Henry III nominated the bishop of Hereford and John Maunsel to negotiate the arrangements for the wedding with Alfonso, and on the fourteenth of the month Edward's apanage was confirmed in expectation of his marriage. It included Gascony and the county of Chester, both of which his mother had worked hard to attain for him.

Eleanor of Provence fitted out 300 ships in preparation for the voyage, but her grand departure was spoiled by a violent outbreak of jealousy between the men of Winchelsea, who were furnishing the Queen's ship, and the shipwrights of Yarmouth, who were responsible for Edward's. The Winchelsea men attacked their rivals, some of whom were killed, and the mast of Edward's ship was stolen and attached to Eleanor's. In early June, Edward and Eleanor arrived without further incident in Bordeaux, where Eleanor presented three gold cloths to the churches of St André, St Séver and St Croix. It is not certain when the two Eleanors first met, as Edward travelled on to Castile for his wedding, which almost certainly took place on 1 November at the convent of Las Huelgos, near Burgos. Edward and his bride were back in Gascony later that month, but by then Eleanor and Henry had left for Paris.

In spite of its inauspicious start, this journey was probably one of the most pleasant of Eleanor's life. For once she and her husband were travelling unburdened by war or politics and could relax in the knowledge that Gascony was settled and Edward's marriage accomplished. They even found time for a little sentimental tourism, visiting the abbey of Fontevrault, where Henry would request that his heart be sent for burial, and the shrine of Edmund of Abingdon, who had married them nearly twenty years before at Pontigny. They moved on to Chartres, where they visited the cathedral, an experience that greatly influenced Henry's ambitions for Westminster Abbey, and where Eleanor was reunited not only with her mother and youngest sister Beatrice but also with Marguerite, Queen of France, and Sanchia, who had travelled from England. The agreement then forged between Henry and Louis IX, known as the treaty of Paris, might officially have been an arrangement between men, but it was brought about by five women. If the relationships between these sisters and their mother had on occasion been strained by the diplomatic entanglements of their husbands, their meeting in 1254 suggests that they were bound by a strong, even atavistic loyalty – a loyalty on which Eleanor would depend during the greatest crisis of her queenship.

Practically, the treaty of Paris did not in fact change a great deal in the long term, but it was regarded by contemporaries as a breakthrough in Anglo–French relations. Henry was to pay homage for his remaining French possessions and renounce his claims to Anjou, Poitou, Maine and Touraine in return for the grant of Gascony as a fief, lands in Cahors, Limoges and the Périgueux and funds for 500 knights for two years. The unofficial agenda, which may well have been managed by the Provençal women, included the marriage of Eleanor's daughter Beatrice to John, Duke of Brittany, agreements of financial and diplomatic aid from France and promises to protect Eleanor's interests against the Lusignans who, to the English Queen's irritation, were very much in the ascendant after the Gascon campaign, where their provision of Poitevin knights through local affinities had greatly aided Henry.

After the success in France Eleanor turned to another project close to her heart: the establishment of her second son, Edmund, as king of Sicily. At this time, Sicily comprised not only the eponymous island but also a large tranche of southern Italy, known together as the Regno. The plan, or 'the business of Sicily', as contemporaries called it, had been in train for some time, since the death of the Emperor Frederick II in 1250. Frederick had controlled the Regno, but when he was succeeded by his son Conrad, the Pope decided to install his own candidate. Edmund was suggested, along with his uncle by marriage Charles of Anjou. In 1254, Henry accepted the proposal and the Pope conveyed his formal agreement, followed by a confirmation of the grant of Regno in May. Again, the hand of the Savoyards can be seen in what has been mooted as the first stage in the creation of a Mediterranean empire. The papal chaplain who acted as a go-between for Henry and the papal nuncio, John d'Ambléou, was a Savoyard close to Peter of Savoy, and Eleanor's uncles Peter, Philip and Thomas were among the nine proctors appointed to manage Edmund's succession. Even the Pope had Savoyard connections – his niece, Beatrice di Fieschi, was married to Thomas of Savoy. However, Eleanor's hopes were thwarted when Conrad died just a week after the confirmation and the Regno was seized by Manfred, Emperor Frederick's illegitimate son. In December, Pope Innocent also died, and it appeared that the only means of acquiring Sicily for Edmund would be a military campaign. Both Eleanor and the new Pope, Alexander IV, pushed for armed intervention, but the pontiff insisted that any campaign would have to be financed by Henry. To the great resentment of the English clergy, he ordered a diversion of the crusading tax from the English Church for five years to raise funds. In 1255, Edmund was invested as King of Sicily at Westminster, looking somewhat foolish in traditional Sicilian dress, but his prospects of success appeared even more remote when Thomas of Savoy failed to put down a rebellion in Turin and was taken prisoner by his own subjects.

It is quite possible that the Savoyards, whose complex trans-European involvements always geared towards the bigger picture, had never seriously intended a war to be fought on Edmund's behalf, and had supported the scheme merely to gain leverage with the Holy See to extract concessions in matters with which they were more closely concerned. Now the priority was raising the ransom for Thomas's release, but Eleanor's funds had been exhausted by the pursuit of Sicily, and Gascony had eaten too much crown revenue. To both help her uncle and keep her ambitions for Edmund alive, she was obliged to borrow. She did so with the help of her clothes merchant, William, one of a group of businessmen who arranged to lend Eleanor, Henry and Edward a total of 14,500 marks against the religious foundations of Cirencester, Chertsey, Abingdon, Hyde and Pershore, to be raised through letters of obligation issued in the names of Eleanor and Peter of Savoy.

Dear though it was to Eleanor, the 'business of Sicily' and the costs it incurred were seen as another instance of the Queen and her foreign relatives attempting to enrich themselves at the expense of the English people. Neither Henry nor Eleanor had taken account of the volatile atmosphere in their kingdom, and it has been suggested that they saw diplomacy as simply a family matter (which in fact it was) and England as little more than a piggy-bank to dip into to fund their schemes. But the mood in England in the mid-thirteenth century was angrier and more restless than they realised. In addition to the resentment over the hated crusading tax, the clergy were weary of Henry's interference in ecclesiastical elections and courts and of his holding sees open to profit from their revenues. The combination of the costs of Gascony and the papal commitment in Sicily led the King to push his sheriffs to extortionate measures in the shires, which affected smaller landowners badly. Their disgruntlement was compounded by Henry's favouritism towards his own relatives – Richard of Cornwall, Peter of Savoy and the Lusignans were, for example, exempt from any writs in Chancery, which effectively meant that there was no recourse against them if they chose not to honour any debts. Eleanor's management of her finances was also making her unpopular.

The queen's council had existed as an independent body since at least the early thirteenth century. The three Matildas had held and managed their own dower lands in their husbands' lifetimes, whereas Eleanor

William the Conqueror (above): his queen, Matilda of Flanders, was not flattered by his proposal. She could not know that she was to become the consort of a legendary king.

Below: 'Good Queen Maud' was popular with the people, but the court mocked her for her frumpy dress sense.

Right: The White Ship disaster which claimed Henry I's heir had profound dynastic implications for the English crown.

Above: A great general and a great diplomat, Matilda was invaluable to King Stephen in his struggle to retain the crown.

The magnificent mausoleum of the Angevin Empire at Fontevrault.

The most famous woman of her age, Eleanor of Aquitaine ended her scandalous career as a nun at Fontevrault.

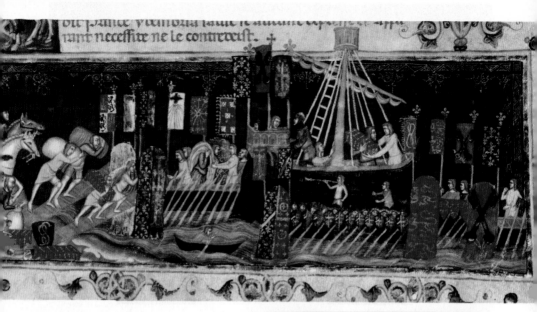

Three English queens made the thrilling, perilous journey to the Holy Land.

Neglected and cheated of her rights, Richard I's queen, Berengaria of Navarre, has been overshadowed by the Lionheart legend.

Isabelle of Angoulême may have gone to war with the English, but she never forgot her royal status.

Eleanor of Provence's partnership with Henry III was successful, but she never learned to understand the English.

Eleanor of Castile was immortalised as a beloved queen, but despised for her rapacity in her own lifetime.

Piers Gaveston was the third party in the doomed marriage of Isabella of France and Edward II.

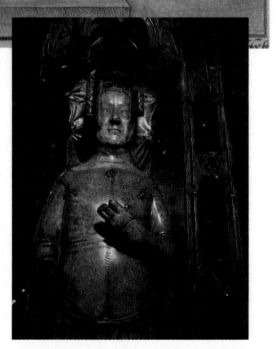

Prolific and placid, Philippa of Hainault juggled parlous finances and an unruly family.

A hidden painting provides a clue to the mystery of Richard II's marriages.

Opposite: Richard II mourned so deeply for Anne of Bohemia that
he had her favourite palace destroyed.

Overleaf: Mother to two English queens, Isabeau of Bavaria's story
epitomises the suspicion and fear provoked by foreign consorts.

La requeste con
templation z plai
sance de tresshut
et noble prince
mon tresscher seigneur z maistre
Guy de chastillon conte de blois
seigneur dauesnes de chymay
et de beaumont de schonehone
et de la hode · ⁌ Ie iehan fuis
sair prebstre et chappelain a mon

treschier seigneur dessus nôme
Et pour le tampz de lore tresorie
et chanonne de chynay et de lille
en flandres ille suis de nouuel
resueillie et entre dedens ma fo
rte pour ouurer et fortuer en sa
haulte et noble matiere de la
quelle du tampz passe re me
suis ensonne Laquelle traitte
et propose les fais et aduenues

of Aquitaine and Berengaria of Navarre had theoretically been able to administrate their dower property only as widows. From Eleanor of Provence's time, the queen of England had the unique legal status of *'femme sole'* while her husband was living. She could control her property, grant and acquire land and bequeath her own possessions, including crops grown on her estates. The queen's council also had jurisdiction over local officials and, contrary to general practice, the queen's tenants could not take her to court, leaving the council as the ultimate arbiter of disputes. The queen, on the other hand, could serve writs in her own name, (Eleanor's lawyer, Gilbert de Chalfont, represented her in several such suits). The only place where the queen could be held to legal account was the king's court. This was obviously a highly advantageous position, and one neither Eleanor of Provence nor several of her successors was above abusing.

Before passing judgement on Eleanor's governance of her finances, it is worth remembering how qualities that were seen as being merely businesslike in a man were quickly interpreted as a sign of unfeminine avarice in a medieval woman. Eleanor was a strict manager, impressively well informed about her sources of income and unembarrassed about extracting her due. She 'evidently condoned ruthless exploitation of estates in her wardship'[3] and her steward William of Tarrant was widely hated. Despite Matthew Paris's disapproval of the 'loss and peril' Tarrant caused to Eleanor's tenants, she was prepared to make excuses for him, whether through expedience or indifference. As public discontent with the King's financial exigency began to mount, Eleanor was named in a complaint by the sheriff of Buckinghamshire, who claimed he was unable to obtain dues on certain lands because of the protectionism that sheltered their owners. Perhaps Eleanor's grasping way with money could be attributed to her father's perennial financial difficulties, but Henry, too, seemed blind to the way in which his fund-raising was perceived. Even on Edward's birth, the joyful citizens of London were so offended by Henry's demands for increasingly grand celebratory gifts that a saying doing the rounds was: 'God gave us this child, but the King sells him to us.'

Eleanor's indifference to her lesser subjects is unfortunately typical of a rather crass political attitude towards her husband's realm that characterised her daily life in the 1250s. She was simply not very interested in the English. She ordered books and elegant headgear from Paris, the cloth for her dresses was imported from Florence and her carpets from Spain. To the Queen of England, fresh from a visit to her sister the Queen of France and her wondrous court at Paris, her own country might well have seemed a pinched, prejudiced sort of place, and Eleanor was far too sure of her own status to bother to try to hide her feelings. The messenger evidence from her household bears out the supposition that beyond the Savoyard network, Eleanor had very little contact with even high-ranking English people. She and Sanchia did exchange books with the countesses of Arundel and Winchester, but beyond the formal intercourse of court ceremony, Eleanor's relationships with the magnate class were relatively limited.

If the Queen saw herself as rather too grand for the parochial concerns of her husband's barons, the events of the 1260s forced a change in her perceptions. She and Henry had hoped to prevent the spread of further factionalism, by resolving their differences after the ecclesiastical dispute, but by 1258 the mood was once more turning against the Lusignans. In April, a group of magnates marched on Westminster and issued an ultimatum, demanding the exile of all Poitevins and the inauguration of a council of twenty-four men chosen to assist the King. In June, the Parliament held at Oxford enumerated a list of 'provisions' which called for all castles to be held by Englishmen, all alienated lands to be restored to the crown and a new arrangement for the government, consisting of three annual Parliaments, an elected council of fifteen served by twelve representatives from the baronage, the annual appointment of local sheriffs and a justiciar to travel the country hearing complaints. Further reforms (the Provisions of Westminster) had a personal impact upon Eleanor. The sale of wardships in the King's gift was to be decided by a committee of five and that same committee was to determine in which areas the tariff of queens-gold should apply. An oath of allegiance, upon pain of excommunication, was imposed, and at some point Eleanor swore it, which indicates how powerful her contemporaries considered her to be. Constitutionally, a queen had only a customary relationship with government, since she did not take an oath on coronation, but in Eleanor's case, her allegiance was formally required along with the King's.

Eleanor was deeply affronted by what she saw as the Provisions' attack on her prerogative, and from the start she was intent on overthrowing them. In November 1259 she left for France to witness the confirmation of the treaty of Paris and to attend her daughter Beatrice on her journey to marry John, Duke of Brittany. Before she embarked, she defiantly made a gift of the first available wardship with a value of forty to sixty pounds to her steward, Matthias, completely ignoring her promise to the committee. The treaty of Paris was published on 4 December, but the family celebrations were marred by the death of the Dauphin, Prince Louis.

Henry was one of the coffin-bearers at his funeral, and Beatrice's marriage, which had been scheduled for the same day, had to be put back a week. Eleanor and Henry remained in France until April, but already they had sought a papal dispensation to absolve Henry from his oath of allegiance to the Provisions.

The chroniclers of Waverley, Tewkesbury and Bury St Edmunds all lay the blame for Henry's repudiation of the reforms at Eleanor's door. She was seen as 'the root, the fomentor and disseminator of all the discord which was soon between her husband King Henry and the barons of his kingdom'.[4] In May, the papal bull cancelling the threat of excommunication over Henry was issued at Winchester. The King had made three statements to the barons in Parliament to try to establish his own position, but the publication of the bull prompted them to call an independent Parliament at St Albans on the same day as Henry summoned them to Windsor. Neither Parliament was held, but it seemed that armed conflict was now inevitable, and Henry and Eleanor withdrew briefly to the Tower. War was avoided by Henry's acquiescence to the treaty of Kingston in November and for a while it appeared that the 'Queen's party' was back in control.

The next spring, however, the violence began in earnest and Eleanor and those loyal to her provided a focal point for the rebels. Those among them who sincerely promoted reform objected to her obstruction of the Provisions, while many English lords had long resented the Savoyard usurpment of royal patronage. Attacks on Eleanor's supporters began in the west of the country in Gloucester and Hereford, spreading to Bristol, Worcester and Shrewsbury, and then as far as Peter of Savoy's lands in East Anglia. By June, Henry and Eleanor were back in the Tower, where Henry received a delegation of Londoners who demanded that he reinstate and swear to the Provisions. The letter had been sealed by Simon de Montfort.

By July, the whole of south-east England was in rebel hands. If Eleanor had refused to accept responsibility for her own part in bringing about this situation, she was rudely reminded of the hatred she had provoked when she attempted to flee the Tower and ride to Prince Edward at Windsor. She was mobbed on London Bridge by a howling, jostling crowd who pelted her with rubbish and pursued her, jeering, back to the Tower, where Henry refused to allow her to enter. The Queen was forced to seek asylum in the home of the bishop of London. As seems to have been the case with the St Thomas's squabble ten years earlier, Henry apparently felt that only the strongest measures could force his stubborn wife to submit to his will, and the fear and shame of London Bridge cowed Eleanor sufficiently for her to appear with him at Westminster three days later, Henry having used her absence to accept the barons' terms. The incident was deeply shocking, not just to Eleanor, but to her family, and especially to the King and Queen of France. That the people should so far forget the deference owed to an anointed queen as to physically threaten her was terrifying: it was revolutionary. Eleanor was to have the last word with the Londoners, though. After the wars had ended Henry gave London Bridge into her keeping and she was too stingy, or too vengeful, to repair it. The nursery rhyme 'London Bridge is Falling Down' commemorates the city's protests.

Family discord now had to be forgotten in the pursuit of a greater interest – the preservation of the crown. Three areas of support were open to the royal house: the Pope, the French and mercenary troops. An agreement was negotiated with the barons whereby Henry and Eleanor would be permitted to leave for France to seek arbitration from King Louis, on condition that they returned. In January 1264, Louis pronounced his judgement at the Mise of Amiens. His decision was attributed by several chroniclers to Eleanor's influence – he was held to have been 'deceived and beguiled by the serpentlike fraud and speech of a woman: the Queen of England'[5] – and unsurprisingly comprised a rousing defence of Henry's prerogative. Equally unsurprisingly, Montfort, who had been kept away from Amiens by a riding accident, entirely rejected Louis's conclusions. Despite Louis's support and that of the Pope, whom Eleanor was urging to appoint a special legate, Henry was not really any stronger. He and Edward returned to England as they had agreed, but Eleanor remained proudly at her sister's court. This was a war of arms, not words, and accordingly the Queen set about raising an army.

Eleanor's understanding of the probability of military engagement was extremely prescient. As early as 1259, she had engaged her distant relative Isabella de Fiennes to distribute rings among knights in Flanders with a view to calling on their services if necessary. In the first months of 1260, when she and Henry were in France, Eleanor had begun to cultivate contacts that would provide her in future with a force of French and Flemish mercenaries. That these activities were known of in England certainly contributed to her unpopularity, and gave the lie to any gestures of acquiescence she made in the interests of maintaining (if not actually winning) support for Henry when he was at his lowest ebb. Her refusal to keep her promise and return to England was also crucial. She was able to call on her family network, her sister Marguerite and her mother Beatrice of Provence in mustering men and money. She even went as far as to pawn the King's jewels. Her foresight was confirmed when both Henry and Edward were taken prisoner by Montfort's rebels after the battle of Lewes in May 1264, leaving Eleanor as the leader of the royalist party.

Eleanor had known Montfort for a long time and she understood his hatred of Henry, his ambition and his ruthlessness. But she did not allow herself to be overcome by fear. Instead, she sold off three bishoprics, borrowed from Henry of Castile, persuaded Peter of Savoy to guarantee substantial loans and called up men from France, Burgundy, Gascony, Poitou, Flanders, Normandy, the Brabant, Germany, Brittany, Spain and Savoy. With her invasion force stationed at St Omer, she requisitioned English ships from Gascon ports to carry her soldiers to liberate the King. She worked ceaselessly – 'insudeuarit', notes The St Albans Chronicle, literally, 'she sweated at it' – but as her funds dwindled, so did her support. She had paid no mind to the papal legate, Guy Foulquois, who strongly opposed the invasion from his base at Boulogne and rather feebly pronounced sentences of interdict and excommunication before returning to Rome to get himself elected Pope Clement IV, but her determination faltered as, over the winter of 1264, her unpaid men began to desert. In 1265, she made a strategic retreat to Gascony.

Eleanor had not given up, but all her efforts had come to nothing. Still, it is pleasing to think that one of her well-placed gifts had a tiny bearing on the next stage in the conflict. On 28 May, Edward escaped with the help of Roger de Mortimer, whose wife Maud had received a girdle from the Queen in the New Year gift-giving of 1253. When Montfort was finally defeated at the battle of Evesham on 4 August, his head and testicles were given to Maud Mortimer as a rather more grisly trophy of loyalty. Eleanor herself returned to England in late October 1265, tactfully accompanied by the new papal legate, Ottobuono de Fieschi, the brother of her aunt Beatrice. By arriving with De Fieschi, Eleanor was demonstrating that she came in a spirit of peace, though in fact this was not fully achieved for another two years.

From 1265 to 1267, Eleanor actively supported Henry in the reassertion of royal authority. A policy of disinheriting the rebels drove them to a last, desperate push under the leadership of Robert Ferrers and Adam Gurdon, who were imprisoned in Eleanor's care at Windsor Castle. In 1267, the Earl of Gloucester fomented an uprising in the northern and eastern counties, and in the spring and summer of that year Eleanor was at Dover Castle, ordering supplies in the event of a siege and overseeing the stockpiling of weapons. Gloucester succeeded in entering London with an army and, for a brief period, as the Londoners attacked 'royalist' property and even the Palace of Westminster, it looked as if Henry's rule was once more severely threatened, but Eleanor's groundwork on the Continent now bore fruit, in the shape of the arrival of a mercenary force of a hundred knights in May, and by early July Gloucester had surrendered.

At the same time, Eleanor was busily making good her parlous financial situation. The Pope had sanctioned a triennial levy of one tenth of clerical incomes, from which she personally obtained 15,000 pounds to pay off the debts she had incurred while maintaining her army at St Omer. Her clerk, Henry Sampson, pursued her claims diligently, even though the tax was inevitably unpopular. Eleanor was also determined to compensate Prince Edmund for the loss of the Sicilian crown, which had eventually been presented to her brother-in-law Charles of Anjou. De Montfort's death had provided Edmund with the forfeited earldom of Leicester and the honour of Lancaster, but Eleanor was involved in some unscrupulous machinations to provide him with an even greater inheritance. The imprisoned rebel Robert Ferrers, the Earl of Derby, was theoretically permitted the restoration of his lands on the payment of 50,000 pounds, a deliberately unfeasible sum. The custodian to whom the debt was to be paid was, conveniently, Edmund. On 9 April 1269, Edmund married Aveline de Forz, the heiress to the Aumale and Devon earldoms, for which Eleanor had negotiated with her guardians, her mother Isabella and grandmother Amice, who had received 1,000 pounds apiece. It appears that the three women had conspired to defraud Ferrers, who was, of course, in Eleanor's custody, of the initial payments of his fine to enable Edmund to get his hands on Ferrers' lands as well as Aveline's.

This degree of ruthless ambition for her son is an unattractive aspect of Eleanor's character, but her relationships with her children also provide an insight into a gentler facet of her nature, one that connected her emotionally with both Henry and her daughter-in-law Eleanor of Castile. Medieval motherhood for women of her class has proved a vexed issue for scholars, notably in the case of Eleanor of Aquitaine, but Eleanor of Provence's aspirations for and interest in her children was not confined to their roles in adulthood; she also exhibited a relatively involved concern for them as infants. For example, from July 1252 to July 1253, she spent thirty weeks at Windsor with her children which, given her demanding itinerary, suggests a genuine commitment to devoting time to them.

Her accounts illustrate her participation in her children's day-to-day lives, showing orders for gowns for Beatrice, a silk tabard for Edward, tunics and robes for both boys. And, like any modern mother, Eleanor found herself constantly buying shoes. An order of hawking gloves for herself and Beatrice suggests that she took her children hunting with her when they were old enough. Introducing them to activities appropriate to their status was a significant part of their education, as was ensuring that they were dressed according to the pageantry expected of the royal family on formal occasions. At Margaret's wedding, the mother of the bride is depicted in silk robes trimmed with gold and an ermine cloak, while the twelve-year-old Prince Edward wears a gold tabard decorated with the royal leopards of England. Eleanor also initiated her children into the ritual of jewel-giving, providing them with gifts to present graciously to their attendants. In 1253, Beatrice and Edward were supplied with brooches to give to their respective nurses, Lady Agnes and Lady Alice, and to their cousin Edmund, Sanchia's son.

When Edward fell ill on a visit to the monastery of Beaulieu in 1246, Eleanor insisted on remaining with him for the three weeks it took him to recover, in flagrant contravention of the house's male-only rule. Although Edward by now had his own household, Eleanor sent for three of her own doctors to attend him and paid for his medicines herself. She was obviously displeased with the monks' response to her anxieties, because the prior and cellarer of Beaulieu were dismissed once Edward was well again.

There is no more touching illustration of the speciousness of the argument that royal mothers' concern for their children was predominantly a matter of political expediency than the reaction of Eleanor and Henry to the death of their youngest child, Katherine, in 1257. Katherine had suffered from some form of disability since birth – Matthew Paris cruelly describes her as 'muta et inutilis' – and during her last illness her parents were desperately worried. Eager for news of her condition, Henry presented a messenger from his wife with a robe and had a silver statue of Katherine placed on St Edward's shrine. When she died, both Henry and Eleanor were reported as being ill with grief. They built her a beautiful tomb at Westminster and engaged a chaplain to say a daily Mass for her soul, a sincere if conventional gesture of mourning, but their real feelings were expressed more poignantly in the presents they made to the nurses who had tended to little Katherine on her deathbed. Eleanor's empathy with other mothers is shown in a late letter to Edward, after he had become King, on behalf of Margaret de Nevile, the mother of a royal ward. 'We pray you, sweetest son, that you may command and pray the aforesaid Margaret de Weyland, that she will suffer that the mother may have the solace of her child after her desire,' she wrote. 'I know well the longing of a mother to see a child from whom she has long been parted.'

Eleanor was close to both her elder daughters, Margaret and Beatrice. When, in 1251, Margaret, aged eleven, had been married to Alexander III of Scotland, the tension between the two countries made visiting difficult. In 1252 Henry asked that Margaret might be permitted to come to the English court, but his request was denied, so in 1255 Eleanor sent an envoy, Reginald of Bath, to investigate her daughter's situation and report back. Reginald was allegedly poisoned by the Scots after advising that Margaret was miserable, and Eleanor and Henry immediately set off for Scotland, accompanied by troops. Margaret and Eleanor were able to spend time together at Wark in Northumberland, and the next year she and her husband came to London and Woodstock. In 1260, Margaret was at Windsor, with Eleanor in attendance, for the birth of a grandchild. Eleanor was considerate towards Margaret's servants in Scotland, Matilda Cantilupe and Geoffrey de Langley, who received New Year gifts of dishes and a goblet.

Beatrice, as Duchess of Brittany, was even further away than Margaret, but evidently trusted her mother: she sent some of her children to live with Eleanor while she was away on crusade with her husband. Eleanor had to endure the grief of outliving both her surviving daughters, who died within a month of one another in 1275. Beatrice's request to be buried in the Franciscan convent in London, a place Eleanor favoured and where her own heart was placed after her death, suggests that they enjoyed a religious connection which may have given Eleanor some consolation. A surviving book of hours, probably presented to Beatrice by Eleanor on her marriage, also points to a spiritual affinity. Edmund's first wife, Aveline, too, died early, after giving birth to twins in 1274.

Eleanor took comfort in her closeness to her brood of grandchildren after the loss of her daughters. Edward and Eleanor had fourteen children in total, though many of them died young. After the demise in 1272 of Richard of Cornwall, who had been left *in loco parentis* while they were away on crusade, their daughter Eleanor and son Henry lived with their grandmother, and thereafter Eleanor continued to stay with her for long visits when she was not travelling with her father and mother. Henry's death in the sad year of 1274 was also attended by Eleanor of Provence, and, as John Carmi Parsons remarks, 'it was perhaps better that the dying boy ... was supported by the grandmother he knew intimately, not the mother he had met for the first time in his memory only some ten weeks earlier'.[6] Eleanor founded a Dominican priory at Guildford in Henry's memory.

The two Eleanors were united in their concerns for the children's welfare and, one suspects, in deploring the English climate: a letter from the elder to the younger in 1290 warns of the dangers of a long visit to the north. They went on a pilgrimage together to St Albans in 1257, attended the consecration of Salisbury Cathedral in 1258 and held court together at Mortlake in 1259. The most notable instance of the two women working together was their successful prevention of an early marriage for Edward's eldest daughter. Both women had been married in their early teens, and their collaboration here suggests they had discussed their experiences intimately. Perhaps Eleanor of Provence took pains to avoid causing the kind of difficulties mothers-in-law could create after hearing about the experiences of her sister Marguerite of France with the overbearing Blanche of Castile. And for her part, Eleanor of Castile was a support to her mother-in-law when she herself became Queen in 1272.

When Henry III died at Westminster that November, Eleanor of Provence found herself suddenly isolated. Sanchia had died in 1261, Peter of Savoy in 1268, her mother and Boniface were also dead and all her children were abroad. Though Prince Edward's succession passed uncontested, the grievances of the past still lingered. The King had passed away to the sounds of riots outside his palace. He was buried on 20 November, after which Eleanor travelled to Windsor to join her grandchildren Eleanor, Henry and John of Brittany. Edward and the new Queen joined her there when they returned to England in December.

For the next decade, Eleanor lived mainly on her dower properties at Guildford, Marlborough and Ludgershall, though she also spent time at Clarendon, Westminster and Windsor. By the mid-1280s, now in her early sixties, she was considering a retreat to the cloister. Curiously, for one who had had such a cold and troubled relationship with the country of which she had been queen for nearly forty years, Eleanor chose to spend her last years in England. Her choice of retreat was Amesbury, a daughter house of Fontevrault, though Fontevrault itself would have seemed a more obvious destination. Perhaps Eleanor's determination to die in England was a gesture of reconciliation.

Like Berengaria of Navarre, Eleanor changed her title when she entered the convent, styling herself 'a humble nun of the order of Fontevrault of the convent of Amesbury', but typically, she did not choose to retire altogether humbly. Fifty-seven oaks were used in making the improvements to Amesbury she considered essential for her arrival, and she never became a fully professed nun, choosing to retain both her wealth and a degree of influence in the outside world. Although she entered the monastery in July 1286, she was still exchanging letters with her daughter-in-law that year about the murage rights of Southampton, which had been passed on in dower to Eleanor of Castile. She also maintained a correspondence with Edward and kept a sharp eye on her lands and business. The fact that she still had one foot firmly planted in the world gave rise to a degree of mockery, yet it was her removal to Amesbury that led to the only known conflict with Eleanor of Castile. Beatrice's daughter Eleanor of Brittany took the veil there in March 1285, eventually rising to become abbess of Fontevrault itself, and while her vocation may well have been genuine, this was not the case with Edward's little daughter Mary, who was enclosed at Amesbury at the age of six in August the same year. Eleanor of Castile objected to the move, probably because Mary was too young to know her own mind, but Eleanor was selfishly bent upon keeping her granddaughter with her. (Mary showed that her vocation was not all it might have been when, after her grandmother's death, she took to visiting her father's court and developed a taste for extravagant gambling. There were also slanderous rumours of a liaison with the Earl of Surrey, her nephew by marriage.)

Eleanor of Provence died at Amesbury on 24 June 1291, and was buried there on 8 September with Edward, Edmund and a large gathering of magnates and clergy in attendance. *The Westminster Chronicle* described her as '*Generosa et religiosa virago*', a rare accolade for a woman. Eleanor had not been popular, but she was respected. Her informal role in government had been essential during the Montfort revolution and her position had been affirmed internationally even as De Montfort was issuing writs in Henry's name, as a powerful counter-influence to the depleted command of her imprisoned husband and son. Eleanor's resourcefulness, intellligence and above all her conviction of her own authority emphasised the implicit power of English queenship. After the uneven career of Eleanor of Aquitaine and the almost total lack of influence of Berengaria of Navarre and Isabelle of Angoulême, Eleanor of Provence re-established the role of consort on its great Anglo-Norman model. Her financial acuity did not make her lovable, but the thousands of pounds she disbursed in 'secret gifts and private alms'[7] had created a discreet diplomatic network on which she drew in crisis. Her snobbery and lack of sympathy for her husband's magnates contributed directly to a pivotal struggle for power between lords and crown, but it was her perspicacity and energy that also helped to solve it. At the end of her life, despite its many defeats and disappointments, Eleanor had made her peace with the English. The differences between the posthumous reputations of Eleanor and her daughter-in-law exemplify the way in which monarchs could manipulate posterity, to the extent that Eleanor of Castile is the better remembered of the two. Yet it was the first of three southern princesses who was the greater English queen.

CHAPTER 9

ELEANOR OF CASTILE

'Wise, religious, fruitful, meek?'

Of all England's medieval queens, Eleanor of Castile is celebrated more for her death than for her life. The twelve 'Eleanor crosses', three of which survive, built by Edward I to commemorate the staging posts of her body's last journey from Lincoln to Westminster for burial have enshrined her image as a beloved wife and devoted consort. As time passed, Eleanor's reputation became bound up with the crosses themselves: they represent her as 'pillar of all England', whose death was 'tearfully mourned'.[1] Their magnificence, though, is as much a testament to Edward's conception of the dignity of his kingship than to Eleanor's own qualities. Her contemporaries had a more ambivalent attitude to their Spanish queen, who was by no means as revered in life as she became in death. Her reinvention through the propaganda of her husband's memorials provides an interesting example of the way in which commemoration, traditionally a responsibility of royal women, could be effectively manipulated into an immortalisation of majesty.

Until the outbreak of the civil wars of the 1260s, Eleanor occupies a modest place in the chronicles. After her marriage in 1254, she appears mainly in relation to her mother-in-law's activities, as when Eleanor of Provence appointed her own clerk John de Loundres, to set up the Princess's wardrobe in 1255, or at New Year 1259, when she was provided with two sapphire rings to present as a gift to a knight of Gaston de Béarn's household at Mortlake. It is possible that she crossed to Brittany for the marriage of her sister-in-law Beatrice in 1260, in which case she would have been reunited with her mother, Jeanne, and brother Ferdinand; she was certainly in Aquitaine with her husband from 1260 to 1262, returning to England in June.

During the crisis of 1263, Eleanor of Castile, like Eleanor of Provence, drew on her maternal inheritance to assist her imprisoned husband. She summoned archers from Ponthieu for the garrison at Windsor, where she remained until after the defeat at Lewes. Suspected by Simon de Montfort of trying to raise mercenary troops in Castile, she was obliged on 17 June, along with her first child, Katherine, to rejoin King Henry's household. The extent to which she was marginalised at this time can be seen in the fact that with Eleanor of Provence in France, Edward imprisoned and the King on forced progress with De Montfort, she was effectively abandoned. When Katherine died that September Eleanor, isolated and grieving, was forced to borrow forty pounds for her expenses from Hugh Despenser. Perhaps it is not going too far to suggest that this period, in which Eleanor herself is barely more than a footnote to broader events, carries the key to some aspects of her future character. Acquisitiveness can be a defence against insecurity, a way of cheating fortune, and Eleanor proved herself determined never again to experience the humiliating poverty and frustrating ineffectuality that had threatened to overturn the status on which her sense of self had been constructed for a decade.

Brightness returned with the victory at Evesham, with which Henry III was restored and Edward and Eleanor reunited. Four more children, Joan, John, Henry and Eleanor, were born in rapid succession, though little Joan did not live out her first year. As the King and Queen worked to consolidate peace with the magnates, Eleanor and Edward were preparing for a real adventure: a crusade to the Holy Land. The crusader states in Outremer were still struggling on, but the ascendance of the Egyptian Mamluk dynasty signified a newly aggressive commitment to jihad, and in 1266 King Louis IX of France, who had already fought one crusade, resolved to embark on another, taking the Cross in March 1267. Ottobuono, the papal legate who had travelled to England with Eleanor of Provence, was promoting the crusade around the country throughout 1266, and in 1268, as Jaffa fell and the kingdom of Antioch collapsed, Edward decided that he, too, should take the Cross, in the face of the objections of both his father and Pope Clement IV. Despite his misgivings, Henry took the precaution of transferring lands and castles to his son for a period of five years which, in the event of the King's death while the heir was abroad, could be held for him against his return.

Edward's allegiances during the Lusignan–Savoyard disputes had illustrated the potentially troublesome relationships between royal parents and a new generation keen to establish their own rights, and his preparations for his crusade offer clues to his feelings about the direction of his future. Having chosen to take his wife with him to the Holy Land, he pointedly excluded his mother from the arrangements he made for their absence.

Edward and Eleanor gave their children into the care of their great-uncle Richard of Cornwall, rather than their grandmother. In comparison with the instructions of Edward's younger brother Edmund, who was to accompany Edward on the expedition and made his mother the governor of his affairs for the duration, this plan suggests a residual anxiety about leaving the heirs to the throne in the care of a woman whose 'foreign' loyalties had been the cause of so much dispute. The danger of factionalism created by the importation of a queen's relatives was one Eleanor of Castile treated more prudently than had her mother-in-law. The need for supportive royal kin had to be balanced against the sensitivities of the magnates, sensitivities to which Eleanor of Provence had shown herself imperiously oblivious. Eleanor of Castile had to find a means of promoting royal affinity without imposing her alien status too obviously on the English. She had already seen how easily that status could be negatively manipulated.

At the time of her marriage, the young Eleanor's brother Sancho had advised Henry on how he could make her feel welcome, and the King, rather as he had done for his own wife, had kindly tried to make her apartments comfortably familiar, decorating them in Castilian style with rich carpets on the floors. This immediately led to accusations of extravagance, if not oriental depravity, and Eleanor showed herself attuned to English suspicions of Spanish ways in both her choice of attendants, nearly all of whom came from relatively modest, gentle families and in her match-making strategies. She did not involve herself in importing husbands for English heiresses, and though she did promote her Picard connections, finding English husbands for cousins from Ponthieu, she avoided provoking criticism among the chroniclers as Eleanor of Provence had done.

Eleanor did, however, remain close to her natal family; indeed, one of the reasons for her presence on the crusade was a plan to travel via Gascony to join Alfonso of Castile, but the project was prevented by the death of Boniface of Savoy. Instead, when she and Edward set off for France on 20 August 1270, their month-long journey south took them to Louis IX's beautiful crusader port of Aigue-Mortes, where they embarked to rendezvous with the French forces who had mustered in Sardinia. En route Louis decided on an attack on Tunis, which he thought would be a strategic loss to the Mamluks, but five days after the English ships put out, the French King died, and Edward's Uncle Charles of Anjou replaced him as commander. Much to Edward's disgust, when he arrived a week later, Charles quickly came to an accommodation with the Tunisian emir, and the French turned round and went home. Edward refused to make any treaty with a ruler he saw first and foremost as an infidel, and defiantly set off for Sicily, where he and Eleanor remained until the following May. With a small flotilla of thirteen ships they then sailed to Cyprus and on to Acre.

The crusade, which lasted a year, was a largely fruitless exercise that achieved very little beyond a small English garrison at Acre. What it did produce was a legend that contributed to Eleanor's posthumous reputation. A fifteenth-century Spanish chronicler, Rodrigo de Arevalo, recorded an incident (retold in English by Robert le Bel in 1579), in which a Muslim assassin lurking in Edward's tent managed to stab him with a poisoned dagger. Edward killed his assailant, but the wound rotted and Edward's life was despaired of until 'Queen Eleanor, who had accompanied him on that journey, endangering her own life, in loving affection saved him and eternalised her own honour. For she daily and nightly sucked out that rank poison, which love made sweet to her ... to his safety, her joy, and the comfort of all England.'² What, asks Le Bel, 'can be more rare than this woman's expression of love?' The whole story is more than likely to be apocryphal. One version casts the assassin as a turncoat spy whom Edward himself had employed, while *The Guisborough Chronicle* has Eleanor led sobbing from Edward's tent by Edmund so as not to see the doctor cut out the putrefying flesh, though Edmund had in fact left the crusade by the time the incident supposedly took place. The preference of later writers for the Spanish version, which gives it as fact, rather than those of other chronicles, which mention it as a legend, is an example of the way Eleanor's memory was consciously manipulated to her posthumous advantage.

The reference to Eleanor's having endangered her life does contain some truth, however: she had become pregnant in the summer of 1271 and gave birth to a daughter, another Joan, at Acre in spring 1272. Childbirth was perilous in the best of circumstances, but in the ramshackle conditions of crusader quarters, hot and disease-ridden, it was terrifying. After Joan's birth, Eleanor and Edward stayed on in Acre until September, when the baby was deemed strong enough to travel. Pausing at Trapani on Sicily on their return, they received the news that their son John had died and, shortly afterwards, that Henry III, too, was gone.

Edward returned to England as the only living king in Europe who had made the pilgrimage to the Holy Land, a distinction that hugely augmented his international standing. The expedition had cost a fortune which, as ever, the English crown didn't have, but compared to the unrest of the 1260s, it represented a certain political advancement. The subsidy of 30,000 pounds granted to Edward for the crusade, the first such since 1237, was an acknowledgement of the new authority obtained by Parliament in relation to the economy. Though Edward's force had been small, about 1,000 men in total, 225 of them were knights, all drawn from families closely associated with the court, and the expedition served as a means of unifying the aristocracy after the divisions of the wars. And although Edward was no Lionheart, he could identify himself afterwards as that glorious figure, a crusading king, and proclaimed his eagerness to return to the Holy Land until his dying day.

Returning through Rome, Orvieto – where they met Pope Gregory X – Lombardy and Milan, Edward and Eleanor reached Savoy. Here they stayed at the castle of St Georges d'Esperande in the Isère with Edward's great-uncle Philip, ruler since 1268. By July they were in Paris, where Edward performed homage for his French holdings to the new king, Philip III, and in August 1274 they finally arrived back in England after an absence of four years. It was a sad homecoming. Edward was deeply affected by his father's death – he had rather callously remarked to Charles of Anjou that he mourned less for his son John than for Henry, as sons could be replaced. There was also a quarrel with Edmund about precedence rights at the coronation, which took place on 19 August. Edmund was so offended by the rebuttal of his claim to carry the Curtana, the ceremonial sword, that he stayed away. At least, Edward wrote to his uncle Charles, he felt a greater closeness to his mother since losing his father.

Eleanor had given birth to another son, named for her brother Alfonso, in 1273. Her three eldest children had died, but four were living at her coronation (Henry would be lost shortly afterwards). She would go on to have six more: Margaret in 1275, Berengaria (1276), an unnamed child who died in infancy in 1278, Mary (1279), Elizabeth (1282) and Edward (1284). Another baby whose name is not recorded had died in 1271, and there may have been a further daughter, born soon after Eleanor's marriage, whom some sources name as Blanche. Eleanor's fertility attests to a consistent sexual relationship with Edward, which confirms the closeness of their relationship. A family tradition was the 'kidnapping' of the King in his bed by seven of Eleanor's ladies on Easter Monday morning. Sexual intercourse was forbidden during the period of Lenten abstinence, and Edward had to pay a fine of two pounds to his captors before he was released to indulge himself with the Queen. But if she was fortunate in her marriage Eleanor was very unlucky with her children, even in an age of high infant mortality. Eleanor, the second Joan, Margaret, Mary and

Elizabeth survived to adulthood, but of the boys only Edward reached his majority.

In the past, one of the commonplace assumptions about medieval childhood was that parents were less attached to their offspring because the prospect of losing them was so great, and though as a generalisation this was manifestly untrue, Eleanor does seem to have had a cooler relationship with her children than several of her predecessors. Six-year-old Henry died at Guildford in 1274 while the King and Queen were in London, no great distance away, yet there is no evidence that they visited him. Great hope was held out for Alfonso, who survived until he was ten, but there is no mention in the household accounts of a Mass for his death in 1284, or of anniversary Masses for his lost brothers and sisters. The quarrel with her mother-in-law about Mary's early enclosure at Amesbury demonstrates that Eleanor was not indifferent to her children's welfare, but what little evidence there is presents a broad picture of a dutiful rather than a loving mother.

Early matrimony was one area where Eleanor did show exceptional concern. As has been noted, she lobbied with Eleanor of Provence to postpone the marriage of her eldest daughter, Eleanor, and Joan of Acre, who became the wife of Gilbert de Clare, Earl of Gloucester, and Elizabeth, who married Count John of Holland, did so at the relatively late ages of eighteen and fifteen respectively (Elizabeth remained at court for a further nine months after her wedding). Eleanor's children were brought up with all the privileges of their rank, yet their father and mother were thoroughly occupied elsewhere, which is entirely typical of the period, if not an especially sympathetic approach to child-rearing. Some evidence of parental interest is shown in the miniature castles and siege engines ordered for Alfonso and Edward, and the King indulged the girls in the matter of dresses, carriages and jewels, but the Queen's emotional priority was very much the King.

Both duty and inclination meant Eleanor was often away from her children as she accompanied Edward on his travels. Indeed, with the exception of his military campaigns and her lyings-in, they were rarely separated. Royal excursions were no more comfortable than they had been in Eleanor of Aquitaine's time, and Eleanor, who was almost permanently pregnant, was beset by overturning carts, lost baggage and accidents such as the fire that nearly killed the royal couple at Hope Castle in 1283. She was renowned for her Castilian addiction to comfort, which might be better figured as an objection to freezing. Where the Queen went, glazed windows and lead roofs quickly followed. She stayed loyal to her carpets, buying seven in 1278, paying five pounds to the carpet-maker John de Winton in 1286 and ordering 26s 8d-worth of painted cloths from Cologne in 1290. Eleanor tried to make her lodgings cheerful with colourful candles, Venetian glass, ivory mirrors and brightly painted walls, and she shared a southern love of scented gardens with Eleanor of Provence. Food was another connection to her native culture. Most eccentrically, the Queen ate lots of fresh fruit: English pears, apples and quinces and exotic pomegranates, figs, raisins and dates. Her cooks used olive oil and citrus fruit, and cheeses were ordered from Brie and Champagne. It is tempting to suggest, though impossible to prove, that the distinctly Arabic flavour that characterised grand English cookery in the fourteenth and fifteenth centuries may have been influenced by Eleanor's household, as she had grown up with the flavours of Moorish cuisine. Keeping up standards in the travelling circus of the court, she ate from silver or gold plate using knives with gold and jasper handles.

Like her mother-in-law, Eleanor loved gardens. Just as she was true to the flavours of her childhood, she may also have tried to recreate the sophisticated, Islamic-influenced gardens she had known in Castile. At Westminster, a system of pipes from the Thames filled the Queen's pond, surrounded by a lawn set with vines and roses, while a herb garden wafted scents through the window of her chapel. At Langley, which she bought in 1275, Eleanor employed Aragonese gardeners to create wells, perhaps for fountains. Her partiality to fragrant blossom and fruit led her to send for French apple cuttings to be spliced by her vine-tender, the aptly named James Frangipane.

Eleanor and Edward had several interests in common. Both were keen hunters, though Eleanor preferred hounds, keeping her own pack, while Edward's passion was falconry. The King's hawks had a marvellous mews in London, with a garden and a bath fed by a fountain. For Eleanor, there was an aviary with nightingales and Sicilian parrots. They were also avid chess players, and Edward, certainly, played for money. A gift to Eleanor of jasper and crystal chessmen was eventually inherited by her daughter-in-law Isabella of France. Eleanor's brother Alfonso was an enthusiast who commissioned a chess manual; Eleanor borrowed one from Cerne Abbey and became competent enough to manage 'Four Kings', the four-player version of the game.

Eleanor's queenship was not a political one, and this may have been in part a reaction to Eleanor of Provence's talent for interfering. However, as a product of the 'aggressively literary' court of Castile,[3] one area in which she did make her mark was the creation and dissemination of books.

Henry III's interests had inclined more to architecture than literature, and his son was no great reader. The only evidence of his literary patronage is the commission of Rustichello de Pisa's *Meliadus*, the source for which was a book of Arthurian legends Edward lent the writer while passing through Sicily on crusade. Eleanor sent the *Meliadus* to her brother Alfonso, and thus the book in turn influenced *Tristan de Leonis*, the first Arthurian romance written in Castilian. Alfonso followed his father in his love of vernacular literature and he and Eleanor exchanged books, including a French translation from the Arabic of *The Ladder of Mohammed* (the subject suggests that Eleanor, with her Moorish-influenced childhood, took a more sophisticated view of 'infidels' than did her husband).

Books were a matter for the women of the family, and Eleanor of Castile and Eleanor of Provence were associated in two valuable texts which connected them with the traditions of English queenship. *La Estoire de Seint Aedward le Rei*, a history of Edward the Confessor, was dedicated to Eleanor of Provence in recognition of Henry III's rebuilding of the Confessor's foundation of Westminster Abbey. The text is based on Aelred's twelfth-century *Vita Sancti Edwardi*, itself based on Osbert of Clare's *Vita Beati Eadwardi Regis Anglorum*, which is derived from a late eleventh-century *Vita Aedwardi Regis* dedicated to the Confessor's Queen, Edith. The first text thus envisions a line of female patronage fulfilled by the version made for Eleanor of Provence in the thirteenth century. The dedication of the *Estoire* is another symbol of the special protection the Confessor afforded to the King and Queen, represented also in the coronation Mass, in which the wine was drunk from the saint's chalice. Eleanor of Castile is shown on the first page of the 1270 *Douce Apocalypse*, an illustrated treatment of the Revelation of St John, next to her husband, for whom it was made. Eleanor's centrality to the production of *Douce* and the dedication of the *Estoire* to her mother-in-law link them both to the holy queens of the Anglo-Saxon tradition and, in their didactic purpose, illustrate the special relationship between patron queens and pious education.

Eleanor of Castile was concerned with literacy and education on a personal scale as well as a symbolic one. She bought writing tablets for her daughters to practise on and sponsored the production of her own texts. Her unique contribution was her scriptorium, an innovation she introduced which did not survive her. Eleanor's artist, Godfrey, and her clerk of the scriptorium, Roger, bought the vellum, ink, quills, colours, gold leaf and glue needed to create the Queen's books, and her accounts show that they travelled as part of Eleanor's household, even venturing as far as Aquitaine in 1286. Roger and Godfrey were permanent staff, but other artisans were hired for specific commissions. Richard du Marche, for example, made a psalter for Eleanor in 1289. Her interest in vernacular literature connects Eleanor with a tradition of women's patronage in which her predecessors had participated, and with one of the more positive aspects of 'foreign' queenship, whereby 'migratory brides could act as unique and powerful conduits for cultural exchange'.[4]

Sadly, none of the fruits of Eleanor's scriptorium have survived, but other books known to have been associated with her are a history of military kings, produced for her at Acre by a royal clerk, Mr Richard, and a redaction by Archbishop Pecham of 'De Celesti Hierarchia', the primate's only vernacular work of theology. Though her own interests were more varied and cosmopolitan, she encouraged Edward's enthusiasm for all things Arthurian, accompanying him in 1278 to the 'tomb' of Arthur and Guinevere at Glastonbury, which had been luring the tourist trade since 1190. Edward has, however, been over-identified with Arthur. While he was not slow to profit from comparisons with the mythical king, he was less obsessed with them than his grandson Edward III. Eleanor may have benefited from her mother-in-law's penchant for French romance. The Dowager Queen, whose chambers were still adorned with scenes from Geste d'Antioc, was a collector of French books, some of which she could have exchanged with her daughter-in-law. Multilingual and multicultural, Eleanor of Castile was truly extraordinary in that her scriptorium was the only personal institution of its type known to have existed in northern Europe at the time. She was a highly active participant in the cultural change, 'at once gradual and revolutionary'[5] that women's patronage was bringing about in literature.

As a religious patron, Eleanor's activities were equally impressive, making her 'the most active royal foundress since the twelfth century'.[6] She especially favoured the Dominican order, which admitted the Queen and her children to the benefits of their charity at Oxford in 1280, and from whose friars the children's tutors were chosen. She founded Dominican priories at Chichester and London and contributed to the foundations of Rhuddlan, Salisbury and Northampton. She also donated gold for statues of two saints particularly venerated by her husband, St George and the Confessor, and made gifts of vestments from her chapel to Bath and Lichfield cathedrals. The chaotic lifestyle of the travelling court is illustrated by her successful application for a dispensation for a portable altar in 1278. The Queen's intellectual bent encouraged the private devotions advocated by the Dominicans, such as the saying of the rosary and the use of books of hours, and there is none of the evangelical immediacy of a Matilda of Scotland in Eleanor's piety. She preferred her charity to be dispensed by her priests and almoners rather than in person.

This picture of Eleanor as a respected wife and capable mother, surrounded by beautiful things and quietly cultivating her intellect and her gardens, suggests a serene, benign lady graciously fulfilling her duties. It appears, though, that Eleanor of Castile was really rather a horrible woman. She had a notoriously vile temper and in her relations with those with whom she did business, she seems to have been regarded as a 'grasping harpy', vengeful and vindictive. Edward may have actively sheltered his wife from any political controversy, but his insistence on her prerogative was something Eleanor knew she could twist to her own advantage, and she made sure that others knew it, too. Archbishop Pecham wrote letters of warning to the nuns of Hedingham and the church of Crondall, advising that they had better accept the Queen's nominations for positions, or risk her wrath. The prior of Deerhurst was obliged to sack a newly appointed chaplain and replace him with Eleanor's man on the advice of the bishop of Worcester, who had received threatening letters from her. She threatened to prosecute the bishop himself over a debt of 350 marks which he claimed he had never owed her. The advice given by the chancellor, who had experience of Eleanor's rages, was that he should pay up and shut up.

If she could make herself personally unpleasant, it was nothing compared to the 'outcry and gossip' she provoked in her relentless pursuit of wealth. In 1283, she was rebuked by Archbishop Pecham: 'For God's sake, Lady, when you receive land or manor acquired by usury of Jews, take heed that usury is a mortal sin to those who take the usury and those who support it ... you must therefore return the things thus acquired to the Christians who have lost them ... My Lady, know that I am telling you the lawful truth and if anyone gives you to understand anything else he is a heretic.'

And three years later, the archbishop wrote to Eleanor's clerk of the wardrobe: 'A rumour is waxing strong throughout the Kingdom of England and much scandal is thereby generated because it is said that the illustrious Lady Queen of England ... is occupying many manors, lands and other possessions of nobles ... lands which the Jews extorted with usury under the protection of the royal court.' This was exactly what Eleanor was doing. The archbishop continued: 'There is public outcry and gossip about this in every part of England. Wherefore, as gain of this sort is illicit and damnable, we beg you and firmly command and enjoin you as our clerk that when you see an opportunity you will be pleased humbly to beseech the said Lady on our behalf that she bid her people entirely to abstain from the aforesaid practices ...'

A snippet of popular doggerel put the case more succinctly:

> The king would like to get our gold,
> The queen our manors fair to hold.[7]

In twenty-five years as Queen, Eleanor of Castile acquired lands worth 2,500 pounds, more than half the value again of her dower assignment as fixed in 1275. Her avarice provoked public outrage as well as the archbishop's concern for her immortal soul. She attracted claims of eviction and ruthless dispossession – one charge, later proved, was that her men had thrown a household into prison and left the family's baby abandoned in the road. From her deathbed, Eleanor requested that all the wrongs done in her name be righted and the subsequent evidence from the king's council that investigated her acquisitions found ample evidence of the oppression, injustice and extortion that pertained on her lands.

What Eleanor was doing might have been ethically unsavoury, but it was perfectly legal; indeed, the responsibility she bore in her own lifetime for the actions of her officials was unfair, since the augmentation of her estates was encouraged and guided by Edward as part of a policy to increase the crown lands after the Angevin losses under King John. When Henry III died, Eleanor could not come into her dower estates as they were already in the possession of her mother-in-law, and prerogatives such as queens-gold, which Eleanor of Provence made over to her, and debts granted by the King were unreliable and inadequate. Edward needed to provide for his queen and he found a way of doing so that allowed her to acquire lands which would then revert to the crown on her death.

Between 1269 and 1275, Edward exploited the relationship between the Jews and the crown to provide a means of channelling Jewish wealth to Eleanor. The receipt of Jewish debt was forbidden except with a royal grant or licence. Jewish families had to pay a tax on a deceased Jew's possessions at a third of their value and Jews were also liable for tallage, effectively random taxation. When they were unable to pay, they could transfer their debts to be exacted by the receiver, who would also pocket the interest paid by the original debtor. The Statute of Jewry of 1275 outlawed the practice of usury and permitted Jews to enter trade or farming, but the crown retained exclusive control over such exchange of debt. Between this date and 1290, when they were expelled from England, the Jews were Eleanor's moneybox.

The Queen took advantage of her monopoly principally to fund the purchase of lands, and although, in fairness, the number of 'Christians' she dispossessed through Jewish debt was misunderstood by the archbishop, it may certainly be inferred that there was a painful human cost to her hunger for real estate. Edward's sanction of this policy is evident in the fact that he created it, but it may have been that he was also giving her an occupation which would distract her from meddling in politics. The alacrity with which Eleanor took to business was offensive not only to the Church but to the magnates, too. There was something rather middle-class about her efficiency in grabbing at wealth, and the briskness of her administration had a whiff of the parvenue.

In this light, Edward's burial and commemoration of his wife may be read as something of a public-relations campaign. Eleanor died aged forty-nine at Harby, in Nottinghamshire, en route to Lincoln, on 28 November 1290. She was suffering from marsh fever, or quartain, which she had contracted on her last visit to Gascony with Edward in 1287. Her body, stuffed with barley, bound, then embalmed in linen, travelled in twelve solemn stages to Westminster. Her heart was buried with that of her son Alfonso at the Dominican church in London, while her viscera were splendidly entombed at Lincoln. Her body lay at Westminster, but though her tomb there is impressive, it is the crosses Edward erected to mark the stages of her final journey that were most influential in creating her eventual reputation. Two others were put up after 1291 in memory of Edward's sister Beatrice and his mother, but stylistically, Eleanor's represent a complete innovation: nothing like them had been seen before in England. Inspired by the *montjoie* crosses built for the funeral of Louis IX, they share a three-tiered structure with a closed first storey, an open second storey and a spire, originally surmounted with a cross. Within the open section, Eleanor's statue gazes out calmly, her hair loose as she had worn it at her coronation, her right hand holding a sceptre. She is aloof, yet not haughty, her countenance gracious, her sceptre invoking the intercession of Mary, Queen of Heaven as well as her earthly power. In addition to her three tombs, the presence of the Eleanor crosses throughout England replaced in local memory the nasty remnants of her reputation with an image of authoritative feminine spirituality and benevolence.

Commemorative arrangements for Eleanor were exhaustively elaborate, and exhausting for the weary chaplains to carry out. On the anniversary of her death, the office was sung on the hour for twenty-four hours, while less than six months after her funeral the archbishop of York proudly reported to the King that over 47,000 Masses had already been said for her. Positive associations were encouraged by indulgences, as at York in 1290, where forty days' exemption from penance was given to anyone who said the Pater Noster and Ave Maria for the Queen, a measure repeated at Lincoln in 1291. At Westminster, according to the rules Edward set out in a statute of 1292, Eleanor's tomb was to be surrounded by thirty candles, two of them constantly burning and all thirty on feast days. Monday, the day of her death, was marked with high Mass and the tolling of bells, and after Mass on Tuesday 140 paupers were each to receive a silver penny, reciting the Pater Noster, the Credo and the Ave Maria for the Queen's soul before and afterwards. Edward personally founded three chantries for Eleanor and services were held for her at St Albans, Bath and Coventry. Licences and land grants to support foundations for the Queen's soul continued until well into the reign of her son Edward II.

Later characterisations of Edward I's reign show just how effective his magnification of Eleanor had become, in that the nature of his rule is judged to have changed after 1290 as a consequence of the loss of her benign influence. In fact, Eleanor was blamed for the King's harshness in his lifetime. Edward did love Eleanor: his most famous comment about her was made in a letter to the abbot of Cluny in 1291, in which he referred to his wife as she 'whom living we dearly cherished and in death we cannot cease to love'. The year after she died he glumly went through the motions of paying his Easter 'ransom', even though there was no warm, welcoming bed for him to jump into. Yet Edward did recover from the loss, despite later affirmations that he never ceased to mourn her, and in a sense his commemoration of Eleanor serves to subsume the woman she truly was, first in terms of the remaking of her reputation and secondly in fashioning it into a representation of the might and spiritual dignity of the Plantagenet kings. Edward took a woman whom no one except himself had much liked and made her into a virtual saint, exquisitely celebrated in a novel fusion of sculpture and symbolism that attested far more to his own glory than to her achievements as a queen.

The success of the crosses in reinventing Eleanor is most poignantly evoked in the continuation of *The St Albans Chronicle* of Matthew Paris in 1408. Edward II, Eleanor's last child, barely knew his mother – she had left England for three years when he was two, remaining in Gascony between May 1286 and August 1289, and in the final months of her life she hardly saw him. Brought up mainly at Langley, which was his favourite residence as King, Edward would often have seen his mother's cross at nearby St Albans, and would probably have attended her annual commemorative Mass there. In 1305, he asked the abbot of St Albans to take in John le Parker, a former servant of Eleanor's who had worked at Langley, who wished to spend his last days in prayer for the late Queen's soul. The continuation of *The St Albans Chronicle*, in essence a history of the reign of Edward I, would have been seen by Edward (if it was not intended specifically for him), and the writer may have hoped to please him by idealising the mother he had never really known. According to the continuation, Eleanor's influence was one of a transcendental purity: 'As the dawn scatters the shadows of the waning night with its rays of light, so by the promotion of this most holy woman and Queen, through-out England the night of faithlessness was expelled.'

One might suspect the chronicler of a little sarcasm at the royal expense. The 'faithless' Jews had indeed been expelled from England in the year of Eleanor's death, but only, as her subjects were well aware, after she and Edward had bled them dry.

CHAPTER 10

MARGUERITE OF FRANCE

'Dame Marguerite, good withouten lack'

Marguerite, Edward I's second wife, was the first French queen of England. Her marriage, like that of her predecessor, Eleanor of Castile, was largely determined upon as a consequence of the continued insecurity of the English position in Gascony, though the sixty-year-old King's decision to take a much younger wife may well have been influenced by the need to provide additional heirs, as despite the fecundity of his union with Eleanor, Edward of Carnarvon was their only surviving son. Marguerite was one of four children of Philip III of France, the second of his second queen, Marie of Brabant. She probably remembered little of her father, who had died in 1285, when she was only three. She was brought up at the court of her brother, Philip IV, under the guidance of her mother and Philip's queen, Jeanne of Navarre, both of whom were involved in the negotiation of the double betrothal of two French princesses, to Edward I and his heir respectively, which was ratified by the treaty of Montreuil in 1299.

In 1296, King Philip had successfully invaded Gascony, which, naturally, the English were desperate to recover, but Edward's determination to subdue Scotland in a campaign that had been ongoing since 1290 had greatly depleted his military resources, and a diplomatic solution to Gascony seemed preferable to a war he was unlikely to win. In 1298, Pope Boniface VIII suggested the double marriage of Edward senior to Marguerite and his heir to Isabella, Philip's three-year-old daughter, and in May the Earl of Lincoln was sent to open talks with the French. By the spring of the next year, after the conditions had been discussed by Parliament, Lincoln, accompanied by the Earl of Warwick and Amadeus of Savoy, returned to conduct the proxy betrothals. Amadeus reported back to Edward that seventeen-year-old Marguerite was possessed of the obligatory qualities of beauty, piety and virtue, though it is not known how he responded to Edward's more intimate inquiries about the span of her waist and the size of her feet. Under the treaty of Montreuil (signed by the English and French monarchs respectively in July and October 1299), Marguerite was to have a dowry of 15,000 livres. This offer of a cash sum, rather than lands, set a precedent for a policy that Charles V would cement by ordinanace in the next century as a way of preserving the French royal dominions intact. In return, Edward would give Marguerite the lands held by his first queen, Eleanor, in dower. These estates represented only a portion of the vast holdings Eleanor had obtained through royal grants and her unscrupulous acquisitions, but they were nevertheless worth 4,500 pounds per year and included land, farms and forest in Buckinghamshire, Cambridgeshire, Derbyshire, Dorset, Essex, Hampshire, Huntingdon, Leicestershire, Lincolnshire, Norfolk, Northamptonshire, Oxfordshire, Somerset, Suffolk, Wiltshire and Yorkshire, as well as the towns of Bristol, Lincoln, Grimsby, Tickhill and Heddon. The value of Marguerite's dower lands was similar to that of the two previous English queens, and this sum was accepted as the rate for a queen's dower throughout the fourteenth century, though Marguerite was exceptional in that the dower was decided quite precisely at her marriage, there being no queen dowager already in possession of it. These lands, the 'terre regine', formed the backbone of royal dower assignments into the next century.

The background to Marguerite's married life was always to be the rhythm of the Scots campaign. In 1296, Edward had taken Berwick, captured John Balliol, originally his own candidate for the Scottish throne, removed the sacred Stone of Scone and conquered the country to the north of Aberdeen. After defeating the rebel Scots leader William Wallace at Falkirk in 1298, Edward did not campaign in the year of his marriage, but in 1301 he wintered at Linlithgow after taking Bothwell. In 1302 Robert the Bruce negotiated a truce with England. The celebrated hero of Scottish nationalism campaigned effectively for the English in 1303–4, and after the siege of Stirling that summer, Edward was able to return to England. Wallace was surrendered in 1305, but a disgruntled Bruce turned back to Scotland in 1306 so that year and the next Edward was again leading his army in the north.

Edward and Marguerite were married at Canterbury on 10 September 1299. Though Edward had been a handsome man in his youth, Marguerite had high standards when it came to looks – her brother Philip was so exceptionally attractive he was nicknamed 'the Fair' – and it is rare for seventeen to look kindly on sixty. Still, both parties evidently did their duty, as Marguerite became pregnant almost immediately. Perhaps they were temperamentally suited. Edward ordered two crowns for his new bride, a plain gold circlet for £22 10s and a grand, bejewelled state piece from the goldsmith Thomas de Frowick for over 400 pounds, but he was so keen to get back to his northern campaign that there was deemed to be no time for a coronation and, despite her condition, Marguerite gamely accompanied him. That she too was energetic and had no truck with physical weakness is demonstrated by the fact that she continued hunting until late in her pregnancy. Indeed, she was riding to hounds in Wharfedale, Yorkshire when her labour pains began, and just managed to get to nearby Brotherton for the safe delivery of her first son. The boy was named in honour of Thomas à Becket, to whom Marguerite had prayed during the delivery, and was known as Thomas of Brotherton for his last-minute birthplace. Edward was so delighted that he rushed 'like a falcon' to his wife's side and baby Thomas was presented with two cradles, one in scarlet and one in blue, each draped with thirteen ells of cloth. Edward personally ordered striped draperies for his room and gilded hangings decorated with heraldic devices. The King was an old hand at fatherhood but, like many men who have children late in life, he seems to have found a new pleasure in the role, and when Marguerite's second boy, Edmund, was born at Woodstock the following August, the purveyors were so rapacious in their pursuit of goods for her that merchants were known to avoid being in the vicinity of her household.

Edward and Marguerite were united by their interest in their children and surviving information about the household set up for little Thomas and Edmund (a third child, politely named Eleanor, lived with them in 1305, but died young) gives an unusually intimate picture of medieval royal childhood. The boys were attended by a 'family' of fifty to seventy people, at a cost of approximately 1,300 pounds per year. The 'family' was overseen by a couple, Sir Stephen and his wife Lady Eveline, who supervised the female servants, among them chambermaids, washerwomen, Thomas's wet nurse Mabille and Edmund's cradle-rocker, Perrette. Lady Eveline, Mabille and Perrette were given presents of money by Marguerite in 1305, and the two nurses remained six years in the household, until the boys were ready for more masculine instruction. William de Lorri was appointed chaplain in 1301, and the children's religious education was managed strictly. They were expected to sit patiently through high Mass from a young age – in September 1302 Edward ordered that the boys hear divine service at Canterbury and make an offering of seven shillings apiece and the keeper of their wardrobe, John de Weston, was briefed to report back to the King on the conduct of the toddlers. At Easter, offerings of clothes, shoes and money were made to the poor on the princes' behalf. Queen Marguerite had a particular love for the Franciscan order, and was one of the main benefactresses of the new Franciscan foundation at Newgate in London. Regular payments to Franciscan friars show that she encouraged this association in her boys.

Like their parents, Thomas and Edmund played chess and also enjoyed 'tables'. Skilled riding was a necessity, not a leisure activity, and they were each provided with a palfreyman to attend to their horses. Yet there was also time for fun. Marguerite, who was fond of music and employed her own minstrel, Guy de Psaltery, also hired musicians to entertain her sons on the zither, viola and trumpet. The boys made their own musical efforts, playing the drum of their minstrel Martinet with such enthusiasm that it had to be repaired in 1305. Music was part of the hospitality laid on for visitors, too, and as Thomas and Edmund, like their parents, journeyed between royal houses, they received noblemen, clergy and their rakish half-sister Mary, who had been enclosed at the Amesbury convent with their grandmother Eleanor of Provence, but who seemed to relish any opportunity to escape.

In common with other royal mothers, Marguerite was obliged to spend time away from her children, often on campaign with Edward in the north, but the details of the boys' accounts indicate that she took a precise interest in their wellbeing. She was informed as to their diet, which was very healthy by medieval standards and included fresh fruit and vegetables as well as the usual quantities of meat and fish spiced with saffron, ginger, cinnamon and pepper. Treats included almonds, dates, figs and twisted candy sticks of spun sugar. Stephen the tailor made their clothes, always styled to reflect their royal rank. They had silk and wool cloaks, mantles and tabards, galoshes for wet weather and fur-lined robes with silver buttons and beaverskin hats for travelling in the cold. There is a tenderness to such touches as the broken drum and silver buttons that suggests Marguerite had both an intimate and a joyful relationship with her sons, and that this contributed to the happiness of her marriage to Edward.

For his part, the King's satisfaction with his wife was evident from his unfashionable fidelity, and from his interest in the minutiae of her life. Marguerite was accused of extravagance by the St Albans chronicler, and apparently loved fashion: in 1302 she owed 1,000 pounds to Balliardi of Lucca for fabrics, not to mention 3,000 pounds-worth of other debts. Edward provided for their payment through grants of wardships and marriages, and managed to do so without attracting undue criticism of Marguerite. He was concerned about her health, corresponding with her doctor on her recovery from measles and recommending bloodletting. The man who told Charles of Anjou that sons could always be got may be glimpsed in his clumsily kind-hearted advice to Marguerite's confessor on the death of her sister Blanche. The priest, Edward suggested, should break the news to the Queen as gently as possible, but if she became very upset he was to say that she mustn't mind as Blanche, who had married the Duke of Austria, had been as good as dead for a long while.

Contentment and warmth between the couple is also evident in Marguerite's success not only as a provider of heirs but in another essential of the queenly dynamic: intercession. Though the queen's role as 'peace-weaver' was to some extent becoming ritualised (as will be seen in the case of Philippa of Hainault in the reign of Edward III), it was still effective, as Marguerite proved when she pleaded that the citizens of Winchester be pardoned for having allowed an important hostage to escape, or in the case of Geoffrey de Coigners, a goldsmith who had had the temerity to manufacture a crown for Edward's sometime arch-enemy, Robert the Bruce, King of the Scots, and who was pardoned only through Edward's love of his 'dearest' wife. Marguerite also attempted to intercede for the Earl of Atholl, who had been taken prisoner while guarding the Scottish royal ladies at Kildrimny Castle in 1306. Edward responded harshly that Atholl would only be hanged higher than the rest. The siege of the same castle provoked Edward to the exceptionally ungallant punishment of two high-ranking ladies, Bruce's sister Mary and the Countess of Buchan, who were imprisoned in cages within their chambers and per-mitted only English attendants and a niggardly fourpence per day for their maintenance.

Perhaps Marguerite's most important intercessionary initiatives were directed at keeping the peace between her husband and his heir, since 1301 the Prince of Wales, Edward of Carnarvon. Of Edward's living children, as well as Mary, Joan, now Countess of Gloucester, and Elizabeth, the wife of Humphrey de Bohun, Earl of Hereford, were still in England. Edward had lost his mother at the age of six, and though Marguerite was only a few years his senior, she seems to have developed a maternal relationship with him and he wrote to her on at least eight occasions in 1305, frequently requesting her intercession with his father. Usually this was on relatively small matters, such as a prebend for his clerk, Walter Reynolds, or a settlement of land rights near Westminster Abbey for his cousin Henry de Beaumont. In September, however, Edward wrote to her of 'business', sending Sir Robert de Clifford to the Queen in advance of his letter to explain it and listen to her advice, and asking Clifford to convey any requests Marguerite wished to make of him. The frequency of Edward's letters and his respect for Marguerite's opinion point to a strong relationship touched by gratitude on the prince's side. And it was to Marguerite that the future King Edward II made one of the most revealing emotional statements of his troubled life: a plea for the return of his favourite, and some said his lover, Piers Gaveston.

The question of the supposed homosexuality of Edward II is far more vexing than that of Richard I. That he 'loved' Piers Gaveston is beyond doubt, but the nature of that love has exercised generations of scholars. Such efforts have been deemed 'both anachronistic and futile: anachronistic because medieval attitudes to sexuality were so different from our own and futile because the nature of the evidence makes it impossible to tell what Edward actually did'.' What Edward got up to with Gaveston is actually less important than what his contemporaries thought he did, and the implications this held for their understanding of his failed kingship.

That the Prince was passionately involved with Gaveston was apparent from their first meeting in 1300, when Gaveston was appointed a member of his household, one of ten young men selected by the King to provide his heir with knightly companionship. Gaveston was clearly capable of making an impression, as this son of minor Gascon gentry was chosen despite having no claim to nobility. It was generally agreed that he was good-looking, intelligent and proficient on the battlefield – indeed, he distinguished himself on one of the Scottish campaigns in 1303 – but he was also arrogant, conceited and made spiteful use of his wit. His lack of respect for the King's values was demonstrated in 1305 when he casually left the Scottish battlelines for a tournament in France, and his contempt for authority when he, Edward and a gang of friends ravaged the estates of the bishop of Chester, driving off his game. The King was so disgusted by Edward's impertinent response to his remonstrances that he disbanded his household, forbade him to see Gaveston and sent him to Windsor Castle with a single manservant. It was at this point that Edward sought the Queen's intercession, and in August he wrote to thank her for the restoration of the majority of his household: 'We know well that this was done at your request, for which we are dearly grateful to you, as you know.' He continued to plead for her good offices, asking her to petition for the return of his cousin Gilbert de Clare and the disgraced Gaveston himself. 'But truly, my lady, if we should add those two to the others, we would feel much comfort and alleviation of the anguish we have endured and continue to suffer, by the ordinance of our aforementioned lord and father. My lady, will you please take this business to heart, and pursue it in the most gracious manner you may, so dearly as you love us.'[2]

The Prince of Wales clearly felt he could trust his stepmother with this intimate declaration, and his trust in her power to sway his father was well-judged, for by Whitsun 1306 Gaveston was back in favour and being knighted at Westminster alongside his dear friend. By February 1307, however, the King was so anxious about the 'inordinate affection'[3] between Gaveston and his son that he banished the knight to Gascony. In fact, he went only as far as Eleanor of Castile's county of Ponthieu where, in the summer, he received the news that the man who called him 'brother'[4] was now King of England.

Marguerite had accompanied King Edward north once more for the now-customary summer campaign. Usually, she would remain at Tyne-mouth, on English soil, for her own protection, but this time she was with her husband at Burgh-on-Sands, because the King had become so ill he could not rise from his bed. On 7 July, he died.

The very first act of the new King was to summon Gaveston. At this point, the grieving Marguerite could not have imagined she had anything to fear from the favourite's return. She and Edward had a strong rela-tionship and he was in her debt for her positive efforts on Gaveston's behalf. But suddenly her own interests appeared to be threatened. In early August, before Gaveston had even set foot in the kingdom, Edward made him Earl of Cornwall. This was both undutiful and, frankly, stupid, and it immediately provoked the anger of the magnates and the enmity of the Dowager Queen. Cornwall was a royal earldom, and Edward's right to bestow it was dubious; moreover, Marguerite had understood it to be intended for one of her own sons. Edward was also foolish and insensitive in the semi-royal marriage he arranged for Gaveston a few months after his return to England. Gaveston's bride was Margaret de Clare, the daughter of the King's sister Joan of Acre and her husband Gilbert de Clare, the Earl of Gloucester. Joan had been mocked for marrying beneath her station for love, but she was still a royal lady and Margaret was the King's own niece. Despite Gaveston's new title, this marriage, too, was 'disparaging', one of the offences to the social order the medieval nobility found so threatening. Gaveston made matters worse by insulting his brother-in-law, calling him 'whoreson' in reference to Joan's disparaging match. As a French princess and Margaret's relative, Marguerite would have been highly sensitive to the insult to the royal family, and King Edward compounded it by insisting that the marriage was held at Berkhamsted Castle, one of Marguerite's properties.

Edward had also failed to respect his father's wishes for his funeral. The story was put about that the late King had left instructions for the flesh to be boiled from his body so that his bones, at least, could head a victorious army into Scotland. This tale is most likely a product of the ever-fertile imagination of the chronicler Froissart, but it supposedly caused Robert the Bruce to remark with some accuracy that there was more to fear from the dead Edward's bones than the living Edward's sword. In any event, Edward I was buried, intact, at Westminster on 27 October, and the Scottish campaign was apparently forgotten. A month later, Edward, who took no more than a token interest in tournaments, organised a great joust at Wallingford as an opportunity for his favourite to display his skills. Gaveston's party carried the day, to the great resentment of the older magnates, and

> from these and other incidents, hatred mounted day by day, for Piers was very proud and haughty in bearing. All those whom the custom of the realm made equal to him he regarded as lowly and abject, nor could anyone, he thought, equal him in valour. On the other hand, the earls and barons of England looked down on Piers, because, as a foreigner and formerly a mere man at arms raised to such distinction and eminence, he was unmindful of his former rank. Thus he was an object of mockery to almost everyone in the kingdom.[5]

It may have given Marguerite some satisfaction that Edward was obliged to issue orders reminding the court to style Gaveston with his proper title of Earl of Cornwall, but she had to contend with the fact that the favourite she had herself protected was now dangerously powerful. The award of the earldom, the Clare marriage and the funeral showed that Edward had no respect for his father's memory. Would this neglect extend to Marguerite? Such fears were confirmed when Edward gave Berkhamsted to Gaveston. Marguerite was till only twenty-five, and at this point she might have made a second marriage, or even have returned to France. That she did not do so suggests both a genuine love for her husband and a need to protect her interests under the new regime, interests which were now allied to those of her niece, Isabella, the twelve-year-old girl who was about to become the next queen of England.

The terms of the treaty of Montreuil were fulfilled on 25 January 1308, when Isabella and Edward were married at Our Lady of Boulogne. For Queen Marguerite, the ceremonies, which lasted nine days, were a chance to see her brother and her mother, Marie, once more. She may have been hopeful that, as well as affording her the pleasure of a family reunion, the wedding would encourage her stepson to assume his proper role and diminish Gaveston's influence. A silver casket engraved with Marguerite and Isabella's arms, now in the British Museum, may have been a gift for the bride from Marguerite, intended to emphasise their potential alliance. When the English party returned to Dover on 3 February, however, it was soon clear that Edward still had eyes only for Gaveston.

For twelve-year-old Isabella, the first weeks in England were confusing. All her life she had expected to become queen of England, and her impeccable lineage (she was royal on both sides, her mother Jeanne having been Queen of Navarre in her own right), her magnificent 18,000-pound dowry and the splendour of her wedding, which was attended by five kings and three queens, led her to assume she would be treated with every honour. Yet supervising the ladies who would form her retinue, she found this Gaveston, a nobody, who very shortly was seen peacocking about in Isabella's own jewellery. As Marguerite was still in possession of the Queen's dower lands, Edward was supposed to make separate provision for his wife, but despite pressure from King Philip, he refused to declare his terms, and Isabella discovered that she had nothing with which to maintain herself. Even before she was crowned, his furious bride was writing to her father to complain of her impoverished and 'wretched' position.

Thanks to Gaveston, even the coronation was in danger of collapsing into farce. According to the *Annales Paulini*, one magnate was so enraged by the indignity of the proceedings that he had to restrain himself from challenging Gaveston in Westminster Abbey itself. With the blindness characteristic of his favourite, Edward had put him in charge of the coronation ceremonies. From the start, the assembled nobility were incandescent when Gaveston appeared in purple robes, a colour only the King had the right to wear, and a deliberate insult to the earls in their own carefully ranked cloth-of-gold. Worse still, he carried the sacred crown of Edward the Confessor, an honour to which he had so little right it was almost sacrilegious. Perhaps, in fairness to Gaveston, it should be recalled that coronation disasters were practically an English tradition, hard to avoid when huge numbers of people were crammed into limited space, on this occasion the joint coronation was marred by the death of a knight under a tumbling wall. Nevertheless, it was Gaveston's fault that the banquet at Westminster Hall was served so late and was so poorly prepared that the guests could hardly eat it. The representatives of the French royal family were disgusted not only by the food, but by the fact that Edward sat next to Gaveston, not Isabella, and that it was Gaveston's arms that were displayed next to the King's on the tapestries decorating the chamber.

Marguerite decided to retire to her castle at Marlborough after the coronation. If, in effect, she abandoned her lonely and bewildered niece, she may well have done so for political reasons. Resentment of Gaveston had risen to such a degree that 'it was held for certain that the quarrel once begun could not be settled without great destruction'.[6] Many magnates had united in a vow to depose the favourite, and when Parliament met on 28 April, having been postponed from 3 March, the assembled lords arrived in arms. They accused Gaveston of embezzling crown revenues and alienating the King from those who ought to have been his closest counsellors, and demanded that he be exiled. Three chronicles suggest that Isabella's father, King Philip, angered not only by the reports of Gaveston's ascendancy but by the continuing uncertainty over his daughter's income, was conspiring with the English lords to bring him down, and Marguerite was also named in connection with the plan. According to Robert of Reading, Edward, desperately playing for time, was informed in mid-May that Philip and Marguerite had sent 40,000 pounds to the earls of Lincoln and Pembroke, who were among Gaveston's most vocal opponents, to fund his deposition.

Aymer de Valence, Earl of Pembroke, was a grandson of John's queen, Isabelle of Angoulême, the son of Henry III's Lusignan half-brother William. He had been a close friend of Edward I and also enjoyed a warm relationship with Marguerite. In 1303, Pembroke had asked Marguerite to write to the then chancellor, William Greenfield, to petition for a postponement of the trial of two men accused of trespass in her parks, as at the time they had both been absent on campaign in Scotland. In her letter, Marguerite refers to Pembroke as her 'dear cousin', and wrote again to Greenfield a month later, mercifully requesting that since one of the men, Robert Parker, had paid his fine, he should be 'quit of all manner of exigencies and other demands'. Marguerite's closeness to Pembroke is demonstrated by her bequest of Hertford Castle, a significant enough portion of the Queen's dower lands for Isabella of France to repossess it from Pembroke's widow in 1327.

That Marguerite should have been able personally to raise even half the huge sum quoted by Robert of Reading seems implausible, but if she was in correspondence with Philip about the treatment of her niece and the vicious influence of Gaveston, she may well have been a conduit from the French King to Pembroke for his support of the anti-Gaveston party. Rumours abounded that Philip had sent envoys to declare his commitment

to Gaveston's banishment. It has been suggested that Isabella was conspiring against Gaveston, and certainly the magnates used her as a sort of
figurehead, but given her immaturity and impecuniousness, if the earls
did have a female ally in one of the French queens of England, it is far
more likely to have been Marguerite. In response to the report of his
stepmother's involvement, Edward declared the same day that Isabella
should be dowered with the counties of Ponthieu and Montreuil and be
'honourably and decently'[7] provided with the necessities to set up her
household. If Philip was mollified by this, the English earls remained
adamant, and on 18 May, Edward was forced to order that on pain of
excommunication, Gaveston would leave England on 24 June.

Gaveston's exile was however, short-lived. Edward made him Lieutenant of Ireland, where he stayed for just a year, appropriating the Crown
revenues for his own enrichment, until the King's wheedling lobbying of
the Pope, the barons and even his father-in-law produced a bull quashing
the sentence of excommunication. Gaveston returned triumphantly in
June 1309, and Edward received him joyfully at Chester. They kept
Christmas together that year at Edward's favourite manor of Langley
in Hertfordshire, with Queen Isabella an awkward third. For his own
protection, Gaveston went north when Parliament met in February 1310,
while Isabella accompanied Edward to Westminster. By the end of March,
Edward had been forced to accept the election of twenty-one 'Lords
Ordainers', Pembroke among them, whose job would be to reform the
government. It was particularly galling for Edward that a prominent
member of this group was his cousin Thomas, Earl of Lancaster, the most
powerful magnate in the country and, until the Gaveston debacle, a firm
supporter. The barons declared that if the King refused to accept their
new rules, they would consider themselves free of the oath of loyalty they
had sworn at his coronation. Edward announced his intention of resuming
the Scottish campaign, in order to both reunite the barons and give him
an opportunity to create a base of support in the north, but soon after he
and Isabella arrived to join Gaveston at Berwick on 18 September, it
became clear that hatred of Gaveston had superseded even the magnates'
pleasure in Scot-hunting and, humiliatingly, only three earls turned out
to fight for Edward. Bruce commanded far more impressively than the
English King, and his guerrilla tactics left the Scottish lowlands stripped
of resources, forcing the invaders back over the border.

Edward and Isabella remained in the north until the following July,
but all the Scottish campaign yielded was an opportunity for the Ordainers
to consolidate their position. When Edward eventually appeared at

Westminster on 13 August 1311, he was presented with a list of forty-one injunctions. As with the Provisions of Oxford in Henry III's reign, it was announced at the public proclamation of the injunctions on 27 September that disloyalty would be punished with excommunication. Isabella, unlike Eleanor of Provence, was not obliged to swear to the ordinances, confirming that her contemporaries at this juncture saw her political influence as minimal. The Queen was in communication with Marguerite, who was on a tour of her properties in Devizes, and a letter of 4 September suggests that she was keeping her aunt informed of events in London. Not surprisingly, one of the principal demands of the Ordainers was the removal, again, of Gaveston, whom they declared 'a public enemy of the king and the kingdom'.[8] Gaveston duly left the country in early November, but Edward clearly had no intention of keeping his promise. It is notable that at this point Edward restored Berkhamsted Castle to Marguerite, who kept Christmas there that year. Perhaps he hoped to enlist her support for Gaveston's return, as he had done in the past.

By Christmas, Gaveston was back at Westminster. Interestingly, Queen Isabella now took a conciliatory attitude to him. Her New Year gifts diplomatically included presents of game to leading Ordainers, but she also sent a Brie cheese to Isabella de Vescy, whose husband Henry de Beaumont had been dismissed from court as a Gaveston supporter, and other delicacies to Margaret de Clare, Gaveston's wife, who was expecting a child. If Isabella was naïvely hoping for some sort of reconciliation, even Edward appreciated that Gaveston's presence in the capital was impolitic, and in January, followed by Isabella, he removed himself, with Gaveston in tow, to York. It was here that Margaret de Clare gave birth to her child – her churching was celebrated by 'King Robert's' minstrels, who received forty marks – and despite the fact that Isabella's husband was behaving with insane carelessness, this York court was a happy time for the Queen, too. She was able to write to Marguerite with the news that after four years she had become pregnant.

But the Ordainers were arming themselves in the south. Edward's blatant defiance in recalling Gaveston was essentially a declaration of war, and by April the King was forced to move on to Newcastle, with an army commanded by the Earl of Lancaster in pursuit, so hurriedly that many of Isabella's possessions were left behind. Edward's lack of consideration for his wife's condition was shown when, just two days after her arrival in Newcastle, she was obliged to move again, to Tynemouth Priory on the coast, ostensibly for her own safety. Lancaster's men were in Newcastle on 4 May, and the King and the favourite made a scrabbling, undignified retreat to Tynemouth, but a few days later, despite Isabella's tearful pleas, they departed for Scarborough, leaving the Queen alone again (poor Margaret de Clare and her new baby having been left to fend for themselves in Newcastle). Entrusting the castle at Scarborough to Gaveston, Edward returned to York, where he summoned Isabella. But the favourite who had incurred such loathing with his boasts of military prowess surrendered to Pembroke on 19 May.

Gaveston's good time was over. Pembroke accompanied him to Deddington in Oxfordshire. He swore that Gaveston would be treated honourably, on the pain of forfeiting his own estates, but the Earl of Warwick was less moderate. While Pembroke was absent on a visit to his wife, he abducted Gaveston and took him to Warwick, where the prisoner was forced to walk barefoot to the castle. 'Blaring trumpets followed Piers, and the horrid cry of the populace. They had taken off his belt of knighthood, and as a thief and a traitor he was taken to Warwick.'[9] On 19 June, Gaveston was beheaded on Blacklow Hill, saved from the full horror of a traitor's death by his family connection to the Earl of Gloucester. The body was left in the dirt until a group of Dominican friars found it, sewed the head back and embalmed it. They carried the corpse to Oxford, but were chary of giving it burial because Gaveston was excommunicated as a consequence of defying the ordinances. The writer of the *Vita Edwardi Secundi* declared: 'I may assert with confidence that the death of one man ... had never before been so acceptable to so many.'

Both Isabella and Marguerite had a part to play in the aftermath of Gaveston's execution. Despite the satisfaction felt by many at the news of the favourite's death, the magnates were divided over the legality of the killing and Pembroke, in particular, was furious that Warwick had caused him to break his word. He now returned to Edward's party and pressured the King to take up arms against Warwick and Lancaster. After corresponding with Marguerite and meeting Pembroke in France, King Philip, mindful that Isabella was carrying an heir of his blood, tried to settle the dispute. The Queen entertained Philip's envoy, her uncle the Comte d'Evreux, on 15 September, before he met the bishops and the Earl of Gloucester, who was also acting as a mediator. By December, a fragile, face-saving settlement had been reached, with the assassins formally requesting a royal pardon and Gaveston's treasury, which had been captured at Newcastle, to be handed over to the King. Edward and Lancaster dined together in public, but Edward was still aching for revenge and Lancaster had no intention of abandoning the ordinances.

For the royal women, the birth of an heir to the throne on 13 November

1312 could not have been better timed. Edward experienced a surge in popularity, Isabella was finally confirmed in her role as Queen and the treaty of Montreuil had achieved its purpose. Isabella had moved to Windsor soon after her meeting with Evreux, and she remained there for the rest of her pregnancy, along with her aunt. Marguerite assisted at the birth of Prince Edward, and attended the christening in the chapel of St Edward on 17 November. After Isabella's churching at Isleworth on Christmas Eve, the royal family kept Christmas at Windsor, removing to Westminster in late January. Londoners had already enjoyed a week of celebrations when the prince was born, but for the return of their Queen they organised a number of ceremonies, including a pageant by the Guild of Fishmongers, who contrived a fully fitted-out ship, which 'sailed', presumably on wheels, from Cheapside to Westminster, attended by the guild members in their finery.

Queen Isabella was unique among her predecessors in having a close family member near to her who had also been queen. There is simply not enough evidence to justify claiming that Marguerite's queenship had a formative influence on the early years of Isabella's, but both women's households and practices were shaped by those of previous queens and their experiences of daily life were similar in many respects. Some details from Isabella's surviving 'household book' give a sense of their routines as they moved between the twenty-five royal residences, many of which had been improved under Henry III and Edward I. Life was not necessarily entirely comfortable, but the innovations provided for the southern queens Eleanor of Provence and Eleanor of Castile had certainly made it more pleasant than once it had been. Two fires had destroyed many of the renovations at Westminster, and on her marriage Marguerite had been obliged to stay at York Place instead of in the queen's apartments, afterwards occupying Eleanor of Provence's apartments at the Tower when she was in London.

Edward II began restoring the Westminster rooms in 1307 in anticipation of Isabella's arrival, rebuilding Eleanor of Castile's garden, pool and aviary and adding two white chambers for himself and his wife. The lavatory system at Westminster had been updated with plumbing, while at Woodstock double doors were fitted to the privies, though private conveniences would have to wait until the reign of Richard II at the end of the century. One of the few attractive aspects of King John's character was his fondness for baths (he took the remarkable number of eight in the first six months of 1209 and travelled with his own bathrobe), while Eleanor of Castile had been a staunch adherent of the dubious foreign habit of bathing regularly. Isabella's book records the transport of tubs and linen for the Queen's bath, and other legacies from Eleanor were carpets and fruit trees in the Queen's gardens. Marguerite and Isabella both slept in beds draped with dimity, and Isabella's tailor, John de Falaise, made scarlet hangings for her bed as well as cushions for her chambers and cloths for her chapel. Isabella kept John extremely busy and, like Marguerite, had a fondness for prized Lucca silks. In 1311 and 1312, John produced one Lucca tunic, fifteen gowns, thirty pairs of stockings, four cloaks, six bodices and thirty-six pairs of shoes for Isabella. Many of Eleanor of Castile's personal possessions had been sold on her death, though some of her jewellery remained and gifts of this were made to both Marguerite and Isabella. Both women also ordered new jewels in extravagant quantities – a girdle worn by Isabella for the wedding of one of her ladies in 1311 featured 300 rubies and 1,800 pearls. The French queens took their duty to display their magnificence seriously. When they rode through the countryside in chariots draped with gold tissue, wrapped in furs and jewel-coloured Lucca silks, they must have seemed to the grubbing labourers in the fields like creatures from another world.

Dress was a state matter, but Marguerite and Isabella also shared spiritual interests. Their mutual ancestor Blanche of Artois, the second wife of Eleanor of Provence's son Edmund, had introduced the order of the Poor Clares, the sisters of the Franciscan friars, to England, and both women were patrons of the Franciscans, as Eleanor of Provence had been. Marguerite sponsored the altar of the Greyfriars church founded by Edmund at Newgate and Isabella presented three advowsons and two pounds for food supplies to the Poor Clares at Aldgate in 1358. They both chose to be buried in the Franciscan church, in the habits of the third order, to which they were admitted before they died. For lay members, the third order stressed penitence as well as a certain asceticism, and though Isabella was to have considerably more to repent of than her aunt, both of these women who had lived so luxuriously seem to have been attracted at the end of their lives to the Franciscan's dynamic new message of simplicity and poverty.

Marguerite died in retirement at Marlborough on 14 February 1318. She did not achieve a great deal as Queen, and her reputation has been obscured by the notoriety of her niece, yet she was not irrelevant. Her interventions had been important in maintaining some degree of civility between her husband and his heir in the years before Edward I's death. In 1301, he had relied on her judgement to advise the treasurer, Walter Langdon, of any amendments required in the letters of authority for truce with the Scots. Her co-operation with Pembroke shows that she was capable of drawing on her natal connections to try to guide her stepson away from controversy. And her own sons, Thomas and Edmund, had significant and tragic roles to play in the career of their mother's successor. Edward I's famed uxoriousness was immortalised by his opulent memorialisation of his first queen, Eleanor of Castile, but although Marguerite had to accept a secondary role in his life and reputation, that role appears to have been both happy and productive.

PART FOUR

DEPOSITIONS, RESTORATIONS

CHAPTER 11

ISABELLA OF FRANCE

'The Iron Virago'

E dward II was fond of low company. 'Shunning the company of nobles, he sought the society of jesters, singers, actors, carriage drivers, diggers, oarsmen, sailors and the practitioners of other mechanical arts,' sniffed Ranulph Higden. Though as Prince of Wales he had shown official support for the aristocratic pursuit of tourneying, taking personal care over the supplies and equipment of his jousters, his own leisure interests were startlingly eccentric for a king. He enjoyed digging ditches, rowing and swimming, even in winter, none of which were acceptable pastimes for a man of his status. In 1325, he entertained a bargemaster, Adam Cogg, in his own room for four days, and ten sailors and two carpenters dined with him on other occasions. Whether Edward took a sexual interest in the fourteenth-century equivalent of 'rough trade' can be neither proved nor disproved, but his contemporaries certainly linked his unsuccessful kingship with his love of 'rustic pursuits',[1] which they attributed to sexual degeneracy. This explanation may, however, have provided a rationale for what might have been an even more shocking idea: that the King's rejection of social convention was a matter of taste. Here was true heresy. Enjoying the company of a peasant was far more disturbing than buggering a favourite.

With the exception of his passion for music and mechanicals, Edward was 'conventional and perhaps even rather dull'.[2] He had inherited his love of music from his father, who always had his four harpists in attendance, but the young King preferred the newer, bowed instruments, such as the Welsh crowth, and sent his own minstrel, Robert the Rymer, to Shrewsbury Abbey to take lessons from a player there. It was suggested that Edward's promotion of his clerk, Walter Reynolds, for whom he asked his stepmother Queen Marguerite to secure a post, and who eventually rose to become archbishop of Canterbury, was encouraged by Reynolds' skill in devising the musical entertainments he so enjoyed. They corresponded about music, in one letter discussing two young trumpeters, a kettle-drummer named Franklin and a trumpeter called Jankin, who remained some years in royal service. Edward liked the organ, giving one as a present to his sister Mary and installing another at his favourite residence of Langley, where it was repaired with fifteen pounds of tin in preparation for a visit from his father and Queen Marguerite. He shared an enthusiasm for horses with his stepmother, receiving a present of foals from her, and even his enemies conceded he had a beautiful seat, though this did not compensate in the eyes of the peers for his sorry lack of military skills, the proper objective of the accomplished rider.

Edward was not, in fact, as 'uncourtly' as the chroniclers suggested. Recent research has confirmed that as well as being interested in music, he loved hawking and hunting with his greyhounds, and his early military career was worthy, if not brilliant. It was with hindsight, after Bannockburn and the deposition, that contemporary writers emphasised his inappropriate pleasures. Nevertheless, there was nothing innovatory about his court, nothing notable in terms of literary, artistic or architectural achievement, and the elegant manners to which his culture paid lip service, at least, was nowhere in evidence in his entourage, who were more given to gambling and drinking themselves into nightly stupors than to the practice of knightly courtesy. What place was there for Queen Isabella in Edward's world?

During the ascendancy of Gaveston, Edward had largely ignored his young wife. That he fulfilled the minimal requirements of a husband is shown by the birth of Prince Edward, followed by John of Eltham in 1316, Eleanor in 1318 and Joan in 1321, but Edward took little more than a conventional interest in his queen's life and the English court could not compare with the home Isabella had left. Paris, where she had spent much of her childhood, was the intellectual capital of Europe, and her mother, Queen Jeanne, had been a notable artistic patron, founding the College de Navarre as part of the city's celebrated university. Isabella employed a minstrel, Walter, and collected painted panels of 'Lombard work'; she had a library which included eight religious books, among them a French Apocalypse, eight volumes of romances and a collection of Arthurian legends bound in white leather, as well as the exquisite 'Isabella Psalter' which may have been a wedding gift. These surviving possessions suggest the young queen was literate (or least that she could read; it is not known whether she was able to write) and cultivated, and certainly had nothing in common with the companions her husband appeared to prefer. For a while after Gaveston's murder, Isabella had enjoyed a warmer relationship with her husband, but in the year of her aunt Marguerite's death it became clear to her that Edward's tendency to blind passion for his favourites had merely been in abeyance. His vulnerability to 'evil counsellors' and his 'unseemly works and occupations'[3] were leading to another crisis. The King's curious tastes, so alien to his elegant, educated French princess, were the first manifestations of a wilful political madness that Isabella could not share and which eventually she would be driven to destroy.

Roger Mortimer, the eighth Baron Wigmore, was a very different man from Edward. Knighted alongside the then Prince of Wales, and Gaveston, in 1306, he was married to Joan de Grenville, one of the ladies appointed to serve Isabella when she first arrived in England as Queen. Mortimer's lands lay on the Welsh marches, between Wigmore and Ludlow, and his family had a history of service to the crown, in reflection of which Mortimer had carried the royal robes at Edward's coronation. From 1306 he had served as the royal governor in Ireland, and had also lent his considerable military skills to campaigns in Wales and the marches. Mortimer was a dynamic commander with a taste for luxurious living, accumulating rare furniture and carpets, plate and gorgeous clothes of silk and velvet. In the years of his ascendancy, he treated himself to silk sheets and the finest armour from Milan and Germany, but though he shared an appreciation of beautiful things with his master, there was nothing effete about him. He was a hard man, physically courageous and dominating, and it is unsurprising that Isabella, spurned and neglected for so long, eventually found him irresistible.

But how did the Queen, whose conduct had been irreproachable for nearly twenty years, come to be involved in an openly adulterous relationship which scandalised the whole of Europe? Her behaviour left such a 'dark stain on the annals of female royalty'[4] that her prim nineteenth-century biographer Agnes Strickland could barely bring herself to write about it. Harridan, unnatural woman – she-wolf, even – are some of the epithets used by contemporaries and subsequent writers to describe the erstwhile virtuous French Princess who ruled England with her lover for three years. Much of Isabella's conduct is inexcusable, but it is not inexplicable, and it may be argued that her actions, driven by desperate circumstances, ultimately protected and even saved the English crown during a period of great vulnerability, a state of affairs created in large part by the behaviour of the King himself.

In August 1318, Edward agreed to the treaty of Leake, which bound him to observe the Ordinances under a council of seventeen headed by the Earl of Pembroke. Included on this council were the Despensers, father and son, both able men with a particular talent for finance, but whose hold over the king was by now becoming a source of concern. Hugh Despenser the younger had joined Edward's household when he was Prince of Wales, and Edward favoured him enough to marry him to his niece Eleanor de Clare, the sister of Gaveston's wife Margaret and one of the most eligible heiresses in England. In 1313, three years after the death of Eleanor's father, the Earl of Gloucester, at Bannockburn, his inheritance was finally divided between his three daughters, Margaret, Eleanor and Elizabeth, but not equally: Edward permitted Hugh to take Glamorgan, the lion's share of the lands, and it was not long before Hugh was scheming to get his hands on the whole Gloucester inheritance. Edward had no objection to this, as he was by now apparently as besotted by Hugh as he had been by Piers Gaveston. Despenser had become 'the King of England's right eye and his chief counsellor against the earls and barons, but an eyesore to the rest of the kingdom. His every desire became a royal command.'[5] Hugh's current desire was the lordship of Gower, which was the property of John Mowbray, and in 1320 he persuaded Edward to confiscate Mowbray's lands and add them to his own affinity of Glamorgan.

The lordships of the Welsh marches had traditionally enjoyed a unique position in English law. Marcher lords governed their lands as mini-kingdoms, exempt from many of the obligations of their peers, in return for keeping the peace on the ever-fractious border. John Mowbray had followed tradition when he acquired Gower, which he had bought from his father-in-law without obtaining formal permission, but in order to justify the confiscation, Hugh claimed he had acted illegally. When Mowbray objected, Edward sent men to take Gower for Hugh by force. Outraged by what they perceived as an attack on their rights, a group of Marchers, which included Roger Mortimer, 'made a sworn conspiracy with the Earl of Lancaster to banish, persecute, condemn and perpetually disinherit the Despensers, father and son'.[6] Mortimer was at Westminster in November 1320 to try to make Edward see reason but, as he had done over Gaveston, Edward dithered, and by the spring, he was preparing for war.

Whatever her own feelings about the Despensers may have been, Isabella, like her husband, was not prepared to countenance any attack on the royal prerogative. Neither she nor Edward seemed to understand that the Marchers were staunch royalists, and that in many respects the situation mirrored that of the Gaveston debacle, with Edward's heedless promotion of his favourite making unwilling enemies of those most bound to support him. Isabella demonstrated her commitment to Edward by handing Marlborough Castle to Hugh Despenser the elder, though she could not join her husband on his campaign to meet the Marchers as she was approaching the delivery of her last child, Joan, who was born in the Tower of London that July. As Isabella waited out the last months of her pregnancy, the Marcher forces, commanded by Mortimer, moved steadily eastwards, taking Newport, Cardiff, Caerphilly and laying waste to much of Gloucestershire. By the time the Queen's baby was born (a more than usually miserable experience since her apartments in the Tower had been neglected and the roof leaked on to her bed), the Marchers were moving on London. On 29 July, the citizens of London closed the city gates. Mortimer's response was to encircle the walls, and when Despenser sailed up and down the Thames in show of bravado, the 'contrariants' threatened to torch every ward of the city between Charing Cross and Westminster. Edward was anxious enough to hand over the custody of the Great Seal to Isabella and two royal clerks, but when Parliament met he refused to listen to the contrariants' demands that the Despensers be banished. Edward's obduracy had brought the country to the very brink of war, but the Earl of Pembroke now suggested that Isabella might make a gesture of intercession, through which Edward could back down without too great a loss of dignity. The Queen obliged by going through the ceremony of pleading on her knees with the King 'for the peoples' sake'.[7] Her action here was not an emotional appeal but a political formula, an example of the ritualisation of the intercession dynamic. Edward was not moved to change his mind out of affection for his wife, rather Isabella's performance was a device, understood by all, by which he could *appear* to change it as a gesture of mercy. On 19 August, the Despensers were duly proscribed and disinherited and a pardon was issued to the contrariants at Westminster the following day. Hugh Despenser made the best of his exile by becoming a pirate, a 'sea-monster' as the *Vita* describes him, but again, as in the case of Gaveston, Edward was determined to restore his favourite and have his revenge on those who had dared to challenge his power. This time, he made direct use of Isabella.

Bartholomew of Badlesmere was a substantial Kentish baron who had until recently been among Edward's supporters (indeed, on Queen Marguerite's death, Leeds Castle in Kent, which she had held in dower and which had for some years been promised to Isabella, had been cavalierly granted to him), but who had now declared for the contrariants, possibly as a result of the marriage of his daughter to Mortimer's son. In

October, Queen Isabella set off with an armed escort on a 'pilgrimage', taking an unusual route to Canterbury. She stopped near Leeds Castle and had her men inform Lady Badlesmere that she wished to rest there for the night. Lord Badlesmere was away, which presumably Isabella knew, and his wife refused to admit her, probably because, as a rebel, Badlesmere had equipped all his castles for defence and his treasure was being stored at Leeds. Isabella then advanced on the castle and ordered her escort to force an entry, at which Lady Badlesmere had her archers fire upon them, killing six members of the Queen's party. If Isabella had been fully party to the plot, she now behaved disingenuously, writing to Edward to request that Lady Badlesmere be punished for the murder of her servants and the insult to her as Queen. Edward responded by sending Pembroke to besiege Leeds. The real point, of course, was not to seek retribution for Lady Badlesmere's impertinence but to provoke the contrariants, and Mortimer fell neatly into the trap by setting off to relieve the castle. This was an open gesture of defiance against Edward. By 27 October Mortimer was at Kingston-on-Thames, where Pembroke wisely met him to dissuade him from advancing any further, and four days later the castle fell. Lady Badlesmere and her children, including Mortimer's daughter-in-law, were lucky. They ended up in the Tower. The constable of Leeds and thirteen of his garrison were hanged in front of the castle gates on Edward's orders.

Mortimer now moved north to join his ally the Earl of Lancaster, but in December the Marchers were forced to return to their own lands, which were threatened both by the Welsh, who had taken advantage of the situation to begin raiding, and the King, who was gathering an army at Cirencester. While Isabella kept Christmas at Langley, Edward, accompanied by his half-brothers Edmund and Thomas, led his troops north along the bank of the Severn, crossing at Shrewsbury in mid-January. Assailed from both sides, the Marcher resistance crumbled and Mortimer's men began to desert. By 22 January Mortimer and his nephew were in chains, and the remaining contrariant castles were quickly taken. For once, Edward had proved himself a shrewd and dynamic commander, but he had displayed these qualities with a total disregard for the law and the need for consensus among his magnates. In the background, Archbishop Reynolds had been working to overturn the Despensers' sentence, and by mid-January father and son were back in England, though Edward did not issue their formal recall for some weeks. The only lord with any power left to object to the reinstatement was Lancaster and, bolstered by his uncharacteristic success against Mortimer, Edward now officially named the Earl as a rebel and pursued him north.

Again, Isabella played her part. She ordered provisions for the castles of York and Carlisle and, according to the Reading chronicler, wrote to the sheriffs of Westmoreland and Yorkshire asking them to move troops to the south to halt Lancaster who, with the royal army behind him, was making for Scotland. Lancaster had been involved in negotiations with Robert the Bruce and his messenger had been granted two safe-conducts by the Scots. This treachery, discovered when Edward's forces raided his abandoned castle of Tutbury, played perfectly into the King's hands.

The period known as the 'tyranny' of Edward II began with the battle of Boroughbridge on 16 March 1322. After a day's fighting, Lancaster surrendered and was tried as a traitor in his own castle of Pontefract. Edward had waited a long time to avenge the death of Gaveston, and Lancaster was sentenced to the full, horrific penalty of hanging, drawing and quartering before Edward conceded that, out of respect for his rank, he might be beheaded. Even so, to execute a great earl set a dangerous precedent. Lancaster died, contemptuously forced to kneel in the direction of Scotland, on 22 March, and in the following days Edward suppressed any remaining rebels with punishments so severe that no one was tempted to rise against him. Over a hundred people were executed, banished or imprisoned, and the Despensers profited eagerly from fines and sequestered lands. In early May, at York, where Isabella had joined him, Edward had the satisfaction of hearing the hated ordinances finally repealed. 'The harshness of the King has increased so much,' commented the *Vita Edwardi Secundi*, 'that no one ... dares to cross his will. The nobles of the realm are terrified by threats and penalties ... whatever pleases the King, though lacking in reason, has the force of law.' Edward was now free to lavish favour on the Despensers, and made Despenser the elder Earl of Winchester, but increasingly it was Hugh the younger who was seen as dominating the King. Indeed, it was Hugh, people said, who was the true governor of the country.

As Hugh became more and more powerful, Isabella slipped from what narrow place she held in Edward's affections. Robert of Reading claimed that the King's 'illicit and sinful unions' caused him to reject the Queen, and it does appear that sexual relations between them ceased after 1321, as Joan was Isabella's last child. But it cannot be inferred from this that Edward and Hugh were having a sexual relationship. The King's accounts for this period show no evidence that Edward was anything other than heterosexual in his tastes, and if he was having an affair, it could equally well have been with Hugh's wife, his niece Eleanor de Clare. Incestuous adultery was certainly 'sinful and illicit', and Eleanor had always been treated very generously by Edward. In 1319, he ordered medicines for her when she was ill, and sugar to make sweets; later he gave her a present of caged goldfinches and, along with money for her expenses, a significant present of one hundred marks. Historians keen to see Edward as homosexual have interpreted these gifts as Edward 'buying off' his lover's wife, but the alternative explanation, that Hugh was prepared to countenance the relationship in order to maintain his hold over the King, is just as plausible. It should also be remembered that Edward had an illegitimate son, Adam, who fought (and died) with him on the Scottish campaign in 1322. Obviously homosexual men can and do have children, but the fact that Edward had willingly entered into a heterosexual relationship, as opposed to confining himself to doing his duty with Isabella, suggests that he had been attracted to women when younger, and perhaps still was. Maybe he was attracted to both men and women. The nature of Edward's sexuality is far from clear; what is relevant, as has been noted, is the way in which it was perceived and the implications drawn by contemporaries with regard to its effect on his kingship. When the time came, Isabella would be able to play on the sympathy of those who sensed there was something unsavoury about the relationship between Edward and Hugh, and she manipulated her position as a slighted wife to great effect.

It was not long after Boroughbridge that Isabella began to feel herself persecuted by Hugh Despenser. His plans for the future may have included his own wife, but there was no place for the King's. Isabella was both inconvenient and irrelevant, and as soon as his enemies were destroyed, Hugh allowed her to feel it. He stopped bothering to pay her the 200 pounds a year he owed her for the farm of Bristol, and the two castles she had made over during the contrariant uprising were not returned. Worse was to come. In a curious parallel to Gaveston's flight in 1313, Isabella once again found herself abandoned at Tynemouth Priory while Edward escaped with his favourite. The King had pompously marched into Scotland in August 1322, but by October it was plain that this time he would not even be able to raise a battle, as Bruce's forces had so devastated the countryside that the only available provision was a single elderly cow. Edward recrossed the border to muster more troops and supplies, and was with Despenser at Rievaulx monastery when the news came that the Scots had advanced as far as nearby Northallerton. Isabella and Eleanor de Clare were at Tynemouth, and their husbands rushed off to York, leaving them at the mercy of Bruce's advancing army. Edward wrote Isabella two shoddy letters, assuring her weakly that he was sending men to protect her, but the Scots were closer than the relief troops, and the Queen of England had no one to defend her but the knights of her household. Swiftly, a ship was commandeered and, after a dreadful voyage, during which one of her ladies drowned, Isabella landed at Scarborough. While Edward and Hugh were running away, Bruce had seized the royal treasure abandoned by Edward at Rievaulx and concluded his campaign by defeating the English at Byland. Not only did Isabella have to bear the shame of her husband's cowardice and incompetence, but it had been proved once more that Edward cared more for his favourite than for his wife.

When war broke out with France in 1324, Hugh's attack on Isabella's resources continued. Philip V had died in 1322, to be succeeded by Isabella's youngest brother, Charles IV. Charles immediately requested that the English monarch come to France to pay homage, but Edward used the situation in his kingdom as an excuse, and Charles agreed to postpone the ceremony for two years. When the time came, fighting had erupted in the Agenais, and in the face of Edward's continued refusal to perform the homage, Charles threatened to invade Gascony. When Edward sent his younger half-brother, Edmund, Earl of Kent, to Gascony as his lieutenant, Kent suffered numerous defeats by the French and was gulled into signing a truce which left much of the territory in Charles's hands. Isabella's position as a foreigner was used against her, and her estates were sequestered (as Queen Marguerite's had been in 1317) but, unlike Marguerite, Isabella received no compensation. Edward had ceased to pay certain debts to his wife that spring, and now her allowance was reduced to just 1,000 marks annually. Parliament then ordered the expulsion of all French subjects, which meant Isabella was deprived of members of her household, some of whom had accompanied her to England and had been with her ever since her marriage. Twenty-seven of her servants who dared to remain were imprisoned. In October, Edward diverted her queens-gold to his own household. Isabella was now dependent on Despenser's goodwill for her maintenance, as officially payments to her were now to be managed by the exchequer, which in practice meant that the Despensers doled out her allowance as they saw fit.

Isabella wrote angrily to her brother, describing her condition as no better than that of a maidservant, but Edward was deaf to any remonstrance. Smarting over the invasion of Gascony, he had another reason to resent Charles: the French King was harbouring England's most wanted man, Roger Mortimer. In August 1323, Mortimer had made an adventurous escape from captivity in the Tower, involving drugged wine, a secret passage, rope ladders and a hidden boat. To explain her brother's willing-ness to harbour the rebel, it has been suggested that Isabella was in some way privy to Mortimer's plan, but this is to overstate the inferences that may be drawn from the evidence. Although Charles and Edward were not yet officially at war, relations were contentious, and Charles had every reason to keep a rebel baron about him as a potentially useful card to play in the future. (Agnes Strickland's claim that Isabella and Mortimer were already lovers at this point and that it was the Queen who provided the sleeping draught used to overpower Mortimer's guards is a good story, but nonsense.)

As England and France prepared to fight, Pope John XXII suggested that Isabella go to her brother to attempt to find a peaceful resolution. The Pope was aware of the attacks Despenser had made on Isabella's prestige, and had written a stern letter condemning him for sowing discord between princes. Isabella was 'pleased to visit her native land and her relatives, delighted to leave the company of some whom she did not like',[8] and when she departed for her brother's court in March 1325, it was already believed by many that she would not return as long as Hugh held sway in England. That the French embassy marked the beginning of Isabella's political prominence is attested to by the *Vita Edwardi Secundi*. Interestingly, having been almost entirely absent for three quarters of the chronicle, from this period Isabella gradually moves towards centre stage and becomes the chief protagonist, dramatically holding England's fate in her hands.

Froissart gives a moving, if somewhat embroidered, account of Isabella's reunion with her brother, who refused to allow her to kneel to him and 'took great pity on her' for 'all the injuries and felonies committed by Sir Hugh'. Charles welcomed his sister with every courtesy, and on 1 April the English Queen made a formal entry into Paris, fashionably dressed in a voluminous black velvet riding habit, black-and-white checked boots and a spun-gold headdress. The peace treaty signed in June was not a notable triumph for Isabella, as her attempts to encourage Charles to reach a settlement were no more successful than those of any other envoy, but he did agree, it was said out of affection for his sister, to prolong the truce until August. Officially, her task was now accomplished, and there was nothing to prevent her from going home – indeed, the English exchequer stopped paying her considerable expenses in mid-June – but Isabella clearly had no intention of returning to her degraded conditions under Despenser. Instead she spent the summer touring the royal properties in the Ile de France, including St Germain, Fontainebleau and Châteauneuf. Possibly she expected to join Edward, for the payment of the overdue homage had been implicit in the terms of the extended truce, and it had been decided that the ceremony would take place at Beauvais, but Edward, too, was prevaricating. The rapacious Despensers were now so unpopular that they feared losing the King's protection if he left England – in his absence 'they would not know where to live safely'[9] – and they persuaded him to make yet another excuse, this time that he had fallen ill and could not travel.

The previous year, Charles had suggested that Prince Edward might be sent to perform the homage in his father's place, and now Isabella realised that she had a means of redressing the balance of power against the Despensers. She held a dinner for John de Stratford, the bishop of Winchester, who then put her suggestion to Charles and, with his agreement, returned to England with a safe-conduct for the Prince. Pleased that her plan enabled the King to remain in England, the favourites were stupid enough to fall for it. Though other magnates voiced misgivings, the Despensers' word ruled, and the boy was duly invested as Duke of Aquitaine, to allow him to perform the homage, before sailing for France on 12 September. Mother and son were reunited at Boulogne and, despite the King's strict instructions that they were to depart for England as soon as the ceremony was over, Edward was never to see his wife again.

On the Prince's arrival, Englishmen who objected to the Despenser regime began to coalesce around Isabella into a rebel party, among them Sir John Maltravers, a survivor of Boroughbridge, Lord Ros, the Earl of Richmond, Henry de Beaumont, Lord Cromwell, Richard de Bury and the King's half-brother Edmund of Kent. Initially, Isabella insisted that her only quarrel was with the Despensers. In November, a furious Edward ordered her home, but Isabella wrote to him declaring: 'I feel that marriage is a joining of a man and a woman, maintaining the undivided habit of life, and that someone has come between my husband and myself trying to break this bond; I protest that I will not return until this intruder is removed, but, discarding my marriage garment, shall assume the robes of widowhood and mourning until I am avenged of this Pharisee.'[10] As good as her word, the formerly fashionable Queen now adopted plain black garments and a modest veil. It was an extremely public manifestation of her self-declared status as a wronged wife, designed to call attention to her predicament and engender sympathy. Isabella was a far shrewder manipulator of public opinion than her husband. In casting herself in the role of a weak woman in need of protection, she appealed to the chivalrous ethos of her supporters and emphasised her own quasi-nun-like humility and virtue. Showing an awareness of the language of diplomacy, she even threatened Edward, claiming that she and her sympathisers had no wish to do anything that would be prejudicial to him and that any action they found it necessary to take would pertain solely to Hugh's destruction. Essentially, she was warning Edward that she could raise the forces to invade if he did not get rid of the Despensers.

The situation was now so serious that Edward had to address Parliament on the matter of his wife's continued absence. Isabella had declared that she feared for her life if the Despensers got their hands on her, and Edward tried to counter this allegation by maintaining that she had not seemed 'offended' with Hugh when she departed, but that now '. . . someone has changed her attitude. Someone has primed her with inventions. For I know she has not fabricated any affront out of her own head. Yet she says that Hugh Despenser is her adversary and hostile to her.'[11] Edward went on to claim that Hugh was surprised and hurt by the Queen's behaviour, but that he was prepared to prove his innocence. Isabella's refusal to return was now a public scandal and, at Edward's urging, the bishops of England wrote to her, reminding her of her duty: 'Most dear and potent Lady, the whole country is disturbed by your news and the answers which you have lately sent to our Lord King: and because you delay your return out of hatred for Hugh Despenser everyone predicts that much evil will follow.' Hugh's defence is repeated, and the letter goes on:

Wherefore, dearest Lady, I beseech you as my Lady, I warn you as a daughter to return to our Lord King, your husband, putting aside rancour. You who have gone away for the sake of peace, do not for the sake of peace delay to return. For all the inhabitants of our land fear that many evils will result from your refusal to return . . . Alas! If things turn out thus it may happen that we shall regard as a stepmother her whom we hoped to have as patron. Alas! Clergy and people with complaining voice reiterate their fear that they and theirs will be utterly destroyed through the hatred felt for one man. Wherefore, my Lady Queen, accept wise counsel and do not delay your return. For your longed-for arrival I will restrain the malice of men and restrict all opportunities for evil.[12]

The language of the letter is interesting in the way it formulates Isabella's position when the King is confronted with the prospect of her power. She is reminded of her duty as wife, lady and queen, but also as 'daughter', and threatened with the prospect of becoming a wicked stepmother instead of a good mother or 'patron'. The bishops' plea is in effect a reversal of the intercession trope – the male supplicating, the female resisting – and the focus on the Queen's various feminine roles may be read as an order to demonstrate her abandonment of the power she has adopted and return to those offices. In other words, the bishops were telling Isabella to act like a woman. Their request forms the last section of the *Vita Edwardi Secundi*. Ominously, the writer concludes: 'But notwithstanding this letter, mother and son refused to return to England.'

What were Isabella's intentions as 1325 drew to its close? Her meetings with disaffected Englishmen suggest that her previous loyalty to the royalist cause had been seriously undermined by her determination to oust the Despensers, but was she planning, or being urged on to, more drastic action? In December, she attended the funeral of her uncle, Charles of Valois, in Paris, where among her gathered relatives she met her cousin, Valois's daughter Jeanne of Hainault. Roger Mortimer had been in the county of Hainault on the Flemish border, for the past year, attempting to rally support for an invasion of England, and the acceptance of his presence by the Count and Countess lends credence to the idea that Jeanne proposed an alliance to Isabella. In return for reviving the idea of marriage between Isabella's son Prince Edward and one of Jeanne's daughters, which had been considered in 1319, and an agreement of trading regulations between their two countries, the Count of Hainault would provide the Queen with troops and funds. Isabella had no mandate to negotiate Edward's marriage, and the boy had promised his father that he would accept no such union without the English King's permission. If a Hainault affiance was mooted at this juncture, Isabella may well already have been considering replacing her husband with her son. The reappearance of Mortimer proved a catalyst to her decision.

Mortimer had arrived in Paris in December, possibly accompanying Countess Jeanne, and it was not long before it was common knowledge that 'Mortimer secretly came first in the household of the Queen'.[13] Isabella was not the first English queen to be accused of adultery, nor would she be the last, but she is unique in being the only one of them to live flagrantly with her lover. The scandal was such that the relationship was largely referred to in the most discreet, euphemistic terms, but by the following February, Edward himself was obliged, albeit obliquely, to acknowledge it. In February, mustering troops to set a guard on the coast of England, the King declared: 'The Queen will not come to the King, nor permit his son to return, and the King understands that she is adopting the counsel of the Mortimer, the King's notorious enemy and rebel, and that she is making alliances with the men of those parts and with other strangers with intent to invade.'[14]

In May, Isabella showed just how much she cared for her husband's remonstrations, appearing publicly with Mortimer at the coronation of Queen Jeanne and permitting her lover the considerable honour of carrying the robes of Prince Edward. Isabella was well aware of the impact such a gesture would have on public opinion, and could only have been mindful of the conclusions that opinion would draw. It was not until July that Edward was drawn into a declaration of war, but Isabella had already made her choice, and displayed it to the world in the Saint-Chapelle.

The Queen was prepared not only to defy her husband, but the Pope. Edward had written to Rome to complain of her behaviour, and that of her brother, who was harbouring an adulteress, and the Pope had written to the King of France in no uncertain terms, threatening him with excommunication if he continued to support his sister. Publicly, Charles was obliged to censure Isabella, and ordered her out of his kingdom. Isabella and Mortimer decided that Hainault should become the base from which they would launch the attack on Edward. Isabella made her way there via Ponthieu, and was busy in the county throughout much of August, making use of her dower lands to raise money and support in her own affinity. She spent eight days at the court of the Count and Countess of Hainault at Valenciennes and on 27 August, at Mons, she signed an agreement for her son's betrothal to one of the Count's daughters, requesting a dowry of men, money and ships and promising to hold the wedding within two years and to ratify a new trade agreement between the countries. Already she was acting like a ruler.

Isabella's invading army was small (the largest estimate is 2,500 men, the smallest 500), but oddly, this proved to be one of its strengths. Isabella had been corresponding with English magnates who resented the Despensers' power and had been assured of the support of the earls of Leicester and Norfolk. When news of her arrival reached Edward and Hugh Despenser as they were dining in the Tower, it was her very lack of troops that dismayed them. 'Alas, alas!' reports the *Brut Chronicle*, 'We be all betrayed, for certain with so little power she had never come to land but folk of this country had to her consented.' After a stormy crossing, in weather so violent that the ships were lost for two days, Isabella had reached the Essex coast on 24 September 1326, spending her first night on dry land in a tent made of carpets. The Earl of Norfolk, Edward's half-brother Thomas, then escorted her to his castle at Walton-on-the-Naze. From there she made her way, via Bury St Edmunds and Cambridge, to Oxford, which she reached on 2 October. Meeting no resistance, she then turned back to Baldock, where she issued a letter to the citizens of London, offering a reward of 2,000 pounds for Hugh Despenser's head and calling on the people to support her in effecting his downfall. The letter was displayed for the public at the Eleanor cross in Cheapside, a significant choice of monument in that it associated Isabella with this emblem of pious queenship, her husband's mother, suggesting that her actions were maintaining her fealty to her marital family and seeking to establish the rights of the true heir of Edward I.

By 15 October, Isabella was at Wallingford, where she put out a proclamation condemning the Despensers and explaining her plans. Despenser had 'tarnished and degraded' the country, 'usurped royal power against law and justice' and despoiled and dishonoured the Church. 'We,' announced Isabella,

> ... who have long been kept far from the goodwill of our Lord the King through the false suggestions and evil dealings of the aforesaid Hugh ... are come to this land to raise up the state of Holy church and of the kingdom and of the people of this land, against the said misdeeds and oppressions, and to safeguard and maintain so far as we can the honour and profit of our Holy Church and of our said Lord the King ... For this reason we ask and pray you, for the common good of all and each of you individually, that you come to our help well and loyally ... For be assured that we all, and all those who are in our company, intend to do nothing that does not redound to the honour and profit of the Holy Church and the whole kingdom ... [15]

Officially, Isabella was careful to insist that she was acting as a loyal subject whose only aim was to cleanse the kingdom of the canker of the Despensers.

Edward's attempts at mustering a campaign force provided dismal proof of the unpopularity of his favourite. On learning on 27 September of Isabella's arrival, he attempted to raise resistance in London and had a papal bull proscribing invaders – it had actually been intended for use against the Scots – read at St Paul's Cross. It was heard in telling silence. He wrote to Charles of France, to the Pope and to the university of Oxford; he sought out supporters in the countryside around London and sent envoys to Wales and East Anglia. When none of this produced much of a result, the King left London with as much money as he could carry and a small group of archers and made for the Despenser lands in Wales. En route, he tried once more to summon troops at Gloucester, but again met with very little success.

As Isabella issued her proclamation at Wallingford, riots broke out in

London. The Tower was seized from Despenser's wife, Eleanor de Clare, and Isabella's ten-year-old son John of Eltham was installed as nominal warden. Any Despenser supporters were threatened, the mayor was forced to declare for Isabella at the Guildhall and Hugh's clerk, John the Marshal, was torn to pieces. In the first in a series of horrible executions, Bishop Stapledon was beheaded with a knife at the Eleanor cross. His head was transported to Gloucester, which was by then in Isabella's hands. According to some reports she received it with the relish of a latter-day Salome. By 18 October, the Queen's forces were besieging Bristol, the headquarters of Despenser the elder. The town fell after a week and Isabella was reunited with her two daughters, Eleanor and Joan, who had been living in Despenser's household in their mother's absence. Her manifest joy at recovering her children did not distract her from her pursuit of her enemies, however, and the day she entered Bristol, Despenser the elder, who was tried without right of reply (as the Earl of Lancaster had been) was sentenced to be hanged immediately. His body was given no burial, but was reputedly chopped to pieces and eaten by dogs.

Edward and Hugh Despenser had travelled from Gloucester to Chepstow, arriving a few days before the fall of Bristol. Exhausted and desperate, they set off in a boat, possibly intending to make for Ireland, or simply for Lundy, the little island held by Despenser in the Bristol Channel. But the weather was against them, and they were forced to put back in at Cardiff after four days. This brief voyage, though, was all Isabella needed. Technically, the King had forsaken the country. In council at Bristol on 26 October, fourteen-year-old Prince Edward was made Keeper of the Realm. Edward's Privy Seal was given to Isabella's clerk, Robert Wyville, and she was now in a position to authorise acts in his name.

By mid-November, Edward was an isolated fugitive. Apart from Despenser, there had been only seven men with him when he was taken near Llantrisant in Glamorgan on 16 November. Despenser was immediately sent to Hereford, where Isabella had been staying since the beginning of the month. He tried to cheat her of her revenge by maintaining a hunger strike after his arrest, and at his trial on 24 November he was barely conscious as the long list of charges against him was read out. Two aspects of Despenser's grisly end signal that his accusers were keen to highlight the corrupt sexual nature of his relationship with the King. While the Queen was at Oxford the previous year, Bishop Orleton had preached a sermon in which he accused Edward of sodomy, the first time such allegations had been made so explicitly. He repeated them three weeks later at Wallingford, adding that Isabella was in fear of her life from

Edward, who claimed to carry a knife about him with which to kill her. Among the charges against Hugh, which he was not permitted to answer, was one of maliciously interfering with the royal marriage. And a refinement was added to his hideous traitor's death of being hung, drawn and quartered: castration. His genitals were then burned before his eyes as Isabella watched. In conjuring this gruesomely symbolic connection between Despenser's penis and Edward's knife it was clear what Isabella wanted people to understand about Hugh's crimes. Despenser's execution in Hereford marketplace before a bawling crowd presents a repugnant image of Isabella, a vampiric, castrating beauty looking on impassively as her rival is literally hacked into spewing pieces. His head was delivered to London and lumps of his body distributed around the country.

Having disposed of Hugh, Isabella's final challenge was to replace the rule of her husband with that of her son. But how could such an unprecedented revolution be brought about? She had been exercising official authority since writs had been issued in the names of the Queen and Prince Edward at Hereford in October. Bishop Orleton had been charged with recovering the Great Seal from the King, who was held first at Monmouth Castle then moved to Kenilworth. From 30 November, when Isabella and Edward were made joint Keepers of the Great Seal, the Queen was able to make out writs in her own name. Christmas was kept at Wallingford, where Isabella was at last able to see all her children together, and Parliament was summoned at Westminster for 7 January. At this juncture, there was nothing to prevent Edward II being restored to both his realm and his wife, but though Isabella scrupulously maintained her façade of acting legally and in the King's name, this was obviously the last thing she intended. There was some doubt as to whether it was legally possible to summon Parliament without the King. Isabella put out a story that she had sent two deputations of bishops to Kenilworth to ask Edward to join the session, but that he had responded by cursing them 'contemptuously' and 'declaring that he would not come among his enemies'.[16] Empowered by this convenient refusal, and whipped in by Mortimer, members of the Lords and Commons consented to attend the Guildhall, where the new mayor of London had invited them to swear an oath of loyalty to Isabella and the Prince, to depose Edward II and crown his son.

In November, Isabella had communicated with the Londoners proposing that they elect a new mayor to replace the unpopular 'royalist' Hamo de Chigwell. The man they had chosen was one Richard de Bethune, an old crony of Mortimer's. One theory about Mortimer's escape from the Tower in 1323 has Bethune among the prominent

Londoners who helped him. Certainly Bethune was Mortimer's man and it would be interesting to know how big a part Mortimer's influence played in his election. Isabella and Mortimer recognised that the support of London would be imperative if they wished to push through the deposition of the anointed king, and Bethune was ideally placed to help them paint a gloss of legality over the solemn pantomime of the January Parliament. The consent of the capital would suffice to present their actions as an expression of the common will, and the clamour for the deposition has been described as having 'a distinct London accent'.[7] In return, the oath sworn at the Guildhall included a promise to respect the liberties of the city, and in March 1327 it was granted a charter exempting citizens from the military service whose obligations had provoked such resentment of Edward II.

After the oath-swearing, the sitting resumed at Westminster. Archbishop Reynolds, the clerk for whom Edward had once petitioned a prebend, preached a stirring sermon, then declared that Edward II was deposed, to cries of enthusiasm. A list of Articles of Deposition was read aloud, then Prince Edward was led in and presented as the new King. Queen Isabella was in floods of tears, whether of joy or of sorrow who could say? Several chronicles now concur that the prospective Edward III, misunderstanding his mother's sobs, threw a spanner in the works by refusing to accept the crown in his father's lifetime without his consent. The writers in question were working some time after the events, and though it was obviously preferable that Edward III should be seen to have acted with absolute probity, there is no more reason to suppose that he refused the crown than there is to accept that his imprisoned father refused to come to Parliament. Isabella and Mortimer were making up procedure as they went along. There was no post-Conquest pattern for the deposition of an English king, as no one had ever done it. The processions, deputations, ceremonies and oath-swearings were little more than improvisations, and the roles of the players – sorrowing wife, reluctant prince – were part of the masquerade.

At Kenilworth on 20 January 1327, Edward was informed by Bishop Orleton that unless he accepted the 'invitation' to renounce the throne in recognition of the charges in the Articles of Deposition, he risked his son's inheritance. It was even hinted that Mortimer himself might be invited to take the crown (though the Earl of Lancaster might have had something to say about that), but again, the reports of such persuasions may have been made to give Edward a noble motive for renunciation. Dressed in black, sobbing and finally fainting, Edward gave his consent. The reign of his son officially began five days later. On 30 January, at York, Edward III was married, as his mother had arranged, to the Count of Hainault's daughter Philippa, who had arrived in England in December, and on 1 February he was crowned at Westminster.

However one judges Isabella's methods, and the degree of Mortimer's involvement in her achievements, she had managed to do something practically unthinkable: to depose an anointed king. Her journey from passive, obedient daughter to dutiful wife to vengeful lover required an extraordinary personal transformation, and whether she is celebrated or condemned, she remains exceptional. She had outsmarted the Despensers and succeeded in escaping to France, she had employed diplomacy and raised an invading army, pursued a campaign and seen her son crowned while his father lived. Throughout she had remained alert to the importance of public opinion and had attempted as far as possible to control her 'image' so that she would be perceived sympathetically. If history has been very hard on Isabella, recent attempts to rehabilitate her reputation have veered too far towards the positive. Just because she was brave, intelligent and resourceful does not mean that she could not be devious, ruthless and cruel. And now she was faced with one final problem. What was to be done with her husband?

The answer forms one of the most notorious episodes in English history. In September 1327, Edward II died in Berkeley Castle. Of two contemporary accounts, the *Annales Paulini* is terse: 'The same year, on the Eve of St Matthew ... King Edward ... died in Berkeley Castle where he was held in custody.'

Adam Murimuth gives more detail: 'Afterwards on 22nd September 1327 died Edward King of England in Berkeley Castle, in which as was said before, he was committed to prison or detained unwillingly. And although many abbots, priors, knights and burgesses of Bristol and Gloucester were called to view the body whole and so looked at it superficially, nevertheless it was commonly said that by the orders of John Maltravers and Thomas Gourney he was craftily killed.'

These two reports initiated a deluge of speculation, incrimination and downright fabrication, including the famous detail of Edward being murdered by having a heated poker inserted into his anus. By the time Geoffrey le Baker was writing a generation later, the poker had become 'a plumber's iron, heated red hot [applied] through a horn leading to the privy part of the bowel'. This is the version immortalised by Christopher Marlowe in his glorious tragedy *Edward II*. Edward's death has given rise to a parlour game of historical supposition, and at least two theories that propose he did not in fact die at Berkeley have received serious scholarly attention since the last quarter of the nineteenth century.[18] Neither of these, however, proves conclusively that he was not killed at Berkeley, and scholars have also been attentive to the way in which reports of his death were produced, disseminated and manipulated for changing political purposes. In Isabella's lifetime and that of her son, all chroniclers (however lurid and inaccurate their accounts) agreed that the King was dead, and that he died at Berkeley. Ordinary people certainly believed he was dead, so much so that a cult grew up around his tomb at Gloucester and proved so popular that it financed the rebuilding of the south transept and persisted until the sixteenth century.

In the spring of 1328, Isabelle and Mortimer negotiated the treaty of Northampton with the Scots. With Edward II disposed of they were now in a position to reconfigure England's role in international politics, and they reasoned that a settlement with Scotland was a necessary step. In February, Isabella's last surviving brother, Charles IV, had died, leaving Queen Jeanne pregnant. If the child were a girl, the English argued that legally the French crown should go to Edward III. The French Queen did indeed give birth to a daughter that April. In Parliament in May, Isabella and Mortimer argued that peace with Scotland was intrinsic to Edward's claim to France, but the treaty, signed earlier in the month, was loathed by both the new King and his people. The independence of Scotland was recognised and the border restored to its limits under Alexander III, which left a group of English peers, known as the 'Disinherited', deprived of the land they had held on the marches. Robert the Bruce agreed to pay 20,000 marks compensation (which Isabella and Mortimer promptly spent) and to the marriage of his son David to Isabella's six-year-old daughter Joan. Edward III was so appalled by this 'shameful peace' that he refused to attend the wedding, which took place on 16 July. He also baulked at returning the Stone of Scone, one of the provisions of the treaty, and popular feeling was reflected in the riot that ensued when the abbot of Westminster, on Isabella's orders, tried to give it up.

On 14 April an assembly of the twelve peers of France elected Philip de Valois, Isabella's cousin, as their King. The Plantagenet claim to the French crown has often been seen as an artifice, a mere prop to territorial aggression, but Edward's legal position in 1328 is worth considering, not only in relation to the conflict which became known as the Hundred Years War, but in terms of his relationship with his mother and his actions in 1330. The notion of Salic law, whereby women were excluded from dynastic succession, was not quite as entrenched in French practice in the fourteenth century as is commonly assumed; indeed, the first reference by a Capetian writer to its application in any matter other than the transfer of private property occurs in 1413, and the two precedents for its employment were as recent as 1316 and 1322, on the deaths of Isabella's brothers Louis X and Philip V. The English argued that Edward III's standing after Charles IV's death was unique, that because this was the first occasion on which there was a proximate male heir to France whose entitlement derived from a woman, the assemblies that had produced the statutes of 1316 and 1322 were irrelevant, since they had not anticipated a cognate (i.e. maternal family) claim. This created a question which would become highly relevant to Edward III at the end of his own life. Was the claim of the son of a younger brother stronger than that of a grandson of an elder brother? In 1340, when Edward assumed the title of King of France, the English favoured the latter argument. Yet in 1328, when Edward was still a minor, he was in no position to exercise his right. Moreover, the eminently sensible decision of the French peers to choose an experienced Frenchman over an English boy was also affected by the compromising circumstances of Edward's mother. Internationally, Edward was perceived as the pawn of a pair of adulterers, a horribly humiliating role to inhabit. Added to the shame of Northampton, the election of Philip VI was another confirmation that Edward would have no control over his kingdom as long as Mortimer controlled his mother.

The relative discretion among contemporary sources on the relationship between Mortimer and Isabella does not mean that Edward was unaware of it. Between 1328 and 1330, the young King seems to have been desperately trying to balance his affection for his mother with the need to maintain some stability in the realm, but Mortimer's ambition was making this increasingly impossible. Mortimer was growing ever more unpopular, and Isabella found herself in a similar situation to that of her late husband, obliged to aggrandise her favourite to prevent his enemies from bringing him down, and heaping more disapproval on herself in the process. Mortimer was 'in such glory and honour that it was without all comparison'.[19] He sat in Edward's presence, walked and rode beside, instead of respectfully behind him, and had become 'so proud and high that he held no Lord of the realm his equal'.[20] Mortimer thoroughly alienated his former ally, Henry, Earl of Lancaster, the theoretical head of the regency council, who, along with Edward's uncles Norfolk and Kent, was horrified at his increasing power. In London, the previously loyal citizens had re-elected their former mayor Hamo de Chigwell, and in a meeting at the

Guildhall in September 1328, Isabella's extravagance was denounced and there were calls for Mortimer to be banished from court to his own estates. Mortimer's response to this was to have himself declared Earl of March by an increasingly bullied Edward, and it was once more rumoured that he himself had designs on the crown. In 1330, according to Froissart, it was whispered that the Dowager Queen was pregnant with her lover's child. Scandal and discord were making Edward's position shamefully untenable.

The King's patience collapsed when Mortimer plotted the destruction of his uncle, the Earl of Kent. Mortimer later confessed to the 'sting', in which Kent, who had never shown himself to be terribly bright, was approached by two friars and informed that Edward II was alive and living in secrecy at Corfe Castle. (The fact that Corfe was in the custody of Edward's former keeper Maltravers, and therefore possibly the least likely place for the deposed King to hide, did not stop Kent, or many subsequent writers, for that matter, from believing this tale.) Kent wrote a letter to his half-brother, reassuring him that he was planning to restore him to the throne, and gave it to two of the castle custodians, who had been instructed to send it at once to Mortimer. Kent was arrested for treason on 10 March 1330, and both Isabella and Mortimer cajoled and threatened Edward into signing his death warrant. Kent went to the scaffold at Winchester four days later. Such was the outrage at his execution that the public hangman refused to do his duty, and Edward I's son was left shivering in his shirt until a felon could be found to dispatch him.

The Earl of Lancaster had been absent from politics since January 1329 when, after a series of attempts to undermine Mortimer, he had led his own men against royal forces in Leicestershire and Warwickshire. Lancaster had submitted to the King at Bedford and withdrawn from court, though the huge fine imposed against the retention of his lands had never been paid. Lancaster had been aware of Kent's noble, if misguided conspiracy, but had not incriminated himself, though he, too, was working to overthrow Mortimer. He visited Edward on the birth of his first child in July 1330, and made another appearance for the Nottingham Parliament in October the same year. The Earl was not personally involved in the event that took place at Nottingham castle on 19 October, but twelve of the twenty-one men who helped Edward that night were his close associates, and it was Lancaster who publicly announced their success.

Edward had been planning to move against Mortimer since the summer. His close friend Sir William Montagu had advised him that it was 'better to eat dog than be eaten by the dog' and evidence from the wardrobe accounts shows that Edward acquired a set of matching aketon jackets, usually worn for tournaments, for himself and Montagu. Another batch was ordered later for supporters who had posed as members of Montagu's retinue, and at court these jackets became a very visible emblem of the 'team' which had collaborated with Edward in his liberation. On the evening of 19 October, Edward crept out of his room and opened the door to Montagu, who fought his way into the Dowager Queen's chamber, where Isabella and Mortimer were meeting with three ministers. To the delight of one chronicler, the chancellor, Bishop Burghersh, tried to make his escape down the privy shaft. Three men were killed, and Mortimer was seized by Sir John de Moleyns. Edward stayed outside the room, as it was vital that his life was safe; it was important, too, that Mortimer's should be preserved so he could stand trial. Isabella knew her son was nearby, though she could not see him, and she tried to rush for the door, crying, 'Fair son, have pity on noble Mortimer,' but was pushed inside as Mortimer was led away. At dawn, Lancaster proclaimed:

> Whereas the King's affairs and the affairs of the realm have been directed until now to the damage and dishonour of him and his realm and to the impoverishment of his people ... he wills that all men shall know that he will henceforth govern his people according to right and reason as befits his royal dignity and that the affairs that concern him and the estate of the realm shall be directed by the common counsel of the magnates of the realm and in no otherwise ... [21]

Mortimer was hanged for treason on 29 November. Isabella was sent to Berkhamsted after his arrest, but by Christmas she had joined Edward and Philippa at Windsor, where she spent the next two years under house arrest. Edward supplied her with money and permitted her to retain a household, but it was quite clear that she was in disgrace. The loathing she had provoked posed a difficulty for Edward. His French ambitions depended on his mother's respectability, and he had been urged by the Pope not to expose her shame. The recasting of Isabella's relationship with Mortimer is connected with Edward's need to rehabilitate his father's memory, and sheds much light on the vexed question of Edward II's alleged homosexuality.

The 'anal rape' narrative of Edward II's death gruesomely highlights the way in which his downfall was sexualised, and links his deposition with the atavistic correspondence of sexual potency and kingship in which the sexuality of the queen also played a potentially destabilising part.

Just as later representations of Isabella were 'demonised' to rehabilitate Edward,[22] so, in the 1320s, Edward had to be presented as sexually degenerate to provide grounds for her rule. In her reply to the bishops in 1325, Isabella had emphasised that 'someone has come between my husband and myself'. In the same way as Eleanor of Aquitaine cast doubt on Louis of France's virility to justify a divorce that was in fact desired by both parties, Isabella may have chosen to sexualise her dissatisfaction with Edward in order to rationalise not only the deposition, but her refusal to return to Edward afterwards despite the pleas of the Pope and the bishops. The fact that Edward was presented as a 'political sodomite'[23] does not of course exclude the possibility that he did engage in anal sex, but it is notable that the first reference to such acts was made in the sermon preached by Isabella's ally Bishop Orleton in 1326, in which he referred to Edward as 'a tyrant and a sodomite'. That Edward was obsessed with Piers Gaveston and loved him, in whatever manner, seems beyond doubt, but the specific nature of his relationship with Gaveston, and, by implication, Despenser and others, may be 'entirely and exclusively due to the sermons which Adam of Orleton preached in 1326'.[24] Of the fourteen chronicles that suggest Edward was murdered, eight specifically mention the story of the red-hot horn or poker (though the Bridlington writer claims not to believe it), and of these eight, all were written after 1333.

However Edward II died – and in fact, if only for reasons of practicality and discretion, it is unlikely to have been at the end of an iron brand – the fictionalised versions of his demise may be interpreted in a variety of ways that illustrate contemporary anxieties about the role Isabella played in his deposition. Some scholars have seen the anal rape narrative as a grisly poetic justice, playing on Orleton's unsubstantiated accusations of sodomy to fashion a fitting end for a degenerate King and to shore up Isabella's legitimacy as a ruler. However, given the timing of the story's emergence and its source in the northern and Midlands writers (no London chronicler mentions it), it may also be interpreted as evidence of Isabella's unspeakable, unfeminine cruelty in the context of opposition to her governance from 1329. In this light, the account serves as both an explanation of and a balance to Edward's deposition, preserving the royal dignity to some extent by affirming that the office of King could be attacked only by extreme, inhuman violence, but also locating the King's vulnerability in his own unmasculine practices. Thus, even if the story is read as anti-Isabella, it still confirms Edward's unfitness to rule.

After Mortimer's downfall, Edward's death took on different connotations. Edward III was faced with the need to play down his mother's role in the scandal and simultaneously recover the 'masculinity' of his office. The heterosexual normality of the royal marriage therefore had to be emphasised, but if his father was to be portrayed as sinned against, it left Isabella as the sinner. The solution was to represent Isabella in a more traditional feminine role, as a weak woman led astray by a vile seducer: 'To suggest, as was now done in 1330, that Mortimer had prevented a reconciliation between the royal partners was to ascribe to him the dominant role in the adulterous affair.'[25] The records of Mortimer's trial are discreet about his relationship with Isabella, but one of the charges states: 'The said Roger falsely and maliciously sowed discord between the father of our Lord King and the Queen his companion ... Wherefore by this cause and other subtleties, the Queen remained absent from her said Lord, to the great dishonour of the King and of his mother.' By representing Mortimer as the guilty party and Isabella as his victim, the Queen was confined to an appropriately submissive role, and the regency conflict reconfigured as an assertion of the King's rights over a rebellious male subject.

Some writers accept that a Norman French poem, known as the 'Song' or 'Lament' of King Edward, was in fact written by Edward II himself during his captivity. In conventional language, the poem reflects on the cruelty of fortune:

> The chiefest sorrow of my state
> Springs from Isabelle the fair
> She that I loved but now must hate
> I held her true, now faithless she;
> Steeped in deceit, my deadly foe
> Brings naught but black despair to me
> And all my joy she turns to woe.[26]

Adversity can produce surprising capacities, but it is debatable, to put it mildly, that the ditch-digging King became a poet in Berkeley Castle. The 'Lament' may more plausibly be seen as a product of the court of Edward III. While the poem emphasises Isabella's guilt, it also casts Edward in the role of the courtly – heterosexual – lover, and may be interpreted as 'a kind of admonition to Isabella to accept her subordinate status following the coup of 1330'.[27]

After her release from Windsor, Isabella lived mainly at Castle Rising, which had been built by Adeliza of Louvain's widower William d'Aubigne around 1150, and which Isabella had bought from the widow of Robert de Montalt, one of her supporters during the deposition, in 1327. Initially, she spent little time in London, though she travelled between Eltham and Havering and was present in the capital on a few special occasions. She continued to correspond with Edward about her lands, and in January 1344 was at Westminster on estate business. In November that year she was at the Tower to welcome Edward back from France. Relations with Edward were cordial: they celebrated his birthday together at least twice, once at Castle Rising (Isabella called in eight carpenters to make ready for the visit), and in 1341 Edward ordered a daily Mass to be said for his mother in the chapel at Leeds Castle. Isabella participated in family events such as the Mass for the Round Table feast at Windsor in 1344 and in 1354 she kept Christmas at Berkhamsted with her eldest grandson, Edward, known as the Black Prince.

Isabella's household accounts show that at the end of her life, far from being marginalised, she had been restored to a prestigious diplomatic position. In September 1356 the Black Prince defeated the French at Poitiers, and the French King, Jean, was taken prisoner. He remained in English custody, on the most chivalrous of terms, until 1358. One consequence of Poitiers was the release of King David of Scotland, who returned home after more than ten years with his mistress, Kate Mortimer, in tow. His Queen, Edward III's sister Joan, was so disgusted that she returned to England, where Edward gave her the castle of Hertford in 1357 and an allowance of 200 pounds. Hertford had been in Isabella's possession since 1327, and she had stayed at the castle in the 1340s. Now she and Joan were able to spend much time there together.

In October 1357, Isabella left Hertford on pilgrimage for Canterbury, and on her return entertained Edward, Queen Philippa and the Black Prince at her new house in London. In November and December, she received many high-ranking members of King Jean's entourage, including Jacques de Bourbon, Comte de la Marche, the Comte de Tancarville, Hankyn de Oreby, the marshal of France, Arnaud d'Audrehem, and the seneschal of Toulouse, Regnaut d'Aubigny. She also lent the French King two romances, *The Holy Grail* and, appropriately, *Sir Lancelot*. The royal family kept Christmas at Marlborough, but Isabella remained at home, nearer to London, and the accounts show she kept the feast in style. Her role at this point appears to have been as a mediator in the peace process and the discussions over Jean's ransom. In February, the two main negotiators on these issues in Parliament were her guests Tancarville and Audrehem. While Parliament was in session, Edward and Philippa were staying at King's Langley, and Isabella's base at Hertford conveniently placed her halfway between the King and Westminster. In April, Tancarville was Isabella's guest in London, and on the nineteenth she dined with the chancellor and the treasurer, then held a meeting with Edward and the Black Prince. They all joined the Queen and the royal children for what was the most significant diplomatic and cultural event of the decade, the Garter Feast on St George's Day.

Isabella was not present for the signing of the eventual peace treaty, in which Jean agreed to a ransom of four million gold crowns and recognised Edward III's claims to Isabella's dower counties of Ponthieu and Montreuil, as well as Gascony, Guisnes and Calais. Isabella heard the news in a letter from Queen Philippa on 10 May, and was so delighted she rewarded the messenger with ten crowns. She and Philippa had a celebratory dinner together the next day and on 13 May she entertained the King of France. Isabella's status may have been 'subordinate', but it was certainly not negligible. Nor does it show any sign of mental instability. Nineteenth-century writers depicted a deranged Isabella, howling her sins from the battlements of Castle Rising, but though physician's bills from the first phase of a confinement at Windsor suggest she may have had some sort of nervous collapse after Mortimer's execution, her subsequent activities are very much those of the active, intelligent woman she had always been.

This is not to suggest that Isabella was not penitent. As she grew older, her household acounts show that she had not relinquished her passion for jewellery or given up music or wine, but she was increasingly attentive to spiritual matters. She undertook frequent pilgrimages, including a last visit to Canterbury with her daughter Queen Joan a few months before her death, acquired religious relics, such as a ring which belonged to St Dunstan, and developed her family association with the Franciscans. In 1344, the Pope granted her request for the admission of William of Pudding Norton and twelve other priests to benefices without examination. The fact that the pontiff was prepared to accept Isabella's judgement indicates that her public pieties had gone some way to restoring her reputation.[28] During her period of government with Mortimer, her extravagance and rapacity had been infamous; now, under the guidance of the Franciscan rule, she took a greater interest in the poor. Thirteen poor people were fed each day at her expense and three more on Mondays, Fridays and Saturdays, while she distributed alms to 150 on holy days of obligation and maintained a number of 'poor scholars' at Oxford University. Fourteen paupers were paid twopence a day to pray over her corpse as it lay in state and five were given robes and money by her son to pray for her soul.

Isabella's most distinctive act of contrition was her request to be laid to rest in her wedding cloak alongside a silver casket containing Edward II's heart. Her funeral procession through London three months after her death, on 27 November 1358, was accorded all the dignity befitting a widowed queen. She was interred at Greyfrairs, where Marguerite of France already lay and where Queen Joan of Scotland would be buried, as would Edward III's daughter Isabella. The Dowager Queen's tomb therefore became honoured element of a commemorative site for Plantagenet women. Although her reputation has until recently been almost universally maligned, her queenship was in many ways a success. She deposed a dreadful king and replaced him with an exceptional one. She has been blamed for starting the Hundred Years War, but it was not her vanity that prosecuted it, and it should not be forgotten that the English pursuit of the French crown into the fifteenth century produced Crécy, Poitiers and Agincourt, which, fairly or not, have contributed more to the reputation of English kings and the English identity than the forgotten corpses of its battlefields. Perhaps Isabella was a bad woman, but she was rather a magnificent queen.

CHAPTER 12

PHILIPPA OF HAINAULT

'Good angel of Edward and of England'

Philippa of Hainault's queenship had a difficult beginning. Her arrival in London in December 1327 was marred by the mood in the wake of Edward II's funeral, which had taken place four days earlier, and her wedding, held at the unfinished, leaking cathedral church of St William, York, on 30 January 1328, was a shabby affair, redeemed only by the bride's money. The Londoners had put on a good show, presenting her with a valuable gift of plate during her four days' residence at Ely Place, Holborn, but her long, icy journey north was a lonely one for the young woman who had left her family far away in Valenciennes. Since Lent intervened, Edward and Philippa did not fully celebrate, or consummate, their marriage until Easter, and although Philippa's new mother-in-law staged three weeks of festivities, the presence at the wedding of a hundred Scots who had come to negotiate the 'shameful peace' was a reminder that her adopted country was deeply troubled and divided and that her husband was still the instrument of his adulterous mother and her lover.

Froissart gives a touching account of the first meeting between Edward III and his betrothed during Queen Isabella's visit to Valenciennes in the summer of 1326, but there is some doubt as to whether Edward did in fact accompany his mother to the Count of Hainault's court. If not, then Philippa met her husband for the first time just before their wedding at York, where she stayed for a week at Isabella's lodgings. There is also some uncertainty about her age, her birth year being variously given as 1311 or 1314. Back in 1319, when an alliance with Hainault was first discussed, Walter Stapledon visited Valenciennes and left a detailed pen portrait of the 'daughter of the Count of Hainault'[1] he had been sent to inspect. The girl was reported as being 'nine years old on St John's day to come, as her mother says', which would tally with the earlier date. In 1326, the Count and Countess had three unmarried daughters, Philippa, Isabelle and

Jeanne, as well as a son, but their eldest girl, Sybella, had died some time between 1319 and 1326, and it is possible that Stapledon's description applies to her, in which case the 1314 date would be more plausible. His examination of the prospective bride is notable for the attention given to every physical feature: hair, forehead, eyes, nose, lips, teeth (her adult teeth are whiter than her milk teeth) and her 'brown' complexion; his assessment of her figure, which, 'so far as a man may see', was acceptable, suggests that the bishop was required to take his investigations as far as modesty would permit. If this checklist applies to Sybella, then it cannot of course be assumed that Philippa possessed her sister's black hair, dark eyes and satisfactory figure, but the girl was 'well taught in all that becomes her rank', and upbringing and education was presumably one attribute that was shared by both girls and their sisters.

In any event, Philippa was at most seventeen when she was married, to a boy about her own age whom she may well never have seen. Her husband's unconventional domestic set-up was very different from the atmosphere in which she had grown up. The Count and Countess of Hainault had a successful marriage by contemporary standards in that they produced children, co-operated in government and lived together until Count William's death in 1337, when Countess Jeanne retired to a convent. Philippa and her sisters are described as having been 'sensibly brought up by a sensible mother',[2] though this may be no more than an extrapolation from the characteristics of Philippa herself which, in the eyes of her Edwardian biographer, were deemed 'sensible'. She certainly had a head for figures, perhaps unsurprisingly, since she had grown up in the Low Countries in the period of their ascendance into the greatest trading centre in the world. Hainault, though small, was hugely rich, and Valenciennes in the south of the province (in modern-day France), along with towns such as Lille and St Omer, was a meeting point for traders from all over Europe. For the wealthy, eastern silks, Spanish figs, raisins and leather, dates and spices from north Africa, the latest luxuries from Italy and even furs and ivory from Russia and the Baltic were available to make everyday life more exotic and beautiful. Philippa was very interested in clothes and food and, despite her pedigree, is often presented as something of a 'bourgeois' queen – solid, comfortable, domestic. While this image has much to do with Edward's need to reorient the royal family after the scandal of the regency crisis, it also colours the sparse picture of a girl brought up in a loving, secure family in a wealthy provincial city, a far cry from Mortimer's rackety court and Isabella's vicious glamour.

During her childhood at the palace of Salle-le-Comte and her family's summer residence of Beaumont, Philippa was exposed to an increasingly French-directed literary culture, part of the Valois influence of her mother, Jeanne. Jeanne was a keen reader of romances, as was Philippa's aunt the Duchesse de Bourbon, while her Hainault ancestors, Count Jean and Countess Philippine, were enthusiastic collectors and sponsors of illuminated books. As Queen, Philippa employed her own illuminator, Master Robert, and her accounts record payments to his wife. The owner of two illuminated psalters, she clearly shared her family's interest in elaborate books, and her betrothal gift to Edward was a compilation of Latin and French prayers and romances, including a translation of a pseudo-Aristotelian text, *De Secretis Secretorum*. The book features a picture of a woman displaying the arms of Hainault presenting the text to a man in a coat worked with those of England. Philippa's new husband shared her enthusiasm for reading: the Tower inventory for the period 1322–41 shows 160 volumes in the keeping of the privy wardrobe, a royal library that was augmented and shared through regular exchanges of books within the royal circle. Philippa's interest in learning is also attested by the licence granted in January 1341 to her chaplain, Robert de Eglesfield, for the foundation of a college for scholars in the Oxford parish of St Peter, to be known as the Queen's Hall.

Such patronage lay in the future. For several years, the new Queen was largely subordinate to the Queen Dowager. On 15 May, at Northampton, Edward agreed to assign Philippa's dower lands within a year, but they remained largely in Isabella's hands until 1331. The 3,000 pounds-worth of lands and rents agreed upon at her betrothal were not available, and Philippa received only a series of piecemeal grants until her estates could be fully provided. She did, however, attempt to act her part. Soon after her wedding, as she and Edward journeyed south, she made a traditional gesture of intercession at Stamford, on behalf of Agnes, the daughter of one Alice de Penrith, who had been convicted of robbery and sent to Marshalsea Prison. Philippa sued for a pardon on the grounds that the girl was less than eleven years old. Other interventions were less successful. In 1328, her request to place Joanna de Tourbeuyle as a lay sister in a convent was met with an indignant response from the prioress:

> No Queen has ever asked such a thing of our little house before, and if
> it may please of your debonaire Highness to know of our simple state,
> we are so poor, as God and everybody knows, that what we have would
> not suffice for our little necessities in performing the service of God day
> and night if by the aid of our friends we were charged with seculars

without lessening the number of our Religious, thus to the belittling of our service to God and to the perpetual prejudice of our poor House.[3]

Such meagre attempts at influence constitute most of what is known about Philippa for the first years of her marriage. Even her coronation was delayed to the point of embarrassment.

The fifteenth-century chronicle of John Hardyng gives a hint at why Edward selected Philippa over her sisters to become queen of England. 'We will have her with good hips, I wean/For she will bear good sons at mine intent? To which they all accorded with one assent/And chose Philippa that was full feminine.' Philippa's rather plump figure may have been the consequence rather than the cause of her success as a mother, but she was definitely a great breeder. She had almost as many children as Eleanor of Castile, except that many of Philippa's lived into adulthood, a difference which was to have revolutionary effects on the succession in the next century. Her sons – Edward, two Williams, Lionel, John, Edmund and Thomas – and her daughters – Isabella, Joan, Blanche, Mary and Margaret – were born between 1330 and 1355. It was the arrival of the first, Edward, who would become known as the Black Prince, that finally shamed Isabella into organising Philippa's coronation, which had been put off for two years. The Queen Dowager was patently reluctant to relinquish any part of her status, but by the time Philippa was six months' pregnant, in early 1330, there could be no delaying it any longer. The ceremony, which took place at Westminster on 4 March, had to be shortened so as not to exhaust the new Queen and, after a spring tour of Windsor, Guildford and Winchester, she retired to Woodstock for her first lying-in. It was typical of the financial insecurity with which Philippa had to contend all her married life that the expenses for her birthing chamber were in arrears even as she entered it.

The birth of a son on 15 June was the perfect confirmation of Philippa's queenship. Her valet Thomas, who brought the news to the King, was rewarded with an annuity of forty marks and the baby's cradle-rocker, Martha Plympton, his wetnurse, Joan of Oxenford, and Philippa's nurse, Lady Katherine Haryngton, all received gifts. The Queen had happy memories of this first birth at Woodstock and chose to deliver three more of her children there. The Pope wrote to congratulate her on Edward's arrival and, just months later, in the aftermath of Mortimer's execution, he was corresponding with her again, this time commending her for her treatment of her imprisoned mother-in-law and encouraging her to 'aim at restoring the good fortune of the Queen Mother, which has been undeservedly injured'. Philippa never did anything to contradict the official line on Isabella's position, even, it has been suggested, naming her first daughter after the Dowager Queen in 1332 in a show of family solidarity (though this could be reading too much into the gesture: Isabelle was also her sister's name), but 1331 marked a new beginning for her and Edward. Contrite, Isabella had 'voluntarily' handed over her lands to her son in December, and Philippa's dower could now be settled. Increasing mentions in the Rolls of the royal household demonstrate that Philippa was finally stepping into the role which had been prepared for her five years before.

The Queen's household was expanding rapidly. Childbirth, like coronation, was a rite of passage in which the expectations of the state were ritually enacted on the queen's person in a series of ceremonies which by the fifteenth century had coalesced into elaborate and lengthy protocols. Some weeks before the birth of a child, the pregnant queen would elect to 'take her chamber', attending a special Mass before processing to a splendidly prepared birthing suite where she would be served with wine and spices, as she had been at her coronation. When her attendants progressed to the inner rooms, all the men would be dismissed, confirming their secondary role in the mystic, sacred period of confinement. Traditionally male offices, such as that of butler, would be filled by the queen's women, who would receive supplies from the household at the chamber door. The queen's isolation was a fiction, 'part of the very public role of kingship',[4] serving to focus all attention on the magnitude of the event occurring in the womb-within-the-palace, where the sounds of the outside world were muffled in the folds of rich draperies. Once the child was born, she participated, as we have seen, in the similarly theatrical ritual of churching, in which she was presented to the court reclining on a bed of state. Afterwards she would be offered a candle and proceed to Mass with her women, priests and musicians. At the church door she was sprinkled with holy water before hearing the service and making offerings. As with the ceremony of confinement, the king did not attend. After a solemn, women-only banquet, the queen would re-enter court life. The significance of the churching ritual was understood by many as one of purification (with roots perhaps in Jewish ceremonies surrounding menstruation and childbirth), but it could also be seen as one of blessing and thanksgiving, an opportunity to give praise after an often deadly ordeal. Churching after a successful confinement emphasised and celebrated the centrality of queenly fertility to the sacred sanction of royal continuity.

Philippa gave birth to Princess Isabella in 1332, preferring Woodstock to Clarendon, which her husband had had prepared. For the formal reception of the court after her churching, tiny Isabella wore a fur-trimmed robe of Lucca silk, while her mother was dazzling in red and purple pearl-embroidered velvet, seated on a green velvet bed adorned with mermaids bearing the arms of England and Hainault. Later churching regalia featured hangings of red cloth decorated with gold leaf and a tunic for Philippa embellished with golden birds in a circle of pearls, worn over a dark blue costume. Isabella, as was customary, was given her own household, with John Bromley, her tailor, Joan Gambon, her rocker, and Joan Pyebrook, her nurse, but the children's bills were met through the central organisation of Philippa's own wardrobe. In the first of many money-spinning schemes, Edward granted his wife the right to cut down any leafless oaks in her dower parks to the value of 1,000 pounds to keep up with expenses. The previous year, Philippa had also been granted some of Mortimer's seizures, in the form of the issues of the county of Chester, for the maintenance of her son, who held the earldom, and her thirteen-year-old sister-in-law Eleanor, who had joined her household after Dowager Queen Isabella's 'retirement'.

Preparations were made that summer for Eleanor's marriage to Reginald II, Count of Gueldres and Zutphen, and Philippa had the pleasure of welcoming her mother, Countess Jeanne, who was instrumental in negotiating the betrothal. Edward staged tournaments for the entertainment of his guests at Dartmouth, Stepney and Cheapside, where a wooden tower was built to accommodate the royal party and Edward and his retinue appeared in exciting 'Tartar' costumes, with fur cloaks and tall hats. Unfortunately, the 'sensible' proportions of the Flemish ladies proved too much for the tower, which collapsed. Eleanor set off to join her bridegroom at Nijmegen after Christmas at Eltham, where Edward settled her dowry of 15,000 pounds and presented her with a gold cup and her trousseau. She had a green bed, six gold altar cloths, accoutrements for her private chapel, a furred robe, a wedding outfit of cloth-of-gold and crimson, Spanish leather shoes, sugar, rice, raisins, figs and pepper and an up-to-the-minute purple chariot with a waxed-cloth rain hood. In spite of these splendid celebrations and accoutrements Eleanor's marriage was troubled. Her husband disliked her and, after she had given him two children, tried to get an annulment by claiming she had leprosy. She refuted this charge in some style by riding into court wearing the skimpiest of shifts to display her healthy body, and Reginald was obliged to return to her.

Between 1332 and 1337 Philippa's life was dominated by babies and Scots. Edward had always resented the 'shameful peace' of the treaty of Northampton, and chose to ignore the alliance Isabella had forged through the marriage of his sister Joan with David of Scotland. David had become king, aged four, in 1329, and neither Edward nor his mother attended the children's joint coronation at Scone Abbey in 1331 (Edward could hardly appear as he persisted in refusing to give back the Stone). Edward now began to question the treaty, suggesting that he had only agreed to it under duress, and that he had been too young to understand what was happening. He decided to support the campaign of Edward Balliol, the son of John Balliol, deposed by his grandfather Edward I as King in 1296, to regain the crown. Balliol and his English troops defeated the Scots at Duppin Moor in August 1332, and the next July Edward won a great victory at Halidon Hill. Balliol succeeded in having himself crowned as Joan and David fled to France, where they were received by Philip VI, remaining there until 1341.

Philippa accompanied Edward to Northumbria in 1332, staying at Bamburgh, twenty miles from the front, and, since Edward had moved the government temporarily to York, was able to remain in the north until the end of the following year. As Edward was besieging Berwick, Philippa found herself under attack by the Earl of Douglas in an attempt to draw the English King back. Edward coolly waited until Berwick fell before returning to rescue his wife. After Halidon, where Edward's brother John of Eltham also commanded, Philippa began to make her way south for her next lying-in, and Joan was born at Woodstock in February 1334. Soon after the birth, Philippa returned north to York, but this time she took her three children with her. During the Berwick campaign mismanagement in their household had run up a debt of 500 pounds and she had been obliged to ask Edward to meet it. Edward was no miser, indeed he was extravagant when it came to display, but one has the sense, looking at the accounts of Philippa's dealings, that he resented what he saw as dreary, petty expenses, mundane matters such as food and travel.

The royal family remained at York, with Philippa making excursions to visit Newcastle-on-Tyne and Carlisle before moving down to Norfolk for the summer. Philippa was always a great traveller, and Edward's Scottish campaign was an opportunity for her to become more familiar with the north than her predecessors, whose progresses had been mainly confined to the south and west. Another son, William, was born at Hatfield, but he lived only a short time and was buried at York minster the following spring. A little girl, Blanche of the Tower, survived for only a few minutes after her birth, and these two losses were followed by that of Philippa's father, Count William, in 1337. This period, then, was a very sad one, and the Count's death additionally meant that funds from Hainault dried up and Philippa was burdened with money worries.

A letter in the Madox collection concerning a debt of queens-gold on the estate of one Sir Richard de Cressiwil shows that Philippa tried to balance the prosecution of her own rights with the display of charity that was one of the obligations of queenship. She asked that the executors pause so that 'we and our Council may be able to be advised which of the said writs are to be put into execution for our profit and which of them to cease for the relief of our people, to save our conscience'. Yet she was also keen to manage her lands efficiently in order to obtain the funds she needed, and in 1337, and again a decade later, she was involved in a number of lawsuits: 'Many a case was fought on her behalf against certain bold poachers who had broken into her parks, felled her trees, fished in her fisheries, hunted her deer, carried away royal goods and wreck of sea, conies [rabbits], pheasants and partridges from her warrens, depastured her grass and crops and assaulted her servants.'⁵ Philippa's willingness to go to law made her unpopular, and people vented their feelings on her lands and goods. A particular source of resentment was purveyance, whereby her household representatives were sent out to obtain provisions for the Queen as she moved between her residences. Such goods were meant to be paid for, at 'cost' price, but even these debts often went unsettled for years. In April 1348, two carts carrying provisions for the Queen, forty pounds-worth of wine and twelve horses, were impounded and held for so long that the wine spoiled and the horses starved. Richard Hegham, appointed to purvey oats and hay for her stables at Nottingham, was the victim of a vicious assault. Philippa's promptness in collecting her rents even led to the disgruntled vicar of Lincoln, John le Tailleur, publishing a sarcastic libel against 'the horror and scandal' of the King's 'dearest consort', for which he was sent to prison.

Why was Philippa constantly short of money? There were two contributory factors. The first was the vast debts Edward III was running up to finance the first phase of what later became known as the Hundred Years War; the second was the dispute over her rights, and those of her sisters, to Hainault. Philippa followed the example of Eleanor of Castile in keeping her connections with her native country relatively discreet. Unlike Eleanor of Provence, she did not attract criticism for her promotion of foreigners, indeed her household has been described as old-fashioned and offered few opportunities for ambitious courtiers to make their fortunes. Most of Philippa's Hainault servants had left after her wedding, but Wantelet de Maunay, who had been her page at Valenciennes, stayed to become her carver, and later, anglicised as Sir Walter Manny, was admitted to the order of the Garter. Among the Queen's ladies, Emma Priour, the wife of Philippa's valet, Amiciua de Gaveston, Mabel Fitz-Waryne, Elena de Maule and Joan de Carne were Hainaulters, and were later given grants of land for their long service. However, Philippa did resemble Eleanor of Provence in that she made use of the connections of her natal family on the international stage. The most important of these was Louis of Bavaria, King of the Germans and since 1328 Holy Roman Emperor, who had married her sister Margaret in 1324.

Edward's interest in pursuing the Scottish campaign was diverted in 1337 when Philip VI confiscated Gascony. The duchy, which has been wonderfully described as the Jarndyce and Jarndyce of the fourteenth century, was the inevitable pressure point for yet another outbreak of hostilities after Philip's disputed succession to the French crown in 1328. Under the newly established Salic law, the crown could not be transmitted through a female claimant, but Edward felt his own rights, as the son of the last surviving child of Philip IV, were superior to those of a mere cousin. In October 1337, he declared war on France. The states that made up the Low Countries were concerned about encroachments from the aggressive French King and united in an alliance with England against France. Two features of this alliance were Edward's receipt of the honour of vicar of the Holy Roman Empire from his brother-in-law and the betrothal of four-year-old Princess Joan to Frederick, heir to Duke Otho of Austria.

In July 1338, Edward and Philippa set off for Antwerp. Anxious to make a splendid impression, Edward provided over 500 pounds-worth of 'saddles, silver vases, purses, silk and jewels' for the expedition, as well as the poignant provision of a 'pallet for the Lady Joan the King's daughter on her passage to foreign parts in a ship'. Their arrival in Flanders was not auspicious. Their host was so anxious to prepare a grand feast that the overtaxed kitchens caught fire, the house burned down and the royal family was obliged to retreat to the nearby abbey of St Michael, where Philippa stayed to await the birth of another child (Lionel, born on 29 November) while Edward set off for the crowning ceremony in Cologne.

Philippa said goodbye to little Joan at Herenthals. Her daughter was to travel with Lord John de Montgomery and her governess, Lady Isabella de la Mote. Philippa was in correspondence with her sister Margaret, the Empress, who would superintend the journey to Austria, where Joan was to be educated at her fiancé's court. Despite Philippa's frequent letters, Margaret was a negligent guardian and it was reported that Joan sometimes did not even have enough to eat. Philippa was so concerned that she eventually asked Edward to write to Montgomery and have him remove Joan from the imperial household. No sooner had Joan arrived at the ducal court than Otho died, leaving his own son and Joan in the care of his pro-French brother. At this point, the business was given up and Joan was returned to her parents, setting off in April 1340 with two chariots and twelve horses, for which Philippa had to pay out £132 10s, and rejoining her mother at Ghent. Philippa had remained between Antwerp and Cologne for this period, and had given birth to another son, John of Ghent (Gaunt) in December 1339. Her children Edward and Isabella had sailed from England to join their parents, an anxious crossing as the French had been raiding the English coast. The convoy was indeed attacked on one occasion, but the children's escort of 800 men succeeded in keeping the French at bay.

By 1340, the alliance between Edward and the Low Countries was beginning to disintegrate. Although the English King had borrowed heavily from his Italian bankers, the Bardi and the Peruzzi, to subsidise his supporters, funds were running short. Edward's 'great crown' was at the pawn shop, and Philippa's was pledged for 5,500 florins to Anthony Bache, a merchant of Cologne. By the time she returned to England, the King's payments to her household were over 7,000 pounds in arrears. Another worry was the French invasion of Hainault in 1340. In June, the English overpowered the French fleet in a naval battle off Sluys, but Edward was frustrated by Philip's refusal to engage on land. After an inconclusive siege at Tournai, a nine-months truce was agreed and Edward was free to go home to his family.

Edward was never a faithful husband to Philippa, but then, infidelities were expected of kings. They were nevertheless a close couple, and Edward was happy to display the unity and contentment of his family life. On his arrival back at the Tower in 1341, Edward gave a party for the children, with music by one of his own minstrels, Godelan. Predictably, the result of too much paternal spoiling was a visit from the royal physician, Master Philip. A picture of the daily life of Edward's children is to be found in the accounts for Isabella and Joan, who shared a household after Joan's return from her unsuccessful betrothal. She had two maids, Isabella, the elder sister, had three, and they each had a lady-in-waiting, Alexia de la Mote for Isabella and Lonota de Werthyngpole for Joan, as well as a chaplain apiece. Both girls were given a penny a day to offer in church. They had a joint waiting staff, and a minstrel, Gerard de Gay, who received a present of a winter coat in 1339, as did Isabella's valet, Thomas de Bastenthwaite. Whatever Philippa's money worries, she was determined that her daughters live in befitting style, sending them green robes edged with fur from Ghent and authorising the making of new clothes and scarlet stockings for Church feasts, as well as party dresses for a tournament, which took eighteen men nine days to sew with eleven ounces of gold leaf. The girls slept together in a bed hung with green silk and velvet and ate off silver plate. Philippa also bought gold thread and silk for Joan, who enjoyed needlework. Outdoor entertainments included trips to 'the gardens' across the river, for which the girls personally rewarded John the bargeman and his sailors. It sounds a charming existence, and soon there were more children to share it. Edmund was born in 1341, and Lionel was betrothed to Elizabeth de Burgh, Countess of Ulster in her own right, who joined the royal nursery to be brought up with her toddling husband. Philippa gave birth to another princess, Mary, in 1343 at Waltham, followed by Margaret in 1346, soon after her husband had embarked for France with young Edward, now created Prince of Wales, and a huge invasion force.

The size of this army does much to highlight the uncertainty of medieval battle estimates, for though Edward was said to have set off with over 30,000 men, by the time he had taken Caen and pitched camp near a windmill at Crécy in August, a good number of them appear to have been mislaid, as there were only 8,000 to 12,000 left to face the forces of the French and their Genoese mercenaries. Crécy was the first in a series of legendary victories which assured Edward's reputation as the ideal medieval king and quietened, if they did not entirely silence, the disconcerted mutterings of a Parliament overburdened by the cost of war. The unwieldy, laden French *destriers* were undone by what Froissart records as a 'snow' of arrows from Edward's Welsh longbowmen and, despite the disparity in numbers, many of the French nobility were killed. Edward oversaw the battle from the 'little windmill hill',[6] but his sixteen-year-old son won his spurs that day as a commander of one of the three battle divisions.

Crécy was also the occasion on which Edward adopted his only French motto, the famous '*Honi soit qui mal y pense*'. The sources and use of this motto, and its associated chivalric order, the Garter, give an insight into Edward's skill at blending the arts and their relationship with the peacetime ethos of the tournament to encourage the coherent mentality among his magnates that was one of the great achievements of his reign. The origin of the order of the Garter is a matter of both legend and scholarly dispute, but it must be understood as 'an integral part of Edward's Norman campaign from its inception, not merely a retrospective (that is, post-Crécy) commemoration of its success.'[7] As has been noted, Edward shared his wife's pleasure in romances. An order for 1335 shows 100 marks being paid to a nun, Isabella de Lancaster, 'for a book of romances purchased for the King's use',[8] while Philippa's New Year gift to her husband in 1333 was a silver cup, ewer and basin, the ewer decorated with figures of Julius Caesar, Charlemagne, King Arthur and Lancelot, a combination indicating the easy familiarity of Edward and his household with the vocabulary and characters of romance and *chanson de geste*. The use of romance figures as exemplars for conduct plays chimed with the ornate '*ludi*' costumes worn for court festivities. Those for the family Christmas spent at Guildford after Crécy featured swan, peacock and dragon headdresses with matching wings, and at various times lions, elephants, a Saracen's head, griffons and even flower pots were on show. The exact significance of these costumes is uncertain, but their elaborate theatricality links them to the themes of disguises and mottos displayed in tournaments. Edward's sense of costume as a unifying device of loyalty had been seen in the aketon jackets devised for the Mortimer coup; now, with the order of the Garter, he was able to give fuller expression to his romance-driven ideal of knighthood.

The device of the garter was first used by the twenty-four companion knights in April 1349 (since Queen Philippa is found offering cloth-of-gold at the tomb of Hugh de Courtenay, one of the original members, in September that year, 1349 is the most likely date for the order's foundation, though the College of St George at Windsor was established in 1348, and dating is further confused by Froissart's conflation of the 'Round Table' tournament at Windsor in 1344 with the Garter ceremonies). The year is significant in that it casts doubt on one legend of the order's origin: Edward's relationship with Catherine Montague, Countess of Salisbury. Two Continental sources, *The Hainault Chronicle* and that of Jean le Bel, claim that Edward had seen the Countess in 1341 while on campaign in Scotland, invited the Salisburys to a tournament in 1342 and then, when she resisted his advances, raped her, causing a bitter quarrel with the Earl. The Garter legend glosses the story politely by suggesting that the Countess's garter slipped while she danced with the King at Eltham, provoking the bon mot that became the order's motto. The tale has been definitively dismissed as no more than an attempt to blacken Edward's character during the French campaigns, but its persistence is notable in that it links sexual misconduct with political illegitimacy – in this case, Edward's claim to France. It might be considered, though, that Edward's choice of '*Honi soit*' as an announcement of the purity of his motivations in the conquest of France *did* have some relation to sexual misdemeanours, not his own, but his mother's. Edward chose to deliver his political message, uniquely, in French. 'Shame on he who thinks evil of it' is an assertion of his rights to France in spite of Isabella's adultery, a resonance to which he and his romance-steeped courtiers, whose sensibilities had been educated into romance symbolism well before the foundation of the Garter, would have been highly alert. In this respect, it is notable that Queen Isabella herself was never admitted as a Lady companion of the Garter, though Philippa, her daughters Isabella and Mary and all subsequent medieval queens were to be received.

During Edward's absence on the Crécy campaign, six-year-old Lionel had been installed as Guardian of the Realm under the supervision of Philippa and her council. King David of Scotland had sneaked back into his country five years before and, taking advantage of Edward's absence, he sacked York with the encouragement of his ally the King of France. Philippa immediately set off for Durham, where she ordered a muster of English troops and received a challenge from David. According to Holinshed, the Queen rode among her men on a white horse, the same colour as her husband's at Crécy, to rally the men, then returned to Durham to await news of the battle of Neville's Cross. The Scots were thoroughly routed, and David was captured by John Copeland, but despite Philippa's demands – Copeland had displeased her by carrying off her prisoner' – he refused to surrender the defeated Scots King to anyone but Edward himself. Philippa wrote to Edward at Calais, and the King summoned Copeland, knighted him and gave him a large grant of lands, after which he was persuaded to give up his hostage. (One wonders, given Philippa's reputation for being close with money, whether Copeland feared she might demur in the matter of David's ransom.) Philippa took charge of David at York, and he was received at the Tower of London by Lionel, perching solemnly on his father's throne.

Flanders had pursued a policy of neutrality during the first period of Edward's alliance against the French, but with Count Louis I having died fighting for Philip VI at Crécy, Edward and Philippa now saw an opportunity to make another attempt at a pact by betrothing Isabella to the new Count, Louis II. Louis had no intention of marrying Isabella, as he had already fixed upon Margaret, daughter of the Duke of Brabant, as a bride, but he played for time, and in November 1346 Philippa and Isabella crossed to Calais. In March, the families met at Bergues, near Dunkirk, and Louis promised to marry Isabella within a fortnight of Easter Day, accepting 25,000 pounds in rents and the massive sum of 400,000 gold deniers as her dowry, until such time as her father could recover on her behalf her grandmother's county of Ponthieu. The reluctant bridegroom then made off on horseback during a celebratory hunting party and Isabella found herself jilted.

Isabella and her father were very close, and after this embarrassment, Edward tried to compensate by spoiling her. He allowed her to preside at tournaments and one, at Canterbury, was even given in her honour. She had more attendants than her sisters, and by the time she was nineteen was allowed her own household, whereas Margaret and Mary had to make do with twenty marks' pocket money. As Edward lavished attention on his eldest daughter, she and Philippa became estranged, to the point where they avoided one another's company. Eventually, Isabella announced that she did wish to take a husband: Bernard Ezzi, the son of a minor Gascon lord. It was a shoddy match for the daughter of Edward III, but her parents made the best of it and a grand wedding was planned at Windsor. A week before the ceremony, Isabella capriciously changed her mind, though she kept the money her father had settled on her (not to mention the clothes, descriptions of which run to pages in the accounts), and continued at court with all the advantages and none of the responsibilities of a married woman. Poor Bernard renounced his inheritance and died in a monastery. Whether Philippa felt guilty that she had not handled the Louis fiasco better, or resented the relationship between her husband and her vain, extravagant daughter, she and Isabella were to remain on poor terms until the mid 1360s.

Philippa's visit to Calais in August 1347 was the setting for the most famous and symbolically resonant incident of her queenship. Edward had successfully besieged the city and as punishment for its resistance had finally elected to execute six token townsmen, who carried the keys to the city to the King with ropes about their necks. According to Froissart:

> The noble queen of England, who was heavily pregnant, humbled herself greatly and wept so tenderly that none could bear it. The valiant and good lady threw herself on her knees before the King and said 'Ah, my dear Lord, since I came across the sea in great peril as you know, I have asked nothing of you nor required any favour. Now I humbly pray and request of you a favour, that for the Son of the Holy Mary and for the love of me, you shall wish to have mercy on these six men.' The King waited a little before he spoke and he looked upon the good Lady his wife, who was very pregnant and wept so tenderly on her knees before him. A change of heart came over him as she knelt there before him and when he spoke he said 'Ah, Lady, I would have much preferred

you were anywhere but here. You have prayed so strongly that I dare not refuse the favour you ask of me.'

The first point to be made about this account is that it cannot be factually accurate. Philippa gave birth to her next child, the second William, in May 1348. She could have been just pregnant, could, as an experienced mother, have known herself to be so, but she could not have looked 'heavily pregnant'. Why does Froissart make her condition the focus of her entreaty? The connection between intercession and fertility was made very explicit for English queens in their coronation ritual, yet this poignant image of the cumbrously child-laden woman weeping on her knees, much beloved of Victorian artists as 'Queen Philippa Pleading for the Burghers of Calais', strikes an odd, stagey note. There is no reason to believe that Philippa did not make her successful intercession, but Froissart's description points to something having changed in the power that intercession represented. Recall Isabella's intervention for the banishment of the Despensers, a formulaic gesture that allowed Edward II to carry out a necessary policy without appearing to back down. Philippa's supplication marks another stage in the process by which intercession ceased to be a manifestation of real political strength, albeit one enacted in the context of a symbolic paradigm, and became an allegorical performance, a brief manifestation of the feminine side of the body politic. Philippa's pleas are transgressive, in that they contradict the King's stated plan, but permitted because of her status as queen and the resonance of her pregnancy. As Paul Strohm puts it, 'Without any disrespect to the force of [Edward's] male ire, his wife has contributed a supplementary perspective that will enhance the reputation of his kingship.'9 Philippa is all femininity – tear-sodden, begging and fulsomely maternal. In case anyone should miss the point, she invokes the Virgin and draws attention to her condition – 'I came across the sea in great peril' – and thus the special position of her unborn child, hovering between the spiritual and earthly realms. Her whole body is a representation of Edward's power, not just her kneeling, mentioned, like her pregnancy, three times, but her belly, the proof of his virility and of the future security of his kingdom. Edward, by contrast, is cast as the perfect embodiment of male authority: upright, stern, omnipotent. Together, the King and Queen act out a little mystery play of royal might tempered by royal mercy. Philippa's actual power is reduced while her symbolic usefulness increases. The Queen's spontaneous gesture has become carefully contrived, absorbed into, rather than a reaction against, the King's ultimate authority.

★

Philippa's brother-in-law Louis of Bavaria died in October 1347. Philippa's share in the inheritance of Hainault had been in dispute since the death of her brother William in 1345. William had left no heirs, and Edward was keen that Philippa's rights be recognised along with those of her living sisters, Margaret, Jeanne and Isabelle. On William's death, Louis, as Emperor, had conferred Hainault on Margaret and then on their son William, but when his father died, William resisted his mother's claim to the county and refused to offer her any compensation for its resignation. By 1351, the inheritance dispute had escalated into civil war between the 'Cods', William's supporters, and the 'Hooks', who declared for his mother. Edward sent military aid to Margaret, as her victory was obviously in Philippa's interests, but the Cods defeated the Hooks at the battle of Vlaardingen, and Edward was obliged to pursue a policy of conciliation. He offered an alliance in the person of Maud, the co-heiress to the Duke of Lancaster, in 1352, but this could not prevent William from taking over Hainault after his mother's death in 1356. William got his just deserts – he went mad and had to be locked up for the next thirty years – but Philippa was no better treated by his successor, her nephew Albert. She has been unfairly characterised as being hopeless with money, but with Edward constantly borrowing from her randomly paid allowance and the Hainault inheritance deadlocked, it is hardly surprising that she found herself perpetually running into debt.

Eleanor of Provence and Eleanor of Castile had both been castigated for their harsh management of their lands and their determination to squeeze every penny they could from their tenants, and they had died rich. Philippa was a less effective manager in that she attracted the criticism without the profits. Still, her Hainault blood showed in her enterprising spirit. The Scots wars had stalled coalmining in the valleys near Newcastle, but Philippa asked Edward to permit her bailiff, Alan de Strothere, to work a mine at Aldemstone, with a degree of success. In February 1351 she appointed Thomas de Clogh keeper at her castle of High Peak in Derbyshire and set him to work at a lead mine. John de Moneyasse was also chosen to 'find lead from time to time as required by the King and Queen for their works in London' and to arrange for shipment. For the management of her business affairs, Philippa was granted La Reole in the London ward of Vintry as a seat for her wardrobe. She attempted to exercise her unique queen's prerogatives – her council can be seen, for example, considering a plan to let the farm of Bristol to its mayor and commune for ten years – but she frequently found herself in trouble for taking excessive advantage of her legal status. In 1352 a special commission was set up under Sir John Moleyns to investigate 'too grievous fines and amercements' on the Queen's lands.

On Philippa's return from France in 1347, funds were needed for the preparation of a new marriage for her daughter Joan, this time to the heir to the throne of Castile. Joan was kitted out with two folding chairs and a copper warming pan, as well as more glamorous gifts of scarlet and purple saddles inlaid with pearls, two sets of tapestries patterned with birds and roses and a cloth-of-gold bridal dress. The wedding was arranged for November, and Joan left Westminster in January to sail from Plymouth to Bordeaux, where she would spend the summer before travelling to Bayonne for the ceremony. In September, in the village of Loremo, she contracted the Black Death, and died aged fourteen.

The spread of bubonic plague, which had entered England by June 1348, was described by Thomas Walsingham as 'the great mortality', spreading 'throughout the world from south to north, so catastrophic that hardly half the population remained alive. Towns once full of men were left forsaken until the epidemic had left scarcely enough men alive to bury the dead.'[10] Estimates of the death rates in England suggest that as much as one third of the population was wiped out in the first phase of the plague, which broke out periodically until the seventeenth century. The royal family immediately left London. At Windsor in October, Philippa received Edward's younger sister, Queen Joan of Scotland, on a visit to her imprisoned husband. In the ensuing months she stayed at Clarendon, Woodstock and Langley in an attempt to avoid the plague, but in the wake of the loss of Joan she had to bear that of another child, her youngest boy, William. He was buried at Windsor beside his sister Blanche in St Edmund's chapel.

As ever in Philippa's life, personal events took place against the background of her husband's wars. In 1350 she was an eyewitness to one of the most exciting naval battles of the century, in which Edward and the Black Prince took on a fleet of Castilian pirates. The Spanish were allies of the French, though at sea the difference between military activity and privateering was barely discernible. An English flotilla had been captured off the coast of Flanders by a Castilian commander, Carlos de Cerda, the ships taken and the crews thrown unceremoniously into the sea. Edward resolved to recover his ships as the Spaniards returned home, and as they neared Rotherhithe, he was waiting for them with a fleet of fifty, including his own galleon, the *Cog Thomas*. Philippa and her ladies watched from Winchelsea convent as the ships broadsided one another, and Edward had a dramatic escape, climbing on to a speared Spanish vessel just before the

Cog Thomas went down. His heavy household galley, *La Salle du Roi*, and the battle, looked lost when a Spanish ship bore down on it, but both were saved by the quick thinking of a Flemish squire, Robert of Namur, who boarded the Castilian vessel and slit her rigging. The battle of 'Espagnols' was another greatest hit for the century's most glamorous warrior, the Black Prince, who achieved immortality with his victory over the French in 1356, as Lieutenant of Aquitaine, at Poitiers, where he captured the French King himself. King Jean was given the palace of the Savoy as a most comfortable prison, and he praised the Queen for the elegance and warmth of his reception.

In 1355, Philippa gave birth to her last child, Thomas, at Woodstock. Margaret and John were married in 1358, Margaret, aged twelve, to the Earl of Pembroke and John to Blanche of Lancaster. John's bride, also twelve, would eventually bring him the Lancaster estates of her father, the first Duke, upon which wealth he would found his dynasty. (Blanche's father, Henry, and his elder brother Thomas of Lancaster, were the sons of Edward I's younger brother Edmund.) Isabella was still single at the advanced age of thirty. She gave Blanche a wedding gift of silver buckles worth thirty pounds but characteristically neglected to pay for them. Soon afterwards, Edward and his four elder sons sailed for France, this time leaving Thomas as Guardian of the Realm. Philippa's particular concern during this period was a French invasion, as Edward had attempted to muster practically every able-bodied man in England. She had King Jean removed to the Tower, garrisoned the castles at Pevensey, Old Sarum and Marlborough and ordered beacon fires to be prepared along the coast. One party of invaders did land at Winchelsea, where they managed some burning and pillaging before being driven off

Deaths and weddings continued to mark the following years. Mary married the Duke of Brittany in 1360, but less than a year later was buried at Abingdon Abbey next to her sister Margaret, Countess of Pembroke. Joan of Scotland, Maud of Hainault and Lionel's wife Elizabeth of Clarence succumbed in 1362. Two further weddings brightened Philippa's grief, though neither was the splendid royal match she and Edward had hoped for. In 1361, the Black Prince secretly married his cousin, Joan of Kent, daughter of the Earl of Kent, Marguerite's son Edmund, who had been executed by Isabella and Roger Mortimer. Joan, whom Froissart called 'the most beautiful woman in all England', had grown up in Philippa's care, and apparently the Black Prince had always been attracted to her. However, she had a dubious marital history. Aged twelve she had been married to Thomas Holland without the permission of her guardian,

Edward III. When Holland departed on crusade she was married again to William Montacute, heir to the Earl of Salisbury. When Holland returned, he quite reasonably asked for his wife back, and after much scandal the second union was annulled in 1349. Joan and Thomas went on to have four children together, but shortly after Thomas became Earl of Kent, in right of his wife, in 1360, he died, and with somewhat indecent haste his widow married her childhood sweetheart. The ceremony was declared invalid, as the couple were related within the prohibited degrees, but when the Black Prince refused to abandon his bride the King, against his better judgement, had to arrange for a swift dispensation and a public remarriage at Windsor, which he was too furious to attend.

So Joan might have been beautiful, but obviously she was no royal virgin, and her past history, not to mention her negligible diplomatic connections, made her a shabby choice for the next queen of England. Philippa, though, seems to have been content that her son was happy. She did attend the wedding, along with Isabella and Joan of Scotland. The Prince and Princess of Wales removed themselves from Edward's bad temper by leaving the next year to govern Aquitaine, where Joan gave birth to two sons, Edward, who died young, and Richard of Bordeaux, Edward III's eventual heir.

To Philippa's evident satisfaction, her only living daughter Isabella was finally married off three years later, to Enguerrand de Coucy, a grandson of the Duke of Austria. Again, it was not a brilliant match, but Edward, ever-indulgent where Isabella was concerned, made the best of it and created De Coucy Earl of Bedford and Knight of the Garter. Isabella received a dowry of 4,000 pounds and 300 pounds-worth of jewels, and De Coucy an annuity of 300 marks. After Isabella's first child, a daughter named Mary, was born in France in 1265, she and her mother, who had been on frosty terms for so long, grew closer. Isabella came back to England for her second lying-in, at which Philippa assisted, and the child, born at Eltham in 1367, was named for her grandmother.

Another namesake, Philippa of Clarence, Lionel's daughter with Elizabeth de Burgh, married the Earl of March, Roger Mortimer's great-grandson. Edward had revoked the attainder against the family in 1354, and Philippa's union was to prove of crucial dynastic significance in the fifteenth century. Lionel himself was back on the matrimonial market, and in June 1368 he travelled to Italy as the betrothed of Violante Visconti, the daughter of the immensely rich Duke of Milan. Their wedding, in the city's pink marble cathedral, was one of the social events of the century. Unfortunately, Lionel enjoyed la dolce vita too much, and died in October at Alba, having 'addicted himself . . . to untimely banquetings'.[11]

Philippa had remained active well into middle age. She dislocated her shoulder hunting at Cosham two years after Thomas's birth and during Edward's absences moved constantly between the royal palaces of the south-east, but Lionel's death seemed to break her spirit. She had already suffered an attack of dropsy in 1367, and was now increasingly unwell. Yet she continued to support her husband with her Hainault connections, writing to her nephew Albert and sending him a gift of jewellery that had belonged to Maud of Hainault as a sweetener to his support for Edward in yet another assault on the French. She also wrote and sent gifts to the King of Cyprus. John of Gaunt left for Paris in early summer, while Philippa lay ill at Windsor, and on 15 August 1369 she died, with Edward and Thomas beside her.

Froissart's description of her death is worth quoting at length, as despite his tendency to embroider, it reflects something of the way in which Philippa was perceived:

When the good Lady perceived her end approaching she called to the King and extending her hand from under the bedclothes, put it into the right hand of the King, who was very sorrowful at heart, and thus spoke. 'We have enjoyed our union in happiness peace and prosperity, I entreat therefore of you on our separation that you will grant me three requests.' The King with sighs and tears replied 'My Lady, ask, whatever you request shall be granted.' 'My Lord, I beg you will acquit me of whatever engagements I have entered into with merchants for their wares as well on this as on the other side of the sea. I beseech you also to fulfil whatever gifts or legacies I may have left to churches here or on the continent where I have paid my devotions as well as what I may have left to those of both sexes who have been in my service. Thirdly, I entreat that when it shall please God to call you hence you will not choose any other sepulchre than mine and will lie by my side in the sepulchre at Westminster.' The King in tears replied, 'Lady, I grant them!' Soon after the good Lady made the sign of the Cross on her breast and having recommended to God the King and her youngest son Thomas, who was present, gave up her spirit, which I firmly believe was caught by the Holy Angels and carried to glory in Heaven for she had never done anything by thought or deed which could endanger her losing it.

Presumably Froissart did not mean to be comic, but it is typical that Philippa's first dying thought should be of her debts.

CHAPTER 13

ANNE OF BOHEMIA AND ISABELLE OF FRANCE

'The Little Queens'

When the Black Prince and his family returned to England in 1371, Joan of Kent still had reason to hope that she would be the next queen of England. The Maid of Kent was in truth more fat than fair these days, and her ailing husband was a decrepit shadow of his former gallant self, but the aura of glamour surrounding the couple persisted in the face of reality. As Princess of Wales, Joan could expect to be the first lady at court now that Philippa was gone, but the Queen's death had provoked a slump in standards for the most chivalrous of kings and Edward, now ill and often confused, was very publicly in the clutches of his mistress, Alice Perrers. Philippa had turned a blind – and, in the light of her incessant pregnancies, perhaps rather relieved – eye to her husband's infidelities in the past, but Alice Perrers was different. The relationship had begun in 1364, and two years later Alice was installed as a maid of the Queen's bedchamber, which suggests that either Philippa sanctioned the liaison, or Edward simply no longer cared about his wife's dignity. If the hostile *St Albans Chronicle* is to be believed, the latter would appear to have been the case, as Alice was reported to be the daughter of a tiler and a maidservant, hardly a suitable background for such a prestigious position. More probably she was the daughter of Sir Richard Perrers, a Hertfordshire member of Parliament, but this was still a very modest rank, and it could only have been galling for Joan to find Alice taking very public precedence in Edward's court. Even more incomprehensible, to a legendary beauty, was the fact that Alice was famously ugly, though even *The St Albans Chronicle* conceded she was intelligent. The Prince and Princess of Wales were to spend the next six years living in semi-retirement at Kennington and Berkhamsted, largely because of the Prince's poor health, but conceivably also because Joan was appalled by the degenerate atmosphere that now prevailed at Edward's once glorious court.

To a far greater extent than Henry II's 'Fair Rosamund', Alice Perrers was the first mistress of an English king to enjoy a semi-official position. She acquired manors in seventeen counties, valuable property in London and the castle of Egremont – and, inevitably, a reputation for being grasping and litigious. In a dispute over St Albans Abbey involving her likely father, Sir Richard, she was accused of threatening the judges, but she was clearly a capable manager, going to law to defend her holdings until her death in 1400 and dealing with such prestigious figures as William of Wykeham and John of Gaunt. The King was sufficiently in love to overturn Philippa's bequest of jewels and goods to her lady Euphemia de Heselarton and make them over to Alice, and he had no qualms about appearing with her in public, as at a Smithfield tournament in 1374, when she rode next to him in the royal chariot, got up as 'the Lady of the Sun'. She became a great crony of Philippa's daughter Isabella, whose husband had by now been mislaid, and together they took the leading female roles in court ceremonial, to general disgust.

Any plans Joan may have had for putting La Perrers in her place suffered a setback when the Black Prince died in 1376. Life had proved a miserable disappointment for the young warrior who had shown such magnificent promise, and although, in his broken state, he may have been an ineffective king, the succession now depended on the vulnerable figure of the nine-year-old Richard of Bordeaux. As Queen Mother-in-waiting, Joan could now anticipate a position of considerable power, and this was reflected in the grants made to her after her husband's death which, along with her own holdings in Kent, provided her with an income nearly equivalent to that of a dowager queen. Almost at once, Joan found herself involved in political controversy. The Black Prince's death occurred as Parliament was sitting, with John of Gaunt representing the elderly King. Parliament had taken measures to correct the sorry state of national affairs, impeaching several members of the royal household for financial corruption and demanding that Alice Perrers be exiled and her property sequestered. Prominent among the reformers were the Speaker, Peter de la Mare, and the bishop of Winchester, William of Wykeham. There was much anxiety as to the security of the succession, as it was feared that Gaunt might try to take the crown for himself. Those fears were confirmed when Gaunt, on his own authority, declared the 1376 proceedings void and recalled Alice Perrers. De la Mare was imprisoned and the bishop had his revenues confiscated and was forbidden to approach within twenty miles of London.

When Parliament was reconvened in January 1377, riots broke out.

Gaunt and the Earl of Northumberland escaped by boat to Joan's house at Kennington. Joan sent three envoys, including her son's tutor Sir Simon Burley, to negotiate with the Londoners, but they would be satisfied only by an audience with the King himself. William of Wykeham was not too proud to bargain with an adulteress, and paid Alice Perrers to conspire behind Gaunt's back for the restoration of his income. Triumphant, she remained at court for the last few months of her lover's life. Avaricious to the end, when Edward III died at Havering on 21 June 1377, his mistress was accused of pulling the rings from his fingers before his body was cold.

Joan and Richard were at Kingston-on-Thames as Edward lay dying. The Londoners showed their allegiance to his heir Richard by sending a deputation to Kingston before the King expired, signalling their intentions in advance to Gaunt who, if he had ever been minded to try for the crown, now had to accept that this would be impossible. The passing of the man Froissart called the greatest English king since Arthur was overshadowed by the swift preparations for his grandson's coronation and, on 16 July, Richard was crowned at Westminster. Almost immediately, Joan began to make arrangements for the boy king's marriage. One of the first offers came from the Holy Roman Emperor, Charles IV, who proposed the hand of his eleven-year-old daughter Anne, but Joan was also considering princesses of France, Navarre and Scotland as well as the daughter of the Visconti Duke of Milan.

In 1378, the successive elections of two rival popes affected the direction of English matrimonial policy. Urban VI, at Rome, had the support of the Italian, German and English rulers, while Clement VII, in Avignon, was championed by the French, Scots and Castilians. Urban's support was geographically disparate, and he planned to consolidate it through an alliance between the King of England and the imperial house. Urban's envoy, the bishop of Ravenna, Pileo de Prata, visited Charles IV's son Wenzel (known as the King of Bohemia), in Prague to advise on the advantages of a marriage between Richard and his sister, and Wenzel duly wrote to the King to affirm their holy duty in reuniting Christendom. Richard's envoys, at that time in Milan discussing the possible betrothal to the Duke's daughter, were now sent to Prague, but the talks were delayed when they were kidnapped on their return journey and detained abroad until their ransom was paid. Negotiations finally resumed in June 1380, and it was not until January the following year that the English and imperial representatives met. On 2 May, a month after the imperial envoys, under the Duke of Teschen, had been received by John of Gaunt at the

Savoy, Richard was able to agree to the treaty for his marriage with Anne of Bohemia.

This 'little scrap of humanity', as the Westminster chronicler described her, had spent much of her childhood at the Hradschin Palace in the flourishing city of Prague, which under her father's rule had been transformed with the building of new districts, the awe-inspiring cathedral of St Vitus and a university. Charles IV, who aspired to emulate Charlemagne and St Louis, was a pious, exceptionally learned man, a traveller and collector of Carolingian art. He was a patron of Petrarch, while his grandfather had promoted the work of Dante. Influenced by the new Italian philosophy of humanism, Charles inaugurated a '"new age" in all the domains of social, artistic and literary advance'[1] and he was also innovative in his attitude to sovereignty. Anne would have witnessed, and perhaps participated in, a court ceremonial that elevated even acts of everyday business to an almost holy status, 'sanctifying' the embodiments of state power through a cultivated association with religious imagery. Anne lived mainly at the court of her elder brother Wenzel while their father toured his scattered empire, and after Charles's death in 1379, it was Wenzel with whom the English dealt. In terms of her breeding and extensive cosmopolitan connections, Anne was an ideal bride. Her elder sister Margareta was Queen of Hungary and Poland, her aunt Bona had been Queen of France and her father's first wife had been a Valois princess. Richard himself was to try to emulate the stately ceremonial and sophisticated atmosphere his bride had known at the imperial courts. But she was embarrassingly poor.

Initially, discussion of Anne's dowry had been diplomatically postponed, but it was soon obvious that Wenzel simply could not afford one. Nevertheless, the marriage was considered sufficiently important for Richard to effectively buy Anne from her brother for 'loans' totalling 15,000 pounds. Acquiring Anne was less a matter of healing the rift in Christendom than of detaching the imperial powers from their links with the French, and Richard was prepared to pay dearly for it, yet Anne's impecuniousness immediately aroused dissent.

She set out from Germany with her retinue in September 1381, chaperoned by her aunt the Duchess of Brabant. They travelled from Ghent to Bruges, where they were greeted by the Count of Flanders, then on to meet the earls of Devon and Salisbury at Gravelines, protected by an impressive company of 500 men-at-arms. Anne's escort now left her, and she continued on to Calais with the English party, crossing to Dover on 18 December. Her arrival was inauspicious – a storm raised huge waves in the harbour, smashing the ships against one another and destroying the vessel in which the new queen had sailed – but she reached Canterbury safely three days later, accompanied by John of Gaunt, and then moved on to spend Christmas at Leeds Castle before leaving for London in mid-January. Already people were complaining that the King would have been better advised to marry the rich Visconti princess. Anne had been obliged to linger at Leeds while money was raised for her ceremonial entry into the capital through loans from the abbot of Westminster, the bishop of Worcester and a grocer turned mayor of London named Nicholas Brembre. After a pageant at Blackheath, Anne and Richard progressed through the city, but the people made their feelings apparent by ripping down the royal arms crossed with the imperial ones that had been hung on a fountain to welcome her.

Anne's foreign entourage also provoked antagonism. Richard was keen to display his magnanimity, and gave an annuity of 500 pounds to the Duke of Teschen, while two other envoys were granted 250 pounds apiece and numerous other gifts of between five and 200 florins were distributed. To make matters worse, the primates of London and Canterbury argued about which of them should be given precedence at her wedding and coronation, a quarrel resolved by sharing the honours. The bishop of London conducted the wedding on 20 January and the archbishop the coronation two days later. It is testament to Anne's judgement and a certain sweetness of character that she was eventually able to make herself beloved of the Londoners, but the awkward circumstances of her marriage highlighted an uneasy relationship between the King and his people which would eventually result in desperate conflict.

The previous year, Richard had confronted a rebellion. Conflict between a king and his magnates was nothing new, but the 1381 revolt was revolutionary in that it was orchestrated by the peasants. In the years after the Black Death, agricultural labourers had seen the potential for an improved standard of living, as the scarcity of men made their work more valuable. Their hopes were dashed by a combination of taxation and legislation to return wages to pre-plague levels and resentment soon turned to violence, culminating in a union of peasants from Kent and Essex marching on London. The image of Richard the blond boy-king riding bravely out to calm his rioting subjects is familiar from school textbooks, but his involvement in the Peasants' Revolt was a source of contemporary disagreement which sheds light on his complex and contradictory character. In the pro-Richard version of events, the King retreated from the Tower, where the rebels were planning to 'slay all the lords and ladies of great renown', diverted their attention by agreeing to meet them at Mile End, where he granted freedom from villein status (essentially a prevailing form of slavery whereby men were bound to the land they worked and to those who owned it), confronted the peasant leader, Wat Tyler, at Smithfield and, when a scuffle broke out resulting in Tyler's death, personally led the peasants away from the danger posed by his bodyguard. The other version has Richard opening the doors to the Tower, making craven concessions at Mile End and behaving with unpleasant duplicity at Smithfield. The granting of manumission and the guiding to safety of the rebels at Smithfield are the points on which the chronicles concur, but was Richard 'marvellously impelled by cleverness beyond his years and excited by boldness',[2] or a sneaking coward who permitted the protestors to take liberties with his mother at the Tower and shrilly declared he wished the villeins would be 'incomparably more debased'?[3]

Inevitably, hindsight invites comparisons between Richard II and his great-grandfather Edward but, as in Edward's case, it is imperative to attempt to disentangle the perceptions of his contemporaries from those of a broader history. The variance of chronicle accounts of the Peasants' Revolt is just one instance of how Richard's mercurial tendencies were interpreted in different ways from different standpoints. He had his 'Gaveston' in Robert de Vere, Earl of Oxford, with whom he was accused of enjoying perverse intimacies and, like Edward II, he was fond of late-night drinking parties. He also had an exaggerated, doomed sense of his own prerogative and a persistent belief in his right 'arbitrarily in his own mad counsels to exercise his own personal will obstinately'.[4] Following the accusation that he was timid in war, Richard has been presented as an arty rather than a hearty king, his reign a 'watershed in English art',[5] yet Christine de Pisan described him as 'a true Lancelot', while his personal contribution to the flowering of late fourteenth-century court culture has been questioned. The King was a dedicated setter of fashion, something of a gourmand, even a voluptuary, but he was also profoundly pious and engaged with the pageantry, if not the activity, of chivalry. John Gower saw the Peasants' Revolt as the germ of Richard's tyranny and ultimate deposition, a warning from God which he ignored, but it was, and is still, a matter of debate whether he did so through arrogance or weakness, or whether he was simply a martyr to the dishonourable ambition of the coming age.

The man Anne of Bohemia married in 1382 was fair-haired and self-consciously youthful, keeping his face clean-shaven when it was conventional for grown men to wear a beard. He was 'abrupt and somewhat stammering in his speech, capricious in his manners . . . prodigal in his gifts, extravagantly splendid in his entertainments and dress . . . haughty and too much devoted to voluptuousness'.[6] If his ideal was what he saw as the re-establishment of the royal prerogative, his daily preoccupation was the manifestation of the royal dignity. Perhaps more than any other northern European king until Louis XIV of France in the seventeenth century, he strove to make a pageant of every moment of his existence. He developed elaborations on court protocol, insisting on more complex ceremonial and new forms of address such as 'Your Highness' and 'Your Majesty' which had never before been used in England. The peerage was expanded with new ranks in its hierarchy: the title of marquess was introduced in 1385, baronies by patent formalised in 1387 and all of the King's relations, the royal earls, were elevated to the rank of duke in 1397. Forever in the shadow of his father's legend, Richard was obsessed with chivalry and an expert manipulator of the propaganda generated by great tournaments, though he did not joust himself but watched from his throne. It was noted that at formal crown-wearings he would remain seated in silent splendour all day long, and those to whom he inclined his royal gaze were expected to fall to their knees. With hindsight, Richard's emphasis on his own regality seems rather pathetic, pompously empty, but his own age regarded him differently. He certainly provoked criticism, but the size and splendour of his court also inspired awe.

The Smithfield tournament of 1390 is typical of the kind of chivalric display in which Richard revelled. Attended by his brother-in-law Waleran of Luxembourg, the Count of St Pol and William of Bavaria, it featured the King himself taking out the honours in a new badge, his emblem of the white hart. After the jousts, the company moved to Westminster, where they heard service and midnight Mass and then processed to high Mass with the King and Queen in their crowns. The celebrations continued at Kennington, where Richard presided – crowned – over a banquet, and after that at Windsor, with another feast. At every stage of the festivities, rich colours and jewels, music and rare delicacies combined in a concetto of regality. 'The sensory overload engendered by the overlapping layers of exquisite creations was part of the magic that distinguished the realm of the great from the drudgery of the rest,' writes Marina Belozerskaya. 'Great princely celebrations were also international events, epicentres whence ideas and tastes radiated across Europe.'[7]

On the surface, at least, then, Anne's new life was one of elegance and luxury. Londoners may have grumbled at her lack of a dowry, but she was greeted in the capital with novel displays of magnificence, including a pageant featuring a gilded castle made by the city goldsmiths. Chaucer remarked on the new glass windows installed in royal residences, and though many of Richard's building projects, such as the reconstruction of the Great Hall at Westminster or the thirteen statues of English kings commemorating their descent from Edward the Confessor (an inheritance on which William the Conqueror had insisted all along), were emphatically grandiose, they also had a private character, motivated by increasingly sophisticated notions of comfort and privacy. At Eltham, Richard installed a bath house, a painted chamber, a ballroom and a garden for the Queen. Another was made for her at King's Langley, while at Sheen he chose the island of La Neyt in the Thames for the royal lodging, which featured a bathroom with 2,000 coloured tiles and private lavatories. Chaucer's directions in the prologue to 'The Legend of Good Women' suggest that Eltham and Sheen were Anne's preferred residences, and she perhaps linked these smaller palaces with the meditative seclusion he glorifies in his poem.

At Eltham, Richard constructed a spicery and two sauceries to serve another of his enthusiasms, eating. In this as everything else, Richard was determined to appear a perfect king, and the prologue to *The Forme of Cury*, his recipe book, describes him as 'the royallest viander' in Christendom. The book contains 196 recipes, divided into first courses, main courses and puddings, and shows that court food was heavily spiced with ginger, cloves and cardamom, and similar in flavour to modern Arabic food, with meats cooked in sugar, spices and fruits. Richard, who is credited with inventing the handkerchief for his personal use, did not go in for coarse great lumps of meat. Spoons were used, and there are recipes for pâtés, galantines and stews, hare with almonds, oysters with rice and ginger and fruits baked with honey and wine. Spices were a tremendous luxury, and their prodigal use may have had as much to do with status as with preservation or flavour.

Richard was passionate, too, about fine clothes, and set the fashion for all the men at court. Clothes were more than a form of indulgence, they were an essential part of the image of royal power: 'A king who was poorly attired or accoutred would sooner or later forfeit the allegiance of his subjects, as Henry VI was to find in the next century.'[8] Courtiers were obliged to emulate the King if they wished to get ahead, a challenge encountered in the poem 'Richard the Redeless', which describes a man who wears the whole of his wealth on his back. New trends included the codpiece, worn over tight hose, embroidered doublets with padded shoulders and the 'houpelande', a long, coloured robe with a high neck, often set with jewels, which replaced the more functional cloak. Such fashions were designed to display the male physique to perfection, emphasising long legs, a slim waist and powerful shoulders; others were more frivolous, including the 'shoon in long pikes' that Anne's Bohemian entourage was credited with introducing: shoes so long and pointed they had to be supported with chained garters wrapped round the knee and attached to the toes. Women wore fitted gowns that flowed at the hem, with beautiful collars sewn into the neck of their houpelandes. Anne owned at least two such collars bearing her emblems, an ostrich feather and a branch of rosemary, and ornamented with pearls.

Anne's jewellery is also of interest in that it in all likelihood connects her with Chaucer, the most celebrated poet of the age. The 'F' version to the prologue of 'The Legend of Good Women' begins with the poet asleep in a garden, dreaming of the God of Love and a queen, Alcestis, who reproaches the poet with his previous work, 'Troilus and Criseyde'. Alcestis claims that 'Troilus' is unjust to women and to love, since its subject is inconstancy, and commands him to write a history of faithful women which shall be delivered to the (real) Queen at Eltham or Sheen:

> Thou shalt, where thou livest, year by year
> The most part of thy time spend
> In making of a glorious legend
> Of good women, maidens and wives,
> That were true in loving all their lives.

It seems obvious to identify the God and Queen of Love with Richard and Anne – the god, like the King, has golden hair – but the comparison has been disputed. It has been suggested that Alcestis may have been intended as a compliment to Joan of Kent but, leaving aside the fact that the Fair Maid was dead when the poem was written, the inventory of the royal jewels in 1499 presents new evidence that Alcestis is a tribute to Anne of Bohemia. The inventory features a crown enamelled in red and blue with white enamel flowers, red and blue gems and pearls. Its origins are uncertain, and the workmanship may be French, but the crown was used as part of the dowry of Henry IV's daughter Blanche of Lancaster on her marriage to Ludwig of Bavaria in 1401, and it has been associated with collars that were certainly Anne's. The detail of the white flower is the key. Isabelle de Valois, Richard's second wife, was presented with two crowns after her marriage in 1396, one of which was decorated with jewels, pearls and white daisies. During the negotiations for the marriage,

Isabelle was referred to as 'our young marguerite, our precious stone, our beautiful white pearl'.[9] Pearls and daisies were potent iconographic symbols of purity and innocence, highly appropriate for a young bride. Given the uncertainty as to when the crown was acquired and its provenance, it is possible to posit that it was made for Isabelle, but this would be to neglect its similarity to the crown in the poem. Alcestis is described as wearing

> A fret of gold next her hair
> And upon that a white crown she bear
> With flowers small, and I shall not lie
> For all the world, right as a daisy
> Crowned is with white leaves light
> So were the flowers of her crown white.

The image is extended so that the Queen of Love's whole body appears as a daisy, in a green dress with 'the white 'wered crown' on her head. The 'F' version of the prologue was written in Anne's lifetime, and Chaucer, who spent a long period as a servant of the court, would have had the opportunity to see her wearing such a crown. The daisies in the crown suggest that he did, strengthening the case for Anne as the model for Alcestis (and potentially an involvement with the commissioning of the poem), and indicating that the crown given to Queen Isabelle was passed on from Anne's possessions.

Anne imported more to England than shoes and jewels. Her literary activities place her within the tradition of culturally innovative queens. The extent and influences of Richard's artistic patronage is still a matter of dispute, as has been noted, but there is no doubt that his reign encompassed one of the most important periods in English literature, a blossoming in which Anne played a small but significant part.

She is credited with introducing Bohemian craftsmanship in the field of manuscript illustration, specifically with regard to the *Liber Regalis*, the manual for royal coronations produced at Westminster in 1383 whose illuminations have been identified as Bohemian work. Bohemian influence has also been proposed in the Great Missal of Westminster (1384) and the Carmelite Missal made for the London Whitefriars in 1393. Anne's badge, an ostrich crowned and chained (ironically, far more appropriate to her husband), appears in the margin, and the work of the second master of the Missal, one of three artists who worked on it, is very similar to that of the *Liber Regalis* illuminator. The extent of Bohemian influence on English art in general is, again, a matter of debate, but even if the *Liber Regalis* represents an exception, it is an extremely significant one.

Vernacular literature, especially religious literature, had been strongly linked with English queens since Matilda of Scotland commissioned the French version of 'The Voyage of St Brendan' for her ladies' enjoyment. Anne's father, the Emperor, had been an active patron of religious works in Czech and German. By the fourteenth century, queens' traditional patronage of literature can be linked with another important dynamic of queenship, that of Marianism. Increasingly, the Virgin was depicted by artists as a keen reader, even leafing through a book on the back of the donkey as she flees with Joseph and Jesus to Egypt. The first such image appears in the eleventh century, and they were common by the fourteenth. Symbolically, the literacy of the mother of God celebrated her wisdom and her fitness to receive in her body the Word made flesh, and it is notable that a rise in the numbers of women book-owners through the period corresponds with the growth of portrayals of the Virgin reading, both a model for and a reflection of daily life. In a fourteenth-century annunciation painting, the Bohemian Master of Vissi Brod shows Mary seated at a table with two books before her.

Anne came from a part of Europe where the law specifically linked women with the transmission of culture, 'especially lay religious culture'.[10] In the early thirteenth century, a collection of Saxon customary laws was produced with reference to the 'Sachsenspiegel', an area of land stretching from Magdeburg, the first capital of the Holy Roman Empire, into modern Russia. 'The Way of the Saxons' sets out which objects are to be inherited by women, including geese, linens, kitchen utensils – and books, particularly those concerned with religious practices. As Anne had been educated in a place where women's role in trans-generational religious inheritance was official and vernacular religious texts had the support of the highest lay authority, Charles IV, and at a time when women's reading was increasingly associated with the Virgin, a powerful symbol for queens, it is unsurprising to find that she brought with her to England the New Testament in Latin, Czech and German, and that translations of the Gospels were made for her in English, perhaps as an aid to her education in the language. Her commitment to pious reading was celebrated at her funeral, as was her desire to overcome her foreignness 'so great a lady and also an alien would so lowlily study in virtuous books', praised Archbishop Arundel.

Yet Anne's English gospels also involved her in a theological controversy that contained some of the seeds of the Protestant Reformation. John Wycliffe, the Oxford theologian, promoted and translated the Bible in the vernacular, and his project is connected (though not to be conflated) with Lollardism, the movement that called for reform of the Church and emphasised the authority of faith rather than the worldly hierarchies of Rome. Accessible translations of the Bible were considered heretical by many, but not by Anne. When Wycliffe petitioned in favour of his translation in 1383, he observed: 'It is lawful for the noble Queen of England the sister of the Emperor to have the Gospel written in three languages ... and it would savour of the pride of Lucifer to call her a heretic for such a reason as this! And since the Germans wish in this matter reasonably to defend their own tongue, so ought the English to defend theirs.'[11] The Lollards seized on Archbishop Arundel's commendation of Anne's possession of the English texts in a tract published in 1407. It is not absurd to claim that this royal example endorsed a movement which was to come to its revolutionary fruition in the time of the next Queen Anne.

The connection between piety and literature also had a deeply personal significance for Anne of Bohemia. Soon after her arrival in 1382, she sought papal permission for greater solemnity in the celebration of the feast day of her namesake St Anne, the mother of the Virgin. In the early fifth century, St Jerome had highlighted the important role of mothers in teaching their daughters to read. 'Have a set of letters made for her ... and tell her their names ... let her every day repeat to you a portion of the Scriptures as her fixed task.' Reading the scriptures, Jerome explained, was the best way to prevent girls from wasting their time in idle pursuits, or succumbing to the vanities of the flesh. Alongside the growing tendency to portray the Virgin reading, the fourteenth century popularised depictions of St Anne teaching her daughter. Anne of Bohemia's veneration of the saint could be associated with her own longing to bear a child, as St Anne and her husband Joachim had waited twenty years before being so blessed. Anne's petition to the Pope at the time of her marriage could possibly suggest that she felt an affinity with St Anne, believing she would wait a long time for a child because her marriage was not consummated.

This is speculation. There is absolutely no evidence that Richard and Anne did not enjoy a normal sex life and only some reason to suspect the opposite. In his lifetime, Richard was accused of homosexuality. He identified with his great-grandfather Edward II, and the same analogy was made politically at the end of his reign when Adam Usk's chronicle accuses him of 'perjuries, *sacrileges, sodomitical acts*, the reduction of his people to servitude, lack of reason and incapacity to rule' (the italics are this author's), though, as in the case of Edward, this does not necessarily mean he committed homosexual acts – sodomy was a politicised perversity, used as grounds for unfitness. Richard liked the company of women, in fact the cost of the retinues of his female courtiers was a source of complaint, but he also enjoyed passionate friendships with men, particularly Robert de Vere, Earl of Oxford. Such friendships, again, do not necessarily indicate homosexuality (indeed, De Vere proved himself inconveniently straight). However, a persistent accusation levelled against Richard was that he was childlike. Obviously, he had come to the throne as a child, but such observations dogged him to the end of his reign, and he may have encouraged them in cultivating infantile appearance. If it is dabbling in psycho-history to theorise that Richard preferred loving, romanticised friendship to mature sex, it is notable that in his second wife, a six-year-old girl, he consciously chose a bride with whom he could not hope to have sexual relations for some years. Given that his relationship with Anne was childless, the need for an heir by 1396 was imperative, yet he chose to ignore it. Possibly Richard was infertile, which might account for the fact that, as far as is known, he had no illegitimate children, but there is some evidence that he was committed to chastity. In the hauntingly exquisite Wilton Diptych, the double-panelled painting that is one of the artistic glories of his reign, Richard's arms are impaled with those of Edward the Confessor, suggesting that, like the saint, he had rejected sex for a spiritual marriage with his country. This, and the marriage with Isabelle de Valois, may have been connected with his grief for Anne, as the diptych was made in 1395, a year after her death, but it is certainly possible that his first marriage was also electively chaste.

There is another reason to suspect that Richard had little hope of a child from his marriage to Anne. By 1385, the Scots were causing trouble again. Their allies, the French, were menacing English ships in the Channel and the northern marches were subject to yet more raids. That summer, at York, Richard called out the final feudal force ever to be summoned in England. It was one of the greatest armies ever seen in the country, and the last to include fighting priests. Edinburgh was taken, but little else was achieved beyond the siege of Stirling Castle and the destruction of a few religious houses. The campaign did quell unrest on the border for three years but, despite Froissart's sycophantic assurances that Richard had achieved more than the Black Prince or Edward III, it was neither an answer to Edward II's dismal rout at Bannockburn nor a challenge to Edward I's conquests in the north. In a gesture that attracted comparisons with Edward II's promotion of Piers Gaveston, Richard elevated Robert de Vere to Marquess of Dublin on his return, but more significantly, in terms of his marriage and the future of England, he named eleven-year-old Roger Mortimer as his heir.

Queen Anne was nineteen in 1385. She and Richard had been married just three years. Why would Richard make such a pessimistic statement so publicly? The rumours of John of Gaunt's ambitions for the throne had not abated in the decade since Richard's coronation. As Edward III lay dying at Havering, he had naturally been troubled by the question of the succession. If his grandson were to die, which branch of the royal family would have the better claim? Should the English crown pass through the heirs general, in which case the succession would belong to Philippa, the daughter of Edward III's second son, Lionel, Duke of Clarence, or through the heirs male, in which case it would go to Gaunt as the third son? Philippa Plantagenet had married Edmund Mortimer, Earl of March and, in 1385, Richard declared his support for the heirs general argument by naming Philippa's son Roger. The transmission of a claim via a woman was one Edward himself had endorsed; it had been the foundation for his bid for the French crown through his mother Isabella, and a reversion to the Salic law of heirs male as practised in France would effectively undermine the English position in the Hundred Years War. However, at the end of 1376, Edward attested a letter patent entailing the crown in the male line, with only a remainder to the heirs general. According to this document, the house of Lancaster, not Mortimer, stood to inherit if Richard had no children.

Richard's statement naming Mortimer may have been a stalling tactic. As well as promoting his friend De Vere, Richard raised his two other royal uncles, Edmund of Langley and Thomas of Woodstock, to the dukedoms of York and Gloucester, a move that diluted the preeminence of Gaunt as the only royal duke. Gaunt was still unpopular, and Richard needed to curb his aspirations. This may also have been the motivation for his support of Gaunt's attempt on the throne of Castile. Walsingham asserted that John had petitioned Parliament for a confirmation of the entail to heirs male, but this did not prevent him from claiming the throne of Castile in right of his second wife, Constance. Richard acknowledged this claim on his return from Scotland and in March 1386 placed him at his own right hand and declared he should be addressed as King. Gaunt departed to fight for his Spanish kingdom that July, remaining abroad three years. Richard had therefore done what he could to neutralise a potential Lancastrian threat, and in this context his naming of Mortimer can be seen as part of a tactical pattern. Yet why was he seemingly so certain he would not have children himself? In January 1394, when Anne was still living, Richard permitted his close friend Thomas Mowbray to use the crest of a crowned leopard, a badge traditionally reserved for the eldest son of the king. The use in the grant of the pluperfect tense '*si quem procreassemus*' 'if we had begotten the same'[12] has been highlighted as evidence that Richard accepted his childless condition. Officially, the subject was taboo – 'Who is it that dares to suggest that the King will have no issue?' asked Parliament the same year – but it is possible that Richard himself knew that he would not. By 1394, it could of course have become apparent that Anne was unable to bear a child, but no such diagnosis could have been conclusive in 1385. So it is plausible that Richard and Anne did not consummate their marriage, and that Anne, like her namesake saint, continued to hope for a miracle.

Richard's Scottish expedition had not been a total failure, but the mood in Parliament was hostile. The King had promoted another friend, Michael de la Pole, to the earldom of Suffolk, and Pole and De Vere were given the posts of chancellor and chamberlain. The Scots war had been an attempt on Richard's part to assert his majority, now that he was eighteen, and it was natural that he should seek to create a circle of loyal magnates from among his peers, but he was criticised for ignoring the advice of the older magnates. The royal finances were overstretched, and the cost of the campaign, as well as the truce with France that had made it possible, was also unpopular. Robert de Vere had caused a scandal by having an affair with one of the Queen's Bohemian ladies, Agnes Launcecrona, and was trying to repudiate his wife. Richard's sanctioning of this relationship was perceived as a great insult by his uncles, as De Vere was married to their niece Philippa de Coucy, the daughter of Edward III and Philippa of Hainault's eldest girl, Isabella. Adultery was one thing, but such an affront to a woman of royal blood was shocking, and it fuelled more general criticisms that Queen Anne's household had introduced suspicious foreign 'abuses'. Money, favouritism and the whiff of sex scandals were all creating dissent between the King and his magnates, but Richard refused to accept any correction.

The obduracy of the lords in their demands for financial reform gathered force throughout the following year. When Parliament met in October 1386, the lords demanded that the chancellor, the new Earl of Suffolk, be removed, a motion that was carried despite Richard's furious objections. Suffolk was impeached and imprisoned at Windsor and Richard, outraged, left London, first for his county of Cheshire and then on a prolonged tour of the provinces. Anne accompanied him, and they were together for the initiation of Richard Scrope to the see of Lichfield in June. Richard was planning to strike at the lords and in August he summoned his chief justice, Robert Tresilian, to Nottingham, where he inquired into the legal status of Parliament's actions. In 1352, Edward III's Treason Act had set out five counts on which treason could be defined, which did not include challenge to the royal prerogative, but Richard was keen that the judicial advice should favour the cause of the crown, and though Tresilian did not claim that the lords' actions were treasonous, in a neat bit of casuistry, he did assert that Richard had the right to execute as traitors those who had hindered that prerogative.

After Richard had flounced off on progress, a council of fourteen lords had been convened to administer the realm in the King's name. When Richard returned to London in November 1387 he summoned its leaders, his uncle Thomas of Woodstock, Duke of Gloucester, Richard FitzAlan, the Earl of Arundel and Thomas Beauchamp, the Earl of Warwick. They attended him at Westminster on 17 November, with a small but threatening company of 300 men-at-arms, and charged De Vere, Suffolk, Tresilian, Archbishop Neville of York and the obliging Nicholas Brembre with treason. Their collective name, the Lords Appellant, derives from their offer to prove their charge by the trial of 'appeal', or accusation, in single combat. The situation was already too grave for such chivalrous posturing. Henry of Bolingbroke, the eldest son of John of Gaunt, and Thomas Mowbray, Richard's former friend, joined the Appellants, and Robert de Vere was raising troops in Oxfordshire. On 20 December, he was defeated by a force captained by Bolingbroke at Radcot Bridge. De Vere escaped by swimming his horse over the river and fled to Louvain, and Richard and Anne were placed under house arrest in the Tower.

For several days, it was claimed later, the Lords Appellant had considered deposing the King, but when Parliament resumed in February, Richard took his place on his throne. However, the 'Merciless Parliament' was not inclined to be lenient to those who, the Lords Appellant alleged, had 'seduced' the 'King into bringing the country to the brink of war. Tresilian was dragged out of his hiding place in Westminster Sanctuary and executed, as was Brembre. Queen Anne interceded on her knees for Sir Simon Burley, who had been her husband's tutor and a close member of her late mother-in-law's circle, but her pleas succeeded only in sparing Burley the full agony of a traitor's death. Three other knights of Richard's chamber did endure being hung, drawn and quartered. Although Richard renewed his coronation oath and received the homage of his magnates, there had been a perceptible shift in the balance of power in England. The Lords

Appellant had made it clear that Parliament, and not the king, was sovereign. Richard never forgave them.

Thomas Mowbray was restored to favour in May, but Richard refused to countenance a reconciliation with Gloucester and Arundel until the return of John of Gaunt in 1389. The Castilian challenge had failed, and though Richard had been pleased to have his uncle out of the way, Gaunt's presence now bolstered the shaken and divided royal family. In the summer of 1390 Anne and Richard paid a long visit to him at Leicester Castle, and they were all together again at Eltham for Christmas. Richard appeared to have stabilised his government, or at least stage-managed the appearance of stability. On the last day of the 1391 Parliamentary session, the Rolls record that the King was formally petitioned by the commons to be 'as free in his regality, liberty and royal dignity in his time as his noble progenitors, formerly kings of England, were in their time, notwithstanding any statute or ordinance made before this time to the contrary, and especially in the time of Edward II'. The reference to Edward II makes the petition's authorship clear.

If all was respectful concord between the magnates, the citizens of London were not quite so particular about the King's dignity. The year 1391 was a hard one for the city, struck by plague and serious food shortages due to a poor harvest. By November, a curfew had been imposed, and the next month Richard forbade public assemblies as a threat to the peace. London was alive with seditious rumour: that the King was incapable of government, that the King was planning to renege on his promises of reform and recall De Vere. In Fleet Street, a crowd rioted for bread, and the alarmed court heard of armed gangs on the loose. Richard had no reason to favour the Londoners. They had done nothing to help him against the Lords Appellant, and the city had recently refused two royal requests for loans. In May 1392, Richard relocated the court of common pleas to York, and after a ten-day visit there with Anne, went on progress in the Midlands. The mayor, aldermen and sheriffs of London, along with twenty-four citizens, were summoned to appear on pain of death before the King at Nottingham on 25 June. Richard dismissed and imprisoned the mayor and two sheriffs, appointed his own warden and set up a committee to investigate abuses. London's liberties were revoked and a collective fine of 100,000 pounds imposed. According to Walsingham, Queen Anne had attempted to soften Richard's heart towards the Londoners, on her knees, at Westminster, Windsor and Nottingham. Practically, such gestures were useless, but Anne took part in the ceremony for the formal submission of London, a hugely elaborate performance in which the intercession of the Queen featured as the climax.

On 21 August, Richard and Anne crossed London Bridge from South-wark to receive the keys of the city from the mayor, the first time such a ceremony was performed. They processed via St Paul's to Westminster through streets decorated with gold cloth and crimson banners, pausing at Cheapside to receive two gold crowns and two golden cups from a boy and girl who hovered precariously on pulleys above a castle set in painted clouds. The Londoners presented gifts of horses and holy images of St Anne and the Trinity, and two altarpieces featuring scenes from the crucifixion. When Anne had made her first entry into London before her wedding, she had been given a charter begging her intercession on behalf of the city, 'just as our other lady Queens who preceded Your most Excellent Highness, may it be pleasing to your most clement and pre-eminent nobility to mediate with our Lord the King in such wise with gracious words and deeds'. Now, prior to entering Westminster Hall, where the banquet was arranged, Anne proclaimed that she would do her duty for the city. Having changed her dress, she knelt before her enthroned husband and begged him to restore the city's liberties, emphasising that no king, not even Arthur himself, had been so loved and honoured by his people. Richard then returned the city keys and its ceremonial sword.

If the practical authority of English queens can be said to have declined since the twelfth century, then intercession had undergone a concomitant diminution in status. Where the Anglo-Norman queens had shared and participated in their husbands' governments, the conciliar role of the consort since then had been reduced to one of supplication. The way intercession had lost its meaning through ritualisation, becoming a staged means of permitting a king to act in a 'feminised' manner – to change his mind or show mercy – without compromising his masculinity, has been traced here through Isabella of France's intercession for the banishment of the Despensers in 1321 and Philippa of Hainault's pleas for the citizens of Calais in 1347. The failure of Anne's intercession for Simon Burley shows that as a device it now had no spontaneous power, but merely modified the perception of a decision that had already been taken. Intercession had always been predicated on weakness, the idea of the queen as subversive, in that she was challenging the king's judgement, contained by the queen as vulnerable petitioner. In London in 1392, her special intercessory status as the intimate of the king's bed was made erotically explicit. Queens' sexual relationships with their husbands had frequently been presented as threatening, but the description of the 1392 ceremony in the *Concordia* indicates that Anne's (presumed) intimacy with Richard was used as an allegory for the submission of the city itself. The *Concordia* casts Richard as a bridegroom come to take possession of his wife, giving, as one critic has remarked, 'a whole new meaning to the phrase 'royal entry'.[13] The body of the kneeling queen becomes a conduit for the city's 'eroticised abjection', Richard's possession of her person a symbol of his possession of his city. The scripted success of Anne's submission earned her the presumably unironic compliment of '*virgo mediatrix*', inviting comparison with the Virgin in her representation as Maria mediatrix.

Anne's Christmas gift from the grateful Londoners was a pelican, again a symbol of self-sacrificing femininity, as the bird will feed its young with blood from its own breast. Richard got a camel. In spring, Gaunt and Gloucester left to discuss terms for extending the French truce, though the English continued to despise the idea of peace with their old enemy. When the extension was achieved in June, there were outbreaks of violence in Yorkshire and Cheshire, where fighting the French was practically the local industry. That summer, Anne and Richard stayed at Sheen, and the next year made pilgrimage to Canterbury, where they received the news of the death of Anne's mother, the Empress Elizabeth. A requiem was sung for the Empress at St Paul's, and in July the King and Queen heard another for Joan of Kent at Corfe. In August Richard staged a joint crown-wearing at Salisbury, then he and Anne set off for Beaulieu Abbey, followed by Titchfield, where the abbot entertained them to a fine supper featuring twelve dressed pike. They were together at Westminster for the opening of Parliament in 1394, when Richard made his sad grant of arms to Thomas Mowbray.

Anne had spent much of her marriage travelling at her husband's side. They were rarely separated, and whatever their private relationship may have been, Richard loved her. She died at Sheen on 7 June 1394, aged just twenty-seven, and Richard ordered that the palace to which he had devoted so much attention be ripped down. He vowed that for a year he would enter no building except a church in which he had spent time with the Queen. Anne's funeral was delayed for two months while Richard prepared in characteristically grand style, ordering a hundred wax torches from Flanders. On 3 August, her body was carried from Sheen to St Paul's and then to Westminster Abbey. Determined that the ceremony should be fully attended, Richard had summoned the magnates to London for 29 July, but Richard FitzAlan, the Earl of Arundel, still managed to arrive late and the overwrought King hit him so hard that he fell bleeding to the ground.

Anne's childlessness excluded her from participating in one of the key dynamics of queenship, but by the end of her life she had attracted affection and respect. Richard's court was one of the glories of the age, and Anne had an influential role in the continuation of the presentation of English royal magnificence that had begun with the efforts of Edward III. Her epitaph, produced for Henry V's reburial of King Richard, remembered her as a merciful intercessor whose intervention had resolved disputes. Like Adeliza of Louvain, she had sublimated her lack of children into a maternal concern for the poor, and was celebrated for her charity and her kindness to the sick and the widowed. Most poignantly, Anne of Bohemia's epitaph particularly recalled her care for pregnant women.

Soon after Anne's death, Richard departed for a seven-month campaign in Ireland, but the search for a new queen had already begun. As early as August 1394 embassies were sent to the King of Scots, the Duke of Bavaria and the King of Aragon. Keen to prevent a Spanish alliance, and to continue the peace between France and England, Charles VI sent envoys to Ireland to propose his own daughter, six-year-old Isabelle, in May 1395. In an attempt to encourage Richard, Charles commissioned a long treatise from Philippe de Mezières, a distinguished writer now living in retirement in the Celestine convent in Paris, which discussed the advantages of the match. De Mezières chose to emphasise the consequences of an earlier royal marriage, that of Isabella of France and Edward II, which had been intended to bring peace between the two nations but had instead resulted in the onset of the Hundred Years War: 'Call to mind, and sadly, the marriage, then thought a fortunate one, of the mother of the valiant King Edward, your much loved ancestor, from which you are descended, and of the deadly and penetrating thorns resulting from that union, which have been active in such a way that the beautiful lilies from which you spring have been horribly trampled underfoot.'[14] A marriage to a second Isabelle, De Mezières asserted, would heal what marriage to the first had wounded. His treatise indulges in some confusingly mystic language – 'the rich diamond through the holy sacrament of marriage should become son to the shining carbuncle and so shut the mouths of all those who ask for the five-footed sheep' – but sought to offer some homespun wisdom on the main problem with the match, namely the bride's age. Richard had no heir, and legally could not hope to consummate his marriage for six years, and it could take still longer for Isabelle to be ready to bear a child. But women, declared De Mezières, were, like horses, all the better for being broken young, and Richard would have the satisfaction of a wife who had been educated to his tastes.

Joanna of Navarre and Henry IV: a prestigious foreign bride for a parvenu monarch.

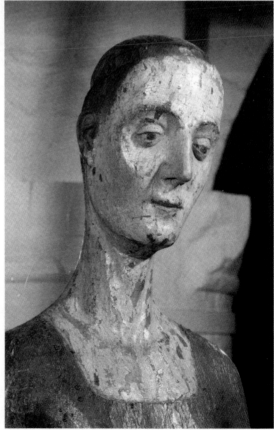

Catherine de Valois was the ancestress of a great royal dynasty, but by a servant, not a king.

Omine ne in furo
re tuo arguas me
neq; in ira tua cor
ripias me.

A glimpse of the secrets of the queen's chamber. The birth of a son to Catherine de Valois was supposed to unite England and France.

Valiant but fatally cautious, Marguerite of Anjou struggled to take the place of a king who could not grow up.

Opposite: Catherine was the perfect princess for England's model warrior, Henry V.

ur moost goode and graciouse. Queue d

The love match between Edward IV and the beautiful widow
Elizabeth Woodville (above and opposite) scandalised Europe. But was
Elizabeth a grasping arriviste or a courageous and tragic queen?

Anne Neville had two chances at the crown, but she barely lived to enjoy it.

Anne Neville's northern affinities were essential to her husband's successful usurpation.

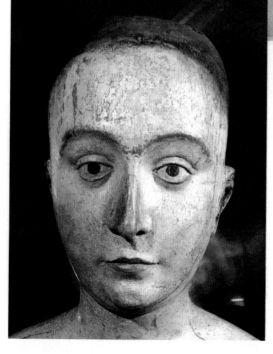

Did Elizabeth of York conceal an affair with her murderous uncle Richard?

Henry Tudor was desperate to conceal the fact that his wife's royal claims were far superior to his own.

The allusion to Isabelle's education is a discreet reference to her unfortunate domestic circumstances. Better, De Mezières suggests, that a bride should be removed from her parents before habits which may prove displeasing to her husband can become ingrained. Isabelle's mother, Isabeau of Bavaria, was notorious for her debauched lifestyle and undiscriminating love life and had received warnings about the neglect of her regal and maternal duties from everyone from the Pope to the celebrated scholar Christine de Pisan. Isabeau and Charles had married in 1385, and the French Queen's arrival in Paris had set a new standard for royal pageantry, but the success of their relationship, which produced twelve children, was compromised when, in 1392, the King went mad, and the periodic fits of insanity he suffered for the rest of his life overshadowed the marriage. One of the first consequences was the assumption of the regency by Charles's uncle, Philip of Burgundy, which led to dissent between the crown and the duchy that would influence English policy in the next century. More immediately, it had a personal impact on the French royal children.

Isabeau of Bavaria might not have been a perfect mother, but a glance at the 'facts' of her life reveals that, as in the case of Eleanor of Aquitaine, many of them are legends, if not downright fabrications. Since much of the criticism levelled by French accounts is politically motivated, it is not surprising that these are particularly hostile. Although Isabeau was extravagant and unwise in her choice of allies, her accounts belie accusations that she was a neglectful mother.[15] Purchases of books, toys and clothes for her children, as well as the commissioning of memorial Masses for those who died show that she was at least as involved with their upbringing as other women of her rank, but this has not stopped her detractors from claiming that, caught between their mother's frivolity and their father's bouts of madness, the royal children lived a ramshackle, abandoned life in conditions of squalor that scandalised witnesses. It was said that it was only thanks to the pity of their servants that the sons and daughters of France managed not to die of starvation. While there is no evidence for such extreme allegations, the atmosphere in which Isabelle was raised might well have been an unpleasant and confusing one.

Charles's madness often caused him to shrink from his wife and children in confusion and fear, and he frequently did not recognise them. He could be violent, smashing and burning furniture, tearing his clothes, and such rages were severe enough for it to be considered unsafe for the Queen to sleep with him. A mistress was procured for the King, perhaps as some sort of therapeutic measure, but this led to accusations that the Queen of

France was pimping for her husband. When he was sane, Charles was a handsome, intelligent man, but when the fits came over him, 'It was a great pity to see him, as his body was all eaten away with dirt and ordure'.[16] The French court was condemned for immorality and drunkenness, and Isabeau's reputation was not helped by dreadful incidents such as the 1393 'Bal des Sauvages', a party in 'primitive' costumes which went horribly wrong, resulting in the death by fire of five of the King's friends. Charles himself was saved only by a quick-thinking duchess who threw her dress over him to stifle the flames. Yet Isabeau did try to help her husband. During his first illness, she promised she would dedicate the child she was then carrying to God if He would spare the King, and Isabelle's sister Marie duly became a nun at Poissy at the age of six. Isabeau also organised holy processions in Paris and in 1409 sent her children to pray for their father's recovery at Mont St Michel. A combination of the frenzied hedonism of the court, her mother's anxious piety and a father who was by turns gentle and terrifying could not have formed a very stable background for a little girl, even a privileged princess of France. Perhaps this explains Isabelle's own rather sad enthusiasm to leave home to be married, as, according to Froissart she expressed her gladness at the prospect: 'For I am told that then I shall be a great lady.'

Isabelle's age may well have accorded with Richard's own inclinations towards chastity which, if they did not precede Anne's death, were affirmed by the crossing of his arms with those of the Confessor in the Wilton Diptych and the announcement of the King's assumption of the new arms on 13 October, the feast of the saint. A sexless marriage fitted into the splendid vision carefully conjured by De Mezières, of Richard as a new Arthur and Charles as Charlemagne, uniting not only European Christendom but the kingdoms of the east in 'royal and imperial splendour'. In Monmouth's *History of Britain*, Arthur is said to have begun his reign with a campaign in Ireland, where Richard received Charles's proposal, and the combination of the Irish expedition and the French marriage played seductively into a grandiose projection of Richard as the king who would finally lead England to the new Jerusalem. *The Verses of Gildas*, a prophecy written in Edward II's reign, describes the 'king now ruling' as being married to a princess of France. After a serious crisis, the king would conquer Ireland and Scotland, settle the Gascon question and restore unity to England. France, Spain and North Africa would fall to his might, he would recover the Holy Land and accept an imperial crown from the Pope. De Mezières' use of Edward II's story, and his casting of Richard as the conquering redeemer of the past through his alliance with Isabelle, could be seen as corroborating the Gildas prophecy. An alliance with Isabelle would chastely connect Richard not only with the heroes of Arthurian romance, but with the crusaders: the Grail could be glimpsed only by the pure, while the attainment of the Holy City had been linked with sexual abstinence (or not) since Eleanor of Aquitaine had been maligned for subverting Louis VII's hopes for Jerusalem. The distinction between the private and the public man could never be clear for any medieval king, and in Richard's case it is quite characteristic that what may have begun as an idiosyncrasy, or a personal religious commitment, had to be transformed into transcendental destiny.

Of course, it was also a matter of money. This time, Richard would not be accused of taking a pauper bride. In July, he sent his own envoys to Charles to demand two million gold francs as Isabelle's dowry, though they were permitted to allow the French to haggle them down to one million if necessary, with an initial payment of 400,000 and the balance to be paid annually over three years. Eventually the English settled for 800,000 with a 3,000 down payment. If the match were to be broken off, Charles would be liable for a three million-franc forfeit, and he was to bear the expense of bringing his daughter to Calais for the wedding. Should Isabelle die before she was thirteen, Richard was to marry a relative, possibly one of her sisters Mary or Michelle, and retain 400,000 francs of the dowry. If Richard died before Isabelle was twelve she would receive 500,000 francs, as well as her dower settlement of £6,666 13s 4d per year. Some provision was made for the fact that Isabelle was below the canonical age of consent: if she refused the marriage when she was twelve the dowry was forfeit, and if Richard rejected her he would return it with 800,000 francs' compensation. Any jewels Isabelle was given could also return with her to France in the event of Richard's death.

Thus, on 9 March 1396, a twenty-eight-year truce was sealed between England and France. One clause of the marriage settlement has attracted particular interest: the assurance of French military assistance for Richard against his own subjects if necessary. Given that many English magnates, notably Gloucester, objected to the French peace, this clause has been seen as indicative of Richard's future plans, but in fact it was dropped when the first payment of 300,000 francs was accepted. A proxy marriage was conducted at the Sainte-Chapelle in Paris three days later, with the Earl of Nottingham substituting for the King, and Isabelle prettily made her first formal intercession as Queen of England, a plea for an imprisoned debtor named Peter de Craon.

In October, Isabelle and her father left Paris with a retinue that included the dukes of Berry, Bourbon and Orleans and the counts of Harcourt and Sancerre. On 26 October Richard and Charles met at Ardres, where Charles wore a green gown whose decoration commemorated Richard's first wife Anne, a respectful gesture of family solidarity echoed in the livery of Richard's companions. On 30 October, Isabelle rode to meet her husband in a blue gown and a jewelled crown, curtsied to Richard, who kissed her, and was formally handed into his care by her father. Froissart recorded that when Charles expressed his disappointment that Isabelle was too young to become his wife in the full sense, Richard declared that the love he valued best was that of the King of France, and of his people, 'for we shall now be so strongly united that no king in Christendom can in any way harm us'.

The meeting between the kings of England and France was Richard's first international embassy, and neither party was prepared to concede anything to the other when it came to display. The courtiers were housed in a city of tents, with ornate pavilions for the monarchs, between which ran an ever more competitive exchange of extravagant gifts, featuring a gold cup and basin, a gilt ship carved with tigresses and set with mirrors, a pearl collar, a crystal bottle encrusted with jewels, a buckle worth 500 marks and a horse with a silver saddle. Charles was judged to have come out on top in the present-giving, but Richard bested him in the fashion stakes, for the French King wore the same red velvet each day, while Richard's array of outfits included a red velvet robe with a gold collar, another of red and white velvet and one of blue with gold ornaments. For the wedding itself, in the church of St Nicholas on All Saints Day, Isabelle was carried to Calais in a cloth-of-gold litter. The whole business cost Richard between 10,000 and 15,000 pounds, but it was considered an essential investment in royal prestige.

After hearing Mass together on 3 November, Richard and Isabelle sailed for England. Despite a fair wind, the curse of the English queens' arrival fell on Isabelle, and some of the ships were wrecked. From Dover, the couple travelled through Rochester and Canterbury to Eltham, where they rested before the Queen's entry into London. At Calais, Isabelle had been given into the care of the duchesses of Gloucester and Lancaster, and it was between their households that she could expect to spend the rest of her married childhood. Eleanor de Bohun, the thirty-six-year old Duchess of Gloucester, was the elder sister of Mary de Bohun, the wife of John of Gaunt's son Henry Bolingbroke. The Duchess of Lancaster, Bolingbroke's stepmother, Katherine Swynford, had married Gaunt in January 1396. She was notorious for having been Gaunt's mistress before, during and after his second marriage to Constance of Castile, and for having four children by him. Katherine was of Hainault descent, her father Paen de Rouet having served as a herald under Edward III, and her sister Philippa had attended Edward's Queen before her marriage to the poet Geoffrey Chaucer. Katherine's first husband, Sir Hugh Swynford, was a member of Gaunt's household, and after the death of Gaunt's first wife, Blanche of Lancaster in 1369 (commemorated by Chaucer in his *Book of the Duchess*), Katherine had acted as governess to Blanche's daughters. Her relationship with Gaunt was an open secret, but the marriage, and Richard's subsequent legitimisation of his Beaufort cousins, was a scandal. However, Gaunt was the premier English magnate and there could be no question of excluding his wife from her proper role. In Eleanor, Isabelle might have found a more maternal figure, and a playmate in her daughter, another Isabelle, aged ten. Queen Isabelle was given her own French governess, Margaret de Courcy, who received an annuity of a hundred pounds on New Year's Day 1397.

Isabelle arrived in London for her coronation on 3 January that year, spending the night in the Tower. Her formal entry into the city the preceding November had been spoiled by a great crush on the bridge between Southwark and Kennington, where the eager crowds swarmed so tightly that several people were killed, but the coronation, conducted according to the *Liber Regalis*, went smoothly. On 4 January Isabelle rode in procession along Cheapside with twenty ladies leading twenty knights in red gowns emblazoned with the King's badge of the white hart to meet Richard at Westminster. She was crowned the next day, and two weeks of tournaments were held in celebration, although, as in Anne of Bohemia's case, there were mutterings about the expense. It seemed cruel to make a little girl the focus of political conflict which had been fomenting for a decade, but the unpopularity of the peace with France was reflected in a certain discourtesy in Isabelle's reception. Markedly, neither Warwick nor Arundel presented the Queen with New Year gifts, and Isabelle's new uncle, the Duke of Gloucester, made plain his objections to the truce in Parliament, which convened on 22 January.

It would be unreasonable to expect Isabelle to have made any mark at the beginning of her queenship, and within three years circumstance deprived her of the opportunity forever. The chronicler Adam of Usk was convinced that Richard had married Isabelle only as a means of obtaining French support for a long-planned revenge on his enemies Gloucester, Arundel and Warwick. Froissart reports a conversation between the King and the Count of St Pol in the summer of 1396, as arrangements for the wedding were being finalised, in which Richard expressed his fear that Gloucester's hatred of the peace would provoke him and his allies to another rebellion. St Pol's advice was to bribe and flatter Gloucester into acquiescence until the marriage had taken place, after which Richard could depend on the help of the King of France to 'crush all your enemies or rebellious subjects'. If Richard believed that his second marriage was to inaugurate a form of Arthurian apotheosis, he certainly needed to silence his opponents first, but neither Isabelle nor his actions of 1397 can be entirely explained by his personal animus against the Lords Appellant.

The January Parliament revived the criticisms of the King of a decade before. A bill presented by one Thomas Haxey outlined four areas of grievance: the length of office of sheriffs, Richard's failure to secure the Scottish border, the distribution of badges of office or affinity by the King and the excessive cost of the royal household. Richard particularly objected to the final point, which he saw as touching on his 'regality', and Haxey was arraigned as a traitor. Yet he was given no stricter punishment than house arrest. Many writers[17] have seen Haxey's bill as a ruse instigated by Richard to establish a fresh mandate for the defence of his 'regality' in preparation for his next move, a theory substantiated by Richard's recall of the exiled judges who had ruled in his favour in 1387. The King also seemed to be courting the support of his powerful uncle, as on 6 February he legitimised Gaunt's Beaufort bastards and made the eldest, John, Earl of Somerset. When he left with Isabelle for a pilgrimage to Canterbury at the end of the month he was accompanied by Gaunt and his son Henry Bolingbroke, who also joined the court at Windsor in February. The Haxey bill, the recall of the judges and the cultivation of Gaunt fit a pattern of Richard's increasing frustration at opposition to his prerogative. There were rumours at court of plots against him, and Walsingham focuses on a sharp remark made in relation to the King's ambition to be elected Holy Roman Emperor. An embassy from Cologne had given him hope of achieving this, and he sent envoys of his own to sound out the electors, one of whom dissented with the suggestion that Richard was hardly fit to be emperor since he was incapable of controlling his own subjects. It is notable that Richard resumed his wooing of the imperial electors less than two weeks after the July coup.

On 10 July, Richard invited Warwick, Gloucester and Arundel to dinner. Only Warwick accepted, and after they had dined together with apparent cordiality, Richard had him arrested and sent to the Tower. Men were then sent to detain Arundel while Richard himself rode to Pleshy for his uncle Gloucester. On 13 July the King sent out proclamations announcing the arrests and forbidding any assembly as treasonous. He was careful to stress that the three men had been detained not for past offences but on the evidence of a new plot dating back to the previous summer. Parliament was summoned to judge the Appellants in September, and Walsingham describes how Richard spent the summer gathering supporters as though for a war. On 17 September the King opened Parliament surrounded by 1,000 Cheshire archers and 500 men-at-arms. By that time, Gloucester had been murdered on his orders in prison in Calais. A confession was read out in which he admitted his guilt in the events of 1386–7, though inconveniently it contained no new evidence and the date had to be left off as Gloucester had apparently written it after his death in August. Arundel was tried and beheaded as a traitor on 21 September, defiant to the last, while Warwick made such a convincing show of contrition that his life was spared and he was condemned only to imprisonment and the forfeit of his goods.

Having dealt with his enemies, Richard now cemented his control with vast land grants of their properties to those who had supported him and promoted five new dukedoms, including his cousin Henry Bolingbroke to Hereford. On the second day of the Parliament, it had been 'ordained that anyone who should in future be convicted of violating, usurping or undermining the King's regality should be adjudged a false traitor and should be sentenced to suffer appropriate penalty for treason'.[18] After high Mass on 30 September, Richard sat enthroned in his crown as the lay lords swore to observe the rulings of the Parliament and to adhere to them in perpetuity, condemning any who sought to repeal or annul them as traitors. It is not certain that little Queen Isabelle attended the banquet and ball that followed at Westminster Palace. The prize for best dancer and singer was won by the new Duchess of Exeter.

Isabelle and her husband were, however, together for Christmas at Lichfield. On 24 January they moved to the abbey of Lilleshall, where they received the Chamberlain of France, Viscount Perellos, who had visited the Queen two months earlier at Woodstock. Isabelle may have enjoyed Perellos's adventurous tales of his Irish Christmas at the court of the 'wild' King O'Neill. They then moved on to Shrewsbury for the opening of Parliament on 29 January. The next day Richard chose to examine a curious piece of business: the accusations of his cousin Henry Bolingbroke against his friend Thomas Mowbray, Duke of Norfolk. In his early thirties in 1398, Bolingbroke was the fourth child and only living son of John of Gaunt by his first wife Blanche of Lancaster. He had been admitted to the order of the Garter by Edward III alongside his cousin

Richard in 1377 and their relationship had always been an odd mixture of loyalty and mistrust. Henry had been pardoned for his membership of the Appellants in 1387, but he had tactfully elected to spend the period between 1388 and 1391 on an extended martial grand tour, which included fighting with the Teutonic knights (a sort of early Foreign Legion) in Lithuania, tournaments in France, a pilgrimage to Jerusalem and visits to Prague, Vienna, Venice, Milan and Savoy. His return to London with a leopard, a gift from his distant Lusignan cousin the King of Cyprus, had caused a great stir.

As Gaunt's heir, Henry was one of the most significant magnates in the land, a position that had been augmented by his marriage in 1381 to Eleanor de Bohun's sister Mary, co-heiress to the wealth of the Earl of Hereford. Mary had given him seven children, of whom four sons and two daughters were living, before her death in 1394. Henry had acted as his father's deputy in the Duchy of Lancaster while Gaunt was in Aquitaine in 1394, and his political rehabilitation after Radcot Bridge was signalled by his place on Richard's regency council during the King's first Irish expedition after the loss of Anne of Bohemia. It was as a loyal subject, then, that Henry approached Richard at the house of the bishop of Lichfield on 22 January 1398 to report a conversation between himself and Norfolk, in which the latter claimed that Richard intended them to suffer the same fate as Gloucester, Warwick and Arundel, the other Lords Appellant. Henry observed that they had been pardoned, but Norfolk claimed there was a plot against the house of Lancaster and that he did not trust the King's word. Bolingbroke claimed that Norfolk had been trying to trick him into sedition and into joining a counter-plot against Richard.

At Shrewsbury, Henry's accusation was formalised. Mowbray was removed from his office as the marshal of England and the case was eventually heard at Windsor on 28 April. In the intervening months, Richard's increasingly tyrannical behaviour was making itself felt through-out the country. A priest was arrested for preaching against him at Shrews-bury and there were armed uprisings in Oxfordshire and Berkshire. Despite his proud assertion to the envoys of the Byzantine Emperor in April that 'when we could no longer endure their rebellion and wantonness, we collected the might of our prowess and stretched forth our arm against them our enemies and at length, by the aid of God's grace, we have trodden on the necks of the proud and the haughty',[19] Richard was growing increasingly paranoid. He sent out proclamations demanding that traitors be rounded up, he pursued the unfortunate retainers of the Lords Appellant, he forbade the sending of letters abroad and demanded that incoming foreign mail to magnates be intercepted. His main fear was the resentment provoked by his financial policies. In contravention of Magna Carta, Richard had introduced a fine known as 'la pleasaunce' through which the King's goodwill, or 'pleasure', could be purchased. Supporters of the Appellants had to buy their safety. By Easter 1398 over 20,000 pounds had been raised through la pleasaunce, through forced 'loans', across seventeen counties. As his subjects suffered, Richard's court grew ever more deliriously magnificent: 'Though he abounded in riches beyond all his predecessors [he] nonetheless continued to busy himself amassing money, caring not at all by what title he could acquire it from the hands of his subjects.'[20]

In the quarrel between Norfolk and Bolingbroke, Richard saw the opportunity to help himself to even more wealth. At Windsor, it was decided that the dispute should be settled in the old-fashioned way by single combat. On 16 September, at Coventry, Henry appeared in green velvet decorated with gold antelopes and swans on a white charger. His opponent faced him in crimson with silver lions. With characteristic dramatic timing, Richard waited until the men had actually started riding towards one another before calling a halt to the duel and, after two hours' deliberation, sentenced both men to exile. Rather than having one Appellant left standing, he had decided to get rid of them both and appropriate their lands for his own use After John of Gaunt died in February 1399, Richard also took possession of his estates in council at Westminster, and parcelled up the Mowbray inheritance on the death of Edward I's granddaughter Margaret, Duchess of Norfolk.

Isabelle, of course, had no part to play in any of this. The majority of her time was spent at Eltham, where she continued her education with her governess, Lady de Courcy. In the spring of 1399, Richard visited her at Windsor before his departure for his second Irish campaign. The mood of the country could be gauged by the sparsity of the crowds that turned out for the splendid tournament he had arranged to celebrate St George's Day. Richard had made his will, though without nominating a successor. He played with Isabelle in the gardens at Windsor, holding her hand and picking her up to kiss her. He promised that she should join him soon in Ireland. What Isabelle did not know was that her husband had already planned for Lady de Courcy, whose extravagance was unpopular, to be commanded to pay her debts and leave for France. For all his petting, Richard did not give a thought to his nine-year-old wife's loneliness and isolation. He did not keep his promise to send for her from Ireland. In fact, she never saw the King again.

Richard set sail for Ireland at the end of May. By July, Henry Bolingbroke, now Duke of Lancaster, was back in England. During his French
exile Henry had acquired the clandestine backing of Charles VI's brother
the Duke of Orléans (which the Duke later vehemently denied), and had
been sounding out the disaffected English magnates. In the north, the
men of his Lancastrian affinities began to mobilise. On 4 July, Henry
landed with no more than a hundred men at Ravenspur on the Humber
estuary. Five days later he was at Knaresborough, moving on to Pontefract
for a muster of Lancastrian troops. At Doncaster he was joined by Henry
Percy, heir to the Earl of Northumberland, the 'Harry Hotspur' of Shakespearean fame, with 30,000 men. By the time Henry reached Warwick on
24 July, his supporters were so numerous that he was obliged to send some
of them home. Adam of Usk estimated that 100,000 had turned out for
Lancaster. Richard's uncle, Edmund, Duke of York, was Keeper of the
Realm during the King's absence in Ireland. He chose swiftly between
his nephews. On 27 July York and Lancaster met with a certain dramatic
irony at Berkeley, where the Duke assured Henry that he had no wish to
fight against him.

The King had managed to reach the coast at Milford Haven on 24 July.
With a small company, he rode for Chester, where the Earl of Salisbury
was waiting with an army, but by the time he arrived at Conway, his men
were already deserting, helping themselves to the royal baggage as they
left. Disgruntlement was so widespread that, according to one story, even
the King's greyhound defected and joined Henry at Shrewsbury. On 9
August, Henry was at Chester, his troops having laid waste to Richard's
most loyal county. The Earl of Northumberland was sent to bring Richard
in. The King decided on a mad plan to meet Henry, escape and raise an
army in Wales, but Northumberland took him to Flint Castle, strongly
garrisoned with Lancastrian soldiers. Mindful of Richard's passion for
elegant dining, Henry courteously allowed him to finish his supper before
entering the castle to arrest him, though his understanding of his cousin's
character was also evident in the refined little cruelty of not permitting
Richard to change his clothes on the journey south.

As a precedent for the second deposition of an English king in a century,
Henry had only the innovations of Isabella of France to look to. In a
propaganda campaign of 'bogus genealogy, false prophecy, anti-Ricardian
fabrication and novel ceremonial',[21] the process by which Henry Bolingbroke turned himself into Henry IV shared its latter two characteristics
with Isabella's routing of Edward II. Using Isabella's strategy of serving
writs in the King's name, he summoned the estates of the realm on 19

August 1399. After convening a meeting of ecclesiastics to debate the succession, he announced his claim on 30 September. Officially, Richard, like Edward, abdicated willingly, though *The Hardyng Chronicle* reports that, according to the Earl of Northumberland, 'Henry made King Richard under duress of prison in the Tower of London in fear of his life to make a resignation of his right to him.' After hearing thirty-three 'Articles of Deposition', Parliament declared that there was 'abundant reason for proceeding to deposition for the greater security and tranquillity of the realm and the good of the kingdom'. 'Richard of Bordeaux', as he was henceforth known, was sentenced to imprisonment.

On 13 October, Henry IV was crowned at Westminster. He was anointed with the sacred chrism, believed to have been given to St Thomas à Becket when the Virgin appeared to him, and which had been used for the coronation of Edward II. Richard had been relieved of the oil, which he had removed in its golden eagle vessel from the Tower prior to his departure for Ireland, perhaps planning a recrowning on his return. All his life, Richard had consciously identified himself with Edward II. It was therefore appropriate that after Henry had him murdered at Pontefract Castle, probably in February 1400, he was laid to rest not with his beloved Anne, as he had requested, but in the chapel at King's Langley built by Edward for his favourite, Piers Gaveston.

Queen Isabelle had been waiting at Sonning in Berkshire for news of her husband, whom she was not permitted to see. During the rebellion, the house had been stormed and her attendants' badges ripped off. In December, she received a visit from the earls of Kent and Salisbury, who reassured her that Richard was free and the imposter hiding in the Tower. Their conspiracy failed. Even as they proclaimed to the men of the west that Richard was in the field, he may already have been dead. Richard had been sent to Pontefract at the end of October, and in early February he was officially still alive, though by this time Henry's council were discussing what to do with his body if the 'rumours' of his death proved to be true. Isabelle's fear, confusion and sense of isolation can only be imagined. Henry attended Richard's requiem at St Paul's, but it is not certain that Isabelle was allowed to see the body.

The Queen was now a diplomatic problem. According to the original agreement, the French argued, her dowry, the last instalment of which had been paid in 1399, ought to be returned, as she was not technically a queen dowager and had not in any case reached the age of canonical consent. Stalling, Henry sent to Paris to open discussions for a new marriage with his eldest son, now Prince of Wales, who was eventually to marry Isabelle's younger sister Catherine. The English simply had no money to repay the dowry, but they could not risk their already delicate position in France. In a treaty signed at Leulinghem in May 1401, Henry agreed that Isabelle would be repatriated with her jewels and property, though in fact he never did give back the dowry. In 1406, Isabelle was married to her first cousin Charles, Count of Angoulême, who became Duke of Orléans when his father was murdered by the Duke of Burgundy in 1407. Shortly afterwards she died giving birth to her daughter, Jeanne. Perhaps the most that can be said of Isabelle is that, like so many of Richard's grandiose gestures, her symbolic value was huge. But as a means of retaining and governing a kingdom, she had been virtually pointless.

PART FIVE

LANCASTER AND YORK

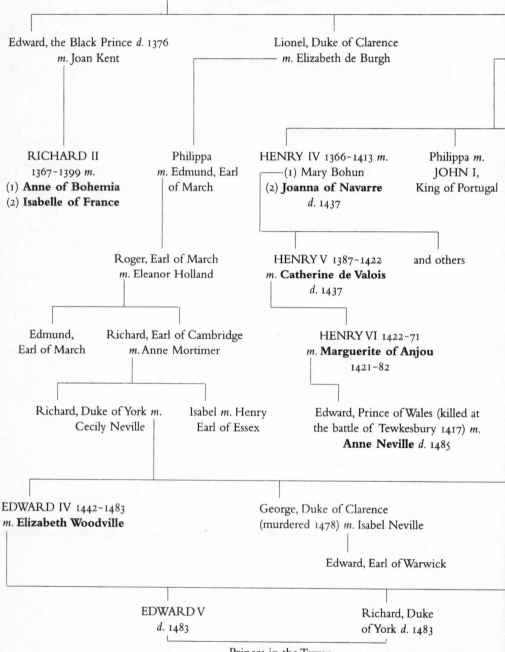

EDWARD III 1312-1377 _m._ **Philippa of Hainault**

Edward, the Black Prince _d._ 1376
_m._ Joan Kent

Lionel, Duke of Clarence
_m._ Elizabeth de Burgh

RICHARD II
1367-1399 _m._
(1) **Anne of Bohemia**
(2) **Isabelle of France**

Philippa
_m._ Edmund, Earl
of March

HENRY IV 1366-1413 _m._
(1) Mary Bohun
(2) **Joanna of Navarre**
_d._ 1437

Philippa _m._
JOHN I,
King of Portugal

Roger, Earl of March
_m._ Eleanor Holland

HENRY V 1387-1422
_m._ **Catherine de Valois**
_d._ 1437

and others

Edmund,
Earl of March

Richard, Earl of Cambridge
_m._ Anne Mortimer

HENRY VI 1422-71
_m._ **Marguerite of Anjou**
1421-82

Richard, Duke of York _m._
Cecily Neville

Isabel _m._ Henry
Earl of Essex

Edward, Prince of Wales (killed at
the battle of Tewkesbury 1417) _m._
Anne Neville _d._ 1485

EDWARD IV 1442-1483
_m._ **Elizabeth Woodville**

George, Duke of Clarence
(murdered 1478) _m._ Isabel Neville

Edward, Earl of Warwick

EDWARD V
_d._ 1483

Richard, Duke
of York _d._ 1483

Princes in the Tower

THE HOUSES OF LANCASTER AND YORK

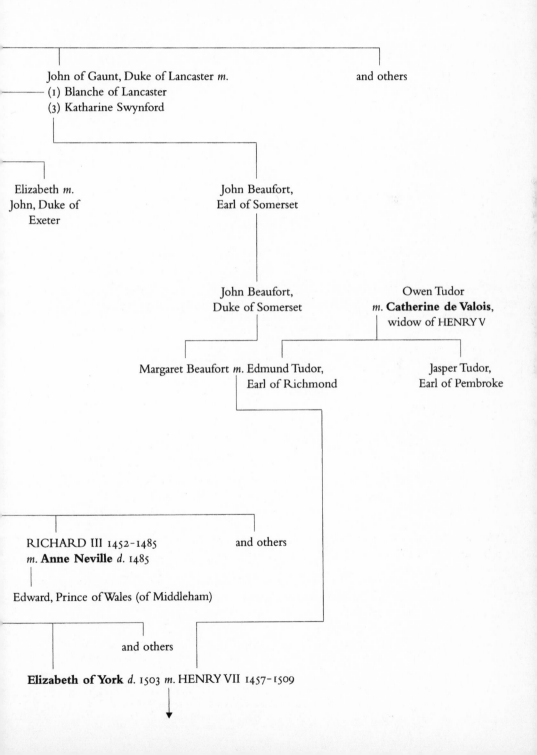

John of Gaunt, Duke of Lancaster *m.*   and others
(1) Blanche of Lancaster
(3) Katharine Swynford

Elizabeth *m.*   John Beaufort,
John, Duke of   Earl of Somerset
Exeter

John Beaufort,   Owen Tudor
Duke of Somerset   *m.* **Catherine de Valois**,
                                            widow of HENRY V

Margaret Beaufort *m.* Edmund Tudor,   Jasper Tudor,
                        Earl of Richmond   Earl of Pembroke

RICHARD III 1452-1485   and others
m. **Anne Neville** *d.* 1485

Edward, Prince of Wales (of Middleham)

                    and others

Elizabeth of York *d.* 1503 *m.* HENRY VII 1457-1509

CHAPTER 14

JOANNA OF NAVARRE

'A royal witch'

As the fifteenth century opened, what the new Lancastrian dynasty needed above all was money. The succession was about the only thing of which Henry IV could be certain; indeed, sons were the only thing he had plenty of. Having lost his wife, Mary de Bohun, five years before becoming king, he was short of a queen. He required a woman whose birth and connections could validate his newborn title to the crown, and, most importantly, a rich one. Once her pedigree was unravelled, the Dowager Duchess of Brittany appeared to be the perfect choice. Joanna of Navarre was born at Evreux, Normandy in 1368, to Jeanne de Valois, daughter of Jean II of France, and Charles 'The Bad', King of Navarre. Jeanne's great-great-grandmother was the mother of Edward II's Queen Isabella, Jeanne de Navarre. On the death of Jeanne's son Louis X, his daughter, Charles's mother, was excluded from the French succession, but renounced her claim only on condition she was able to take up her right to rule Navarre. Jeanne was thus descended on her father's side from a queen of France and two queens of Navarre in their own right, while her mother, a daughter of France, was descended from the imperial house through her mother Bona, aunt to Anne of Bohemia and daughter of Emperor John I.

So Joanna's blood was of the purest, and better yet was the promise of her money. Charles the Bad had fought on the right side in the French wars and was enormously wealthy. His reputation, however, was unfortunate, a career as a murderer and reputedly a sorcerer having ended with him being sewn up in a sack and set on fire. In 1386, a year before this alarming event, Charles had provided a dowry of 120,000 livres with an annual pension of 60,000 for the marriage of his eighteen-year-old daughter Joanna to the Duke of Brittany. He also pushed a hard bargain with his forty-seven-year-old son-in-law, demanding one third of the Duke's assets as Joanna's dower. The dowry had not been paid in full when Charles met his grisly end, but the dower, which was renegotiated in 1396, remained unchanged, and when Duke Jean died in 1399, thirty-one-year-old Joanna found herself a very rich woman.

As a descendant of female rulers, she appeared to relish her independence, and governed Brittany competently as regent for her eldest son Jean until he assumed his title in 1401. When Henry IV proposed for her early the next year, her offspring proved to be one of the first of several difficulties. Of the nine children Joanna had given Duke Jean, seven were still living in 1402: thirteen-year-old Jean, Artur, Gilles and Richard, aged nine, eight and seven respectively, and two girls, ten-year-old Marguerite and five-year-old Blanche. A third daughter, Marie, was already married to the Duke of Alençon. Jean could not leave his duchy, but although Marguerite and Blanche would be permitted to travel to England, the Breton magnates objected to the prospect of Joanna taking the younger boys out of the country and she found she would be obliged to leave them under the guardianship of the Duke of Burgundy. The other problems were canonical. Henry and Joanna would require a papal dispensation to marry as they were related within the prohibited degrees. Joanna had been Duke Jean's third wife: his first had been Henry's aunt, Edward III's daughter Mary, and his second Joan Holland, daughter of Henry's aunt-by-marriage Joan of Kent. This already complex situation was further complicated by the papal schism in which Europe was still embroiled. The division that the marriage of Richard II and Anne of Bohemia had been supposed to heal had passed into a new generation with the see of Rome occupied by the English-supported Boniface IX and that of Avignon by the French- and Burgundian-backed Benedict XIII. Notwithstanding their political disputes with France, the Bretons supported Benedict, so another dispensation was required for Joanna and her daughters to go and live among schismatics.

Despite these obstacles, both Henry and Joanna at first pursued the match urgently. Joanna's envoy Anthony Rhys was sent to the English King on 14 March 1402, and the papal dispensation granted less than a week later. In April, Henry underwent a proxy ceremony at Eltham, swearing fidelity unto death to the papal envoy. Legally, the couple were now married, but Joanna waited until December to set out for England. Why the delay? The most obvious answer is that Joanna was making suitable arrangements for her young sons and the handover of the government to her eldest, but might she have wished to change her mind? What were her motivations for the match in the first place? So little is known of Joanna's early life that it is impossible to get any sense of her character other than retrospectively. Aside from her place of birth and payments made to the convent of Santa Clara at Estella in Navarre, where she was educated, she is virtually absent from the records until her first marriage. As a well-dowered ducal mother, why did Joanna want to get away from Brittany so badly that she was prepared to leave her sons behind? Some clue may be found in her later political affiliations, but the simplest explanation is perhaps that, as a rich and marriageable (if not, by the standards of her day, young) woman, she, like Eleanor of Aquitaine after her divorce, was extremely vulnerable. As Queen of England Joanna would not only have one of the most powerful protectors in Europe, but also the unique legal position of a consort. It was this determination to maintain control of her own affairs which would lead to one of the most extraordinary situations in the life of any English queen: her imprisonment on suspicion of witchcraft in 1419.

Henry's enthusiasm for the marriage is perhaps easier to understand. He was reputedly very attracted by descriptions of Joanna and, in addition to the status and funds with which he believed she would provide him, there was also the possibility of benefit to English trade and military operations through access to Breton ports, of an increased English influence in the duchy and of an Anglo-Breton alliance against the French. Joanna's importance to Henry is reflected in the status accorded her in the depiction of her coronation, an amalgamation of traditional Marian associations of queens consort with the sense of a new definition for English monarchs adopted from Richard II's self-fashioned kingship.

After the now-traditional rough crossing, Joanna arrived at Falmouth at the end of December 1402 and met her husband at Exeter. Their marriage took place at Winchester on 8 February 1403, and she was crowned at Westminster on 26 February. In spite of the fact that she was a widow, Joanna wore her hair loose at her coronation to signify virginity, also an identification with two potent images of the Virgin, Mary, Queen of Heaven and Maria mediatrix. The connection of the consort with the merciful intercession of the Virgin was one that she had already enacted as Duchess of Brittany: in a well-known incident she had intervened in her husband's arrest of the French ambassador. According to the *Chronicle of St Denis*, a pregnant Joanna, 'setting aside her womanly modesty ... taking her children in her arms ... entered the chamber of the Duke', and on her knees 'earnestly pleaded that he reconsider', if only for the sake of their children, who would require French support after his death. As in the case of Philippa of Hainault at Calais, Joanna's plea permitted her husband to pursue the course of action it was necessary for him to take without risking the concomitant embarrassment of appearing to change his mind. The 'spontaneity' of such gestures was by this point more theatrical than emotional, as has been observed, notably in the case of Anne of Bohemia's intercession for London, yet though the autonomous political agency of the intercessory gesture was reduced, Joanna's invocation of it shows it retained a meaningful symbolic power outside the conventions of male-directed action.

Joanna's coronation ceremony was 'unusually extravagant'.[1] An illustration of the event shows the Queen seated alone on a throne under a canopy with the archbishop of Canterbury and the abbot of Westminster beside her, instead of the more conventional position enthroned below the King. This gestures towards Joanna's individual authority as the descendant of so many rulers, as does the orb she holds in her left hand. Before Philippa of Hainault, queens were depicted with only a sceptre, or virga, in the right hand, but in the funeral effigy commissioned by Richard II for his double tomb with Anne of Bohemia, there is an orb between the couple, implying a novel degree of shared authority. The presence of the orb projects a queenly participation in a more explicit relationship between England and the Mother of Christ, that of the realm itself as the Virgin's dowry.

In the Wilton Diptych, Richard II is pictured in red and cloth-of-gold robes decorated with rosemary (one of Anne's emblems) and eagles, the symbol of the empire. To the King's right are the Virgin and Child, with one of eleven angels proffering a banner topped with an orb and cross, which have been painted over with a larger orb. Examination of the painting has shown that the first orb contains a tiny illustration of a green island with a boat at sea and a white tower, an image that connects the Wilton orb with another (now lost) depiction of Richard made in Anne's lifetime. Details of this painting, part of a five-panelled Roman altarpiece, survive only in seventeenth-century descriptions, in which Anne, in a cope emblazoned with imperial eagles, stands beside Richard, five saints and the Virgin. St John is introducing the couple to the Virgin, and they are presenting her with a globe on which is a map of England: 'This is your dowry, O Holy Virgin, wherefore, O Mary, may you have rule over it.' In terms of Richard's conception of his destiny after Anne's death, the Wilton Diptych has been interpreted as the King giving his realm over to the Virgin and then receiving it back from her in the form of her dowry, evoking a spiritual marriage between Mary and England in his person. The implications of this for Richard's possible commitment to chastity have been discussed, but there is also a connection between the map in the Rome altarpiece, the Wilton orb, Joanna's coronation portrait and the Lancastrian adoption of the concept of England as the Virgin's dower.

As a new dynasty, legitimacy was essential for the Lancastrians. The marriage between Henry and Joanna was part of establishing this, as was the conscious appropriation of Ricardian symbolism. In a letter to the bishop of London in 1400, Thomas Arundel states: 'We are the humble servants of her own inheritance and liegemen of her especial dower, as we are approved by common parlance, ought to excel all others in the fervour of our praises and devotions to her.'[2] By Henry V's reign, England was being referred to as the *Dos Mariae* (dowry of Mary), the title by which the Roman altarpiece was known. The globe in the Roman painting establishes the idea, the Wilton orb elaborates it, the tomb of Richard and Anne reiterates it. Thus the orb held by Joanna of Navarre associates the queen, already linked to the Virgin, with this new contribution to England's unique destiny; even, it would not be going too far to say, casting her, in her marriage with the king, as its conduit.

Henry's respect for Joanna's status was demonstrated practically as well as symbolically. In 1403, he dowered her to the immense sum of 10,000 marks, payable from the exchequer until such a time as rents could be collected from her assigned lands in the duchy of Lancaster holdings. This was far more than the government could afford, even though the rents had to be supplemented for a further six years. Eventually, Joanna received many traditional queens' lands, including the manors of Woodstock, Ludgershall, Geddington, Langley, Havering, Gillingham and Rockingham and the castles of Bristol, Hertford, Nottingham and Leeds. She also received a reversion from the Lancaster estates after the death of Gaunt's last duchess, Katherine Swynford. Joanna's administration of these properties represented a significant new direction for the office of the Queen's Council. With the absorption in 1399 of the lands, but not the independent practices of the Lancaster duchy, into the crown estates, it was possible to establish a certain continuity for the management of the queen's dower which, throughout the fifteenth century, derived in the main from Lancaster. On 10 December 1404, Joanna was granted the use of a new tower opposite the main palace gate to house her council, directed by her treasurer, John Chandeler, who became bishop of Salisbury, her receiver-general, William Denys, her chancellors, John Tubbay and John Mapleton, and her steward, Henry Luttrell. Working closely with the council of the duchy of Lancaster, these officials kept Joanna's accounts, met to determine policy and preserved the Queen's charters and records.

Much of their business was concerned with Joanna's Breton holdings, for despite Henry's hopes of her fortune, Joanna had brought him no dowry and continued to manage her dower. The King did not get a penny.

Joanna's management of her revenues presents her as 'a woman bent on exercising a significant degree of fiscal self-determination'.[3] Lobineau's *Chronicle of Brittany* notes that she continued to take payments from the Breton dower as set out in 1396, including 12,000 crowns from the sale of the rents of Nantes to Olivier de Clisson. She also received deliveries of provisions from her former home at Vannes. Perhaps Henry was allowed to sample them. If so, they were the only tangible benefit he obtained from the marriage. Joanna's financial independence might have been laudable, but it smacks of miserliness, and while Henry may have felt that her symbolic value was worth the vast expense of her dower, his subjects disagreed. Anti-Breton feeling ran high. With Joanna's sons in the custody of the Duke of Burgundy, there was little chance of England increasing its influence in Brittany, and in a matter of months after the marriage the two states were at war. Yet Joanna's loyalties remained firmly with her son. In 1404 she delivered up to him 6,000 livres of Norman land rents and claims to 70,000 which remained due from her first marriage. As had so frequently been the case with foreign queens, she attracted hostility for the size and cost of her Breton entourage. In the same year as she made the grants to Duke Jean, Parliament heard a petition that 'all French persons, Bretons, Lombards, Italians and Navarrese be removed out of the palace'. Joanna was initially permitted to retain only her daughters Blanche and Marguerite and one lady-in-waiting, Marie de Parency, though the lords eventually relaxed enough to let her keep twelve others, including her daughters' nurse.

The Queen maintained close links with her distant children. Her son Artur visited England in 1404, and in 1407 she negotiated the marriages of her daughters, Marguerite to Alain, Viscount Rohan, and Blanche to Jean, heir to the Count of Armagnac. Blanche and Jean visited her in 1409, as did her son Gilles. She disseminated the work of English artisans, sending an alabaster monument to the cathedral of Nantes in 1408 and a jewelled reliquary, which may be seen today in the Louvre, across the Channel for her eldest son, but politically as well as financially, she was pro-Breton. Having persuaded Henry to give her custody of a group of Breton sailors who had been captured raiding the Devon coast near Dartmouth, she then provoked more English hostility by releasing them without claiming a ransom. Her influence has also been identified in the two Anglo-Breton truces negotiated in 1407 and 1417, but her later peace-weaving efforts had to contend with the suspicion and dislike she had aroused from the start.

The main focus of this was Henry's over-generous provision for her dower, which had been a source of dispute since 1404 and which gathered force after his death in 1413. As a couple, Joanna and Henry appear to have been happy, if not extravagantly so. It might be posited that theirs was a companionable rather than a passionate marriage: they spent a good deal of time together and she was able to establish amiable relations with her stepchildren. A letter to Henry IV's third son, John, Duke of Bedford, written from Langley in 1415, describes him as 'our dearest and best beloved son' and concludes: 'If there be anything on our part that we can do to your pleasure, be pleased to signify it, and we will accomplish it with a very good heart, according to our power.' Joanna was also on excellent terms with her eldest stepson, Henry, with whom she shared a love of music, but this did not stop him conspiring to cheat her of her rights.

As Prince of Wales, Henry had a famously difficult relationship with his father, though their differences were more substantial than is implied by the older man's disapproval of the roistering 'Prince Hal' of Shakespeare's *Henry IV.* Elevated to the full heir's apanage of Wales, the duchies of Cornwall, Lancaster and Aquitaine and the earldom of Chester in 1399, Henry was given a seat on his father's council in 1406. In 1410 the King fell seriously ill, and for a year his son acted as regent. At the time, France was involved in a civil war prompted by the mental instability of Charles VI and the consequent struggle between the Duke of Burgundy, who had assumed the regency in 1392, and the house of Orléans, headed by the Count of Armagnac, for control of the provisional government. In 1407, Charles VI's younger brother, Louis of Orléans, was assassinated by the Duke and his son, Charles, made a second marriage to the daughter of Bernard VII of Armagnac in order to raise a league against Burgundy. Joanna had both political and personal connections with the Armagnac wars. Brittany had long been at odds with Burgundy, and her son Duke Jean supported the Armagnacs. Moreover, her daughter Blanche was now sister-in-law to Charles of Orléans. As head of the council, Prince Henry had supported Burgundy, but once his father regained control he switched his allegiance to Armagnac. Although Joanna advised a neutral policy, which she was well placed to do, when it came to choosing sides, she supported Prince Henry against her husband.

In March 1413, Henry IV died in the Jerusalem chamber at Westminster. The King had particularly desired to be buried at Canterbury, where Joanna commissioned the tomb she would eventually share with him. Poor Mary de Bohun, who had given Henry her fortune and nine children, was relegated to the relatively humble church of St Mary, Newark. Henry might have gained no material advantages from Joanna, but he emphasised the value of his royal bride even in death. At first, it seemed that Henry V was prepared to honour his father's provisions for Joanna, but his commitment collapsed in the face of his ambitions in France. Henry was intent on reviving the Plantagenet claim to the French crown, on the grounds that his rights had been systematically denied through the series of truces and alliances that had obtained since Edward III's death. In almost every one of the opening addresses to Parliament he made during his reign, the just cause of the war was stressed, and Henry insisted until the end of his life that he had only ever been trying to bring peace after more than thirty years of failed diplomacy. Since the French had betrayed the 1360 treaty of Bretigny by encroaching on English sovereignty in Aquitaine, Henry asserted that he had every entitlement to pursue his great-grandfather's claim to the crown.

In August 1415, Henry left England at the head of the largest invasion force to have been mustered since the time of Edward III. Before his departure, he had granted the castles of Wallingford, Berkhamsted and Windsor to Joanna, and his formal leave-taking of the Queen Dowager was, according to *The London Chronicle*, one of the official ceremonies prior to his embarkation, between offering at St Paul's and praying at the shrine of St George. On arriving in France, the English spent five weeks successfully besieging Harfleur and then marched towards Calais. Henry had left with a force estimated at 9,000 to 12,000 men, but by October, ravaged by fever and dysentery, this number had sunk to between 6,000 and 8,000. On 24 October, they found their route blocked by a huge French army, commanded by the constable of France (Charles VI was mad again) and the leading magnates of the Armagnac faction. Half-starved, sick and freezing, there was nothing the English could do but stand and fight.

Agincourt is the *ne plus ultra* of medieval battles, immortalised by Shakespeare and romanticised on film. The reality was muddy, brutish and short. For three hours the two armies glared at one another across a sodden wheatfield, then, as the French van moved, Henry advanced in an avalanche of bow fire. The arrows devastated the oncoming French, who had little room for manoeuvre and found themselves immured in the mud. Henry charged his cavalry over the first corpses, using the bodies as duckboards, while his men-at-arms heaped up the dead to serve as improvised forts. When the French rearguard rallied and pushed forward, all the prisoners, including the dukes of Orléans and Bourbon were promptly slaughtered, an order which has compromised Henry V's chivalric reputation ever since. The Marquise de Sevigne callously commented in the seventeenth century that the only consolation for the French was that, unlike at Crécy, relatively few of the dead prisoners were 'born'. Practically, Agincourt achieved very little, as Henry lacked the men and resources to make good his advantage and merely pressed on to Calais, but historically, it was priceless.

Queen Joanna took part in Henry's victory procession in London on 24 November 1415, but she cannot have been wholeheartedly joyous. Her son Artur had been one of the lucky prisoners to survive Agincourt, but her son-in-law, Marie's husband Jean d'Alençon, had been killed, as was her brother, Charles of Navarre. The highly nationalistic mood at the time of the triumph had also manifested itself in another attack on her household, this time in the form of accusations that Breton spies were eavesdropping and selling government secrets (which suggests that, though the Duke of Bedford, not Joanna, acted as regent while Henry was in France, she was still closely associated with the centre of power), and that they were trafficking in stolen money and jewels. Hatred of Bretons persisted until 1425, when a petition was made for their definitive expulsion.

Joanna's connection with Agincourt also produced an unusual piece of anti-Lancastrian propaganda in the mid-fifteenth century. Afterwards her son Artur took the opportunity to visit her and, according to an account by Guillaume Gruel, Joanna played a rather cruel trick on him, installing one of her ladies in her place and then berating him when he failed to recognise that she was not his mother. They 'both began to cry because they were so dear to each other. And the Queen his mother gave him a thousand nobles ... and also gave him shirts and garments, and he did not afterwards dare to speak to her or visit her, as he would have wished.'[4] If this odd story is true, it figures Joanna as a callous mother, who torments her 'abandoned' child and then palms him off with gifts. Rather paltry gifts, considering that the previous year Artur had lost his title to the earldom of Richmond, associated with the ducal family of Brittany since Norman times, to John, Duke of Bedford. The writer, Guillaume, served Artur when he became constable of France after 1324, which suggests that Artur may have conveyed this bitter memory personally. But there is another, more stylised interpretation of the story. At the time Guillaume was writing, Henry V's son was not only officially failing to make good his inheritance of the French crown, but was struggling to maintain his right to his English one. The 'recognition trick' is a classic device of French romance, invoked, for example, in the legend of Joan of Arc's identification of Charles VII at Chinon. Artur's inability to recognise his mother thus becomes an indictment of the Lancastrian dynasty, as he is not able to discern which woman is the 'true queen'. Since Joanna could not be distinguished by the ineffable aura of royalty, it follows that Henry IV, and therefore his grandson, were not 'true' kings.

Henry V was not troubled by such doubts, but he was concerned at the exorbitant cost of the renewal of the French wars. For years, the Dowager Queen's dower had been a source of contention, and in 1419 the financial pressure was increased by the need to find 40,000 crowns to dower Henry's betrothed, Catherine de Valois. So, in September that year, Joanna was arrested on suspicion of witchcraft. On the twenty-fifth of the month, the archbishop of Canterbury wrote a circular requiring English priests to pray for the safety of the King, who was at risk from the 'superstitious deeds of necromancers'. Fear of witchcraft was a perennial anxiety. Twenty years before, Queen Isabelle's secretary, Pierre Salmon, had reported a conversation with Richard II at Woodstock in which the King claimed that Charles VI's madness had been conjured by the sorcery of his brother the Duke d'Orléans. Richard, Salmon claimed, offered a handsome reward if the secretary could make a 'drink' for Orléans that would prevent him from further harming Charles or anyone else. In a deeply religious and superstitious culture, witchcraft seemed very real, but it was also invoked as a political weapon. A person accused of 'necromancy' could be easily deprived of his rights. The archbishop's letter, designed to create an atmosphere of rumour in which the accusations against Joanna would seem more plausible, was followed up on 27 September by an order from the royal council depriving the Queen of her dower and possessions on the basis of evidence from John Randolf, a friar in her household. Randolf claimed Joanna had 'compacted and imagined the death and destruction of our lord the King in the most high and horrible manner that could be recounted'. On 1 October, Joanna was arrested at Havering for 'treasonous imagining', or, in the words of *The London Chronicle*, for seeking 'by sorcery and necromancy to have destroyed the King'. No one appeared to know precisely what form Joanna's magic had taken, and the 'witnesses', Randolf himself and two other members of Joanna's household, Peronell Brocart and Roger Colles, were swiftly imprisoned, but the end had been achieved. Joanna lost not only her dower, but also her servants and property.

Joanna was never tried for witchcraft, but that meant she could never be acquitted. Her rank offered no protection against the ruthless exploit-ation of her fortune. Since queens' power was consensual and customary, rather than constitutional, her abrupt fall from grace also illustrates the inherent vulnerability of even the most powerful woman in the land. Eleanor of Aquitaine and Isabella of France had been imprisoned for political offences, and their sex and status had arguably preserved them from the sterner punishment that such behaviour in a man would have merited, but Joanna's only crime was having her own money and, given the nature of the charge, not even the legal protections afforded her council could save her. If she had pushed for a trial, she risked losing her life as well as her fortune, and though Henry could not have been expected to go as far as to burn an anointed queen at the stake, there were other, more discreet methods available to silence a troublesome woman. Divine right had proved no ultimate aid to Edward II or Richard.

So Joanna went quietly. From Havering she was taken to Rotherhithe, then to Pevensey, where she spent the first months of 1420, and finally on to Leeds Castle. There she remained, in the custody of Sir John Pelham, until six weeks before the King's death. The conditions of her captivity indicate, though, that even the royal council tacitly acknowledged their accusations were spurious. In the first months of her imprisonment at Pevensey, the average expenditure for Joanna's upkeep was thirty-seven pounds a week, including twelve to sixteen shillings for her stables (which suggests she had the freedom to ride out), wages for nineteen grooms and seven pages, a harp, aquavit to keep up her spirits and a cage for her songbird. She also continued to dress in royal style, ordering furs, silks and delicate linens from Flanders. She had a gold girdle, silver gilt buckle, gold chains, a gilt basin, silver gilt knives, a silver candlestick and a gold rosary. Medicines were ordered from her Portuguese physician Pedro de Alcoba. The period after March 1420 shows Joanna less well provided for, with an average expenditure of eleven pounds per week, but she still had her carriage and was able to enjoy delicacies such as green ginger, rosewater (which was used as a cosmetic as well as in cookery) and cardamom. Among the foodstuffs and household goods recorded in the accounts are 'wheat, barley, beans, peas, oats, wine, ale, cows, calves, sheep, lambs, pigs, little pigs, capons, hens, poultry, geeses, ducks, pheasants, partridges, coneys, salt and fresh fish ... hay, litter, coals, firewood, rushes'.[5] She was also able to keep up with some business matters. She employed a clerk, Thomas Lilbourne, and two sergeants-at-law were paid to pursue claims for queens-gold.

There is even a tiny hint that Joanna profited from her unusual privacy and seclusion. At Leeds, she received her stepson Humphrey, Duke of Gloucester, and Henry Beaufort, bishop of Winchester. Wine was provided for the guests and they were entertained with music by Joanna's minstrel, Nicholas. Another visitor was Thomas, Lord Camoys, who enjoyed his stay so much he prolonged it for ten months, from April 1420 to January 1421. Camoys is discreetly described as a 'close friend', and when he died shortly after leaving Leeds, in March 1421, mourning clothes were ordered for the Queen: seven yards of black cloth at 7s 8d per yard, a satin cape and fur for a collar. It was once assumed that these luxury garments were purchased for the death of Henry V, but that did not take place until the following year. Their richness suggests that Camoys was a very close friend indeed.

The exchequer certainly profited from the scurrilous treatment of the Queen. In total, Joanna cost the crown only 1,000 pounds per year during her imprisonment, while 8,000 pounds was realised from her dower for the period June 1421 to August 1422 alone. Even so, the King remained terribly short of money. Adam Usk reports the 'unbearable extortions' to which Henry resorted, and comments darkly on the profound 'though private' resentment they provoked. In 1420 and 1421 the King was too wary of his critics to risk asking Parliament for yet more subsidies for the war, and in 1421 no new taxes were collected and Parliament was pushing for the King to return to England. If Joanna could not have been expected to have much sympathy for her stepson's predicament, her condition was clearly weighing on Henry's mind, because before his death he paid her dower arrears and restored her lands and, in July 1422, the King's *carissima mater* was freed.

It seemed, though, that the devil was not done with Joanna. In 1429, she took the unusual step of leaving the accoutrements of her chapel to the mistress of her stepson Humphrey of Gloucester. Eleanor Cobham had been Gloucester's lover for some years, and in 1431 his marriage to Jacqueline of Hainault was annulled and he married Eleanor. The 1429 bequest indicates that Joanna knew Eleanor well and was publicly attached to her, despite her irregular status at the time. After the deaths of Henry IV's second and third sons, Thomas, Duke of Clarence in 1421 and John, Duke of Bedford in 1435, Gloucester became the next heir to the throne in the event that Henry V's son did not produce a child, and thus Eleanor was prospectively the next Queen of England. In 1441, a whispering campaign began against the Duchess of Gloucester, accusing her of using witchcraft to seduce her husband. Ultimately, Eleanor was arrested for procuring potions from a witch named Margery Jourdemayne and of employing two corrupt priests to cast spells to predict whether Humphrey would succeed to the throne. Eleanor and her fellow sorcerers were tried, and the Duchess supposedly admitted to some of the charges against her, though she pleaded pathetically that a wax effigy produced as evidence was only a charm she superstitiously hoped would help her bear a child.

Margery was burned, one of the priests hanged and the other died in prison, while Eleanor was forced to do public penance, walking barefoot and bareheaded through London with a candle. Her marriage was dissolved by the archbishop of Canterbury and she spent the rest of her life shut up in prison of the Isle of Man. Her conditions were much less comfortable than Joanna's had been: she was permitted only twelve attendants and an annual allowance of one hundred marks. Like Joanna, Eleanor had been the highest-ranking woman in the land before her disgrace, and like Joanna she was powerless to help herself. Eleanor was unpopular, but the campaign against her seems to have been no more than an attempt to curb her husband's aspirations before the marriage of Henry VI.

The use of allegations of witchcraft as a means of curtailing the power of prominent women continued throughout the fifteenth century. After the battle of Edgecote in 1469, Jacquetta, Duchess of Bedford, the mother of Queen Elizabeth Woodville, was accused of sorcery by Thomas Wake. Wake was a servant of the Earl of Warwick, who was at this point holding King Edward IV prisoner. Though Warwick was determined to smash the rule of the Woodville family, Wake's accusations couched Jacquetta's witchcraft 'loyally' in terms of a plot against the King and Queen. He claimed he had discovered a model of a man-at-arms, smashed and bound with wire. The case was dismissed when the witnesses withdrew their evidence, but Jacquetta was charged once more – posthumously, in 1483 – this time for supposedly having used the black arts to procure her daughter's controversial marriage to the King. Polydore Vergil has Richard III accusing Elizabeth Woodville herself. Richard claimed he was unable to eat or sleep, and that his arm was wasting away, 'which mischief verily proceedeth from that sorceress Elizabeth who with her witchcraft has so enchanted me that by the annoyance thereof I am dissolved'. Any gains from the allegations against Elizabeth and Jacquetta were propagandist, rather than financial, as in Joanna's case. What all their stories illustrate is the potency of rumours of witchcraft to tap into contemporary anxieties about the 'unnaturalness' of powerful women, a suspicion to which queens, that legal anomaly, were acutely prey.

There was little time for Joanna to restore relations with Henry V before his death, though he did make her a rather cursory gift of cloth for five or six gowns. Prior to her arrest, Joanna had appeared as Queen on ceremonial occasions, but this role was now taken by Henry's widow, Catherine, and for the rest of her life Joanna lived in semi-retirement, first at Langley, until the palace burned down in 1431, and then at Havering. Though she was not active at his court, Henry VI treated her courteously, presenting her, for example, with a New Year gift of jewellery in 1437.

Joanna was perhaps more interested in business than cultural matters. Her council continued to be active on her behalf in the management of her estates and she was apparently frustrated by the poor management of Havering Manor, but aside from the innovations in the queen's administration, she left no remarkable legacy, with the exception of her signature as 'Royne Jahanne' – the first of any English queen to survive. During Henry IV's lifetime she had shown some interest in the promotion of scholars at Oxford and Cambridge, and in her captivity she possessed at least two books, a mid-thirteenth-century psalter and a contemporary book of hours, but she made no major foundations and was not a notable patron. She is more remarkable for what she suffered than what she achieved. On her death in 1437, a woman who had been among the wealthiest of English queens was living on 500 marks a year. She was the first in a line of fifteenth-century consorts whose careers were to prove that while queenship made a woman exceptional, it by no means rendered her invulnerable.

CHAPTER 15

CATHERINE DE VALOIS

'Very handsome, of high birth and of the most engaging manners'

S amuel Pepys was a great one for the glamour of royalty. On 23 February 1669, the celebrated diarist noted that he had viewed the embalmed body of Catherine de Valois on the anniversary of her coronation at Westminster, 'and here we did see by particular favour the body of queen Katherine of Valois, and had her upper part of her body in my hands. And I did kiss her mouth, reflecting upon it that I did kiss a queen.' The macabre eroticism of this image says a good deal about Samuel's own tendencies, but it also recalls that Catherine, whose body continued to be periodically displayed at the abbey until the eighteenth century, was a queen whose sexuality, both sanctified and transgressive, had dominated not just her own life but that of the royal dynasty of England.

Traditionally, one of the most glamorous English royal marriages began with two young men arguing about the size of their balls. In the second year of his reign, Henry V sent

> to France two Ambassadors in State, a Bishop, two Doctors and two Knights in fitting array. They deliberated with the King of France and his council concerning a marriage to be celebrated between King Henry of England and the noble Lady Catherine, daughter of the King of France, but these envoys of the English King had only a brief discussion with the French on this matter, without arriving at any conclusion consistent with the honour or to the advantage of our King and so they returned home.[1]

Henry's honour was apparently insulted by a gift of tennis balls from Catherine's brother the Dauphin, who said that he could play with the 'little balls' until he had come to a man's strength. Henry countered that he 'would play with such balls in the Frenchmen's own streets', or, as

Shakespeare told it, until he had 'turn'd his balls to gun-stones'. There is no French confirmation for this story, though it is corroborated by four English chronicles, but beneath the relish for thumping innuendo, it shows something of the mood that surrounded Henry's eventual marriage to Catherine in 1420, and perhaps something of Henry's self-projection as England's most celebrated warrior king since Richard the Lionheart.

At the coronation banquet held for Catherine de Valois in February 1421, even the pudding was political. The dessert course, or 'subtleties', featured four angels each bearing a 'reason' as to why the Queen's marriage had ended the French wars. The conflict was not over, but its purpose – the provision of an heir to both England and France – was the final resolution to a century of violence. The tennis-ball anecdote highlights Henry's masculinity, his virility, emphasising (not to put too fine a point on it) that he will prevail not just through his balls of steel, but through the seed they carry. After the siege of Harfleur in 1415, Henry offered to settle the succession to France once and for all in single combat with the Dauphin. Even then, it was a slightly absurd gesture, but the story also foregrounds the element of personal challenge in Henry's ambitions for conquest, casting himself and Louis as rival knights, with Catherine the waiting maiden in the tower. Many chronicles concur that Henry, as King, had undergone a remarkable change of character since his days of 'riot and wild governance'[2] as Prince of Wales. According to the *Brut Chronicle*, one of his first acts was to assemble his companions from his drinking and whoring days, reward them and dismiss them. From then on, until his marriage to Catherine, he reputedly remained chaste. Potency thus becomes a condition of abstinence, vigour dependent upon purity. The symbolism of Catherine's coronation pageantry was therefore both pious and romantic: her queenship, as well as creating her role as peace-weaver and mother to the future King, was confirmation that God had smiled on Henry, her true knight.

Catherine de Valois was the youngest daughter and eleventh child of Charles VI of France and Isabeau of Bavaria – the younger sister, by fourteen years, of Richard II's second queen, Isabelle. Isabelle died in 1409, the same year that the marriage was first proposed, when Catherine was eight. Talks and battles continued for a decade, but in 1419 Catherine was granted the unusual opportunity of meeting her future husband when she travelled with her mother and Duke John the Fearless of Burgundy to rendezvous with Henry at Meulan.

The French royal family was in crisis. The four elder sons of Charles and Isabeau had died, and Catherine's younger brother Charles had become Dauphin in 1417. Since 1403, Isabeau had been the head of the regency council formed to govern when the King ran mad, but she was not well equipped to deal with the factionalism of the French magnates. According to her detractors, she had demonstrated her support for the Armagnac side during the civil war by sleeping with both Louis de Valois and Bernard, Count of Armagnac, but Armagnac ambition eventually led to her being imprisoned at Tours for six months in 1317 on charges of corruption. Isabeau was rescued by John the Fearless, Duke of Burgundy (who was also accused of being her lover), by which time the Armagnacs, supported by the Dauphin, had control of both Paris and the King. In 1418, John of Burgundy succeeded in ejecting them from the capital. While not actively pro-English at this juncture, John saw it was in his interests to allow Henry V's armies to continue their ongoing conquest of northern France. Charles VI was in no condition to be useful, so it was left to Isabeau to try to broker a deal with Henry at Meulan through which the capital might be recovered. A king of Henry's chivalric reputation could do nothing less than fall in love at first sight, and the 'flame of love' duly blazed in his 'martial heart'.[3] But not quite fiercely enough, it seems, as the talks collapsed and he went back to making war in Normandy. In August, the Dauphin played neatly into his hands by murdering John the Fearless, while Rouen fell to the English. Much of northern France was now under English control and Paris was exposed. Henry was prepared to make an alliance with John's heir, Philip the Good, so the French faced the prospect of seeing their kingdom eaten up between England and Burgundy. In 1521, a monk showed the broken skull of John the Fearless to the then King François I, explaining that this was the hole through which England had entered France.

Anti-Isabeau writers maintain that she now betrayed her son Charles by casting doubts on his paternity and persuading her husband to repudiate him in order to hand the kingdom to Henry. In fact, Charles had been disinherited by his father before the treaty of Troyes was ratified on the grounds that his ordering of the Duke of Burgundy's murder proved him unfit to govern. On 20 May 1420, Henry V and Philip of Burgundy arrived at the camp of the displaced and diminished French court at Troyes. The treaty was ratified in the cathedral of St Peter, where the English conquerors embarrassed their dingy hosts with the splendour of their accoutrements. In Charles VI's name, Isabeau agreed that on his marriage to Catherine, Henry and not her son, would become his heir, and that the French crown would duly pass to their offspring. The treaty does not declare that the Dauphin was illegitimate, and the single allusion to him refers only to the moral grounds for his disinheritance. But it was Troyes that destroyed the reputation of Catherine's mother for future French historians as her signature on the treaty perpetuated the claim that she was solely responsible for giving France away. In truth Isabeau was only fulfilling a decision made earlier by her husband (and confirmed by him in a joint *lit de justice* he held with Henry V in Paris in December that year), and her presence without him at the signing was necessary simply because he was in no state to appear in public. Isabeau is another example of the dangers to which foreign royal brides were susceptible, the complexities of her situation subsumed beneath the treacherous disloyalty to which, because she was not French, she was seen as inevitably subject. French historians, it is suggested, have found it 'safer and more emotionally satisfying to blame all the trouble on foreign women rather than take sides among internal factions that often manipulated queens as their puppets'.[4]

For the English, at least, Troyes was naturally a triumph. Henry kissed Catherine's hand 'joyfully', as well he might, and on 2 June 'the King of the English married Lady Catherine and he willed that the ceremony should be carried out entirely according to the custom of the France'.[5] Henry gave 200 nobles to the church of St John, and the bride and groom were feasted before being ceremonially put to bed, but Henry was in such a hurry to get back to his war that he didn't bother with a tournament to mark the occasion.

Catherine had a honeymoon of sieges. Henry, who had now taken over from Isabeau as head of the French regency council, was now effectively fighting a civil war against his new brother-in-law the Dauphin. That was certainly the opinion of the English Parliament, who felt that from now on the conflict should be financed by Henry's French subjects. Catherine was with the King for the surrender of Sens on 11 June, then returned to her parents at Troyes while Henry starved her brother's prisoners to death in trenches dug around the besieged fortress of Melun. On 1 December the King and Queen of France returned to Paris with their new son-in-law, his brothers Bedford and Clarence, Philip of Burgundy and Catherine. They processed from the St Denis gate to Nôtre Dame through brightly decorated streets filled with Parisians wearing celebratory red. The Christmas festivities again highlighted the mortifying differences in circumstances between the two kings. At the Hôtel de St Pol, Charles VI received 'a small number of old servants and persons of low degree',[6] while over at the Louvre Henry and Catherine kept the holiday in style: 'It is scarcely possible to tell in detail of the state they kept that day, the feasts and ceremony and luxury of their court.'[7] On 27 December, Catherine accompanied Henry on his ceremonial entry into Rouen, the Conqueror's capital, and then they moved on to Amiens and Calais before embarking for England.

If Parliament was complaining about the expense of the whole business, Henry's subjects were in rapture. The *Brut Chronicle* claims that 30,000 people were waiting to greet the King and Queen when they arrived at Blackheath to process to London in February. Finally, here was a queen to worship. Anne of Bohemia had been poor, Isabelle de Valois a child, Joanna of Navarre an expensive widow, but Catherine was a beautiful blonde virgin who brought the kingdom of France as a dowry. If contemporary descriptions bear any relation to the truth, Henry and Catherine were almost divinely lovely. Henry was tall, fair-haired and clear-skinned, with an athletic body and white teeth (truly an extraordinary attribute in medieval times). Catherine, who took after her father in his better moments, was slim and fair. In the *Bedford Hours*, Catherine and Henry are pictured with golden hair, wearing red gowns covered with blue cloaks, a combination of colours in which the Virgin was most frequently illustrated, the red representing her 'worldly' nature and the blue its 'heavenly' counterpart. Blonde hair was something of an ideal, particularly for queens, as it carried implications of spirituality (the light of the halo) and fertility (the colour of ripe wheat). Since the beginning of the thirteenth century, in both Italian and northern European painting, the Virgin had been depicted with golden hair, and in another example of the myriad Marian associations of idealised queenship, all four of Catherine's fifteenth-century successors were shown with bright blonde locks, though Marguerite of Anjou, at least, was almost certainly a brunette.

Catherine rode to her coronation on 23 February through streets lined with cloth-of-gold. Henry did not attend, but his absence did not stem from a waning of affection, as has sometimes been suggested, but as a result of a more sophisticated concept of the significance of the public body of the king. Traditionally, English kings did not attend their predecessors' funerals as, until the corpse was entombed, the public body of the monarch was contained in the funeral effigy lying upon the coffin. Since there could never be more than one king, the new king could not appear beside the effigy of the old.[8] In the fifteenth century, it has been suggested it was at the point of coronation that the queen became part of the king's public body, as she was anointed with the holy oil, and therefore the king could not be simultaneously visible.

After the celebrations were over, Henry turned his mind to his greatest love, the war. Catherine stayed behind as he departed on a fund-raising progress through Bristol, Kenilworth and Coventry, and joined him for Easter at Leicester. This was the period when Catherine became pregnant with her son, though Henry was not inclined to linger in her company and set off again soon afterwards for Lincoln and York. Catherine returned slowly to London through Stamford, Huntingdon, Cambridge and Colchester, receiving gifts of gold and silver to contribute to the war effort. In June, by which time the Queen was aware of her pregnancy, Henry left once more for France.

Catherine spent just five months in England with her husband during a marriage that lasted a total of twenty-six, for much of which time Henry was away on campaign. It is posited that 'Catherine had beauty to recommend her, but neither intelligence nor personality to captivate for long a man of Henry's qualities'.[9] The fact that Henry preferred fighting to his wife does not necessarily confirm that she was boring and stupid, as Henry was fonder of war than of anything else. (If they didn't get on, it was perhaps because Catherine, judging from her later behaviour, was a rather jolly person, whereas Henry in his post-Prince Hal incarnation was notably abstemious, if not something of a prig.) They certainly had one thing in common, which was an appreciation of music. Henry had learned the harp as a boy, and in October 1420 new harps were ordered for both the King and his wife. The royal chapel was a celebrated centre for the development of English music, and Henry's clerks of the chapel, who included the composers John Cooke, Thomas Damett and Nicholas Sturgeon, produced celebrations of Agincourt, the royal marriage and the treaty of Troyes in Mass pieces and motets. Henry brought thirty-eight musicians and sixteen singers to perform at his wedding, and Sturgeon may have accompanied him when he returned to France in 1421.

As far as their contemporaries were concerned, Catherine and Henry had a fairytale marriage, and its perfection was crowned with the birth of the heir to England and France, Henry VI, at Windsor on 6 December 1421. Catherine crossed to France the following May, escorted by the Duke of Bedford, and though by July the King had fallen ill, he did not send for her. She spent some time near Paris and visited the tombs of her ancestors at St Denis, then joined her parents at Senlis. Even when Henry knew he was dying, Catherine was not summoned, and she was not present at his deathbed at Vincennes on 31 August. This certainly suggests that something had soured between them, or perhaps that, like Richard I, Henry was so preoccupied with his battles he was largely indifferent to his wife. The Queen travelled back to England with her husband's embalmed body from Vincennes to Dover, a journey which took over two months. The hearse was accompanied by the King's entire household, wearing black and white mourning, surveyed by his life-sized effigy laid upon the coffin. In England, there was another week of solemn ceremony before the funeral. By the time Henry was finally buried at Westminster in November, Charles VI of France was also dead. On 22 October 1422, Catherine's ten-month-old child became King of England and France.

The matter of Catherine having a role in the regency during Henry's minority was barely discussed. The last English queen to serve as regent while her husband was abroad had been Eleanor of Provence, and only Isabella of France had assumed the office as Dowager Queen, during the minority of Edward III. In the cases of the two kings who succeeded as children before and after Edward, Henry III and Richard II, the government was directed by a regency council until they came of age. Catherine's mother's experience as regent had hardly been a success and, like Isabeau's, Catherine's foreign status might well have made her a suspect choice given that England was still at war with her brother. Before leaving on his last journey for France, Henry had made provision for government by council, and Catherine, as Queen Mother, showed no wish to challenge his arrangements, leaving the management of the country to Henry's brothers. John, Duke of Bedford, was the senior regent, with governance over France and the pursuit of the continuing war, while Humphrey of Gloucester was the first member of the council while his brother was out of England.

In terms of her own resources, Catherine was able to profit from the new administrative arrangements for the queen's council inaugurated for Joanna of Navarre. Like Joanna's, her dowry had been set at 10,000 crowns (40,000 marks) on funds derived from the Lancaster estates. Initially, Catherine's income was provided from the sequestration of Joanna's, her ladies receiving 'ten livres apiece out of the funds of Queen Joan'[10] and her confessor John Boyars twenty. Catherine was given Anglesey, Flintshire, Leicester, Knaresborough and the castles and manors of Wallingford, Hertford and Waltham. Since, after her release from custody, Joanna was obliged to live on a reduced income and in 1332 Catherine's was over 3,000 marks short of what had been promised to her, it appears that even the hugely wealthy Lancaster estates were not sufficient to provide full dower assignments for two queens.

Catherine's personal rather than her political life has been emphasised during the period of her widowhood and second marriage, but her dynastic importance remained crucial to the English in the period between 1422 and 1431. Her brother Charles refused to cede his claim to the

French crown (which, if Salic law were applied, was stronger than Henry VI's), though his activities after Troyes were at first concentrated south of the Loire. In 1429, thanks to the miraculous efforts of Joan of Arc, the tide of English success was reversed, and after the fall of Orléans and the battle of Patay, Charles was crowned King of France in July 1429. Paris, though, was still held for Henry VI, and a reassertion of the English claim was now vital. After his English coronation in November 1429, the boy king was proclaimed in the French capital in 1431. The challenge to the English government under Bedford post-1429 was to assert the justice of Henry's claim to France while selling its advantages to the English, propaganda efforts in which the Queen Mother was essential.

The Plantagenet claim deriving from Isabella of France had been contested in the Hundred Years War whereas Henry's claim, through Catherine and Charles VI, had been ratified at Troyes. As early as 1423, Bedford commissioned a set of verses from Lawrence Cabot to accompany an illustrated genealogy designed to be exhibited in churches throughout northern France. The family tree shows Henry's dual descent from St Louis of France and Edward I of England, concluding with portraits of Henry V and Catherine de Valois and a miniature of the boy king receiving two crowns from two angels, one from each royal house. This image is another example of the Lancastrian adoption of Ricardian symbolism, as well as an allusion to French traditions of the divine presentation of the crown to Clovis. At Richard II's coronation in 1377, a castle had been erected by the guild of goldsmiths on Cheapside from which a mechanical angel descended to present a crown to the King. The *Bedford Hours* contains a version of the popular French story of Clovis, the fifth-century Frankish King who united the country, converted to Christianity and founded the Merovingian dynasty, receiving the Fleur de Lys from St Clotilde. In Henry's coronation banquets, as at his mother's, the 'subtleties' featured pastry 'reasons', showing, among other images, Edward I and St Louis, with Henry as the 'inheritor of the Fleur de Lys' and St George and St Denis, the patron saints of the two countries, presenting the King to the Virgin and Child as 'Born by descent and title of right/Justly to reign in England and in France'. This attentiveness to French, as well as English royal traditions is testament to the English administration's 'determination that Henry VI's French antecedents should receive all possible publicity'.[11] Catherine was certainly not the least of these antecedents, and the political symbolism invoked by the English to bolster Henry's claim to the dual monarchy was significantly dependent upon the Queen's role in having provided the resolution to the promises of Troyes.

Catherine's visibility was therefore of importance. Perhaps because she had no political role she was able to spend a good deal of time with her son when he was small, both at her preferred residences of Hertford and Waltham and at Windsor. She accompanied him to Parliament and attended his English coronation. Until 1427 she maintained a separate household, but is then found living with her son, paying for her keep with seven pounds per day at the wardrobe. This move was not, however, motivated entirely by maternal affection, because by then the government had decided that it needed to keep its eye on her.

The French commentators who so maligned Isabeau of Bavaria might well have said that Catherine was her mother's daughter. Her presence in Henry's household was a consequence of her inability 'to curb fully her carnal passions'.[12] In 1426, Catherine had begun an affair with Edmund Beaufort, the younger brother of the Duke of Somerset. For a family whose origins were still being sneered at in the nickname 'Fairborn' at the end of the century, John of Gaunt's bastards had done extraordinarily well. In the first generation, John Beaufort had been made Earl of Somerset and had married one of the Holland heiresses, a granddaughter of Joan of Kent. Henry Beaufort, cardinal bishop of Winchester, was chancellor and Thomas, the third of Katherine Swynford's sons, became Duke of Exeter. John Beaufort died in 1410 after which his title, which became a dukedom, passed to his eldest and then second sons, Henry and John. His third son, Thomas, became Count of Perche, and his daughter Margaret, Countess of Devon. Margaret's sister Joan scooped the jackpot, marrying James I of Scotland in 1423. Their brother Edmund, who inherited the ducal title in 1444, was therefore highly eligible, and, as a nineteen-year-old war hero, highly attractive.

James of Scotland had been a prisoner in England since he was twelve, when he had been captured for Henry IV en route to France. His regent, the Duke of Albany, found this a most satisfactory situation, and the Scots did not agree to pay James's ransom for fourteen years. Catherine received James at Windsor and made a formal intercession for his release with her son, but given James's relationship with Joan Beaufort, whom he married before he returned to Scotland, and Catherine's with Joan's brother, it is possible to think of them as forming a 'younger set' at Henry VI's nominal court. Catherine herself was twenty-five, and though her marriage had been a political triumph, it has left no record of particular affection. Her son's government was run by old men, and according to evidence of Marguerite of Anjou's resurrection of court life when she became Queen in 1445, high society was not what it had been under Richard II. Catherine was young and beautiful and had nothing much to do except fall in love.

Naturally, Catherine and Edmund caused a scandal. The Dowager Queen's behaviour was wildly compromising. Given the importance of preserving the propaganda value of Henry V's legacy, the widow of the hero of Agincourt could hardly be seen to be carrying on with a younger man. There was also the fear that Catherine and Beaufort could marry and have children. Since the King was still only five years old, there was every chance he might not reach his majority, in which case the heir in 1426 was Bedford, but a child with Plantagenet and French royal blood could prove extremely troublesome. The only Dowager Queen to have remarried an English subject was Adeliza of Louvain in the twelfth century, but she had not been the mother of Henry I's children and had elected for a quiet life. In the fifteenth century, the government desperately needed the young King's mother to remain respectable. In the 1427–8 session, Parliament passed a pointed bill dealing with the remarriage of dowager queens. The fact that Joanna of Navarre was still alive provided a screen of decorum, but there was no doubt at whom it was directed.

The bill determined that if a dowager queen should remarry without the consent of the King, the lands and possessions of her husband would be declared forfeit, though any children would be acknowledged as members of the royal family. The latter clause is both highly pertinent to the future royal line of England and evidence of the bill's purpose, given that Joanna of Navarre had no children by Henry IV, and any offspring would not therefore have had the status of uterine (from the same mother) siblings of the king. Since permission to remarry could only be given by the king himself when he came of age, Catherine was in theory prevented from doing so at all for some years. She was also obliged to live in Henry's household, where her conduct could be supervised. Catherine remained there until 1432, and may have been permitted to attend Henry's French coronation. It is not certain that she did so, but given the situation with Charles VII, it would have been surprising if her presence had not been sought to support her son's assumption of his claim. Quite how Catherine acquired a reputation for dullness is hard to understand, since soon after the coronation she left the King's household to do precisely what she had been forbidden to do. Evidently the loss of Edmund Beaufort had not broken her heart irreparably, because, in defiance of the bill passed four years earlier, without seeking the King's consent, Catherine got married.

The circumstances in which Catherine de Valois met and fell in love with Owen ap Maredudd ap Tudor are obscure. What is clear, despite Henry VII's best efforts to demonstrate otherwise at the end of the century, is that, compared with the Queen, he was absolutely nobody. The earliest reference to Owen, after 1483, places him as a servant in Catherine's chamber. The origin of this story could be one Owen Meredith (a possible anglicisation of his name) who travelled to France in the retinue of Sir Walter Hungerford, Henry V's steward, in 1421. That he was in some way connected with Catherine's household is suggested by one of the most popular versions of their meeting which has him collapsing merrily into her lap at a ball. Owen himself supposedly alluded to this when he died and, writing after Owen's death in 1461, Robin of Anglesey described the incident: 'He once on a holiday clapped his ardent humble affection on the daughter of the King of the land of wine.' This luscious description of Catherine sounds as though she was less averse to the effects of her vinous inheritance than was her first husband. The sexiest version of the story has the Queen catching sight of her young Welsh servant stripped to go swimming. Intrigued, she disguises herself as a maid and arranges an assignation, but when Owen, mistaking her status, takes the liberty of kissing her cheek, she recoils, wounded (does he bite her?). Owen, seeing the mark on her face when he serves her at dinner later, realises her true identity and understands that she loves him.

What became essential to Catherine's grandson Henry Tudor was that no one doubted the legitimacy of Catherine and Owen's marriage. His father, Henry VI, certainly accepted it. It is suggested that Catherine selected a commoner as a means of circumventing the council's threats to her husband's estates, which had successfully deterred the ambitious Beaufort. Owen Tudor could hardly have been worried about forfeiture since he had nothing to forfeit. But if Catherine's choice was a calculated one, she had neglected one important factor, which was that Owen Tudor was Welsh. From 1394 to 1400, the Welsh, unified under Owen Glyndwr, had once again resisted the English, initially with marked success. In 1402, Henry IV had enacted penal statutes against them, elaborated in the Charter of Brecon after Henry V's successful Welsh campaign. Welshmen were prohibited from carrying arms, assembling, living in certain towns, owning land to the east of the ancient border of Offa's Dyke or holding government office and denied the liberties of Englishmen under the law. However, 'Queen Catherine, being a Frenchwoman born, knew no difference between the English and the Welsh nations until her marriage being published Owen Tudor's kin and country were objected, to disgrace him'.[13] In the May Parliament of 1432, Owen was given the status and rights of an Englishman, which suggests that wherever and whenever the marriage had taken place, the council had been obliged to acknowledge it as fact and make some provision for the preservation of the wayward Queen's dignity. The Tudor antiquary John Leland claimed to have seen a genealogy which Catherine had been required to produce in Parliament to prove Owen's descent.

Two years after Owen was naturalised, Catherine gave him custody of her lands and the crown profit on the marriage of John Conway, an important landowner. She clearly trusted her husband and was attempting to give him a measure of financial independence. Catherine and Owen had four children in six years, and the timing of their births indicates that she may have been pregnant with the first one before her wedding, in which case Parliament's decision was even more explicable: according to the Charter of Brecon, any man who was not judged to be English or to have an English father would be subject to the penal statutes, potentially an embarrassing position for the brother of the King. The proximity of the births of Edmund, Jasper, Owen and a daughter who died in infancy point to the marriage being a happy one, at least in bed, but little evidence survives of the circumstances in which the couple lived. Catherine was apparently surprised that Owen came from such a very different culture: 'He brought to her presence John ap Maredudd and Hywel ap Llewelyn ap Hywel, his near cousins, men of goodly stature and personage, but wholly destitute of bringing up and nurture, for when the Queen had spoken to them in diverse languages and they were not able to answer her, she said they were the goodliest dumb creatures that she ever saw.'[14]

Incidentally, this anecdote casts doubt on one reason offered for Catherine's political inactivity during her reign: that she found herself 'linguistically isolated'[15] in a court that increasingly identified itself as, and spoke, English. The description of her meeting Owen's Welsh relatives implies that she knew several languages other than French; moreover, given that she had been betrothed to Henry on and off for much of her life, and had lived in England for a decade, it would be surprising if she did not have some grasp of English.

The birthplaces of Catherine's children indicate that she and Owen continued to reside in and around her dower properties in Hertfordshire. Edmund was born at the bishop of London's manor at Much Hadham, and Jasper at Hatfield, the house of the bishop of Ely, locations that also suggest the couple had attained a degree of social acceptance. Yet after Catherine's death in 1437, Owen had to confront the consequences of his impudence. John of Bedford having died in 1435, Humphrey of Gloucester was next in line for the throne, and Owen was so fearful of the Duke that he took sanctuary at Westminster Abbey. He appeared before the regency council, which acquitted him of breaching the 1428 statute, but as he tried to return to Wales, he was arrested and his possessions, including a small fortune in gold and silver plate, were confiscated. Imprisoned in Newgate Jail, with only his confessor and a servant for company, Owen made a botched attempt at escape and was committed to custody at Windsor in 1438, where he remained for a year before being released on bail the following July and pardoned in November 1439. His sons Edmund and Jasper were taken into the care of Katherine de la Pole, the sister of the Earl of Suffolk, who was abbess at Barking Abbey (the third boy, Owen, became a monk at Westminster), until 1442.

The Tudor luck turned when Henry VI decided to take an interest in his half-brothers. At twenty-one, the sensitive, pious young King was lonely. Jasper and Henry were invited to join his household and, ten years later, Henry decided he wished to ennoble them. He had married Marguerite of Anjou in 1445, but as yet the couple had no children. On 5 January 1453, Edmund was invested as Earl of Richmond and Jasper as Earl of Pembroke by the King at the Tower of London. In March they took their seats in Parliament, where a formal acknowledgement of their position as the King's uterine brothers was heard. On 24 March, Henry gave the wardship and marriage of ten-year-old Margaret Beaufort to his brothers. It was one of the few independent decisions of his life, and it provided the means by which the grandson of a Welsh servant ascended the throne of England. Margaret was the greatest marital prize of her generation, the sole heiress of John, first Duke of Somerset and through him to the Holland fortune of her grandmother Margaret. After John's death in 1444, Margaret's wardship had been given to the Earl of Suffolk who, shortly before his death in 1450, married her to his own heir, John de la Pole. Henry VI dissolved the marriage in 1453 and Margaret was swiftly married to Edmund Tudor. Henry's wife, Marguerite of Anjou, was actually in the early stages of pregnancy at this time, but it is possible that even the Queen herself was unaware of this, as it is considered likely that Henry was considering adopting Edmund as his heir in right of Margaret's descent from Edward III through John of Gaunt.

A chance for a Tudor grab at the crown receded with the birth of Henry's own son, but Edmund and Jasper were still in an extraordinarily advantageous position, given the circumstances of their birth. In 1455, as the conflict which became known as the Wars of the Roses began to rumble, Edmund was made the King's deputy in Wales and he and Margaret moved to Lamphey in Pembrokeshire. Edmund seems to have been more concerned with ensuring a lifelong interest in Margaret's money than with the health of his wife, as he slept with her as soon as she attained the canonical age of twelve. Shortly after Margaret ascertained that she was pregnant, he was captured by the forces of the Duke of York and imprisoned at Carmarthen Castle, where he died of plague on 1 November 1456. Margaret took refuge with her brother-in-law Jasper and her child, ambitiously named Henry for his uncle, was born at Pembroke Castle in January 1457. In the coming years, Jasper's loyalty would prove a vital asset to the Lancastrian cause, while Henry VI's gift of a few essential drops of Plantagenet blood saw the Tudors to the throne.

Thus, as predicted by the treaty of Troyes, Catherine de Valois was the ancestress of a great royal dynasty – if not quite in the form Henry V had planned. In the manner of her death, though, she appeared to be looking to the past rather than the future. Some months before she died, Catherine had elected to enter Bermondsey Abbey, returning in this to a tradition of pious queenship shared with Adeliza of Louvain, Eleanor of Aquitaine and Eleanor of Provence, a tradition she had so daringly flouted with her second marriage. Catherine knew she was unwell. Given the mental illness of her father, and later of her son, it is possible that the 'long and grievous malady' from which she suffered was mental rather than physical in origin. As a child she had prayed with her brothers and sisters at Mont St Michel for their father's recovery, and perhaps she hoped that in the convent her mind would be spared long enough to bring her closer to God.

One picture of medieval women, now thankfully dismissed, presents them as scarcely more than 'animated title deeds',[16] their existence entirely determined by the transmission of property. Catherine's queenship, more than that of any of her predecessors, might be said to be contained by this very limited concept. She did very little as a consort except to transmit the kingdom of France, a claim whose vanity was to prove devastating for her son. Yet in this Catherine may also be seen as the model for the perfect princess, the royal heroine who waited patiently for her true knight and confirmed God's grace in her offspring. As a woman, however, Catherine was considerably more interesting. She was courageous, independent-minded and astonishingly audacious in the pursuit of her desire. Hers was an extraordinarily vivid life, blighted by war and madness, elevated by marriage to the hero of the age and a love affair which really did change the course of history. It is a pity, perhaps, that only hints of the colour of that life can be found beyond the stilted, jewel-like radiance of her portraits as the beautiful bride of England's greatest warrior prince.

CHAPTER 16

MARGUERITE OF ANJOU

'An hault courage above the nature of her sex'

In his book of hours for March 1430, René of Anjou noted on the twenty-fourth that his second daughter, Lady Marguerite, had been born. The winter that year had been so bitter that wolves stalked the suburbs of Paris, a fitting symbol for the battleground that western Europe had become. The ancestral Anjou heritage of baby Marguerite was as grand as it was complex. The Plantagenet branch of the house of Anjou had taken England to the height of its recent Continental power under Henry V, whose son Henry VI asserted his right to the crowns of both England and France. Marguerite's great-great-grandfather was the King Jean of France who had been entertained so courteously by Edward II's queen; his second son, Louis I, had brought up various hereditary claims and eventually styled himself Emperor of Constantinople, King of Jerusalem, Mallorca and Cyprus, titles 'that were as grandiloquent as they were devoid of substance'.[1] Interfamilial networks also related Marguerite to the rulers of Sicily, Naples, Provence, Hungary, Poland, Moldavia, Wallachia and the Dalmatian provinces. Her immensely capable paternal grandmother, Yolande of Aragon, the bride of Louis II, succeeded in betrothing her only daughter to Charles VII of France, who was thus Marguerite's uncle by marriage as well as her third cousin, but the royal connection by which she was more significantly affected was the contentious claim of her father, René of Anjou, to the kingdom of Naples.

The Angevin claim in Naples had been established by Charles of Anjou, King of Sicily, the husband of Eleanor of Provence's sister Beatrice. By the early fifteenth century, two branches of the house of Anjou were contesting the crown, but a resolution was offered by Queen Joanna II of Naples, who adopted Louis III of Anjou, René's elder brother, as her declared heir. Louis III died in 1434, followed the next year by Queen Joanna, so all his rights devolved upon René. The father of four-year-old

Marguerite was hardly in a position to celebrate at the time, being imprisoned on the orders of the Duke of Burgundy, but luckily for him, he had chosen in his wife Isabelle of Lorraine a woman as adventurous and loyal as his own mother, and the twenty-four-year-old Queen of Naples set off to reclaim her husband's birthright. Some stories have it that she was accompanied by her young daughter, but Marguerite stayed at home in Anjou with her grandmother Yolande and her nurse, Tiphaine la Majine, who had also cared for her father and aunt Marie, and whose tomb may be seen at Saumur, holding them as swaddled babies.

By 1438, both Marguerite's parents were successfully established in Naples, where they enjoyed four glorious years until the city fell to Alfonso of Aragon, and the erstwhile royal couple shuffled back to their impoverished French estates, exhausted and penniless. It was essential that a good match be arranged for their daughter, and the early negotiations surrounding Marguerite's betrothal provide a particularly naked example of the way in which aristocratic women were used as bargaining tools. One candidate was the Count of St Pol, whose father, Jean of Luxembourg, was engaged in buying the county of Guise from René for 20,000 pounds; another was the Count of Charolais, to whom René owed part of the ransom for his release from the Duke of Burgundy's incarceration, a debt that could be offset by a marriage settlement. The recently elected Emperor, Frederick of Hapsburg, also showed some interest in twelve-year-old Marguerite, and was received at Saumur by Yolande, who touchingly put on the best display she could muster, ordering 330 crowns-worth of gold, violet and crimson cloth and fur trimmings for Marguerite's dresses. Yolande died that autumn, content in her belief that she had arranged a great match for her granddaughter.

However, in April 1444, René met William de la Pole, the Earl of Suffolk, at the court of his brother-in-law Charles at Montils, near Tours, where Suffolk proposed for Marguerite on behalf of King Henry VI of England. Such a match would gain René Charles's support in dealing with discontented subjects. Metz had recently rebelled in protest at excessive taxation and the non-payment of interest on the loan René had raised to pay off his ransom to the Duke of Burgundy, and an English marriage, with the corollary of a truce between England and France, would release Charles's forces to help him. Charles was famously stingy (when he became Dauphin he had no treasury, barely the scraps of an army and it was said he could not even afford shoes), and the price he demanded from the English for his niece was high: the counties of Maine and Anjou itself were to transfer their allegiance to the French crown. Moreover, Henry would have to meet the costs of Marguerite's wedding journey and accept the farcical dowry of René's claims to Mallorca and Menorca, which he might conquer in right of his wife if he got round to it. René was a king without a country, and his reverses in Italy had absorbed what little of his fortune and future revenues were not mortgaged to pay the Burgundy debt.

Nevertheless, the wedding was a splendid affair. Marguerite and her mother had arrived at Tours from Angers, where they stayed at the abbey of Beaumont les Tours. The night before, 22 May 1444, a treaty securing a truce between England and France was signed, guaranteed until 1 April 1446. The betrothal was celebrated in the church of St Martin, attended by the King and Queen of France, René of Anjou and Isabelle of Lorraine, the Dukes of Calabria, Brittany and Alençon, the Dauphine, Margaret of Scotland, the Counts of St Pol and Vendôme and Marguerite's uncle, Charles Count of Maine, though not by the bridegroom. After curtseying to the King of France, Marguerite was presented with the marriage licence (a provisional document allowing the couple to marry even though they were within the prohibited degrees; the real licence took one year), by the papal legate, Monsignor de Mont Dieu, bishop of Brescia, and the ring was placed on her finger. At the feast afterwards, at the abbey of St Julien, the fourteen-year-old bride was treated with the status of an English queen.

Marguerite remained at home long enough to see Metz submit satisfactorily to 30,000 French troops sent by Charles VII and to witness the marriage of her sister Yolande at Nancy. She then set off on the journey to her new country with an escort of 1,500. Two leagues from Nancy, she wished her uncle Charles a tearful goodbye, then continued on to Bar-le-Duc to see Isabelle and René. In Paris in mid-March, she heard Mass at Nôtre Dame and was presented with relics from the treasury. At St Denis she was formally handed over to Suffolk and the party sailed to Rouen, the capital of the English territories in northern France, where she was saluted by 600 archers as Richard, Duke of York and regent of France, came to meet her. Marguerite was presented with a gift from Henry, a beautiful palfrey draped in crimson velvet sewn with gold roses, then rode in a carriage to the Hôtel de Ville for yet another banquet, although she was unwell and her place had to be taken by Lady Suffolk. On 9 April, Marguerite's ship, captained by one Thomas Adam, arrived at Portchester. The vessel had inevitably endured a terrible storm, losing both its masts, and though the people of Portchester had tried to provide a welcome, heaping carpets on the beach, the new Queen was able only to stagger, ill and raggedly dressed, to a nearby cottage, where she promptly fainted.

Marguerite of Anjou met her husband, King Henry VI, for the first time on 14 April 1445 at Southampton. A week later they were married privately, at Titchfield Abbey by William Aicough, bishop of Salisbury and royal confessor. What did they make of each other in their earliest days as a couple? At twenty-three, Henry had been king for his entire life. Unlike other aristocratic boys he had not been brought up among his peers, but had lived a rather sad, solitary life, lonely among the older men who made up his household. He was already displaying the deep piety and lack of worldliness that made him seem more fit for life as a monk than as a king, a view expressed by a papal envoy as early as 1437. Marguerite's mother and grandmother had provided her with examples of strong, influential women who had fought hard for their husbands' rights. Not unlike Henry, René was a dreamy character. He particularly loved painting – he worked on a portrait of Philip of Burgundy even while detained in the man's prison – and it was said that he was so underwhelmed when he heard the news of his inheritance that he barely glanced up from the manuscript he was illuminating. Yolande and Isabelle of Lorraine had made the best of what power they had in an essentially masculine world, so perhaps quiet, docile Henry aroused a protective instinct in his young wife, a desire to offer the decisive support she had seen provided by her female relatives. If Henry responded to an incipient dominating tendency in her personality, it may have reassured him, as he had been bossed about for ever. By the time Marguerite made her formal entry into London on 28 May, Henry is described as being 'wildly in love'.[2]

One romantic story about the couple's first meeting comes from Raffaelo de Negra, a correspondent of the Duchess of Milan. Henry supposedly disguised himself as a squire and brought Marguerite a letter 'from the King', so that he could gaze at her while she read it, as he believed that watching a woman read was the best way to observe her.

Marguerite was crowned at Westminster on 30 May. For her journey from the Tower she wore a white damask dress decorated with gold and a gold and pearl coronet set with jewels set on her loose hair. The fact that the pageants enacted to celebrate her arrival were in English indicates that Marguerite could understand something of her new country's language, but they were perhaps more remarkable for the two themes on which they concentrated: peace and power. A figure of 'Plenty' welcomed her as a bringer of 'wealth, joy and abundance' and she was compared to the dove who came to Noah after the Flood and to the Virgin as Mary, Queen of Heaven. Comparison with the Virgin was a frequent theme of such pageants, but it is notable that those prepared for Marguerite concentrated less on the queen's maternal role and focused so strongly on that of 'peace-weaver'. At Leadenhall, Marguerite was greeted by 'Dame Grace', who announced herself as 'God's Vicar General'. The personification of such an important figure as a woman suggests that Marguerite was expected to be more than a humble supplicant for the King's grace, rather someone who might be capable of assisting him in his judgements. Does this betray a degree of uneasiness about Henry's qualities as king, and a hope that Marguerite might be able to compensate for his deficiencies? At least one scholar has concluded that 'the surprisingly powerful image of queenship conveyed in these particular pageants may have reflected contemporary concerns about Henry's inability to govern'.[3]

The political purpose of Marguerite's marriage became even more explicit with the arrival of a French embassy just a few months after her coronation, in July 1445. Its purpose was the cession of Maine, which Suffolk had conceded as part of Marguerite's marriage contract. Henry dithered, unable to entirely resist the aggressive elements in his council, though the French demands were reasonable: usufruct of Maine for Charles of Anjou's life in exchange for ten years' revenues. Eventually, a twenty-year alliance was proposed, and a second French party arrived in October to discuss this, but this time Suffolk prevaricated. Impatiently, Marguerite wrote directly to her uncle in December, and on the twenty-second an agreement was finalised, whereby the truce would continue and Maine would be handed over in April 1446. The letter was given under the King's signet and contained the phrase: 'To please the King of France and at the request of his wife'. Margaret's precise role in this is not known, but it has been suggested that the peace initiative was not Henry's and that the letter was supervised, if not written, by Suffolk himself.[4] Marguerite's name might be present as a diplomatic courtesy, showing that she was fulfilling her intended role in her marriage, or she may indeed have been working to bring Henry round.

Certainly, the next year finds Marguerite writing to Charles regarding the idea that Edward, Earl of March, son of the Duke of York, should marry Princess Madeleine of France: 'In that you pray and exhort us perseveringly to hold our hand towards my most redoubted Lord that on his part he may still be inclined to the benefit of peace, may it please you to know that in truth we are employed at it and shall be with good heart so far as it shall be possible'. Elsewhere, Marguerite concentrates her efforts on the restitution of Maine and on maintaining Henry's commitment to peace. In these early gestures at diplomacy, however unsubstantiated her real influence at the time, Marguerite reveals a degree of naïveté, an impatience with ambassadorial feints, that betrays a failure to understand how delicate mendacity can be part of the art of negotiation. In trying to achieve her ends explicitly and directly, she appears not to realise that her actions could easily be misconstrued as treacherous meddling.

As Marguerite took her first steps into politics, she was becoming aware of a situation which had slowly dawned on the English magnates in the years before her marriage, and which may well have been hinted at in her coronation pageant. Quite simply, King Henry was never going to grow up. In the 1440s, the chroniclers John Hardyng and John Capgrave were already commenting on the King's peculiar lack of energy and decisiveness, while records of 'treasonable' statements show that many people – even if they only said so when they were drunk – thought he was retarded. Modern historians have debated the implications of his alleged apathy, and there is some consensus that he did make his own wishes heard in both foreign affairs and domestic grants during the 1440s. A case can be made either for Henry pursuing a considered strategy of peace or for his apparent pacifism being merely the consequence of inertia. Either way, it was becoming increasingly evident that it was Suffolk who was governing, Suffolk who presented an appearance of authority to the world – an authority that the King himself conspicuously lacked.

Marguerite found herself in an unusual and isolated position. As the symbolism of her coronation had made clear, the primary duty of the queen was to produce an heir to the throne, but two years after her wedding she had not yet become pregnant. Whether Henry was a saint or merely a simpleton, he did not seem very interested in sex. His chaplain, John Blackman, recounts an incident at Christmastime when: 'A certain great lord brought before him a dance or show of young ladies with bared bosoms who were to dance in that guise before the King, perhaps to prove him or to entice his youthful mind. But the King was not blind to it, not unaware of the devilish wile, and spurned the delusion, and very angrily averted his eyes, turned his back upon them and went out of his chamber, saying "Fie, fie, for shame."'

Blackman's description of Henry needs to be viewed with caution, as it was written under the auspices of Henry VII, who had an interest in demonstrating that his Lancastrian predecessor had saintly tendencies. Hagiography aside, if Henry's piety was offended by cavorting hussies, he was also suspicious of relations with his legal wife. His spiritual counsellor, the bishop of Salisbury, was accused by some of interfering in the royal marriage by advising the King not to go near his wife. Marguerite would have been highly conscious of the imperative to produce a child, and thus frustrated by any sexual neglect on her husband's part. Henry's pious vagueness was not unaffectionate, but while there was no heir, her own position remained uncertain. Suffolk was in every way a contrast to her husband, a decisive, paternal figure, and moreover one of the few people to whom she had been close since her wedding. There were rumours that they were lovers, and though again these are unsubstantiated, Marguerite was careless in allowing their political alliance to be displayed so openly.

Humphrey, Duke of Gloucester, the King's uncle and the only living brother of Henry V, was a potential threat to both Marguerite and Suffolk. As heir presumptive, he stood to gain the crown if Marguerite remained childless and, as one of the strongest opponents of the 1444 peace settlement, he was angry and resentful of the Maine agreement, seeing it as a betrayal of his brother's glorious legacy. On 10 February Henry and Marguerite opened Parliament in Bury St Edmunds, away from Gloucester's centre of support in London and one of the focal points of Suffolk's interest. When Gloucester arrived on 18 February, he was arrested by the Queen's steward, Viscount Beaumont, and taken into custody to await trial. Five days later he was found dead in his lodgings. Suffolk had the body exposed to prove that Gloucester had not been injured, and possibly the Duke had died of a stroke, but rumours of hot spits and smothering with feather beds were more satisfactory to political gossips. Marguerite's role in the Gloucester plot was soon perceived as the fruit of her relationship with Suffolk. She had 'asked, then cajoled, then begged'[5] Henry to have his uncle arrested, on Suffolk's advice that he had been planning to seize Henry and herself, imprison them and take the crown for himself.

Gloucester was not the only one to be disgusted at the 'sorry tale of dishonesty, underhand dealing, vacillation and mismanagement' of French affairs.[6] Still favouring Suffolk's policies (or complying with them), Henry made him a duke, but by 1449 Charles VII had grown weary of English promises and machinations. He took matters into his own hands by invading Normandy in July. By October, Rouen was lost, in April the following year the English suffered a devastating defeat at Formigny and by August the whole province had fallen. In spite of Marguerite's vigorous opposition to attempts to impeach Suffolk, who was formally named in Parliament as the culprit of this national disgrace, in January 1450 he was imprisoned in the Tower to await trial in February, though Henry did rouse himself to intervene and persuade Suffolk's accusers to accept a five-year banishment.

By now, the country was in uproar. In January, Adam Moleyns, bishop of Chichester, keeper of the Privy Seal and one of Suffolk's two closest associates, was murdered by a mob at Portsmouth. The men of Kent had taken up arms, and the terrified government banned the carrying of weapons in London and the south-east, an order as fearful as it was impractical. Suffolk was attacked as he left the Tower, but permitted a six-week respite before embarking on his exile on 30 April. On 2 May, his ships were surrounded and he was taken aboard the *Nicholas of the Tower*. A rusty sword proclaimed his last privilege as a peer and his headless body was delivered to Dover.

Officially, Suffolk's death was treated as a crime, just as Humphrey of Gloucester's had not been, and the unruly rabble of Kent was blamed. The Kentish response was the uprising that became known as Jack Cade's rebellion. In June, the bishop of Salisbury, the last living member of the Suffolk 'triumvirate', was hauled from the Wiltshire church where he was saying Mass and killed. The rebels were in London in early July, brandishing their manifesto, the 'Complaint of the Commons of Kent', while Henry and Marguerite took refuge at Kenilworth. Two thousand pardons were issued to the rebels who massed at Blackheath, which gives a sense of the numbers involved, and though Jack Cade himself was put to death on 12 July and order restored, the first six months of 1450 had provided a horrifying example of how precarious Henry's authority had become, and how easy it might be to overturn it.

On the Feast of the Epiphany 1451, the King and Queen were about to take their seats for dinner when the steward of the household regretfully informed them that there was none, as the court purveyors refused to deliver any more food on credit. The deplorable state of Henry VI's finances was a consequence of the political and administrative incompetence that had brought about the crisis on the Continent and the frightening unrest in England. The truce negotiated on the King's marriage ought to have permitted England to reassert its strong position in Normandy, but Henry's poor leadership and the mangled diplomacy of long-term peace arrangements wasted this opportunity. A tax had been voted in for 1445–9 with a view to providing an extra 30,000 pounds a year to pay for defence, but taxpayers were infuriated to discover that this had dribbled away into the household accounts and were disinclined to pay more. Revenues fell as expenses increased and funds were divided incompetently between Normandy and the other French territories with the result that by 1449 the garrison of Calais, the King's most powerful standing force, was owed 20,000 pounds in wages.

Marguerite was both directly and indirectly involved in this state of affairs. Suffolk had spent the incredible sum of £5,573 17s 5d during the period he had spent in France organising her wedding and overseeing her return journey, the magnificence of which was designed to impress Henry's dignity upon the French, but which he could ill afford. Further expenses were incurred by the preparation of Marguerite's lodgings: there had been no queen in England for twenty years and the royal apartments at Westminster presented a rather sorry appearance. Henry engaged William Cleve, the clerk of works at Westminster, to build a new suite of rooms at Eltham, 'honourable for the Queen's lodging',[7] comprising a hall, scullery, saucery and serving area, so that Marguerite would have somewhere to entertain.

Marguerite had no dowry to offset such extravagance, and her management of her household suggests an almost defiant pride, a refusal to economise and thus to acknowledge her relatively impoverished status. In 1444, household expenses rose from 8,000 pounds to 27,000, and while a great proportion of this vast expenditure had nothing to do with Marguerite, it is notable that expenses for the Queen's chamber in the year 1452 were 1,719 pounds in comparison with 919 for 1466 in the following reign. Marguerite was not the first queen to be plagued with debt, but it seemed at first that she was well provided for financially. Her dower settlement brought her 3,000 pounds in total from various resources of the duchy of Lancaster estates, 1,000 from the customs at Southampton, just over 1,000 from the duchy of Cornwall and a direct allowance of £1,657 17s 11d from the royal exchequer. In addition, she could claim queens-gold and, after Gloucester was removed, she was given a further 500 marks from his duchy of Lancaster holdings. However, none of these resources was particularly reliable: in 1452–3, for example, Marguerite received only £53 1s 14d in queens-gold, and a large part of this was unpaid debt carried over from previous years. Of fifty-nine claims for that period, only sixteen were paid. She constantly battled to stabilise her income, attempting to trade her rights at the exchequer for the more solid security of land, and even venturing into trade with a licence to transport wool for sale tax-free. The customs payments from Southampton were tardy, and Marguerite was obliged to write sternly to John Somerton, one of the officials, to remind him of his duty: 'We desire and pray you and also exhort and require you, that, of such money as is due to us, at Michaelmas term last past, of our dower, assigned to be paid of the customers of Southampton by your hands, you will do your pain and diligence that we may be contented and paid in all haste ... and that you fail not hereof as we trust, and you think to stand in continuance of the favour of our good grace and to eschew our displeasure.'

Marguerite was justifiably active in pursuing her financial rights, but in the process she inevitably acquired a reputation for both avarice and extravagance. However, this judgement should be considered against one of the achievements of that 'extravagance': the restoration of the royal court. One of the Queen's wedding gifts was a French-made collection of romances presented to her by the Earl of Shrewsbury, John Talbot. The frontispiece features Henry and Marguerite crowned, with Talbot kneeling before them, the King's chamberlain and counsellors grouped behind him and Marguerite's ladies watching the presentation. Peeking from behind the chamber walls are enormous daisies, Marguerite's emblem. After the frequent illnesses of Henry IV, the long absences of Henry V and the minority of Henry VI, the court had dwindled to little more than the King's place of business, rather than the fascinating, cultured and romantic environment Talbot's frontispiece imagines. As J.L. Laynesmith comments: 'The combination of romances and treatises on chivalry and government within the book itself were ... entirely appropriate as a wedding gift to a woman whose marriage signified her King's entry into mature kingship and with that the re-establishment of the English court.'[8]

In August and September of 1450, the 'new' court received two men who would dominate the struggle for power around the King in the next few years. Edmund Beaufort, whose love affair with Catherine de Valois had caused such a scandal twenty years before, had now succeeded to the dukedom of Somerset and was the King's closest living male relative. Like Somerset, Richard, Duke of York was descended from Edward III, and given the attainder on descendants of John of Gaunt's mistress Katherine Swynford inheriting, his claim to the throne was arguably stronger than Somerset's, despite the fact that he was descended from Edmund of Langley, the younger brother of Somerset's grandfather Gaunt. With Suffolk disposed of, Somerset and York were set for a bitter rivalry as to which of them should control the King and, in the event that Marguerite remained childless, the succession. York was disgusted by the losses in France, for which he held Somerset responsible as lieutenant, a post he himself had coveted. There was a strong feeling, reflected in the November Parliament, that York, who had been absent as lieutenant of Ireland during the Normandy debacle, should now take up his rightful place as the nation's premier aristocrat and its greatest magnate, but it was Somerset who was awarded the post of constable of England, and York's attempts to advise Henry were ignored.

Events in France could only add to York's rancour. By 30 June 1451, Bordeaux had surrendered to the French, Gascony was almost lost and the French armies were moving north to Calais. Henry was sufficiently galvanised to declare that he would lead an expedition to recover his Aquitainian inheritance himself, but it came to nothing, and York was increasingly convinced that Somerset was poisoning the King against him and leading England towards chaos. York attempted to win supporters for reform in a series of open letters that were sent around the country, inveighing against the 'envy, malice and untruth' of the Duke of Somerset and setting out York's manifesto against him: 'To the intent that every man shall know my purpose ... I, after long sufferance and delays, it not being my will or intent to displease my sovereign lord, but seeing that the said Duke ever prevails and rules about the King's person and that by this means the land is likely to be destroyed, am fully determined to proceed in all haste against him with the help of my kinsmen and friends.'[9]

It was not quite a declaration of war, but York was risking a charge of treason. On 1 March 1451, his party met Henry and Somerset at Black-heath. Despite his wealth, the extent of his support and the popularity of his cause, York made a poor showing. The magnates, with the exception of Lord Cobham and the Earl of Devon, had come out for Henry. York made his case against Somerset, demanding that the Duke be arrested and tried for his mismanagement of the French war. Henry made some gesture of consent, but Somerset remained obstinately by his side, and in fact it was York who was escorted back to London like a prisoner and made to swear a humiliating public oath of allegiance at St Paul's.

After this defeat, York withdrew from politics for a time, but it seemed as though his concerns were justified. The lack of any real central authority meant landowners felt justified in taking the law into their own hands and disturbances broke out in Derbyshire, Warwickshire, Gloucestershire, East Anglia, Devon and Bedfordshire. In South Wales Richard Neville, the new Earl of Warwick, was engaged in what amounted to a private war against Somerset, while the two great northern dynasties, the Nevilles and the Percies, were at daggers drawn in the North Riding of Yorkshire. There was no comfort to be found in Gascony. In August 1453, despite an earlier English rally which had retaken Bordeaux, the English were subjected to another crushing defeat. Worse still, Henry appeared to have finally lost what little there was of his mind.

For Marguerite, this should have been a joyful year, as it became clear in the spring that, finally, the Queen was expecting a child. The state of catatonic insensibility that overcame her husband during her pregnancy suggests that it may have been linked to his inability to cope with the ramifications of his sexuality, but whatever the reason for his 'madness', he was utterly unavailable to support or counsel Marguerite as the birth drew near. Descriptions of his symptoms suggest his disease was inherited from his grandfather, Charles VI, as for two months Henry remained at Clarendon, unable to move or speak and apparently incapable of recognising anyone. Meanwhile, Somerset scrabbled desperately to discover an alternative to the correct procedure, which would have been to invite York to take the King's place in the government. On 13 October Marguerite gave birth to a son, Prince Edward. Defiantly, she chose Somerset as godfather.

That autumn, York had come to an accommodation with the ambitious Earl of Warwick. York offered to help him in his feud with the Percies in the north in return for the backing of the mighty Neville family. In December, Somerset was seized in Marguerite's apartments and imprisoned in the Tower to answer the old charges of his conduct of the war in France. York's successful manoeuvrings now brought Marguerite to centre stage. As mother of the future king, she could now expect to have some authority in the government and, with Somerset locked up, his supporters adopted her as their leader. Marguerite was deeply suspicious of York, who would be heir presumptive if her baby were to die, and she was determined that he should not act as regent while Henry remained incapable. Boldly, she made a list of provisions for the forthcoming February Parliament, the first of which was that she, not York, should govern the country. She demanded control over the appointments of the chancellor, the treasurer and the keeper of the Privy Seal as well as all officers for the shires. A party of twelve councillors rode to Windsor, where the King was being cared for, to see if they could get some kind of answer from him, but it was useless. He did not even know his own child.

Marguerite's hopes were thwarted when the increasingly desperate council appointed York as 'Protector'. Baby Edward had been created Prince of Wales, but for the next year Marguerite had to live in isolation at Windsor, with the uncertainty of whether Henry would be restored to health and the pain of his inability to acknowledge their heir. At Christmas, however, Henry at last came to his senses. He asked his son's name, thanked God for his recovery and was able to resume his religious devotions. But even after such a long rest his political sense had become no more acute. Somerset was soon released from the Tower and restored to his post as constable and York's protectorate was at an end. The Duke, accompanied by Warwick and the Earl of Salisbury, left London soon afterwards without taking formal leave of the King, a subtle but telling gesture.

By mid-May, Somerset realised that York had gone north to raise an army. On 21 May the court set off to confront the rebels at St Albans, sending Marguerite and her ladies to Greenwich for safety. After some discussion, Henry, in an atypical but predictably unintelligent show of decisiveness, determined that the royalist troops should set up their battle base in the centre of the town. At first, it seemed that their barricades would hold off the Yorkists, but Warwick had a party of men creep through the gardens and demolish a group of houses, through which they broke into the marketplace. Henry's immediate entourage now came under attack. The King's only contribution to the action was to sit in his armour in his pavilion, praying, but even then he managed to get an arrow wound in the neck and had to run away and hide in a cottage with Somerset. York had Henry removed to more suitable quarters, but for Somerset there was no hope. Cornered in the Castle Inn, Somerset resolved to go down fighting, and rushed on his attackers, taking four of them with him. With his enemy destroyed, York went through the motions of asking Henry's pardon, which the King had no choice but to grant.

It would be unwise to see St Albans as dividing 'Yorkists' and 'Lancastrians' into two neatly defined opposing factions, gearing up for the Wars of the Roses. The battle had been motivated by York's passion to be rid of Somerset, but it was also an opportunity for the Nevilles to settle private grievances; the only other two important magnates killed that day were Neville enemies. With Henry still unfit even to go through the motions of government, York found it easy to have himself declared protector once more, but his troubles had not died with Somerset. The garrison of Calais had mutinied and there were ongoing disturbances in the west country. York's challenge was to patch up a consensus in a situation where Henry's failure as a king had permitted essentially local disputes to fatally undermine national unity.

Marguerite, it must be said, was no politician. She saw things in black and white. She had been outraged when, as part of York's Act of Resumption in his first Parliament, her expenditure was ordered to be reduced to 10,000 marks and she was deprived of the power to bequeath duchy of Lancaster revenues. If she had ever had any faith in her husband, it was gone. She now had to protect him, and their child, from the threat York represented, and she saw herself as the successor to Somerset. In 1456 Henry was sufficiently sensible to attend Parliament and York was officially relieved of his commission as protector, but York and the Neville party managed to keep the King away from any serious business, and Marguerite was keen to get him out of London in order to influence him for his own good.

Accordingly, she left for Coventry Castle with Prince Edward, moving north towards Chester. Henry joined her in August at Kenilworth, and soon Marguerite had persuaded him to replace York's men with supporters of her own in the offices of treasurer and chancellor. Marguerite's private chancellor, Laurence Booth, became keeper of the Privy Seal and was then promoted to the see of Durham. As she began to gain some grip in government, Marguerite also concentrated on augmenting her power base in two areas, the duchy of Lancaster lands in the Midlands, where she held the honours of Tutbury and Leicester, and Prince Edward's earldom of Chester and principality of Wales. She took Edward on a tour of Cheshire and the Midlands, showing him to the people and reminding them that she was the mother of their future King. Little Edward now had his own household, and Marguerite was beginning to draw around her those men she believed would faithfully support his succession when the time came. These included the new Duke of Somerset and his brother, the Percy Earl of Northumberland and Lord Clifford, whose fathers had died at St Albans, lords Grey and Wiltshire, the bishop of Winchester and the Duke of Buckingham, whose son, Henry Stafford, was married to Margaret Beaufort, herself the strongest claimant to the throne after Prince Edward through her descent from John of Gaunt. The Beaufort connection was heightened by the fact that Margaret was the widow of Edmund Tudor, Catherine de Valois's son, whose brother Jasper, the Earl of Pembroke, was to be a staunch champion of the Lancastrian cause, acting as the King's lieutenant in central and southern Wales and receiving the constableship of Carmarthen and Aberystwyth in 1457.

In March 1458, Henry believed he had inaugurated a reconciliation ceremony whose bombastic symbolism might make even a present-day political spin-doctor cringe. The 'Loveday' featured Marguerite pro-gressing hand in hand with the Duke of York to St Paul's, accompanied by the main protagonists on both sides. The Queen's clumsy emphasis on York-Lancaster unity now brought into focus what everyone until this point had found it convenient to ignore: that there in fact existed two opposing camps. 'It is perhaps at this point, ironically at the most overt moment of conciliation,' remarks Christine Carpenter, 'that the Wars of the Roses can be said to have begun.'[10]

Still, it seemed that Marguerite was regaining control of the situation and at this juncture it is interesting to ask why she seemed so determined to alienate the Earl of Warwick. Warwick had held the captaincy of England's most important remaining Continental garrison since 1455, though wrangling over wages arrears had meant he had been unable to enter the city for a year. Now, Marguerite pushed the exchequer to starve him of the funds he needed, and as his resources dwindled Warwick resorted to piracy to pay his men. The Queen returned to London in the autumn and attempted to have Warwick deposed and indicted on the charge of attacking the Hanseatic Bay fleet, a crime of which he was entirely guilty but which nevertheless her own policies had provoked. Warwick retreated to Calais after fighting his way to his barge on the Thames. However, Marguerite could still have recognised the possibility of negotiation with the powerful Neville family who, up to November 1458, were not overtly partisan. It was not until the Earl of Salisbury, Warwick's father, held a family meeting at their seat at Middleham to declare his intention of taking 'full party with the noble prince the Duke of York' that the Nevilles were definitively alienated. Why did Marguerite not have the sense to make an ally of Warwick? As events were later to prove, she held a tremendous lure to Warwick's ambition in the person of Prince Edward. Was it pride or obstinacy that pushed her to force those magnates who remained neutral to take sides?

It was apparent that England was headed for war. Marguerite was raising troops in Cheshire and the Wirral and in May 1459 3,000 bows were ordered for the royal armoury. Marguerite and Henry were at Coventry, from where they summoned the men of the shires to muster at Leicester. A council was announced for June, but York, Salisbury, Warwick and their supporters were excluded. In response, the Yorkists decided to hold their own council at Ludlow, with Warwick bringing a contingent from Calais. Warwick arrived safely, and from Ludlow York published another of his open letters, declaring his loyalty and asking Henry's pardon, but insisting that he had been driven to extremity for the good of the realm. Warwick's father, however, was intercepted by Marguerite's supporters, and gave the lie to the Ludlow protestations. Very little is known about the encounter between Salisbury and a group of Cheshire men led by Lord Audley at Blore's Heath that September, but Salisbury had the better of it and Audley was killed. A local tradition claims that Marguerite herself watched the battle from the nearby church tower of Mucclestone, then escaped by reversing her horse's shoes to lay a false trail. There is no reliability to this story, but it is perhaps the first of the legends that grew up around Marguerite as a warrior queen. Salisbury pushed on to Ludlow, but on 12 October the Yorkist leaders had to face the fact that they were hopelessly outnumbered. Henry himself was there at the head of his troops, and such was the power of majesty that the Calais division, the Yorkists' crack fighting corps, promptly changed sides. There was little point in a confrontation. York fled to Ireland, his eldest son, Edward, Earl of March, galloped off into the night with his Neville cousins, and Warwick and Salisbury, assisted by a Devon man named John Dinham, got away safely to Calais. There could now be no pretence that either side sought a peaceful resolution to England's problems. This would be a fight to the death.

Ludlow taught Marguerite the essential lesson that power lay with whoever controlled the person of the king, as the innate respect for the anointed monarch inspired a powerful reluctance to take up arms against him. Her enemies scattered, the Queen triumphantly summoned a council at Coventry which issued attainders depriving Yorkist supporters of their lands and bestowing them on Marguerite's men. But Calais was still controlled by Warwick, despite Somerset having been appointed captain in his place. Somerset took up quarters at the port of Guines, from where he launched repeated but unsuccessful attacks against the garrison. The royalists tried to come to his aid by preparing a fleet at Sandwich, but suffered a huge setback when Lord Rivers, the commander, his wife, the Duchess of Bedford, and their son, Anthony Woodville, were taken by a raiding party sent by Warwick and all the ships commandeered. In June 1460 the Yorkists succeeded in taking the port itself, and Marguerite had to accept that an invasion would follow.

It was shockingly swift. By 26 June, Warwick's forces were at Canterbury and two days later they marched towards London. Marguerite and Prince Edward remained at Coventry while the King and his supporters made for the capital. They paused at Northampton and set up camp while the Yorkist forces, now sure of Henry's whereabouts, swung north after only two days in the city. The battle that followed lasted only half an hour. Buckingham was killed in the King's tent and Henry himself was taken prisoner by Warwick. Marguerite and Edward were attacked as they fled from Coventry, but with the help of Owen Tudor they managed to reach the safety of Harlech Castle in Wales.

York arrived in London in September, and though Warwick had protested his loyalty to the imprisoned Henry over the summer, it was obvious that the Duke was intent upon the crown. Notably, he displayed the arms of Clarence for the first time as he entered the city. York was descended from Edward III through both his father and his mother, who was a great-granddaughter of Lionel, Duke of Clarence, Edward's third son. He was clearly eager to exercise the female, as well as the male claim to his right to rule, and to emphasise at this crucial moment that in this respect his position was actually stronger than Henry's own, since Salic law, which permitted succession only through the male line, did not apply in England as it did in France. York entered the palace of Westminster and 'went straight through to the Great Hall until he came to the chamber where the King ... was accustomed to hold his Parliament. There he strode up to the throne and put his hand on its cushion just as though he were a man about to take possession of what was rightfully his'.[11] He did not receive the rapturous reception he clearly anticipated; indeed, his audacity was greeted with offended silence, but in the Act of Accord of 24 October 1460, he had his way. Parliament decided that Henry would keep the throne for life, but that it would then devolve to York and his heirs. Prince Edward was disinherited, and it would be York's son, Edward, Earl of March, who would wear the crown in the next generation.

Marguerite's cause was now precisely defined. Until this point, she had obviously been acting in Prince Edward's interests, but with this act her defence of his rights became official. Even operating under duress, it was despicably pathetic that Henry should have concurred with the annulment of his own son's rights, and unsurprising that Marguerite refused to answer her weak husband's summons to London. Instead she managed to get a ship for Scotland, where she negotiated with King James II for reinforcements and funds. On her own authority, she offered to trade the stronghold of Berwick for Scottish aid. Meanwhile, Somerset was active in the southwest, and the Percy lands in the north were still loyal. By December, the Lancastrian forces were gathered at Pontefract under the command of Somerset and Northumberland, while the Yorkists were holed up at York's castle of Sandal near Wakefield.

The battle of Wakefield was a huge victory for the Lancastrians but a disaster for Marguerite's reputation. One of her influential biographers has it that she led her troops in person (having boned up on her Livy – apparently her tactics mirrored those of Hannibal at Cannae), and had the head of the Duke of York brought to her, whereupon she slapped the dead face, stuck a paper crown on its head and spiked it on the gates of York. Shakespeare's version, in *King Henry VI Part III*, has Marguerite stabbing York with her own hands. York did die on the battlefield, the Earl of Salisbury was executed at Pontefract and the heads of the losers were displayed on the walls of York, but Marguerite herself took no part in the Wakefield executions, though she may well have rejoiced at them. As in the case of Eleanor of Aquitaine, Marguerite's exceptional qualities not only counted against her posthumously but also with her contemporaries. What people were prepared to say and believe of her gives an insight into how she was perceived, and the aftermath of Wakefield portrayed her as terrifying.

Marguerite led her troops south, but lack of discipline and the perennial problem of supplies soon had the troops stripping the countryside. The Scottish soldiers had a fearsome reputation, and panic began to spread through the Midland counties. *The Croyland Chronicle* gives a picture of what was rapidly being seen less as a royal campaign than as a barbarian invasion from the north.

> The northmen, being sensible that the only impediment was now withdrawn ... swept onwards like a whirlwind from the north, and in the impulse of their fury attempted to overrun the whole of England. At this period too, fancying that everything tended to ensure them freedom from molestation, paupers and beggars flocked forth from those quarters in infinite numbers, just like so many mice rushing forward from their holes, and universally devoted themselves to spoil and rapine without regard for place or person ... Thus did they proceed with impunity, spreading in vast multitudes over a space of thirty miles in breadth ... covering the whole surface of the earth just like so many locusts.[12]

Yorkist propaganda seized on Marguerite's inability to control her advancing army, to the point where one historian suggests it was their 'excesses' that were decisive in the outcome of the conflict. As the Lancastrians made their lawless way down the country, Edward, Earl of March, now the Yorkist leader and heir apparent, encountered Jasper Tudor and his troops en route to Hereford. The battle of Mortimer's Cross was the first of an impressive series of victories for the young Earl, and also provided the badge he was to adopt as the symbol of his house, the golden sun of York, inspired by what appeared to be three suns in the sky as the armies engaged. Owen Tudor was among the Lancastrian prisoners who were executed at Hereford after the battle. He was reported to have said, 'That head shall lie on the stock that was wont to lie on Queen Catherine's lap,' before the executioner gave the stroke.

The next confrontation came on 17 February 1461 at St Albans, where Warwick was faced with another Duke of Somerset. For all his subsequent reputation as a kingmaker, Warwick lost the battle, misplacing the captured King Henry in the process. Marguerite and Prince Edward were sheltering in the abbey, and Henry managed to make his way to join them, apparently quite unmolested. Two days later the Lancastrians were prepared to march for the gates of London. The city authorities were terrified that the soldiers would sack the town, and the lord mayor sent a deputation of aristocratic ladies to negotiate the terms of entry. 'The Duchess of Bedford ... went to St Albans to the King, Queen and Prince, for to entreat for grace for the city,' recorded *The London Chronicle*. 'And the King and his council granted that four knights with four hundred men should go to the City and see the disposition of it, and make an appointment with the Mayor and the Aldermen.' Unusually, this agreement was essentially negotiated between women, so it is disappointing that it proved such a strategic disaster. Marguerite and the Duchess of Bedford were very much on the same side (the Duchess and her husband, Lord Rivers, had, after all, been kidnapped by Warwick during preparations for the attack on Calais, and her son-in-law, John Grey, had just lost his life at St Albans), yet Lady Bedford and her companion Lady Buckingham were so convincing in conveying the fears of the Londoners that Marguerite, fearful of losing their goodwill, lost her nerve instead. She ordered her troops to retreat to Dunstable as a gesture of good faith and in doing so she may well have set the crown on Edward of March's head. The panic inspired by the advance of the northmen had done its work and the mood of the citizens was staunchly pro-Yorkist, but Marguerite had the King and she had an army, as well as a group of loyal nobles within the city. The Duchess of Bedford has been praised for 'saving' London, but as far as her own side was concerned, it was an own goal.

In contrast with Marguerite, Edward of March proved himself quick and resolute at this moment of crisis. He joined forces with Warwick in the Cotswolds and together they entered London on 26 February. The people had had enough of Henry's ditherings and they were exhausted by terror. Prince Edward was a child of seven, but Edward of March was a man, and a big, handsome, fighting man at that. An Italian correspondent reported that there was a 'great multitude who say they want to be with him to conquer or die'. On 4 March, the nineteen-year-old Earl was proclaimed as King Edward IV.

The Lancastrian cause was not entirely lost at this juncture. If Marguerite were able to hold out, there was a good chance that Edward, perceived by many as a usurper, would waste his forces and his popularity pursuing her. Edward knew that he had to attack, and do so decisively. In mid-March he set off towards Yorkshire and at the end of the month the two sides met once more at Towton. Chronicle figures are notoriously misleading when it comes to the size of medieval armies, but in this case, even a conservative estimation of the numbers involved gives 50,000 men apiece to both Yorkists and Lancastrians. Towton was perhaps the bloodiest battle of a bloody century, though no eyewitness description has survived.

Perhaps the greatest asset the Yorkists had was Edward himself, who fought on foot after his cavalry was routed by Somerset and Lord Rivers. Prepared to go to the death beside his standard, he cut a magnificent figure in the hand-to-hand combat at the core of the battle, all the more so for the conspicuous absence of his opposite number. It was claimed that 28,000 men fell at Towton, and even if this figure is exaggerated, it was felt as a calamity, 'a last, appalling commentary on the misrule of Henry VI'.[13]

Edward IV was crowned at Westminster on 28 June, three months after Towton. Marguerite, Henry and Prince Edward were now in Scotland, from where, in April, Marguerite had made good her promise of giving up Berwick, which did nothing for her popularity even among Englishmen who were sympathetic. In fact, one of Marguerite's greatest disadvantages had been her inability to understand the consensual structure of English society, particularly the vital role of the gentry in the shires whose support was essential to the crown in times of need. It was these lesser men, rather than great magnates like Warwick or Somerset, who were embittered by the local unruliness and financial instability that had threatened them throughout the 1450s, and Marguerite had alienated them from the beginning by her aggressively partisan approach. The recent wars had not been expressly fought to get rid of Henry, but many people were glad to see the back of Marguerite. She had also gained a bloodthirsty reputation, however undeservedly, and her mishandling of her northern troops had terrified many potential loyalists into the Yorkist camp.

However, Marguerite is to some extent a victim of hindsight. Just as Suffolk had been made the scapegoat for the disastrous losses of the 1440s, so Marguerite was blamed for her husband's shortcomings. If Henry were to be a saintly figure, pious, humble and unworldly, then it was necessary for someone to take the responsibility for the whole mess of his reign, and many writers chose the traditional option of *chercher la femme*. Marguerite may not have been possessed of brilliant understanding but she was 'a great and intensely active woman, for she spares no pains to pursue her business towards an end and conclusion favourable to her power'.[14] Moreover, unlike many of her contemporaries, such as her former chancellor Laurence Booth, who now became confessor to the new King, she had remained staunchly loyal to the cause of her husband and son. She had been dealt a dud hand with Henry, and perhaps, like Suffolk, should be 'given credit for taking on an impossible job'.[15] Undaunted, she continued to battle for her rights for the next decade.

CHAPTER 17

ELIZABETH WOODVILLE

'Neither too wanton nor too humble'

In July 1461 the new King set off on progress, to show himself to the people and emphasise his regal authority. Pausing to hunt in the forest of Whittlewood near Grafton in Northamptonshire, Edward met a young widow, Lady Elizabeth Grey, née Woodville, whose husband had died fighting for the Lancastrians at St Albans. Lady Grey had apparently deliberately thrown herself in the King's path to beg for the restoration of her husband's lands to provide for their two small sons. Thomas More later imagined the meeting: 'This poor lady made humble suit unto the King that she might be restored unto such small lands as her late husband had given her in jointure. Whom when the King beheld and heard her speak, as she was both fair and of a good favour, moderate of stature, well made and very wise, he not only pitied her, but also waxed enamoured on her. And taking her afterward secretly aside, began to enter in talking more familiarly.'[1]

Beauty is a difficult quality to draw out from the evidence of medieval chroniclers, who attributed it to most women of high birth and particularly to many queens. Elizabeth Woodville seems to have been possessed of the genuine article, a feature her contemporaries found unsettling and for which she was rewarded and punished in equal measure. Even allowing for the stilted artistic style of the period, her portrait at Queens' College, Cambridge is captivating, the delicacy of the mouth and chin contrasting with the large, dark, sensuous eyes, her blonde hair gathered beneath an elaborate headdress.

Though the sylvan meeting of the King and the ravishing supplicant owes a good deal to local legend, there is no doubt that Edward was utterly smitten. Elizabeth was beautiful enough for him to defy his mother, the Duchess of York, his chief commander, Warwick, and his council in order to possess her.

Elizabeth's marriage to Edward IV was that extraordinary thing, a love match. It initiated a series of problems within the already tangled skein of ambition and political loyalties that knotted into the Wars of the Roses. It also created an ambiguous perception of the Queen and her family which persists until the present day. Was Elizabeth a low-born adventuress who promoted the interests of the Woodville family at the expense of the nation, or a passionately loyal wife who showed exceptional fortitude and skill in surviving two political revolutions to ensure the final survival of the Yorkist dynasty? Elements of both interpretations are periodically valid; perhaps neither Elizabeth's accusers nor her apologists have fully taken her measure as an individual in exceptional circumstances, in exceptional times.

Elizabeth was one of fifteen children born to Jacquetta, the dowager Duchess of Bedford, and her second husband, Sir Richard Woodville. The status of her family was one of the principal sources of objection to her marriage to Edward in the 'lethally competitive'[2] world of the fifteenth-century aristocracy. Traditionally the Woodvilles have been depicted as minor country gentry, living unostentatiously on their estates at Grafton in Northamptonshire, but a minimally attentive look at Elizabeth's ancestors proves that this was far from being the case. Her mother, Jacquetta, was the daughter of Pierre, Count of St Pol, Conversano and Brienne, and Marguerite, daughter of Francesco de Balzo, Duke of Andrea in Apulia, who claimed descent from Charlemagne. Admittedly, her paternal lineage was of no particular distinction among the European aristocracy of the time, but the Counts of St Pol, on her mother's side, were one of the most prestigious houses in Europe, as evinced by the magnificent marriage Pierre arranged for Jacquetta who, in 1433, married Henry V's brother John, Duke of Bedford. Thus for two years, until Bedford's death, Jacquetta was England's second lady after her sister-in-law, Queen Catherine, and she was permitted to use her royal title until the end of her own life.

If Sir Richard's ancestors were not quite so illustrious, they could hardly be termed obscure. They had held their land in Northamptonshire since the twelfth century and Richard's father had served Henry V as an esquire of the body and Henry VI as seneschal of Normandy. He was knighted on Palm Sunday 1426 in the same ceremony as Edward IV's father, the Duke of York. Another post, the one that brought him into Jacquetta's orbit, was chamberlain to the Duke of Bedford during his captaincy of Calais. When Jacquetta was widowed, she was granted her dowry in February 1436 on condition that she did not marry again without Henry VI's permission. Nevertheless she and Richard married in a clandestine ceremony the same year and the couple were forced to ask for a royal pardon, which they received in October 1437, the year of Elizabeth's birth, subject to a huge fine of 1,000 pounds, which Jacquetta raised by selling property in the west country to Cardinal Beaufort. The circumstances of her parents' marriage are interesting when compared with Elizabeth's own story. Jacquetta and Richard were prepared to defy royal authority to marry, and did so in hurried secrecy. That they were pardoned so quickly suggests the King held them in high regard, and the fact that the dower agreement, marriage and the granting of the pardon took place in such a short space of time indicates that Richard and Jacquetta truly loved each other, that they took a serious gamble, and that they won.

The Woodvilles continued to be closely associated with the court. Isabel, Jacquetta's sister, was aunt by marriage to Marguerite of Anjou and in 1444 Richard and Jacquetta had formed part of the new Queen's escort to England. In 1448 Richard was created Baron Rivers, and in 1450 made a knight of the Garter. Jacquetta and Queen Marguerite exchanged those politically charged New Year gifts, with Jacquetta receiving jewellery from Marguerite to welcome her in 1452. It has been strongly mooted that Jacquetta's eldest daughter also held a position among the Queen's ladies, and that Edward IV, then Earl of March, first saw her at the Reading Parliament of 1454. The interpretations of the subsequent conduct of both queens differs if they are believed to have known one another well, but the evidence that Elizabeth had a role at court is not definitive.

Both Thomas More and *Hall's Chronicle* concur that Elizabeth waited on Marguerite which, given their access to eyewitness accounts and Jacquetta's position, seems highly probable, but it is not absolutely certain. At the age of about seven, Elizabeth had been betrothed to John Grey, son of Sir Edward Grey of Groby and his wife, Lady Ferrers, and, as was customary, went to live with her groom's family at their home in Leicestershire. In 1452–3 there are references to 'Isabelle Domine Grey' and 'Domine Elizabeth Grey' as holding the post of lady-in-waiting and receiving gifts of jewellery. Elizabeth was fifteen at the time and not yet married, so it seems odd (though not unheard of) that she should be described by her future husband's name. Moreover, the references might well relate either to John Grey's mother, another Elizabeth, or to Elizabeth the widow of Ralph Grey, who appears as an attendant in 1445. The opinion of a recent biographer of Elizabeth (the italics are this author's) that 'the adolescent Edward ... *surely* observed more than political ceremony at the various court affairs. Among the Queen's attendants, the sophisticated Elizabeth ... *must have* ignited Edward with all the passion typical of adolescent boys'[3] seems rather optimistically romantic. It is possible that Elizabeth Woodville served Queen Marguerite, but there is as yet no direct proof that she did so and, given the calumnies heaped on her for her lack of royal connections, it seems odd that her contemporary supporters do not mention it.[4]

From the first, Elizabeth's relationship with Edward was controversial. If their meeting is correctly placed in 1461, then the idea of Edward's marriage as 'impulsive'[5] must be dismissed, as it did not take place until May 1464. Edward already had a reputation as a ladies' man. He was gloriously attractive, with the Plantagenet height, strawberry-blond hair and an impressively honed physique. With his good looks, his position and his appetites, he was already something of a connoisseur of beautiful women, and he was not accustomed to rejection. As Thomas More tells the story, he tried to seduce Elizabeth, but when she presented him with a dagger and begged him to kill her rather than despoil her honour, his desire was even more inflamed. Reports of this version of the incident were spread as far as Milan, but even if Elizabeth had defended her virtue so passionately, it seems unlikely that she would have had the energy to do so for three years. Her detractors also seized on the story, claiming she played at virtue to push Edward into marriage (a tactic that later worked most effectively for Anne Boleyn, the mother of Elizabeth's great-granddaughter). Edward himself acknowledged this controversy by keeping his marriage secret for four months, not announcing it until a council meeting at Reading in September. The ceremony had been witnessed only by Jacquetta, Elizabeth's mother, the priest and a clerk to sing the office. It was altogether an embarrassing, rather sordid affair, but Edward put the best face he could on his defiance. Again, Thomas More puts words into Edward's mouth, suggesting that his choice of Elizabeth was a patriotic one: 'He reckoned the amity of no earthly nation so necessary for him as the friendship of his own. Which he thought likely to bear him so much the more hearty favour in that he disdained not to marry with one of his own land.'[6]

However respectable Elizabeth's connections might have been, notwithstanding Jacquetta having disparaged herself with her second marriage and the fact that Richard's barony was a recent creation, she was irrefutably not royal. Luchino Dallaghiexa, an Italian diplomat in London, described her as 'a widow of this island of quite low birth', while Jean de Waurin observed that Edward 'must know well that she was no wife for such a high prince as himself'. Warwick had been planning a dynastic marriage for Edward with a French princess and, since in his own eyes it was he who had placed Edward on the throne, it was disturbing that the King should simply have ignored him. Moreover, Warwick already had a reason to dislike Elizabeth, for it was her father who had refused him entry to Calais back in 1455. When Queen Marguerite tried to have Warwick arraigned for piracy, Lord Rivers was among the commissioners and Warwick, one of England's greatest aristocrats, was disgusted that he should be obliged to defend himself before a 'mere baron'. (Warwick has been accused of hypocrisy here in that he held the Warwick earldom merely in right of his wife, but his critics neglect to mention that he was also heir to the Salisbury title in the male line, a far grander inheritance than anything the Woodvilles could boast.)

To counter the nasty rumours that he had demeaned himself in his choice of bride, Edward was determined Elizabeth's coronation should be as splendid as their marriage had been simple. First, on 30 September 1464, she was formally presented as queen by a grudging Warwick and Edward's brother the Duke of Clarence. Edward then sent to the Duke of Burgundy requesting a suitable delegation of guests, including Elizabeth's uncle, Jacques de Luxembourg. The sum of 400 pounds was advanced to the treasurer of the household to cover coronation expenses, including £27 10s for silkwork on Elizabeth's chairs, saddle and pillion, 108 pounds for a gold cup and basin, 280 for two cloths of gold and twenty to Sir John Howard, who provided the plate. Elizabeth rode into London on 24 May 1465, where she was greeted by the mayor, aldermen and representatives of the city's guilds, who had spent 200 marks on decorations. A pageant on London Bridge featured the boys from the choir of St Magnus church dressed up as angels in blond wigs.

As in Marguerite's case, the ceremonies around the coronation were shaped to be appropriate to an individual woman, and to highlight the qualities that could be hoped of her as queen. For Elizabeth Woodville, the emphasis was placed on her impeccable foreign connections and her already proven fertility. Elizabeth was met by 'St Paul', in reference to her mother's St Pol descent, and surrounded by the Burgundian delegation, which presented her in the context of her noble Continental family. Two saints, St Elizabeth, mother of St John the Baptist, and St Mary Cleophas, half-sister to the Virgin Mary and mother to four of the disciples, were also featured. Since these three saintly relatives were often depicted together in psalters and books of hours, 'when Elizabeth Woodville arrived beside them, very probably with her blonde hair loose beneath a jeweled coronet . . . she would immediately have reminded onlookers of the Virgin Mary'.[7]

While Elizabeth's obvious fertility favoured her in one sense, it was also proof of her 'blemished' sexual status. More claimed that Edward's mother had berated him for 'befouling' himself with a 'bigamous' marriage, while at least two other commentators noted that English custom demanded the King marry a virgin (they had obviously forgotten about Joan of Navarre). By going 'in her hair' to Westminster and very probably wearing a white dress similar to that of Marguerite of Anjou, in which she is shown in the royal window of Canterbury Cathedral, Elizabeth was asserting a spiritual purity which in her new role as queen transcended her physical reality.

At her coronation banquet, the newly dubbed knights of the Bath, who included Elizabeth's brothers, Richard and John, brought in the dishes and the Duke of Clarence accompanied each course to the table on horseback. At the tournament next day in the sanctuary of Westminster, Edward specially requested that some of the Burgundian knights took part, though Elizabeth handed the winner's prize of a ruby ring to Lord Stanley.

Elizabeth was now an anointed queen, and the next year she cemented her success with the birth of her first child by Edward, Elizabeth, in February, quickly followed by Mary in 1467 and Cecily in 1469. Yet there were still many who refused to accept her, portraying her as a devious interloper concerned only with the interests of her own family. According to Luchino Dallaghiexa: 'Since her coronation she has always asserted herself to aggrandise her relations, to wit her father, mother, brothers and sisters. She had five brothers and as many sisters and had brought things to such a pass that they had the entire government of this realm.'[8]

There was nothing unusual about a queen's family receiving advantages from her marriage, and nothing unusual about it provoking resentment, as had been the case with Eleanor of Provence and the Savoyards. The particular difficulty with the Woodvilles was that there were simply so many of them. Two of Elizabeth's siblings had died in infancy, but that still left John, Anthony, Lionel, Edward, Richard, Jacquetta, Martha, Margaret, Katherine, Mary, Anne and Joan. Anthony had established himself independently, acquiring the title of Lord Scales in right of his wife, Lionel entered the church, aided by a grant of the issues of the archdeaconry of Norwich, and Richard remained unmarried, while Edward's circumstances are unknown. The other Woodville siblings did tremendously well out of their royal sister's influence. Margaret married Lord Maltravers, the heir to the Earl of Arundel; Katherine married Henry, Duke of Buckingham; Mary, the Earl of Pembroke; Anne, Lord Bourchier, heir to the Earl of Essex; Jacquetta, Lord Strange of Knocklyn;

Joan, Lord Grey of Ruthin and Martha, less dazzlingly, Sir John Bromley. Perhaps the most talked-about match was that of John with Catherine Neville, Dowager Duchess of Norfolk, Edward IV's aunt. John was twenty and the Duchess a spring chicken of anywhere between sixty and eighty, depending on the bitchiness of the chronicler. Elizabeth's father also benefited from his daughter's new dignity, obtaining the post of treasurer of England in 1466 and being created Earl Rivers in May that year, with the title to revert to his son Anthony. So prominent did the Woodvilles become that it became a court joke: Edward's fool appeared one day in boots, carrying a walking staff, and when the King inquired about this costume answered: 'Upon my faith, sir, I have passed through many countries of your realm, and in places that I have passed, the Rivers have been so high that I could barely scape through them!'

Not everyone found such laboured humour terribly funny. The Earl of Warwick was infuriated that the Woodvilles seemed to be infiltrating the network of Neville power he had worked so hard to build up. He had two daughters of his own, Isabel and Anne, to marry off, yet between 1464 and 1470 every English earl with an available heir selected a Woodville bride. He was particularly incensed by the wedding of Henry Stafford to Katherine Woodville and that of Anne, heiress to the Duke of Exeter, to Thomas Grey, Queen Elizabeth's son by her first marriage, in 1466. It has been suggested that Edward was using the availability of Woodville spouses to create a new centre of loyalty at court, associated primarily with himself and not the Neville connections that had been so instrumental in bringing him to power. If so, it was a sensible enough strategy, but there is no doubt his treatment of Warwick at this time was ill judged, and Warwick's alienation began to make him feel he had been cheated of the right to rule which had appeared implicit when Edward first claimed the crown.

Warwick's anger at the Woodville marriages was compounded by the prominent role the family now played in facilitating the union of Edward IV's sister Margaret to Charles, Duke of Burgundy, an alliance expressly contradictory to Warwick's own policy, which was a dynastic marriage with France (perhaps to compensate for the one Edward denied him in his own case). In 1467, the Queen's brother Anthony was the King's champion at a magnificent five-day tournament at Smithfield against the Comte de la Roche, known as 'The Bastard of Burgundy'. The tournament was followed by a supper offered by the Mercers' Company, and an invitation from the Comte to the Queen 'and especially her sisters', which included Margaret of York. Warwick was permitted to leave for France to open talks for a French marriage with Louis IX, but Anthony

Woodville led a similar embassy to Burgundy, and that match was confirmed at Kingston-upon-Thames in October 1467.

Warwick had certainly been outraged when Edward married Elizabeth Woodville, but *The Croyland Chronicle* emphasises that it was the Burgundian marriage that proved the last straw. 'Indeed it is the fact that the Earl continued to show favour to all the Queen's kindred until he found that her relatives and connections, contrary to his wishes, were using their utmost endeavours to promote the other marriage.' Now, on his return from France, he sulked at his northern seat of Middleham for several months and did not return to court until January. Ever the courtier, he concealed his animosity and led Margaret's wedding procession in June. The bride spent a night with her brother and sister-in-law at Stratford Abbey before travelling to Canterbury and embarking for Burgundy with an entourage dominated by the Queen's family. Both Anthony and John Woodville sailed in the same vessel, and John was awarded the honour of Prince of the Tournament at the nine-day jousts held to mark one of the most splendid royal weddings of the century.

As early as the preceding spring, a messenger apprehended en route to Harlech Castle, which still defiantly held out for the Lancastrians, had claimed that Warwick was in contact with Marguerite of Anjou. Whether or not he had begun to plan a rebellion at this stage, Warwick's attitude to Edward now showed itself explicitly disobedient. Warwick had proposed a marriage between Edward's brother the Duke of Clarence and his own elder daughter Isabel, a suggestion the King refused to countenance. Persisting in spite of the royal veto, Warwick pursued a papal dispensation (the couple were within the prohibited degrees), which was granted in March 1469. In June that year, Edward made a progress to the shrine at Walsingham while Queen Elizabeth, who had recently given birth to her third child, Cecily, met her husband at Fotheringhay Castle towards the end of the month, after which Edward departed to deal with yet another Lancastrian uprising in the north and Elizabeth set off for Norwich.

The Queen's visit to Norwich provides a touching glimpse of the excitement generated among ordinary people by the glamour of royalty. The mayor of the town declared that 'because this should be her first coming hither ... she will desire to be received and attended as worshipfully as ever was Queen afore her'.[9] A committee was organised to repair the church tower and Robert Horgoner was sent out to supervise the Queen's route into Norwich, while John Sadler instructed her servants to enter by the Westwick Gate. Parnell's company were hired for twelve days to provide pageants on a stage decorated with red and green worsted.

Elizabeth was met by the mayor and corporation as well as two wooden giants stuffed with hay, and heard a speech of salutation performed by Mr Gilbert Spirling. Other entertainments included the angel Gabriel and sixteen virgins in hooded cloaks. The 'great chair' of St Luke's Guild was brought from the cathedral to the abbey of the Friars Preachers for the Queen to sit on, and Mr Farckes's choir of boys sang. In typically English fashion, the whole event was rather spoiled by heavy summer rain.

While Elizabeth was at Norwich and Edward at Nottingham, Isabel Neville was married to the Duke of Clarence at Calais by Warwick's brother the archbishop of York, attended by her younger sister Anne Neville. The wedding celebrations lasted five days, but the Earl himself left almost immediately to raise an army in Kent. Maintaining the pose of a loyal subject, Warwick released a letter in which he denounced the Woodvilles as the 'evil counsellors' so often invoked by potential traitors:

> The deceivable covetous rule and guiding of certain seditious persons, that is to say the Lord Rivers, the Duchess of Bedford his wife, Sir William Herbert Earl of Pembroke, Humphrey Stafford Earl of Devonshire, the Lords Scales and Audley; Sir John Woodville and his brothers ... and others of their mischievous rule, opinion and assent, which have caused our said Sovereign Lord and his said realm to fall into great poverty of misery, disturbing the ministrations of the laws, only intending to their own promotion and enriching.

As the Yorkists had done during the crisis of 1450, Warwick emphasised the interdependence of the King and his great magnates, focusing on the ultimate criterion of medieval hierarchy: blood.

> First, where the said Kings estranged the great lords of their blood from their secret counsel, and not advised by them; and taking about them others not of their blood and inclining only to their counsel, rule and advice, the which persons take not respect nor consideration to the weal of the said princes, nor to the commonweal of this land, but only to their singular lucre and enriching of themselves ... by which the said princes were so impoverished that they had not sufficient of livelihood or of goods, whereby they might keep and maintain their honourable estates and ordinary charges within this realm.

Pro-Woodville writers have chosen to oppose Warwick's obsession with 'blood' with the more 'meritocratic' tendencies of the Woodville family, figuring Warwick as the harrumphing reactionary and the Woodvilles as proto-modern, achieving distinction by service rather than birth. This simplistic opposition overlooks the fact that we know nothing of how much or how little the Woodvilles, or indeed Warwick himself, truly believed in the ineffable qualities of breeding. Nor had the Woodvilles proved averse to allying themselves with some of the most prestigious families of the nobility. Warwick was not alone in considering them a pack of parvenus and upstarts, but equally, he and the Woodvilles were playing the same game, and when it appeared that they might best him, it was logical that he should employ a conventional form of outrage against them, whether or not he himself cared for the principle. 'Blood' was a concept to which fifteenth-century society paid a great deal of attention but, as became evident in the reign of Edward IV's son-in-law, Henry Tudor, it was a flexible commodity, a very little of which could be made to go a very long way.

By 20 July, Warwick and his troops had left Canterbury for London. Edward remained at Nottingham, awaiting support from the Earl of Pembroke, but Pembroke's army was attacked and defeated by a pro-Warwick force of northerners at Edgecote, and on Warwick's orders their commander and his brother were executed. Queen Elizabeth was still at Norwich when she heard the appalling, incredible news that the King himself had been taken prisoner and was being held at Warwick Castle. Edward had barely advanced out of Nottingham when he received word of the Edgecote defeat, and had submitted himself to George Neville's keeping on 29 July. Following a short spell at Warwick he was taken to the Nevilles' northern power base of Middleham. After a two-week wait at Norwich, Elizabeth had to endure even more terrifying tidings. Her father, Earl Rivers, and her brother John had been beheaded at Coventry, again on Warwick's orders. Elizabeth was in an extremely vulnerable position. She could not have known what Warwick's intentions were, but she knew that if the 'kingmaker' were to depose her husband as he had done Henry VI, the next in line to the throne was Warwick's new son-in-law, Clarence and, after the treatment of her father and brother, that her family could expect no mercy from either. Nevertheless, she set off for London.

Perhaps Warwick's intentions were not entirely clear even to the Earl himself. He had claimed to be fighting for the reformation of the government, not the deposition of the King, yet he had acted entirely illegally in the executions of the Pembrokes, Earl Rivers and John Woodville, who served the man he still acknowledged as his master. Warwick's supporters had no wish to dethrone Edward, and Warwick himself did not intend the restoration of Henry VI, who was by this time languishing in the Tower. It was rumoured that he had been thinking of having Edward declared illegitimate and was conspiring to replace him with Clarence, but now that he was on the way to creating his puppet king he appeared at a loss to know what to do next. In this light, Edward's seemingly inexplicable passivity might be seen as a stroke of political genius. Had he attempted to flee and raise another army, the whole grisly process of battling towards the crown would have started up again. As it was, he played the role of the polite prisoner until his captors were embarrassed into releasing him. By 10 September, Edward was back in London, and everybody acted as though nothing much had happened.

Outwardly, all was peace and concord. Edward even went so far as to betrothe his three-year-old daughter Elizabeth to Warwick's nephew, creating him Duke of Bedford to mark the occasion. The Queen and her family suppressed their outrage at Warwick's unjustifiable savagery, and for some months Edward and Warwick held councils together, but both the King and the Earl were planning their next moves. In March, Edward travelled north to put down a rebellion in Lincolnshire, while Warwick was supposedly mustering troops in the Midlands to come to assist him. When Edward confronted the Lincolnshire men, their war cry 'For Clarence! For Warwick!' told him all he needed to know about the Earl's latest conspiracy. The King continued northwards, and while Clarence and Warwick maintained appearances of loyalty in their letters, they refused to join the King as promised. On 24 March Edward issued a proclamation against them, announcing that if they came within four days to York they could be reconciled with him, but if they failed to do so they were to be considered traitors. Needless to say, they did not appear. The rebel list later compiled in Salisbury shows that at this point support for the rebels was weak – only four lords, fewer than twenty knights and twenty esquires were arraigned – and Warwick realised that it was time to flee. Edward's army was now pursuing him to the west country, but Warwick, his wife, Clarence, Isabel and the second Warwick daughter, Anne, succeeded in taking ship at Dartmouth. The Earl attempted to supplement his fleet with a raid on Portsmouth, but was repelled by a force led by Anthony Woodville, now Earl Rivers.

Warwick headed for his old stamping ground of Calais, but found the guns of the garrison, which had appealed to Edward's brother-in-law the Duke of Burgundy for support, turned against him. Nineteen-year-old Isabel was heavily pregnant, and went into labour on board ship, but though Warwick was able to obtain some wine for her, the birth was difficult and her baby died. The Earl now put to sea again, encountering and taking a large Burgundian convoy, and on 1 May he arrived in Normandy. Officially, Louis IX was unable to offer him any help. He did extend an offer of hospitality to the Countess and her daughters, but the family chose to stay together at Vulognes, near Barfleur, where Warwick came to the conclusion that his only remaining hope lay with his old enemy, Marguerite of Anjou.

After the battle of Towton, Marguerite had stayed in Scotland until 1462. She received some support from Mary of Guelders, acting as regent for her son James III, who was the same age as Prince Edward, and it was Mary who paid for Marguerite's passage to France. Marguerite's uncle Charles VII had died the previous July, and she now persuaded her cousin, the new French King Louis XI to supply her with money and troops in return for the promise of Calais. Louis lost interest after the Duke of Burgundy refused French forces access to the port across his lands, and in the end Marguerite had returned to Scotland with just 800 men. She was able to advance as far as Bamburgh which, along with the other important Marcher castles of Alnwick and Dunstanburgh, had reverted to the Lancastrians, but when she heard the news that both Edward and Warwick were heading north, she retreated, suffering the misery of a shipwreck on the way. Marguerite herself arrived safely at Berwick, but many of her little force were marooned on Holy Island, where they had nothing to do but wait for the Yorkist army. Still, she soldiered on.

Over the winter of 1462–3, the three castles changed hands again, first to York and then back to Lancaster, so by March it seemed plausible that Henry VI's supporters could attempt a more ambitious attack. Marguerite had worked hard to retain the support of the Scottish regency council, this time wildly promising them seven English counties if they should succeed, and in July 1463 the young James III led an attack on the castle of Norham, accompanied by his mother, King Henry and Marguerite. The expedition ended hopelessly, with the invaders fleeing Norham for their lives and Warwick harrying the undefended Scottish marches. The Scots had now had enough, and in August Marguerite embarked once more for France with Prince Edward.

Everyone felt very sorry for her, and did all they could to avoid her. France had supported Henry VI in the conflict, but it now seemed clear to Louis XI that there was nothing to be gained from maintaining such an alliance any longer. He was keen to come to an accommodation with the Duke of Burgundy, who had supported the Yorkists, concerning lands in the Somme, and both rulers were ready to make terms with Edward, the new English King. Marguerite pleaded in person with the Duke, but came away with no more than a sum of money and a few courteous commonplaces. Neither Burgundy nor France were overly concerned about a dethroned queen or her dispossessed son.

What remained of Marguerite's hopes was signed away at Hesdin in October 1463. In exchange for the cession of the Somme towns by Burgundy, the King of France renounced all help to the Lancastrians, along with the traditional French protection of Scotland. Edward IV had been funding a conspiracy by the 'Black Douglases', whom James II of Scotland had stripped of their power, to foment civil war, and the Scottish regency council, isolated and abandoned by the French, was prepared to come to terms with England if Edward ended his assistance to the rebels. The Lancastrians were still pushing hard in the north, and there was a brief resurgence of optimism when the Duke of Somerset, who had been pardoned by Edward, turned his coat again and joined Henry VI, who was now imprisoned at Bamburgh. Despite an attack led by Somerset, Scottish envoys reached York in April 1464, and once an agreement was reached with Edward, Scotland would no longer offer a refuge. Somerset brought Henry to Bywell Castle, close to where the royal army, commanded by Warwick's brother John Neville, was camped, but any hope that his presence would garner enough support to overwhelm the Yorkists was disappointed by a swift, sudden defeat at Hexham on 15 May. Somerset was executed immediately, but by the time soldiers arrived at Bywell, Henry had vanished, leaving behind his coroneted helmet. It had never been much use to him. For a year, the former King of England wandered the north country until he was finally taken the following July at Ribblesdale and shut up in the Tower of London, but not before Warwick and Edward had paraded him with tasteless cruelty through the city streets, denounced as a usurper.

Marguerite now had little choice but to return to the protection of her own family. René of Anjou eventually provided her with the castle of Koeur near Verdun and a pension of 2,000 livres. By 1470, Marguerite and Prince Edward had been in France for seven years. Time did not reconcile her to her position. Henry lived, her son was the rightful heir to the throne and there were still many loyal to her cause. (Perhaps it is permissible to imagine Marguerite heaving a sigh of relief every time Elizabeth Woodville was delivered of a girl). But the Lancastrians were poor. They had no means to attempt another invasion, and meanwhile politics was moving on. Harlech, the last castle in Lancastrian hands, fell in 1468, Edward was establishing his family and a new court party and cementing his European alliances. If it was difficult to imagine that the situation would ever change, certainly no one could have foreseen what actually happened.

The Lancastrian cause was revived by the most wonderful and improbable of marriages: that between Edward, Prince of Wales and Anne Neville, the fourteen-year-old daughter of the kingmaker.

Marguerite and Warwick had little cause for mutual trust, but perhaps they had one thing in common: their shared hatred of Elizabeth Woodville. Certainly, they were both determined to depose Edward IV, and to achieve this they had to depend not only on one another but on King Louis of France. Louis was careful to portray himself as a reluctant mediator, rather than the instigator of this extraordinary alliance, but he was nevertheless instrumental in bringing it about. He was determined to bolster his power against Charles of Burgundy, who still retained control of the disputed Somme territories, and he was prepared to gamble on Charles's reaction to his support for Warwick in the confidence that the marriage could bring about the restoration of a Lancastrian king and a subsequent pact against Burgundy.

When Warwick's battered, miserable family arrived at Honfleur in May 1470, Louis sent an invitation to Marguerite to come to court. By June, the betrothal between Anne and Edward had been proposed. Marguerite had little choice but to favour the match, even though she risked Warwick's treachery if he planned to worm his way back into Edward IV's favour by delivering up the Lancastrian's principal bargaining tool in the person of the Prince. She also had her dignity to think of. Warwick took care of that by grovelling on his knees for a full fifteen minutes at Angers Cathedral on 22 July, and on the twenty-fifth both parties swore themselves to the proposal over sacred fragments of the True Cross.

What Edward and Anne thought of their marriage is unknown, though both seem to have accepted it dutifully. Warwick was clearly prepared to forget that he had accused the Prince of being illegitimate when he was born, manipulating rumours of Marguerite's adultery and Henry's inability to recognise the baby to support his campaign to bring Edward to the throne. To be married to the daughter of the man who had deposed his father, forced his mother into humiliating exile and called him a bastard might have been a very bitter pill for a sixteen-year-old boy to swallow, but 'the very little we perceive of Edward of Lancaster ... is of a boy who had been brought up to think of himself as a prince and who was keen to have his opponent's heads off'.[10] Edward, like Marguerite, was clearly prepared to accept whatever distasteful necessities fate presented in the quest for the restoration of his rights. Nor was Anne necessarily a demeaning bride. She was a great heiress, five of her ancestral lines gave her a share of royal blood, she also had connections with European dynasties and (inevitably) Charlemagne, and was described as 'the most noble Lady and Princess of the royal blood of diverse realms lineally descending from princes, kings, emperors and many glorious saints'.[11]

Anne had been four years old when Edward IV was crowned. She had been born at Warwick in 1456, but had spent the first few years of her life in Calais, when her father was captain there. Unusually for medieval children of high rank, she and her sister Isabel had remained with their parents until their teens. There had been no queen's household for them to enter until Edward's marriage in 1464, and there is no evidence that Anne or Isabel waited on Elizabeth Woodville, though they were mentioned as being present, along with the King's younger brother Richard, Duke of Gloucester, at the consecration of Anne's uncle, George Neville, as archbishop of York in 1465. Anne spoke French, and possibly Flemish – the former language may have eased her introduction to her formidable future mother-in-law – but little else is known of her education. What Anne was aware of were the vicissitudes of fortune so beloved of medieval moralists. She had seen her father as almost a ruler in his own right in Calais, then as the greatest man at Edward's court, then as an exile, and according to the aggrieved Burgundians, a pirate. She had watched her sister, in theory one of the highest-ranking women in England, endure a miserable childbirth at sea, with her father reduced to begging for supplies. Now Anne was to displace her sister in Warwick's putative succession, and Isabel's was not a happy precedent. Though the Duke of Clarence was tactfully kept away from the betrothal proceedings, his newly bereaved Duchess was not. Anne saw her mighty father creeping on his knees to his former enemy, and yet he planned to make her Queen of England. It could only have been bewildering. The events of the following months were to prove even more dramatic.

At the same time as Anne's betrothal was taking place, Queen Elizabeth, once again pregnant, moved into the safety of the Tower of London with Henry VI. King Edward had left for the north, to put down yet another rising, this time led by the Earl of Warwick's brother-in-law, Lord Fitzhugh. The King's fleet was patrolling the Channel, and Elizabeth's removal to the Tower with her three daughters was one more indication that invasion was inevitable. Through the lucky chance of a huge storm which scattered Edward's fleet, Warwick and Clarence were able to land at Dartmouth in mid-September. When she heard the news, Elizabeth began preparing for a siege.

Like King Harold in 1066, Edward now had to swing his army round and head south to face Warwick who had mustered 30,000 men at Coventry. His own troops were gathering at Nottingham, and John Neville was rallying a northern contingent. Edward was dining with his brother Gloucester and brother-in-law Lord Rivers at Doncaster when he received word that Neville had betrayed him and marshalled the northern levy in favour of Henry VI. Edward was caught between two advancing hostile armies and there was no time to think of fighting. The King and his immediate entourage rode for the coast and on 2 October set sail in three borrowed ships. Somehow a message was carried to the Queen in the Tower, and on the night before Edward's escape, Elizabeth, Jacquetta and the princesses were rowed up the Thames to Westminster, where they took sanctuary. The atmosphere in London was terrifying. With the King gone so suddenly, the authorities had no idea how to keep order. Debtors and criminals scuttled out of sanctuary and swarmed over the city. It was an opportunity for general anarchy, with prisons broken open and mobs of looters declaring they were supporters of Warwick. The Earl himself, accompanied by the Duke of Clarence, appeared on 6 October. Poor Henry VI, confused and shuffling, was fetched from prison and set once more upon his throne.

It is curious that at this juncture Marguerite did not rush over to Westminster to join her husband. Initially this was due to a delay in the marriage between Anne Neville and Prince Edward. The ceremony eventually took place at Amboise on 13 December, held up by bureaucratic tanglings and the last-minute discovery of a need for the dreaded papal dispensation (Anne and Edward shared a great-great-grandfather in John of Gaunt). In the meantime Anne, Isabel of Clarence and the Countess of Warwick remained with Marguerite, leaving for Paris after the wedding. Louis XI was finally prepared to open his purse now that Marguerite was useful to him once more, and provided over 6,000 livres for 'the furnishing of their silver ware' and their 'pleasures', but even a return to luxurious living could not have been much of a temptation to Marguerite to linger, given that what she had fought and schemed and yearned for had finally been achieved.

In March 1471, Marguerite's party were once more at Harfleur, but were kept ashore for seventeen days more by adverse winds. This dithering was highly prejudicial to the Readeption, as the restoration of Henry

VI is known. Warwick had difficulty in creating any coherent sense of government, and without the presence of Marguerite and, more importantly, Prince Edward, there was no prospect of stability in England. Henry's inadequacies were common knowledge, and returning Lancastrians were resentful at the ascent of one who had so recently been their enemy, when they, not he, had suffered for their King's cause. So why did Marguerite wait? She may have been reckless in speech but, as she had shown in retreating from London in 1461, she had a tendency to hesitate at crucial moments. She had to delay until her son's marriage had taken place to give herself some security, but she still had no guarantee that Warwick might not decide Clarence was a more malleable successor to Henry. Either way, he would still have a daughter on the throne.

Marguerite's indecisiveness once again allowed events to get the better of her. In November, Queen Elizabeth had given birth to a son, Edward, in Westminster sanctuary. A greater contrast to the hushed ceremonial of her previous lyings-in could hardly be imagined. Henry VI had behaved considerately, providing a salary of ten pounds for Elizabeth, Lady Scrope to wait on her, and permitting a butcher named William Gould to send in a half of beef and two muttons every week for her household. There was even a fishmonger to provide for Fridays and fast days. But the sanctuary quarters in Westminster Close were disgustingly crowded and insanitary, with the many debtors, thieves and beggars sharing space with fifty monks and the hundred servants who waited on them, as well as shopkeepers and cookshops. The public latrine, situated to the west of the abbey, filled the whole area with its stink and there was little space for outdoor exercise. Anyone who has spent a rainy day indoors with small children might pity Elizabeth, who was confined here for six months with a newborn to nurse. For her labour, Elizabeth had been allowed the company of Marjory Cobbe, the midwife who had attended her at Cecily's birth, and a physician, Dominic de Sergio. The Prince was christened in the abbey with Abbot Millyng and the prior of Westminster as godfathers and Lady Scrope as godmother. It was an inauspicious, indeed ominous beginning, but still a joyful one. The new baby was the heir to the house of York and now Elizabeth, like Marguerite, had a son to fight for.

If Warwick was disadvantaged by Marguerite's hesitancy, Edward IV was saved by Louis XI's impatience. On 3 December, the French King declared war on Burgundy. Until this point, Charles of Burgundy had refused to see his exiled brother-in-law, who was living under the protection of the governor of Holland, Lord Gruuthuyse. Charles's main concern was that he should have an ally against Louis in the English, and now that Edward had been deposed it was more sensible of him to seek an accommodation with the new government. However, as Warwick was pro-French, Louis's aggressive stance now meant Charles had an interest in helping Edward, and the Duke had nothing to lose by acknowledging him openly. He provided Edward with 20,000 pounds to finance an invasion, and Edward and his brother Gloucester also had an interview with their sister, Duchess Margaret, who raised further money and ships from bankers and merchants and 6,000 florins from five Dutch towns. In March, Edward set sail with thirty-six ships, landing at Ravenspur on the fourteenth. Arriving at York, Edward, like Henry IV before him, declared that he had not come to claim the crown, but only the duchy that had belonged to his father. He swore an oath on the high altar at York Minster that he would never again make an attempt on the throne of England, then promptly set about raising an army. At this stage, though, he looked unlikely to succeed. He had brought about 2,000 troops from Burgundy, but Warwick had reputedly gathered 7,000 at Coventry. The crucial intervention came from the Duke of Clarence.

Clarence was not tremendously intelligent, but he finally realised that Warwick had used him and that he had little to gain by Henry's restoration. In a dramatic scene on the Banbury road, the two brothers, each with their army behind them, came forward and embraced. Thus Clarence, and more importantly 4,000 men, were firmly engaged on Edward's side. By 9 April, Edward was able to send a reassuring message to his supporters in London and Queen Elizabeth in sanctuary, and two days later he entered the city. After a quick pause at St Paul's to thank God and St Edward and feel the crown once more on his head, Edward went to Westminster to retrieve his wife and daughters and see his son for the first time. The *Historie of the Arrivall* pictures Edward comforting Elizabeth, and praises her fortitude in 'right great trouble, sorrow and heaviness, which she sustained with all manner of patience that belonged to any creature, and as constantly as has been seen at any time any of so high estate to endure', and describes his joy as he was presented with the baby prince.[12] Henry VI was once more stowed away in the Tower. He had been produced by Warwick's brother George Neville to march in a propaganda procession in a last attempt to hold the city, but had made a poor showing in a scruffy blue velvet gown, and he was apparently quite relieved to see Edward again, shaking his hand and expressing gratitude to his 'cousin of York', whom he trusted to spare his life.

The next day was Good Friday, and Edward and Elizabeth, who had spent the night with Edward's mother, the Duchess of York, heard Mass together. Elizabeth, Jacquetta and the children then returned to the Tower while Edward prepared for the final showdown with Warwick. The King and the kingmaker met at Barnet on the morning of Easter Sunday, 14 April 1471. The battle began at dawn, and once again Edward fought at the centre of his men, his tall figure rearing out of the mist, 'turning first one way and then another he so beat and bore down that nothing might stand in the sight of him'[13] After three hours of close fighting, Warwick was dead and the field was Edward's. A few hours later Marguerite, with her son Edward and his Neville bride, landed at Weymouth.

The news of Warwick's death reached Marguerite the next day at Cerne Abbey in Dorset. There is something magnificent in her refusal to surrender, her clear belief that there was still a chance of victory. From Cerne she moved to Exeter, where the troops of Devon and Cornwall were called out for Henry VI. Marguerite was supported by the third Duke of Somerset to fight for the Lancastrian cause (Edmund, the younger brother of Henry, who had been executed after Hexham in 1464), and the earls of Wiltshire and Dorset, while Jasper Tudor was gathering a Lancastrian army in Wales. Now began a cat-and-mouse hunt that lasted almost three weeks, with Marguerite moving cautiously north via Wells, Bath and Bristol and Edward leaving London to the west then turning north, marching in parallel with the Lancastrians, as Marguerite sent out small parties of troops in different directions to confuse Edward's spies. Conditions were hard for both armies, with hot sun and scant supplies of water for the heavily laden men and gasping horses. On 3 May as Edward's troops approached faster and faster to the rear, the Lancastrians camped at Tewkesbury while Marguerite and Anne took shelter in the abbey house.

On Saturday 4 May, Edward's trumpets blared out the attack and his guns and archers started to pound the Lancastrian defence. Somerset managed to lead a contingent round the side of the central Yorkist division and attack downhill. As usual, Edward had placed himself in the centre and now he and his soldiers shifted to face the oncoming Lancastrians, trying to force them, hand to hand, back up the slope. Meanwhile, the Yorkist vanguard, under the command of Richard of Gloucester, had been liberated by Somerset's feint and now bore down on the Lancastrians. Edward had stationed 200 men-at-arms on his flank and they rushed forward so that Somerset's men were boxed in, with no option but to try to flee. Few succeeded. The second Lancastrian division, led by the inexperienced Prince Edward, was coming up, and the King wheeled his troops again to face them head on. The Yorkists knew they were winning and the remaining Lancastrians had little spirit for the fight. Many of them ran away, pursued enthusiastically by Edward's troops, who had been given permission to chase, kill and rob them. Most disastrously of all for Marguerite, Prince Edward was killed.

Until recently, it has been accepted that Prince Edward died in the field while attempting to escape to the town, as confirmed by the *Arrivall, The Tewkesbury Abbey Chronicle* and *The Warkworth Chronicle*. Another story of his death exists in *Hall's Chronicle* which, since it was written under the Tudors, was dismissed for some time as propaganda. In this version, Prince Edward was captured and brought face to face with Edward IV before being executed by Gloucester and Clarence some days after the battle. However, an illustrated version of the *Arrivall* from 1471 suggests that Hall's version may indeed be correct. Clarence had been in the field with Edward, but where was Isabel? The Countess of Warwick had taken refuge at Beaulieu Abbey, but there is no mention of Isabel having joined her. Did this mean that Anne Neville had to wait with her sister while her brother-in-law murdered her husband?

The aftermath of Tewkesbury brought very different consequences for the once, present and future queens of England. Both Anne and Marguerite were formally pardoned at Tewkesbury as Edward passed through on 7 May, having sought refuge in a convent on the Worcester road. Anne was given into the custody of the Duke of Clarence. Marguerite was treated more severely. When Edward made his triumphal entry into London, she was exhibited as a penitent captive in the rear of his train, then sent straight to the Tower. She was not permitted to see her husband. Henry VI died that night. The highly partisan account in the *Arrivall* has him expiring of 'ire and indignation', unlikely indeed for such a passive character, and the consensus is that he was murdered, though how or by whom is a matter for speculation. However, 'no matter who carried it out, the responsibility of the deed was Edward's'.[14] Edward's decision was harsh and treacherous, but the upheavals of the last years had taught him that the violence could not end as long as Henry or his heirs were living. (Anne Neville, it must be assumed, was not considered to be pregnant with Henry's grandchild.) To confirm the refoundation of his dynasty, Edward created his baby son Prince of Wales that July, in the presence of two archbishops, eight bishops and as many magnates as could be assembled, all swearing their allegiance to a Yorkist future.

Marguerite remained in prison for the next four years. Agnes Strickland speaks with determined optimism of the amelioration of her 'rigorous' confinement brought about by the 'compassionate influence' of Elizabeth Woodville, but as with so many of Strickland's accounts, this is agreeable fantasising. There is no record that Queen Elizabeth visited or saw Marguerite during her imprisonment, nor do her expenses show any personal favours. Marguerite had worked for years to destroy Elizabeth's husband and family, and though she was no longer a political risk, Elizabeth, understandably, left no documented trace of compassion towards her. Strickland's embroidering has been accepted by at least one of Elizabeth's biographers, who has suggested that she was motivated by 'a grateful remembrance of the benefits she had received from her royal mistress',[15] but the evidence of Elizabeth having served Marguerite is very flimsy, and her true feelings seem more apparent in the fact that in 1475 she had Marguerite's arms removed from Queens' College, Cambridge, and replaced with her own and those of England.

After a period in the Tower, Marguerite was moved to Windsor, then Wallingford and eventually to Ewelm in Oxfordshire, the seat of Lady Suffolk, who received a weekly sum of eight marks for the maintenance of the royal prisoner. Now that Henry was dead, the King of France had no purpose for Marguerite, while her father, René, seemed content to let her linger in captivity. It was a cruel reminder that despite all her struggles and suffering, she remained merely a woman, only as valuable as her alliances, and they were no more. Finally, in 1475, when Louis XI and Edward met at Picquigny to ratify an Anglo-French truce (one of the provisions of which was a second betrothal for Edward's eldest daughter, Elizabeth of York, this time to the Dauphin), Louis agreed to ransom Marguerite. She had to renounce all claims to her jointure and any English inheritance, and Louis handed over 50,000 crowns for her freedom. In January 1476 she landed at Dieppe and travelled to Rouen, where she was received by the King's representative, Jean d'Haguet, the receiver general of Normandy. The motivation behind Louis's magnanimity soon became apparent: he invaded Anjou the next year. Since Marguerite's brother John of Calabria had died in 1470, she was rightfully an heiress, but on 29 January 1476 she was obliged to sign away her rights in Lorraine, Barrois, Anjou and Provence, describing herself in the document as 'I Marguerite, formerly married in the Kingdom of England'.

Marguerite's father gave her the use of a castle and a small pension, but in 1480, he died. *Bourdigne's Chronicle* mourned: 'No prince ever loved his subjects as he loved his, nor was in like manner better loved and well-wished than he was by them,' but René's 'love' does not seem to have extended to his widowed, bereaved and dispossessed daughter. He had ceded his own inheritance to his nephew Charles of Maine, who had sold it on to King Louis, so now that he was gone, there was no one to pay

Marguerite's pension. She was forced to beg, writing plaintively to one of Louis's ministers that 'it may please him to take my poor case in the matter of what can and should belong to me, into his hands to do with it according to his good will and pleasure and still keep me in his good grace and love'.[16] Louis obliged her by insisting she confirmed the 1476 donation and then permitting her to go to law with her living sibling, Yolande, for the resignation of her rights to the Barrois. By this time, Marguerite was living in penury and, having manipulated her for his own territorial gain, Louis simply abandoned her. She was compelled to leave her castle of Reculée as she could no longer maintain her household, and it was only the charity of François Vignolles, Lord of Morains and one of her father's former vassals, that protected her. He provided her with a home in his castle of Dampierre, about three miles from Saumur on the River Loire. The final indignity came when Charles of Maine died and Marguerite was pressured to sign a will in Louis's favour. It included a request that he provide funds for her funeral and burial with her parents at St Maurice d'Angers. Marguerite had her wish and was interred with her father who, despite his careless treatment, she seems to have loved to the end.

Marguerite died aged fifty-two in August 1482. The last decade of her life had been one long fall from grace. There were some who still considered her a champion of the Lancastrian cause, and she had received a party of exiled Lancastrian lords in 1479, but the year of her death saw Edward IV's dynasty apparently firmly established on the throne. At her coronation she had been hailed as a bringer of peace and plenty; she died an isolated exile, an impoverished symbol of war. King Louis demanded her hunting dogs be given to him as, pathetically, they were the only thing of value that she owned. No record exists of her funeral. It is possible that no one troubled to write one.

The decade after Edward IV's ultimate recovery of his kingdom had been peaceful and productive, both for the country as a whole and for Elizabeth Woodville. She gave Edward three more daughters, Anne, Katherine and Bridget, and a second son, Richard, Duke of York. Two other children, Margaret and George, died as infants. Her public activities reflected both pious and scholarly interests whose pattern had been disturbed by the upheavals of the Lancastrian insurrection. In 1466, she had received a grant from the city of London for a tract of land adjacent to Tower Hill, on which to build a chapel or college, and though no more is heard of this project, by 1479 Elizabeth had founded a chapel to St Erasmus at Westminster Abbey. She made grants to Holy Trinity, Syon Abbey to the

Carthusians at Sheen and went on pilgrimage to Canterbury with her husband and eldest daughter. The Pope saw fit to make particular mention of her devotion to the Virgin and St Elizabeth, and granted exceptional indulgences to worshippers who recited the Hail Mary three times a day at the encouragement of the Queen. Elizabeth adopted Marguerite of Anjou's foundation of Queens' College, Cambridge and, along with her brother Lord Rivers, was a benefactress of Henry VI's college at Eton.

Two accounts of Elizabeth's participation in public rituals give a sense of her conduct and, again, of how the way her background influenced perceptions of that conduct. One is the description of her churching banquet after the birth of her first child as queen. It was held in 'an unbelievably costly apartment', where she sat on a golden chair. Jacquetta and Edward's sister Margaret stood apart and knelt when she spoke to them. They were not permitted a seat until the first dish had been placed on the table, while the other sixty ladies at the women–only event remained on their knees in silence until the Queen had dined. Elizabeth's silence and the formal protocol of the event have been attributed to her 'haughti-ness' and 'arrogance' (characteristics that may well have been seen as appropriate had she been a royal princess), but this strange, soundless ballet was part of a sacred ritual, and in no way expressed her own preferences.

A warmer image is provided by Elizabeth's role as hostess to Lord Gruuthuyse in 1472. Gruuthuyse had been Edward's host during his Flemish exile, a sojourn that provided the King with an opportunity to experience the magnificence of the Burgundian court lifestyle and which was to be highly influential on his own tastes and cultural ambitions. Edward was keen to reward Gruuthuyse, and invited him to England, where he created him Earl of Winchester at Windsor. After supper, Edward conducted his guest to Elizabeth's rooms, where she was playing at bowls with her ladies, a sight Gruuthuyse found charming. Following the bowls there was dancing and next day Elizabeth had a banquet prepared in her apartments. She had created three 'chambers of pleasance' hung with silks and floral tapestries, which featured a tented bath and a fine down bed for Gruuthuyse, complete with a cloth-of-gold and ermine counterpane, gold canopy, white curtains and sheets and pillows 'of the queen's own ordinance'. Elizabeth's gilt-and-ivory beauty would have been set off to full advantage by such a backdrop, and here she appears as the perfect picture of graciousness and condescension, regal and courteous, yet simple enough to concern herself with cushions. Nothing in either of these accounts suggests that she was anything less than fully capable of fulfilling her royal role in public.

Privately, Elizabeth's situation was less satisfactory, as she was learning that even great beauty is not enough to hold a philandering man. Her sexual relationship with the King certainly continued until 1480, since she gave birth to Bridget, her last child, in November that year. But Thomas More noted that Edward was 'greatly given to fleshly wantonness', and few women could resist the attentions of a handsome king. Dominic Mancini, an Italian cleric in the service of one of Louis XI's ministers, added that Edward generously passed on his mistresses to his friends when he tired of them. The King had a bastard son, Arthur, by his lover Elizabeth Lucy, and two daughters, the tactlessly named Elizabeth and Grace (with whom Elizabeth Woodville obviously had some sort of relationship, as Grace attended her funeral). Anti-Woodville writers have made a vice even of Elizabeth's dignified silence in the face of her husband's many infidelities, citing it as evidence of her 'cold' and 'designing' character.[17] A similar twisting occurs in the case of Edward's best-known mistress Jane Shore, a source of misconceptions about Elizabeth's relationship with the chamberlain, William, Lord Hastings, which would affect the interpretation of her role in the events surrounding her son's thwarted succession. Many commentators have accepted that Elizabeth hated Hastings, with whom she had a long history of disputes dating back to the 1460s, though there is some evidence that they collaborated with one another in the 1470s. The reason for this 'hatred' was supposedly the pleasure Hastings shared with Edward in 'wanton company', a tendency which, according to Mancini, spilled over into a quarrel with Elizabeth's son by her first marriage, Thomas Grey, Marquess of Dorset. Dorset planned to take over from his stepfather in Jane Shore's affections, but Mistress Shore wasted no time in throwing herself on the protection of the chamberlain. Thomas More bulks out Mancini's gossip with a political motivation for the ill will between Hastings and the Woodvilles with the suggestion that Edward preferred Hastings for the governorship of Calais over the Queen's candidate, her brother Lord Rivers, in 1482. The enmity between Hastings and the Queen's family has been seen as a crucial stalling point in Edward V's accession, though Elizabeth's personal responsibility for it is 'the most uncertain factor of all'.[18]

Malicious rumour also placed Elizabeth Woodville at the centre of another controversy of the 1470s: the execution of the Duke of Clarence. Isabel Neville died in January 1477, yet the King was reluctant to allow his untrustworthy brother to marry again. Matches were proposed with Mary, the heiress to the Duke of Burgundy, and Margaret, the King of Scotland's sister, but the former would have prejudiced Edward's concord with Louis of France and the latter given Clarence a power base disturbingly proximate to England. A truculent Clarence began to display his contempt for Edward's authority and in May 1477 expressly defied the King with his support of one Thomas Burdet, who was hanged for treason, sorcery and the spread of sedition that month. There were whispers of another rebellion plot, which the Duke compounded by claiming that he and his heirs had the true right to Henry VI's crown and encouraging some of his men to swear fealty to him. Clarence was becoming dangerous, and by June Edward felt he had no choice but to arrest him. The Queen was reported to be using her influence to destroy the Duke, for fear that her son would never reign while his uncle was alive, but the decision to execute Clarence in February 1478 was Edward's and Edward's alone. Elizabeth may never have forgiven Clarence for conspiring with Warwick, so it is possible that she did perceive him as a threat and welcomed his demise, but her purported responsibility in the matter proves nothing more than the readiness of her critics to attribute her husband's unpleasant political actions to the powers of persuasion of his wife, a trope with which English queens had had to contend since Eleanor of Provence's day.

Despite the shadows of Edward's infidelity and the bitterness of Clarence's death, it appeared that by 1482 the royal couple had finally overcome the horrors and sufferings of years of war. *The Croyland Chronicle* presents an idyllic picture of the family at Christmas that year: 'You might have seen, in those days, the royal court presenting no other appearance than such as fully befits a most mighty kingdom, filled with riches, boasting of the sweet and beautiful children, the issue of [Edward's] marriage with Queen Elizabeth.' As ever for Elizabeth, though, peace and security proved to be short-lived.

CHAPTER 18

ANNE NEVILLE

'I'll have her, but I will not keep her long . . .'

Despite being born to great wealth and married to even greater estate, Anne Neville appears until 1472 as a victim. Her marriage had annealed one of the most implausible alliances in English history, but its brokers had failed in their purpose and she found herself a widow having barely been a wife, a princess without a title and an heiress without an estate. But after eight months as the reluctant ward of the Duke of Clarence, Anne took an extraordinary step. She arranged her own marriage and moreover, if Hall's account of the aftermath of Tewkesbury is credited, she chose for her second husband the man who had murdered her first.

The motivation behind Anne's strike for independence lay in her unusual legal position. As a widow, she enjoyed the status of a *femme sole* with the legal right to conduct her own affairs, but whatever hopes she may have had of regaining her inheritance were thwarted. Any prospective dower settlement she could have expected as Dowager Princess of Wales was now void, but she was entitled to a half share of her father's Neville lands. The other half was held by Clarence through his wife, Anne's sister Isabel, and now the couple stalled Anne's attempts to assert her rights. She wrote to Queen Elizabeth, the Duchess of York, Princess Elizabeth and Jacquetta, Duchess of Bedford to try to persuade them to intercede with her with the King, who refused to allow her safe conduct to make her case in court. They did nothing. Isabel was now a part of the royal family, with Clarence's treachery officially forgotten – for the moment, at least – and Anne, despite the fact that she had been pardoned, excluded from favour. The Countess of Warwick did little to help her daughter, and indeed there was little she could do, as the Warwick earldom had been attaindered. If Anne could marry, she would have a champion to uphold her rights, but she needed a partner powerful enough to counter

Clarence's influence. The natural choice was Edward IV's second brother, Richard of Gloucester.

It has been suggested that Anne and Richard had actually fallen in love when Richard was a member of the Earl of Warwick's household in his teens, yet though they knew each other well, having grown up together, their marriage was one of mutual convenience, a convenience Anne was the first to perceive. The Clarences were opposed to Anne making any marriage, as that would mean they would have to give up their claim to her half of the inheritance, but when, after a Christmas visit by Richard, they suspected Anne's precise intentions, they were furious. The Milanese ambassador confirmed the gossip that Clarence opposed a match because 'his brother King Edward had promised him Warwick's country, he did not want [Gloucester] to have it by reason of marriage with the Earl's second daughter'.[1] *The Croyland Chronicle* is responsible for the famous story that the Clarences disguised Anne as a kitchen maid in their London home at Coldharbour to prevent Richard from carrying her off, and though the type of costume is unlikely, the idea that they attempted to hide her is deemed plausible. Somehow, Anne got the better of them and between December 1471, when Richard arrived in London, and February 1472, when her presence is recorded there, she defiantly fled the Clarences' house and took sanctuary at St Martin's, near St Paul's Cathedral.

Anne's escape was a courageous, if not strictly romantic act, but its object may seem psychologically repugnant to a modern mind. Leaving aside the rather tiresome matter of Richard III's true appearance (he may have been born with teeth but he was probably not hunchbacked, let alone the deformed creeping gargoyle of hammier Shakespearean representation), how could Anne have countenanced marriage to the man who was responsible, perhaps personally, for her husband's death? This is simply the wrong question. Rather, how could Anne have chosen to ignore the fact that marriage to Richard was deeply sinful? Richard and Anne were both distantly related to Prince Edward, they were first cousins once removed and brother- and sister-in-law. The papal degrees were often treated as no more than tedious necessities requiring dispensation, but in this instance Anne's relationship with her intended husband was considered genuinely incestuous. To anyone with a conscience in the late fifteenth century, it was just plain wrong. But Anne was clearly desperate, as was borne out by the fact that she was prepared to accept no dower when the marriage and inheritance settlement was finalised in 1474.

Anne's wedding to Richard was simple enough for it to have left no record, but it probably took place in the spring of 1472, since in April that year a dispensation granting them licence in the third and fourth degrees of kinship was granted (though this was not in itself sufficient to validate the marriage). Anne had been living under Richard's protection since leaving sanctuary after Clarence grudgingly consented to the match. The King attempted to reconcile the feuding brothers by declaring that they could divide the whole of the Warwick inheritance, to the disadvantage of the Countess, and acknowledged the inadequate dispensation by giving Richard his share for life in the event that he and Anne were obliged to divorce, which anticipatory claim confirms that his interests in the enterprise had little to do with affection for Anne. If the correct dispensation were sought and denied, it would also mean that any children ran the risk of being declared illegitimate, but once again Anne was prepared to face this possibility. Altogether, it was an ugly marriage, even for a time when marriage was essentially a matter of business. Anne colluded with her husband in cheating her mother of her rights, and entered knowingly into a marriage that risked disgraceful dissolution. But it was also a successful union, in that both parties got what they wanted, even if that was not necessarily one another.

As well as wealth, Anne brought Richard a dowry that would prove essential in his eventual rise to power, the Neville affinity of the northern march. Anne's great-grandfather, Ralph, Earl of Westmoreland, had married as his second wife a daughter of John of Gaunt by Katherine Swynford, Joan Beaufort. His elder son by his royal bride, Anne's grandfather Richard, Earl of Salisbury, came to hold the wardenship of the west march against the Scots and, along with their rivals, the Percies, the Nevilles governed what was almost a mini-kingdom on the northern border. The power struggles of the two great families had played an influential part in the turmoil leading to the deposition of Henry VI. Now, with Warwick gone, Richard claimed the Earl's northern allegiances as his own. Recognising the potency of the Neville association, Edward made Richard his regent in the north from 1472, formalising his position with an appointment to lieutenant general in 1480. The couple, especially Anne, spent much of their time during the first decade of their marriage at Middleham, in modern-day Wensleydale, and though the eleventh-century castle there is a ruin, it remains impressive even today. It was at Middleham (according to local lore, in the south-west tower), that their son Edward was born in the mid-1470s.

Records of Anne's activities until 1483 are extremely scant. She represented her husband at York during his absence in France in 1475–6, and it may be assumed she did so on other occasions, just as it may be assumed she conducted her household in the typical, unexceptional manner of other great ladies of her class. The nature of her relationship with Queen Elizabeth is unknown, but their stories entwine again in the summer of 1483. Edward IV fell sick at the end of March that year, and on 9 April he died at Westminster. Anne did not arrive in London until 5 June. How much she knew of her husband's plans at this point is uncertain, but the fact that she did not make this journey sooner suggests she was aware that the planned coronation of Prince Edward was not going to take place in May, as scheduled. Indeed, it was just a few weeks later that Anne found herself once again in the position of prospective Queen of England.

With hindsight, the main protagonists of the rapid events following Edward IV's death have been too easily sorted into the categories of heroes and villains. Anti-Richard writers have him immediately plotting to seize the throne, while his apologists have him battling an attempted coup by the Queen's relations, the Woodvilles. With regard to Elizabeth herself, we may imagine first that she was still reeling from the shock of her husband's death, for though Edward was no longer the beautiful man she had married, his tall figure now marred by a bulging stomach and his features coarsened through dissipation, he had still been only forty years old, and no one had expected him to die so suddenly. Secondly, her entirely reasonable aim was to have her son crowned and the succession smoothly assured. It was perhaps unwise of her to depend so closely on the counsel of her supporters, her nearest relatives, but it is nevertheless hardly surprising that she did.

Edward's extant will, made in 1475, named Elizabeth 'his dearest and most entirely beloved wife', as his chief executor and guardian of his children, but a subsequent codicil named Richard of Gloucester as lord protector. (In fact, neither instruction was binding, as legally only the council and Parliament could decide on the governance of the realm in the minority of the King.) In the absence of the amended will, it has been suggested that Elizabeth was excluded from her role as executor, as is supposedly confirmed by the fact that she did not attend an executors' meeting on 7 May. Her absence was due to the very good reason that she was in Westminster Sanctuary, so nothing can be proved either way. It has also been mooted that Elizabeth personally worked to prevent Richard of Gloucester from taking up his position as protector. According to Alison Weir, 'The Woodvilles were firmly entrenched and meant to stay that way, having determined to resist all attempts to make Gloucester protector.

Their intention was to ignore Edward IV's will and use Edward V as a puppet.'² The Woodvilles certainly knew that their power was threatened, but until later in the month they had no reason to fear a direct attack from Richard.

The Croyland Chronicle emphasises that when the council met after the funeral, the desire to see Edward V crowned was unanimous, but the company was divided as to the most appropriate arrangements for his guardianship, and that of the realm, until he reached his majority. Prominent among the anti-Woodville contingent was Lord Hastings. *Croyland* suggests that Hastings feared the Woodvilles because 'if power slipped into the grasp of the Queen's relatives they would avenge the injuries they claimed he had done them'. If Edward were crowned quickly, the role of protector could be dispensed with and the Woodvilles could then rule through the King. *Croyland* adds that the situation was saved by the 'benevolence' of the Queen, who seems to have grasped that this was no time for personal antagonisms. Hastings was supported by the prominent Cheshire magnate Lord Stanley, the third husband of Margaret Beaufort, but the large pro-Woodville faction, as well as neutral figures such as the Archbishop of Canterbury, overruled the 'wiser' element and the coronation was fixed for 4 May.

Hastings had, however, been able to effect one modification to the Woodville plans, which was the size of the escort that would accompany Edward south from Ludlow. Hastings threatened to return to Calais if the Prince's escort were not reduced to 2,000 men. This is an indication of just how intimidated the anti-Woodville party felt. Edward's arrival with a large army would be perceived as highly aggressive and Hastings was prepared take an equally aggressive position (holing up at Calais with the country's only standing army) to counter it. It was Elizabeth who persuaded her supporters that Hastings was right. This gesture has been interpreted as an enactment of her 'peace-making' role, and of her sensitivity to the feelings of the magnates, but it could equally well have been a piece of realpolitik: Calais was loyal to Hastings and he had made powerful friends at the courts of France and Burgundy during his governorship. The new King could not afford to have him as an enemy.

Richard of Gloucester was in the north at the time of his brother's death, and it was Hastings who wrote to him with the news, which he received on 13 or 14 April, at the same time as the messengers to Ludlow informed the twelve-year-old Edward he was now King. One view of Richard's feelings at this time comes from Dominic Mancini, who asserts that Richard had sequestered himself in the north to avoid the 'jealousy' of the Queen and the 'insults' of her 'ignoble family'. Mancini also claims Hastings advised Richard that he could 'avenge' such insults if he took the young King under his protection before the boy arrived in London. Mancini's reports are valuable in that he wrote down the information he picked up about London, that is, what people believed to be happening, but for the same reason there is inevitably a strong element of hearsay in his accounts. He claimed Gloucester hated Elizabeth because of Clarence's execution, and vowed to be avenged, but this seems excessively simplistic, given the brothers' feud over the Neville inheritance and Clarence's earlier history of treachery to the crown.

Gloucester had made a great public show of grief, true, but this had not prevented him from scooping up his brother's share of the Neville booty. On the surface, Richard, unlike Hastings, appeared to have no quarrel with the Woodvilles in 1483, nor did Elizabeth seem to have any especial dislike of him. Indeed, Lord Rivers had requested Richard's arbitration in a property dispute in Norfolk just a few months before. And whatever his private feelings, Richard had been quick to write a letter of condolence to the Queen, assuring her of his loyalty. Richard did come to give the Woodvilles cause to hate and fear him, but even then there is no reason to assume it was personal. He merely turned on them, as on so many others, when they got in his way.

It is not necessarily correct then, to suppose that Richard's actions were the result of a longstanding grudge against the Woodvilles. Much has been made of the fact that it was Hastings, rather than the Woodville faction, who informed Richard of Edward's death, with the implication that the Woodvilles were trying to crown Edward before he had a chance to take up his role as protector, but in Hastings' capacity as lord chamberlain, it was appropriate that he should break the news, and Richard would have had ample time to reach London for 4 May, if he had intended to accede to the arrangements. Recall that Edward's death had come as a great surprise. Even Richard's enemies had to concede that he was an out-standing military commander, as he had so often proved in the service of his brother. He was used to making difficult decisions quickly. One reading of the evidence, then, is that Richard made his choice in the days between receiving Hastings' letter and setting off for Northampton. This would also explain why Anne Neville came to arrive in London as late as 5 June. If she knew before her husband departed that the coronation would be delayed, it made sense to put off her journey rather than start for the capital at once.

Whatever the case, by 29 April, Richard had concluded that the

Woodvilles had to go. In this he was aided by a magnate who *did* hate the Queen's family, even though he was her brother-in-law. Henry Stafford, Duke of Buckingham, was the grandson of the Duke of Buckingham who had died fighting for Henry VI at Northampton. He had been married aged eleven to Elizabeth's sister Katherine and, as a descendant of Edward III through Thomas of Woodstock, his pride smarted under the disparagement. Buckingham loathed the Woodvilles. Like Hastings, he saw Richard as a natural ally now that it appeared the family was poised to take control of the King, and the two men had been in rapid correspondence since hearing of Edward IV's death.

On 29 April, Richard and Buckingham met at Northampton. Lord Rivers, Elizabeth's second son Sir Richard Grey and the new King had passed by on their route from Ludlow and were resting at Stony Stratford, fourteen miles closer to London. In a further example of the Woodvilles' confidence in Richard at this point, Rivers and Grey now rode back to meet Richard and spent a pleasant evening dining and talking with the two dukes. Grey's presence has been interpreted as Elizabeth's last, desperate attempt to prevent Richard from assuming the protectorship. 'Soon after his arrival [at Northampton] the King was joined by Sir Richard Grey, hot-foot from London and probably bearing orders from the Queen to Rivers, urging him to press on to the capital without delay,' suggests Alison Weir.[3] If Grey were carrying any such orders, whether as a warning or in an attempt to rush Edward to London for his coronation, why did he and Rivers turn back after they had conveyed Edward to Stony Stratford? If they feared Richard, and were conspiring to deprive him of the protectorate, why have dinner with him? If their cordiality was a feint, it backfired. In the morning, Richard had Rivers and Grey arrested and imprisoned.

News of the arrests reached London that night. Elizabeth panicked. Her first thought was to attempt to raise an army with her son the Marquis of Dorset, but they found little support, as it was not considered odd or threatening that the King should be in the company of his only uncle, his official protector. Desperate to safeguard herself and her children, Elizabeth decided once more to take sanctuary at Westminster. Thomas More gives an imaginative picture of her flight, of the 'rumble, haste and busyness, carriage and conveyance of her stuff into sanctuary, chests, coffers, packs, fardels, trusses, all on men's backs, no man unoccupied, some loading, some going, some discharging, some coming for more'. Distraught, the Queen herself could do little more than slump to the floor and weep, and when the archbishop of York tried to comfort her with a reassuring message from Hastings, More has her hissing bitterly, 'Woe worth him, for he is one of them that labours to destroy me and my blood.' Elizabeth, her daughters Elizabeth, Cecily, Anne, Katherine and Bridget, her brother Lionel Woodville and her sons Richard, Duke of York and Thomas Grey were received into sanctuary by the abbot of Westminster, John Easteney, and housed in his own quarters. By morning, the river was ominously full of the patrolling barges of Gloucester's men, ensuring that no one left or entered the sanctuary's precincts.

Was Elizabeth's flight a mistake? Richard's imprisonment of Rivers and Grey made it clear that he intended to take up the protectorship, but Elizabeth was the Dowager Queen. Had she really so much to fear? Once again, her reaction has been interpreted as evidence that she had been planning to exclude Richard from the government all along, and was now terrified of his discovering this. But such a response could equally have been prompted by the arrests alone. Elizabeth had lived through the Readeption, and she may have believed that it was her decisive action in taking sanctuary then which saved her life and those of her daughters and her unborn child. But now, she too, was effectively a prisoner, cut off from her eldest son and with limited means of communication with the outside world. And in removing herself from Richard's clutches, she also deprived herself of one of her most powerful weapons: her symbolic presence as queen.

At least Elizabeth's accommodation in the sanctuary had improved since her first visit. For the eleven months she lived there, she had the use of the abbot's Great Hall with its minstrels' gallery, a private chamber and courtyard and for audiences and the grand Jerusalem Chamber, hung with tapestries. Elizabeth was able to receive visitors, and after Richard arrived in the capital with Edward V on 4 May, news began to filter through of his propaganda campaign against her family. When Richard had taken possession of the King, he had claimed that the Woodvilles were plotting to assassinate him to deprive him of the regency, and that he had evidence of ambushes prepared on the London road. He also wrote to the council, explaining that he had rescued Edward and the country from 'perdition' and hinting that the Woodvilles had been involved in the death of Edward IV. When the King's party arrived in London, four carts of weapons were dragged through the streets to demonstrate to the people the 'proof' of the Woodvilles' evil plans. There is something painfully modern about Richard's disregard for the truth at this point. He had chosen his lie very effectively, and he stuck to it adamantly. By 10 June, he was writing to the representatives of the city of York asking for a muster of men to be sent south 'to aid and assist us against the Queen, her blood adherents and affinity, which hath intended and doth daily intend to murder and utterly destroy us'. The notable aspect of Richard's request is that it is a public one. The Woodvilles by this stage posed very little threat: the King himself was with Richard, the Queen and Dorset were in sanctuary, Rivers and Grey were being held captive and Elizabeth's brother Sir Edward Woodville, the commander of the fleet, had been forced to flee. Richard was using the perceived menace of the Woodvilles to raise men for his own purposes.

Officially, his aims were still peaceful. A new date of 22 June had been set for Edward's coronation, and Richard had already held an oath-swearing at the King's temporary lodging of the Chapter House of St Paul's, where lords and citizens gathered to profess their loyalty to the new monarch. On 10 May, Richard had been formally invested as protector until the coronation, after which a regency council was to be selected. Edward was moved to his new lodgings in the royal apartments at the Tower, so recently vacated by his mother. Elizabeth's continued residence in the sanctuary was now proving an embarrassment to Richard, particularly as some members of the council were expressing concern, according to *Croyland*, that 'the Protector did not, with a sufficient degree of considerateness, take fitting care for the preservation of the dignity and safety of the Queen'. Richard now began a campaign to persuade Elizabeth to leave the abbot's quarters, sending members of the council to visit her and reassure her that she and her children had nothing to fear, but Elizabeth remained obdurate.

Richard now grew impatient, and his next act began to reveal his true plans. On 13 June Lord Hastings, the archbishop of York, the bishop of Ely and the King's secretary were suddenly arrested during a council meeting at the Tower. Hastings was dragged outside and immediately beheaded. Why would Richard so ruthlessly dispose of one of his chief allies? If he was now scheming to seize the crown, then he needed both heirs to the throne in his power. Professor Gillingham's hypothesis is that Hastings had opposed the use of force to remove the Duke of York from sanctuary, but since he was unaware of Richard's ultimate ambition, would not have realised the significance of his opposition.[4] This would explain why Richard needed to eliminate him, and why Hastings was apparently caught unawares. Richard put out a story that Hastings had been plotting against him, and now, with the council silenced, he could move against Elizabeth.

On 16 June, the Queen handed over her son Richard to the protector. Why did she do so, particularly as the news of Hastings' execution was now common knowledge? For weeks, Elizabeth had been pressured to deliver the boy. One of Richard's main advocates was Thomas Bourchier, the cardinal archbishop of Canterbury, the man who had crowned Elizabeth and Edward and who had been for years a trusted friend, not to mention the highest spiritual authority in the country. Bourchier swore to the Queen that he would defend Richard if he was released from sanctuary. Morever, the protector had made it clear that if necessary he would use force. With the sanctuary surrounded by troops and the archbishop's well-meaning promises in her ear, Elizabeth, sobbing, gave up her child. It was probably the greatest mistake of her life.

Now that he had both princes in his control, Richard no longer troubled to disguise his intentions. He rounded up the last male claimant, Clarence's son, the eight-year-old Earl of Warwick, and gave him into the keeping of his aunt, Anne Neville. Richard had stayed at his mother's home, Baynard's Castle, when he first arrived in London, but on the day Anne arrived they took up residence at Crosby Place, Bishopsgate, so it was here, in the city, that Anne stayed with Warwick. Her own child, Edward, was still at Middleham. The removal from Baynard's Castle was politic, for the Duchess was in town for the coronation, and Richard's next step was to accuse her in public of adultery. On Sunday 22 June, the day set for Edward V's anointing as king, Dr Ralph Shaa, the brother of the mayor of London, preached a sermon at St Paul's entitled 'Bastard Slips Shall Never Take Deep Root'. He declared that Edward IV and the Duke of Clarence had been illegitimate, that Edward had therefore never been qualified to rule and that the only true heir to the house of York was now Richard of Gloucester.

Needless to say, the eighty-year-old Duchess of York, whose life was seen as a model of piety and who was well known for her strict religious observance, was less than delighted at her son's preposterous conduct. Other sermons preached that day declared that the marriage of Elizabeth and Edward had been invalid, as Edward had agreed a pre-contract with one Lady Eleanor Butler (who was conveniently dead), and that therefore Edward V, his brother and all his sisters were illegitimate. On 24 June the Duke of Buckingham addressed prominent citizens at the Guildhall and confirmed the pre-contract accusation.

The fact that no one believed these stories was by now immaterial. Richard had been very clever in choosing to resurrect the memory of Elizabeth's marriage, even going so far as to have Lady Eleanor's story mirror Elizabeth's own. She was described as a young widow who had petitioned Edward IV for the restoration of her lands in 1461. In digging up the old scandal of the King and the widow, Richard spread doubt and confusion. The arrests of the thirteenth, and Hastings' execution without trial, had also done their work. Finally, it appeared that Richard had soldiers everywhere. His troops were occupying the houses of his prisoners, parading at Westminster, and Simon Stallworth, one of the chancellor's clerks, reported in a letter that a fearsome army of 20,000 was expected any day from the north. Richard's manipulation of the public alarm was very sophisticated. Even before the northern forces arrived, people were afraid that soldiers could be hidden everywhere, so that 'the possibility . . . was more fearsome than the fact'.[5] On 25 June, the lords who were in London for the aborted coronation gathered at Westminster to hear Buckingham request a modestly hesitant Richard to take the crown. Meanwhile, at Pontefract Castle, Earl Rivers and Sir Richard Grey were beheaded. The next day, Richard III was proclaimed king.

Anne Neville had waited a long time for her crown. She had suffered a good deal, but it would be fascinating to have an insight into the state of her conscience. She knew that she had no right to be queen this time round, in the first place because her marriage was illegitimate in the eyes of the Church. And did she really believe the pre-contract story? Richard had provided an official justification for his usurpation, but it was intellectually barren. What information can be gleaned of Anne's spiritual life shows that she was a conventionally pious woman. In 1476 she became a member of the sisterhood of Durham Cathedral Priory (the cathedral had strong associations with the Neville family), and the next year she and her husband were admitted to the Guild of Corpus Christi at York, and founded a chantry at the Queens' College, Cambridge. They also established two colleges, at Barnard Castle, Durham and Middleham, but these activities were as much an appropriate means of enhancing family prestige as reflective of any profound spiritual commitment. As Queen, Anne formed a close relationship with her mother-in-law, Cecily, Duchess of York, who was a national example of piety. Cecily forgave Richard for branding her an adulteress and was a frequent visitor at court, where she and Anne discussed religious books such as *Ghostly Grace*, by the thirteenth-century German mystic Mechtild of Hackeborn, of which they both owned a copy. Such interests aside, Anne left no record of notable acts of more personal dedication and her religious patronage was negligible. If she did entertain private doubts about her new position, she did not feel the need to make public amends.

Anne's most significant cultural association is with the *Beauchamp Pageant*, a magnificent illustrated life of her grandfather Richard Beauchamp. The identity of the *Pageant's* patron is uncertain, but it is widely believed to have been commissioned by Anne's mother, either as an attempt to curry favour with Henry VII or as a 'mirror' (in the manner of the *Life of St Margaret of Scotland)* for Edward of Middleham. Given the meagre resources of the Countess of Warwick, it has also been proposed that Richard and Anne commissioned the work. Though this seems less likely, the fact that Anne and her mother could both have been involved in this monument to the greatness of the Queen's maternal family allows the possibility that their relationship was collaborative, if not cordial, even after the Countess had been dispossessed by her son–in–law.

While the anointed Queen of England lingered in sanctuary, Richard and Anne made rapid preparations for their coronation. Many of the arrangements were already in place in anticipation of Edward's crowning, including his small robes, but now there was a great rush to ensure that Richard and Anne's ceremony would be a faultless display of their legitimacy to rule. It was essential that all the rituals be performed correctly, and a special book, *The Little Device*, was drawn up for their coronation, which also followed the provisions set down in the *Royal Book* or *Liber Regalis*. On 3 July, the couple exchanged gifts of over fifty yards of purple velevet and cloth-of-gold, worked with garters and roses, and on the next day they made the traditional journey to the Tower, possibly by water. Anne Neville entered Westminster Abbey on 6 July with a magnificent crimson train, her fair hair loose under a gold circlet, evoking the virginity that had become part of the coronation symbolism (though of course she, like Elizabeth Woodville, was both a widow and a mother) and walked in her stockinged feet up the aisle as a display of humility, before prostrating herself at the altar. She and Richard were crowned by Archbishop Bourchier, who did not, however, attend the banquet for 3,000 that followed the ceremony.

Anne's short, hurried journey to the Tower gave no scope for the personally tailored pageants that had represented the hopes of the country for the queenships of her predecessors Marguerite of Anjou and Elizabeth Woodville. Given that this was a moment to show queens as 'individuals with particular contributions to make to kingship at different times',[6] the absence of such pageantry negated Anne's own character and her significant pedigree and family history, suggesting that in the public mind she was little more than 'the female body that bore the king's heirs and sat beside him in public'.[7] And unlike Marguerite, who had forty, and Elizabeth who had thirty-eight, Anne was accompanied to Westminster by only seventeen newly dubbed knights of the Bath, though forty-nine men had been summoned to enter the order for Edward V. Had the remainder discreetly made themselves scarce rather than be so closely associated with the new regime?

'Being now desirous, with all speed, to show in the north ... his high and kingly station',[8] Richard and his Queen now set off on progress, to display themselves to their new subjects. Anne took a more leisurely route than Richard, travelling from Greenwich to Windsor, where she stayed for two weeks before moving on to join the King at Warwick. There they received an important mark of international acknowledgement of their rule: a delegation from King Ferdinand and Queen Isabella of Spain proposing a betrothal between their son Edward and an infanta of Spain. In mid-August they set off for the north, arriving at Pontefract on the twenty-eighth and the next day at York, where Edward joined them. There, on 8 September, he was created Prince of Wales. The ceremony was followed by a four-hour crown-wearing and accompanied by 'gorgeous and sumptuous feasts and banquets for the purpose of gaining the affections of the people'.[9] In breaking the convention of investiture at Westminster, Richard was offering a gesture of prestige to the northern affinity he had consolidated with his marriage and ensuring its loyalty to his family for the future.

According to Polydore Vergil, when Queen Elizabeth heard the news that Anne's son was created Prince of Wales, she 'fell in a swoon and lay lifeless a good while; after coming to herself she wept, she cried out loud and with lamentable shrieks made all the house ring. She struck her breast, tore and cut her hair and ... prayed for her own death ... condemning herself as a madwoman for that (being deceived by false promises), she had delivered her younger son out of sanctuary to be murdered by his enemy.'

The mystery of the princes in the Tower has generated a literature of its own, its ambiguities providing tantalising space for the insertion of all manner of conspiracy theories. Depending on which account is believed, twelve-year-old Edward and ten-year-old Richard were stabbed, poisoned, drowned in wine, walled up alive, thrown into the Thames, buried alive in a chest or smothered. Other rumours, exploited by later pretenders, held that they had escaped and been spirited away in secrecy, still others that they lived to adulthood under assumed identities. What is certain is that they disappeared, and the balance of evidence suggests that they were murdered some time after the coronation – at which point *The Croyland Chronicle*, supported by other accounts, asserts that they were alive – and Edward of Middleham's investiture as Prince of Wales on 8 September.

Elizabeth Woodville, for all that Vergil's account is dramatised, believed her sons were dead. She knew that her husband had had Henry VI killed, and may have been personally involved in the death of his son. She was all too well acquainted with the exigencies of civil war. It made no sense for Richard III to allow the boys to live, for as long as they did his throne would always be in jeopardy. Elizabeth had now lost her father, her first husband, two of her brothers and three of her sons in the battles for the English throne. Her subsequent actions can therefore be seen as a fight to preserve her own life and those of her daughters, whatever the cost.

In 1483, the only living Plantagenet heirs male were Richard III himself, his son Edward, his weak-minded nephew the Earl of Warwick, who was living in the household of Queen Anne, the Duke of Buckingham and Henry, the son of Edmund Tudor. Of them all, Henry Tudor's claim to the throne was the slightest. He had inherited a tincture of English royal blood through his mother, Margaret Beaufort, the great-great-grand-daughter of Edward III, and his grandmother Catherine de Valois gave him descent from Charles VI of France. Since 1471 he and his uncle Jasper had been living at the court of François II of Brittany. Their status in the duchy was precarious, varying from that of minor diplomatic pawns to 'honourable prisoners',[10] and Henry had narrowly avoided being sent back to England by faking an illness when Edward IV tempted François in 1476 with a marriage proposal for Henry, once again offering the hand of his eldest daughter, Elizabeth of York. That such a marriage was proposed so early is borne out by the fact that Margaret Beaufort and Edward IV held talks about potential problems of consanguinity. Lady Margaret had been determined for years to restore her son to the earldom of Richmond, his father's title. She had discussed the possibility with Richard before his coronation, raising the suggestion of a marriage between Henry and Elizabeth once again afterwards with the 'King's favour',[11] and she had shown her loyalty to the new Queen by carrying her train at her cor-onation. Despite their Lancastrian connections, Lady Margaret and her husband Lord Stanley were officially in favour – Stanley, a supporter of Hastings, was appointed steward of the royal household – but Richard did not entirely trust them. Stanley's heir, Lord Strange, had married a niece of Queen Elizabeth, and it was as much out of caution as a need for his services that Stanley was commanded to accompany the King on his northern progess.

Even as Richard III triumphantly celebrated his accession in the north, he was aware that conspiracies against him were simmering. His supporter the Duke of Buckingham had already been rewarded with significant offices in Wales and the marches, and on 13 July 1483 he had received a grant for a share of the Bohun inheritance (to which he was entitled through his great-grandmother Eleanor, wife of Thomas of Woodstock and sister to Mary de Bohun, Henry IV's first wife and mother of Henry V), a longstanding source of grievance to the Duke, as some of the Bohun lands had been given to Elizabeth Woodville. Buckingham had every reason to be satisfied with the fruits of his loyalty. But as the 'rumour was spread that the sons of King Edward had died a violent death', Buckingham 'repented of his former conduct'.[12] He may have been motivated by moral repugnance, or by the possibility that if Richard were deposed he himself would have a chance at the crown. Whatever the reason, he now, extra-ordinarily, became involved in a plan for an uprising led by Lionel Wood-ville and Thomas Grey, Marquis of Dorset. The Marquis had been in hiding after making a dramatic escape from Westminster sanctuary pursued by soldiers and hunting dogs, but the rumours of the Princes' death galvanised him into attempting to organise the disparate groups of Rich-ard's opponents into a coherent force for rebellion.

Someone else who had grasped the significance of the murder of the direct heirs was Margaret Beaufort. She perceived that her son Henry could now aspire to much more than the restoration of his earldom. The Duke of Buckingham had last seen Richard at Warwick on 2 August, from where he had travelled to Brecon to take custody of John Morton, bishop of Ely, who had been arrested with Hastings. Many later chroniclers attribute Buckingham's change of heart to Morton's influence. Lady Margaret sent her servant Reginald Bray to Brecon to parley with the Duke. She had also found a means of communicating with Elizabeth Woodville in the heavily guarded sanctuary. The two women used the same physician, Lewis Caerleon, who was still permitted to visit the Dowager Queen. Together, Margaret and Elizabeth formulated a plan based on Henry's marriage, a concerted rising by the English rebels and an invasion by Henry himself. Margaret, however, was playing a double game with Buckingham, leading him to believe that it was his claim she was supporting. Why else would Buckingham have been prepared to take the suicidal risk of rebelling in favour of a man who was virtually unknown? Furthermore, if Henry became king, the Woodvilles would have been assured of a return to power. According to Michael Jones and Malcolm Underwood, 'serious consideration must be given to the possibility that Margaret duped Buckingham, encouraging him to claim the throne him-self'.[13] This suggestion is given weight by the fact that when Buckingham declared himself by writing to Henry Tudor on 24 September, it was to invite him to join the rebellion without any reference to accepting Henry as king or to his future marriage.

In the event, the rebellion was a failure. The men of Kent rose on 10 October 1483, followed by groups in Newbury, Salisbury and Exeter. Richard was informed on the eleventh and ordered a muster at Leicester for 21 October. He offered free pardons to any rebels who were prepared to surrender and set rewards for the capture of Buckingham, Dorset and Lionel Woodville. Buckingham began an advance along the Wye Valley towards Hereford, but violent floods and Richard's blandishments kept many hoped-for supporters away, and he was reduced to escaping in disguise. Betrayed by one of his own supporters, he was taken into the custody of the sheriff of Shropshire. With news of the Duke's capture, the rebellion collapsed and Richard marched via Salisbury, where Buckingham was beheaded, to Exeter, arriving by 8 November, without meeting any resistance. Meanwhile Henry Tudor had sailed from Brittany and reached Plymouth, but on hearing of the disaster he had prudently turned back.

Margaret Beaufort was now in great danger, but she and her husband, Lord Stanley, had worked out a brilliant insurance policy. While Margaret had sided with the rebels, Lord Stanley had retained his allegiance to the King and, along with the Percys and their northern supporters, had marched in pursuit of the rebels with Richard. It was in recognition of Stanley's service that the Parliament of 1484 spared Margaret from attainder, and though Richard's proceedings against her were punitive, including the loss of her right to inherit her mother's lands, they were softened by many of her forfeited properties being regranted to Stanley. Moreover, Margaret remained in contact with Henry. After the failure of the rebellion, he had been joined in Brittany by many fleeing rebels, including the Marquis of Dorset and his son Thomas Grey and Lionel Woodville, who died soon afterwards. Edward Woodville had been part of Henry's circle since escaping Richard's routing of the fleet with his two ships the *Trinity*, and the *Falcon*. Other members of Henry's growing court were Sir John Cheyne, a former knight of the chamber to Edward IV, Peter Courtenay, a former royal secretary and now bishop of Exeter, and Sir William Berkeley, William Brandon and Sir Giles Daubeney, who had also served in Edward's household. It was before these men that Henry swore to marry Elizabeth of York in the cathedral of Rennes on Christmas Day. He also received the sworn homage of his supporters.

With Buckingham dead, Henry Tudor still exiled and Margaret Beaufort confined to her husband's household on the King's instructions,

Queen Elizabeth remained in sanctuary, reduced to living on charity and with her paltry resources stretched even further by the arrival of Buckingham's widow, her sister Katherine. In January 1484, Parliament confirmed Richard's rule and (to the disgust of the *Croyland* commentator), the illegitimacy of the marriage between Edward IV and Elizabeth Woodville. Richard took care to distribute the attaindered lands of the rebels between his northern supporters, further shoring up his now apparently unassailable power.

Elizabeth decided the time had come to accept the new order. The only leverage left to her was the embarrassment her continuance in sanctuary caused Richard, and before she was prepared to quit the abbey, the new King was obliged to swear an oath to the mayor and aldermen of London, in the presence of numerous magnates. On 1 March 1484, he announced that if 'the daughters of the said Dame Elizabeth Grey, lately calling herself Queen of England, will come out of the sanctuary at Westminster ... then I shall see that they shall be in surety of their lives and also not suffer any manner hurt by any manner person or persons ... nor any of them imprison within the Tower of London or any other prison'. Elizabeth, Cecily, Anne, Katherine and Bridget were now offi- cially bastards, and Elizabeth herself was forced to relinquish her rightful rank as Queen Dowager. Richard cancelled her dower and arranged that she would receive 700 marks annually, in quarterly payments, through the offices of John Nesfield, diminishing her to the status of a royal pensioner. Elizabeth's critics had always remarked on her excessive pride, yet now she was forced to humble herself and disparage her daughters before the man who had murdered her sons and her brother. But her remaining children were free, and they would live. That month, before her first year of mourning for her husband was over, Elizabeth and her daughters joined Richard's court.

In April 1484, the court was at Nottingham when the news arrived that Edward of Middleham, the newly created Prince of Wales, had died. He had always been delicate, and had been so ill at his investiture at York that he had had to be carried on a litter. Richard had deliberately left him behind in the north as a symbol to his most loyal adherents of the new regime to which they owed allegiance, but it was likely that he was also too ill to travel. He may have been suffering from tuberculosis, the disease that had killed his aunt Isabel of Clarence and would also claim his mother's life. Richard and Anne were described as being in a state 'almost bordering on madness, by reason of their sudden grief'.[14] To contemporaries, young Edward's death was seen as proof of the ungodliness of his father's rule. Did it give Elizabeth Woodville a certain bitter satisfaction?

From the available evidence, it appears that however much their marriage had been a calculation on both sides, Anne and Richard were united in being loving and interested parents. Edward had been wet-nursed by Isabel Burgh, then lived in the nursery at Middleham in the care of Anne Idley. Her story suggests that Anne Neville may have been concerned with modern theories of education. She was the widow of Peter Idley, an Oxfordshire esquire who had died around the time of Edward's birth. She had agreed to leave her marital home, Drayton Manor, in favour of her stepson William in return for an annuity of five marks, which William then refused to pay. When Anne became mistress of the nursery at Middleham, Richard himself wrote to the commission of the peace for Oxfordshire, ordering them to summon 'William Idley and Elizabeth his sister and demand them the cause why they contest and pay not to our right well beloved servant Anne Idley ... her annuity of five marks and advise them, as they would avoid our grievous displeasure, to see that she is as well thereof yearly contented as of that she is behind unpaid of the same'.[15] The letter shows an unexpected human side of one of history's most celebrated tyrants, the great northern magnate who was concerned enough about his son's governess to interfere in a few marks-worth of arrears. The Gloucesters may have particularly valued Anne because she had moved in educated circles. Her husband Peter had written a book, *Instructions to His Son*, a collection of verses with adaptations from the English writer Lydgate as well as Latin poets which gave tips on cleanliness, modest dress and manners and the importance of keeping respectable company. Little Edward could have been frightened into good behaviour with tales such as 'The Witch and her Cow-Sucking Bug'.

It is amply evident that Richard III was a man who valued power, and the strategies to obtain it, far above feeling. When Edward died, Anne had to confront her incapacity to fulfil one of the Queen's primary functions, the provision of heirs. Richard himself was confident of his fertility, and he now urgently needed another child, preferably a son. He had at least two acknowledged bastards, Katherine Plantagenet, who was betrothed in 1484 to William Herbert, Earl of Huntingdon, and died three years later, and John of Pontefract. Richard knighted John at York in 1483 and gave him the titular captaincy of Calais in 1485. John's mother was Alice Burgh (possibly a relation of Richard's wet nurse), who received an annuity of twenty pounds from Middleham revenues. This suggests that Alice was a local woman, and that Richard had therefore begun his affair with her after coming to Middleham on his marriage. Anne had little choice but to accept this blatant adultery, which was not, after all, uncommon, and the fact that she and Richard continued to sleep together until 1485 is another indication that their marriage was reasonably contented. However, when, after the loss of his heir, it became obvious that Anne could not do her duty, and provide him with another, Richard made it obvious he had no use for her. Early in 1485, he announced that he had been advised by her doctors to discontinue marital relations.

There is a convincing argument that Anne had inherited fertility problems from her own mother, who had given birth for the first time, to Isabel, at the advanced age of twenty-five, at least six years after her marriage was consummated, and bore her second child, Anne herself, aged thirty. The Earl (whose own family were famously prolific) and Countess of Warwick continued to live together until his death, but had no more children.

Anne's mother had received a papal dispensation in 1453 to permit her to eat eggs and meat in Lent while pregnant, as she was weakened by sickness and childbearing. This, and the fact that she lost the child she was carrying when the dispensation was granted, points to a history of miscarriage, and the brevity of her successful childbearing years could also be a sign of the late onset of puberty and an early menopause. Isabel of Clarence suffered a premature birth early in the Readeption, and she had two live births in seven years of marriage. Both Isabel and Anne died from tuberculosis, a disease which can affect the genitals and cause a condition known as tuberculous endometritis, an infection of the uterus and fallopian tubes which leads to infertility. This manifestation of the disease creates no obvious symptoms, so if Anne was suffering from it, her frustration would have been exacerbated by the absence of any sign that anything was wrong.

Richard's announcement that he had stopped sleeping with Anne was a dreadful humiliation. By this time everyone knew the Queen was ill; now the King was effectively declaring that she had failed as a wife, that he was waiting for her to die. It even appeared he had already selected her successor. At that year's Christmas court, something was noticed that 'caused the people to murmur and the nobles and prelates to greatly wonder thereat'. During the games, a great many 'vain changes of apparel'[16] were presented to Queen Anne and Elizabeth of York, and many jokes were made about the similarity of complexion and figure between the

Queen and her niece. The gossips were quick to suggest that Richard was planning to make Elizabeth his next queen before his ailing wife was yet in her grave. And, scandalously, horribly, Elizabeth of York was delighted.

The evidence for Elizabeth of York's direct involvement in a scheme to marry her uncle before Queen Anne was dead rests on a famously disputed account by the seventeenth-century historian Sir George Buck, a descendant of Sir John Buck, who died fighting for Richard at Bosworth. Buck's 1619 *History of King Richard III* contains a third-person version of a letter Buck claimed to have seen in the family collection of Thomas Howard, Earl of Arundel. The letter was written by Elizabeth of York to John Howard, the Duke of Norfolk, in an attempt to win his support for her projected marriage. Buck was a pro-Richard writer, and his history, particularly this aspect of it, has been questioned by many historians, as the original letter is lost and Buck's work was largely rewritten by his nephew before its eventual publication in 1646. To make matters even more complicated, the original manuscript was badly damaged by fire in 1731. Despite the fact that Buck dedicated his History to Arundel, who would therefore have been in a position to object to any invention or forgery, Buck's evidence of Elizabeth's active enthusiasm for the marriage was dismissed for a long time. However, a recent edition of the original manuscript has led to the conclusion that 'one can hardly doubt that Buck saw the letter and that his version is broadly correct'.[17] So what did Elizabeth write?

'She prayed for him [Norfolk] as before to be a mediator in the cause of her marriage to the King, who, as she wrote, was her only joy and maker in this world, and that she was in his heart and thoughts, in body, and in all. And then she intimated that the better half of February was passed, and that she feared the Queen would never die.'[18]

Apart from the obviously distasteful evidence of Elizabeth's eagerness for Anne's death, the letter implies two things. First, that this was not her first discussion of the subject with Norfolk. Given that she writes in mid-February, the words 'as before' support the rumours surrounding the plan at or just after the Christmas court where *Croyland* had remarked upon it. Secondly, the oddly indecorous phrase 'in body and in all' could be read as confirmation that she and Richard had already begun a sexual relationship. Perhaps Elizabeth meant that she intended to dedicate herself to the King and refuse any other suitor (her betrothal to Henry Tudor was a well-known secret), but if Buck's rendering is accurate, 'in body' seems quite physically explicit. Following *Croyland*,

Richard made his declaration that he had stopped sleeping with Anne in mid-February, just as Elizabeth was writing that her body belonged to him. Whether or not they were lovers, Elizabeth was clearly very pleased with the possibility of marrying the man who had injured her family so terribly.

Anne Neville died on 16 March 1485. Given the gossip, this was just too convenient. 'Why enlarge?' was *Croyland*'s cryptic comment, using the same device of turning enigma to emphasis employed by hostile chroniclers against Eleanor of Aquitaine. Such caution was politic, too, but it was widely believed that Richard had given his lingering Queen a helping hand. By the end of the month the scandal had spread so far that Richard was forced to issue a public denial. He had been advised by two of his most trusted counsellors, Sir Richard Ratclyffe and William Catesby, that Anne's Neville connections in the north would never stand for a marriage to Elizabeth of York, and that they would take it as evidence that Richard had murdered one of their own. Ratclyffe and Catesby also called for the opinion of twelve divines, who confirmed that the Pope could never grant a dispensation for such a clearly incestuous union. The unambiguousness of the caution his advisers were prepared to give the King, that 'if he did not abandon his intended purpose ... opposition would not be offered to him merely by warnings of the voice',[9] suggests that marrying Elizabeth was indeed his purpose, and that he cried off for fear of repercussions amongst his essential northern allies.

On 30 March 1485, Richard announced to the mayor and aldermen of London, who were assembled in the hall of St John's Hospital, Clerkenwell:

Whereas a long saying and much simple (foolish) communication among the people by evil disposed persons contrived and sown to very great displeasure by the King, showing how that the Queen as by consent and will of the King was poisoned for and to the intent that he might marry and have to wife Lady Elizabeth, eldest daughter of his brother ... the King ... showed his grief and displeasure aforesaid and said it never came into his thought or mind to marry in any such manner wise nor willing or glad of the death of his Queen ... For the which he admonished and charged every person to cease of such untrue talking on peril of his indignation.

To further rout rumour, Richard sent a message to Sir Walter Herbert, proposing for his sister. (Richard seems to have had a propensity for incest.

Walter, a son of the first Earl of Pembroke, was the brother of William, Earl of Huntingdon, who was betrothed to Richard's illegitimate daughter Katherine. The King would thus have become his daughter's brother-in-law.)

Queen Anne was buried in the sanctuary of Westminster Abbey. If Richard intended to raise any monument to her, events overtook his plans, and today the precise location of her grave is unknown.

Holinshed's *Chronicle* reports that Elizabeth of York was not permitted to attend Queen Anne's funeral. 'Her only joy' had sent her away from court, to Lord Stanley's estate in Lancashire. The choice of destination suggests that Margaret Beaufort had heard the whispers, possibly even that Elizabeth was pleased by the match, and wished to have her son's betrothed under her control. Canny as ever, Lady Margaret used the embarrassment of Elizabeth's continued residence in Richard's household as an excuse to take charge. Her prospective daughter-in-law's rashness had jeopardised her ambitions: Henry was insulted enough to consider a different marriage, but Lady Margaret wrote to reassure him. She recognised that marriage to Elizabeth was crucial to any hope he had of the crown, even if his own wounded pride did not. Elizabeth was then moved to Sheriff Hutton, one of the late Queen's Neville properties in Yorkshire, with her cousin the Earl of Warwick to keep her company.

Even before the Elizabeth scandal, Henry Tudor was making Richard nervous. In October 1484, Henry had moved to the court of the new French King, Charles VIII, in response to Richard's offers of military aid to his former protector the Duke of Brittany. With Richard as an ally, the Duke could no longer be trusted. In December that year, Richard ordered an investigation into the military capacities of his magnates, to ascertain how many men each could muster at twelve hours' notice, and issued a proclamation against Henry. Even as Richard flirted with Elizabeth at the notorious Christmas court, *The Croyland Chronicle* claims he knew that Henry was planning to invade the following summer. When Henry did indeed land at Milford Haven, on 7 August 1485, Richard professed himself joyful 'that now the long wished-for day had arrived, for him to triumph with ease over so contemptible a faction'. For both sides, the prospect of battle was a relief.

Henry's troops were at Lichfield shortly after 17 August. Richard set off from Nottingham on the twentieth after summoning a muster at Leicester. It was obvious that his support was waning, as of thirty-five peers who might have responded, only seven turned up. Both commanders employed contingents of foreign mercenaries, and though neither army was large, Richard's is estimated to have been the greater, over 5,000 men. On 22 August, they faced one another at Bosworth Field, an uncertain location on the Redmoor Plain between Sutton Cheney and Upton. For Henry, all depended on which way his mother's husband, Lord Stanley, would turn. Stanley had a force nearby but had not yet declared for either party, while his son, Lord Strange, was with Richard, a hostage to his father's good behaviour. Tudor mythologising portrays the events of Bosworth as the ultimate chivalric encounter, with Henry and Richard pitched against one another in single combat and the victor scooping the crown from the mud of the battlefield. Richard and Henry did not quite take one another on personally, but they came close. After an unenthusiastic start from both sides, Richard spotted Henry's banner and brought his own household troops around the perimeter of the field to launch a charge. Perhaps the rivals' swords actually touched; certainly both men had to stand and fight for their lives. The Stanley force now had to declare one way or the other. Sir William, Lord Stanley's brother and commander, was faced with an extraordinary individual choice, truly a choice that would change the course of history. With Richard cut off from the body of his men, engaged with Henry's bodyguards, Sir William made his decision. He brought down the full force of his 3,000 troops in a sweeping charge against Richard's men.

There is an oddly elegiac quality to Polydore Vergil's account of Richard's death. Bosworth is taken as one of those convenient, and contested, points of English history, the moment at which the medieval age ended and a new era began. To contemporaries, this would have been less than obvious. Bosworth was just one more skirmish in a conflict which had seen the reigning dynasty overturned four times since the start of the century, and historians have been arguing ever since about the accuracy and relevance of slotting this battle too neatly into a periodic categorisation. Yet there is an inevitably appealing neatness about Bosworth, a resonance of Hastings, of two men on a battlefield staking their lives for their claims to the crown, a beginning and an end. 'King Richard alone was killed fighting manfully in the press of his enemies ... his courage was high and fierce and failed him not even at the death which, when his men forsook him, he preferred to take by the sword, rather than by foul flight, to prolong his life.'

Richard's son Edward, the short-lived Prince of Wales, had been educated in the belief that his supreme duties were to his God and his king. His father had defied both. Peter Idley had warned of the dangers of trusting to fortune:

Shining as glass, that soon is broken . . .
Beware of that maid, for she is unstable,
Flee from her fast, and trust her never . . .
She is flattering and false and double of deed
And faileth a man ever at his most need.

CHAPTER 19

ELIZABETH OF YORK

*'A faithful love that did us both combine
in marriage and peaceable concord'*

Almost nine months to the day after her marriage to Henry Tudor, Elizabeth of York gave birth to a son at Winchester. Henry's choice of name for this first Tudor prince made the clearest possible statement of his ambition for his newly established dynasty. The baby was called Arthur. After Bosworth, Elizabeth had been instructed to make her way to London to join her mother, escorted by Sir Roger Willoughby. Meanwhile, apartments were prepared for her in Margaret Beaufort's house in Coldharbour Lane. Her betrothed husband had been in the capital since September, but it was not until 18 January that their marriage had taken place, after Thomas Lovell, the speaker of the Lords, had made a statement in the December Parliament requesting that Henry make good his promise. Why did Henry wait so long? Was he concerned about the stories of Elizabeth's relationship with her uncle and if so, did he decide to stall until there was no possibility that she was carrying Richard's child? Or was the King determined to separate his claim to the throne from his wife's, which, after all, was far stronger than his own?

The delay in crowning Elizabeth of York indicates the strength of the latter argument. Henry could not be seen to be assuming the crown through his wife. He had not quite snatched it from the bloodied earth of Bosworth Field, but it was essential that it appear his by right of conquest, rather than claimed through the line of Edward IV. A double coronation could be too easily interpreted as a sign of joint sovereignty. There could be no doubt that Elizabeth and Henry's marriage represented an alliance between two battling dynasties, as the papal bull read out in churches on Trinity Sunday 1486 made clear:

Understanding of the long and grievous variance, contentions and debates that have been in this Realm of England between the house of the Duchy of Lancaster on the one party and the house of the Duchy of York on the other party. Willing all such divisions following to be put apart by the council and consent of his college of Cardinals approves, confirms and establishes the matrimony and conjunction made between our sovereign lord King Henry the Seventh of the House of Lancaster of that one party and the noble Princess Elizabeth of the house of York of that other with all their issue born between the same.[1]

Henry, however, was keen to play down Elizabeth's blood claim and accordingly the commemorative medals struck for their wedding referred to 'a virtuous wife' being 'a sweet rose' and an 'ornament of her house'. Though clearly there were reminders here of her birth, the priority was to celebrate her virtue over her lineage.

Elizabeth was not crowned until November 1487, more than a year after the birth of her first child. By this time Henry had already had to deal with two plots against his rule, but 1487 produced the most serious challenge, the Lambert Simnel conspiracy. At the beginning of the year, it was rumoured that Elizabeth's cousin, Clarence's son the Earl of Warwick, who had been kept at the Tower since Henry's accession, had escaped and was hiding in Ireland. With Lambert Simnel – a nobody who had been persuaded by a priest named Richard Simons to impersonate Warwick – being acknowledged as the Earl by Margaret of Burgundy, Edward IV's sister, and John de la Pole, the Earl of Lincoln, Henry's exhibition of the real Warwick in London in February did nothing to scotch the story. Neither Margaret nor Lincoln necessarily believed that Simnel was in fact the Earl: for them the plot was simply a means of striking against Henry. Margaret supplied 2,000 troops for Lincoln, who arrived in May 1487 in Dublin, where Simnel was crowned 'Edward VI' on the twenty-fourth. By June Simnel had landed on the Lancashire coast. Henry raised a large army and defeated Lincoln's forces at Stoke on 16 June. The first Tudor king is usually remembered as a dour man, but his treatment of Simnel displayed a streak of humour. The pretender was put to work in the royal kitchens as a scullion, and eventually became quite popular, rising to become the master of the King's hawks. Lincoln had died at Stoke, and though Margaret of Burgundy was to prove a threat for years to come, it was only after the suppression of this last military challenge to his rule that Henry felt secure enough to anoint his queen.

The pageantry of Elizabeth of York's coronation was in keeping with the aim of minimising the significance of her personal claim. Henry had made a ceremonial entry into the city some days before, watched in secret by Elizabeth and his mother, so that when she made her formal arrival by barge from Greenwich (itself a departure from custom), he was able to welcome her to the city almost as though she were a foreign bride. Elizabeth was attended by her mother-in-law, Margaret Beaufort, rather than any of her own family, and there was a notable absence of Yorkist badges and decorations. One feature did signal a connection with Edward IV: a model of a huge, red, fire-breathing dragon, the symbol of the last of the ancient British kings, Cadwaladr. Contemporary genealogies show that Edward IV had been interested in proving his descent through the Mortimers from Cadwaladr who, in legend, was visited by an angel who told him that only the true King of Britain would one day recover the realm. Henry VII co-opted even this idea, also claiming descent from Cadwaladr and decorating the horse of Elizabeth's champion at her coronation banquet – Jasper Tudor, now promoted Duke of Bedford – with red dragons. In accordance with the practice of Catherine de Valois's coronation, Henry was not present for Elizabeth's crowning or her banquet, surveying both from behind a latticed screen draped with cloth of arras. In this concealment he was reinforcing her status by melding his public body with hers at the moment of translation, even though his choice of timing for her coronation struck a blow at queenly authority. In the fourteenth century, it had been considered essential to crown Philippa of Hainault before she gave birth to the heir to the throne. By delaying Elizabeth's ceremony until a year after Arthur's arrival, Henry undid nearly 500 years-worth of accumulated customary power. With the exception of Marguerite of France, whose husband already had an heir, and Anne Neville, whose queenship had not been foreseen, Elizabeth was the only English queen since 1066 to give birth to the King's child without first being crowned. It was marriage to him, he emphasised, that legitimated his heir, and that alone.

The continuation of the papal declaration of 1486 had affirmed that it was Henry's blood, and only Henry's, that could transmit a claim: 'If it please God that the said Elizabeth . . . should decease without issue between our sovereign lord and her of their bodies born than such issue as between him and her whom after God shall join him to shall be had and born heritors to the same crown and realm of England.'[2]

The aggrandisement of the Tudor line also extended to twitching at the details of the past. Henry had the headstone of Catherine de Valois's tomb replaced with one that mentioned her second marriage, to Owen Tudor, a gesture which retroactively endorsed his own family claim to royal blood. Officially, then, the Yorkist entitlement had died with the princes in the Tower. But suspicion and paranoia was to haunt the succession of Elizabeth's descendants for the duration of her husband's dynasty.

A week after Henry VII's coronation on 7 November 1485, an act of Parliament repealed the statute of invalidity against his mother-in-law's marriage and restored the Queen Dowager to her full status. Elizabeth Woodville attended her daughter's wedding, after which Henry confirmed her dower rights. The royal women then moved to Winchester for the spring while the King was on progress, and Elizabeth Woodville stood godmother at Prince Arthur's christening at the cathedral, which was also attended by her daughters Anne and Cecily, Edward Woodville and the Marchioness of Dorset. For once the Woodvilles had no need to feel like parvenus, for the new King's pedigree was more dubious than their own. Finally, after all her struggles, it seemed that Elizabeth Woodville was safe. Yet just a few months later, in February 1487, the royal council assembled to deprive Elizabeth of 'all her possessions. This was done because she had made her peace with King Richard, had placed her daughters at his disposal and had, by leaving sanctuary, broken her promise to those ... who had, at her own most urgent entreaty, forsaken their own English property and fled to Henry in Brittany.'[3] On 20 February Parliament granted her 400-mark annuity and she was registered as a boarder at Bermondsey Abbey. The Benedictine convent of Bermondsey was a sister house of the Cluniac foundation of 1082. Since the Cluniacs looked to William, first Duke of Aquitaine, as their tenth-century founder, Elizabeth, as the widow of one of the Duke's descendants, was entitled to a special offer of free board and lodging.

Officially, Elizabeth Woodville had voluntarily surrendered her lands and decided to follow the tradition of widowed queens by retiring to the contemplative life. But if this was truly the case, why would the partisan Vergil put out a report that reflected so badly on Henry? Francis Bacon's suggestion was that Elizabeth thought her daughter disparaged by the marriage to Henry 'not advanced, but depressed', and that she had therefore collaborated in the Simnel plot. One of the more absurd conclusions of at least one of Elizabeth's biographers is that 'it seems certain that she was actively working for Henry's overthrow'.[4] In February 1487, when Henry showed the true Earl of Warwick in the streets of London, he was clearly concerned about rumours of an invasion, but why would Elizabeth have involved herself in such a conspiracy? She had worked for her daughter's marriage, if not actually suggested it. Warwick was the son of her erstwhile enemy Clarence, the son, moreover, of Anne Neville's sister, and Anne's husband had murdered her sons. Elizabeth was far too seasoned in political intrigue to have believed in Simnel. There is strong evidence that Henry never seriously doubted her loyalty, either. Edward Woodville commanded 2,000 troops in Henry's van at the battle of Stoke (this factor is evaded by the suggestion that Elizabeth was acting alone), but why would Henry have proposed a third marriage to Elizabeth, as he did as part of the three-year Scottish truce signed in 1486, if he believed her intention was to overthrow him, and thereby her own daughter?

If the question of treason is dismissed, we are left with the theory that Elizabeth had deliberately impoverished herself and withdrawn from court at the very point of her daughter's triumph. Apologists for this explanation have claimed that Elizabeth's dower lands were in the right of the reigning queen, which is not only inaccurate but implausible, given that Henry had handed over the lands himself, and that Elizabeth was ill, of which there is no record whatsoever. The fact that Henry officially remained on good terms with his mother-in-law, suggesting her as a bride for James III, referring to her affectionately in official documents as 'our right dear and right well beloved Queen Elizabeth, mother of our dear wife the Queen', inviting her to court and making occasional grants such as fifty marks in 1490 for Christmas, does not necessarily indicate that Elizabeth's decision to live at Bermondsey was her own, merely that Henry knew any public appearance of disunity would be damaging to the royal family. He could keep Elizabeth at arm's length by inviting her to attend court in the full knowledge that he had made her too embarrassingly poor to do so.

Elizabeth was not even permitted to attend the 1487 coronation. Jealousy of Margaret Beaufort would hardly have kept her away. Her presence would have been an all-too-visible reminder of the past, and of the fact that Elizabeth of York was far closer by right to the throne than her husband. Even Elizabeth Woodville's champions have too easily accepted the theory that her retreat to Bermondsey was an elective choice to follow tradition of pious queenship, when all the evidence suggests that she, like Joanna of Navarre, was simply inconveniently rich. Henry wanted her dower and he shut her up in the convent to get it. Given what Elizabeth Woodville had endured, Henry's treatment of her was appalling, and it does not reflect well on Elizabeth of York that she apparently acquiesced so passively in his plans.

The last five years of Elizabeth Woodville's life were spent at Bermondsey. She did attend her daughter's next lying-in at Westminster in 1489, but aside from this her only notable excursion was in response to an invitation to meet the French ambassadors and her kinsman François of Luxembourg in November the same year. In April 1492, Elizabeth made her will:

> I Elizabeth, by the grace of God Queen of England, late wife to the most victorious Prince of blessed memory Edward the Fourth, being of whole mind, seeing the world so transitory and no creature certain when they shall depart from hence, having God Almighty fresh in mind ... bequeath my soul into his hands ... I bequeath my body to be buried with the body of my said Lord at Windsor according to the will of my said Lord and mine, without pompous interring of costly expenses thereabout. Item, where I have no worldly goods to do the Queen's Grace, my dearest daughter, a pleasure with, neither to reward any of my children according to my heart and mind, I beseech Almighty God to bless her Grace with all her noble issue and wish as good heart and mind as is to me possible. I give her Grace my blessing and all the foresaid my children. Item, I will that such small stuff and goods that I have to be disposed truly in the account of my debts and for the health of my soul as far as they will extend. Item, if any of my blood will of my stuff or goods to me pertaining, I will that they have the preferment before any other.[5]

It is a heartbreakingly pathetic document for anyone to leave, let alone a woman who had been a reigning queen consort. Two years later, Elizabeth died at Bermondsey on 8 June. On the tenth, the twenty-seventh anniversary of her coronation, her body was transported by boat to Windsor, accompanied by her friends Dr Brent and Prior Ingilby, the executors of her will. Also in attendance were two 'gentlewomen', one of whom was Grace, the illegitimate daughter of Edward IV. Only one priest and a clerk waited to receive the coffin. Two days later Dorset, princesses Anne, Katherine and Bridget and Edmund de la Pole arrived to hear a funeral service conducted by the bishop of Rochester. A clerk who witnessed the ceremony left a concerned account. 'There was nothing done solemnly for her saving a low hearse such as they use for the common people with wooden candlesticks about it ... never a new torch, but old torches, nor poor men in black gowns nor hoods but upon a dozen old men holding torches and torches ends.'[6] It was not customary for the King to attend funerals, and the Queen was about to give birth, but neither were the senior magnates represented and the dean of Windsor, though in attendance, took no part in the service. No one even bothered to ring the bells for the Dowager Queen. The sum of Elizabeth's memorial was forty shillings paid out in alms by Dorset.

Even if the family were complying with Elizabeth's request for a humble funeral, their negligence in arranging no Masses for her soul was extraordinary. By the late fourteenth century, the chantry tradition, which had been flourishing by the time of Eleanor of Castile's death 200 years before, had reached its peak. An increased attention to the doctrine of Purgatory, in which the soul was believed to linger before attaining the purity required to enter Heaven, meant that intercessory prayers and Masses were vital to the safe passage of a loved one's soul to Paradise. Fifteenth-century religious practice is characterised by this 'obsessive anxiety'.[7] Chantry foundations, essentially small chapels where funds could be willed to support intercessory Masses, were a form of private post-mortem insurance for the wealthy. Elizabeth herself had founded a chantry for two priests at her chapel of St Erasmus, Westminster, in the 1470s to pray for the royal family. To leave no such provision was a serious risk; indeed, 'to make a will without thought for intercessory prayer was near to heresy'.[8] Elizabeth's hope that her meagre possessions might serve 'for the health of my soul as far as they shall extend' gestures towards such provision, but given her evident poverty and the extravagant measures taken for most people of rank (47,000 Masses for Queen Eleanor in the first six months after her death, 10,000 for Cardinal Beaufort), it is literally rather damning that her family apparently made no efforts to augment her minimal arrangements.

Henry VII has always had a reputation as a grasping, miserly king, and his treatment of his wife's family does nothing to dispel it. Elizabeth of York's sisters, Bridget, Cecily, Anne and Katherine, were entitled by their Mortimer descent to a share of the Mortimer-Clare inheritance, but Henry quietly absorbed those lands into his own estates and did nothing to provide the princesses with dowries. This explains the relatively humble matches made by the daughters of Edward IV, for without dowries, diplomatic foreign matches were out of the question. Bridget gave up and became a nun at Dartmouth Priory, from where she corresponded with her sister for the rest of her life. Katherine married the heir of the Earl of Devon, William Lord Courtenay, and Cecily John, Viscount Welles, half-brother of Margaret Beaufort. For each of these marriages Elizabeth supplied her sisters with allowances of fifty pounds a year and £120-pound annuities for their husbands from her own privy purse. Katherine's marriage was tainted with scandal – her husband was imprisoned for conspiracy with the Earl of Suffolk – and Elizabeth arranged for the education of her children under Lady Margaret Cotton and provided them with clothes and necessities. When her elderly husband died, Cecily made a love match with a squire, Thomas Kyne of Lincolnshire, which outraged Henry, though he had only himself to blame, and Elizabeth and her mother-in-law stepped in to support the couple. Thomas and Cecily lived for some time at Margaret Beaufort's great country house, Collyweston, near Stamford, but they and their two children were eventually obliged to retreat for economy's sake to the Isle of Wight, where reportedly their circumstances were less than royal. When Cecily died in 1507, Margaret Beaufort paid for part of her funeral expenses at the abbey of Quarre, which was more than anyone had done for poor Elizabeth Woodville.

Elizabeth of York's relationship with her ambitious, domineering mother-in-law has been described politely as 'tinged with ambiguity'.[9] Publicly, their relationship was cordial – they even went so far as to have identical outfits made up for the Christmas court of 1487 and their award of Garter robes the following year, with a celebratory song composed for the occasion, and rooms were kept for the Queen at Collyweston. Elizabeth's first daughter, born in 1489, was named Margaret. The two women also worked together, as Eleanor of Castile and Eleanor of Provence had done, to protect Margaret from the perils of an early marriage when her betrothal to King James of Scotland was arranged in 1498. Margaret was just nine, and her grandmother particularly spoke from bitter experience when she expressed her fear that 'the King of Scots would not wait, but injure her and endanger her health'. Yet it is hard to imagine that a woman as jealous of her son, ambitious and interfering as Margaret Beaufort could have been anything other than an insufferable mother-in-law. In 1498, the Spanish ambassador reported the dislike between the two women and the 'subjection' the Queen was obliged to tolerate. Elizabeth and Henry apparently had a warm, loving and faithful relationship, but there was no question who was the first woman in the King's life. There was one interest in which the two women collaborated with apparent enthusiasm, and which, for Elizabeth, was a means of maintaining the traditions of her cultivated, literary-minded mother and her family: the development of printing.

The main figures in the Buckingham rebellion of 1483 had been Buckingham himself, Elizabeth Woodville, Margaret Beaufort and Henry Tudor, but their supporters were largely drawn from men who had served in Edward IV's household. Among the 1,100 gentry and merchant figures who petitioned for Richard III's pardon after the rebellion was the printer

William Caxton. It was Elizabeth's uncle, Anthony, Earl Rivers, who had done more than anything to promote Caxton's revolutionary printing innovations in England. Caxton's patron in the Low Countries had been Margaret of Burgundy, Elizabeth's aunt, and the first-ever printed book in English, the *Histories of Troy* shows Caxton presenting the text to Margaret in Bruges. The first book to be printed in England itself was Lord Rivers's translation of a collection of maxims in French and Latin by Jean de Teonville, published as *Dictes and sayings of the Philosophers*, followed by his translation of Christine de Pisan in 1478 and a book known as the *Cordial* in 1479.

Elizabeth Woodville was a keen literary patron, purchasing books from, among others, the chancellor of Cambridge University. Her copy of *The Romance of the San Graal* was passed down to her elder daughter, while Caxton's *History of Jason* was dedicated and presented to Prince Edward in 1477 to help him learn to read. Caxton noted Elizabeth Woodville's encouragement as 'the supportacion of our most redobted liege lady'.[10] The most intriguing connection with Caxton is his dedication to her of *The Knight of the Tower* while she was in sanctuary in 1484. In 1483, Margaret Beaufort had requested a copy of a French romance, *Blanchardin and Eglantine*, from Caxton, a text which remained with her throughout Richard III's deposition and which she asked Caxton to translate and print in 1489. Since Caxton's shop was located near Westminster sanctuary, it has been suggested that Lewis Caerleon, the physician used as a go-between by Margaret Beaufort and Elizabeth Woodville, may have smuggled the book to Elizabeth of York and her mother. The plot of *Blanchardin and Eglantine* closely mirrors the situation in which the imprisoned Princess found herself in 1483. With her betrothed husband in exile, Elizabeth, like Eglantine, had to remain steadfast in the face of her enemies while her beloved staked his life to fulfil his promise. In this, the transmission of books between royal women, which had always formed part of an informal network of patronage and power, becomes an instrument of female conspiracy in a gesture worthy of courtly romance. By later publicising the book, Margaret Beaufort was able to gloss over Elizabeth's unfortunate carry-on with her uncle and augment her family's prestige by guiding readers instead towards a romantic story which had parallels in fresh contemporary memory.

Elizabeth of York was also a customer of Caxton's (though Margaret, typically, took credit for introducing him to the King), as well as of his successor, Wynkeyn de Worde. *Eneydos* was dedicated to Arthur, Prince of Wales, and Caxton's final book, *The Fifteen Oes*, an appropriate selection of prayers from St Bridget of Sweden, was made for Elizabeth and her daughter Margaret. There is thus a connection between Margaret of Scotland's earliest vernacular commissions and Elizabeth of York's patronage of the first English printer, placing the patronage of English royal women at the centre of a movement whose impact, during the Renaissance, was to be felt all over the world.

The baby whose birth had prevented Elizabeth from attending her mother's funeral was named for her lost mother, but she died in infancy. Elizabeth was to lose two more children, Edmund in 1499 and her last child, Catherine, in 1503, but she gave Henry two healthy sons, Arthur in 1486, and Henry, Duke of York, in 1491, and two daughters, Margaret in 1489 and Mary in 1495. Henry may have been niggardly towards his sisters-in-law, but he was determined that the marriages of his children should consolidate the Tudor dynasty by connecting them to the greatest houses in Europe. Plans for Arthur's marriage began when he was just a year old, and in 1489 the treaty of Medina del Campo provided for an alliance between England and the united Spanish kingdoms of Aragon and Castile with the Prince's marriage to Catalina (Catherine), the youngest daughter of Ferdinand and Isabella of Spain. For Henry, this was not only a diplomatic coup, but an essential validation of his kingship. Catherine of Aragon, twice descended from John of Gaunt and the daughter of their Most Christian Majesties, was the most prestigious English royal bride since Catherine de Valois.

Arthur was the only one of Elizabeth's children she would live to see married, and the arrangements for the wedding are a further indication of her marginalisation at the court so effectively dominated by Margaret Beaufort. After a decade of diplomatic stalling, Arthur was married in a proxy ceremony to the Spanish ambassador Dr de Puebla at Woodstock in 1499. Elizabeth wrote fulsomely to Isabella of Spain:

Although we before entertained singular love and regard to your Highness above all other queens in the world, as well for the consanguinity and necessary intercourse which mutually take place between us, as also for the eminent dignity and virtue by which your Majesty so shines and excels that your most celebrated name is noised abroad and diffused everywhere; yet much more has this love increased and accumulated by the accession of noble affinity which has recently been celebrated between the most illustrious Arthur, Prince of Wales, our eldest son and the most illustrious Princess the Lady Catherine.

But it was Margaret Beaufort who sent instructions to advise the Infanta on English customs and behaviour, and who made a list for the 'convenience' of Elizabeth's household over the arrangements for the marriage. It was Margaret Beaufort who suggested that Catherine learn French as a means of communicating with her new family. Elizabeth of York already spoke French well, a reminder of the days of her early betrothal, after the treaty of Picquigny, when her father had teased her by calling her 'Madame la Dauphine', but it is often overlooked that she also spoke and wrote Spanish. Margaret Beaufort did not speak Spanish, and she was not prepared to be left out, so the Infanta and her mother-in-law would speak French. Margaret's intention to control the new Princess of Wales is also reflected in the arrangements she made for Catherine's household, in which several officials, the clerk of the signet, almoner and usher were shared with her own.

Before the marriage could take place, Henry was obliged to employ ruthless measures to convince the Spanish that he was able to maintain his rule over the kingdom. Lambert Simnel was not the only royal imposter. Since 1491, a young man named Perkin Warbeck, with the connivance of Margaret of Burgundy, the King of France and James of Scotland, had been presenting himself as Elizabeth's vanished brother, Richard, Duke of York. As in the case of Simnel, it is impossible that any of the powerful movers of the plot actually believed in Warbeck, what mattered was keeping alive the image of Henry VII as a usurper and its attendant insecurities. Warbeck was received in Scotland by James IV after a brief appearance on the Kent coast, where he failed to attract any supporters, and in 1499 he was arrested in Hampshire. For a short period he was permitted to live in Elizabeth's household, but Henry then committed him to the Tower. In a perfectly contrived piece of political theatre, Warbeck was then discovered to have been helping the Earl of Warwick, previously impersonated by Lambert Simnel, to escape. Warwick's claim had always been an embarrassment to Henry, and now he created an excuse to execute both fake and true pretenders. Elizabeth was hardly unaware of the brutalities of realpolitik, but Warwick's execution was a reminder that her husband could, if necessary, be as cruelly ambitious as her uncle.

Catherine of Aragon arrived in England in 1501, after a crossing that was dreadful, even by the standards of previous queens-in-waiting. She and Arthur were married on 14 November at St Paul's, after a nod to the Yorkist origins of the groom's mother in a progress down the Thames to the home of the indomitable Duchess of York, Cecily Neville. The wedding was followed by a week of pageants and tournaments, in which challengers hung their shields on a Tree of Chivalry, watched by the royal ladies from a specially erected stand in Westminster yard. Henry's famous meanness made itself apparent in the pageants, which featured great emphasis on four model beasts, two lions, a hart and an elk, with two men inside each. These were not new: Henry had simply had them painted up from previous celebrations. Relentlessly, throughout the week, the beasts appeared.

For Christmas at Richmond, though, Henry was prepared to spare no expense. Elizabeth of York might be paying her tailor a regular twopence to turn her gowns, but Richmond Palace (on the site of Sheen, which Richard II had destroyed in memory of Anne of Bohemia) was to impress the world with the very latest in Tudor taste and convenience. Inspiration for Richmond had come from Elizabeth's family. Edward IV's stay at the Burgundian court as the guest of Lord Gruuthuyse had been extremely influential. Fifteenth-century Bruges was far from the tiny outpost of civilisation in a barbarous land that Matilda of Flanders had known: 'The inhabitants are extraordinarily industrious, possibly on account of the barrenness of the soil, since very little corn is grown, and no wine, nor is there water fit for drinking, nor any fruit. On this account, the products of the whole world are brought here.'[11]

Burgundy was the capital of the Christian world for luxury, and Edward IV had come back to England intent upon replicating its magnificence. The reorganisation of the royal household in the 1470s was inspired by Olivier de la Marche, whom Edward had commissioned to write *L'Etat de la Maison de Charles de Bourgogne* (1473), a text upon which Margaret Beaufort drew for her own codification of etiquette for the Tudor court. As well as clothes, jewels and tapestries, Edward's building projects demonstrated Burgundian influence. At Nottingham, the royal apartments were constructed on several storeys, attached by a staircase modelled on that of the Princehof in Bruges, and at Eltham Edward built a gallery and a raised garden with a view of the river. At Richmond, Henry VII included the 'donjon' design for the royal apartments, enclosed gardens and open-loggia galleries. A new chapel featured a private closet for Elizabeth to the left of the altar, with the King's on the right.

In the Christmas celebrations floats shaped like ships, lanterns, castles and mountains carried costumed dancers and actors in direct imitation of Burgundian pageants. One wonders whether Elizabeth found her husband's over-earnest imitation of the Burgundian dukes slightly embarrassing. She had been born royal, he had not. As an exile, Henry had little experience of dealing with, or impressing, his English magnates. Surrounding himself with churchmen and civil servants may have earned him the accolades of posterity for his modernity, but his eagerness to follow his mother's strictures on court practice and his incessant money-grabbing was frankly rather middle-class. Edward had made his court 'the house of very policy and flower of England'. Elizabeth would have remembered the celebrations for the marriage of her lost brother Richard to the five-year-old heiress to the duchy of Norfolk in 1478, one of the great pageants of her father's reign, when St Stephen's Chapel at Westminster was hung in blue and gold, coins were thrown to the crowd from gold and silver basins and Princess Elizabeth had presented a gold 'E' set with rubies to the winner of the tournament. She knew a good deal more about regal display than her cautious husband and his fussy, exacting mother.

Whatever Elizabeth's private feelings about her Henry, she was publicly never less than entirely loyal to him. Her political involvement was minimal, as he evidently wished it to be, and she confined herself to educating her children in the exceptional tradition from which she herself had benefited and making small gestures of reconciliation towards former Yorkists, such as payments to servants of her father and a man who had assisted her uncle Anthony in 1483. However, she was prepared on occasion to defy the Tudors, as when a tenant of the Duke of Bedford appealed to her in a property dispute and she wrote to Henry's uncle using the sternest, most formal eloquence of her position. She practised small, rather touching economies – the gown-turning, wearing cheap shoes that cost under a pound and paying her ladies seven pounds per year less than they had received under Elizabeth Woodville. How much of Elizabeth's modest, pious, maternal image was due to her own nature and how much to Henry's fashioning is hard to judge, but her queenship was very different in style from her mother's.

If Edward IV was England's last medieval king, then Elizabeth Woodville was his ideal consort. Sifting the calumnies and fabrications which have dogged her reputation, she presents a picture of an intriguing, impetuous, tremendously courageous woman in contrast with whom her daughter is inevitably prosaic, very much a consort rather than a queen. Generalisations being a disease of conclusions, it perhaps does not do to compare Elizabeth of York too unfavourably with her mother, but perhaps it is not going too far to say that Elizabeth Woodville applied her energies to a tradition of queenship that stretched back to Emma of Normandy, while her daughter anticipated an era in which, for the first time in more than 500 years, queens were reduced to little more than decorative dynastic appendages. And yet Elizabeth of York was the grandmother of England's first queen regnant, Mary Tudor, and of her unique namesake, Elizabeth I. It is fair to say that there remains work to be done on her influence on both these women. Like her husband, Elizabeth of York had been educated in a hard school. It is unsurprising that she chose to live quietly, and keep her own counsel.

After Arthur's marriage in 1501, he and Catherine were sent, against Elizabeth's wishes, to Ludlow to play at government. But by 2 April 1502, Arthur was dead. Riding through the night, a messenger from the marches arrived at Greenwich at midnight, and Henry immediately sent for Elizabeth to break the news to her. Bravely, she told him: 'God has left us yet a fair prince and two fair princesses ... and we are both young enough.'[12] She then retreated to her chamber where she collapsed with grief, and Henry took his turn at comforting her. The Queen lived to receive her bewildered daughter-in-law, Catherine, back into her household and, just as she had promised, she conceived again. In January 1503 she travelled by barge from Hampton Court to the Tower for her final confinement. She died there, on 11 February, her thirty-eighth birthday, in the White Tower, shortly after giving birth to her last child, Catherine, who was not to survive. Henry 'privily departed to a solitary place and would no man should resort unto him'.[13]

On 11 June 1509, Elizabeth's second son, Henry VIII, married Catherine of Aragon.

CONCLUSION

The first text of Thomas Malory's *Morte d'Arthur* was printed by William Caxton a month before Bosworth field. If Bosworth may be taken, simply, as the date for the passing of the medieval age in England, then *Morte d'Arthur*, the chronicle of the rise and fall of Camelot, is that age's fitting elegy. Romance does battle with treacherous, grasping reality, and reality wins. Sir Lancelot, the greatest knight who has ever lived, dies grovelling in shame, starved and shrunken, on the tomb of his lord, while the only four knights remaining of Arthur's great brotherhood are dispatched to the Holy Land to die in battle with the Turks. Other kings will come, but as one Malory critic bluntly puts it, 'We are not interested.'[1] And the source of this desolation and decay? The catalyst for the fall of Camelot? A queen.

'And so . . . in a May morning, they took their horses with the Queen and rode a-Maying in woods or meadows as it pleased them.' Finely mounted in her green silks, Guinevere appears to us as vividly as a jewel-like figure in a book of hours, the perfect embodiment of queenly grace and courtesy. Yet the consequences of her adulterous affair with Lancelot bring about knightly failure and political collapse. What does Guinevere's portrait tell us about perceptions of queenship at the end of the fifteenth century? One way of answering this question is to compare Malory's image of queenship with that of a writer from the very beginning of the period, the Anglo-Saxon 'Beowulf' poet. His protagonist is a lone warrior with the strength of thirty men who defeats two monsters and is ultimately defeated by a third. While initially it may appear that the two texts are divided by a whole culture, as well as seven centuries, both stories consciously invoke a lost past, myths or romances which were familiar to contemporary audiences, both investigate and criticise that past's sense of 'heroic' values and both seek to make such questioning applicable to their contemporary audiences. 'Beowulf', too, is elegiac, in that it celebrates the passing of the pagan warriors and their monster foes whose time is over. Yet 'Beowulf' proposes an alternative, optimistic form of a new heroism, one that is characterised by the 'feminine' values of its queenly characters. In a sense, it anticipates the chivalric tradition that Guinevere's adultery dismantles.

But how does the analysis of these texts help us to an overview of English queenship from the period of the Conquest to the beginning of the sixteenth century? Surely 'Beowulf' and *Morte d'Arthur* are fantasies, escapist entertainments that served as distractions from ordinary life in the way that Hollywood films might do today? Yes and no. There is no reason to believe that Saxon or medieval audiences were any less sophisticated in their relationship with such entertainments than modern cinemagoers. They knew perfectly well that knights and dragons were not 'real', even if their world had more of magic and miracles in it than ours. Their fears, hopes and comforts were dramatised for them in storytelling and reading just as they are for us, and the creators of those stories were alive to the inferences and resonances that would be drawn from them. Malory, for instance, who had been in Warwick's company in the north in the 1460s, has the wizard Merlin foresee the early death of King Arthur's father, Uther Pendragon, and the consequent dangers to young princes represented by the ambitions of great lords – as topical a reference as one could wish for. Similarly, although the exploits of Beowulf take place in an ostensibly pagan world, the   poet adjusts the inclinations of his characters to the expectations of his audience, rendering them 'natural' Christians. What makes these texts relevant, when read against each other, to English queenship, is how both centralise queens as instruments of the ideal, for better for worse, and this in turn suggests a distinct shift in values with regard to the always anomalous status of feminine power within a patriarchal culture between the eighth and fifteenth centuries.

Though there are more female characters in 'Beowulf' than in any other Old English poem, it can hardly be said to be 'about' women. The exploits of Beowulf and his thanes explore an almost exclusively masculine world. Yet of all the female characters, the five referred to by name are all queens, who observe rather than participate in the enthusiastically bloodthirsty violence of Beowulf s adventures. Nevertheless, by their presence, their gestures and their position as victims of the heroic ethos, they are in a powerful position to offer both a comment on that ethos and an alternative to it. Essentially, they challenge the values of Beowulf's world, both as emblems of their human cost and as transmitters of a

Christianised world view which posits a new ideal of the heroic, in which battles are not fought against giants but against sin: 'The "Beowulf" poet mobilises feminine voices to prescribe a new model of heroism premised on turning the violent energies of heroic self-assertion inward.'[2] How is this argued in the poem? At first, the roles of the queens appear to be conventional. The women are presented as participating in traditional heroic life in three ways, as the gracious hostesses in their lords' halls, as the bestowers of treasure and as the peace-weavers. After Beowulf has slain the man-eating monster Grendel, Queen Wealtheow appears at the celebratory feast, elegant in her golden collar, reminding her husband to speak 'words of gratitude' and declaring that 'Here, each warrior is true to the others/gentle of mind, loyal to his lord? The thanes are as one, the people all alert/the warriors have drunk well/They will do as I ask.' She presents Beowulf with a collar, bracelets and rings, treasures which diplomatically evoke ancestral memories for Beowulf's people, the Geats.

But Wealtheow's poise is counterpointed by the examples of two other women. Before she appears, the warriors hear the story of Queen Hildeburh, whose political marriage collapses in the tensions between her marital and natal kin. She is pictured singing 'doleful dirges' over the corpse of her son, and is stripped of her treasure and returned to her own people. Hildeburh has failed as a peace-weaver, and the poet predicts the same fate for Wealtheow's daughter, Freawaru, whose marriage will fail to effect concord between the Danes and their enemies the Heathobards. Although women have a crucial role in the maintenance of the social order, the price of adherence to the old-fashioned ethos of heroism is simply too high. Beowulf himself refuses to marry, as for him incessant warfare is incompatible with domesticity, but this has severe spiritual and practical consequences. When Beowulf divests himself of his weapons in order to fight hand-to-hand with Grendel, it seems initially that his gesture is heroic, but in a sense he is reducing himself to the level of a monster – 'life within a cultural group ruled by the logic of the sword's edge is ultimately dehumanising'.[3] Beowulf's lack of a wife reflects his insistence on the 'old' heroic model, but he is left without sons, and with no woman to pass the mead cup in his hall he is unable to establish the necessary affective bonds between lord and thane. In his final encounter with the dragon, his men desert him and he is killed. His death is all the more poignant because he has no children, his heroic virility to all intents and purposes fails him at the last and, just as he had no queen to love him, there is no woman to mourn him.

In this reading of the poem, Beowulf is ultimately shown as an anachronism, albeit a glorious one. What is the alternative to the 'toxic'[4] violence of the heroic code? If traditionally 'feminine' attributes can be incorporated into heroism, then heroes can reinvent themselves. This is not to suggest that Beowulf is best advised to stay at home and take up weaving, but to absorb the more fluid understanding of gender roles that typified Anglo-Saxon culture. It has been proposed that sexual difference in the Anglo-Saxon world was less a result of biological distinction than of the way in which the individual accessed and interacted with power – sex was effectively dependent on status. In the 'old' code, such status was predicated on aggression, but it could, potentially, be spiritual. Spiritual militancy was a means of transcending gender: women could be *geworht werlice* (made male), through faith. Anglo-Saxon hagiography is rich with examples of 'transvestite saints', women who have overcome their biological femininity by attaining spiritual masculinity. The wisdom which was traditionally associated with women in Germanic culture, and which is frequently referred to in 'Beowulf was, when combined with Christian faith, a route to power and thus a crossing of gender boundaries. As the tenth-century divine Aelfric put it, 'If a woman is made manfully and strong in accordance with God's will, she will be counted among the men who sit at God's table.'[5] But what constituted spiritual as opposed to martial strength? In the section of 'Beowulf' known as Hrothgar's 'Sermon', the aged King advises Beowulf that the real enemy is not monsters and dragons, but 'secret temptation' and 'the seeds of arrogance'. Beowulf must 'learn the nature of nobility' if he wishes to achieve 'gain everlasting'; that is, battles are no longer to be fought only with swords, but with the will. If 'heroic' maleness can in this manner be associated with the 'feminine' qualities of the mind, the gender distinctions might meld into a new definition of 'heroic femininity' which offers a positive prospect for the future when compared with the deadly code of the fading Germanic twilight. If the arena of battle is relocated to the spirit, then peacefulness is rendered heroic, and 'Beowulf' can be seen as gesturing 'toward a new model of masculine heroism, one rooted less in external proficiency in war than in a cultivation of the inner self'.[6] As observers and critics, the queens of 'Beowulf' posit and endorse such a model.

In the centuries between the composition of 'Beowulf' and the *Morte d'Arthur*, it could hardly be said that pacifism acquired heroic status. The splendours of war bedazzled the fear of death and the elites of Europe continued slaughtering one another (and their unfortunate retainers) with familiar gusto. Norbert Elias offers a picture of the practical psychology of the warrior of the Middle Ages. '(He)not only loved battle, he lived in it. He spent his youth preparing for battle. When he came of age he was knighted and waged war as long as his strength permitted . . . His life had no other function. His dwelling place was a watchtower, a fortress . . . If by accident he lived in peace, he needed at least the illusion of war. He fought in tournaments and these tournaments often differed little from real battles.'[7] Several critics have pointed out the 'chronic form' of war and the 'universal uncertainty' it produced,[8] and the tension between knightly Christianity and its clerical form is at the centre of scholarly discussion on the definition, meaning and uses of chivalry. The world of *Morte d'Arthur*, for which Malory drew on the French romances that had been such popular reading matter with many English queens, largely endorses the 'knightly' version in its tales of gallant warriors, beautiful women and conveniently flexible aristocratic morality. (Casual encounters are one thing, but ladies of *family* quite another.) Early on, Sir Lancelot's view of the 'feminine' world of marriage is similar to Beowulf's own: 'But for to be a weddyd man, I thynke it not, for then I must couche with hir and leve armys and turnaments, batelys and adventures'. For Lancelot and his fellows, women might be a good excuse for fighting, but there is nothing feminine about heroism.

Then something odd happens. In Book Six, 'The Tale of the Sankgreal' (the Holy Grail), Malory abruptly shifts the moral focus of the Arthurian world to incorporate a version of heroism which looks very much like the one posited by the 'Beowulf' poet. Suddenly, earthly valour is shown as inferior to spiritual might; 'Goddys workis' take the place of 'worldly workis'. Chastity is now imperative, and even killing is off the menu: Lancelot declares that 'sith that he wente into the queste of the Sankgreal he slew never man nought shall, tylle that he come to Camelot again'.

Yet even as he raises the possibility of such a new form of heroism, Malory disenchants his reader. Lancelot fails in the Grail quest because of his sinful relationship with Queen Guinevere, and from that sin springs the disaster which overwhelms the world of the knights. As in 'Beowulf', it is the private world, the interior world, that is the real enemy, but whereas in 'Beowulf' the private is figured as a new battleground to be conquered, in *Morte d'Arthur* it is the imprudence of allowing the private into the public realm that brings destruction. Lancelot and Guinevere fail at the challenge the 'heroic femininity' laid down in 'Beowulf'. Malory does not quite condemn their relationship, but their love gives an opportunity for evil to slip into Camelot, just as Lancelot (in one of the sexiest passages in medieval literature) breaks the iron bars protecting the Queen's bedroom. The lovers are trapped and discovered, and now the world of 'private ambition and greed' represented by the wicked Mordred pollutes Arthur's kingdom with avarice and ambition, treachery and dissent. The values of chivalry no longer apply, the public good is overwhelmed by the personal and private. When Mordred and Arthur confront one another in their final showdown, Malory offers a vision of a world in which battle is anything but noble: 'That pyllours and robbers were corn into the fylde to pylle and robbe many a full noble knight ... And who were not dead all out they slew them for their harneys and their riches.' *Morte d'Arthur*, like 'Beowulf', takes place in a mythicised past; what Malory is presenting here is a window on the future, in a sense, his present.

If the queens of 'Beowulf' anticipate a form of feminine power, then Guinevere's end closes off the possibility of its achievement. She sees out her life as a nun at Amesbury, redeemed, but enclosed and powerless. Her spirituality is penitent rather than militant. Her laments recall the *geomuru ides*, the 'sad women' of Anglo-Saxon literature who, like Hildeburh in 'Beowulf', can do nothing but weep and mourn the destruction their men have wrought. Like Beowulf, Guinevere is barren. Beowulf's lack of heirs can be read as positive, as making way for the new type of hero the poem envisages through its queens, but Guinevere's childlessness can only confirm the ignobility of the future anticipated by the thieves who stream over the battlegrounds. If, then, we see these two 'historical' texts as casting a question and an answer, how does Malory's response in the fifteenth century allow us to examine the paradigm of queenship from the Conquest onwards?

The tension between the heroic potentiality of the 'Beowulf' queens and the ambiguous presentation of Guinevere in Arthurian literature corresponds with several of the dynamics discussed in relation to the lives of English queens. The source of this tension has been identified as the 'structural misogyny'[9] that characterised the era, in which powerful women were increasingly defined in terms of their 'masculine' attributes. Women could, and did, participate in politics, economic and religious matters at the highest level, but such participation was consistently figured in relation to the superiority of a masculine model. Hence the trans-gender poss-ibilities offered by heroic femininity anticipate the cultural case for the medieval virago, a 'third sex' of women whose power traversed the traditional confines of their role, a position which was 'unconsciously addressed in the legislation of the era, but that had never been overtly categorised'.[10] The sixth-century *Life of the Holy Radegund* confirms the potential of spiritual militancy signalled in 'Beowulf'. 'He wins mighty victories through the female sex and despite their frail physique He confers glory and greatness on women through strength of mind. By faith, Christ makes them strong who were born weak so that . . . they garner praise for their creator who hid heavenly treasure in earthen vessels.'[11] Yet while such possibilities were recognised, the figure of the virago remained troublingly anomalous, and it might be argued that in the period between 'Beowulf' and the *Morte d'Arthur* its connotations were increasingly negative.

A skilful queen could negotiate the ambiguities of the 'virago' label to her advantage. Confronted with rebellious French magnates during the minority of her five-year-old son, Eleanor of Aquitaine's granddaughter Blanche of Castile met with them on her bed, holding her child. This image – maternal, intimate, sexual and beseeching – convinced the magnates to support her, placing them in the position of chivalrous protectors, after which Blanche governed as actively as any man. In post-Conquest England, Matilda of Boulogne was able to manipulate the stereotypes of femininity in such a manner that in her case, 'virago' became a term of praise, in contrast with its negative use by the detractors of her rival, the Empress Matilda. Eleanor of Provence was positively commemorated as a 'virago', but anxieties about Isabella of France's sexuality and ruthless ambition again saw the description used pejoratively. By the fifteenth century, Marguerite of Anjou's desperate struggle for her rights earned her the sobriquet 'shrill virago'.[12] Considering Guinevere's portrayal in the fifteenth century, it would seem that the virago had descended from a richly able figure whose role as counsellor, peace-weaver and ruler in post-Germanic culture was accepted and honoured (if not unequivocally) to a transgressive fomentor of dissent who needed to be kept in her place. Malory is careful to display Guinevere as less an individual woman than the occupier of a role. His portrait of her exists because of the purpose it serves 'at the heart of the public/private clash which heralds and provokes the downfall of the realm'.[13] In a sense, she exists at all only insofar as she is a queen. When Lancelot rescues her from being burned at the stake, he rides 'straight unto Queen Gwenyver and made caste a kurtyll and gown upon her'. Lancelot cannot speak to her as a woman before he has restored her fitting apparel as a queen; she has no power of her own, merely that with which her role, literally, in this instance, covers her. Her position has superseded her personality, and when, as Lancelot's lover, Guinevere casts it off, the ramifications are terrible.

Morte d'Arthur's answer to the question posed by 'Beowulf' summarises a model of queenship from the eleventh to the fifteenth centuries in which queens' active authority slowly declines while their ceremonial, ritual role becomes increasingly complex and codified. The move from actual to symbolic efficacity of the intercession dynamic, as we have observed in the examples of Philippa of Hainault and Anne of Bohemia, the elaboration of ceremonies such as coronation, childbirth and churching fix the queen ever more firmly in her place, reducing her, like Guinevere in her kirtle, to a powerless image. Malory refuses the possibilities of heroic femininity opened up by 'Beowulf' just as he despairs at the passing of the chivalric world he celebrates. *The Morte d'Arthur* is, as we have seen, coloured by contemporary events. It is theorised that Malory diverted from his sources in the tale of the 'Knight of the Cart' to reflect Marguerite of Anjou's 'Queen's gallants', who died for her at Blore's Heath, in Guinevere's company of 'Quene's knyghts'.[14] This is not to suggest that Malory believed the violence and conflict of 1485 was brought about by a queen, but, as noted in the case of Eleanor of Provence, a foreign queen was always the preferred scapegoat in times of conflict, and perhaps it is not going too far to say that the diminution in queens' actual power by the fifteenth century, as best exemplified by Elizabeth of York, was correlated to the anxieties provoked by the paradoxical figure of the virago.

And yet. The sixteenth century was to see England's first queen regnant, and in the figure of Elizabeth Tudor its most heroic female of all. Any dynamic of slow decline in queenly power from the Anglo-Norman period to the fifteenth century is abruptly arrested by a peek into the future. Compared with Wealtheow at the beginning of the period, Guinevere is a pessimistic queenly model for its end, but while Thomas Malory may have been despondent about the possibilities of queenship, the political and cultural legacies of all the women discussed combined to inaugurate perhaps the greatest period of female power in England before the twentieth century.

SELECT BIBLIOGRAPHY

PRIMARY SOURCES

Adam of Eynsham, *Magna Vita Sancti Hugonis*, ed. D.L. Douie and D.H. Farmer (Oxford, 1985)

Adam of Usk, *Chronicon Adae de Usk*, ed. Edward Thompson (London, 1866)

Adams, N. and Donahue, C. (eds.), *Select Cases from the Ecclesiastical Courts of the Province of Canterbury* Donohue (London, 1981)

Aelred of Rievaulx, '*Genealogia Regum Anglorum*' in *Chronicles of the Reigns of Stephen, Henry II and Richard I*, ed. Richard Howlett (Rolls Series, London, 1884)

Ambroise, *Histoire de la Guerre Sainte*, ed. G.Paris (Paris, 1897)

Andreas Capellanus, *Tractatus de Amore et de Amoris Remedio*

Anselm, *Opera: S. Anselmi Opera Omnia* (6 vols.), ed. F. S. Schmitt (Edinburgh, 1938–61)

Aungier, G. (ed.), *The French Chronicle of London* (London, 1844)

Bacon, Francis *The History of the Reign of King Henry the Seventh*, ed. R. Lockyer (London, 1972)

Le Baker, Geoffrey, *Chronicon Galfridi le Baker de Swynebroke*, ed. E. Maunde (London, 1909)

Bates, David (ed.), *Regesta Regum Anglo-Normannorum: The Acta of William I* (Oxford, 1998)

Bernard of Clairvaux, *Letters*, trans. B.S. James (Stroud, 1998)

Blackley, F.D. and Hermansen, G. (eds.), *The Household Book of Queen Isabella* (Edmonton, 1971)

Bliss, W.H. (ed.), *Calendar of Papal Registers Relating to Great Britain and Ireland* (London, 1893)

Bond, E.A. (ed.), *The Chronicle of Meaux* (3 vols.) (Rolls Series, London, 1866)

Bouquet, M. (ed.), *Recueil des Historiens des Gaules et de la France* (24 vols.) (Paris, 1869–1904)

Brie, F.W.D. (ed.), *Brut Chronicle* (2 vols.) (London, 1906)

Brown, R. (ed.), *Calendar of State Papers – Venice 1202–1509* (London, 1864)

Bruce, J. (ed.), *Historie of the Arrivall of Edward IV in England and the Final Recoverye of his Kingdomes from Henry VI* (London, Camden Society, 1838)

Calendar of the Close Rolls, Edward I, Edward II and Edward III, preserved in the Public Record Office (24 vols.) (London, 1892–7)

Calendar of the Close Rolls 1447–1500 (London, 1941)

Campbell, Alistair (ed. and trans.), *Encomium Emmae Reginae* (3rd Series, London, Camden Society, 1949)

Capgrave, John, *Chronicle*, ed. Peter J. Lucas (Oxford, 1983)

Charters and Custumals of the Abbey of Holy Trinity, Caen (ed.) (London, Oxford University Press for the British Academy, 1982)

Chibnall, Marjorie, *The World of Orderic Vitalis* (Oxford, 1984)

Childs W.R. and Taylor, J. (eds.), *The Anominalle Chronicle, 1307–1344* (Leeds, 1991)

Cole, H. (ed.), *Documents Illustrative of English History in the Thirteenth and Fourteenth Centuries* (London, 1844)

De Commines, Philippe, *Mémoires* (3 vols.), ed. J. Calmette and G. Durville (Paris, 1923)

Courthope, W.H. (ed.), *The Rows Rolls* (1859)

Crawford, Anne (ed.), *Letters of the Queens of England, 1100–1547* (Stroud, 1994)

Creton, Jean, *Histoire du Roi d'Angleterre Richard, Archaelogia* Vol. 20 (1824)

Croyland Chronicle: Ingulph's Chronicle of the Abbey of Croyland, trans. Henry Thomas Riley (London, 1908)

Delisle, L. and Berger, E. (eds.) *Recueil des Actes de Henry II, Roi d'Angleterre ed Duc de Normandie* (4 vols.) (Paris, 1909)

Delisle, Leopold (ed.), *Catalogue des Actes de Philippe Auguste* (Paris, 1856)

Denholm Young, N. (trans.), *Vita Edwardi Secundi* (London, 1957)

De Deuil, Odo, *De Ludovici VII Francorum Regis*, trans. and ed. Virginia D. Berry (New York, 1948)

Devon, F. (ed.), *Extracts from the Issue Rolls of the Exchequer* (London, 1837)

Dickinson, William Croft (ed.), *The Chronicle of Melrose Abbey* (London, 1936)

Douglas, D.C. and Greenaway, G.W. (eds.), *English Historical Documents* (Vol. 2, c. 1042–1189) (London, 1953)

Eadmer of Canterbury, *Historia Novorum in Anglia*, ed. Martin Rule (London 1866)

Edwards, E. (ed.) *Hyde Chronicle (Liber Monasterii de Hyda)* (London, 1866)

Ellis, Henry (ed.), *Three Books of Polydore Vergil's English History* (London, 1844)

De l'Estoile, Pierre, *Mémoires* (11 vols.), ed. G. Brunet (Paris, 1888)

Fabyan, Robert, *The New Chronicles of England and France* (London, 1811)

Farrer, William (ed.) *An Outline Itinerary of Henry I* (Oxford, 1919)

Fauroux, M. (ed.), *Recueil des Actes des Ducs de Normandie* (Rouen, 1961)

Foedera, Conventiones, Literae et cujuscumque generis Acta Publica 1066–1383 (Rymer's

Foedera) (20 vols.), ed. Thomas Rymer, 1704; 4 vols. ed. Adam Clarke, J. Caley, F. Holbrooke, J.W. Clarke, T.Hardy (London, 1816)

Froissart, Jean, *Chroniques* (4 vols.) (Paris, 1869–1966)

Gairdner, J. (ed.), *Memorials of King Henry the Seventh* (RS10, London, 1858)

Galbraith, V.H. (ed.), *The Anominalle Chronicle 1331–1388* (Manchester, 1927)

Geoffrey of Monmouth, *History of the Kings of Britain*, trans. L. Thorpe (Harmondsworth, 1966)

Gervase of Canterbury, *The Historical Works of Gervase of Canterbury*, ed.W. Stubbs, (2 vols.) (London, 1879)

Gesta Stephani, ed. R.C.H. Davis (London, 1976).

Giles, J.A. (ed.), *Incerti Scriptoris Chronicon Angliae (Giles's Chronicle)* (London, 1948)

Giraldus Cambrensis, *Opera*, ed. J.S. Brewer, J.F. Dimmock, G.F. Warner (Rolls Series 21, London, 1861)

Giry, Arthur (ed.), *Les Etablissements de Rouen Etudes sur l'histoire des institutions municipales de Rouen* (Vol. 55) (Bibliothèque de l'Ecole des Hautes Etudes, Rouen, 1883)

Given-Wilson, Chris (ed. and trans.), *Chronicles of the Revolution 1397–1400* (Manchester, 1993)

Gower, John, *The English Works of John Gower*, ed. G.C. Macaulay (London, 1901)

Gransden, Antonia (ed. and trans.) *The Chronicle of Bury St Edmunds (Chronica Buriensis) 1212–1301* (London, 1964)

Hall, Edward, *Chronicle*, ed. H. Ellis (London, 1809)

Hamilton Wylie, J. (notes by), 'Memorandum concerning a proposed marriage between Henry V and Catherine of France in 1414', *English Historical Review* (No. 114, Vol. 29) (April 1914)

Hardyng, John, *The Chronicle of John Hardyng*, ed. H. Ellis (London, 1812)

Hector, L.C and Harvey, Barbara (eds. and trans.), *The Westminster Chronicle* (Oxford, 1982)

Henry of Huntingdon, *Historia Anglorum*, ed. Thomas Arnold (London, 1879)

Herald of Sir John Chandos, *The Life of the Black Prince*, ed. M.K. Pope and E.C. Lodge (Oxford, 1910)

Higden, Ranulph, *The Polychronicon*, ed. C. Babington and J.R. Lumby (Rolls Series 41, London, 1864)

Hinds, A.B. (ed.), *Calendar of State Papers and Manuscripts Relating to English Affairs Existing in the Archives and Collections of Milan* (London, 1912)

Holinshed, Raphael, *Holinshed's Chronicles of England, Scotland and Ireland* (6 vols.) (New York, 1965)

Idley, Peter, *Instructions to his Son*, ed. Charlotte d'Evelyn (Lancaster PA, 1935)

Jeanroy, Alfred (ed.) *Les Chansons de Guillaume IX* (Paris, Honoré Chapman, 1913)

John of Reading, *Chronica*, ed. J. Tait (Manchester, 1914)

John of Salisbury, *Historia Pontificalis*, ed. Marjorie Chibnall (Oxford, 1986)

The Letters of John of Salisbury, ed. C.N.L. Brooke and W.J. Millor (Oxford, 1979)

John, Fenn and Hind, Archer (eds.) *The Paston Letters* (2 vols.) (London, J.M. Dent & Sons, 1938)

Kingsford, C.L. (ed.), *The First English Life of Henry V* (Oxford, 1911) *The Chronicles of London* (London, 1905)

English Historical Literature in the Fifteenth Century (Oxford, 1913)

Langtoft, Pierre, *The Chronicle of Pierre de Langtoft* (2 vols.), ed. T. Wright (Rolls Series 47, London, 1866)

Legg, L.G.W. (ed.), *English Coronation Records* (London, 1901)

London Society of Antiquaries, *A Collection of Ordinances and Regulations for the Royal Household* (London, 1790)

Luard, H.R. (ed.), '*Annals of Waverley*' in *Annales Monsatici* (5 vols.) (Rolls Series, London, 1864)

Lumby, J.R. (ed.), *Knighton Chronicle* (Rolls Series, London, 1889)

Mancini, Domenico, *The Usurpation of Richard III*, ed. C.A.J. Armstrong (Oxford, 1969)

Map, Walter, *De Nugis Curialium*, ed. C.N.L. Brooke and Roger Mynors (Oxford, 1983)

Maxwell, Herbert R. (ed. and trans.), *The Chronicle of Lanercost* (Glasgow, 1913)

De Mezières, Philippe, *Letter to King Richard II*, ed. G.W. Coopland (Liverpool, 1975)

Michaud and Poujouillet (eds.), *Histoire de Charles VI, Roy de France* (Paris, 1836)

More, Thomas, *The History of Richard III*, ed. Richard S. Sylvester (New Haven, 1963)

Morey, Adrian and Brooke, C.L. (eds.), *Gilbert Foliot and his Letters* (Cambridge, 1965)

Muhlberger, Stephen, *Chronicle of St Denis* (2001), trans. *Chronique du Religieux de Saint-Denys*, ed. M.L. Bellguelet (Paris, 1839)

Murimuth, Adam, Chronicon and Continuatio chronicarum, ed. E.M. Thompson (Rolls Series, London, 1889)

Myers, A. R. (ed.), *The Household of Edward IV* (Manchester, 1959)

Nicholas, H. (ed.), Chronicle of London 1089–1483 (London, 1827)

Nichols, J. (ed.), *Wills of the Kings and Queens of England* (London, 1780)

Nicholson, H. (trans.), *Chronicle of the Third Crusade (Itinerarium Peregrinorum et Gesta Regis Ricardi)* (Aldershot, 1997)

Nicolas, N.H. (ed.), *Privy Purse Expenses of Elizabeth of York* (London, 1830)

Noble Stone, Edward (trans.), 'The Chronicle of Rheims' in *Three Old French Chronicles* (Seattle, 1939)

Opus Chronicorum Chronica Johannis de Trokelowe, ed. Henry Thomas Riley (London, 1866)

Orderic Vitalis, *The Ecclesiastical History of Orderic Vitalis*, ed. Marjorie Chibnall, (Oxford 1969–80)

Paris, Matthew, *Matthaei Parisiensis, Monachi Sancti Albani, Chronica Majora* (7 vols.), ed. H.R. Luard (London, 1872)

Historia Anglorum (3 vols.), ed. Frederick H. Madden (Rolls Series, London, 1866)

De Perseigne, Adam, *Lettres*, ed. J. Bonet (Paris, 1960)

Three Chronicles of the Reign of Edward IV, ed. Keith Dockray (Gloucester, 1988)

De Pisan, Christine *The Treasury of the City of Ladies*, trans. S. Lawson (Harmondsworth, 1985)

Le Poitevin, Richard, *Ex Chronico, Recueil des Histoires de Gaules et de la France* (24 vols.), ed. Leopold Delisle (Paris, 1738–1904)

De Poitiers, Guillaume, *Histoire de Guillaume le Conquérant*, ed. R. Foreville (Paris, 1952)

Pollard, A.F. (ed.), *The Reign of Henry VII from Contemporary Sources* (London, 1913)

Pronay, N. and Cox, J. (eds.), *The Croyland Chronicle Continuations* (London, 1986)

Ralph of Coggeshall, *Chronicum Anglicanum*, ed. J. Stevenson (Rolls Series 66, London, 1875)

Ralph of Diceto, *Opera Historica*, ed. W. Stubbs (Rolls Series 68, London, 1876)

Ramsay, H., *Lancaster and York: A Century of English History* (2 vols.) (Oxford, 1892)

Richard of Devizes, *Chronicon de Tempore Regis Ricardi Primi*, ed. R.G. Howlett (Rolls Series 3, London, 1886)

Robert of Torigny, 'Chronica' in *Chronicles of the Reigns of Stephen, Henry II and Richard I*, ed. Richard Howlett (Rolls Series, London, 1884)

Roger of Howden, *Gesta Henrici II et Ricardi I* (2 vols.), ed. W. Stubbs (Rolls Series 49, London, 1868)

Chronica (4 vols.), ed. W. Stubbs (Rolls Series 51, London, 1867)

Roger of Wendover, *Flores Historiarum*, ed. H.G. Hewlett (Rolls Series 84, London, 1887)

Rothwell, H. (ed.), *English Historical Documents* (Vol. 3) (London, 1975)

Round, J.H. (ed.), *Calendar of Documents preserved in France, illustrative of the History of Great Britain and Ireland* (Vol. 1) (London, 1899)

St Albans Chronicle (Gesta Abbatum Monasterii Sancti Albani) (3 vols.), ed. Henry Thomas Riley (London, 1867)

De Saussure Duls, Louisa, *Richard II in the Early Chronicles* (The Hague, Mouton, 1975)

Scott Moncrieff, C.K. (trans.), *The Letters of Abelard and Heloise* (New York, 1974)

Shirley, J. (ed.), *Parisian Journal 1406–1449* (London, 1968)

Sinclair, Alexandra (ed.), *The Beauchamp Pageant*, (Donington, 2003)

Smith, David M. (ed.), *Guide to the Bishops' Registers of England and Wales* (London, 1981)

Sneyd, Charlotte (trans.), *A Relation of the Island of England about the Year 1500* in

C.H. Williams (ed.), *English Historical Documents 1485–1558* (London,1967)

Stubbs, W. (ed.), *Annales Londonienses* (Rolls Series, London, 1882)

Annales Paulini (Rolls Series, London, 1882)

'*Gesta Edwardi*' *de Carnarvon auctore Canonico Bridlingtoniensi*' in *Chronicles of the Reigns of Edward I and Edward II* (2 vols.) (Rolls Series, London, 1882)

Swanton, Michael (trans. and ed.), *The Anglo-Saxon Chronicles* (London, 2000)

Taylor, Frank (ed.), *The Chronicle of John Strecche for the Reign of Henry V 1414–1422 from the 5th Book of the Historica Regnum* (London, 1932)

Thomas, A.H. and Thornley, I.D. (eds.), *The Great Chronicle of London* (London, 1938)

Thompson, Peter E. (ed. and trans.), *Contemporary Chronicles of the Hundred Years' War from the Works of Jean le Bel, Jean Froissart and Enguerrand de Monstrelet* (London, 1966)

De la Tour-Landry, Geoffrey, *The Book of the Knight of the Tower*, trans. W. Caxton, ed. M.Y. Offord (London, 1971)

Des Ursins, Juvenal, Histoire de Charles VI, Roy de France' in *Nouvelle Collection de Mémoires sur l'Histoire de France* (Paris, 1836)

Walsingham, Thomas, *Historia Anglicana*, ed. H.T. Riley (London, 1862)

Walter of Guisborough, *The Chronicle of Walter of Guisborough*, ed. H. Rothwell (London, 1957)

Warkworth, John, *A Chronicle of the First Thirteen Years of the Reign of Edward the Fourth*, ed. James Orchard Halliwell (London, 1839)

Whitelock, D. (ed.), *English Historical Documents* (Vol. 1, c. 500–1042) (London, 1953)

William of Jumièges, *Gesta Normanorum Ducum*, ed. and trans. E. Van Houts (Oxford, 1992)

William of Malmesbury, *Gesta Regum Anglorum*, Vol. 1 ed. and trans. R.A.B. Mynors (Oxford, 1998); Vol. 2 ed. R.M. Thomson and M. Winterbottom (Oxford, 2002)

Historia Novella, trans. K.R. Potter, ed. Emund King (Oxford, 1999)

Gesta Pontificum Anglorum, trans. David Preest (Oxford, 2002)

William of Newburgh, '*Historia Rerum Anglicarum*' (2 vols.) in *Chronicles and Memorials of the Reigns of Stephen, Henry II and Richard I*, ed. R.G. Howlett (Rolls Series 82, London, 1884)

William of Tyre, *A History of Deeds Done Beyond the Sea*, ed. E. Babcock and A.C. Krey (New York, *1943*) *Guillaume de Tyr et ses Continuateurs* (2 vols.) (Paris, 1879)

Woodruff, C. Eveleigh (ed.), *Canterbury Cathedral Chronicle (Archaelogia Cantania)* (London, 1911)

Wright, Thomas (ed.), *Political Poems and Songs relating to English History, composed during the Period from the Accession of Edward III to that of Richard III* (London, 1861)

SECONDARY SOURCES

VOLUMES

Aries, Philippe, *Centuries of Childhood*, trans. Robert Baldick (London, Jonathan Cape, 1962)

Ashe, G., *The Virgin* (London, 1976)

Backhouse, J., *The Bedford Hours* (London, 1990)

Baldwin, David, *Elizabeth Woodville: Mother of the Princes in the Tower* (Sutton, Stroud, 2002)

Bard, Rachel, *Navarre, The Durable Kingdom* (Reno, 1982)

Bartlett, Robert, *England under the Norman and Angevin Kings* (Oxford, Clarendon Press, 2000)

Bautier, Robert-Henri, *Etudes sur la France capetienne* (London, 1992)

Belozerskaya, Marina, *Rethinking the Renaissance: Burgundian Arts Across Europe* (Cambridge University Press, 2002)

Bennett, Michael, *Richard II and the Revolution of 1399* (Stroud, 1999)

Binski, Paul, *Westminster Abbey and the Plantagenets* (New Haven, Yale University Press, 1995)

Blamires, Alcuin, *The Case for Women in Medieval Culture* (Oxford, 1997)

Bloch, Howard R., *Medieval Misogyny and the Invention of Western Romantic Love* (Chicago, 1991)

Boase, Roger, *The Origin and Meaning of Courtly Love* (Manchester University Press, 1977)

Bothwell, J.S., *The Age of Edward III* (York, 2001)

Du Boulay, F.R.H., *An Age of Ambition: English Society in the Late Middle Ages* (London, 1970)

Bouton, A., *La Vie Tourmentée de la Reine Berengere*, Vie Mancelle No. 45 (1964)

Brooke, Christopher N.L., *The Medieval Idea of Marriage* (Oxford, 1989)

Brooks, Janice Young, *The Plantagenets of England* (New York, 1975)

Brown, Allen R., *The Normans and the Norman Conquest* (London, 1969)

Brown, Elizabeth A.R., 'Eleanor of Aquitaine: Parent, Queen and Duchess' in *Eleanor of Aquitaine, Patron and Politician*, ed. Kibler

Brundage, James, 'Sex and Canon Law' in *The Handbook of Medieval Sexuality*, ed. Bullough and Brundage (New York, 1996)
Law, Sex and Christian Society in Medieval Europe (Chicago, 1987)

Carmi Parsons, John *Eleanor of Castile: Queen and Society in Thirteenth Century England* (New York, 1995)
Medieval Queenship (ed.) (Stroud, 1994)

Carmi Parsons, John and Wheeler, Bonnie (eds.), *Eleanor of Aquitaine: Lord and Lady* (Basingstoke, Palgrave Macmillan, 2002)
Medieval Mothering (New York, 1996)

Carpenter, Christine, *The Wars of the Roses: Politics and the Constitution in England c. 1437–1509* (Cambridge, Cambridge University Press, 1997)

Chambers, James, *The Norman Kings* (London, 1981)

Chaplais, Pierre, *Piers Gaveston* (Oxford, 1995)

Chardon, Henri, *Histoire de la reine Berengere, femme de Richard Coeur de Lion* (Le Mans, 1866)

Chibnall, Marjorie, *Anglo-Norman England* (Oxford, 1986)
The Empress Matilda: Queen Consort, Queen Mother and Lady of the English (Oxford, Blackwell, 1993)

Collins, Roger, *Early Medieval Spain* (New York, 1995)

Colvin, H.M. (ed.), *The History of the King's Works* (6 vols.) (London, 1963)

Cosandey, Fanny, *La reine de France* (Paris, Gallimard, 2000)

Coss, Peter, *The Lady in Medieval England* (Stroud, 1998)

Cox, E. L., *The Eagles of Savoy: The House of Savoy in Thirteenth Century Europe* (Princeton, 1974)

Crouch, David, *William Marshal: Court, Career and Chivalry in the Angevin Empire* (London, 1990)
The Normans (London, 2002) *The Birth of Aristocracy: Constructing Aristocracy in England and France 900–1300* (Harlow, Pearson, 2005)
The Image of the Aristocracy in Britain (London, 1992)
The Reign of King Stephen (Pearson, Harlow, 2000)

Dewindt, A.R. and E.B. (eds.), *Royal Justice and the Medieval English Countryside* (2 vols.) (Toronto, 1981)

Dockray, Keith, *Henry V* (London, 2004)

Dodd, Gwilym and Musson, Anthony (eds.), *The Reign of Edward II: New Perspectives* (Woodbridge, York Medieval Press, 2006)

Doherty, Paul, *Isabella and the Strange Death of Edward II* (London, 2003)

Douglas, David C., *William the Conqueror* (London, 1964)

Duby, George and Perrot, Michelle, *Histoires des Femmes en Occident*, Vol. 2, *Le Moyen Age* (series ed. Christiane Klapisch-Zuber) (Paris, Perrin, 2002)

Duggan, Anne J. (ed.), *Queens and Queenship in Medieval Europe* (Woodbridge, Boydell Press, 1997)

Dvorakova, V., Krasa, Josef, Merhautoua, Anezka, Stejskal, Karl, *Gothic Mural Painting in Bohemia and Moravia 1300–1378* (London, Oxford University Press, 1964)

Edwards, Cyril, 'The Magnanimous Sex Object: Richard the Lionheart in the Medieval German Lyric' in *Courtly Literature: Culture and Context*, ed. Keith Busby and Erik Cooper (Philadelphia, 1990)

Edwards, R., *The Itinerary of King Richard III 1483–1485* (Richard III Society, 1983)

Elias, Norbert, *The Civilizing Process: The History of Manners* (Oxford, Blackwell, 1978)

Elliott, Dyan, *Spiritual Marriage: Sexual Abstinence in Medieval Wedlock* (Princeton, 1993)

Erlanger, Philip, *Margaret of Anjou: Queen of England* (London, Elek, 1970)

Evergates, Theodore (ed.), *Aristocratic Women in Medieval France* (Philadelphia, 1999)

Fleming, Peter, *Family and Household in Medieval England* (Basingstoke, Palgrave Macmillan, 2001)

Fowler, Kenneth, *The Age of Plantagenet and Valois* (London, 1967)

Freeman, E.A., *The History of the Norman Conquest of England* (5 vols.) (Oxford, 1870)

Fryde, Natalie, *The Tyranny and Fall of Edward II, 1321–1326* (Cambridge University Press, 1993)

Gillespie, James T. (ed.), *The Age of Richard II* (Sutton, Stroud, 1997)

Gillingham, John, *The Wars of the Roses* (Baton Rouge, Louisiana State University Press, 1981)

'Some Legends of Richard the Lionheart: Their Development and Their Influence' in *Richard Coeur de Lion in History and Myth*, ed. Janet L. Nelson (London, King's College London Centre for Late Antique and Medieval Studies, 1992)

Given-Wilson, Chris, *The English Nobility in the Late Middle Ages* (London, 1987)

Le Goff, Jacques, 'What Did the Twelfth Century Renaissance Mean?' in *The Medieval World*, ed. Peter Linehan and Janet L. Nelson (New York, Routledge, 2003)

Goldberg, P.J.P., *Medieval England: A Social History* (London, 2004)

Golding, Brian, *Conquest and Colonization: The Normans in Britain: 1066–1100* (Basingstoke, 2001)

Griffiths, Ralph A. and Thomas, Roger S., *The Making of the Tudor Dynasty* (Stroud, Sutton, 2005)

Guy, John, *Tudor England* (Oxford, 1988)

Hardy, B.C., *Philippa of Hainault and her Times* (London, 1910)

Harvey, J., 'Political and Cultural Exchanges between England and the Iberian Peninsula in the Middle Ages' in *Literature, Culture and Society of the Middle Ages*, ed. M.M. Lopez (Barcelona, 1989)

Haskins, Charles H., *The Renaissance of the Twelfth Century* (Cambridge, MA, Harvard University Press, 1927)

Heslop, T.A. (ed.), *English Romanesque Art 1066–1200* (London, 1984)

Hicks, Michael, *Anne Neville, Queen to Richard III* (Stroud, 2006)

Horrox, Rosemary (ed.), *Fifteenth Century Attitudes: Perceptions of Society in Late Medieval England* (Cambridge, 1994)

Howell, Margaret, *Eleanor of Provence: Queenship in Thirteenth Century England* (Oxford, 1998)

Huneycutt, Lois L., *Matilda of Scotland: A Study in Medieval Queenship* (Woodbridge, The Boydell Press, 2003)

Hyams, P.R., *Kings, Lords and Peasants in Medieval England* (Oxford, 1980)

Johns, Susan M., *Noblewomen, Aristocracy and Power in the Twelfth Century Anglo-Norman Realm* (Manchester University Press, 2003)

Johnson, Paul, *Edward III* (London, 1973)

Jones, Michael K. and Underwood, Malcolm G., *The King's Mother: Lady Margaret Beaufort, Countess of Richmond and Derby* (Cambridge, 1992)

Kantorowicz, E. H., *The King's Two Bodies: A Study in Medieval Political Theology* (Princeton, 1957)

Kendrick, Laura, *The Game of Love: Troubadour Wordplay* (Berkeley, University of California Press, 1988)

Keynes, Simon and Smyth, Alfred P. (eds.), *Anglo-Saxons* (Portland, Four Courts Press, 2006)

King, Edmund (ed.), *The Anarchy of Stephen's Reign* (Oxford, 1994)

Kirby, J.L., *Henry IV of England* (London, 1970)

Klein, Stacey S., *Ruling Women: Queenship and Gender in Anglo-Saxon Literature* (Indiana, University of Notre Dame Press, 2006)

Kristeller, Paul Oskar, *Renaissance Thought and the Arts* (Princeton, 1990)

Lamonte, John L., *The World of the Middle Ages* (New York, 1949)

Laynesmith, J.L., *The Last Medieval Queens: English Queenship 1445–1503* (Oxford University Press, 2004)

Lenz Harvey, Nancy, *Elizabeth of York* (London, Weidenfeld & Nicolson, 1973)

Lewis, Katherine J., Menuge, Noel James and Phelps, Kim (eds.), *Young Medieval Women* (Stroud, 1999)

Leyser, Henrietta, *Medieval Women: A Social History of Women in England 450–1500* (London, 1995)
Medieval Women (London, Weidenfeld & Nicolson, 1995)

Lieber Gerson, Paula (ed.), *Abbot Suger and St Denis: A Symposium* (New York, 1986)

Linehan, Peter and Nelson, Janet L. (eds.), *The Medieval World* (Abingdon, Routledge, 2003)

McCarthy, Conor, *Marriage in Medieval England: Law, Literature and Practice* (Woodbridge, Boydell, 2004)

McCash, June Hall (ed.), *The Cultural Patronage of Medieval Women* (Athens, GA, University of Georgia Press, 1996)

MacFarlane K.B., *The Nobility of Later Medieval England* (Oxford, Clarendon Press, 1973)

McLynn, Frank, *Lionheart and Lackland: King Richard, King John and the Wars of Conquest* (London, 2006)

McMurray Gibson, G., 'Blessing from Sun and Moon: Churching as Women's Theatre' in *Bodies and Disciplines: Intersections of Literature and History in Fifteenth Century England*, ed. B.A. Hanawalt and D. Wallace (Minneapolis, 1996)

McNamara, J.A. and Wemple, S., 'The Power of Women through the Family in Medieval Europe' in *Women and Power in the Middle Ages*, ed. M. and M. Kowaleski (Athens, GA, 1988)

McNamara, J.A., Halborg, John E. and Whatley, E. Gordon (eds.), *Sainted Women of the Dark Ages* (Durham, NC, 1992)

Martindale, Jane, *Eleanor of Aquitaine: The Last Years*
'Eleanor of Aquitaine' in *Richard Coeur de Lion in History and Myth*, ed. Janet L. Nelson (London, King's College London Centre for Late Antique and Medieval Studies, 1992)
'Eleanor of Aquitaine: The Last Years' in *King John: New Interpretations*, ed. S.D. Church (Woodbridge, Boydell Press, 1999)

Masson, Gustave, *Medieval France from the reign of Hugues Capet to the beginning of the Sixteenth century* (London, T. Fisher Unwin, 1888)

Mathew, Gervase, *The Court of Richard II* (London, 1968)

Mattingley, Garrett, *Catherine of Aragon* (London, Jonathan Cape, 1950)

Mitchell, Linda E., *Portraits of Medieval Women: Family, Marriage and Politics in England 1225–1350* (New York, 2003)

Mortimer, R., *Angevin England* (Oxford, 1994)

Nicholas, David, *Medieval Flanders* (London, Longman, 1992) *Trade, Urbanisation and the Family: Studies in the History of Medieval Flanders* (Aldershot, 1996)

Okerlund, Arlene, *Elizabeth Wydeville* (Stroud, Tempus, 2005)

Ormrod, W.M. (ed.), *England in the Thirteenth Century: Proceedings of the 1989 Harlaxton Symposium* (Stamford, 1991)

Pollard, A.J., *Late Medieval England* (Harlow, 2000)

Powicke, F.M., *The Loss of Normandy* (Manchester, 1913)

Prestwich, M., *Edward I* (London, 1988)

Reynolds, P.L., *Marriage in the Western Church: The Christianization of Marriage During the Patristic and Early Medieval Periods* (London, 1994)

Richard, Alfred, *Histoire des Comtes de Poitou* (Paris, 1903)

Rigby, S.H., *English Society in the Later Middle Ages: Class, Status and Gender* (New York, St Martin's Press, 1995)

Rosenthal, Joel, *Nobles and the Noble Life: 1295–1500* (London, 1976)

Sassier, Yves, *Louis VII* (Paris, 1991)

Saul, Nigel, *Richard II* (New Haven, Yale University Press, 1997)
The Three Richards (London, Hambledon and London, 2005)

Scase, Wendy, 'St Anne and the Education of the Virgin' in *England in the Fourteenth Century: Proceedings of the 1991 Harlaxton Symposium*, ed. Nicholas Rogers (Stamford, 1993)

Schatzmiller, J., *Shylock Revisited: Jews, Moneylending and Medieval Society* (Los Angeles, 1990)

Schramm, P.E., *A History of the English Coronation*, trans. L.G.W. Legg (Oxford, 1937)

Simpson, Amanda, *The Connections Between English and Bohemian Painting During the Second Half of the Fourteenth Century* (London, 1978)

Sivery, G., *Marguerite de Provence: Une refine aux temps des cathedrals* (Paris, 1984)

Stafford, Pauline, *Queens, Concubines and Dowagers: The King's Wife in the Early Middle Ages* (London, 1983)

Starkey, David, *Monarchy Volume 1: The Beginnings* (London, 2004)

Stow, K., 'Hatred of the Jews and Love of the Church: Papal Policy Towards the Jews in the Middle Ages' in *Antisemitism through the Ages*, ed. S. Almog (London, 1988)

Strickland, Agnes, *Lives of the Queens of England* (11 vols.) (London, 1841)

Strohm, Paul, *England's Empty Throne: Usurpation and the Language of Legitimisation 1399–1422* (New Haven, Yale University Press, 1998)

Hochon's Arrow: The Social Imagination of Fourteenth Century Texts (Princeton, 1992)

Strong, Roy, *The Spirit of Britain: A Narrative History of the Arts* (London, 1999)

Thomas, Alfred, *Anne's Bohemia: Czech Literature and Society 1310–1420* (Minneapolis, 1998)

Thomas, H., *The English and the Normans: Ethnic Hostility, Assimilation and Identity 1066–1220* (Oxford, 2003)

Tolley, T., 'Eleanor of Castile and the "Spanish" Style in England', in *England in the Thirteenth Century*, ed. W.M. Ormrod

Trindade, Ann, *Berengaria: In Search of Richard's Lost Queen* (Portland, Four Courts Press, 1999)

Tyerman, Christopher, *God's War: A New History of the Crusades* (London, 2006)

Vale, Juliet, *Edward III and Chivalry* (Woodbridge, Boydell, 1982)

Verdon, Jean, *Le Moyen Age: Ombres et Lumieres* (Paris, 2005)

Vincent, Nicholas, 'Isabella of Angoulême: John's Jezebel' in *King John: New Interpretations*, ed. S.D. Church (Woodbridge, Boydell Press, 1999)

Voaden, Rosalynn (ed.) *Prophets Abroad: The Reception of Continental Holy Women in Late Medieval England* (Cambridge, 1996)

Ward, J., *English Noblewomen in the Later Middle Ages* (London, 1992)

Warner, Marina, *Alone of All her Sex: The Myth and Cult of the Virgin Mary* (London, Vintage, 2000)

Warren, W.L., *Henry II* (New Haven, 2000)

Weir, Alison, *Eleanor of Aquitaine* (London, Pimlico, 2000)

Isabella: She-Wolf of France, Queen of England (London, 2005)

The Princes in the Tower (London, 1992)

Williams, Gwyn, *Medieval London: From Commune to Capital* (London, 1970)

Winters, W., *The Queen Eleanor Memorial, Waltham Cross* (Waltham Abbey, 1885)

Wolffe, B.P., *The Royal Demesne in English History: The Crown Estate in the Government of the Realm from the Conquest to 1509* (Athens, OH, 1971)

Wood, Charles T., 'Queens, Queans and Kingship: An Inquiry into the Theories of Royal Legitimacy in Late Medieval England and France' in *Order and Innovation in the Middle Ages: Essays in Honour of Joseph R. Strayer*, ed. William C. Jordan, Bruce McNab, T. Teofilo (Princeton, 1976)

Woodbridge, Linda, *Women and the English Renaissance: Literature and the Nature of Womankind* (Urbana, 1984)

Women and the English Renaissance (Brighton, Harvester, 1984)

Woolgar, C.M., *The Great Household in Medieval England* (New Haven, 1999)

Wylie, J. H., *History of England under Henry the Fourth* (4 vols.)

JOURNALS

Ashdown-Hill, John, 'Edward IV's Uncrowned Queen', *The Ricardian* No. 139, Vol. 11 (December 1997)

Baldwin, J.W., 'The Rise of Administrative Kingship, Henry I and Philip Augustus', *American Historical Review* 83 (1978)

Bandel, Betty, 'The English Chroniclers' Attitude Towards Women', *Journal of the History of Ideas* No. 1, Vol. 16 (January 1955)

Barratt, Nick, 'The Revenue of King John', *English Historical Review* No. 443, Vol. 111 (September 1996)

Bates, David, 'Normandy and England after 1066', *English Historical Review* No. 413, Vol. 104 (October 1989)

Bennett, Michael, 'Edward III's Entail and the Succession to the Crown', *English Historical Review* No. 452, Vol. 113 (June 1998)

Boase, J., 'Fontevraud and the Plantagenets', *Journal of the British Archeological Association*, 3rd series, Vol. 34 (1971)

Brown, Elizabeth A.R., 'The Political Repercussions of Family Ties in the Early Fourteenth Century: The Marriage of Edward II of England and Isabelle of France', *Speculum* No. 3, Vol. 63 (July 1988)

Burgwinkle, William E., 'Troubadour Song and the Art of Juggling', *Pacific Coast Philology* Nos. 1–2, Vol. 26 (1991)

Chambers, F.M., 'Some Legends Concerning Eleanor of Aquitaine' *Speculum* No. 16 (1944)

Cherry, John, 'Late Fourteenth Century Jewellery: The Inventory of 1399', *The Burlington Magazine* No. 1019, Vol. 130 (February 1988)

Clarke, P.D.. 'English Royal Marriages and the Papal Penitentiary in Fifteenth Century England', *English Historical Review* Vol. 120 (2005)

Clover, Carol, 'Regardless of Sex: Men, Women, and Power in Early Northern Europe', *Speculum* No. 68 (1993)

Crawford, Anne, 'The Queen's Council in the Middle Ages', *English Historical Review* No. 469, Vol. 116 (November 2001)

Crawford, Katherine B., 'Love, Sodomy and Scandal: Controlling the Sexual Reputation of Henry III', *Journal of the History of Sexuality* No. 4, Vol. 12 (October 2003)

Cressy, D., 'Purification, Thanksgiving and the Churching of Women', *Past and Present* No. 141 (1993)

Cron, B.M., 'Margaret of Anjou and the Lancastrian March', *The Ricardian* No. 147, Vol. 11 (December 1999)

'The Duke of Suffolk, the Angevin Marriage and the Ceding of Maine, 1445', *Journal of Medieval History* No. 20 (1994)

Crook, D., 'The Last Days of Eleanor of Castile: The Death of a Queen in

Nottinghamshire, November 1290', *Transactions of the Thoroton Society* 94 (1990)

Cuttino, G.P. on T.W. Lyman, 'Where is Edward II?', *Speculum* No. 53 (July 1978)

Davis, R.H.C., 'William of Jumièges, Robert Curthose and the Norman Succession', *The English Historical Review* No. 95 (1980)

Davis, R.H.C. and Prestwich, J.O., 'The Treason of Geoffrey de Mandeville', *The English Historical Review* No. 407, Vol. 103 (April 1988)

De Hemptinne, T., '*Les Epouses des Croises . . . l'exemple des Comtesses de Flandres' in Autour de la Premiere Croisade'*, *Actes du Colloque de la 'Society for the Study of the Crusades'* (1996)

Di Clemente, Kristi, 'The Women of Flanders and their Husbands', *Essays in Medieval Studies* Vol. 23 (2006)

Dionnet, A.C., 'La *Cassette Reliquaire du Bienheureux Jean de Montmirail'*, *Revue Française d'heraldique et de Sigillographie* No. 65 (1995)

Facinger, Marion, 'A Study of Medieval Queenship', *Studies in Medieval and Renaissance History* 5 (1968)

Fallows, David, 'The Coutenance Angloise', *Renaissance Studies* No.2, Vol. 1 (June 1987)

Farmer, Sharon, 'Persuasive Voices: Clerical Images of Medieval Wives', *Speculum* No. 61 (1986)

George, R.H., 'The Contribution of Flanders to the Conquest of England', *Revue Belge de Philologie et d'Histoire*, V (1926)

Gibbons, Rachel, Isabeau of Bavaria, Queen of France (1385–1422): The Creation of An Historical Villainess', *Transactions of the Royal Historical Society*, 6th series, Vol. 6 (1996)

Gill, Louise, 'William Caxton and the Revolution of 1483', *English Historical Review* No.445, Vol. 112 (February 1997)

Gillingham, John, 'Love, Marriage and Politics in the Twelfth Century', *Forum for Modern Language Studies* 25 (1989)

Gordon, Dillian, 'A New Discovery in the Wilton Diptych', *The Burlington Magazine* No.1075, Vol. 134 (October 1992)

Gransden, Antonia, 'The Alleged Rape by Edward III of the Countess of Salisbury', *English Historical Review* vol. 87 no. 343 (April 1972)

Grierson, Philip, 'The Relations of England and Flanders before the Norman Conquest', *Transactions of the Royal Historical Society*, 4th series, Vol. 23 (1941)

Groag Bell, Susan, 'Medieval Women Book Owners: Arbiters of Lay Piety and Culture', *Signs* No.4, Vol. 7 (Summer 1982)

Guilloreau, L., '*Marie de Woodstock, une fille d'Edouard I moniale a Amesbury'*, *Revue Mabillon* 9 (1914)

Hampton, W.E., 'Witchcraft and the Sons of York', *The Ricardian* No. 68, Vol. 5 1980)

Heimann, Adelheid, '"The Douce Apocalypse" by A.G. Hassall', *Burlington Magazine* No. 722, Vol. 105 (May 1963)

Helmholz, R.H., 'Usury and the medieval English church courts', *Speculum* No. 61 (1986)

Hilpert, H.E., 'Richard of Cornwall's Candidature for the German Throne and the Christmas 1256 Parliament at Westminster', *Journal of Medieval History* 6 (1980)

Hilton, G.M., 'The Chronicle of John Strecche and its place in medieval historical records of England and Kenilworth Priory', *Bulletin of John Rylands Library* Part 1, Vol. 85 (2003).

Hollister, C.Warren, 'The Anglo Norman Succession Debate of 1126', *Journal of Medieval History* 1 (1975)

Hooper, N., 'Edgar the Aetheling: Anglo-Saxon Prince, Rebel and Crusader', *Anglo-Saxon England* xiv (1985)

Horrox, Rosemary, 'The History of KRIII (1619) by Sir George Buck, Master of the Revels' (review), *English Historical Review* No. 382, Vol. 97 (January 1982)

Howell, Margaret, 'The Resources of Eleanor of Provence as Queen Consort', *English Historical Review* No. 403, Vol. 102 (April 1987)

Huneycutt, Lois L., 'The Idea of the Perfect Princess: The "Life of St Margaret" in the Reign of Matilda II', *Anglo-Norman Studies* 12 (1990)

Kettle, Andrew, 'Parvenus and Politics', *The Ricardian* Vol. 15 (2005)

Kliman, Bernice, 'Women in Early English Literature, "Beowulf" to the "Ancrene Wisse"', *Nottingham Medieval Studies* 21 (1977)

Labande, Edmond-René, '*Pour une Image Véridique d'Alienor d'Aquitaine*', *Bulletin de la Société des Antiquaires de l'Ouest*, 4th series, No. 2 (1951)

Lee, P. A., 'Reflections of Power: Margaret of Anjou and the Dark Side of Queenship', *Renaissance Quarterly* 29 (1986)

Legge, M.D., '*Les origines de l'Anglo-normand litteraire*', *Revue de Linguistique Romane* 31 (1967)

Leyser, Karl, 'The Anglo-Norman Succession 1120–1125', *Anglo-Norman Studies* 13 (1991)

Lulofs, Maaike, 'King Edward IV in Exile', *The Ricardian* No. 44, Vol. 3 (March 1974)

McCash, June Hall, 'Marie de Champagne and Eleanor of Aquitaine: A Relationship Re-Examined', *Speculum* No. 4, Vol. 54 (October 1979)

McKenna J.W., 'Henry VI of England and the Dual Monarchy', *Journal of the Warburg and Courtauld Institutes* Vol. 28 (1965)

Michael, Michael A., 'A Manuscript Wedding Gift from Philippa of Hainault to Edward III', *Burlington Magazine* No. 990, Vol. 127 (September 1985)

Michalove, Sharon D., 'The Reinvention of Richard III', *The Ricardian* No. 130, Vol. 10 (September 1995)

Milner, John D,. 'The Battle of Bauge', *Journal of the Historical Association* No. 304, Vol. 91 (October 2006)

Morgan D.A.L., 'The Political After-Life of Edward III: The Apotheosis of a Warmonger', *English Historical Review* No. 448, Vol. 112 (September 1997)

Morgan, Nigel, 'Early Gothic Manuscripts 1250–1285', *Speculum* No. 1, Vol. 68 (January 1993)

Musset, L., *'La reine Mathilde et la fondation de la Trinité de Caen'*, *Mémoires de l'Académie nationale des Sciences, Arts et Belles Lettres*, Vol. xxi (1984) *'Les Actes de Guillaume le Conquérant et de la reine Mathilde pour les abbeys Caennaises'*, *Mémoires de la Société des Antiquaires de Normandie* XXXVIII (1967)

Myers, A.R., 'The Captivity of Royal Witch: The Household Accounts of Queen Joan of Navarre 1419–21', *Bulletin of the John Rylands Library* Vol. 24 (1940)

Nip, Renée, 'Political Relations between England and Flanders 1066–1128', *Anglo-Norman Studies* XXI (1998)

O'Regan, Mary, 'The Pre-Contract and Its Effect on the Succession', *The Ricardian* No. 54, Vol. 4 (June 1976)

Ormrod, W.M., 'Edward III and His Family', *The Journal of British Studies* No. 4, Vol. 26 (October 1987)

Painter, Sidney, 'The Houses of Lusignan and Chatellerault 1150–1250', *Speculum* No. 30 (1955)

Post, J.B., 'Ages at Menarche and Menopause: Some Medieval Authorities', *Population Studies* 25 (1971)

Reid, W. Stanford, '"Edward III and the Scots: The Formative Years of a Military Career", by Renald Nicholson', *Speculum* No. 1, Vol. 41 (June 1966)

Rhodes, W.E., 'The Inventory of the Jewels and Wardrobe of Queen Isabella (1307–08)', *English Historical Review* No. 12 (1897)

Richardson H. G., 'The Marriage and Coronation of Isabelle of Angoulême', *English Historical Review* No. 241, Vol. 61 (September 1946)
'King John and Isabelle of Angoulême', *English Historical Review* No. 256, Vol. 65 (July 1950).
'The Letters and Charters of Eleanor of Aquitaine', *English Historical Review*, Vol. 74 (1959)

Richardson, J., 'The Letters and Charters of Eleanor of Aquitaine', *English Historical Review* No. 74 (1959)

Ridgeway, H.W., 'Foreign Favourites and Henry III's Problems of Patronage', *English Historical Review* No. 104 (1989)

Robinson, Fred C., 'The Prescient Woman in Old English Literature', *Philologia Anglia* (1988)

Saul, Nigel, 'The Despensers and the Downfall of Edward II', *English Historical Review* XCIX (1984)

Stones, E.L.G., 'The Date of Roger Mortimer's Escape from the Tower of London', *English Historical Review* LXVI (1951)

Strayer, Joseph P., ' *"Enquetes sur les droits et revenues de Charles Ière d'Anjou en Provence"* by Edouard Baratier', *American Historical Review* No.3, Vol. 76 (June 1971)

Sutton, A. and Visser-Fuchs, L., 'A Most Benevolent Queen,' *The Ricardian* No. 129, Vol. 10 (June 1995)

'The Device of Queen Elizabeth Woodville', *The Ricardian* No. 136, Vol. 11 (March 1997)

'Royal Burials at Windsor', *The Ricardian* No. 144, Vol. 11 (March 1999)

Tatlock, J.S.P., 'Muriel: The Earliest English Poetess', *Publications of the Modern Language Association of America* 48 (1933)

Turner, Ralph V., 'Eleanor of Aquitaine and Her Children: An Inquiry into Medieval Family Attachment', *Journal of Medieval History* 14 (1988)

'The Problem of Survival for the Angevin "Empire": Henry II and His Sons' 'Vision versus Late Twelfth Century Realities', *American Historical Review* No. 1, Vol. 100 (February 1995)

Valente, Claire, 'The Lament of Edward II: Religious Lyric, Political Propaganda', *Speculum* No. 2, Vol. LXXVIII (April 2002)

Van Houts, E., 'Latin Poetry and the Anglo-Norman Court', *Journal of Medieval History* 15 (1989)

Walker, Curtis H., 'Eleanor of Aquitaine and the Disaster at Cadmos Mountain on the Second Crusade', *American Historical Review* No. 55, Vol. 4 (1950)

Wertheimer, L., 'Adeliza of Louvain and Anglo-Norman Queenship', *Haskins Society Journal* No. 7 (1997)

Williams, Barrie, 'Elizabeth of York's Last Journey', *The Ricardian* No. 83, Vol. 6 (March 1988)

NOTES

For brevity, primary sources are cited only where they are not previously referenced in the text. All quotations from letters, except where otherwise stated, are from Anne Crawford's Letters of the Queens of England, 1100–1457 *(Stroud, 2002).*

INTRODUCTION

1. Cited in Lois L. Huneycutt, *Matilda of Scotland: A Study in Medieval Queenship* (Woodbridge, 2003), p.35.
2. Dorothy Laird, *How the Queen Reigns* (London, 1959), p.35.
3. Pauline Stafford, *Queens, Concubines, Dowagers: The King's Wife in the Early Middle Ages* (London, 1983), p.34.
4. Alcuin Blamires, *The Case for Women in Medieval Culture* (Oxford, 1997), p.20. Peter Abelard's comments are in 'The Authority and Dignity of Nuns', Letter 7, *The Letters of Abelard and Heloise*, trans. C.K. Scott Moncrieff (New York, 1974).
5. Blamires, op. cit., p.89
6. Philippe Aries, *Centuries of Childhood*, trans. Robert Baldick (London, 1962), p.368.
7. J.L. Laynesmith, *The Last Medieval Queens* (Oxford, 2004), p.77.
8. Conor McCarthy, *Marriage in Medieval England: Law, Literature and Practice* (Woodbridge, 2004), p.99.
9. Linda Paterson, 'Gender Negotiations in France During the Central Middle Ages: The Literary Evidence', in *The Medieval World*, ed. Peter Linehan and Janet L. Nelson (New York, Routledge, 2003), p.250.
10. Margaret Howell, *Eleanor of Provence: Queenship in Thirteenth Century England* (Oxford, 1998), p.77.
11. Peter Coss, *The Lady in Medieval England 1000–1500* (Stroud, 1998), p.12. See also Theodore Evergates, 'The Aristocracy of Champagne in the Mid-Thirteenth Century', in *Journal of Interdisciplinary History*, No. 1, Vol. 5 (Summer 1974).

PART ONE

CHAPTER 1: MATILDA OF FLANDERS

1. David C. Douglas, *William the Conqueror* (London, 1964) p.79.
2. Orderic Vitalis.
3. Douglas, op. cit., p.76.
4. Orderic Vitalis.
5. Adam of Eynsham.
6. Agnes Strickland, *Lives of the Queens of England* Vol. 1 (London, 1851), p.9.
7. Exeter Book.
8. Quoted in Nicholas Vincent, 'Isabella of Angoulême: John's Jezebel', in *King John: New Interpretations*, ed. S.D. Church (Woodbridge, 1999), p.20.
9. Nicholas, op. cit., p.41.
10. David Starkey, *Monarchy* (London, 2004), p.80.
11. Pauline Stafford, 'Emma: The Powers of the Queen in the Eleventh Century', in *Queens and Queenship in Medieval Europe*, ed. Anne J. Duggan (Woodbridge, 1997), p.4.
12. *Anglo-Saxon Chronicle*.
13. *Anglo-Saxon Chronicle*.
14. Henrietta Leyser, *Medieval Women: A Social History of Women in England 450–1500* (London, 1995), p.20.
15. Ibid., p.34.
16. From P.J.P. Goldberg, 'Women', in *Fifteenth Century Attitudes: Perceptions of Society in Late Medieval England*, ed. Rosemary Horrox (Cambridge, 1994), cited p.123.
17. J. Ward, *English Noblewomen in the Later Middle Ages* (London, 1992), p.57.
18. Quoted in John Gillingham, *The Wars of the Roses* (Baton Rouge, 1981), p.49.
19. Orderic Vitalis.
20. David Crouch, *The Normans* (London, 2002), p.83.
21. Douglas, op. cit., p.85.
22. Huneycutt, *Matilda of Scotland*, op. cit., p.50.
23. *Anglo-Saxon Chronicle*, 'D' version.
24. Pauline Stafford, 'Chronicle D, 1067 and Women: Gendering Conquest in Eleventh Century England', in *Anglo-Saxons*, ed. Simon Keynes and Alfred P. Smyth (Portland, 2006), p.209.
25. James Chambers, *The Norman Kings* (London, 1981), p.17.
26. Orderic Vitalis.
27. William of Jumièges, *Gesta Normanorum Ducum*.
28. *Recueil des Actes des Ducs de Normandie*.

CHAPTER 2: MATILDA OF SCOTLAND

1. Huneycutt, *Matilda of Scotland*, op. cit., p.165.

2. Ibid., p.17.
3. Eadmer.
4. *Anglo-Saxon Chronicle.*
5. Ibid.
6. Anselm.
7. Eadmer.
8. Ibid.
9. Aelred of Rievaulx.
10. Anne Crawford, *Letters of the Queens of England* (Stroud, 2002), p.20.
11. Anselm.
12. On Henry's absences from England see, for example, Robert Bartlett, *England Under the Norman and Angevin Kings 1075–1225* (Oxford, 2000), pp. 38–41, and William Farrer, *An Outline Itinerary for Henry I* (Oxford, 1919).
13. Huneycutt, *Matilda of Scotland*, op. cit., p.74.
14. Ibid., p.80.
15. Ibid., p.38.
16. *Life of St Margaret of Scotland*, 'The Idea of a Perfect Princesse in the Life of St Margaret Queen of Scotland' (Paris, 1661).
17. Huneycutt. op. cit., p.26.
18. Lois L. Huneycutt, 'Proclaiming her Dignity Abroad: The Literary and Artistic Network of Matilda of Scotland', in *The Cultural Patronage of Medieval Women*, ed. June Hall McCash (Athens, GA, 1996), p.155.
19. Roy Strong, *The Spirit of Britain: A Narrative History of the Arts* (London, 1999), p.38.
20. See Jacques Le Goff, 'What Did The Twelfth Century Renaissance Mean?', in Linehan and Nelson, op. cit., pp.635–47.
21. Susan M. Johns, *Noblewomen, Aristocracy and Power in the Twelfth Century Anglo-Norman Realm* (Manchester, 2003), p.37.
22. William of Malmesbury, *Gesta.*
23. Huneycutt, *Matilda of Scotland*, op. cit., p.128.
24. *Liber Monasterii de Hyda.*

CHAPTER 3: ADELIZA OF LOUVAIN
1. Marjorie Chibnall, *The Empress Matilda: Queen Consort, Queen Mother and Lady of the English* (Oxford, 1993), p.37.
2. Alison Weir, *Eleanor of Aquitaine* (London, 2000), p.134.
3. Quoted in Bartlett, op. cit, p.41.
4. William of Malmesbury, *Gesta.*

CHAPTER 4: MATILDA OF BOULOGNE
1. David Crouch, *The Reign of King Stephen* (Harlow, 2000), p.24.
2. Warren Hollister, 'The Anglo-Norman Succession Debate of 1126: Prelude to Stephen's Anarchy', in *Journal of Medieval History* 1 (1976), p.25.

3. Crouch, *The Reign of King Stephen*, op. cit., p.31.

4. Ibid., p.318.

5. Orderic Vitalis.

6. Heather J. Tanner, 'Queenship, Custom or Ad Hoc? The Case of Matilda III of England', in *Eleanor of Aquitaine: Lord and Lady*, ed. John Carmi Parsons and Bonnie Wheeler (Basingstoke, 2002), p.139.

7. Crouch, *The Reign of King Stephen*, op. cit., p.89.

8. Ibid., p.77.

9. Marjorie Chibnall, *The Empress Matilda*, op. cit., p.87.

10. Crouch, *The Reign of King Stephen*, op. cit., p.126.

11. For illumination compare Marjorie Chibnall, *The Empress Matilda*, p.85, with David Crouch, 'Robert of Gloucester and the daughters of Zelophehad', *Journal of Medieval History*, No. 11 (1965).

12. See John Carmi Parsons, 'Mothers, Daughters, Marriage, Power: Some Plantagenet Evidence 1150–1500', in *Medieval Queenship*, ed. John Carmi Parsons (Stroud, 1994).

13. *Gesta Stephani*.

14. Johns, op. cit., p.19.

15. Chibnall, *The Empress Matilda*, op. cit., p.115.

16. Crouch, *The Reign of King Stephen*, op. cit., p.261.

17. Betty Bandel, 'The English Chroniclers' Attitude Towards Women', in *Journal of the History of Ideas*, No. 1, Vol. 16 (January 1955), p.114.

PART TWO

CHAPTER 5: ELEANOR OF AQUITAINE

1. W.L. Warren, *Henry II* (New Haven, 2000), p.121.

2. Christopher Tyerman, *God's War: A New History of the Crusades* (London, 2006), p.275.

3. Constance Brittain Bouchard, 'Eleanor's Divorce from Louis VII: The Uses of Consanguinity', in Carmi Parsons and Wheeler, *Eleanor of Aquitaine*, op. cit., p.230.

4. See Andrew W. Lewis, 'The Birth and Childhood of King John: Some Revisions', in Carmi Parsons and Wheeler, *Eleanor of Aquitaine*, op. cit.

5. Weir, *Eleanor of Aquitaine*, op. cit., p.34.

6. Bernard of Clairvaux, *Letters*, trans. B.S. James (Stroud, 1998), No. 323.

7. Tyerman, op. cit., p.328.

8. See Alfred Richard, *Histoire des Comtes de Poitou* (Paris, 1903).

9. William Stubbs, quoted in Curtis H. Walker, 'Eleanor of Aquitaine and the Disaster at Cadmos Mountain on the Second Crusade', in *American Historical Review* No. 55, Vol. 4 (1950).

10. Peggy McCracken, 'Scandalizing Desire: Eleanor of Aquitaine and the

Chroniclers', in Carmi Parsons and Wheeler, *Eleanor of Aquitaine*, op. cit., p.247.

11. Tyerman, op. cit., p.333.

12. Otto of Freising, *The Deeds of Frederick Barbarossa*, trans. C.C. Mierow (Columbia, 1953), p.27.

13. John of Salisbury.

14. Brittain Bouchard, op. cit., p.224.

15. John of Salisbury.

16. Christopher N.L. Brooke, *The Medieval Idea of Marriage* (Oxford, 1989), p.125.

17. William of Newburgh.

18. Weir, *Eleanor of Aquitaine*, op. cit., p.89.

19. Elizabeth A.R. Brown, 'Eleanor of Aquitaine Reconsidered' in Carmi Parsons and Wheeler, *Eleanor of Aquitaine*, op. cit., p.9.

20. Lois L. Huneycutt, 'Alianora Regina Anglorum: Eleanor of Aquitaine and her Anglo-Norman Predecessors as Queens of England', in Carmi Parsons and Wheeler, *Eleanor of Aquitaine*, op. cit., p.128.

21. Edmond-René Labande, '*Pour Une Image Véridique d'Alienor d'Aquitaine*' in *Bulletin de la Société des Antiquaires de l'Ouest*, 4th series, No. 2 (1951), quotation trans. Lisa Hilton.

22. Robert-Henri Bautier, '*Etudes sur la France capetienne*', Art. 5 (London, 1992), p.33.

23. Marie Hivergneaux, 'Queen Eleanor and Aquitaine 1137–1189', in Carmi Parsons and Wheeler, *Eleanor of Aquitaine*, op. cit., p.67.

24. See Kathleen Nolan, 'The Queen's Choice: Eleanor of Aquitaine and the Tombs at Fontevrault', in Carmi Parsons and Wheeler, Eleanor of Aquitaine, op. cit.

25. Frank McLynn, *Lionheart and Lackland: King Richard, King John and the Wars of Conquest* (London, 2006), p.43.

CHAPTER 6: BERENGARIA OF NAVARRE

1. Brown, op. cit., p.13.

2. Ann Trindade, *Berengaria of Navarre: In Search of Richard's Lost Queen* (Portland, 1999), p.44.

3. Ambroise.

4. William of Newburgh, Ranulph of Higden, Pierre de Langtoft.

5. Karl Brunner (ed.), *Der mittelenglische Versroman über Richard Lowenherz* (Vienna, 1913), B version ll2456.

6. Trindade, op. cit., p.59.

7. Roger of Howden, *Gesta*.

8. Ibid.

9. See J. Brundage, 'Sex and Canon Law' in *The Handbook of Medieval Sexuality*, ed. J. Brundage and V. Bullough (New York, 1996), pp.33–50; also Brundage, *Law, Sex and Christian Society in Medieval Europe* (Chicago, 1987).

10. McLynn, op. cit., p.267.
11. Ibid., p. 267
12. *Cartulaire de l'Eglise du Mans: Livre Blanc du Chapitre*, ed. Lottin (Archives Departementales de la Sarthe, 1848), p.123.
13. *Honorii III Romani Pontificis Opera Omnia*, ed. J. Horoy (Paris, 1879). Book II, Letter CXCV.
14. Weir, *Eleanor of Aquitaine*, op. cit., p.321.
15. A. Bouton, '*La Vie Tourmentée de la Reine Berengere*', in *Vie Mancelle* No. 45 (1964), p.26.

CHAPTER 7: ISABELLE OF ANGOULÊME

1. McLynn, op. cit., p.287.
2. Andrew W. Lewis, 'The Birth and Childhood of King John: Some Revisions' in Carmi Parsons and Wheeler, *Eleanor of Aquitaine*, op.cit., p.166.
3. McLynn, op. cit., p.244.
4. Vincent, op. cit., p.173.
5. H.G. Richardson, 'King John and Isabelle of Angoulême' in *English Historical Review* No. 256, Vol. 65 (July 1950).
6. Giraldus Cambrensis.
7. McLynn, op. cit., p.316.
8. Matthew Paris, *Chronica Majora*.
9. Quoted in Vincent, op.cit., p.195.
10. Paul Strohm, *Hochon's Arrow: The Social Imagination of Fourteenth Century Texts* (Princeton, 1992), p.3.

PART THREE

CHAPTER 8: ELEANOR OF PROVENCE

1. McLynn, op. cit., p.43.
2. Margaret Howell, *Eleanor of Provence*, op. cit., p.48.
3. Ibid., p.274.
4. *The Chronicle of Melrose Abbey.*
5. *Tewkesbury Chronicle.*
6. John Carmi Parsons, *Eleanor of Castile: Queen and Society in Thirteenth Century England* (New York, 1995), p.39.
7. H. Johnstone, 'Poor Relief in the Royal Households of the Thirteenth Century', in *Speculum* No. 4 (1929).

CHAPTER 9: ELEANOR OF CASTILE

1. *Opus Chronicorum.*
2. The story may have originated with Ptolemy of Lucca's *Historia Ecclesiastica*, in which it is reported as rumour.

3. John Carmi Parsons, 'Of Queens, Courts and Books: Reflections on the Literary Patronage of Thirteenth Century Plantagenet Queens', in June Hall McCash, *The Cultural Patronage of Medieval Women*, op. cit., p.177.

4. Ibid., p.178.

5. Susan Groag Bell, 'Medieval Women Book Owners: Arbiters of Lay Piety and Culture', in *Signs* No. 4, Vol. 7 (Summer 1982).

6. John Carmi Parsons, *Eleanor of Castile*, op. cit., p.57.

7. Walter of Guisborough.

CHAPTER 10: MARGUERITE OF FRANCE

1. W.M. Ormrod, 'The Sexualities of Edward II', in *The Reign of Edward II: New Perspectives*, ed. Gwilym Dodd and Anthony Musson (Woodbridge, 2006), p.22.

2. J.S. Hamilton, 'The Character of Edward II: The Letters of Edward of Caernarfon Reconsidered', in Dodd and Musson, op. cit., p.17.

3. *Annales Paulini*.

4. *The Chronicle of Lanercost*.

5. *Vita Edwardi Secundi*.

6. Ibid.

7. *Foedera*.

8. *Vita Edwardi Secundi*.

9. Ibid.

PART FOUR

CHAPTER 11: ISABELLA OF FRANCE

1. *Vita Edwardi Secundi*.

2. Michael Prestwich, 'The Court of Edward II', in Dodd and Musson, op. cit., p.74.

3. Articles of Deposition in *Foedera*.

4. Strickland, op. cit., Vol. 1, p.471.

5. *Chronicles of the Reigns of Edward I and Edward II*.

6. *Vita Edwardi Secundi*.

7. *Annales Paulini*.

8. *Vita Edwardi Secundi*.

9. Ibid.

10. Ibid.

11. Ibid.

12. Ibid.

13. Geoffrey le Baker, *Chronicon*.

14. *Foedera*.

15. Ibid.

16. *Brut Chronicle*.

17. Gwyn Williams, *Medieval London: From Commune to Capital* (London, 1970), p.298.
18. Both Paul Doherty, *Isabella and the Strange Death of Edward II* (London, 2003) and Alison Weir, *Isabella: She-Wolf of France, Queen of England* (London, 2005) give credence to the idea that Edward II was not murdered at Berkeley Castle. G.P. Cuttino on T.W. Lyman, 'Where is Edward II?', in *Speculum* Vol. 53 (July, 1978), gives a rather less breathless account of this strenuously contorted conspiracy theory. No good evidence exists to support either Doherty or Weir, though both are ingenious in their justifications.
19. *Brut Chronicle.*
20. Ibid.
21. *Calendar of Close Rolls 1330–3*, p.158.
22. Ormrod, 'The Sexualities of Edward II', op. cit., p.43.
23. Ian Mortimer, 'Sermons of Sodomy: A Reconsideration of Edward II's Sodomitical Reputation', in Dodd and Musson, op. cit., pp.52–3
24. Ibid., p.52.
25. Ormrod, 'The Sexualities of Edward II', op. cit., p.44.
26. Robert Fabyan, *The New Chronicles.*
27. Claire Valente, 'The Lament of Edward II: Religious Lyric, Political Propaganda', in *Speculum* No.2, Vol. LXXVIII (April 2002).
28. *Calendar of Papal Registers.*

CHAPTER 12: PHILIPPA OF HAINAULT
1. *The Register of Walter de Stapledon, Bishop of Exeter* (London, 1981).
2. B.C. Hardy, *Philippa of Hainault and her Times* (London, 1910), p.30.
3. *Exeter Diocese Register* (Canterbury and York Society).
4. Laynesmith, op. cit., p.118.
5. Hardy, op. cit., p.112.
6. Froissart, *Chroniques.*
7. Juliet Vale, *Edward III and Chivalry* (Woodbridge, Boydell, 1982), p.77.
8. Hardy, op. cit., p.126.
9. Paul Strohm, 'Queens as Intercessors', in *Hochon's Arrow*, op. cit., p. 103.
10. Walsingham.
11. Hardy, op. cit., quoted p.293.

CHAPTER 13: ANNE OF BOHEMIA AND ISABELLE OF FRANCE
1. V. Dvorakova et al, *Gothic Mural Painting in Bohemia and Moravia 1300–1378* (London, 1964), p.49.
2. Walsingham.
3. Ibid.
4. *Knighton Chronicle.*
5. Gervase Mathew, *The Court of Richard II* (London, 1968), p.38.

6. MS Reg., 13d fol.117b, cited in Louisa De Saussure Duls, *Richard II in the Early Chronicles*, p.8.

7. Marina Belozerskaya, *Rethinking the Renaissance: Burgundian Arts Across Europe* (Cambridge, 2002), p.144.

8. Nigel Saul, *Richard II* (New Haven, 1997), p.457.

9. Philippe de Mezières, *Letter to King Richard II*.

10. Susan Groag Bell, 'Medieval Women Book Owners: Arbiters of Lay Piety and Culture' in *Signs*, No. 4, Vol. 7 (Summer 1982).

11. John Wycliffe, *De triplici vinculi amors*, in M. Deanesley (ed.), *The Lollard Bible and Other Medieval Biblical Versions* (Cambridge, 1920), p.248.

12. *Foedera*.

13. Strohm, *Hochon's Arrow*, op. cit., p.108.

14. Philippe de Mezières, op. cit.

15. Rachel Gibbons, 'Isabeau of Bavaria, Queen of France (1385–1422): The Creation of An Historical Villainess' in *Transactions of the Royal Historical Society*, 6th series, Vol. 6 (1996)

16. Juvenal des Ursins, '*Histoire de Charles VI, Roy de France*' in *Nouvelle Collection de memoires sur l'histoire de France* (Paris, 1836), quotation trans. Lisa Hilton.

17. See Gervase Mathew, op. cit., and also Michael Bennett, *Richard II and the Revolutions of 1399* (Stroud, 1999).

18. *Chronicles of the Revolution 1397–1400*, ed. and trans. Chris Given-Wilson (Manchester, 1993), pp.56–7.

19. *English Historical Documents* IV, p.174.

20. Walsingham.

21. Strohm, *Hochon's Arrow*, op. cit., p.59.

PART FIVE

CHAPTER 14: JOANNA OF NAVARRE

1. Paul Strohm, *England's Empty Throne: Usurpation and the Language of Legitimisation 1399–1422* (New Haven, 1998), p.160.

2. Cited in Dillian Gordon, 'A New Discovery in the Wilton Diptych', *Burlington Magazine* No. 1075, Vol. 134 (October 1992).

3. Strohm, *England's Empty Throne*, op. cit., p.157.

4. Guillaume Gruel, *Chronique d'Artur de Richemont*, ed. le Vavasseur, Achille (Paris, 1890)

5. A.R. Myers, 'The Captivity of a Royal Witch: The Household Accounts of Queen Joan of Navarre 1419–21', in *Bulletin of the John Rylands Library* Vol. 24 (1940).

CHAPTER 15: CATHERINE DE VALOIS

1. Strecche, *Chronicle*.

2. *The Great Chronicle of London*.

3. *The First English Life of Henry V.*

4. Gibbons, op. cit.

5. Juvenal des Ursins, op. cit.

6. *Parisian Journal 1406–1499.*

7. Ibid.

8. See E.H. Kantorowicz, *The King's Two Bodies: A Study in Medieval Political Theology* (Princeton, 1957), p.240.

9. Anne Crawford, *Letters*, p.116.

10. Ibid.

11. J.W. McKenna, 'Henry VI of England and the Dual Monarchy', in *Journal of the Warburg and Courtauld Institutes* Vol. 28 (1965).

12. *Incerti Scriptoris Chronicon Angliae (Giles's Chronicle).*

13. Ralph A. Griffiths and Roger S. Thomas, *The Making of the Tudor Dynasty* (Stroud, 2005), p.38.

14. Sir John Wyn of Gwydir, cited in Griffiths and Thomas, ibid.,p.38.

15. Laynesmith, op. cit., p.41.

16. David Crouch, 'Noble Women: The View from the Stands' in *The Birth of Nobility: Constructing Aristocracy in England and France 900–1300* (Harlow, 2005), p.316.

CHAPTER 16: MARGUERITE OF ANJOU

1. Philippe Erlanger, *Margaret of Anjou: Queen of England* (London, 1970), p.29.

2. Ibid., p.80.

3. Laynesmith, op.cit., p.84.

4. See Christine Carpenter, *The Wars of the Roses: Politics and the Constitution of England c. 1437–1509* (Cambridge, 1997), pp.92–4.

5. Erlanger, op. cit., p.113.

6. Gillingham, op. cit., p.62.

7. H.M. Colvin, *The History of the King's Works* Vol. ii (London, 1963) p.936.

8. Laynesmith, op. cit., p.242.

9. Cited in Gillingham, op. cit., pp.72–3.

10. Carpenter, op. cit., p.143.

11. Gillingham, op. cit., p.116.

12. *London Chronicle.*

13. Gillingham, op. cit., p.135.

14. Ibid., p.99.

15. Carpenter, op. cit., p.113.

CHAPTER 17: ELIZABETH WOODVILLE

1. Thomas More, *The History of Richard III.*

2. A.R. Myers (ed.), Introduction to *The Household of Edward IV*, p.2.

3. Arlene Okerlund, *Elizabeth Wydeville* (Stroud, 2005), p.15.

4. In their article 'Most Benevolent Queen', A. Sutton and L.Visser Fuchs confirm that Elizabeth Woodville was 'too young ever to have been a lady-in-waiting'.
5. This view of the marriage is taken by, among others, David Baldwin.
6. More, op. cit.
7. Laynesmith, op. cit., p.88.
8. Luchino Dallaghiexa, *Calendar of State Papers Existing in the Archives and Collections of Milan*, No. 131.
9. David Baldwin, *Elizabeth Woodville: Mother of the Princes in the Tower* (Stroud, 2002), p.41.
10. Michael Hicks, *Anne Neville, Queen to Richard III* (Stroud, 2006), p.84.
11. *Rows Rolls* No. 62.
12. *Historie of the Arrivall of Edward IV in England and the Final Recoverye of his Kingdomes from Henry VI.*
13. Ibid.
14. Gillingham, op. cit., p.213.
15. See Agnes Strickland and Okerlund, op. cit.
16. Erlanger, op. cit., p.243.
17. Charles Ross, *Edward IV* (1971), p.87.
18. A. Sutton and L. Visser Fuchs, 'Most Benevolent Queen', in *The Ricardian* No. 129, Vol. 10 (June 1995)

CHAPTER 18: ANNE NEVILLE

1. *Calendar of State Papers Existing in the Archives and Collections of Milan* I.
2. Alison Weir, *The Princes in the Tower* (London, 1992), p.64.
3. Ibid. p.77.
4. Gillingham, op. cit., p.223.
5. Ibid., p.224.
6. Laynesmith, op.cit., p.90.
7. Ibid.
8. *Croyland Chronicle.*
9. Ibid.
10. Griffiths and Thomas, op. cit., p.92.
11. Edward Hall, *Chronicle.*
12. *Croyland Chronicle.*
13. Michael K. Jones and Malcolm J. Underwood, *The King's Mother: Lady Margaret Beaufort, Countess of Richmond and Derby* (Cambridge, 1992), p.64.
14. *Croyland Chronicle.*
15. Peter Idley, *Instructions to his Son*, ed. Charlotte d'Evelyn (Modern Languages Association of America, Lancaster PA, 1935), p.31.
16. *Croyland Chronicle.*
17. Rosemary Horrox, '*The History of KRIII* (1619) by Sir George Buck, Master of the Revels', review in *English Historical Review* No. 382, Vol. 97 (January 1982).

18. Ibid.
19. *Croyland Chronicle*.

CHAPTER 19: ELIZABETH OF YORK

1. *Camden Miscellany*.
2. Ibid.
3. Polydore Vergil.
4. Baldwin, op. cit., p.125.
5. J. Nichols (ed.), *Wills of the Kings and Queens of England* (London, 1790).
6. *MS Arundel 26*, British Library.
7. Margaret Aston, 'Death' in *Fifteenth Century Attitudes*, ed. Horrox, op. cit., p.212.
8. F.R.H. Du Boulay, *An Age of Ambition: English Society in the Late Middle Ages* (London, 1970)
9. Jones and Underwood, op. cit., p.161.
10. Gill, Louise 'William Caxton and the Revolution of 1483' in *English Historical Review* No. 445, Vol. 112 (February 1997).
11. Cited in Belozerskaya, op. cit., p.77.
12. *English Historical Documents 1485–1558*.
13. Thomas More.

CONCLUSION

All quotations from 'Beowulf' are from Heather O'Donoghue, (ed.) and Kevin Crossley-Holland (trans.), Beowulf *(Oxford, 1999). Those from* Morte d'Arthur *are from Eugene Vinaver,* Malory:Works *(Oxford, 1971).*

1. Terence McCarthy, *An Introduction to Malory* (Cambridge, 1988).
2. This reading of the heroic feminine in 'Beowulf' is drawn from Stacy S. Klein, 'Beowulf and the Gendering of Heroism' in Stacy S. Klein, *Ruling Women: Queenship and Gender in Anglo-Saxon Literature* (Notre Dame, IA, 2006), pp.87–123.
3. Ibid. p. 98.
4. Ibid. p. 98.
5. Peter Clemoes (ed.), *Aelfric's Catholic Homilies* (Oxford, 1997), p.279.
6. Klein, op. cit., p.113.
7. Norbert Elias, *The Civilizing Process: The History of Manners* (Oxford, 1978), p.95.
8. See Elias, ibid., and J. Huizinga, J., 'The Violent Tenor of Life', in J. Huizinga, *The Waning of the Middle Ages* (London, 1955).
9. Blamires, op. cit., p.231.
10. Linda E. Mitchell, *Portraits of Medieval Women: Family, Marriage and Politics in England 1225–1350* (New York, 2003), p.135.

11. J.A. McNamara, John E. Halborg and E. Gordon Whatley (eds.), *Sainted Women of the Dark Ages* (Durham, NC, 1992), p.70.
12. P.A. Lee, 'Reflections of Power: Margaret of Anjou and the Dark Side of Queenship', in *Renaissance Quarterly* 29 (1986).
13. P.J.C. Field, 'The Life and Times of Sir Thomas Malory', in *Arthurian Studies* No. 6 (1993).
14. Ibid., p.143.

ACKNOWLEDGEMENTS

Firstly I would like to thank Claire Norton, who permitted me to begin this book in her beautiful library in the French countryside, and her father, the late Colin Gordon, for his tremendously generous gift of the original editions of Agnes Strickland's works. Pascal Marichalar in Paris, Mañuel Sagastibelza Beraza in Pamplona and Dr Sally Connolly in Houston were all most generous and helpful in suggesting research materials. I am grateful to the director of the Archivio Statale in Milan for permitting me to see some extremely rare material, to Dr Christopher Tyerman of Oxford University for prompt and constructive advice, to Dr Dorian of the British Library, Professor Kinch Hoekstra at Berkeley, Lady Antonia Fraser, for her continued encouragement and interest and Mr Bashir Malik of HSBC, whose eleventh-hour intervention saved the whole project. Many thanks also to Nicole Martinelli in Milan for bad babysitting.

My agent, Michael Alcock, and Alan Samson at Weidenfeld & Nicolson have as ever been fantastically kind, and I am particularly grateful to Caroline North, who agreed to work with me for a third time.

This book could never have been finished had it not been for the patience and endless support of my parents-in-law, Vittorio and Patrizia Moro.

INDEX